Lecture Notes in Computer Science   2758
Edited by G. Goos, J. Hartmanis, and J. van Leeuwen

Springer
Berlin
Heidelberg
New York
Hong Kong
London
Milan
Paris
Tokyo

David Basin
Burkhart Wolff (Eds.)

Theorem Proving
in Higher Order Logics

16 International Conference, TPHOLs 2003
Rome, Italy, September 8-12, 2003
Proceedings

 Springer

Series Editors

Gerhard Goos, Karlsruhe University, Germany
Juris Hartmanis, Cornell University, NY, USA
Jan van Leeuwen, Utrecht University, The Netherlands

Volume Editors

David Basin
ETH Zentrum
CH-8092 Zürich, Switzerland
E-mail: basin@inf.ethz.ch

Burkhart Wolff
Albert-Ludwigs-University Freiburg
D-79110 Freiburg, Germany
E-mail: wolff@informatik.uni-freiburg.de

Cataloging-in-Publication Data applied for

A catalog record for this book is available from the Library of Congress.

Bibliographic information published by Die Deutsche Bibliothek
Die Deutsche Bibliothek lists this publication in the Deutsche Nationalbibliografie;
detailed bibliographic data is available in the Internet at <http://dnb.ddb.de>.

CR Subject Classification (1998): F.4.1, I.2.3, F.3.1, D.2.4, B.6.3

ISSN 0302-9743
ISBN 3-540-40664-6 Springer-Verlag Berlin Heidelberg New York

Springer-Verlag Berlin Heidelberg New York
a member of BertelsmannSpringer Science+Business Media GmbH

http://www.springer.de

© Springer-Verlag Berlin Heidelberg 2003
Printed in Germany

Typesetting: Camera-ready by author, data conversion by PTP Berlin GmbH
Printed on acid-free paper   SPIN: 10930755   06/3142   5 4 3 2 1 0

Preface

This volume constitutes the proceedings of the *16th International Conference on Theorem Proving in Higher Order Logics* (TPHOLs 2003) held September 8–12, 2003 in Rome, Italy. TPHOLs covers all aspects of theorem proving in higher order logics as well as related topics in theorem proving and verification.

TPHOLs 2003 was co-located with *TABLEAUX*, the International Conference on Automated Reasoning with Analytic Tableaux and Related Methods, and with *Calculemus*, the Symposium on the Integration of Symbolic Computation and Mechanized Reasoning.

There were 50 papers submitted to TPHOLs in the full research category, each of which was refereed by at least 3 reviewers, selected by the program committee. Of these submissions, 21 were accepted for presentation at the conference and publication in this volume. In keeping with tradition, TPHOLs 2003 also offered a venue for the presentation of work in progress, where researchers invite discussion by means of a brief preliminary talk and then discuss their work at a poster session. A supplementary proceedings containing associated papers for work in progress was published by the computer science department at the Universität Freiburg.

The organizers are grateful to Jean-Raymond Abrial, Patrick Lincoln, and Dale Miller for agreeing to give invited talks at TPHOLs 2003.

The TPHOLs conference traditionally changes continent each year in order to maximize the chances that researchers from around the world can attend. Starting in 1993, the proceedings of TPHOLs and its predecessor workshops have been published in the Springer-Verlag Lecture Notes in Computer Science series:

1993 (Canada)	780	1998 (Australia)	1479
1994 (Malta)	859	1999 (France)	1690
1995 (USA)	971	2000 (USA)	1869
1996 (Finland)	1125	2001 (UK)	2152
1997 (USA)	1275	2002 (USA)	2410

We would like to thank members of both the Freiburg and Zürich groups for their help in organizing the program. In particular, Achim Brucker, Barbara Geiser, and Paul Hankes Drielsma. We would also like to express our thanks to Marta Cialdea Mayer and her team for coordinating the local arrangements in Rome.

Finally, we thank our sponsors: Intel, ITT, ETH Zürich, and the Universität Freiburg. We also gratefully acknowledge the use of computing equipment from Universitá Roma III.

May 2003

David Basin, Burkhart Wolff
TPHOLs 2003 Program Chairs

Program Committee

Mark Aagaard	University of Waterloo, Canada
David Basin	ETH Zürich, Switzerland
Yves Bertot	INRIA Sophia Antipolis, France
Alan Bundy	University of Edinburgh, UK
Victor Carreno	NASA Langley, USA
Iliano Cervesato	ITT Industries, Inc., USA
Thierry Coquand	Chalmers University, Göteborg, Sweden
Peter Dybjer	Chalmers University, Göteborg, Sweden
Amy Felty	University of Ottawa, Canada
Jean-Christophe Filliâtre	Université Paris Sud, France
Mike Gordon	University of Cambridge, UK
Jim Grundy	Intel Inc., USA
Elsa Gunter	NJIT, USA
John Harrison	Intel Inc., USA
Douglas Howe	Carleton University, Canada
Paul Jackson	University of Edinburgh, UK
Bart Jacobs	University of Nijmegen, The Netherlands
Sara Kalvala	University of Warwick, UK
Thomas Kropf	Bosch, Germany
Tom Melham	Oxford University, UK
César Muñoz	National Institute of Aerospace, USA
Tobias Nipkow	Technische Universität München, Germany
Sam Owre	SRI, USA
Christine Paulin-Mohring	Université Paris Sud, France
Lawrence Paulson	University of Cambridge, UK
Frank Pfenning	Carnegie Mellon University, USA
Wolfgang Reif	Universität Augsburg, Germany
Konrad Slind	University of Utah, USA
Sofiene Tahar	Concordia University, Canada
Burkhart Wolff	Universität Freiburg, Germany

Sponsoring Organizations

Additional Referees

Sabine Glesner
Martin Wildmoser
Joakim von Wright
Gerwin Klein
Bruno Dutertre
Alfons Geser
Otmane Ait-Mohamed
Mohamed Layouni
Ali Habibi
Amjad Gawanmeh
Paul Curzon
Helen Lowe
Tom Ridge
Graham Steel

Daniel Winterstein
Dominik Haneberg
Michael Balser
Claudio Castellini
Christoph Duelli
Gerhard Schellhorn
Andreas Thums
Jean Duprat
Jan von Plato
Makoto Takeyama
Nicolas Oury
Ashish Tiwari
Harald Ruess

Table of Contents

Click'n Prove: Interactive Proofs within Set Theory

Jean-Raymond Abrial[1] and Dominique Cansell[2]*

[1] Consultant Marseille France
jr@abrial.org
[2] LORIA, INRIA Lorraine France
Dominique.Cansell@loria.fr

Abstract. In this article, we first briefly present a proof assistant called the Predicate Prover, which essentially offers two functionalities: (1) an automatic semi-decision procedure for First Order Predicate Calculus, and (2) a systematic translation of statements written within Set Theory into equivalent ones in First Order Predicate Calculus. We then show that the automatic usage of this proof assistant is limited by several factors. We finally present (and this is the main part of this article) the principles that we have used in the construction of a *proactive* interface aiming at circumventing these limitations. Such principles are based on our practical experience in doing many interactive proofs (within Set Theory).

1 Introduction

We believe that the *modeling* of software systems and more generally that of complex systems is an important phase in their rigorous development. This is certainly very common in other engineering disciplines, where models are sometimes called *blueprints*. We also believe that the writing of such models can only be done by *stepwise refinements*. In other words, a model is built by successive enrichment of an original simple "sketch" and then by some careful transformations into more concrete representations. As an analogy, the first sketchy blueprint of an architect is gradually zoomed in order to eventually represent all the fine details of the intended building and then some decisions are made concerning the way it can be constructed, thus obtaining the final complete set of blueprints. We believe that the usage of some formal language is indispensable in such a modeling activity. It gives you the necessary framework within which such models can be built. This is, in a sense, equivalent to the formal conventions to be used in the drawings of blueprints.

We also strongly believe that using such an approach without *validating* the formal texts which constitute the initial model and its successive refinements, is an error because the texts in question can then just be "read" (which is already difficult and rather boring) without any possibilities for reasoning about them. In fact, as the validation of such models cannot be done by testing (since there is no "execution" for a model: the blueprint of a car cannot be driven!) the only (and far more serious) possibility is to validate them by *proving* them.

Of course there exist many "formal" methods on the market which are not using either refinement nor any kind of proving system for validation. These are said to be

---

* Partly supported by PRST IL/QSL/ADHOC project.

D. Basin and B. Wolff (Eds.): TPHOLs 2003, LNCS 2758, pp. 1–24, 2003.

already sufficient to help the designers. It is our opinion however that it is not sufficient nowadays, in the same way as it is not sufficient to draw a bridge and just observe the drawing in question to be persuaded that it will be strong enough.

The construction of formal proofs has certainly not yet entered the collection of standard techniques used by (software) engineers, although some of them have already used such techniques with great success, showing that it is quite feasible. One of the reasons, which is argued against the generalization of such techniques, is that it is too difficult to master (as an aside, we believe that what is really difficult to master is the technique of modeling rather than that of proving). In case where the proving system at hand performs an automatic proof, this is not a problem of course, but this is clearly not always the case. What seems difficult to master is then the technique of *performing a proof interactively* with the computer. To a certain extent, we agree with that opinion. But we believe that, besides a possible intrinsic (but rare) mathematical difficulty, it is most of the time difficult essentially because the interfaces that are usually proposed to users are not adequate. This is the point where we arrive in this introduction at the purpose of this paper: its aim is to report on an experiment in building such an *interface* for a proving system which is possibly, but not exclusively, used in industry.

Being familiar with the B Method [2] and its industrial tool called **Atelier B** [6], our project consisted of completely reshaping the external aspect of this tool in order to give it a more adequate user interface (we are aware however that the adequacy in question is certainly very subjective). We have chosen to develop this interface under **Emacs** for various obvious reasons, which we are not going to develop here.

Among other things, **Atelier B** is essentially made of two tools: the Proof Obligation Generator and the Prover. The former is able to analyze a formal text and to extract from it a number of mathematical statements expressing what is to be proved in order to make sure that the text in question is "correct". Once this is done, these lemmas are passed to the Prover, which first scans them and tries to prove them automatically as much as it can. But there always remains a number of lemmas that cannot be proven automatically (some of them of course because it is not possible to prove them at all, hence detecting a bug in the corresponding model). This is where interactive proofs may enter into the scene.

The prover of **Atelier B** is made of two independent pieces: the first one is called **pb**[1] (for "prover of **Atelier B**"), whereas the second one is called **pp** (for "predicate prover"). The prover **pb** works directly at the level of Set Theory (the mathematical language used in the B Method), it is essentially made of a large number of inference rules able to discharge a large number of "simple" mathematical statements. These rules have been constructed in a rather experimental way. Historically, **pb** was the only prover of **Atelier B**. The prover **pp** had been developed as an independent project in order to validate the many rules of the other, and it was only later fully incorporated within **Atelier B**. The prover **pp** is more elaborate than **pb**, it is based on a firmer theoretical background: it is essentially a prover for First Order Predicate Calculus with Equality

---

[1] We shall only briefly mention **pb** in this paper, but we must say that most of the features described in section 4 have been borrowed from those existing already in **pb**. So that we have often just make them easy to use.

(and some Arithmetic) together with a Translator from Set Theory to First Order Predicate Calculus.

The organization of this paper is as follows. In section 2, we briefly describe the various parts of **pp**. In section 3 we explain why **pp** may fail to automatically prove some statements and hence requires the presence of an interactive interface. In section 4 (which is quite large) we describe this interface in a progressive way. In section 5 we open a general discussion about the principles we have used in the development of this interface and we also perform a short comparison with other proof assistants. In section 6 we conclude the paper.

2 Set-Theoretic Proofs with the Predicate Prover

2.1 Some Underlying Principles behind the Construction of pp

In this section, we present some ideas and concepts that have driven us in the construction of the Predicate Prover.

To begin with, **pp** has been developed *incrementally* on the basis of a *hierarchy of provers*. Although important, this strategy is, after all, nothing else but a good design practice.

The most important idea, we think, behind the construction of **pp**, lies in the fact that it has been designed around a fixed *wired-in* logical system, which is the most classical of all, namely First-Order Predicate Calculus with Equality (used as the *internal engine*), and Set Theory (used as the *external vehicle*). The prover **pp** also contains some treatment of Arithmetic, which we shall not mention further here.

In no way is **pp** constructed from a meta-prover able to be parameterized by a variety of distinct logics. This contrasts with what can be seen in academic circles where extremely powerful general purpose *Proof Systems* are usually offered: HOL [8], Isabelle [12], PVS [11], Coq [5], etc. Our approach is quite different. It is rather similar to that used in the development of some industrial programs handling symbolic data. For instance, a good C compiler is not a meta-compiler specialized to C; likewise, a good chess-playing program is not a general purpose game-playing program specialized by the rules and strategies of the game of chess.

In our case, we have internalized classical logic because it is clearly that logic which is used to handle the usually simple lemmas which validate software and more generally system developments. This is *not* to say, however, that classical logic is the logic of software and system development. Our view is that the logic of software development is whatever logic one wants (Hoare-logic, wp-logic, temporal logic, etc). Such logics, we think, are not the ones concerned by the "how-to-prove", they are the ones used to generate the "what-to-prove".

We think that it is important to completely separate these two functions in two distinct tools: again, this is what is done in **Atelier B** where you have the, so-called, Proof Obligation Generator based on a weakest pre-condition analysis of formal texts and which delivers the statements to be proved (it tells you the "what-to-prove"), and, as a distinct tool, the Prover which is supposed to discharge the previous statements (it tells you thus the "how-to-prove"). Our view is that, whatever the logic of system development you decide to use, it will generate some final lemmas that are, inevitably, to be proved within classical logic.

Moreover, we do not think at all that the usage of Set Theory restricts you to the expression of elementary mathematical facts only: it is quite possible to encode within Set Theory mathematical statements that are clearly belonging to what is called higher order logic [1] (another example is given in **Appendix 2**). A mathematical analogy which can be used at this point, is the well known fact that some non-Euclidean geometry can be "encoded" (on a sphere) within the Euclidean one.

2.2   A Propositional Calculus Decision Procedure

The prover **pp** essentially first contains a decision procedure for Propositional Calculus. This procedure is very close to what is elsewhere proposed under the technical name of Semantic Tableaux [7].

More precisely, the proof procedure consists of applying a number of simple rules (not detailed here), which *gradually* transform an original sequent with no hypotheses into one or several sequents with hypotheses made of *literals* only (that is, either simple propositions containing no logical connectives or the negation of such simple propositions). Such sequents are discharged as soon as their collection of hypotheses contains a certain atomic proposition together with its negation (such literals are boxed in the example that follows). Next is an example proof of a propositional statement with this procedure:

$$\vdash (A \vee B) \Rightarrow (A \vee (B \vee C))$$

$$\vdash A \Rightarrow (A \vee (B \vee C)) \qquad\qquad \vdash B \Rightarrow (A \vee (B \vee C))$$

$$A \vdash A \vee (B \vee C) \qquad\qquad B \vdash A \vee (B \vee C)$$

$$A \vdash \neg A \Rightarrow (B \vee C) \qquad\qquad B \vdash \neg A \Rightarrow (B \vee C)$$

$$\boxed{A}, \boxed{\neg A} \vdash B \vee C \qquad\qquad B, \neg A \vdash B \vee C$$

$$B, \neg A \vdash \neg B \Rightarrow C$$

$$\boxed{B}, \neg A, \boxed{\neg B} \vdash C$$

2.3   A Semi-Decision Procedure for First-Order Predicate Calculus

The just presented simplified form of **pp** has then been extended to handle First-Order Predicate Calculus statements. Within this new framework, the prover again starts with a sequent with no hypotheses. It then loops through two distinct phases:

1. **Phase 1**: The prover first proceeds by applying some rules as above with the only difference that the collection of hypotheses associated with a sequent in formation not only contains some atomic propositions as before, but also some *universally quantified predicates* that are normalized in a certain systematic fashion. The prover thus gradually transforms the original sequent until the right-hand part of the remaining sequent is reduced to F (for FALSE) unless, of course, it has been discharged in the meantime by discovering two contradicting literals. If the contradiction is not

reached trivially, one has then to prove that the simple hypotheses (the literals) are contradictory with the universally quantified ones: this is the purpose of the second phase.

2. **Phase 2**: This search for contradiction is attempted by means of some *instantiations* of the universally quantified hypotheses. Some "interesting" instantiations are discovered in a systematic fashion by means of the atomic hypotheses. This technique is a special case of the, so-called, "set of support" technique of Otter [10], where the set in question is represented by the atomic hypotheses. The conjunct of the retained instantiations is then moved into the right-hand part of the sequent, where it implies F, thus forming a new sequent. At this point, the second phase is completed, and the prover proceeds again with the first phase, and so on.

Here is a little example of using this "ping-pong" technique to prove a simple statement:

$$\vdash \ \forall x \cdot ((\exists y \cdot R_{xy}) \Rightarrow \forall z \cdot R_{zx}) \Rightarrow \forall (x, y) \cdot (R_{xy} \Rightarrow R_{yx})$$

Phase 1

$$\forall (x, y, z) \cdot \neg (R_{xy} \wedge \neg R_{zx}), R_{xy}, \neg R_{yx} \ \vdash \ \mathsf{F}$$

Phase 2

$$\forall (x, y, z) \cdot \neg (R_{xy} \wedge \neg R_{zx}), R_{xy}, \neg R_{yx} \ \vdash \ \neg (R_{xy} \wedge \neg R_{yx}) \Rightarrow \mathsf{F}$$

Phase 1

$$\forall (x, y, z) \cdot \neg (R_{xy} \wedge \neg R_{zx}), \boxed{R_{xy}}, \neg R_{yx}, \boxed{\neg R_{xy}} \vdash \mathsf{F} \quad \forall (x, y, z) \cdot \neg (R_{xy} \wedge \neg R_{zx}), R_{xy}, \boxed{\neg R_{yx}}, \boxed{R_{yx}} \vdash \mathsf{F}$$

In the example above the effect of Phase 2 is to instantiate x, y, and z in the universal hypothesis $\forall (x, y, z) \cdot \neg (R_{xy} \wedge \neg R_{zx})$ with x, y, and y respectively. This leads to $\neg (R_{xy} \wedge \neg R_{yx})$, which is moved to the right hand side of $\vdash$ in order to resume Phase 1.

2.4   The Translation of Set-Theoretic Statements

The next part of **pp** is the Set Translator. It is built very much in accordance with the spirit of the set-theoretic construction presented in the B-Book [2], where Set Theory just appears as an extension of First-Order Logic. The goal of this extension essentially consists of formalizing the abstract concept of set membership.

Statements involving the membership operator are reduced as much as possible by the translator by means of a number of rewriting rules. It results in predicate calculus statements, where *complex* set memberships have disappeared, the remaining set membership operators being left uninterpreted. For instance, a set-theoretic predicate such as $s \in \mathbb{P}(t)$ is transformed into $\forall x \cdot (x \in s \Rightarrow x \in t)$. The translator then just performs the translation of the various instances of set membership. They correspond to the classical set operators ($\cup$, $\cap$, etc), to the generalization of such operators, to the binary relation operators, to the functional operators (including functional abstraction and functional application), and so on. Next is such a set-theoretic statement expressing that intersection distributes over the inverse image of a partial function:

$$f \in s \rightarrowtail t \wedge a \subseteq t \wedge b \subseteq t \ \Rightarrow \ f^{-1}[a \cap b] = f^{-1}[a] \cap f^{-1}[b]$$

Here is the translation of this statement. It is easily discharged by **pp** using the procedure described in the previous section:

$$\forall (x, y) \cdot ((x, y) \in f \ \Rightarrow \ x \in s \wedge y \in t) \ \wedge$$
$$\forall (x, y, z) \cdot ((x, y) \in f \wedge (x, z) \in f \ \Rightarrow \ y = z) \ \wedge$$
$$\forall x \cdot (x \in a \ \Rightarrow \ x \in t) \ \wedge$$
$$\forall x \cdot (x \in b \ \Rightarrow \ x \in t)$$
$$\Rightarrow$$
$$\forall x \cdot (\exists y \cdot (x \in a \wedge x \in b \wedge (x, y) \in f) \ \Rightarrow \ \exists y \cdot (y \in a \wedge (x, y) \in f) \wedge \exists y \cdot (y \in b \wedge (x, y) \in f)) \wedge$$
$$\forall x \cdot (\exists y \cdot (y \in a \wedge (x, y) \in f) \wedge \exists y \cdot (y \in b \wedge (x, y) \in f) \ \Rightarrow \ \exists y \cdot (x \in a \wedge x \in b \wedge (x, y) \in f))$$

As can be seen, membership predicates such as $(x, y) \in f$, $x \in s$, $y \in t$, etc, no longer play a rôle in this statement. They could have been replaced by $F_{x,y}$, S_x, T_x, etc.

3   Deficiencies of the Automatic Mode of the Predicate Prover

Although **pp** is able to automatically prove some non trivial statements (see **Appendix 1**), it is nevertheless limited in various ways. The purpose of this short section is to analyze such deficiencies. We can detect four kinds of deficiencies.

The first limitation of **pp** is certainly its *sensitivity to useless hypotheses*. In other words, **pp** may easily prove a certain mathematical statement, and fail (or take a very long time) to prove the same statement once prefixed with a large collection of useless hypotheses. The prover **pp** is certainly not the only prover to suffer from such a "disease". Note that this problem of useless hypotheses seems rather strange since, clearly, a mathematician never tries to prove a statement containing such hypotheses, his understanding of the problem usually telling him the relevant assumptions. But in formal developments, as we have mentioned above, the statements to prove are not determined by a human being (this is prone to many errors), they are rather *automatically generated* by some tools. And in this case it is quite frequent to have a large number of irrelevant hypotheses.

A second limitation is due to the fact that **pp** is not good (so far) at *abstracting* the statements to prove. A mathematician can almost immediately detect that a certain statement to prove is in fact a special case of a simpler one, which could have been obtained by replacing some common sub-expressions by various dummy variables. And, again, the mathematician can do so because he has a good understanding of the problem at hand. As above, **pp** can take quite a long time to prove a statement that it could have proved easily once abstracted.

A third factor to take into account is the fact that **pp** is not always very good at *managing equalities*. In other words, it sometimes fails to take advantage of the fact that two (set-)expressions are equal or two predicates are equivalent.

The fourth factor is not so much a limitation of **pp** itself but rather one due to the fact that it is *automatic* . It is the recognition that certain statements to prove require some non-trivial *creative strategies*. Examples of such creative strategies are the following:

- Attempt to prove a lemma which, once proved, will become a new hypothesis,
- Perform a proof by cases,
- Decide for a proof by contradiction,
- Attempt to prove the negation of a certain hypothesis (another form of contradiction),

- Propose a witness for an existential statement to prove,
- Similarly propose a specific instantiation for a universally quantified hypothesis,
- Decide for a proof by induction,
- etc.

As a result, it seems advisable to construct a *layer*, with which a person can intervene in a proof by *preparing* the work to be given to **pp**. This is the purpose of next section.

4   The "Click'n Prove" Proactive Interface

4.1   Enlarging the Usage of pp within an Interactive Proof Assistant

Our proof assistant deals with the proofs of *sequents* of the following form:

$$hypotheses \quad \vdash \quad conclusion$$

where *hypotheses* denotes a possibly empty list of predicates and where *conclusion* denotes a predicate which is not conjunctive and usually implicative. Conducting a proof within this framework leads to the application of some pre-defined *inference rules* able to transform such a sequent into zero, one or more *successor sequents*. Once such a rule is applied to it, a sequent is said to be *discharged* and the successor sequents (if any) have then to be discharged themselves. At this point, the procedure resumes by independently applying some inference rules on each of the remaining sequents, and so on. When a successor-less inference rule is applied on the last remaining non-discharged sequent then we are done. Note that at some point in this procedure, we may have a sequent which **pp** or **pb** could successfully discharge. In this case, **pp** or **pb** could then be considered as "special" and powerful inference rules with no successor sequent.

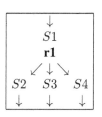

The *trace* of such a procedure, which records the various *states* of a proof (that is, the sequents to be considered at each step), constitutes what is commonly known as a *proof tree*. A node in such a tree is a sequent and the relationship between a node and its set of "offspring nodes" denotes the inference rule which has been applied to this node. In the following diagram, you can see part of such a proof tree with a node $S1$ together with his three "offspring nodes" $S2$, $S3$, and $S4$. Rule **r1** has been applied to $S1$ and produced $S2$, $S3$, and $S4$.

An *automatic* proof is one where the proof tree is constructed entirely automatically from an initial sequent and a set of pre-defined inference rules. In this case the prover is able to choose a correct inference rule at each step of the proof.

An *interactive* proof is one where the prover just correctly applies the rule, which a user tells it to apply at each step. During the proof process, the proof tree may contain some leafs that are "final" because a successor-less inference rule has been applied to them, and several other leafs which are "pending" because some inference rules have yet to be discovered for each of them. In this figure, we have a situation where leaf $S2$ is "final" because the successor-less rule **r2** has been applied to it, whereas leafs $S3$ and $S4$ are still "pending".

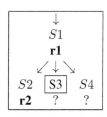

In this situation, the user has the choice to concentrate either on node $S3$ or on node $S4$ in order to discover which inference rule to apply in each case. In the figure, we have "boxed" node $S3$ in order to indicate that the user is now interested in discovering an inference rule for that node.

The proof tree thus appears to be the "object" with which the user has to play during the proof. Unfortunately, such an object is not at all tractable because it is *far too big*. The sequents forming the nodes may contain many large hypotheses and the conclusion may be quite large too. Finally the tree itself can be quite deep. In other words, the full tree does not fit any physical screen (and even the user brain).

In order to help solve this problem we have no choice but to *simplify the proof tree*. This can be done in various ways. First, we may not record the full sequent in each node, only some "significant part" of it. In the figures below we show only simplified sequents[2], namely $G1$, $G2$, $G3$, and $G4$ corresponding respectively to the full sequents $S1$, $S2$, $S3$, and $S4$. This simplified tree is stored in one window: let us call it the *Tree Window*. We also introduce a second window containing the "boxed" full sequent we are interested in at a given moment: this is the *Sequent Window*. In this window, beside the sequent, we may have various buttons (here buttons **[r1] [r2] [pp]**) that are able, when pressed, to activate the corresponding inference rule on the sequent which is currently there. These two windows can be pictured as indicated. We have also shown the dynamics of the proof. You can see how both windows evolves when the user successively presses **[r1]**, **[r2]** (not shown in the figures) and **[pp]**.

What we have presented so far is clearly very sketchy. In fact, these two windows are certainly *not* organized as indicated: what we have shown are just *abstractions* of the real windows at work in the real interface. The rôle of this quick overview was just to set up the scene. It remains now for us to develop the way each of the two windows is organized and how both of them are able to work in cooperation. In sections 4.2 to 4.10 we first study the Sequent Window, and in sections 4.11 to 4.13 we study the Tree Window. Notice that in section 5, we shall present some general principles on which we have based our construction of the interface presented in section 4.

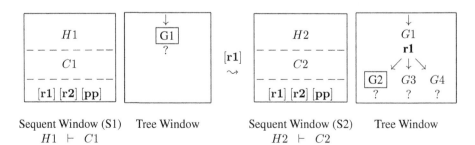

Sequent Window (S1)   Tree Window   Sequent Window (S2)   Tree Window
    $H1 \vdash C1$ $H2 \vdash C2$

---

[2] The exact nature of the simplified sequents with respect to the full ones will be described in section 4.11.

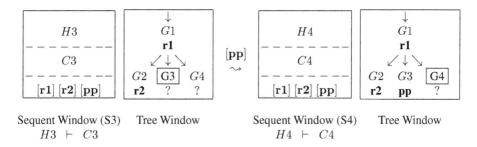

Sequent Window (S3)   Tree Window   Sequent Window (S4)   Tree Window
$H3 \vdash C3$ $H4 \vdash C4$

4.2   Managing the Hypotheses of the Sequent Window: [sh] [sg] [sl] [ds] [dl]

The most natural organization for the Sequent Window would be to split it up in two
parts as shown in the previous section: one part for the *hypotheses* and another one
for the *conclusion*. But the fact that there are *many hypotheses* forces us to structure
the sequent in a richer fashion as follows, where *goal* is a non-conjunctive and non-
implicative predicate and where the other "fields" are possibly empty conjunctive lists
of predicates:

$$\underbrace{hidden \; ; \; searched \; ; \; cached}_{hypotheses} \quad \vdash \quad \underbrace{selected \; \Rightarrow \; goal}_{conclusion}$$

Next are the informal "window" properties of these various kinds of hypotheses:

$$\begin{cases} hidden & \text{Not visible on the window} \\ searched & \text{Visible after some search in } hidden \\ cached & \text{Visible but not part of the conclusion any more} \\ selected & \text{Visible and part of the conclusion} \end{cases}$$

The layout of the window, with which the user can interact with
the prover, reflects the structure of the sequent. It is thus divided
into various areas where each hypothesis is written on a separate
line. This layout evolves as the proof proceeds since each area can
contain a variable number of hypotheses including no hypotheses
at all, in which case the area simply does not exist.

[SH] — — — — — —   *searched*

[KH] — — — — — —   *cached*

[SL] — — — — — —   *selected*

GL — — — — — —   *goal*

This is the reason why each area is indicated on the window with a specific label as shown
in the figure. The first three labels (those surrounded by square brackets) are "buttons"
which, when pressed, make the hypotheses of the area being temporarily hidden until
one presses the button again. Other buttons (not shown here) allows one to show more
(or less) hypotheses in each area.

The idea behind this splitting of the hypotheses into
various areas has been borrowed from the notion of *hierarchy of memories* which is usual in computer systems. We may roughly consider the following analogy
between our areas and various memory media.

hidden	*disk*
searched	*core*
cached	*cache*
selected	*register*

A number of commands, namely [sh], [sg], [sl], [ds], and [dl], allows one to move an
hypothesis from one area to another. A button dedicated to the relevant command is thus
placed *on each line* in front of the corresponding hypothesis as shown in the figure. The

window is thus divided horizontally in a "button area" on the left, and an hypotheses (or goal) area on the right.

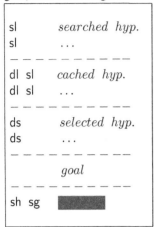

Here are the various functions of these commands:

sh, sg	searching	ds	deselecting
sl	selecting	dl	deleting

Next is the way each command may move an hypothesis from one area to another.

hidden	sh	searched
searched	sg	searched
searched	sl	selected
selected	ds	cached
cached	sl	selected
cached	dl	hidden

The button [sh] requires a search pattern, which is (in first approximation) a character string on which the search is performed. It must be entered before pressing the button. This pattern is either defined by pointing with the mouse to a piece of text anywhere on the window, or by writing it in the editing area (shown in black on the figure). After pressing the button, *searched* (if existing) is first cleared, and then all hypotheses containing an occurrence of the given pattern are moved from *hidden* to *searched*. The button [sg] allows one to search further within the *searched* area itself.

4.3   Launching pp and pb: [p0] [p1] [pb] [it] (*Appendix 3 contains a list of all commands*)

A proof is started in the following situation where the *searched* and *cached* areas are empty:

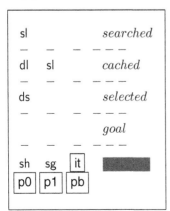

$$hidden \;\vdash\; \underbrace{selected \Rightarrow goal}_{conclusion}$$

Note that **pp** never uses the *hidden* hypotheses nor the *searched* and *cached* ones, it only works with the *conclusion* (but it might be launched even if the *searched* and *cached* areas are present). If, in this initial situation, we feel that **pp** has enough hypotheses (in *selected*), we may launch it by pressing the button [p0] shown at the bottom of the window. The prover **pp** may succeed, in which case we are done, but it may also fail because it needs more hypotheses. In this case, we search for some hypotheses in *hidden* and select those which seems to be most relevant.

This is done by first using the button [sh] together with a certain pattern as explained above: the corresponding hypotheses then appear in the *searched* area. We then use some buttons [sl] of *searched* to move certain hypotheses to *selected* and we press [p0] again.

On the contrary, **pp** may fail because it has too many hypotheses. In this case, we may "De-select" some of them by pressing the buttons [ds] situated in front of them in the *selected* area. Note that in case we remove an hypothesis by mistake, it is easy to select it again as it is still in the *cached* area.

Another common situation is one where the number of needed hypotheses is quite large. In this case, we may follow another technique: rather than searching and selecting some hypotheses, we directly launch **pp** with the button [p1]. This has the effect of automatically enlarging the *selected* area (but for this session of **pp** only) with those hypotheses having some identifier in common with the identifiers occurring in the *selected* and *goal* areas. This is clearly a very straightforward technique, but it may quite often have very spectacular effects. The drawback of this technique is of course that it may select useless hypotheses, and **pp** may then be slowed down (a powerful machine is a good help here!).

In all these cases, instead of launching **pp**, we may do so with **pb** by pressing the corresponding button. Notice that **pp**, as well as **pb**, are not decision procedures. As a consequence, they may sometimes run for ever. In order to circumvent this "difficulty", they are automatically stopped after a certain pre-defined time. But they can also be stopped manually by pressing the button [it] (for "interruption") situated in the bottom part of the window. During a run of **pp** or **pb**, all other buttons are locked except [it], which is highlighted in order to possibly capture the attention of the user: he is then aware that either **pp** or **pb** are working.

4.4   Commands for Reshaping the Conclusion: [ae] [ap] [eh] [he]

As explained in section 3, **pp** may be helped by *abstracting* a common sub-term T in the *conclusion*. For this, we have a button called [ae] (for "abstract expression"). The sub-term T is defined by pointing with the mouse on some piece of text in the window. After pressing [ae], the prover automatically chooses a *free identifier*, say e, and replaces all occurrences of T by e in the *selected* and *goal* areas. It also puts the predicate $e = T$ in the *cached* area. A similar button, [ap], is used to abstract a predicate. These permanent buttons are put next to the *goal* as shown in this figure.

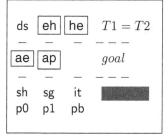

In order to lighten the figure we shall, from now on, only show the *selected* area in the schematic Sequent Window. But the reader should be aware that the other areas may be non-empty.

Another case where **pp** can be helped is by using some hypothesis of the form $T1 = T2$ and either replacing occurrences of $T1$ by $T2$ or vice-versa. This can be done with two commands called [eh] (for "apply equality in hypothesis from left to right") and [he] (for "apply equality in hypothesis from right to left") both placed next to an hypothesis of the required form. The hypothesis in question can be in *searched, cached* or *selected*, but the replacement only occurs in *conclusion*, that is in *selected* and *goal*. In the above figure we have shown such an hypothesis in the *selected* area.

4.5   General Purpose Proof Commands: [ah] [dc] [ct] [mh] [fh]

In this section, we present a number of general commands, which help organizing a proof. The first one, called [ah] (for "add hypothesis"), is used to prove a *local lemma*, which will become, once proved, a new *selected* hypothesis for proving the original goal (this is also called the "cut rule"). This permanent button [ah] is situated in the bottom part of the window. The predicate, say L, to prove is defined by pointing to it with the mouse in the window, or alternatively by editing it in the black field. Notice L will replace the current *goal* so that the collection of hypotheses remains "the same" during its proof.

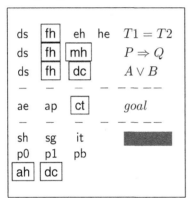

In case L has an implicative form, say $U \Rightarrow V$, then U is automatically moved to the *selected* area whereas *goal* becomes V.

Another general command is called [dc] (for "do case"). It requires a parameter which is a certain predicate C. As for the previous command, this parameter can be defined by pointing to it with the mouse, or alternatively by editing it in the black field. Applying this command results in the successive proofs of *goal* with either C or $\neg C$ as extra *selected* hypotheses. As for the previous button, this permanent button is situated in the bottom part of the window.

Our next command, called [ct] (for "proof by contradiction"), allows one to assume the negation of *goal* as an extra *selected* hypothesis, *goal* itself being replaced by FALSE. This permanent button is situated near *goal* as shown.

We now have two more general commands related to hypotheses with certain forms. When an hypothesis has the form $P \Rightarrow Q$, the command [mh] (for "modus ponens on hypothesis") is proposed. After pressing that button, the *goal* is replaced by P. When P is proved then the new hypothesis Q is *selected* and the original *goal* is put back in place.

When an hypothesis has the form $A \vee B$, another kind of [dc] command (for "do case") is proposed. Pressing that button results in *goal* being successively proved under the extra *selected* hypothesis A and then B. As you can see in the figure, these buttons are dynamically constructed next to corresponding hypotheses.

A last general command is associated with all hypotheses. It is called [fh] (for "false hypothesis"). When pressing that button on an hypothesis H, the goal is simply replaced by $\neg H$. In case of success, this reveals a contradiction in the collection of hypotheses.

4.6   Commands for Instantiating Quantified Hypotheses or Goals: [ph] [se]

Another case where the user can help **pp** is one where he may propose some "interesting" instantiations to be performed on a universally quantified hypothesis. A button

[ph] (for "particularize universal hypothesis") is situated next to an hypothesis with the corresponding form. Note that a small editing field is provided close to the quantified variable definition. Suppose we have an hypothesis of the form $\forall x \cdot (R_x \Rightarrow S_x)$. When pressing the button after filling the field with an expression E, then the lemma R_E is proposed (it replaces the current goal with the same hypotheses). Once R_E is proved, the original goal is put back in place together with the new hypothesis S_E.

ds fh	eh	he		$T1 = T2$
ds fh	mh			$P \Rightarrow Q$
ds fh	dc			$A \vee B$
ds fh	ph			$\forall x \ \blacksquare \ \cdot \ (R_x \Rightarrow S_x)$
—	—	—	— — —	
ae ap	ct	se		$\exists x \ \blacksquare \ \cdot \ (T_x \wedge U_x)$
—	—	—	— — —	
sh sg	it			▬▬▬
p0 p1	pb			
ah dc				

When the universal hypothesis contains several quantified variables, a little editing field is provided next to each variable. By filling some of these fields with a "$\star$", this command results in a *partial instantiation* of the hypothesis. In other words, the resulting new hypothesis is still universally quantified under the "starred variables", whereas the other variables are instantiated within the predicate.

A similar button, called [se] (for "suggest a witness for an existential goal"), is provided in the *goal* field when it has an existential form as shown in the figure. Suppose we have a goal of the form $\exists x \cdot (T_x \wedge U_x)$. If the proposed witness is the expression E then the two goals T_E and U_E are presented one after the other.

Notice that these two commands are indeed the same. For instance, we could "simulate" the command [se] by means of the command [ph] as follows. It is always possible to apply [ct] to the goal $\exists x \cdot (T_x \wedge U_x)$, thus getting the new goal **FALSE** together with the hypothesis $\neg \exists x \cdot (T_x \wedge U_x)$, which can be transformed into $\forall x \cdot (T_x \Rightarrow \neg U_x)$ after pressing [rn] (for "remove negation", see next section). We can then press [ph] with the expression E on this hypothesis. This requires to prove T_E. After this proof, we obtain the new hypothesis $\neg U_E$, still with the Goal **FALSE** to be proved. This hypothesis $\neg U_E$ can then be transformed into the goal U_E by pressing [fh] (for "false hypothesis") !

4.7   Logical Simplification Commands: [ru] [rx] [rn] [rd]

ds fh	eh	he		$T1 = T2$
ds fh	mh			$P \Rightarrow Q$
ds fh	dc			$A \vee B$
ds fh	ph			$\forall x \ \blacksquare \ \cdot \ (R_x \Rightarrow S_x)$
ds fh	rx			$\exists x \cdot (T_x \wedge U_x)$
ds fh	rn			$\neg (C \wedge D)$
—	—	—	— — —	
ae ap	ct	ru		$\forall x \cdot (V_x \Rightarrow W_x)$
—	—	—	— — —	
sh sg	it			▬▬▬
p0 p1	pb			
ah dc				

Although it is not necessary for **pp**, it might sometimes be important for the progress of an interactive proof to remove the quantification of a universally quantified goal or that of an existential hypothesis. Two commands called [ru] (for "remove universal") and [rx] (for "remove existential") are provided for this, as shown in the figure below. Of course, in case the quantified variable is not free in the sequent, an "alpha conversion" takes place when applying such commands. For instance, suppose we have a goal of the form $\forall x \cdot (V_x \Rightarrow W_x)$. By pressing [ru], the predicate V_x (when x is supposed to be free in the sequent) becomes a new *selected* hypothesis, and the goal becomes W_x. Suppose we have an hypothesis of the form $\exists x \cdot (T_x \wedge U_x)$. By pressing [rx], the predicates T_x and U_x become new *selected* hypotheses (when x is free).

An even simpler logical simplification command is provided, it is called [rn] (for "remove negation"). Again, this is not necessary for **pp**, but it can be useful in the progress of the interactive proof. Such negation removals may occur anywhere in the sequent (hypotheses or goal). In the figure, we have shown an hypothesis of the form $\neg(C \wedge D)$. By pressing this button, this hypothesis will be changed to $\neg C \vee \neg D$. Notice that in this case the button [dc] (for "do case") will appear (see section 4.5) next to this new hypothesis. Similar transformations will apply on all other kinds of negated predicates: $\neg \forall x \cdot (P_x \Rightarrow Q_x), \neg \exists \cdot (P_x \wedge Q_x), \neg(A \vee B), \neg(A \Rightarrow B), \neg\neg P$.

A final logical simplification command is provided for a disjunctive *goal* of the form, say, $I \vee J$. It is called [rd] (for "remove disjunction"). When pressing that button situated in the *goal* area, the new hypothesis $\neg I$ is created in the *selected* field, and the *goal* becomes J.

4.8   Set-Theoretic Simplification Commands: [rm] [ri] [rn]

We now propose a number of set-theoretic simplification commands. Again, they are not indispensable for **pp** but sometimes convenient in an interactive proof.

ds fh	eh	he	$T1 = T2$
ds fh	mh		$P \Rightarrow Q$
ds fh	dc		$A \vee B$
ds fh	ph		$\forall x \blacksquare \cdot (R_x \Rightarrow S_x)$
ds fh	rx		$\exists x \cdot (T_x \wedge U_x)$
ds fh	rn		$\neg(C \wedge D)$
ds fh	rm		$E \in \{x \mid F_x \wedge G_x\}$
ds fh	ri		$S \subseteq T$
ds fh	rn		$X \neq$
ae ap	ct	ru	$\forall x \cdot (V_x \Rightarrow W_x)$
sh sg	it		
p0 p1	pb		
ah dc			

The first one, called [rm] (for "remove membership"), works on hypotheses or goals of the form $E \in \{x \mid F_x \wedge G_x\}$ as shown in the figure. Pressing that button results in the predicates F_E and G_E. They become either successive new goals (when [rm] is applied to the goal) or distinct new *selected* hypotheses (when [rm] is applied to an hypothesis).

Another button, called [ri] (for "remove inclusion"), works on hypotheses or goals of the form $S \subseteq T$ as shown in the figure. Pressing that button results in the the predicate $\forall x \cdot (x \in S \Rightarrow x \in T)$ replacing $S \subseteq T$. Such a predicate could be further handled by buttons [ph] (section 4.6) or [ru] (section 4.7).

The button [rn] (for "remove negation") can also be used on predicates of the form $X \neq$ as shown in the figure. When pressing that button, this predicate is replaced by $\exists x \cdot x \in X$, which can itself be further treated by buttons [se] (section 4.6) or [rx] (section 4.7).

4.9   Set-Theoretic Miscellaneous Commands: [eq] [ov]

The next two commands have proved to be quite useful. The first button, called [eq] (for "prove a set membership by an equality") appears next to an hypothesis of the form

$E \in S$ when the goal itself is of the form $F \in S$. By pressing that button, the new goal $E = F$ replaces $E \in S$. This button is then just a short-circuit: it saves attempting to prove the lemma $E = F$ with [ah] (section 4.5) and then applying [eh] on the resulting hypothesis (section 4.4).

The second button called [ov] (for "overriding") generates a proof by cases that is often encountered in set-theoretic statements. This button might be defined on an hypothesis or on the goal. It is present when a predicate P contains a sub-expression of the following form:

$$(f <\!\!+g)(E)$$

where f and g are two partial functions and E is an expression.

The overriding operator $<\!\!+$ is an infix operator taking (in general) two relations as arguments (here it takes two functions). The result of $f <\!\!+g$ in our case is exactly the function g extended with the function f outside the domain of g. So that its application to E is either $g(E)$ when E is in the domain of g or $f(E)$ when E is in the domain of f but not in that of g. The presence of such a sub-expression somewhere in an hypothesis or in the goal strongly suggests a *proof by cases*, where the two cases are $E \in \mathrm{dom}(g)$ (in which case the sub-expression is replaced by $g(E)$) and $E \in \mathrm{dom}(f) - \mathrm{dom}(g)$ (in which case the sub-expression is replaced by $f(E)$). This is exactly what happens when this button is pressed.

ds	fh	eh	he	$T1 = T2$
ds	fh	mh		$P \Rightarrow Q$
ds	fh	dc		$A \vee B$
ds	fh	ph		$\forall x \; \blacksquare \cdot (R_x \Rightarrow S_x)$
ds	fh	rx		$\exists x \cdot (T_x \wedge U_x)$
ds	fh	rn		$\neg (C \wedge D)$
ds	fh	rm		$E \in \{ x \mid F_x \wedge G_x \}$
ds	fh	ri		$S \subseteq T$
ds	fh	rn		$X \neq$
ds	fh	eq		$E \in S$
ds	fh	ov		$P((f <\!\!+g)(E))$
—	—	—	— — — —
ae	ap	ct		$F \in S$
—	—	—	— — — —
sh	sg	it		▮
p0	p1	pb		
ah	dc			

4.10 Beginner and Expert Modes, Online Help: [bg] [xp] hp]

The interface may function according to two distinct modes: either the *expert* mode (this is the default) or the *beginner* mode. While in expert mode, a [bg] button (for "beginner") allows one to switch to the other mode. Likewise in beginner mode, a similar button, called [xp] (for "expert"), is provided.

The difference between the two modes is quite significant. In expert mode, many buttons are "pressed" automatically by the prover itself: these buttons are essentially simplification buttons such as [rm], [ru], [rn] and so on. This is quite efficient but sometimes misleading for the user. He might not understand what is going on, in particular why the *goal* and the *selected* hypotheses have been modified in an unexpected way after pressing a certain button. When this is the case the user can backtrack (see section 4.12), press [bg] and resume the previous command.

ds fh eh	he	$T1 = T2$
ds fh mh		$P \Rightarrow Q$
ds fh dc		$A \vee B$
ds fh ph		$\forall x\, \blacksquare \cdot (\, R_x \Rightarrow S_x\,)$
ds fh rx		$\exists x \cdot (\, T_x \wedge U_x\,)$
ds fh rn		$\neg (C \wedge D)$
ds fh rm		$E \in \{x \mid F_x \wedge G_x\}$
ds fh ri		$S \subseteq T$
ds fh rn		$X \neq$
ds fh eq		$E \in S$
ds fh ov		$P((f \mathbin{<\!\!\!\!+} g)(E))$

| ae ap ct | | $F \in S$ |

sh sg it	hp	
p0 p1 pb	bg	
ah dc		

The prover will then not perform any automatic action "behind the curtain". Once he has understood what was done in expert mode by looking at the behavior in beginner mode, the user may switch back to the expert mode by pressing [xp].

Those buttons, which are normally "pressed" automatically by the prover while in expert mode, are just *highlighted* while in beginner mode, thus suggesting to the user that such buttons might be pressed. There exists a unique [hp] button (for "help"). After pressing that button, all other buttons when pressed do not do anything except producing a short explanation text for the corresponding command. In the mean time the [hp] button is highlighted to make the user aware that he has to press again that button in order to return to the normal mode of operation.

4.11   Representation of the Proof Tree: [zm] [mk]

The proof tree is represented in the Tree Window according to a number of principles which are as follows:

1. Each node is represented by a simplified sequent. In fact, we shall only present the *goal* part of a sequent. The reasons for this are simple:
   a) Usually the goal is not very large. Remember that goals are not conjunctive nor implicative, so that most of the time a goal is just a predicate defined by an equality, a set membership or a set inclusion. But we might have quantified predicates which are larger.
   b) The number of hypotheses (even for those in *selected*) could be quite large.
   c) The hypotheses are usually far less modified than the goal when one goes from one sequent to the next.
   d) The absence of the hypotheses in the Tree Window is compensated by their presence in the current sequent of the Sequent Window.
2. Each simplified sequent is given together with the full command that has been applied to it: that is, the command name and its parameters.
3. In first approximation, the tree is represented vertically, the offspring nodes of a node being slightly shifted to the right (like a Table of Contents)
4. However, this shift is only performed when the simplified " offspring sequent" is different from its simplified "parent sequent". The reason for this is that we want to see at the same level all the commands that have been performed in order to prove a certain goal.

5. Moreover when a simplified "offspring sequent" is the same as its simplified "parent sequent" the former is not written again. The reason for this is to avoid copying again and again the same goal in the proof tree.

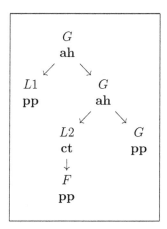
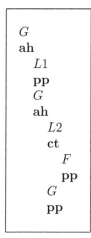
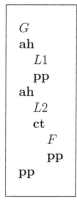

As an illustration of the previous principles, suppose that at some point in a proof, we have a certain goal G. In order to prove that goal we need two lemmas L1 and L2. The first one is proved directly by **pp**, whereas the second one is proved by contradiction and then **pp**. Once these two lemmas are proved, the proof of our original goal G follows immediately by **pp**. This results in the exact proof tree shown on the figure above on the left. Next to it, is its vertical representation, drawn without taking into account points 4 and 5 above. In the last diagram, you may find a vertical representation which takes these two points into account. In the proof tree on the left we can "see" the progress of the proof on G, namely lemma $L1$, lemma $L2$, and **pp**. But this vision is clearly lost in the corresponding vertical representation in the center. Whereas, this structure is clearly visible again on the right-hand side diagram. This is the reason why we have adopted this representation.

$$E \in \{x \mid P_x \wedge Q_x\}$$
rm
$$P_E$$
?
$$Q_E$$

When the application of a certain command results in several offspring sequents, we can see all of them in the Tree Window. We can also see which one is the current node: this is indicated by a "?". This is illustrated in the following example where our goal has the form $E \in \{x \mid P(x) \wedge Q(x)\}$. When applying [rm] (for "remove membership") the two goals P_E and Q_E are generated and the current goal is now P_E.

Two kinds of button are generated with each "line" in the Tree Window. At the beginning of a goal line, we have a button called [zm] (for "zoom/unzoom"). By pressing that button, the part of the proof tree having that goal at its top is hidden. Pressing [zm] again makes the sub-tree reappearing. While a part is hidden the [zm] button is highlighted. Here is an illustration of this mechanism. We have pressed [zm] twice: once for $L1$ and once for $L2$. This results in the tree shown in the right-hand side.

At the beginning of a command line, we have a button called [mk] (for "make an application of the command"). When pressing one of these button and then a second button of the same kind (the second button could be the same as the first one), this results in applying the series of commands situated between these two buttons. This is very convenient to repeat part of a proof.

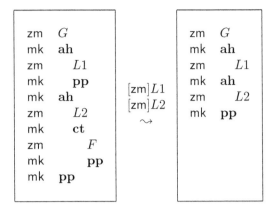

zm	G
mk	ah
zm	$L1$
mk	**pp**
mk	ah
zm	$L2$
mk	ct
zm	F
mk	**pp**
mk	**pp**

$$[zm]L1$$
$$[zm]L2$$
$\rightsquigarrow$

zm	G
mk	ah
zm	$L1$
mk	ah
zm	$L2$
mk	**pp**

4.12 Proof Navigation: [ba] [re] [op] [pt] [st] [qu]

We have several possibilities to navigate on a proof. The basic button is called [ba] (for "backtrack"). It allows one to backtrack one step when we figure out that we have taken a wrong decision. A second navigation button, called [re] (for "reset") is provided to reset a proof. Once it is pressed, the proof done so far is not lost however. In fact, before resetting, the proof tree has been saved and it is now called the "old proof tree". So that, in general, we have always two proof trees, the "current" one and the "old" one.

When pressing the button [op] (for "old proof tree"), the Tree Window splits and we can see at the same time the current proof tree (on top) and the old proof tree (at the bottom). For instance, after doing the proof shown on the Tree Window at the end of the previous section, and then pressing [re] followed by [op], the Tree Window looks the way it is presented in the previous figure. By pressing the button [pt] (for "proof tree"), we may reinstall the current proof tree alone on the Tree Window.

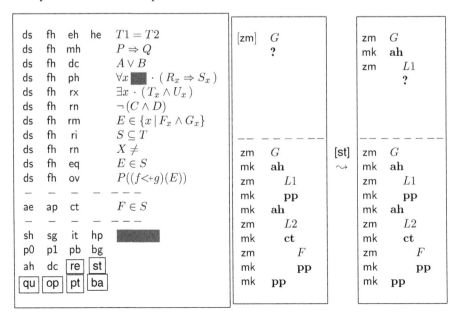

Once the [re] button has been pressed, it is possible to gradually resume the proof by pressing the button called [st] (for "one step") as shown in the figure: we do one step of the old proof tree within the new one. Another possibility in order to replay part of the old proof tree in the new one would be to use the [mk] buttons as explained in the previous section.

Finally, the button [qu] (for "quit") allows one to quit the proof. We can either quit and save the current proof tree or keep the previous proof tree. When we resume the proof in another session, then the previous proof tree automatically becomes the "old" proof tree.

4.13   Proof Refinement: [as] [r1] [r2]

The idea of a proof refinement is very important. In fact this is the way professional mathematicians usually work. The idea is very simple. If at some point in a proof we find a difficulty to prove a certain predicate P (it might be a lemma or any other goal), we would like to jump over it and consider for the time being that we have a proof for it. We then proceed with the main proof and then eventually figure out that this lemma P is what we needed. If this is the case, then we shall come back some time later to perform that part of the proof that was missing (for P) in the middle of the main proof. In doing so, we might find similar difficulties and use the same trick again, and so on.

ds	fh	eh	he	$T1 = T2$
ds	fh	mh		$P \Rightarrow Q$
ds	fh	dc		$A \vee B$
ds	fh	ph		$\forall x \; \blacksquare \; \cdot \; (R_x \Rightarrow S_x)$
ds	fh	rx		$\exists x \; \cdot \; (T_x \wedge U_x)$
ds	fh	rn		$\neg (C \wedge D)$
ds	fh	rm		$E \in \{x \mid F_x \wedge G_x\}$
ds	fh	ri		$S \subseteq T$
ds	fh	rn		$X \neq$
ds	fh	eq		$E \in S$
ds	fh	ov		$P((f \mathbin{<\!\!+} g)(E))$
—	—	—	— — — —	
ae	ap	ct		$F \in S$
—	—	—	— — — —	
sh	sg	it	hp	▬▬▬
p0	p1	pb	bg	
ah	dc	re	st	
qu	op	pt	ba	
r1	r2	as		

zm	G
mk	ah
zm	$L1$
mk	pp
mk	ah
zm	$L2$
zm	?
— — — — — — — —	
zm	G
mk	ah
zm	$L1$
mk	pp
mk	ah
zm	$L2$
zm $\Rightarrow$	as
mk	pp

In order to put this idea into practice, we introduce a "magic" command called [as] (for "assume"). By pressing that button the current goal is proved without any further work. Note that we can press several times [as] in the course of the same proof. If the proof eventually "succeeds" after that, we would like to resume it in order to prove the missing parts. For this, we press the button [r1] (for "refinement of the current proof tree"). When doing this, the Tree Window splits and the former proof (containing occurrences of [as]) becomes the "old" proof. The prover automatically replays the proof from the beginning to the first occurrence of [as]. At this point, it gives back the control to the user as shown in the figure. A little arrow "⇒" indicates where we are in the old proof tree as shown in the figure.

Once the missing part is proved (possibly thanks to some further [as] applications), the prover automatically performs that part of the old proof situated between the current occurrence of [as] in the old proof tree and the next one. It then gives back control to the user as explained, and so on (unless the end of the old proof is reached).

When reentering a proof which was left using the [qu] button (for "quit") with some pending occurrences of [as], we may first decide to restart the proof from scratch and then figure out later that it was a mistake after all. At this point, we may decide to restart our proof from the genuine "old" proof, which was in place when reentering the proof. Pressing the button [r1] then is not what we want to do. There exists for this a second refinement button called [r2] (for "refinement of the old proof tree"), which reinstalls the current proof within the initial old framework.

5   Discussion and Related Works

In this section, we first make precise the main principles which have guided us in the realization of this interface, then we shall briefly compare our work with similar efforts. One of the reasons why we have implemented this interface under **Emacs** is that we consider (with many others) that the making of an interactive proof is a sort of *specialized text editing*. In this context, **Emacs** clearly provides us with a number of features which are not very interesting to reinvent. The main principle that has guided us in the development of this interface is one of *economy*. We have tried to minimize some "gestures" as explained in what follows.

We first tried to *minimize the need for eye movement* of the user so that he can really concentrate on its main proving activity. In fact, we discovered that the obligation to frequently move eyes is a very disturbing activity for someone who is supposed to think. This is the reason why we have banned the use of menus which are very common in all sorts of interfaces. In our case, a menu is very disturbing because it hides for a moment the contents of the screen. It is also disturbing because you have to scan it in order to click on the command you want to launch. A consequence of this choice implies the permanent presence of buttons on the screen.

In order to *minimize the number of clicks* (another very frequent gesture), we have placed these buttons next to the part of the formal text to which they apply. This avoids to first select, say, a specific hypothesis and then apply a command to it. In fact, by its position on the window the button is automatically devoted to the corresponding hypothesis or to the goal. But as the number of buttons placed next to each hypothesis or the goal could then be quite large and most of the time useless, we have made the interface *dynamic-discovering which buttons are applicable* at each proof step. This has proved to be very efficient since it was discovered that *no more than four different buttons* can be used at a given moment on an hypothesis, among the fifteen different ones that could be applied.

To *minimize the moves of the right hand*, which we would like to stay almost permanently on the mouse, we have taken advantage of what is already provided by **Emacs**: the left click is used to point to a piece of text, the central click is used to move a pointed text to the editing field and also to launch a command. We have explicitly programmed the right mouse click to launch [sh] (for "searching hypotheses") so that this very frequent activity is performed in a very efficient way.

We have also managed to *minimize the moves of the mouse*. For example, when a command devoted to a specific hypothesis requires an extra text parameter, we do not need to move the text in question to the editing field: as a short circuit, it is sufficient, if the text fragment is already somewhere on the screen, to point to it with the mouse and then press the desired button. Another way to minimize the moves of the mouse is provided by the presence of specialized editing fields that are close to the quantified variables in a universal hypothesis or in an existential goal. These fields are thus closed to the corresponding buttons, namely either [ph] or [se].

As a result, it is *extremely rare to have to press any key* on the keyboard. As explained above, the right hand stays almost all the time on the mouse, it is not necessary to move it from the mouse to the keyboard and vice-versa. All such small optimizations may seem very superficial at first glance, but we think on the contrary that they are very important in that they allow the user not to be disturbed by many stupid clerical activities.

And last but not least, we want to *minimize the number of syntactic errors*. Our interface, by dynamically producing the buttons associated with a proper goal or hypothesis, guarantees that no button can be pressed wrongly. In fact the only error that may occur is the forgetting of some text parameters, in which case the corresponding button has a void action. For example, if you press [sh] (for "searching hypotheses") without pointing to a text pattern, no search is undertaken. The only visible error that may occur comes from providing a text parameter which is not syntactically correct. In this case, an error is reported.

Another general principles that we have followed in this project was to construct this interface around the concept of *proof*, not that of prover. In other words, we have always tried to discover the sort of features that would help a person doing a (manual) proof within a Sequent Calculus by applying some inference rules in backward mode. This has guided us in the development of the proposed organization with two windows (Sequent and Tree) which are directly connected to the corresponding proof practice as indicated in section 4.1.

As a matter of fact, a certain "proving style" has emerged from using this interface. It can be summarized by the following steps to be performed recurrently:

- Simplify goal and hypotheses: rd, ri, rm, rn, ru, rx, eh, he, ov, ae, ap[3].
- Decide for an "interesting" strategy: ct, fh, dc, mh, eq.
- Propose an "interesting" instantiation: ph, se.
- Invent an "interesting" lemma: ah.
- Decide to temporary postpone the proof of a certain goal: as.

---

[3] We remind the reader that in **Appendix 3** a table contains a summary of the various commands.

- Refine the proof: r1, r2.
- Select "interesting" hypotheses: sh, sg, sl.
- Launch automatic procedures: p0, p1, pb.

Notice that, among these points, the first one (simplification) is partly performed automatically while in expert mode, whereas the ones qualified to be "interesting" require some invention on the part of the user. Note that this "style" covers 28 commands among the 42 we have presented. In fact, the 14 remaining ones (a few more in the real interface) are used at any moment to show more or less of each window or to navigate within the proof.

Our approach could not be compared with some far more ambitious generic interface project such as *Proof General* [4]. Clearly our project is far less "general". This is coherent with what we have said in the introduction about our prover which is also far less general than those to which *Proof General* is applied (Coq [5], Phox [13], LEGO [3], Isabelle [12], etc.). It seems to us that *Proof General* is directed towards *certain kinds of proof assistants* (not proofs), which, in spite of some technical differences between them, are, in a sense, quite close in their appearance and mode of interaction (scripts). What we have in common with *Proof General* however is the fact that our interface (also written under **Emacs**) does not deal with the proof, which remains the realm of the original prover.

Another comparison could be made with the technique of *Proof by Pointing* [14]. Our dynamic handling of buttons situated next to their domain of application (hypothesis, goal) has, in a sense, a similar effect as that of "proof by pointing". Our technique of *Proof by Clicking*, however, can associate several possibilities dedicated to the same piece of formal text. The button is also clearly showing to the user the action which he is going to perform.

A final interesting comparison can be done with the KIV proof assistant [9], which also uses a proof tree window as well as a sequent window. It is not clear however from the documentation at our disposal whether the proof tree could be refined as we have explained in section 4.13 above.

6   Conclusion

In this paper, we have presented an interface to be used with **Atelier B** in order to perform formal proofs of statements written within Set Theory. This interface has been used to teach logic and formal proof to students with a limited background in this area. The result of this experiment was extremely encouraging: students were very quickly acquainted to the tool and able to perform non-trivial proofs in a short time. It seems to us that this kind of approach where you just creatively prepare the work for a rather powerful prover able to perform most of the very mechanical work is an interesting one. On the following web page, you can see more about this interface: www.loria.fr/~cansell/cnp

Acknowledgements. We would like to thank M. Sintzoff for very valuable advice concerning this work, in particular that part devoted to the proof tree. Many thanks also to S. Mertz, P. Gibson, and L. Voisin for their very careful reading of various drafts of this text.

References

1. J.-R. Abrial, D. Cansell, and G. Lafitte. "Higher-Order" Mathematics in B. In *ZB'2002 – Formal Specification and Development in Z and B*, number LNCS 2272 in Lecture Notes in Computer Science, pages 370–393, 2002.
2. J.R. Abrial. *The B Book – Assigning Programs to Meanings*. Cambridge University Press, 1996. ISBN 0-521-49619-5.
3. D. Aspinall. *LEGO Manual version 1.3.1*. Edimburgh University, Edimburgh (UK), 1998. www.lama.dcs.ed.ac.uk/home/lego.
4. D. Aspinall. Proof general – a generic tool for proof development. In S. Graf and M. Schwartzbach, editors, *Proceedings of the 6th International Conference on Tools and Algorithms for the Construction and Analysis of Systems (TACAS 2000)*, number LNCS 1785 in Lecture Notes in Computer Science. Springer, March 2000.
5. B. Barras, S. Boutin, C. Cornes, J. Courant, Y. Coscoy, D. Delahaye, D. de Rauglaudre, J.C. Filliâtre, E. Giménez, H. Herbelin, G. Huet, H. Laulhère, P. Loiseleur, C. Muñoz, C. Murthy, C. Parent, C. Paulin, A. Saïbi, and B. Werner. *The Coq Proof Assistant Reference Manual – Version V6.3*, July 1999.
6. ClearSy, Aix-en-Provence (F).*Atelier B, Version 3.6*, 2001. www.atelierb.societe.com.
7. M. Fitting. *First-order logic and automated theorem proving (2nd ed.)*. Springer-Verlag New York, Inc., 1996.
8. M.J.C Gordon. Hol : A proof generating system for higher-order logic. In G. Birtwistle and P. A. Subrahmanyam, editors, *VLSI Specification, Verification and Synthesis*, pages 73–128, 1988.
9. D. Hutter, B.Langenstein, C.Sengler, J.H. Siekmann, and W. Stephan. Deduction in the verification support environment (vse). In *Proceedings, International Symposium of Formal Methods Europe (FME)*, 1996. Springer-Verlag LNCS 1051.
10. J.A. Kalman. *Automated reasoning with Otter*. Rinton Press, 2001.
11. S. Owre, N. Shankar, and J. M. Rushby. The PVS specification language. Technical report, SRI International, June 14, 1993 1993.
12. L. Paulson. *Isabelle A Generic Theorem Prover*, volume 828 of Lecture Notes in Computer Science. Springer-Verlag, 1994.
13. C. Raffalli. *The Phox proof assistant version 0.8*. Université de savoie, Chambéry (F), 2002.
14. G. Kahn Y. Bertot and L. Théry. Proof by Pointing. In *Theoretical Aspects of Computer Software*, April 1994. Springer-Verlag LNCS 789.

APPENDIX 1: A Sample of Set-Theoretic Statements Proven Automatically by pp

Elementary Set Theory:
$$a \times b \subseteq c \times d \,\wedge\, a \neq \,\wedge\, b \neq \,\Rightarrow\, a \subseteq c \,\wedge\, b \subseteq d$$
Generalized Set Operations:
$$s \in \mathbb{P}(\mathbb{P}(S)) \,\wedge\, t \in \mathbb{P}(\mathbb{P}(T)) \,\Rightarrow\, \bigcup_{x \in s} x \,\cap\, \bigcup_{x \in t} x \,=\, \bigcup_{(x,y)\,\in\, s \times t} x \cap y$$
Operations on Relations:
$$p \in s \leftrightarrow t \,\wedge\, q \in t \leftrightarrow u \,\wedge\, r \in u \leftrightarrow v \,\Rightarrow\, ((p;q);r) \,=\, (p;(q;r))$$
$$r \in s \leftrightarrow t \,\wedge\, a \subseteq s \,\wedge\, b \subseteq t \,\Rightarrow\, r[a] \subseteq b \leftrightarrow a \subseteq r^{-1}[\overline{b}]$$
Operations on Functions:
$$f \in s \to t \,\wedge\, b \subseteq t \,\Rightarrow\, f^{-1}[\overline{b}] \,=\, \overline{f^{-1}[b]}$$
$$f \in s \twoheadrightarrow t \,\wedge\, b \subseteq t \,\Rightarrow\, f[f^{-1}[b]] \,\subseteq\, b$$

Injections and Surjections:
$$f \in b \twoheadrightarrow c \wedge r \in a \leftrightarrow b \wedge s \in a \leftrightarrow b \wedge (r;f) = (s;f) \Rightarrow r = s$$
$$f \in a \rightarrowtail b \wedge \wedge r \in b \leftrightarrow c \wedge s \in b \leftrightarrow c \wedge (f;r) = (f;s) \Rightarrow r = s$$
Equivalence Relations:
$$f \in s \rightarrow t \wedge r = (f;f^{-1}) \Rightarrow \mathrm{id}(s) \subseteq r \wedge r = r^{-1} \wedge (r;r) \subseteq r$$

APPENDIX 2: A Higher Order Statement Proven Interactively

We first give the definition of the set of all *filters* that can be built on a set S:

$$
\begin{aligned}
filter = \{\, f \mid f \in \ & \mathbb{P}(\mathbb{P}(S)) \quad \wedge \\
& \forall (A,B) \cdot (A \in f \wedge B \subseteq S \wedge A \subseteq B \Rightarrow B \in f) \quad \wedge \\
& \forall (A,B) \cdot (A \in f \wedge B \in f \Rightarrow A \cap B \in f) \quad \wedge \\
& S \in f \quad \wedge \\
& \emptyset \notin f \,\}
\end{aligned}
$$

This is followed by the definition of the set of all *ultra-filters*:

$$ultraf = \{\, f \mid f \in filter \wedge \forall g \cdot (g \in filter \wedge f \subseteq g \Rightarrow f = g) \,\}$$

The main very classical completeness theorem that we want to prove is the following:

$$U \in ultraf \wedge C \subseteq S \Rightarrow C \in U \vee \overline{C} \in U$$

where $\overline{C}$ is a shorthand for $S - C$. For this, we first prove the following lemma:

$$U \in ultraf \wedge C \subseteq S \wedge C \notin U \Rightarrow U = \{\, X \mid X \subseteq S \wedge C \cup X \in U \,\}$$

APPENDIX 3: Summary of Commands

ae	Abstract expression	4.4		p1	Apply **pp** on extended conclusion	4.3
ah	Add hypothesis (lemma)	4.5		pb	Apply **pb** on sequent	4.3
ap	Abstract predicate	4.4		ph	Instantiate universal hypothesis	4.6
as	Assume without proof	4.13		pt	Show current proof tree	4.12
ba	Backtrack	4.11		qu	Quit	4.12
bg	Switch to beginner mode	4.10		r1	Refine current proof	4.13
ct	Prove by contradiction	4.5		r2	Refine old proof	4.13
dc	Prove by cases	4.5		rd	Remove disjunction	4.7
dl	Delete hypothesis from *cached*	4.2		re	Reset proof	4.12
ds	Deselect hypothesis from *selected*	4.2		ri	Remove inclusion	4.8
eh	Apply equality (left to right)	4.4		rm	Remove membership	4.8
eq	Try set equality	4.9		rn	Remove negation	4.7
fh	Prove false hypothesis	4.5		ru	Remove universal quantification	4.7
he	Apply equality (right to left)	4.4		rx	Remove existential quantification	4.7
hp	Help	4.10		se	Instantiate existential goal	4.6
it	Interruption	4.3		sh	Search hypotheses in *hidden*	4.2
mh	Modus ponens on hypothesis	4.5		sg	Search hypotheses in *searched*	4.2
mk	Perform a series of commands	4.11		sl	Select hypothesis from *searched*	4.2
op	Show old proof tree	4.12		st	Do one step of old proof	4.11
ov	Treat overriding (by cases)	4.9		xp	Switch to expert mode	4.10
p0	Apply **pp** on conclusion	4.3		zm	Zoom/unzoom on proof tree	4.11

Formal Specification and Verification of ARM6

Anthony Fox

University of Cambridge

Abstract. This paper gives an overview of progress made on the formal specification and verification of the ARM6 *micro-architecture* using the HOL proof system. The ARM6 is a commercial processor design prevalent in mobile and embedded systems – it features a 3-stage pipeline with a multi-cycle execute stage, six operating modes and a rich 32-bit RISC instruction set. This paper describes some of the difficulties encountered when working with a full blown instruction set architecture that has not been designed with verification in mind.

1 Introduction

This paper describes work carried out at Cambridge on the EPSRC funded project 'Formal Specification and Verification of ARM6' (GR/N13135/01). An overview of progress is presented: from earlier work on correctness models (carried out at Swansea), through to the formal verification carried out using HOL. The project has been run in collaboration with a group at Leeds, which was headed by Graham Birtwistle. The Leeds work has focused on the formal specification and simulation of ARM designs using ML.

It is acknowledged that the ARM6 is a comparatively old processor design (early 1990s) and it lacks some of the features of contemporary desktop processor designs – for example, it does not have a superscalar pipeline. However, it is a commercial processor and it has been faithfully modelled at the level of the micro-architecture. Furthermore, many processors used in the mobile and embedded (low-power) markets are only moderately more complicated. One of the main objectives of the project has been to explore the difficulties encountered when one tries to avoid making simplifications and assumptions with respect to the target architecture/processor i.e. when working with designs that were developed without verification in mind. The HOL 4 proof system has been used throughout (`hol.sf.net`). I would like to acknowledge the helpful support of Mike Gordon on this project and in writing this paper.

Several mechanical verifications of complete processors were undertaken during the 1980s and early 1990s. Examples include TAMARACK [16], SECD [11], the partial verification of Viper [6], Hunt's FM8501 and FM9001 [13,14], and Windley [25]. All these processors were simple uniprocessor fetch-decode-execute engines specifically designed for formal verification. Following this work, Miller and Srivas verified the implementation of some of the instructions of a simple real processor called AAMP5 [20]. Complex commercial designs have also

D. Basin and B. Wolff (Eds.): TPHOLs 2003, LNCS 2758, pp. 25–40, 2003.

specified, simulated and verified using ACL2; for example [5,17]. Significant verification work has also been undertaken on specific components: caches, ALUs, floating-point units.

Processors became much more complex from the later 1980s due to the addition of complex multi-stage pipelines, out-of-order execution and coprocessors. Processor designs like the Alpha and Pentium were considered too complex for *complete* formal verification and the introduction of multiple pipelines made their specifications that much harder. Recently progress has been made in verifying academic designs based around Tomasulo's algorithm [24], which is widely used in contemporary superscalar microprocessors; see [18,15,3,21].

2   Correctness

The correctness of a processor's micro-architecture is established with respect to an instruction set architecture (ISA). Examples of architecture families include ARM, SPARC, MIPS, POWERPC and x86. An architecture's instruction set may be extended with new generations of processors but the semantics of the core instructions remains fixed. Any differences in compatibility between processors (whether intended or accidental) must be accounted for when documenting the ISA and in developing compilers. The *micro-architecture* model represents the top level behaviour of a processor's design. In the case of the ARM6, the processor's data path and control logic have been modelled in a cycle accurate manner: it is a 3-stage pipelined design, with fetch, decode and execute stages. To maintain backwards compatibility it is important that new generations of micro-architectures preserve the semantics of existing machine code.

Researchers have used a variety of different correctness models in the verification of microprocessor designs. A framework for categorising correctness statements, as used in the verification of *pipelined* processors, is presented in [1]. Most of the correctness statements are expressed in the form of a commuting diagram, although property-oriented approaches – in which the formal processor model is shown to imply the abstract architecture specification – are an alternative [23]. One way in which approaches differ is in how they account for the temporal properties of pipelined designs i.e. in relating the state components of the pipeline (which processes more than one instruction at a time) with those of a non-pipelined architecture (where instructions are executed one by one). Tahar and Kumar [23] adopt a flexible approach and use Melham style temporal abstractions [19]. A more common approach is to incorporate incremental flushing into the correctness model [15], but this gives a weaker definition of correctness. This was not employed with the AAMP5; they used a temporally skewed data abstraction: "Typically, [in data abstraction] the values for all but the program counter must be obtained from the future state.", [20]. This complicated data abstraction is partly a consequence of their choice of *visible state* (invariant) predicate, which determines the times at which correctness holds.

Data and temporal abstraction maps are used in our correctness statements and these can account for the pipelined behaviour in a much simpler manner.

The data abstraction offsets the pipeline's *program counter* in order to give the address of the instruction being *executed*.[1] The temporal abstraction is used to explicitly identify the times at which the execute stage begins, thus skipping over states in which instruction execution is not complete. One of the advantages of this approach is that our correctness model is strong and generic, and the abstractions are intuitive. The correctness model is not specific to pipelined designs and the abstraction maps can be readily composed when considering more then two levels of abstraction.

3   Approach

An algebraic framework for carrying out processor verifications [12,7] was used as the basis for the ARM6 verification. Systems are modelled with *state functions*: these are functions of the form $F : T \times A \rightarrow A$, where $T = \{0, 1, \dots\}$ is an infinite set of clock cycles and A is a state space (a non-empty set of states). The state of the system at time $t \in T$ from pre-initial[2] state $a \in A$ is $F(t, a)$. A state function is an *iterated map* if, and only if, successive states are given by a *next state* function. Initial states are specified with an initialisation function and this enables specifications to be executed by evaluating the iterated map state function. Iterated maps are primitive recursive functions and they give an operational semantics for the processor's instructions set architecture and micro-architecture. By relating the clocks and state spaces of two state functions (using abstraction maps), one can give a formal and abstract definition of *correctness* that is applicable to a wide range of systems.

It was a straightforward task to transpose this work into higher order logic [8]. Using the HOL system the approach is formalised in an abstract setting, with the natural numbers **num** representing T and a type variable representing the state space. When modelling hardware the state space will invariably be finite but this is not a requirement.

When it comes to verifying correctness, it is advantageous to work with restricted classes of iterated maps and abstraction maps. Our approach encourages the use of *time-consistent* state functions and *uniform* temporal abstractions. Time-consistency and uniformity are defined in HOL and are used as the basis for a *one-step* theorem. This theorem reformulates correctness statements, eliminating the need to carry out an explicit induction over time.

The strength of an initialisation function (number of initial states) determines whether or not a state function is time-consistent. In this context, the rôle of the initialisation function can be likened to that of an invariant and it is closely related to an invariant's characteristic function. For example, if $I \subseteq A$ is an invariant for state space A and $f_I : A \rightarrow \mathbf{B}$ is the characteristic function for I

---

[1] Without this offset the program counter is the address of the instruction being *fetched* which, in pipelined designs, runs ahead of the address of the instruction being executed.

[2] The state $F(0, a)$ is the initial state for the pre-initial state a. All states can be pre-initial but not all states can be initial i.e. not all states can occur at time zero.

(i.e. $f_I(a)$ if, and only if, $a \in I$) then the initialisation function $init : A \to A$ should satisfy:

$$init(a) = \begin{cases} a, & \text{if } f_I(a), \\ x_a, & \text{otherwise.} \end{cases}$$

where $x_a \in I$ can be freely chosen. The invariance condition captured by the initialisation function is only required to hold at times given by a temporal abstraction map. For a more detailed account the reader is referred to [7,8].

4   The Instruction Set Architecture

Instruction set architectures lend themselves well to functional specification with iterated maps. At the *programmer's model* level, the state space of the architecture consists of a main memory and a set of registers. On each cycle, a program counter register gives the address of the instruction (in memory) to be executed. This instruction is decoded by the next state function and the main memory and/or registers are modified in accordance with the type of the instruction.

ARM is 32-bit RISC architecture.[3] The ARM architecture provides a mechanism for extending the instruction set with the use of coprocessors. For example, a system coprocessor may be used to control on-chip functions such as cache and memory management. Floating-point coprocessors are also available. Although the ARM6 supports coprocessor instructions, this functionality has not yet been modelled in HOL. There are seven types of exceptions and two (software interrupts and undefined instructions) have been covered to date. The other exceptions (resets, prefetch aborts, data aborts, and normal and fast interrupts) require one to consider state functions with input; see [7].

There are many areas of the ARM programmer's model where behaviour is allowed to vary from processor to processor. For example, the program counter behaviour of a 3-stage pipeline may differ with that of a 5-stage implementation. To avoid *unpredictable* results, programmer's are encouraged to write code in accordance with a set of guidelines. Most instructions have special cases where behaviour is unpredictable – for example, storing the program counter to memory should be avoided. In some cases the legitimacy of an instruction is dependent on the current *operating mode* of the processor.[4] Therefore, it is incumbent on the programmer to ensure that certain run-time conditions are not violated. Another significant example of processor dependent behaviour is the execution of self modifying code.[5] If a program modifies the memory in such a way as to invalidate fetched and decoded instructions then the ARM6 does not detect this

---

[3] Later ARM designs simultaneously support 16-bit (Thumb) instructions. A load-store RISC architecture only supports simple addressing modes (e.g. memory indirect mode is not supported) and operations are performed only on registers.

[4] For example, one should not try to read a saved program status register when one is in user mode.

[5] The ARM6 implements a 'von Neumann' style architecture i.e. program and data memories are not separated.

and flush the pipeline. This means that the ARM6 will execute an instruction even though it is no longer in memory.

There are numerous versions of the ARM architecture[6] and these differ in the instructions supported (e.g. Thumb), level of backward compatibility (e.g. 26-bit memory addressing) and stipulations about predictable behaviour. Processors that implement the same version of the architecture should be identical in all areas that are deemed predictable. For the purposes of the ARM6 project, the unpredictable parts of the ISA model were tailored to conform with ARM6 behaviour. This works well in most cases – for example, when specifying the results of reading and writing the program counter. This approach has the advantage that one can freely execute machine code at the ISA level, which would be less straightforward if one were working with a property-oriented, non-deterministic or partial specification. However, there may be scope for employing these methods in relating bespoke ISA specifications produced for different processor designs. Specialising the ISA does not resolve the problem of self modifying code because the processor implementation has hidden state components i.e. the state of the pipeline. Approaches to this are discussed in Sect. 5.

4.1   The HOL Specification

The State Space. One of the first tasks in modelling the ARM architecture was to represent the state space of the programmer's model. The main memory is a 32-bit addressable array of bytes. There are thirty one general purpose register which are organised into overlapping banks.[7] There is a current program status register (CPSR) and five saved program status registers. All registers are 32-bits wide and so a suitable model of bit-vectors is required.

When the project began at Cambridge (October 2000) there existed a HOL word theory developed by Wai Wong [26]. However, because HOL does not directly support predicate subtypes this theory did not provide a good means of modelling words of a fixed length i.e. 32-bit words. One of the by-products of this project has been the development of new HOL theory for fixed length words. Wong's theory uses lists as the underlying data type and it provided support for multiple number bases. In contrast, the new theory constructs an equivalence type over the natural numbers (John Harrison's equivalence type package is used to achieve this) and it only supports binary words. An executable `mkword.exe` generates the necessary files – for example, `mkword.exe 32` generates the files for `word32Theory` and `word32Lib`. This has been implemented using an ML *functor*. Some advantages of this approach are:

– HOL terms can be free of word length predicates. There is a concrete type for each length of binary word.

---

[6] Versions of the ARM architecture include: 1, 2, 2a, 3, 3G, 3M, 4, 4T, 5T and 6TEJ.
[7] There is one bank for each operating mode and sixteen general purpose registers (numbered zero to fifteen) are accessible at any one time. Register fifteen is the program counter.

– Ground terms can be evaluated efficiently and this enables specifications to
  be executed and tested.
– One can model a variety of machine operations at a high level of abstraction.
  This includes the ARM arithmetic, logical, and shift operations; as well as
  the bit-field manipulations that are present in the control logic.
– Many theorems about machine operations are readily derived – these include
  commutative ring properties for the arithmetic operations and boolean algebra properties for the logical operations.

The type definition for the ARM state space has been refined a few times.
Both the memory and register banks can be considered as maps from an ad-
dress/name space to a content type, with read and write operations providing
a suitable interface. The precise definition of the state space and associated
primitive operations has subtle implications on the efficiency of term evaluation,
compactness of the specification and the ease of verification. Although a natural type for the main memory is word32→word8 there are clear advantages to
working with word30→word32; since most memory accesses are for 32-bit words
and not bytes. Operating modes complicate the register bank state space and
this also adds an overhead to the verification effort.

The Next State Function. The official ARM reference manual [22] provides a
meticulous and verbose description of the instruction set, with separate entries
for each individual instruction and their main variants. Dominic Pajak's ML
specification (done at Leeds) was used as the initial basis for the HOL specification. However, the HOL specification differs in that instructions are specified
by instruction class, see Table 1.

Table 1. The ARM Instruction Classes.

Class	Instructions
Branch and Branch with Link	B, BL
Data Processing	ADD, ADC, SUB, SBC, RSB, RSC, CMP, CMN, AND, ORR, EOR, MOV, MVN, BIC, TST, TEQ
Multiply and Multiply Accumulate	MUL, MLA
PSR Transfer	MRS, MSR
Single Data Transfer	LDR, STR
Block Data Transfer	LDM, STM
Single Data Swap	SWP
Software Interrupt and Exceptions	SWI

By grouping instructions into classes, the specification is concise and compact – approximately eighty definitions (700 lines of code). During verification
one can case split on the instruction class rather than on a specific instruction

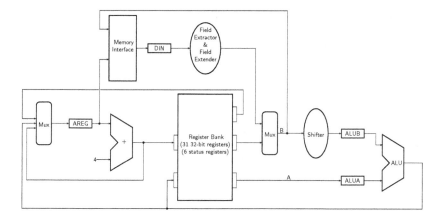

Fig. 1. The ARM6 Data Path.

instance. For each instruction class there is a decoding and next state function. The decoding function splits the 32-bit instruction code into options and parameter fields – these give rise to sub-cases in the verification. All instructions are conditionally executed[8] and an attempt to execute an undefined instruction will cause an exception to be raised. This is resolved by the main next state function, which selects the appropriate next state function by instruction class. A full account of the HOL specification of the instruction set is presented in [9].

5 The Micro-Architecture

The ARM6 is split into data path and control components. The control component contains the instruction decoder and control logic. Figure 1 shows a simplified view of the ARM6 data path. The main functional blocks are:

– The multi-port register bank
– The memory interface
– The address register and address incrementer
– The field extractor/extender
– The barrel shifter
– The Arithmetic Logic Unit (ALU)

There are three main internal buses:

– The A bus (first instruction operand)
– The B bus (second instruction operand and read/write memory data)
– The ALU bus

---

[8] Each instruction can be suffixed by one of sixteen condition mnemonics. For example, an **ADDEQ** instruction will only execute if the Z bit of the CPSR is set. The always condition mnemonic **AL** is optional and the never condition **NV** should not be used.

Consider the following fragment of ARM code:

```
        MOV     r0, #15
        MVN     r1, r0, LSL #16
        EOR     r2, r0, r1
        B       label
        NOP
        NOP
label:  ADDS    r1, r1, r2
        BICHI   r3, r1, r2, ROR r0
        STRB    r3, [r1], r0, ASR #4
```

The pipelined execution of this code is illustrated in Fig. 2. The y-axis shows the order in which the instructions enter the pipeline (through an instruction fetch), and the x-axis enumerates machine clock cycles. The pipeline is full at clock cycle zero i.e. the MOV instructions has been fetched and decoded, and the MVN instruction has been fetched. The execution is shown up until after the completion of the ADDS instruction. With the exception of the branch, each instruction takes a single cycle to execute. The branch takes three cycles to execute: the branch destination is computed on the first execute cycle and the other two cycles are needed to refill the pipeline. Data processing instructions normally take one cycle to execute but shifting by a register value takes an extra cycle and three cycles are needed if the destination register is the program counter. All memory access instructions require more than one cycle to execute but the block data transfer instructions read/write one register per cycle.

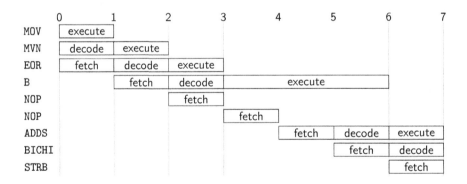

Fig. 2. Pipelined instruction execution.

When verifying the micro-architecture, one must take into account the multi-cycle timing of instructions. The vertical lines in Fig. 2 indicate the points at which the state at micro-architecture level corresponds with an ISA level state after data abstraction. These lines mark the completion of one execute stage and the start of another. Therefore, it is important to know how long each instruction takes to execute. The program counter can be treated just like any other register and so there are many ways in which a branch can be taken, adding an extra two cycles. Block data transfer instructions can take up to twenty cycles to execute.

5.1 The HOL Specification

The HOL specification of the ARM6 micro-architecture was based on specifications produced by Daniel Schostak (Leeds, now at ARM Ltd.) and these were in turn based on ARM6 data sheets supplied by ARM themselves. Schostak's specification is phase accurate (each clock cycle is split into two phases) and gives a high-fidelity description of the ARM6 (covering coprocessor instructions and all exceptions) — he has used it as the basis for an ML simulator. The HOL specification is slightly more abstract (although it is still cycle accurate) and the multiply instruction class has not been modelled. Multiplication is implemented in a CISC style using a modified Booth's algorithm: the data path is used to carry out additions, subtractions and shifts. In most modern processors the ALU can perform multiplication directly and so the multiplication algorithm does not usually encroach upon the main control logic of the processor. Such an implementation would be readily verifiable at the micro-architecture level.

The micro-architecture specification consists of approximately fifty definitions and makes use of a number of definition made at the ISA level; the script file is similar in size to the ISA specification.

The State Space. The state space is split into three main components: memory, data path and control. The memory is identical to the ISA memory. The data path (Fig. 1) contains the (general and program status) register banks together with four 32-bit registers:

- The data input (DIN)
- The address register (AREG)
- The ALU inputs (ALUA and ALUB)

The control contains the pipeline state (three 32-bit registers – pipea, pipeb and the instruction register ireg – each with validity bits) together with an assortment of other latches. In particular, the control contains latches for the next instruction class nxtic and the next instruction sequence nxtis. The next instruction class is computed at the decode stage and it is represented by an enumerated type iclass: there are values for each of the classes from Table 1 (multiplies have been excluded) together with three more – reg_shift for data processing instructions with a register shift amount, unexec for unexecuted instructions, and undef for undefined instructions. The next instruction sequence is represented by an enumerated type with values t3, t4, t5, t6, tn and tm. The instruction sequence is normally incremented during multi-cycle instruction execution. For example, data swap instructions take four cycles to execute and so nxtis will go from t3 to t6 inclusive. The values tn and tm are used to implement block data transfers.

The Next State Function. The next state function at the micro-architecture level is constructed using next state functions for components of the data path and control logic. For example, there is a next state function AREG for the address register; this takes:

- The instruction class (ic)
- The instruction sequence (is)
- The instruction register (ireg)
- The exception vector (aregn, which is part of the control state space)
- Block data transfer status components pencz and oorp.
- The ALU bus, program counter bus and incrementer bus values

The function AREG gives the next value for the areg latch and it implements the leftmost multiplexer shown in Fig. 1.

The main next state function can be decomposed into two functions: one for the first clock phase and the other for the second. The field extractor/extender and barrel shifter both operate in the first phase. By the end of the first phase the values for the ALU registers (ALUA and ALUB) are ready. In the second phase the ALU operates, instruction decode occurs and results are stored.

The Initialisation Function. The micro-architecture state function is defined using an initialisation function. The initialisation function forces the processor to be in a valid state at cycle zero. There must be at least one initial state for each state at the ISA level. Non-initial states are either completely erroneous (the processor should never exhibit such states) or states that the machine passes through in the course of instruction execution. For example, a state in which nxtic = data_proc and nxtis = t5 is erroneous because data processing instructions only take one or two cycles to execute.[9] The states corresponding with cycles four and five in Fig. 2 would be considered intermediate. While these states *could* be considered initial – with the temporal abstraction defined accordingly – to do so would add unnecessary complexity.[10] The initialisation function takes an arbitrary state and sets nxtis to be t3; the rest of the control latches (including the pipeline state) are set in accordance with the pipeline being full as a function of the current program counter value. In Fig. 2 the clock cycles on which initial states arise are marked with vertical lines – these are states at the juncture of execution blocks.

6 Testing the Specifications

The ARM specifications can be executed in HOL both symbolically or with ground (variable free) terms. This means that one can test the specifications by running small programs. HOL's call-by-value conversion CBV_CONV provides an efficient way to execute functional specifications [2]. Testing in this manner provides a vital sanity check prior to attempting a verification. When compared with ACL2 [17], the HOL system is not highly optimised for simulation but the performance is perfectly adequate for small scale testing.

---

[9] If the destination register is the program counter then three or four cycles are needed but while the pipeline refills nxtis is not incremented.

[10] In particular, more cases would have to be considered during verification.

At the ISA level it is important that the specification is able to execute ARM code in a manner consistent with the ARM reference [22]. A handful of bugs have arisen at this level and the absolute fidelity of the ISA specification cannot be guaranteed. However, any lingering bugs are unlikely to be of great significance. The micro-architecture specification is complex and far removed from the ISA description. Here it is important to exercise the control logic, both to ensure that code is being executed correctly and to get to grips with the workings of the design. This is important when designs are not developed by the same individuals that are carrying out formal verifications.

Consider, for example, the program from Sect. 5. The following theorem is generated by executing the ISA specification for five clock cycles – one instruction is executed on each cycle.

```
⊢ STATE_ARM 5 (ARM MEMORY (REG_WRITE ZM usr 15 0x20) RESET_PSR) =
    ARM MEMORY (SUBST (SUBST (SUBST (SUBST ZM (r0,0xF)) (r1,0xFFE1FFEF))
      (r2,0xFFF0FFF0)) (r15,0x3C)) (SUBST ZM (CPSR,0xA0000010))
```

HOL's pretty-printer has been used to display 32-bit words in hexadecimal. The function STATE_ARM is the ISA state function and ARM is the type constructor for the state space. The memory MEMORY is defined such that the program is located at address 0x20.[11] An effective way to define the contents of the memory (which contains machine code) is to make use of an ARM assembler, such as the portable GNU assembler as. The program counter is set to address 0x20 and all other registers have value zero (the zero map ZM is $\lambda x.0x0$). The program status register bank RESET_PSR has the CPSR set to user mode with all the NZCV flags clear; all the saved status registers have a zero value.

State changes are defined in terms of the substitution map:

$$\vdash_{def} \text{SUBST m (a,w) b} = (\text{if a = b then w else m b})$$

Theorems about SUBST are added to the *computation set* and this ensures that multiple substitution are ordered and redundancy is eliminated.

The ARM6 executes the same five instructions in seven cycles, therefore the equivalent machine state is defined by the following theorem.

```
⊢ STATE_ARM6 7 (ARM6 MEMORY
        (DP (REG_WRITE ZM usr 15 0x28) RESET_PSR areg din alua alub)
        (CTRL pipea pipeaval pipeb pipebval ireg iregval ... oareg)) =
    ARM6 MEMORY
        (DP (SUBST (SUBST (SUBST (SUBST ZM (r0,0xF)) (r1,0xFFE1FFEF))
          (r2,0xFFF0FFF0)) (r15,0x44)) (SUBST ZM (CPSR,0xA0000010))
          0x44 0x81C13072 0xFFF0FFFF 0xFFF0FFF0)
        (CTRL 0xE6C13242 T 0xE6C13242 T 0x81C13072 T 0x40 0x40 F T T
          reg_shift t3 2 T F sctrlreg 0x10 0)
```

The state space type constructor is ARM6, and DP and CTRL are the data path and control type constructors respectively. The state passed to the ARM6 state

---

[11] Below this address resides stub exception handling code. The rest of the memory contains zero words.

function STATE_ARM6 is a pre-initial state.[12] The initial state is given at clock cycle zero, which is when the initialisation function is applied and the pipeline is filled with respect to the program counter value. After executing five instructions: the pipeline is full, the next instruction class nxtic has value reg_shift (the ADDS instruction has been decoded) and the next instruction sequence is t3. That is to say, the resulting machine state is a valid initial state. The ARM6 program counter, both before and after execution, is eight bytes (two instructions) ahead of the ISA program counter. Recall that the data abstraction subtracts eight from the ARM6 program counter value.

7   Formal Verification

Correctness is defined by the following predicate.

$$\vdash_{def} \text{CORRECT spec impl imm abs} =$$
$$\text{IMMERSION imm} \wedge \text{DATA\_ABSTRACTION abs (spec 0) (impl 0)} \wedge$$
$$\forall t\ a.\ \text{spec t (abs a)} = \text{abs (impl (imm a t) a)}$$

The immersion predicate ensures that imm is well-defined – it must be a state-dependent and strictly increasing map between clock cycles. The data abstraction predicate ensures that all the initial states at the ISA level are represented by at least one *initial* state at the micro-architecture level. The remaining condition is a commutativity property: this is quantified for all clock cycles (at the ISA level) and for all states at the micro-architecture level. This correctness definition is intentionally abstract, giving no bias to a verification strategy: spec and impl are arbitrary state functions – they need not be iterated maps with next state functions.

The main correctness goal for the ARM6 verification is:

$$\vdash \text{CORRECT STATE\_ARM STATE\_ARM6 IMM\_ARM6 ABS\_ARM6}$$

The data abstraction ABS_ARM6 projects out the memory and registers banks; it also subtracts eight from the program counter value. The immersion IMM_ARM6 is *uniform*, it is defined in terms of a duration map DUR_ARM6: this maps (initial) machine states to a positive number of clock cycles. For example, with the code from Sect. 5 the duration map gives the values: 1, 1, 1, 3, 1, 2, 2. This is the number of machine cycles needed to execute each successive instruction. The corresponding values given by the immersion are: 0, 1, 2, 3, 6, 7, 9, 11.

The one-step theorems [7] are used to reformulate the main correctness goal, giving the following four goals:

$$\vdash \forall a.\ \text{(b = STATE\_ARM6 (IMM\_ARM6 a 0) a)} \Rightarrow \text{(STATE\_ARM6 0 b = b)}$$
$$\vdash \forall a.\ \text{(b = STATE\_ARM6 (IMM\_ARM6 a 1) a)} \Rightarrow \text{(STATE\_ARM6 0 b = b)}$$
$$\vdash \forall a.\ \text{STATE\_ARM 0 (ABS\_ARM6 a) = ABS\_ARM6 (STATE\_ARM6 (IMM\_ARM6 a 0) a)}$$
$$\vdash \forall a.\ \text{STATE\_ARM 1 (ABS\_ARM6 a) = ABS\_ARM6 (STATE\_ARM6 (IMM\_ARM6 a 1) a)}$$

---

[12] The ISA state components are set; the remaining data path and control components are represented with free variables.

The commutativity condition is replaced by cases for cycles zero and one. This now provides a good means in which to tackle the verification – these goals can be readily expressed in terms of next state, initialisation, data abstraction and duration functions. The first two conditions represent an initialisation invariance (closure) property for the pipeline. The first and third goals are easy to verify because the ARM6 initialisation function does not tamper with the ISA state components. The second and forth goals represent the main verification effort.

The proof strategy is conceptually quite simple: evaluate the state functions using term rewriting with appropriate case splitting. However, the complexity of the specifications means that a naïve verification (for example, a single application of HOL's RW_TAC) is not tractable; see [10]. The bulk of the term rewriting was carried out using call-by-value conversion (Sect. 6) with the computation set judiciously chosen. States are evaluated up until applications of read and write operations over the memory and register banks. There are many cases to be explored and this is a product of the ARM instruction set which supports: byte/word access, pre- and post-indexing, register write back (for load-store instructions), conditional updating of the status flags, three shift modes and five shift operations, six operating modes (banked registers), conditional execution, exceptions, and branches through writing to register fifteen. Cases are verified using a set of lemmas – about one hundred were used in total. Most of these were fairly trivial, for example: a small set dealt with register access (write-write, write-read and read-write) and a number deal with data operations (reasoning about bit fields). The block data transfer instructions were the hardest to verify because a number of non-trivial lemmas were required.

The proof strategy simultaneously covers both the control and data aspects of the design. A number of tricky lemmas about 32-bit data operations were need – for example, the field extractor and barrel shifter are used to implement byte memory access. Having a well developed and extensive library of word theorems is of great benefit here. In some instances there was a temptation to cheat – the specifications could have been modified to bring up easier proof obligations. However, this path was resisted: the ISA remains abstract and the micro-architecture is true to the implementation. Verifying these theorems is regarded as being an important part of the formal verification. A decision procedure for the new word theory would be a useful development but this is unlikely to provide a panacea because the specifications incorporate natural number operations.

7.1   Self Modifying Code

Before carrying out the verification it was clear that, in one regard, the ARM6 is not correct (as defined by CORRECT) with respect to our ISA specification. This is because data store instructions can invalidate the pipeline state. For example:

```
STR r0, [pc,#-4]
STR r0, [pc]
```

update the fetched and decoded instructions respectively, but the ARM6 does nothing about this. Consider the first store: if r0 contains an ADD instruction then at the ISA level the store would be followed by the ADD, whereas the ARM6 will execute the instruction originally after the store, which is contained in pipeb. This means that correctness is violated. This problem only arises when writing to the two addresses immediately following the instruction being executed, and so code modification is not a problem *per se*.

To tackle this a number of options can be considered:

1. Modify the correctness condition to contain a predicate asserting the non-presence of destructive self modifying code. This approach has been used by Sawada and Hunt [21].

2. Change the data behaviour of the ISA and ARM6 models. If data store instructions do not write over (clobber) the following two instructions, then correctness holds. This involves minor changes to both specifications and preserves the ARM6 pipeline behaviour. This approach was tried first and has the advantage that our definition of correctness can be easily maintained.

3. Change the pipeline behaviour of the ARM6 so as to correctly implement the abstract ISA behaviour. This has been implemented using data forwarding but it does affect the timing of STR instructions – an extra cycle is sometimes needed.

4. One could no longer regard the memory as part of the ISA and micro-architecture state spaces i.e. just model the processor core. A correctness model with input and output could be used [7] to model interactions with a memory management unit. This has not been implemented but may be in future. This approach may well have advantages, especially if one wishes to introduce more advanced memory models (i.e. caching).

5. Modify the ISA specification to implement the pipelined instruction sequence behaviour. This has been implemented successfully and one advantage of this approach is that the pipelined ISA is an accurate abstract model of the ARM6, which is useful for simulation purposes.

6. The ISA executes instructions given by the ireg component of the ARM6 state space. This has been combined with the previous option to show that the pipelined ISA implements an instruction stream version of the ISA.

Having to deal with disruptive self modifying code is a nuisance from a verification standpoint. In practice, programs never modify instructions that are just about to be executed. This is the reason why ARM has decided not to waste effort in this regard. Any of the above options is reasonable – the choice will depend on the context i.e. the required level of fidelity for the specifications.

8   Conclusion

This paper has identified several elements that are important in the verification of microprocessor designs. The ARM6 verification has benefited from having a pre-existing and mature framework (formalised in HOL) that is suited to the verification of a wide range of computer systems [12,7,8]. This framework gives a clean and strict definition of correctness and a clear verification path through the use of *one-step* theorems. With the addition of a new word theory, HOL provides good support for the production of compact and executable formal processor specifications. Furthermore, being able to verify word theorems was an essential part of the ARM verification. Although the specifications are executable, HOL is not ideally suited to this task – execution is somewhat slow, especially when compared with ACL2 and PVS. This is likely to improve in due course – Konrad Slind (Utah) is working on a mechanism to execute HOL in ML. This would be very useful for simulation but there are still clear benefits in using a fully expansive (logical kernel) approach for the verification.

Working with the ARM architecture raised the question of how to handle *un-predictable* (processor dependent) behaviour. Introducing non-determinism is an obvious solution but this is not ideal from a simulation or verification perspective – deterministic models are easier to work with. Ideally an ISA is developed first and it provides a target for all future processor designs. However, in practice ISAs evolve, are extended and are at best only partial specifications. Processors themselves tend to be the main determiners of semantics, which is why the ARM programmer's model has such a muddled view of the program counter. In this respect the ISA model should simply be viewed as a (relatively) clean and verified abstraction for a given processor. Nevertheless, it is clear that more research can be carried out at this level – showing that the core (predictable) parts of ISA models concur. Furthermore, assemblers introduce another level of abstraction which could also be modelled.

The ARM architecture was not designed with verification in mind but its strong adherence to the RISC ethos makes it reasonably well suited to formal specification and verification. The verification took approximately one man year to complete. It is believed that verifications of later 5-stage designs (ARM7 and ARM9) ought to be quite feasible. The latest model, the ARM11, has parallel pipelines but it is not superscalar (it has single instruction issue) and it might also be a good target for formal verification. The current verification may be widened to include the ARM6's CISC multiplication, which will make the micro-architecture verification instruction set complete.

References

1. M. D. Aagaard, B. Cook, N. A. Day, and R. B. Jones. A framework for microprocessor correctness statements. In *CHARME 2001*, volume 2144 of *LNCS*, pages 433–448. Springer, 2001.
2. B. Barras. Programming and computing in HOL. In M. Aagaard and J. Harrison, editors, *TPHOLs 2000*, volume 1869 of *LNCS*, pages 17–37. Springer, 2000.
3. S. Berezin, E. Clarke, A. Biere, and Y. Zhu. Verification of out-of-order processor designs using model checking and a light-weight completion function. *Formal Methods in System Design*, 20(2):187–222, Mar. 2002.
4. G. Birtwistle and P. A. Subrahmanyam, editors. *VLSI Specification, Verification and Synthesis*. Kluwer Academic Publishers, 1988.
5. B. Brock, M. Kaufmann, and J. S. Moore. ACL2 theorems about commercial microprocessors. In M. K. Srivas and A. Camilleri, editors, *FMCAD '96*, volume 1166 of *LNCS*, pages 275–293. Springer-Verlag, 1996.

6. A. Cohn. The notion of proof in hardware verification. *Journal of Automated Reasoning*, 5(2):127–139, June 1989.
7. A. C. J. Fox. *Algebraic Models for Advanced Microprocessors*. PhD thesis, University of Wales Swansea, 1998.
8. A. C. J. Fox. An algebraic framework for modelling and verifying microprocessors using HOL. Technical Report 512, University of Cambridge, Computer Laboratory, Apr. 2001.
9. A. C. J. Fox. A HOL specification of the ARM instruction set architecture. Technical Report 545, University of Cambridge, Computer Laboratory, June 2001.
10. A. C. J. Fox. Formal verification of the ARM6 micro-architecture. Technical Report 548, University of Cambridge, Computer Laboratory, Nov. 2002.
11. B. T. Graham. *The SECD Microprocessor, A Verification Case Study*. Kluwer International Series in Engineering and Computer Science. Kluwer Academic Publishers, 1992.
12. N. A. Harman and J. V. Tucker. Algebraic models and the correctness of microprocessors. In G. J. Milne and L. Pierre, editors, *Correct Hardware Design and Verification Methods*, volume 683 of *LNCS*, pages 92–108. Springer-Verlag, 1993.
13. W. A. Hunt, Jr. *FM8501: A Verified Microprocessor*, volume 795 of *LNCS*. Springer-Verlag, 1994.
14. W. A. Hunt, Jr. and B. C. Brock. A formal HDL and its use in the FM9001 verification. In C. A. R. Hoare and M. J. C. Gordon, editors, *Mechanized Reasoning and Hardware Design*, pages 35–47. Prentice-Hall, 1992.
15. R. B. Jones, J. U. Skakkebæk, and D. L. Dill. Formal verification of out-of-order execution with incremental flushing. *Formal Methods in System Design*, 20(2):139–158, Mar. 2002.
16. J. J. Joyce. Formal verification and implementation of a microprocessor. In Birtwistle and Subrahmanyam [4], pages 129–157.
17. M. Kaufmann, P. Manolios, and J. S. Moore, editors. *Computer-Aided Reasoning: ACL2 Case Studies*. Kluwer Academic Publishers, June 2000.
18. K. McMillan. Verification of an implementation of tomasulo's algorithm by compositional model checking. In A. J. Hu and M. Y. Vardi, editors, *CAV '98*, volume 1427 of *LNCS*. Springer-Verlag, 1998.
19. T. F. Melham. Abstraction mechanisms for hardware verification. In Birtwistle and Subrahmanyam [4], pages 267–291.
20. S. P. Miller and M. K. Srivas. Applying formal verification to the AAMP5 microprocessor: A case study in the industrial use of formal methods. *Formal Methods in Systems Design*, 8(2):153–188, Mar. 1996.
21. J. Sawada and W. A. Hunt, Jr. Verification of FM9801: An out-of-order model with speculative execution, exceptions, and program-modifying capability. *Formal Methods in System Design*, 20(2):187–222, Mar. 2002.
22. D. Seal, editor. *ARM Architectural Reference Manual*. Addison-Wesley, second edition, 2001.
23. S. Tahar and R. Kumar. A practical methodology for the formal verification of RISC processors. *Formal Methods in System Design*, 13(2):159–225, Sept. 2002.
24. R. M. Tomasulo. An efficient algorithm for exploiting multiple arithmetic units. *IBM Journal*, 11(34):25–33, 1967.
25. P. J. Windley and M. L. Coe. A correctness model for pipelined microprocessors. In R. Kumar and T. Kropf, editors, *TPCD '94*, volume 901 of *LNCS*, pages 33–51. Springer-Verlag, 1995.
26. W. Wong. Modelling bit vectors in HOL: The word library. In J. J. Joyce and C.-J. H. Seger, editors, *HUG '93*, volume 780 of *LNCS*, pages 371–384. Springer-Verlag, 1994.

A Programming Logic for Java Bytecode Programs

Claire L. Quigley

Department of Computing Science,
University of Glasgow.
claire@dcs.gla.ac.uk

Abstract. Using the Isabelle theorem prover [10] we have developed a programming logic for Java bytecode, and demonstrated that it can be used to prove properties of simple bytecode programs involving loops. Our motivation for this was to produce a method by which Java Just-In-Time (JIT) compilers could be assisted to produce more efficient code. This paper discusses the issues involved in the development of the programming logic as it stands, and suggests possible extensions to it. We also describe our experiences of the difficulties inherent in carrying out proof at the level of bytecode instructions, along with the benefits and disadvantages of using a mechanized proof tool.

1 Introduction

One significant disadvantage of interpreted bytecode languages, such as Java, is their low execution speed in comparison to compiled languages like C. The mobile nature of bytecode adds to the problem, as many checks are necessary to ensure that downloaded code from untrusted sources is rendered as safe as possible. But there do exist ways speeding up such systems.

One approach is to carry out static type checking at load time, as in the case of the Java Bytecode Verifier. This reduces the number of runtime checks that must be done and also allows certain instructions to be replaced by faster versions. Another approach is the use of a Just In Time (JIT) Compiler, which takes the bytecode and produces corresponding native code at runtime. Some JIT compilers also carry out some code optimization.

There are, however, limits to the amount of optimization that can safely be done by the Verifier and JITs; some operations simply cannot be carried out safely without a certain amount of runtime checking. But what if it were possible to prove that the conditions the runtime checks guard against would never arise in a particular piece of code? In this case it might well be possible to dispense with these checks altogether, allowing optimizations not feasible at present. In addition to this, because of time constraints, current JIT compilers tend to produce acceptable code as quickly as possible, rather than producing the *best* code possible. By removing the burden of analysis from them it may be possible to change this.

Using the Isabelle theorem prover [10] we have developed a programming logic, and demonstrated that it can be used to prove properties of simple bytecode programs involving loops. Indeed, for any bytecode program involving array update in which the array load instruction is at the very beginning of the body of the loop, it would be

D. Basin and B. Wolff (Eds.): TPHOLs 2003, LNCS 2758, pp. 41–54, 2003.

possible to prove that it would be safe to eliminate the array bounds check contained in the assembly code for that instruction.

This paper discusses the issues involved in the development of the programming logic as it stands, and suggests possible extensions to it. We also describe our experiences of the difficulties inherent in carrying out proof at the level of bytecode instructions, along with the benefits and disadvantages of using a mechanized proof tool.

2   Related Work

A large amount of work has been done in recent years on formalizing aspects of the Java language and the JVM, such as the work of Drossopoulou and Eisenbach [4]— and Syme's treatment of this in an automated prover [13]—and that of Nipkow and von Oheimb [9]. The Extended Static Checking (ESC) Project [3] and the LOOP Project [6]include work done on proving properties of specific Java programs; Moore also describes work done in this area in [8].

Our own work is based on the work described in *Formalizing the Java Virtual Machine in Isabelle/HOL* [11], in which Cornelia Pusch details her formalization of the JVM—which she describes as preliminary—in the theorem prover Isabelle (using the HOL object logic). Pusch's aim is to provide a formal version of the Java Virtual Machine Specification [7] that is not prey to the ambiguities and inconsistencies which tend to creep into informal specifications (and indeed do in the case of the JVM Spec). Although a large subset of the Java language is formalized, there are areas not treated in this implementation. These include exception handling and dynamic class loading.

The paper outlines the formalization of both static aspects of Java programs, e.g. well-formedness of classfiles and relations between classes, and properties of the Java run-time system including object initialisation and the JVM heap. The author also describes an operational semantics for the subset of the JVM instruction set considered.

Our proofs are based on Pusch's formalization, with the addition of the JVM instructions iadd and iinc. Also, the representation of branching instructions was altered to keep all branching proofs in the realm of natural number arithmetic. This avoided situations where it was necessary to cast integers to natural numbers and back again, and greatly simplified the Isabelle proofs.

3   A Programming Logic for Bytecode

to prove properties of the bytecode programs themselves, rather than the corresponding Java source was made based on three factors:

- Java programs are downloaded by consumers as bytecode, not source
- It is perfectly feasible (albeit not common in practice) to produce Java bytecode from another high level language, e.g. C, ML
- It removes the need to verify the Java compiler itself

In order to reason about properties of bytecode programs it is necessary to develop a logical framework that supports this. The fact that bytecode is 'flat' and contains goto instructions presents difficulties not encountered in the standard logic, which deals with a structured programming language. The standard Hoare logic has three main components, however, which can equally be applied to bytecode programs, namely:

- The notion of evaluation of a section of code in the language (which can be based on the operational semantics)
- Definition of a pre- and post-condition relation on execution of code.
- Higher level rules for combining patterns of code

The development of some logical relations corresponding to the first item in this list—the evaluation of bytecode—is discussed in the rest of this section. Section 4 and Section 5 will deal with the remaining two elements of the programming logic.

There are three execution relations for bytecode instructions. The block execution relation (Section 3.1) describes the complete execution of a block of bytecode. The sequence execution relation (Section 3.4) describes the complete execution of a block of bytecode of a very restricted class of instructions. Finally, the execution path relation (Section 3.2) is concerned with the relationship between intermediate states in the execution of a block of bytecode and the initial and final states. All are necessary for the development of the programming logic discussed in Sections 4 and 5.

3.1   Block Execution Relation

The conventional Hoare logic is based on an operational semantics where execution begins at the start of the sequence of commands and finishes at the end (assuming the program terminates). But with bytecode there is the possibility of jumping *into* the code at some point after the start and *out* at a point before the end. One possibility is to state that execution of a sequence of instructions has finished *when the program counter is no longer pointing into the sequence.*

This results in the definition of a relation describing the execution of a list of bytecode instructions in which if execution begins in state σ inside a sequence, it results in state σ', where the program counter of σ' is outside the section.

Suppose that

- *CFS* is a set of Java Classfiles (a classfile contains all the information pertaining to a single Java class)
- The *start* of the bytecode sequence is signified by s, and the *finish* by f, where s and f identify a single instruction in *CFS*
- σ and σ' are JVM states

We write $\langle CFS, \sigma \rangle \xrightarrow{s}_{f} \sigma'$ to mean that executing the sequence of instructions in *CFS* that begins at the instruction identified by s and ends at the instruction identified by f in the state σ results in the state σ', where the instruction identified by σ' is not contained the sequence of instructions in *CFS* bounded by s and f.

The relation is defined inductively (c.f., Winskel [14]) with respect to two rules: the *Stop* rule, referring to the case in which one step of execution results in the program counter being outside the sequence of instructions under consideration; and the *Continue* rule, which pertains to the case where, after one step of execution, the program counter is still within the block of code delimited by s and f. The *Continue* rule constitutes the inductive part of the definition, as the relation is defined in terms of itself.

3.2   Execution Path Relation

The block execution relation can be used to reason about an intermediate state in the execution of a block and the final state. It does not, however, allow discussion of the connection between an intermediate state and the initial state, or between two intermediate states, as both the states in question are inside the block. Since it is clearly useful to be able to do this, a relation that enables us to reason about two states, at least one and possibly both of which, are within a particular sequence of bytecode is needed.

The execution path relation is defined as the set of pairs of states obtained by a successful execution step, where the program counter of the first member of the pair is inside the block in question. This relation is particularly useful in the proof of soundness of the while rule (Section 6), where we must reason about the relationship between the initial state and various intermediate states in the execution of the loop.

3.3   Data-Equality of States

Before describing the third execution relation, it must be noted that it is not possible to talk meaningfully about deterministic execution in terms of an entire JVM state. Pusch's formalization of the JVM aims to mirror as closely as possible the 'real world' in which Java bytecode programs are executed. Consequently, in Pusch's model of the JVM world instructions are not viewed in isolation as independent entities completely isolated from the idea of 'state', but are themselves part of the environment described by a set of classfiles and a JVM state.

Suppose we have a sequence of instructions that appears in two different classes within a set of classfiles. Normally we could prove that executing either sequence starting in a state σ would result in state σ'. In the world of the JVM, however, the differing positions of the sequence within the set of classfiles means that not only would the final not be identical, the initial states would also differ from each other in several places, e.g. program counter, classname, method name. Therefore, in order to discuss determinism in the accepted sense of the word, we must define a different type of 'equality' for states.

Two states are said to be *data-equal* if their exception values (indicating whether an exception has been thrown and consequently causing execution to halt) and the values of the stack and local variables in the top frame of their frame stacks are equal. Of course, this definition of data-equality is not the only possible one. For example, if we wished to talk about a situation involving the execution of instructions which reference the heap, this would have to become part of the definition of data-equality. But, while it is apparent that there may be several equalities of this nature, the above definition will be used throughout this document.

3.4   Sequence Execution Relation

Using the idea of data-equality described above, we now define a relation operating only on the elements of state involved in the definition of data-equality, the relevant instructions as a sequence in its own right, and a pointer into the current position within this sequence. This relation allows us to reason about sequences of instructions independent of their position in a set of classfiles.

Like the block execution relation (3.1), the relation is inductively defined by two rules, one referring to the case in which one step of execution results in the program counter being outside the sequence of instructions under consideration; and the other pertaining to the case where, after one step of execution, the program counter is still within the instruction sequence.

4   A Pre- and Post-condition Relation for Execution of Bytecode

Having defined execution relations for bytecode programs, we now define a pre- and post-condition relation for the execution of such programs. Traditionally, such a relation is defined in terms of the various syntactic patterns of the programming language in question. As bytecode programs are flat, no such patterns are explicit in the code and we must therefore determine what constitutes, for example, a loop or a conditional statement.

We write $\{P\}\ xs\ \{Q\}$ to mean that for all classfiles CFS containing the instruction sequence xs bounded by the instructions identified by s and f (written $CFS[s \dots f] = xs$), if the condition P holds in state σ and $\langle CFS, \sigma \rangle \xrightarrow[f]{s} \sigma'$, then condition Q holds in state σ'. The definition is given by cases on whether or not xs is empty.

$$\{P\}\ [\ ]\ \{Q\} \equiv \forall\ CFS\ \sigma\ \sigma'.\ P(\sigma) \longrightarrow Q(\sigma') \tag{1}$$

$$
\begin{aligned}
\{P\}\ x : xs\ \{Q\} = \forall\, & CFS\ \sigma\ \sigma'\ s\ f. \\
& (\langle CFS, \sigma \rangle \xrightarrow[f]{s} \sigma'\ \wedge \\
& CFS[s \dots f] = x : xs\ \wedge \\
& (pc(\sigma) = pc(s)) \wedge P(\sigma)) \\
& \longrightarrow Q(\sigma')
\end{aligned}
\tag{2}
$$

4.1   Rules

Using this definition and the execution relations described in Section 4, we have derived rules for a number of common bytecode patterns. These include precondition strengthening, postcondition weakening, a rule for combining two consecutive blocks of bytecode (analogous to the sequencing rule in the standard logic), and a rule for joining an unconditional branch forward instruction to its target block while including any intervening instructions.

While the proofs of these rules involve a large amount of detail, the underlying methods do not involve any techniques not previously mentioned in this paper. The discovery of a rule for loops in the bytecode and a proof of its soundness, on the other hand, are not at all straightforward and require the introduction of several new concepts. We therefore describe them at more length in the next two sections. A rule for blocks including a conditional branch forwards instruction (similar to the *if* rule in the standard logic) was also derived using techniques developed in the proof of soundness of the loop rule. This is described in [12].

4.2   A Rule for Loops in Bytecode

Unlike the simple imperative language used in the standard Hoare logic which contains the *while* command, there are no explicit loop constructs in bytecode programs. In order to develop rule for programs containing loops it is therefore necessary to identify the patterns of bytecode instructions that are used to code them. Of course, Java programs may contain loops other than *while* loops—namely *for* loops and *repeat-until* loops. For the purposes of this work, however, we shall restrict our attention to while loops.

A diagram showing the outline of this loop can be seen in Figure 1, where xs represents the instructions making up the body of the loop, and ys the instructions used to prepare the stack for the conditional branch. A general representation of such a loop may now be written as the list of instructions

$$[(UBF\ |xs|\ +\ 1)]@[xs]@[ys]@[(CBB\ |xs@ys|)] \tag{3}$$

where $UBF\ |xs|\ +\ 1$ is the unconditional branch instruction to the head of ys—a jump of one more than the length of xs, and $CBB\ |xs@ys|$ is the conditional branch back to the start of xs—a jump of the length of $xs@ys$. While other possible forms of such loops exist—e.g.

$$[ys]@[CBF\ ||(UBF\ |xs|\ +\ 2]@[xs]@[UBB\ |xs@ys|\ +\ 1] \tag{4}$$

—we shall discuss only loops of the form (3). Treatment of the alternative forms would, however, be similar. The while rule in the standard Hoare logic is

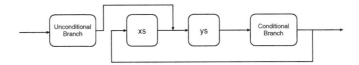

Fig. 1. Loop structure

$$\frac{\{P \wedge S\}\ C\ \{P\}}{\{P\}\ while\ S\ do\ C\ \{P \wedge \neg S\}} \tag{5}$$

Where P is an invariant of the loop and S is the loop guard. In a similar rule for the bytecode representation of a while loop it seems obvious that xs in the diagram above corresponds to C (the body of the loop), and that the invariant P does not depend on the language we are dealing with. This leaves the question of what constitutes S, the loop guard, in the bytecode.

This is not immediately obvious, as the loop guard is not explicit in the bytecode, as it is in the higher level language. One possible candidate is the branching condition of the conditional branch instruction in the loop. But a side effect of the comparison is to pop the values involved in this comparison off the stack, with the result that any predicate involving the top of the stack is meaningful *immediately before execution of the branch instruction.* As we need to be able to talk meaningfully about the loop guard at various other points in the loop, this is clearly not the answer.

In fact, what is needed is to effectively 'wind back' the conditional being tested until we have a condition in terms of actual variables and values rather than items on the stack. We are, in effect, reconstructing the original guard condition present in the Java source code which is concealed in the bytecode instructions. If we look at the bytecode for the loop we can see that the sequence of instructions *ys* is executed prior to the conditional branch every time through the loop. These instructions 'set up' the stack so that the correct values are there ready for the comparison. By taking the *weakest precondition* of these instructions with respect to the condition of the branch we are able to determine the actual guard *S*.

4.3   Data-Equality and the Weakest Precondition

For the purposes of our loop rule, we define a version of the weakest precondition in terms of the sequence execution relation (Section 3.4) rather than the block execution relation. This effectively transforms the definition into that of the conventional definition of weakest precondition, where only the 'non-positional' parts of a state, i.e. the stack and the local variables, are relevant.

This definition does not replace a definition of weakest precondition in terms of the block execution relation, since the sequence weakest precondition can only be used to reason about classfile independent instructions (3.4). But, since the instructions we wish to determine the weakest precondition of in a well-formed while loop *are* classfile independent, this definition is suitable.

It is also necessary to include the fact that all states discussed in relation to the sequence weakest precondition are non-terminating—a condition which requires that the state's list of stack frames is non-empty. As the calculation of the smaller states used in the sequence execution relation (3.4) involves taking the head of the frame list of a JVM state, it is necessary that the frame list contain at least one element.

Data-equality and Loops.   One major difference between the execution of a while loop in an imperative language and a loop sequence in the bytecode is the effect of executing the 'structure' of the loop. As discussed in Section 4.2 a general pattern for loops in bytecode is

$$[(UBF\ |xs|\ +\ 1)]@[xs]@[ys]@[(CBB\ |xs@ys|)] \tag{6}$$

where the instructions xs represent the loop body, and the instructions $(UBF\ |xs|\ +\ 1)$, ys, and $(CBB\ |xs@ys|)$ constitute the structural parts of the loop.

In the imperative language, the rules for execution state that executing a while statement in an initial state in which the loop guard is false results in an unchanged state . In the bytecode, execution of a loop sequence in which the guard is false in the initial state results in a different state, as evaluating the sequences which constitute the structure of the loop means the value of the program counter will have changed. This is shown in Figure 2.

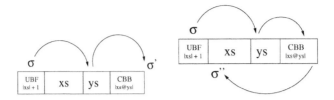

Fig. 2. Evaluation of guard to false (left) and true (right)

Similarly, with the situation where the body of the loop *is* executed, if a while statement is executed in state σ in which the loop guard is true, we can talk of executing the body of the loop in the same state—evaluation of the loop guard does not affect the state. Again, this is not the case in the bytecode sequence. This is shown in Figure 2.

At first glance, this may seem likely to add to the complexity of a proof of the bytecode rule. But closer inspection of the effect of executing the structure of a bytecode loop sequence, shows that the only element of the state affected (assuming the instructions concerned satisfy certain constraints) is the program counter. This means that once again we can use the idea of *data-equality*, discussed in Section 3.3.

As the branch condition does not mention the program counter, and assuming that the loop invariant does not either, data-equal states in the bytecode execution can take the place of equal states in the source code execution. In addition to this the elements of a state involved in data-equality are also the elements that make up the states used in the sequence execution relation, and consequently the sequence weakest precondition.

Currently, the fact that our logic limits certain instructions to those which are classfile independent, means that loop invariants are constrained to predicates that are concerned solely with the operand stack, stk, and local variables, loc, of a method frame. The function $(assert\ Q)$ provides a way of applying such a predicate, Q, to a complete JVM state.

5   Proof of Soundness of the Loop Rule

In light of the issues explored in the previous section, our proposed rule for loops is as follows

$$\frac{\{(assert\ P)\ \wedge\ sequence\_wp(ys,\ branch\_cond)\}\ xs\ \{(assert\ P)\};}{\{P\}\ [(UBF\ |xs|\ +\ 1)]@[xs]@[ys]@[(CBB\ |xs@ys|)]}\ (7)$$
$$\{(assert\ P)\ \wedge\ \neg(sequence\_wp(ys, branch\_cond))\ \wedge\ not\_term\_state\}$$

where not_term_state denotes a state that will not—through the presence of an exception, or the absence of any further instructions—cause execution to terminate.

In the conventional Hoare logic, the proof of soundness for the while often depends on the proof of two subsidiary properties: that the loop guard is false on exit, and that execution of the loop preserves some invariant. In a conventional axiomatic semantics these are very simple to prove as they follow almost immediately from the execution rules for the language ([14]). In the bytecode world, however, they are considerably more difficult to prove and we discuss the methods used to achieve these proofs in some detail.

5.1 Outline of Proof

After rewriting the loop rule with the definition of the pre- and post-condition relation and simplifying, our goal is to show that for the final state σ in the execution of the loop

$$((assert\ P)\ \wedge\ (\neg\ sequence\_wp(ys, branch\_cond))\ \wedge\ not\_term\_state)\ \sigma_n \quad (8)$$

The proof of the second element of the conjunct can be obtained immediately by the theorem stating that the loop guard is false on exit (Section 5.2). Similarly, a proof of the third conjunct can be achieved quite straightforwardly from the fact that the current logic deals only with programs that execute without throwing exceptions. The proof of $(assert\ P)\ \sigma_n$ is slightly more complex, involving a proof that the invariant is preserved by the 'structure' instructions of the loop. The following sections discuss the proof strategies for the two main theorems needed for this result.

5.2 Loop Guard False on Exit

In a well formed loop the conditional branch backwards instruction is executed at least once, and is the only instruction in the loop whose execution can result in a state in which the program counter is pointing outside the loop.

Our proof strategy involves showing that there exists a penultimate state σ_{n-1}, whose program counter points to the conditional branch instruction. Execution of the branch instruction in state σ_{n-1} results in a state σ_n, the program counter of which points to the instruction immediately following the loop.

We know that the branching condition must be false in state σ_{n-1} or we would have branched back into the loop and not reached state σ_n. We then prove that this implies that there exists a state σ_{n-2}, with program counter pointing to the first instruction in ys, in which the sequence weakest precondition does not hold. From the referential transparency of the instructions ys and the operational semantics of the branching instruction, we know that σ_{n-2} and σ_n are data equal.

This means that $\neg\ ((sequence\_wp(ys, CBB\_cond))\ \sigma_n)$, and so we have shown that the guard condition is false on exit from the loop.

5.3 Invariant Preserved by Execution of Loop

It is obvious that, in order to prove that the preservation of an invariant , P, by one execution of the loop body implies its preservation by multiple executions, it will be necessary to use some form of inductive argument. This is the approach used in the proofs of soundness of the while rule for more traditional Hoare logics [14,2], and these proofs are reasonably straightforward as in the inductive definition of the language, one step of execution corresponds to one execution of the body of the loop.

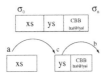

Fig. 3. Decomposition of loop

In the bytecode programming logic, however, this is not the case. The block execution relation works at a much finer grain, i.e. that of individual bytecode instructions, several of which may be needed to represent a single 'higher level' instruction like array assignment. And, although the invariant holds at the beginning and end of the body of the loop, it may not hold anywhere between these points.

In standard inductive definitions of execution like those mentioned above, this is not a problem as the body, C, of a loop many be inductively built up from several commands $C_1, ..., C_n$, but is viewed as a single command in its own right, thereby abstracting away from the finer detail and allowing its execution to be viewed as a single step. In the block execution relation however, a single step of execution is the execution of a single bytecode instruction, and so we cannot use the block execution relation directly to reason about the preservation of P across a loop body consisting of several bytecode instructions.

It is clearly necessary to find a relation describing a 'big step' of execution in the bytecode world. If the execution of the loop can be described in such a manner we can then carry out a successful induction leading to the proof of the invariant's preservation. Of course, this relation must also take into account the fact that we must explicitly execute the 'structure' of the loop, represented by the instructions $ys@[CBB]$.

5.4   A 'Big Step' Execution Relation for Loops

If we consider the section $xs@ys@[CBB]$ of a well-formed loop for which the relation $\langle CFS, \sigma_0 \rangle \xrightarrow[f]{s+1} \sigma_n$ holds, we see that it could be viewed as two separate blocks: xs and $ys@[CBB]$. The states σ_0 and σ_n can then be seen to be members of the set of states

$$\{(a, b) : \exists c. \langle CFS, a \rangle \xrightarrow[s + |xs|]{s+1} c \wedge$$
$$pc(a) = pc(s) + 1 \wedge \tag{9}$$
$$\langle CFS, c \rangle \xrightarrow[f]{s + |xs| + 1} b\}^+$$

as, even if the branch is taken back to the start of xs, the state b is outside the block $ys@[CBB]$ and so the relation holds. This is shown in Figure 3 and Figure 4.

As the pairs of states in this relation span the whole of the block $xs@ys@[CBB]$ we now have a relation upon which we can perform induction. The proof that σ_0, $sigma_n$ are in the block execution relation implies that they are also in the 'big step' relation is described in detail in [12].

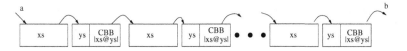

Fig. 4. Loop as transitive closure of blocks

6   Verification Examples

For the simple Java bytecode program

```
 0 bipush 0
 1 istore 1
 2 goto 8
 5 iinc 1 1
 8 iload 1
 9 bipush 5
10 if_icmplt 5
13 return
```

we proved, using our programming logic, that the final value in local variable 1 (written $loc\,!\,1$) is equal to 5. Although this is an extremely small example, the rules would work equally well on larger programs. More significantly, for a loop program containing an array operation as the first instruction in the loop body, it would be possible to prove that it is safe to eliminate array bounds checks.

Unfortunately, the code produced by most Java compilers for an array operation inside a loop does *not* place the array operation at the start of the loop body. In order to deal properly with such 'real life' examples some sort of assertion mechanism would have to be introduced to the logic, whereby it could be asserted that immediately prior to execution of an array instruction the array reference was non-null and the index within bounds.

7   Conclusions

In this section we describe our experience of using a mechanised proof tool in this work, and suggest possible extensions to the programming logic.

7.1   Bytecode Proof and Mechanized Reasoning

The use of a mechanized proof tool is central to our results. It has the benefit of enabling us to keep track of quite complex proofs involving many definitions. Additionally, as mentioned before, it provides an additional degree of confidence in the validity of these proofs. The Isabelle system was considered particularly suitable for our work as it facilitates the definition of logics and subsequent proofs involving them. In the course of the work, however, we did encounter several difficulties which offset these advantages.

As previously discussed, bytecode programs lack the sort of syntactic structure present in the higher level languages for which Hoare logics are more usually defined.

This means that rather than recognising, for example, the keyword while and applying the relevant rule, we must identify 'structural instructions' within a bytecode pattern, check that they conform to certain constraints, and explicitly execute them. This results in a great deal of proof in addition to that necessary in the conventional logics (c.f., Chapter 5).

Possibly the main difficulty we encountered in the course of this work was the sheer length and complexity of the proofs involved. Although the concepts behind the proofs can be communicated in a fairly high-level way to human beings—as we hope we have demonstrated in the preceding chapters—this approach does not work with Isabelle. The JVM world is very detailed; it contains a great deal of information and the Isabelle model must reflect this. It means, however, that there can be no 'glossing over' of the details, and every inference however small, must be spelled out.

The proofs of the various theorems in this report each run to several hundred lines of code, not including the necessary lemmas. The files related to the soundness of the while rule contain in the region of 10,000 lines of code. The complete count for the whole logic is around 22,000 lines. It is likely that this could be reduced to some extent by packaging repeated patterns of proofs as tactics, or by more effective use of the automatic tactics. It gives an idea, however of the amount of detail involved in the proofs.

One other drawback to the structureless form of bytecode programs is the necessity of dealing with a large number of proofs involving lists. Normally this would not be a problem: proofs of list properties can usually be shown by induction, and the Isabelle distribution contains many lemmas about lists already. Unfortunately the lists of instructions we are interested in are often not lists in their own right as such, but slices of a larger list. As we are, in a sense, coming at the list from both ends we cannot use induction: if we induct on the start position we change the length of our list, similarly with induction on the end point; if we try to induct on the slice itself we upset the relationship between the start and end points. This means that we must rely on rewriting with the various lemmas for *take* and *drop*, which can result in some quite tricky proofs.

The fact that instructions are not viewed as independent entities, but rather must be extracted from a set of classfiles and a state, means that a lot of information is contained within the assumptions of each proof. The block execution relation involves two states each of three elements, a set of classfiles, two class name identifiers, two method identifiers, and two program counter values; so an assumption or definition involving quantification over these variables requires thirteen instantiations. Often there are too many possibilities for Isabelle's resolution tactics to work these out automatically, so each variable must be instantiated by hand.

The large number of assumptions in many of the proofs also frequently confuses the automatic tactics. It is often the case that the simplifier will get nowhere with a particular goal if it contains many assumptions not pertinent to the desired conclusion. But if the relevant assumptions are extracted and used in the goal of a separate lemma the tactics succeed almost straight away. This may be a problem that is solved in more recent versions of Isabelle; in particular the rewriting of asm_full_simp_tac so that results do not depend on the order in which the assumptions appear might well have a significant effect on this problem. Unfortunately, one of the more recent versions of Isabelle made significant changes which would have necessitated changes in Pusch's formalization of the semantics, and consequently we made to decision to stay with our current version (Isabelle99) of the prover despite the improved features of newer versions.

Certainly the size and complexity of our proofs was pushing the limits of the computing power available to us. On a machine running at 400 MHz with 256 M of RAM, it was frequently the case that the proof would exceed the available memory and Isabelle would terminate.

These difficulties call into question the wisdom of attempting proofs of bytecode programs. But, as mentioned before, despite its drawbacks, the stack based virtual machine appears to be here to stay, at least for the foreseeable future. Therefore the ability to carry out proofs at this level has a definite value.

7.2   Further Work

Having developed a simple programming logic for bytecode programs, there are a number of ways in which it could be extended. The most obvious first step is the extension of the operational semantics to include all bytecode instructions available in the JVM, rather than the subset currently treated. One possibility would be to transfer the basis of the work to the MicroJava theories [1] which include a larger set of instructions and deal with exception handling.

In terms of the bytecode execution relations, the main drawback is their restriction on states to be all in the same method of a particular class. This means that it is impossible to work with bytecode programs that include method invocation or return, which is obviously not a realistic situation. One possible way of allowing this might be to in effect *inline* the code of the method being called, which would result in a larger block that included the code of all methods called, although this would not work for recursive methods.

The fact that our programming logic relies on the code being executed never throwing exceptions is again unrealistic in a real world situation. Consequently, another useful extension would involve modelling Java's exception handling method in the operational semantics, and altering the programming logic in such a way that it allows reasoning about programs that terminate abruptly as a result of exceptions being raised. The logic described by Jacobs in [5] has this ability.

Finally, it would be useful to add *assertion* statements to the programming logic. This would allow the proof of assertions at intermediate points in a program, rather than just the start and finish.

References

1. Microjava theories. http://isabelle.in.tum.de/library/HOL/MicroJava/.
2. J. Camilleri and T. Melham. Reasoning with Inductively Defined Relations in the HOL Theorem Prover. Technical Report 265, University of Cambridge Computer Laboratory, 1992.
3. David L. Detlefs, K. Rustan M. Leino, Greg Nelson, and James B. Saxe. Extended Static Checking. Technical Report 159, Compaq Systems Research Center, 1998.
4. Sophia Drossopoulou and Susan Eisenbach. Java is Type Safe - Probably. In *Proceedings of the 11th European Conference on Object Oriented Programming*, 1997.

5. M. Huisman and B. Jacobs. Java Program Verification via a Hoare Logic with Abrupt Termination. In *Approaches to Software Engineering (FASE'00)*. Springer, 2000.
6. B. Jacobs. The LOOP Project. http://www.cs.kun.nl/ bart/LOOP/.
7. Tim Lindholm and Frank Yellin. *The Java Virtual Machine Specification*. Addison-Wesley, 1997.
8. J Strother Moore. Proving Theorems about Java-like Byte Code, May 1999.
9. Tobias Nipkow and David von Oheimb. Java$_{light}$ is Type-Safe—Definitely. In *25th ACM Symposium on Principles of Programming Languages, January 19-21, 1998, San Diego*, 1998.
10. Lawrence C. Paulson. Isabelle, a Generic Theorem Prover. *LNCS*, 1994.
11. Cornelia Pusch. Formalizing the Java Virtual Machine in Isabelle/HOL. Technical report, Technische Universität München, June 1998.
12. Claire L. Quigley. *Proof for Optimization, Programming Logic Support for Java JIT Compilers*. PhD thesis, University of Glasgow, submitted October 2002.
13. Don Syme. Proving Java Type Soundness. Technical report, Computer Laboratory, University of Cambridge, June 1997.
14. Glyn Winskel. *The Formal Semantics of Programming Languages*. The MIT Press, 1993.

Verified Bytecode Subroutines

Gerwin Klein and Martin Wildmoser

Technische Universität München
{kleing,wildmosm}@in.tum.de

Abstract. Subroutines are a major complication for Java bytecode verification: they are difficult to fit into the data flow analysis that the Java Virtual Machine (JVM) specification suggests. We examine the problems that occur with subroutines and give an overview of the most prominent solutions in the literature. Using the theorem prover Isabelle/HOL, we have extended our substantial formalization of the JVM and the bytecode verifier with its proof of correctness by the most general solution for bytecode subroutines.

1   Introduction

Bytecode verification is a static check for bytecode safety. Its purpose is to ensure that the JVM only executes safe code: no operand stack over- or underflows, no ill-formed instructions, no type errors. Sun's JVM specification [12] informally describes an algorithm for it: an iterative data flow analysis that statically predicts the types of values on the operand stack and in the register set. Abstractly, the bytecode verifier (BV) is a type inference algorithm.

The relatively simple concept of procedures in the bytecode language does not seem to fit nicely into this data flow analysis. Bytecode subroutines are the center of numerous publications, the cause of bugs in the bytecode verifier, they even have been banished completely from the bytecode language by Sun in the KVM, a JVM for embedded devices.

The contributions of this paper are the following: we advance the field of Java bytecode verifcation with a mechanically verified and executable BV that supports bytecode subroutines; we report on one of the largest applications of the interactive theorem prover Isabelle/HOL [6]; and we make explicit some important assumptions about the type system that remain implicit or are missing completely in pen and paper formalizations.

The formalization we present is the continuation of our work on μJava [8,9], a downsized version of the real Java and JVM. The formalization includes the source language, with operational semantics and a proof of type safety, as well as the bytecode language, with operational semantics, proof of type safety, and executable bytecode verification algorithms. We can only show selected parts of this substantial development here, focusing on the subroutine aspect.

After introducing the JVM (§1.1), bytecode subroutines (§1.2), and the bytecode verifier together with the problems brought forward by subroutines (§1.3), we present the Isabelle/HOL formalization of subroutines in the μJVM (§2), and the bytecode verifier (§3).

D. Basin and B. Wolff (Eds.): TPHOLs 2003, LNCS 2758, pp. 55–70, 2003.

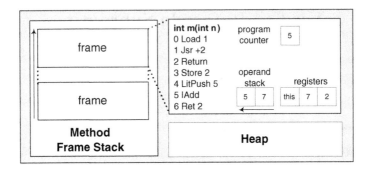

Fig. 1. The JVM.

1.1   Java Bytecode and the JVM

Sun specifies the JVM in [12] as a stack based interpreter of bytecode methods. It comprises a heap, which stores objects, and a frame stack, which captures local data of currently active methods.

When the JVM invokes a method it pushes a new *frame* onto the method frame stack. As Fig. 1 indicates, this frame contains the method's program counter, operand stack, and register set. These and the heap are manipulated by the method's bytecode instructions. For example, the *IAdd* instruction removes the topmost two values from the operand stack, adds them, and pushes the result back onto the operand stack. Register *0* is usually reserved for the *this* pointer of the method. The next p registers store the p parameters, and the rest is dedicated to local variables declared inside the method. The heap stores dynamically created objects while the operand stack and registers only contain references into the heap. Each method has an exception handler table, which is a list of tuples (s,e,pc',C). When an exception E occurs, the JVM searches this table for the first entry (s,e,pc',C) where E is a subclass of C and where the program counter is in the protected area $[s,e)$. Finally it enters the handler by setting the program counter to pc'.

1.2   Bytecode Subroutines

Subroutines can be seen as procedures on the bytecode level. If the same sequence of instructions occurs several times within a bytecode program, the compiler can place this common code into a subroutine and call it at the desired positions. This is mainly used for the try/finally construct of Java: the finally code must be executed on every possible way out of the block protected by try. In contrast to method calls, subroutines share the frame with their caller and manipulate the same register set and stack. Two bytecode instructions, namely *Jsr b* and *Ret x*, handle subroutine calls and returns. The *Jsr b* instruction pushes the return address (the program counter incremented by *1*) onto the stack and branches control to address $pc+b$. To return from a subroutine the bytecode language provides the *Ret x* instruction. It jumps to the return address stored in the

instruction	stack	registers	source
0 Load 0	([], [Int,	Err, Err])	
1 LitPush 0	([Int], [Int,	Err, Err])	int m(int n) {
2 Ifcmpeq +6	([Int, Int], [Int,	Err, Err])	try {
3 LitPush 25	([], [Int,	Err, Err])	if (n==0) {
4 Store 1	([Int], [Int,	Err, Err])	return n;
5 Jsr +6	([], [Int,	Int, Err])	}
6 Load 1	([], [Int,	Err, RA])	int j=25;
7 Return	([Err], [Int,	Err, RA])	return j;
8 Jsr +3	([], [Int,	Err, Err])	}
9 Load 0	([], [Int,	Err, RA])	finally { }
10 Return	([Int], [Int,	Err, RA])	}
11 Store 2	([RA], [Int,	$Int \sqcup Err$, Err])	
12 Ret 2	([], [Int,	Err, RA])	

Fig. 2. Bytecode program with a subroutine.

register with index x (x is a number). For example, Fig. 2 shows a subroutine with its **entry point** at address *11*, its **call points** at *5* and *8*, and its **return points** at *6* and *9*.

1.3   Bytecode Verification

The purpose of the bytecode verifier is to filter out erroneous and malicious bytecode programs prior to execution. It guarantees that all instructions receive their arguments in correct number, order and type. It also guarantees that the operand stack cannot overflow or underflow and that the program counter *pc* never falls off the code range.

These properties are checked by an abstract interpretation, which simulates code execution by manipulating types instead of values. This abstraction views a program as a finite state machine working on so called *state types*. A state type characterizes a set of runtime states by giving type constraints for the operand stack and registers. The state type $([Int], [Int, Err, Err])$ at address *1* in Fig. 2, for example, characterizes all runtime states immediately before execution of the *LitPush 0* instruction: every time execution reaches address *0*, the stack must contain a single integer (Int), register *0* must contain an integer, and the types of the values in registers *1* and *2* are unknown (Err). We call an instruction **applicable** in a state type s if it can be executed safely in all runtime states characterized by s. We call a typing of a method a **welltyping** if all instructions are applicable and if the typing is consistent with execution. A state type s is consistent in *pc* if the state type at each successor instruction correctly characterizes the runtime state after executing the instruction at *pc* (started in a runtime state characterized by s). Bytecode verification is the process of computing welltypings. It is successful if there is a welltyping for each method in the program. In the example in Fig. 2, bytecode verification was not successful, because *Return* at *pc=7* is not applicable (execution might be unsafe; the method would return a value of unkown type).

Computing consistent typings is nontrivial because instructions may have multiple predecessors. The state type at *11*, for instance, must be consistent with the execution of both *Jsr +6* at *5* and *Jsr +3* at *8*. The usual solution is to take the least common supertype (componentwise) of the state types after executing the instructions at *5* and *8*. This is also called *merging*. Here, it results in the state type ([*RA*], [*Int*, *Int*⊔*Err*, *Err*]) at *pc=11*: both instructions put a return address *RA* onto the stack, and both agree on register *0* and *2*. For register *1* the instruction at *5* yields *Int*, while the instruction at *8* yields *Err*. The supremum *Int*⊔*Err* is *Err*. The type system we use for subroutines proposes a different solution. It recognizes the program in Fig. 2 as safe.

Checking code with subroutines poses the following difficulties:

Successor of Ret. The BV has to compute the successors of instructions in order to propagate the resulting state types. The successors of *Ret x* instructions are hard to determine statically, because return addresses are values and not accessible on the type level. For example, in Fig. 2 at address 12, the bytecode verifier has to find out that the values of type *RA* stored in register 2 refer to the addresses 6 or 9.

Polymorphism on Registers. Subroutines may have multiple call points with different types for some registers. We expect that registers not used inside a subroutine have the same type before and after execution of the subroutine. In the example in Fig. 2 at address 11, the BV reacts to the type clash by merging the types *Int* and *Err* to their least common super type. If we merge register types at subroutine entry points, we loose information about their original types. If we propagate the merged type back to the return points, some programs are rejected, because they expect the original, more specific type. For example, bytecode verification fails at *pc=7* in Fig. 2, because the instruction there expects the original *Int* from address 5 in register 1. This problem mainly occurs with registers that are not used inside the subroutine. We call these subroutines *polymorphic over unused registers*.

Subroutine Boundaries. Subroutines are not syntactically delimited from the surrounding code. Ordinary jump instructions may be used to terminate a subroutine. Hence it is difficult to determine which instructions belong to a subroutine and which do not.

Subroutine Nesting. Subroutines can also be nested; a subroutine may call a further subroutine, and so on. This contributes to the difficulty of determining return addresses statically. When we encounter a *Ret x* instruction, we have to find out which of the currently active subroutines is returning. It may be the case that we have a *multilevel return*, which means a subroutine does not return to its caller, but to its caller's caller or further up in the subroutine call history.

The literature offers various solutions to these problems:

Freund [5] labels programs prior to bytecode verification in order to simulate subroutine call stacks statically. Using these labels he specifies typing rules similar to, but more general than those of Stata and Abadi [18]. Leroy [10] proposes a polyvariant analysis which maintains multiple state types per address, ideally one for each control flow route that reaches this address. This avoids type clashes at subroutine entry points. In Coglio's solution [4], state types are not just single types, but rather whole sets of what in the other approaches was the state type. If a program address i is reachable under two different type configurations (st, lt) and (st', lt'), he assigns the state type $\{(st, lt), (st', lt')\}$, a set, to i rather than the single, merged $(st \sqcup st', lt \sqcup lt')$. Uniting type sets instead of merging types is more precise: as the original type information is not lost, polymorphism on registers is not a problem. This is the approach we also use in the Isabelle formalization below. Wildmoser [19] eliminates subroutines by expanding their bodies and proves that this transformation is semantics preserving. Posegga and Vogt [15] take on bytecode verification from the model checking perspective. Basin, Friedrich, and Gawkowski [2] use Isabelle/HOL, μJava, and the abstract BV framework [13] to prove this approach correct. Stärk et al. [17] use Java and the JVM for a case study on abstract state machines. They formalize the process from compilation of Java programs down to bytecode verification. Barthe et al. [1] employ the Coq system for proofs about the JVM and bytecode verification. They formalize the full JavaCard language, but have only a simplified treatment of subroutines.

2   The μJava VM

This and the following section present our formalization of subroutines for bytecode verification in Isabelle/HOL. We begin with an overview of the structure and the operational semantics of the μJVM. In §3 we then develop the bytecode verifier.

As it is one major point of this article to demonstrate not only how a bytecode verifier with subroutines can be formalized, but how it can be formalized in a theorem prover, we will directly use Isabelle/HOL [14] notation. This mostly coincides with the notation used in mathematics and functional programming. We will show some of the basics now and then introduce new notation as we go along.

HOL distinguishes types and sets: types are part of the meta-language and of limited expressiveness, whereas sets are part of the object language and very expressive. Isabelle's type system is similar to ML's. There are the basic types *bool*, *nat*, and *int*, and the polymorphic types α *set* and α *list* and a conversion function *set* from lists to sets.

List operations may be unfamiliar: the "cons" operator is the infix #, concatenation the infix @; head and tail are *hd* and *tl*. The length of a list is denoted by *size*; the i-th element (starting with 0) of list xs is denoted by $xs \mathbin{!} i$. Overwriting the i-th element of a list xs with a new value x is written $xs[i := x]$.

We shall now briefly sketch the operational semantics of the JVM. See [7,9] for a more in-depth discussion.

datatype *instr* =   *Load nat* | *Store nat*
   | *LitPush val* | *New cname* | *Getfield vname cname*
   | *Ifcmpeq int* | *Checkcast cname* | *Putfield vname cname*
   | *Return* | *Dup* | *Invoke cname mname (ty list)*
   | *IAdd* | *Goto int* | *Throw*
   | *Ret nat* | *Jsr int*

Fig. 3. The μJava instruction set.

Fig. 3 shows the instruction set. Method bodies are lists of such instructions together with the exception handler table and two integers specifying the maximum operand stack size and the number of local variables.

The state transition relation $s \xrightarrow{\text{jvm}} t$ is the transitive reflexive closure of one-step execution. Execution halts if the frame stack is empty or an unhandled exception has occurred. In all other cases one-step execution is defined by the function *exec-instr*.

The parameters of *exec-instr* are the instruction, heap, stack, registers, class, signature, and program counter of the top frame, and the rest of the frame stack; the result is the new state (*None* indicates that no exception occurred). For *Jsr* and *Ret* the definition is:

exec-instr (*Jsr b*) *hp stk regs Cl sig pc frs* =
   (*None, hp,* (*RetAddr* (*pc+1*)#*stk, regs, Cl, sig, nat* ((*int pc*)+*b*))#*frs*)

exec-instr (*Ret x*) *hp stk regs Cl sig pc frs* =
   (*None, hp,* (*stk, regs, Cl, sig, the-RetAddr* (*regs ! x*)) # *frs*)

The *Jsr* instruction puts the return address *pc+1* on the operand stack and performs a relative jump to the subroutine (*nat* and *int* are Isabelle type conversion functions that convert the HOL type *int* to *nat* and vice versa). The *Ret x* instruction affects only the program counter. It fetches the return address from register *x* and converts it to *nat* (the destructor *the-RetAddr* is defined by *the-RetAddr* (*RetAddr p*) = *p*).

This style of VM is called *aggressive*, because it does not perform any runtime type or safety checks. It just assumes that everything is as expected, e.g., for *Ret x* that in register *x* there is indeed a return address. It is the task of the bytecode verifier to ensure that these assumptions are met at any time.

For proving type safety it is useful to additionally define a defensive VM that performs safety checks for each instruction. This way it becomes obvious what exactly the bytecode verifier guarantees.

To indicate type errors in the defensive VM, we introduce the datatype

$$\alpha \; type\text{-}error \; = \; TypeError \; | \; Normal \; \alpha$$

Similar to the aggressive machine, we build on a function *check-instr* that performs the safety checks for a single execution step. The definitions for *Jsr* and *Ret* do not contain any surprises. In fact, for *Jsr* we only need the branch target to be inside the method:

check-instr (*Jsr b*) *hp stk regs Cl sig pc maxpc frs* =
$0 \leq$ (*int pc*)+*b* $\land$ *nat*(*int pc*+*b*) < *maxpc*

The *Ret x* instruction requires that the index *x* is inside the register set, that the value of the register is indeed a return address, and that this address is inside the method:

check-instr (*Ret x*) *hp stk regs Cl sig pc maxpc frs* =
x < *length regs* $\land$ *isRetAddr* (*regs*!*x*) $\land$ *the-RetAddr* (*regs*!*x*) < *maxpc*

One-step execution in the defensive machine directly uses the aggressive machine. The function *check* merely unpacks the state *s* into the parameter form used by *check-instr*, *exec* does the same for *exec-instr*.

exec-d TypeError = *TypeError*
exec-d (*Normal s*) = *if check s then Normal* (*exec s*) *else TypeError*

The transition relation $\xrightarrow{\text{djvm}}$ is again the reflexive transitive closure of single step execution.

3   The Bytecode Verifier

Our formalization of the BV consists of an abstract framework for dataflow analysis together with a concrete type system that instantiates the framework. In the following, we will concentrate on the type system for subroutines and we will make explicit the requirements the dataflow analysis places on the type system to be admissible for bytecode verification. Abstractly, the parameters of the framework are a *semilattice* describing types and subtyping and a *flow function* describing the effect of instructions at the type level. The result of the framework is a fully executable BV together with a proof of termination and adherence to the type system. We discuss the semilattice with its restrictions in §3.1 and the flow function in §3.2. Details on the framework itself can be found in [9,7].

Since the BV verifies one method at a time, we can view the context of a method and a program as fixed. The context consists of the following values:

Γ	:: *program*	the program,
ins	:: *instr list*	the instructions of the method,
mxs	:: *nat*	maximum stack size of the method,
mxr	:: *nat*	size of the register set,
mpc	:: *nat*	maximum program counter,
rt	:: *ty*	return type of the method,
et	:: *ex-table*	exception handler table of the method,
pc	:: *nat*	program counter of the current instruction.

The context variables are proper parameters of all functions that use them in the Isabelle formalization. We treat them as global here to spare the reader endless parameter lists in each definition.

3.1 Semilattice

The first parameter of the framework is a semilattice: a tuple $(A, \leq_r, \sqcup_f)$ of a carrier set $A :: \alpha \ set$ (the set of types), a partial order $\leq_r :: \alpha \Rightarrow \alpha \Rightarrow bool$ (the subtyping relation), and a supremum function $\sqcup_f :: \alpha \Rightarrow \alpha \Rightarrow \alpha$ (calculating least common supertypes). The termination proof of the dataflow analysis requires $\leq_r$ to satisfy the *ascending chain condition*. A partial order $\leq_r$ satisfies the ascending chain condition on A iff there is no infinitely ascending chain $x_0 <_r x_1 <_r \ldots$ in A ($a <_r b$ is short for $a \leq_r b \wedge a \neq b$). In this section we shall build up a semilattice suitable for subroutines.

Following the idea of Coglio [4], we use sets as the elements of the semilattice. The order is the usual subset relation $\subseteq$, and the supremum is union $\cup$. The HOL datatype of basic types in μJava is the following:

$$\textbf{datatype} \ \textit{prim-ty} = \textit{Void} \mid \textit{Boolean} \mid \textit{Integer} \mid \textit{RetA nat}$$
$$\textit{ref-ty} \quad = \textit{NullT} \mid \textit{ClassT cname}$$
$$\textit{ty} \qquad = \textit{PrimT prim-ty} \mid \textit{RefT ref-ty}$$

The above means that, in μJava, a type ty is either a primitive type or a reference type. Primitive types can be the usual *Void*, *Boolean*, and *Integer*, but also a return address *RetA pc*. As we do not need to merge types, we can lift the value pc of return addresses into the type system and use it to determine the successors of *Ret* instructions. Reference types are the null type (for the *Null* reference), and class types. For readability, we use the following abbreviations, implemented as *syntax translations* in Isabelle:

$$\textbf{translations} \quad NT \rightleftharpoons \textit{RefT NullT} \qquad\qquad \textit{Int} \rightleftharpoons \textit{PrimT Integer}$$
$$\textit{Class C} \rightleftharpoons \textit{RefT (ClassT C)} \quad \textit{Bool} \rightleftharpoons \textit{PrimT Boolean}$$
$$\textit{RA pc} \rightleftharpoons \textit{PrimT (RetA pc)}$$

To satisfy the ascending chain condition with $\subseteq$, we need to restrict the datatype ty to a finite subset:

$$\textit{types} \equiv \{T \mid \textit{is-type } \Gamma \ T \wedge (\textit{isRA } T \longrightarrow \textit{theRA } T < mpc)\}$$

The predicate *is-type T* holds if T is declared in Γ, *isRA* does the obvious, and *theRA (RA pc)* is pc.

It remains to lift this set to the operand stack and register set structure of the BV. The register set is a list of a fixed length mxr. Apart from basic types, it may contain unusable values that we denote by an artificial top element Err. We write $types_\top$ for the extended set of basic types. The operand stack is a list not of fixed, but of maximum, length mxs. Using *list n A* for the set of lists over A with length n we arrive at:

$$\textit{state-types} \equiv \left(\bigcup \{\textit{list n types} \mid n \leq mxs\}\right) \times \textit{list mxr types}_\top$$

The carrier set *states* of the semilattice in the BV is the power set of *state-types* extended by another artificial error element:

$$\textit{states} \equiv (\textit{Pow state-types})_\top$$

The framework [9,7] provides us with $\subseteq_T$ and $\cup_T$ that extend $\subseteq$ and $\cup$ canonically by treating *Err* as top element. Using these, we have shown the following lemma.

Lemma 1. *(states, $\subseteq_T$, $\cup_T$) is a semilattice and $\subseteq_T$ satisfies the ascending chain condition on states.*

It was easy (automatic) to convince Isabelle of the semilattice property. The ascending chain condition for $\subseteq$ follows directly from the fact that *states* is finite. Since we know that the state types are finite sets, we can replace them by a list implementation in a real BV. We have done so in the ML code generated from the Isabelle specification (using [3]); in the formalization we carry on with sets.

3.2 Flow Function

The flow function of the framework describes the effect instructions have on the type level. It is intuitive to split the definition of this flow function into two parts: a function *app* :: *nat* $\Rightarrow$ *state-type* $\Rightarrow$ *bool* which checks the applicability of the instruction, and *eff* :: *nat* $\Rightarrow$ *state-type* $\Rightarrow$ (*nat* $\times$ *state-type*) *list* which carries out the instruction assuming it is applicable. Going back to the example of §1.3 (Fig. 2), *app* would check for position *1* (*LitPush 0*) that *0* is not an address and that there is enough space on the stack to push the result; *eff* would return $[(2,\{([Int,Int], [Int,Err,Err])\})]$, which says that the effect of *LitPush 0* is pushing one integer onto the stack, and that this result must be propagated to position *2* in the instruction list. Note that there can be a different effect for each successor instruction and that the successors can also depend on the input state type, i.e., the shape of the control flow graph may change during the analysis. Both degrees of freedom are necessary to model the *Ret x* instruction.

For the dataflow analysis to be correct, the framework places the following restrictions on *app* and *eff*:

The semilattice carrier A must be closed under *eff* and the effect *eff* must be bounded by *mpc*:

$$\forall s \in states.\ \forall p < mpc.\ \forall (q,t) \in set\ (eff\ p\ s).\ q < mpc \wedge t \in states$$

Applicability must be monotone:

$$\forall s \in states.\ \forall t \in states.\ \forall p < mpc.\ s \subseteq t \longrightarrow (app\ p\ t \longrightarrow app\ p\ s)$$

The effect must be monotone:

$$\forall s \in states.\ \forall t \in states.\ \forall p < mpc.\ s \subseteq t \wedge app\ p\ t \longrightarrow eff\ p\ s \leq_{\{\subseteq\}} eff\ p\ t$$

where $A \leq_{\{r\}} B \equiv \forall (p,s) \in set\ A.\ \exists t.\ (p,t) \in set\ B \wedge s \leq_r t.$

Note that the monotonicity restriction on *eff* allows the shape of the control flow graph to change in the analysis: if we increase the state type s at a position p, the data flow graph may get more edges (but not less), and the result at each edge may increase (but not decrease).

In the following we instantiate *app* and *eff* for the instruction set of the
μJVM. Both definitions are again subdivided into one part for normal and one
part for exceptional execution.

We begin with the exception handling part of *app*. It builds on a function
xcpt-names that determines which of the exceptions that could occur for instruction *i* have a handler in the method. It returns a list of the exception class
names mentioned in those handlers. For *Getfield* for instance it either returns
the one element list [*NullPointer*], or the empty list if there is no handler for
a *NullPointer* exception. For the *Invoke* instructions all handlers that protect
instruction *i* have to be reported, because an uncaught exception could be propagated up from the invoked method. Applicability for the exception case then
only requires that these class names are declared in the program:

$$xcpt\text{-}app\ i\ \equiv\ \forall\ C\ \in\ set\ (xcpt\text{-}names\ i\ pc\ et).\ is\text{-}class\ \Gamma\ C$$

Remember that *pc* and *et* are part of the context defined in the beginning of
§3. The definition of the effect in the exception case uses *match-ex-table C pc et*
returning *Some handler-pc* if there is an exception handler in the table *et* for
an exception of class *C* thrown at position *pc*, and *None* otherwise. The actual
effect is the same for all instructions: the registers *lt* remain the same; the stack is
cleared, and a reference to the exception object is pushed. The Isabelle notation
f ' A is the image of a set *A* under a function *f*. This effect occurs for every
exception class *C* the instruction may possibly throw.

$$
\begin{aligned}
xcpt\text{-}eff\ &::\ instr\ \Rightarrow\ state\text{-}type\ \Rightarrow\ (nat\ \times\ state\text{-}type)\ list\\
xcpt\text{-}eff\ i\ s\ &\equiv\ let\quad t\ =\ \lambda C.\ (\lambda(st,lt).\ ([Class\ C],\ lt))\ {}^{\backprime}\ s;\\
&\qquad\quad pc'\ =\ \lambda C.\ the\ (match\text{-}ex\text{-}table\ C\ pc\ et)\\
&\qquad in\ map\ (\lambda C.\ (pc'\ C,\ t\ C))\ (xcpt\text{-}names\ i\ pc\ et)
\end{aligned}
$$

This concludes the exception case and we proceed to the applicability of instructions in the normal case. Here, it suffices to look at the elements of the state
type separately: *app'*, defined in Fig. 4, works on one single stack and register
set; *app* then lifts this to sets, i.e., complete state types.

In *app'*, a few new functions occur: *typeof* :: *val* ⇒ *ty option* returns *None* for
addresses, and the type of the value otherwise; *field* looks up declaration information of object fields (defining class and type), while *method* looks up declaration
information for methods (here only used to determine if and in which class the
method is defined); *take* and *rev* are the usual functions on lists known from
functional programming. The subtype ordering ⪯ builds on the direct subclass
relation *subcls Γ* induced by the program *Γ*. It satisfies:

$$
\begin{aligned}
T\ &\preceq\ T\\
NT\ &\preceq\ RefT\ T\\
Class\ C\ &\preceq\ Class\ D\quad\ \ if\ (C,D)\ \in\ (subcls\ \Gamma)^{*}
\end{aligned}
$$

where $(C,D)\ \in\ (subcls\ \Gamma)^{*}$ means that *C* is a subclass of *D*. Note that although
the subtype relation is no longer used as the semilattice order in the BV, it is
still needed to check applicability of instructions.

app' :: $instr \times (ty\ list \times ty\ err\ list) \Rightarrow bool$

$app'\ (Load\ idx,\ (st,lt))$ $\qquad = idx < lt \wedge lt!idx \neq Err \wedge size\ st < mxs$

$app'\ (Store\ idx,\ (t\#st,lt))$ $\qquad = idx < size\ lt$

$app'\ (LitPush\ v,\ (st,lt))$ $\qquad = size\ st < mxs \wedge typeof\ v \in Some`\{NT,\ Bool,\ Int\}$

$app'\ (Getfield\ F\ C,\ (t\#st,lt))$ $\qquad = is\text{-}class\ \Gamma\ C \wedge\ t \preceq Class\ C\ \wedge$
$\qquad\qquad\qquad\qquad\qquad\qquad (\exists\,t'.\ field\ (\Gamma,C)\ F = Some\ (C,\ t'))$

$app'\ (Putfield\ F\ C,(t_1\#t_2\#st,lt)) = is\text{-}class\ \Gamma\ C\ \wedge$
$\qquad\qquad\qquad\qquad\qquad\qquad (\exists\,t'.\ field\ (\Gamma,C)\ F = Some\ (C,t')\ \wedge$
$\qquad\qquad\qquad\qquad\qquad\qquad t_2 \preceq Class\ C \wedge t_1 \preceq t')$

$app'\ (New\ C,\ (st,lt))$ $\qquad\qquad = is\text{-}class\ \Gamma\ C \wedge size\ st < mxs$

$app'\ (Checkcast\ C,\ t\#st,lt))$ $\qquad = is\text{-}class\ \Gamma\ C \wedge isRefT\ t$

$app'\ (Dup,\ (t\#st,lt))$ $\qquad\qquad = 1+size\ st < mxs$

$app'\ (IAdd,\ (t_1\#t_2\#st,lt))$ $\qquad = t_1 = t_2 \wedge t_1 = PrimT\ Integer$

$app'\ (Ifcmpeq\ b,\ (t_1\#t_2\#st,lt))$ $\quad = (isRefT\ t_1 \wedge isRefT\ t_2) \vee t_1 = t_2$

$app'\ (Goto\ b,\ s)$ $\qquad\qquad\qquad = True$

$app'\ (Return,\ (t\#st,lt))$ $\qquad\quad = t \preceq rt$

$app'\ (Throw,\ (t\#st,lt))$ $\qquad\quad = isRefT\ t$

$app'\ (Jsr\ b,\ (st,lt))$ $\qquad\qquad = length\ st < maxs$

$app'\ (Ret\ x,\ (st,lt))$ $\qquad\qquad = x < length\ lt \wedge (\exists\,r.\ lt!x{=}OK\ (RA\ r))$

$app'\ (Invoke\ C\ mn\ ps,\ (st,lt))$ $\quad = size\ ps < size\ st \wedge is\text{-}class\ \Gamma\ C\ \wedge$
$\qquad\qquad\qquad\qquad\qquad\qquad method\ (\Gamma,C)\ (mn,ps) \neq None\ \wedge$
$\qquad\qquad\qquad\qquad\qquad\qquad let\ as = rev\ (take\ (size\ ps)\ st);\ t = st!size\ ps$
$\qquad\qquad\qquad\qquad\qquad\qquad in\ t \preceq Class\ C \wedge as\ [\preceq]\ ps$

$app'\ (i,s)$ $\qquad\qquad\qquad\qquad = False$

Fig. 4. Applicability of instructions.

The definition of app' itself is large, but for most instructions straightforward. Since they are the focus of this paper, we will look at Jsr and Ret in more detail. The $Jsr\ b$ instruction is easy: it puts the return address on the stack, so we have to make sure that there is enough space for it. The test whether pc' is within the code boundaries is done once for all instructions in app below. $Ret\ x$ is equally simple: the index x must be inside the register set, and the value in register x must be a return address.

With app', we can now build the full applicability function app: an instruction is applicable when it is applicable in the normal and in the exception case for every element in the state type. To ensure that eff is bounded, we also require that all successor program counters are in the method:

app :: $nat \Rightarrow state\text{-}type \Rightarrow bool$

$app\ p\ s \equiv \forall\,t{\in}s.\ xcpt\text{-}app\ (ins!p) \wedge app'\ (ins!p,t) \wedge (\forall\,(q,t){\in}set\ (eff\ p\ s).\ q{<}mpc)$

This concludes applicability. It remains to build the normal case for eff and to combine the two cases into the final effect function. In eff we must calculate the successor program counters together with new state types. For the non-exception case, we can define them separately. Fig. 5 shows the successors. Again, most instructions are as expected. Jsr is a simple, relative jump, the same as $Goto$. $Ret\ x$ is more interesting. It is the only instruction whose successors depend

$$succs :: instr \Rightarrow nat \Rightarrow state\text{-}type \Rightarrow nat\ list$$
$$succs\ (Ifcmpeq\ b)\ pc\ s = [pc+1,\ nat\ (int\ pc\ +\ b)]$$
$$succs\ (Goto\ b)\ pc\ s\quad = [nat\ (int\ pc\ +\ b)]$$
$$succs\ Return\ pc\ s\quad\quad = []$$
$$succs\ Throw\ pc\ s\quad\quad = []$$
$$succs\ (Jsr\ b)\ pc\ s\quad\quad = [nat\ (int\ pc\ +\ b)]$$
$$succs\ (Ret\ x)\ pc\ s\quad\quad = (SOME\ l.\ set\ l = (the\text{-}RA\ x)\ `\ s)$$
$$succs\ i\ pc\ s\quad\quad\quad\quad = [pc+1]$$

Fig. 5. Successor program counters for the non-exception case.

on the current state type s. The function $the\text{-}RA\ x\ (st,lt)$ extracts the return address from register x in lt. Since $succs$ returns lists and not sets, we use Hilbert's epsilon operator $SOME$ to pick any list that converts to this set. The result of $succs\ (Ret\ 1)\ \{([],[Int,RA\ 5]),\ ([],(Int,RA\ 7))\}$, for example, is $[5,7]$. Remember that in the implementation we plan to use lists for state types instead of sets, so this $SOME$ will be just the identity function.

As with app we first define an eff' on single stack and registers sets (Fig. 6). The $method$ expression for $Invoke$ determines the return type of the method in question.

$$eff' :: instr \Rightarrow ty\ list \times ty\ err\ list \Rightarrow ty\ list \times ty\ err\ list$$
$$eff'\ (Load\ idx)\ (st,\ lt)\quad\quad = (ok\text{-}val\ (lt!idx)\#st,\ lt)$$
$$eff'\ (Store\ idx)\ (t\#st,\ lt)\quad = (st,\ lt[idx:=\ OK\ t])$$
$$eff'\ (LitPush\ v)\ (st,\ lt)\quad\quad = (the\ (typeof\ v)\#st,\ lt)$$
$$eff'\ (Getfield\ F\ C)\ (t\#st,\ lt) = (snd\ (the\ (field\ (\Gamma,C)\ F))\#st,lt)$$
$$eff'\ (Putfield\ F\ C)\ (st,\ lt)\quad = (tl\ (tl\ st),lt)$$
$$eff'\ (New\ C)\ (st,lt)\quad\quad\quad = (Class\ C\ \#\ st,lt)$$
$$eff'\ (Checkcast\ C)\ (t\#st,lt)\quad = (Class\ C\ \#\ st,lt)$$
$$eff'\ Dup\ (t\#st,lt)\quad\quad\quad\quad = (t\#t\#st,lt)$$
$$eff'\ IAdd\ (t_1\#t_2\#st,lt)\quad\quad = (PrimT\ Integer\#st,lt)$$
$$eff'\ (Ifcmpeq\ b)\ (st,lt)\quad\quad = (tl\ (tl\ st),lt)$$
$$eff'\ (Goto\ b)\ s\quad\quad\quad\quad\quad = s$$
$$eff'\ (Jsr\ t)\ (st,lt)\quad\quad\quad\quad = (RA\ (pc+1)\#st,lt)$$
$$eff'\ (Ret\ x)\ s\quad\quad\quad\quad\quad = s$$
$$eff'\ (Invoke\ C\ mn\ ps)\ (st,lt) = let\ st' = drop\ (1+size\ ps)\ st;$$
$$(\_,rt,\_,\_,\_) = the\ (method\ (\Gamma,C)\ (mn,ps))$$
$$in\ (rt\#st',\ lt)$$

Fig. 6. Effect of instructions on the state type.

While eff' saves the Ret instruction for later (by just returning s), the effect of $Jsr\ b$ is defined there: we put $pc+1$ as the return address on top of the stack. Again remember that eff' is defined in the context we have set up in the beginning of §3, so pc is the program counter of the current instruction. If it was not for Ret, we could apply eff' to every element of the state type and be done. For all other instructions we do just that, for $Ret\ x$ there is special treatment:

if we return from a subroutine to a return position pc', only those elements of the state type may be propagated that can return to this position pc'—the rest originates from different calls to the subroutine. These are the elements of the state type that contain the return address pc' in register x. We use *theIdx*, satisfying *theIdx* $(Ret\ x) = x$, to extract the register index from the instruction and *isRet i* to test whether i is a *Ret* instruction.

> *norm-eff* :: *instr* $\Rightarrow$ *nat* $\Rightarrow$ *state-type* $\Rightarrow$ *state-type*
> *norm-eff i pc' s* $\equiv$
> *if isRet i then* $\{s'|\ s'\in s \wedge$ *the-RA* *(theIdx i)* $s' = pc'\}$ *else (eff' i)* ' *s*

For $s = \{([],[Int,RA\ 5]),\ ([],(Int,RA\ 7))\}$, the result of *norm-eff* $(Ret\ 1)\ 5\ s$ is $\{([],[Int,RA\ 5])\}$ and for *norm-eff* $(Ret\ 1)\ 7\ s$ it is $\{([],[Int,RA\ 7])\}$.

This is the effect of instructions in the non-exception case. If we apply it to every successor instruction pc' returned by *succs* and append the effect for the exception case, we arrive at the final effect function *eff*.

> *eff* :: *nat* $\Rightarrow$ *state-type* $\Rightarrow$ *(nat* $\times$ *state-type) list*
> *eff p s* $\equiv$ *(map* $(\lambda pc'.\ (pc',norm$-*eff i pc' s))$ *(succs i p s))* @ *(xcpt-eff i s)*

If at p, s has for example the value used above, the result of *eff p s* is $[(5,\ \{([],[Int,RA\ 5])\}),\ (7,\ \{([],(Int,RA\ 7))\})]$.

We have shown the following lemma.

Lemma 2. *The functions app and eff are monotone, eff is bounded by mpc, and states is closed under eff.*

The proof that *eff* is bounded is easy, since *app* explicitly checks this condition. For monotonicity we do not even need to look at single instructions to see that the state type set returned by *eff* cannot decrease when we increase *eff*'s argument, and the number of successors, too, can only increase for larger state types. Preservation of the carrier set is a large case distinction over the instruction set, but Isabelle handles most cases automatically.

3.3   Instantiating the Framework

For any given semilattice and flow function, the framework yields a characterization of welltypings. In our case this is the following.

> *wt-app-eff* $\varphi \equiv \forall p{<}size\ \varphi.\ app\ p\ (\varphi!p) \wedge (\forall (q,t)\in set(eff\ p\ (\varphi!p)).\ t \subseteq \varphi!q)$

This is very natural: every instruction is applicable in its start state, and the effect is compatible with the state expected by all successor instructions.

With Lemmas 1 and 2 the framework also provides an executable function *kildall* :: *state-type list* $\Rightarrow$ *state-type list* (implementing Kildall's algorithm) that is a bytecode verifier in the following sense:

Theorem 1. *The algorithm terminates for any start value φ_0 in the carrier set with a result $\varphi = kildall\ \varphi_0$. Moreover, if $\forall p < mpc.\ \varphi!p \neq \top$, then wt-app-eff φ holds true.*

To turn *kildall* into a type checker that accepts or rejects programs, we need to supply a start state type to the algorithm. The JVM specification tells us what the first state type (at method invocation) looks like: the stack is empty, the first register contains the *this* pointer (of type *Class C*), the next registers contain the parameters of the method, and the rest of the registers is reserved for local variables (which do not have a value yet). In the definition of S_0 we use *ps*, the list of parameter types of the method, and *mxl*, the number of local variables (related to *mxr* by *mxr = 1+size ps+mxl*). The state types of the other instructions are initialized with the empty set, the bottom element of the ordering.

$$S_0 = ([], Class\ C\#(map\ (OK \circ Init)\ ps)@(replicate\ mxl\ Err))$$
$$\varphi_0 = (OK\ \{S_0\})\#(replicate\ (size\ ins-1)\ (OK\ \{\}))$$

With this, the function *wt-kil* defines the notion of a method being welltyped w.r.t. Kildall's algorithm.

$$wt\text{-}kil \equiv 0 < size\ ins \land (\forall n < size\ ins.\ (kildall\ \varphi_0)!n \neq \top)$$

Apart from the call to *kildall*, the function *wt-kil* contains the condition of the JVM specification that the instruction list must not be empty.

3.4   Type Safety

If we write $wt\text{-}prog_k$ for *wt-kil* lifted to programs, the type safety theorem is the following: if the bytecode verifier succeeds and we start the program Γ in its canonical start state, the defensive μJVM will never return a type error.

Theorem 2. *If C is a class in Γ with a main method, then*

$$wt\text{-}prog_k\ \Gamma \land (start\ \Gamma\ C) \overset{\mathrm{djvm}}{\longrightarrow} \tau \implies \tau \neq TypeError$$

The proof of this theorem goes by way of an invariant argument that we do not show here formally. It builds on the idea that the runtime states conform to their predicted type in the sense that each stack and register value is of a subtype of the statically predicted one. In this type system, the statically predicted type is a set of types. Conformance here means that the value conforms to one of the elements of the set. The proof of the invariant lemma is then by induction over the length of the execution, and by case distinction over the instruction set. For each instruction, we pick an element s of the static type set, and we conclude from the conformance of the dynamic state together with the *app* part of the BV that all assumptions of the operational semantics are met (e.g. non-empty stack). Then we execute the instruction and observe that the new state conforms to $t = eff\ pc\ s$.

With the additional facts that the start state conforms to Φ if the program has a main method (otherwise the start state is not defined) and that the defensive machine does not produce a type error in conformant states, we can conclude Theorem 2: there will be no type errors in welltyped programs.

4   Conclusion

We have instantiated our previous formalization of an abstract verified data flow analysis with a type system that supports classes, subroutines, and exception handling. The bytecode verifier we have specified is fully executable (as a standalone program) and we have proved in Isabelle/HOL that it is correct.

Our formalization of μJava consists of about 17,000 lines of Isabelle code. This includes all specifications and proofs we mentioned in this article and additionally the source language, a lightweight bytecode verifier, object initialization, and arrays, which we have not shown here.

The type system we use is based on [4]; our formalization is more than a version of [4] in Isabelle/HOL, though: we have shown that the idea scales up to a realistic model of the JVM ([4] did not even have classes). Moreover, using Isabelle has forced us to make explicit the conditions under which type systems are admissible for the data flow analysis of the BV: a generalized notion of monotonicity and the ascending chain condition. These concepts are missing in pen and paper formalizations, or they remain at least implicit.

In theory, the sets we use as state types in the data flow analysis could become very large (up to the full set of all possible types). In practice, this is not the case. Even for contrived examples in our tests most sets were singletons; the maximum size was 4. Leroy [11] proposes an optimization of the type system (using widening steps) that effectively reduces all sets to singletons, and the type system to standard bytecode verification, when no subroutines are present. Our formalization can serve as a basis for the correctness of this optimization. There exists an industrial implementation (by Trusted Logic S.A., France) of this type system, time and space efficient, for use on embedded devices.

The type system presented here is directly applicable to lightweight bytecode verification [8,16], eliminating the need to expand subroutines prior to verification on embedded devices; [7] contains more details on this aspect.

After about 5 years of research (starting with [18]), we can finally conclude that, for bytecode verification, subroutines are not a problem anymore.

Acknowledgments. We thank Norbert Schirmer and Martin Strecker for commenting on and improving drafts of this paper.

References

1. G. Barthe, G. Dufay, L. Jakubiec, S. M. de Sousa, and B. Serpette. A formal correspondence between offensive and defensive JavaCard virtual machines. In A. Cortesi, editor, *Proceedings of VMCAI'02*, Lect. Notes in Comp. Sci. Springer, 2002. to appear.
2. D. Basin, S. Friedrich, and M. Gawkowski. Verified bytecode model checkers. In *Theorem Proving in Higher Order Logics (TPHOLs'02)*, volume 2410 of Lect. Notes in Comp. Sci., pages 47–66, Virginia, USA, August 2002. Springer.

3. S. Berghofer and T. Nipkow. Executing higher order logic. In P. Callaghan, Z. Luo, J. McKinna, and R. Pollack, editors, *Types for Proofs and Programs (TYPES 2000)*, volume 2277 of *Lect. Notes in Comp. Sci.*, pages 24–40. Springer, 2002.
4. A. Coglio. Simple verification technique for complex Java bytecode subroutines. In *Proc. 4th ECOOP Workshop on Formal Techniques for Java-like Programs*, 2002.
5. S. N. Freund. *Type Systems for Object-Oriented Intermediate Languages*. PhD thesis, Stanford University, 2000.
6. Isabelle home page, 2002. http://isabelle.in.tum.de/.
7. G. Klein. Verified Java Bytecode Verification. PhD thesis, Institut für Informatik, Technische Universität München, 2003.
8. G. Klein and T. Nipkow. Verified lightweight bytecode verification. *Concurrency and Computation: Practice and Experience*, 13(13):1133–1151, 2001. Invited contribution to special issue on Formal Techniques for Java.
9. G. Klein and T. Nipkow. Verified bytecode verifiers. *Theoretical Computer Science*, 298(3):583–626, 2002.
10. X. Leroy. Java bytecode verification: an overview. In G. Berry, H. Comon, and A. Finkel, editors, *Computer Aided Verification, CAV 2001, volume 2102 of Lect. Notes in Comp. Sci.*, pages 265–285. Springer, 2001.
11. X. Leroy. Java bytecode verification: algorithms and formalizations. *J. Automated Reasoning*, 2004. to appear.
12. T. Lindholm and F. Yellin. *The Java Virtual Machine Specification*. Addison-Wesley, 1996.
13. T. Nipkow. Verified bytecode verifiers. In F. Honsell, editor, *Foundations of Software Science and Computation Structures (FOSSACS 2001)*, volume 2030 of *Lect. Notes in Comp. Sci.*, pages 347–363. Springer, 2001.
14. T. Nipkow, L. C. Paulson, and M. Wenzel. *Isabelle/HOL – A Proof Assistant for Higher-Order Logic*, volume 2283 of Lect. Notes in Comp. Sci. Springer, 2002.
15. J. Posegga and H. Vogt. Java bytecode verification using model checking. In *OOPSLA '98 Workshop Formal Underpinnings of Java*, 1998.
16. E. Rose and K. Rose. Lightweight bytecode verification. In *OOPSLA '98 Workshop Formal Underpinnings of Java*, 1998.
17. R. Stärk, J. Schmid, and E. Börger. *Java and the Java Virtual Machine – Definition, Verification, Validation*. Springer, 2001.
18. R. Stata and M. Abadi. A type system for Java bytecode subroutines. In *Proc. 25th ACM Symp. Principles of Programming Languages*, pages 149–161. ACM Press, 1998.
19. M. Wildmoser. Subroutines and Java bytecode verification. Master's thesis, Technische Universität München, 2002.

Complete Integer Decision Procedures as Derived Rules in HOL

Michael Norrish*

National ICT Australia
Michael.Norrish@nicta.com.au

Abstract. I describe the implementation of two complete decision procedures for integer Presburger arithmetic in the HOL theorem-proving system. The first procedure is Cooper's algorithm, the second, the Omega Test. Between them, the algorithms illustrate three different implementation techniques in a fully expansive system.

1 Introduction

Integer decision procedures are vital parts of interactive theorem-proving systems. Whether embedded in simplification routines and running automatically, or explicitly invoked by the user, they remove a great deal of tedium from the task of proving goals. Modern interactive systems, including ACL2 [10], Coq [1], HOL [4,11], Isabelle [13], Nuprl [8] and PVS [12], all implement such decision procedures.

There are essentially three procedures implemented in the systems mentioned above: Fourier-Motzkin variable elimination (in HOL, Isabelle and Coq[1]), SUP-INF [15] (in Nuprl) and Shostak's loop-residue algorithm [16] (in PVS). In this paper, I describe two other algorithms. The Omega Test [14] is an extension of Fourier-Motzkin variable elimination, which makes it complete over $\mathbb{Z}$. The second procedure is Cooper's algorithm [3], which is unlike the other algorithms in not requiring formulas to be in DNF before it eliminates a quantifier.

Both of the algorithms I describe differ in scope from the others mentioned: they are both complete over the domains covered by the others (universal Presburger arithmetic), and also complete over the wider language of Presburger formulas with any alternation of quantifiers. I will henceforth take Presburger formulas to be those generated by the grammar given in Fig. 1, and which are also *closed*: all occurrences of variables are bound by a universal or existential quantifier.

The task of the decision procedure is to prove a closed Presburger formula either valid or invalid. If a formula has existential quantifiers outermost and is proved valid, then it may be useful to have the procedure also return a satisfying assignment for the existential variables. Conversely, formulas that are universal at the outermost level, and which are proved invalid might prompt the return of a falsifying assignment. Both

---

* This work was done while supported by the Michael and Morven Heller Research Fellowship at St. Catharine's College, Cambridge.

[1] Coq implements just the first phase of the Omega Test (real shadow elimination), which is Fourier-Motzkin variable elimination.

$$\begin{aligned}
\textit{formula} \quad ::= &\ \textit{formula} \wedge \textit{formula} \ \mid \ \textit{formula} \vee \textit{formula} \ \mid \\
&\ \neg\textit{formula} \ \mid \ \exists\textit{var}.\textit{formula} \ \mid \ \forall\textit{var}.\textit{formula} \ \mid \\
&\ \textit{numeral} \mid \textit{term} \ \mid \ \textit{term relop term} \\
\textit{term} \quad\ ::= &\ \textit{numeral} \ \mid \ \textit{term} + \textit{term} \ \mid \ -\textit{term} \ \mid \ \textit{numeral} * \textit{term} \ \mid \ \textit{var} \\
\textit{relop} \quad\ ::= &\ < \ \mid \ \leq \ \mid \ = \ \mid \ \geq \ \mid \ > \\
\textit{var} \quad\ ::= &\ x \ \mid \ y \ \mid \ z \ldots \\
\textit{numeral} ::= &\ 0 \ \mid \ 1 \ \mid \ 2 \ldots
\end{aligned}$$

Fig. 1. Grammar defining Presburger formulas. Write $c|e$ to mean that c, necessarily a numeral, divides e exactly, or without remainder

algorithms proceed by quantifier elimination, eventually reducing the input formula to an equivalent formula without quantifiers.

This paper is arranged as follows: in Section 2, I describe Cooper's algorithm, including a proof of correctness. In Section 3, I describe the Omega Test, again proving correctness. In Section 4, I describe the techniques that I used to implement these procedures (proofs) within HOL. In the same section, I also briefly compare the two algorithms' performance. In Section 5, I describe extensions to the basic procedures that make them considerably more helpful in the interactive setting.

2   Cooper's Algorithm

The first step in Cooper's algorithm is to normalise the input formula. Negations are pushed inwards, so that they are only found around "divides" and equality leaves, and in front of existential quantifiers. The relations $\leq$, $\geq$ and $>$ are rewritten to forms involving $<$, and universal quantifiers are eliminated by transforming $\forall x\, P(x)$ into $\neg\exists x.\, \neg P(x)$. Note that neither normalisation to DNF nor to CNF occurs. The formula's terms are also normalised, with multiplications distributed over additions, coefficients gathered and other obvious normalisations applied.

The algorithm then arbitrarily picks an innermost (existential) quantifier to eliminate. This quantifier has scope over a formula whose tree structure has conjunctions and disjunctions at its internal nodes. The leaves of this sub-formula are now transformed to equivalent forms, where the quantifier's bound variable is isolated and has a positive coefficient. If a leaf involves the bound variable (x, say) at all, it is transformed to one of the six following forms:

$$\begin{array}{ccc}
cx < e & cx = e & c|dx + e \\
e < cx & \neg(cx = e) & \neg(c|dx + e)
\end{array} \tag{1}$$

where c and d are positive integer numerals, and e is an arbitrary term not including x, but possibly involving other variables.

The algorithm next finds the least common multiple (l say) of all of x's coefficients. Every leaf formula is then multiplied through by an appropriate constant so that every leaf has an occurrence of lx. The formula can then be transformed by appeal to the theorem

$$\exists x.\, P(lx) \equiv \exists x.\, P(x) \wedge l|x$$

ensuring that every occurrence of x implicitly has coefficient one.

The final phase now depends on the generation of two sets of expressions, A and B, based on the leaf expressions in the formula. Table 1 specifies how each leaf generates possible members for each set. For example, a leaf of the form $x < e$ puts e into the A-set, and does not affect the B-set. Leaves involving the divisibility relation, or which do not include the variable x, do not generate members for either set.

Leaf form	A-set	B-set
$x < e$	e	
$e < x$		e
$x = e$	$e + 1$	$e + {}^{-}1$
$\neg(x = e)$	e	e

Table 1. Generation of A and B sets

The algorithm creates two variants on the predicate P underneath the quantifier, $P_{-\infty}$ and $P_{+\infty}$. These new predicates can be understood as versions of the original where the parameter x has been made arbitrarily small (negative) or arbitrarily large, respectively. Therefore, all leaves with x free and which involve $<$ and $=$ are replaced with either true or false. For example, if x is made arbitrarily small, then $x < e$ will be true, $e < x$ will be false, $x = e$ will be false, and $\neg(x = e)$ will be true. Leaves involving divisibility will be unchanged. Finally, let δ be the least common multiple of all the c occurring in leaves of the form $c|x + e$ and $\neg(c|x + e)$.

The algorithm then eliminates the existential quantifier by using one of the two equivalences given in the following theorem. In order to reduce the amount of blow-up in term size, the first equivalence is chosen if the B-set is smaller than the A-set, and the second otherwise. If the sizes of the sets are equal, the set which has fewer occurrences of free variables is chosen.

Theorem 1 (Cooper, 1972). *Let $P(x)$ be a formula constructed of conjunctions and disjunctions of integer relations. Those relations involving x are of the form $x < e$, $e < x$, $x = e$, $x \neq e$, $c|(x + e)$ or $\neg(c|(x + e))$. Then,*

$$\exists x.\, P(x) \;\equiv\; \bigvee_{j=1}^{\delta} P_{-\infty}(j) \;\vee\; \bigvee_{j=1}^{\delta} \bigvee_{b \in B} P(b + j)$$

and

$$\exists x.\, P(x) \;\equiv\; \bigvee_{j=1}^{\delta} P_{+\infty}(j) \;\vee\; \bigvee_{j=1}^{\delta} \bigvee_{a \in A} P(a + {}^{-}j)$$

These equivalences are the heart of Cooper's algorithm. They are sufficiently similar that I will describe the proof of just the first. The equivalence is of the form $L \equiv D_1 \vee D_2$, so I prove it by showing $D_1 \Rightarrow L$, $D_2 \Rightarrow L$, and $L \wedge \neg D_2 \Rightarrow D_1$:

– The first obligation requires a proof of

$$\bigvee_{j=1}^{\delta} P_{-\infty}(j) \;\Rightarrow\; \exists x.\, P(x)$$

This result relies on two further lemmas. The first,

$$\exists y. \forall x. x < y \Rightarrow (P(x) \equiv P_{-\infty}(x)) \qquad (2)$$

states that P and $P_{-\infty}$ coincide once their arguments are small enough. There is a witness for y; the minimum of all the expressions that occur on the other side of a $<$ or an $=$ from the bound variable in the original formula.

The second lemma is

$$\forall x \, \forall c. \; P_{-\infty}(x) \equiv P_{-\infty}(x + c\delta) \qquad (3)$$

which states that the truth value of $P_{-\infty}$ is unaffected by the addition of any number of multiples of δ. Recall that the only leaves in $P_{-\infty}$ involving the bound variable x are of the form, $c|x + e$ or $\neg(c|x + e)$. As δ is the **l.c.m.** of all the c's in the formula, the truth of these leaves will be unaffected by the addition of multiples of δ to x.

The proof of the overall result follows because, from the existence of a witness satisfying $P_{-\infty}$, one can produce another, smaller than the y of (2), and thereby find a witness satisfying P.[2]

– The second obligation is

$$\bigvee_{j=1}^{\delta} \bigvee_{b \in B} P(b + j) \quad \Rightarrow \quad \exists x. P(x)$$

This implication follows immediately because the antecedent provides a witness that satisfies P.

– Finally, the most complicated case is

$$(\exists x. P(x)) \wedge \neg(\bigvee_{j=1}^{\delta} \bigvee_{b \in B} P(b + j)) \quad \Rightarrow \quad \bigvee_{j=1}^{\delta} P_{-\infty}(j) \qquad (4)$$

It is sufficient to prove that

$$\neg\left(\bigvee_{j=1}^{\delta} \bigvee_{b \in B} P(b + j)\right) \Rightarrow \forall x. P(x) \Rightarrow P(x - \delta)$$

This is sufficient because the assumption $\exists x. P(x)$ from (4) provides a witness for which P is true. The new result then provides an infinite sequence of smaller witnesses, each δ smaller than the previous. In particular, there will be one that will be smaller than the y below which $P(x) \equiv P_{-\infty}(x)$ (see (2) above). Then, because $\forall x \, c. P_{-\infty}(x) \equiv P_{-\infty}(x+c\delta)$ (see (3)), there will be another witness for $P_{-\infty}$ that will be between 1 and δ,[3] as required.

---

[2] This is using another theorem about $\mathbb{Z}$, that $\forall d. d \neq 0 \Rightarrow \forall x \, y. \exists c. y + cd < x$.
[3] Using another lemma about $\mathbb{Z}$: $\forall d. 0 < d \Rightarrow \forall x. \exists c. 0 < x + cd \leq d$.

My proof is actually of the stronger statement

$$\forall P.\ Q(x) \land \bigwedge_{j=1}^{\delta} \bigwedge_{b \in B} \neg Q(b+j) \land P(x) \Rightarrow P(x-\delta) \tag{5}$$

so that an induction on the structure of P is possible. The result needed is obtained by picking Q to be P in the above.

There are two inductive steps to the proof, one for formulas constructed by conjunction and one for disjunction. Both are straight-forward: if (5) holds for P_1 and P_2, then it holds for $\lambda x.\ P_1(x) \land P_2(x)$ as well as for $\lambda x.\ P_1(x) \lor P_2(x)$.

There are seven leaf cases to consider, one for each of the forms in (1) and one for the case when the formula P does not mention x at all. The latter is trivially true. The other cases are as follows:

- $x < e \Rightarrow x - \delta < e$
  Follows immediately ($\delta > 0$ as it is the **l.c.m.** of positive arguments).
- $e < x \Rightarrow e < x - \delta$
  Seeking a contradiction, assume $\neg(e < x - \delta)$, i.e., $x \leq e + \delta$. So, for some $j \in 1..\delta$, $x = e + j$. The top-level assumption in (5) is $Q(x)$, so $Q(e + j)$. But e is also part of the formula's B-set, so, by assumption, $\bigwedge_{j=1}^{\delta} \neg Q(e + j)$.
- $(x = e) \Rightarrow (x - \delta = e)$
  $e + {}^- 1$ is in the B-set, so derive a contradiction by noting that both $Q(e)$, and $\bigwedge_{j=1}^{\delta} \neg Q((e + {}^-1) + j)$ (pick $j = 1$).
- $\neg(x = e) \Rightarrow \neg(x - \delta = e)$
  Assume the opposite, so that $x = e + \delta$. Thus $Q(e + \delta)$. But e is in the B-set, so $\neg Q(e + \delta)$ (picking $j = \delta$), another contradiction.
- $c|x+e \Rightarrow c|x-\delta+e$. By construction of δ, $c|\delta$, so the result follows immediately. Similarly for the $\neg(c|x + e)$ case.

$\square$

3   The Omega Test

The heart of the Omega Test operates on formulas of the form

$$\exists x.\ C_1 \land C_2 \land \ldots \land C_m$$

where each C_i is of the form $t_1 \leq t_2$ and involves x. The procedure's initial normalisation must therefore convert input formulas to disjunctive normal form, move boolean negations and existential quantifiers inward and eliminate universal quantifiers. The $<$, $>$ and $\geq$ relations are easily converted to $\leq$ formulas. Sub-formulas $x \neq y$ are converted to $x + 1 \leq y \lor y + 1 \leq x$. The test's treatment of equality and divisibility relations is slightly more involved (see [14] for details), but is straightforward to implement.

Given a normalised formula (as above) sort the C_i into two sets, the lower bounds that are of the form $a \leq \alpha x$ with α positive, and the upper bounds that are of the form $\beta x \leq b$. If either set is empty, then immediately return true. Otherwise, if all of the coefficients of x in either set are equal to one (i.e., if all of the α_i are one, or all of the β_i are one), what Pugh refers to as *exact shadow* elimination can be performed. The original formula is equivalent to

$$\bigwedge_{i,j} a_i \beta_j \leq \alpha_i b_j \tag{6}$$

where i indexes lower bound constraints, and j the upper bounds. The formula (6) is also known as the *real shadow* because the equivalence is true, regardless of coefficients, when variables range over $\mathbb{R}$. The exact shadow result relies on the simpler equivalence

$$(\exists x.\ a \leq \alpha x \wedge \beta x \leq b) \equiv a\beta \leq \alpha b$$

when one of α or β is 1. The implication from left to right is easy to see. From right to left, with $\alpha = 1$, take x to be a; with $\beta = 1$, take x to be b. This result extends to the cross-product of many upper and lower bounds by two successive inductions on the respective sets.

If an exact shadow elimination is not possible, the relevant theorem for quantifier elimination is considerably more complicated.

Theorem 2 (Pugh, 1992). *Let $L(x)$ be a conjunction of lower bounds on x, indexed by i, of the form $a_i \leq \alpha_i x$, with α_i positive. Similarly, let $U(x)$ be a set of upper bounds on x, indexed by j, of the form $\beta_j x \leq b_j$, with β_j positive. Let m be the maximum of all the β_js. Then*

$$
(\exists x.\ L(x) \wedge U(x)) \equiv \quad
\begin{array}{c}
(\bigwedge_{i,j}(\alpha_i - 1)(\beta_j - 1) \leq \alpha_i b_j - a_i \beta_j) \\
\vee \\
\bigvee_i \bigvee_{k=0}^{\left\lfloor \frac{m\alpha_i - \alpha_i - m}{m} \right\rfloor} \exists x.\ (\alpha_i x = a_i + k) \wedge L(x) \wedge U(x)
\end{array}
$$

Following Pugh, the first disjunct of the RHS above is called the *dark shadow*, and the other disjuncts are called *splinters*. Note that as stated, each splinter has as many quantifiers as before. Nonetheless, the extra equality constraint means that the variable x and its quantifier can be eliminated by the normalisation techniques already mentioned, so the theorem does represent a quantifier elimination result. This theorem reduces to exact shadow elimination if all of the α_i or all the β_i are equal to 1.

The theorem is of the form $LHS \equiv D_1 \vee D_2$, with D_1 the dark shadow and D_2 the splinters. I prove the result by proving $D_1 \Rightarrow LHS$, $D_2 \Rightarrow LHS$ and $LHS \wedge \neg D_1 \Rightarrow D_2$:

- $\bigwedge_{i,j}(\alpha_i - 1)(\beta_j - 1) \leq \alpha_i b_j - a_i \beta_j \Rightarrow \exists x.\ L(x) \wedge U(x)$
  Show the result for one pair of upper and lower bound. I.e., that

$$(\alpha - 1)(\beta - 1) \leq \alpha b - a\beta \Rightarrow \exists x.\ a \leq \alpha x \wedge \beta x \leq b$$

Two inductions, on the set of lower bounds and then the upper bounds, give the complete result.
To prove the base case, assume the opposite. Then

$$\neg \exists x.\ a\beta \leq \alpha\beta x \leq \alpha b$$

I.e., there is no multiple of $\alpha\beta$ between $a\beta$ and αb. The other assumption implies $a\beta \leq \alpha b$ as α and β are both positive and non-zero. Take i to be the greatest multiple of $\alpha\beta$ less then $a\beta$. Then

$$\alpha\beta i < a\beta \leq \alpha b < \alpha\beta(i+1)$$

Because $0 < \alpha\beta(i+1) - \alpha b$, conclude $1 \leq \beta(i+1) - b$, and thus $\alpha \leq \alpha\beta(i+1) - \alpha b$. Similarly, $\beta \leq a\beta - \alpha\beta i$. Infer $\alpha + \beta \leq \alpha\beta + a\beta - \alpha b$, or (re-arranging), $\alpha b - a\beta < \alpha\beta - \alpha - \beta + 1$, which contradicts the first assumption.

- $\bigvee_i \bigvee_{k=0}^{\lfloor \frac{m\alpha_i - \alpha_i - m}{m} \rfloor} \exists x.\ (\alpha_i x = a_i + k) \wedge L(x) \wedge U(x) \implies \exists x.\ L(x) \wedge U(x)$
  Trivial, as each splinter disjunct on the left provides an x that will satisfy the weaker requirement on the right.
- $(\exists x.\ L(x) \wedge U(x)) \wedge \neg(\bigwedge_{i,j}(\alpha_i - 1)(\beta_j - 1) \leq \alpha_i b_j - a_i \beta_j) \implies$
  $\bigvee_i \bigvee_{k=0}^{\lfloor \frac{m\alpha_i - \alpha_i - m}{m} \rfloor} \exists x.\ (\alpha_i x = a_i + k) \wedge L(x) \wedge U(x)$
  Let x be the witness to the first assumption. The second assumption means that there exist α, β, a and b such that

$$ab - a\beta \leq \alpha\beta - \beta - \alpha \tag{7}$$

These values occur in constraints from L and U, so $\beta x \leq b$ and $a \leq \alpha x$. Multiplying the former through by α gives $\alpha\beta x \leq \alpha b$, so in conjunction with (7)

$$
\begin{aligned}
\alpha\beta x &\leq a\beta + \alpha\beta - \beta - \alpha \\
\Rightarrow \beta(\alpha x - a) &\leq \alpha\beta - \beta - \alpha \\
\Rightarrow \alpha x - a &\leq \left\lfloor \frac{\alpha\beta - \beta - \alpha}{\beta} \right\rfloor
\end{aligned}
$$

All of the β coefficients are $\leq m$, so

$$\left\lfloor \frac{\alpha\beta - \beta - \alpha}{\beta} \right\rfloor \leq \left\lfloor \frac{m\alpha - \alpha - m}{m} \right\rfloor$$

There is now enough information to pick the appropriate disjunct from the RHS. The α_i is α and k is $\alpha x - a$.

$\square$

Even when exact shadow elimination is not possible, it is still worth checking the real shadow of a formula if all of its variables are bound by existential quantifiers. The latter condition means that performing all of the real shadow eliminations will result in a ground formula. If this formula is false, then so too is the original formula. Thus [14] describes the algorithm for the purely existential case in three stages:

1. Check the real shadow. If it is unsatisfiable, so is the original. If it is satisfiable and the shadow is exact, then the original formula is satisfiable.
2. Check the dark shadow. If it is satisfiable, so is the original.
3. Check the splinters.

4   Implementations in HOL

HOL is a theorem-proving system in the tradition of LCF [5]. Theorems are implemented as an abstract data type in the language SML, exploiting that language's strong typing system, which guarantees that a type's abstraction barrier can not be subverted. The implementation of the type of theorems provides functions, known as the *primitive rules of inference*, for manipulating and creating theorem values. Strong typing then ensures that all such values must ultimately be constructed using just these rules. Rich suites of tools for proving theorems are built on top of this *logical kernel*, but all proofs are *fully expanded* to sequences of primitive inferences. No tool or derived rule has the ability to simply assert a theorem; proofs must be provided.[4]

The implementations of Cooper's algorithm and the Omega Test in HOL illustrate three different techniques for realising decision procedures in a fully expansive setting. Before examining each technique's use in the implementation of the two decision procedures, I will describe each in general terms, as well as giving examples of their use in other applications.

Theorem instance re-proof: This, the simplest but also most naïve technique, plays out the central proof of a decision procedure's core theorem(s) for every problem instance. This approach is used by the implementation of Cooper's algorithm.

For a contrived example, consider a proof procedure to turn a theorem of the form $\vdash P \Rightarrow Q \Rightarrow R$ into a theorem of the form $\vdash P \wedge Q \Rightarrow R$. The ML code implementing this transformation would involve calls to the inference rules given as labels in this inference tree:

$$\cfrac{\cfrac{\cfrac{}{P \wedge Q \vdash P \wedge Q}\text{ ASSUME}}{P \wedge Q \vdash Q}\text{ CONJ2} \qquad \cfrac{\cfrac{\cfrac{}{P \wedge Q \vdash P \wedge Q}\text{ ASSUME}}{P \wedge Q \vdash P}\text{ CONJ1} \qquad \cfrac{\cfrac{\cfrac{\vdash P \Rightarrow Q \Rightarrow R}{P \vdash Q \Rightarrow R}\text{ UNDISCH}}{P, Q \vdash R}\text{ UNDISCH}}{P \wedge Q, Q \vdash R}\text{ PROVE\_HYP}}{P \wedge Q \vdash R}\text{ PROVE\_HYP}}{\vdash P \wedge Q \Rightarrow R}\text{ DISCH}$$

This procedure will run in constant time in terms of number of primitive inferences (nine in this case), but is clearly awkward and inefficient. It is as well that all proof programming in HOL doesn't have to drop to this level. The *pro forma* theorem approach described below is much more appropriate here: prove the equivalence

$$\vdash (P \Rightarrow Q \Rightarrow R) \equiv (P \wedge Q \Rightarrow R)$$

once and then instantiate this theorem as and when necessary.

Theorem instance re-proof is not always so obviously inappropriate. It is particularly useful when it is impossible or difficult to express the generalised theorem in HOL's logic. For example, in a suitable logic about polytypic functions, the following might be true

$$map\ f \circ map\ g = map(f \circ g)$$

---

[4] HOL does not have actual "proof objects". At most, a proof can be regarded a sequence of calls to the kernel's API; only the theorem it creates has any lasting existence.

where map was a polytypic function that mapped functions over the values in appropriate container types, without disturbing the structure of the container. HOL's logic can not give a type to or define such a map. Nevertheless, given suitable definitions of the types and their map functions, it is not difficult to write a proof procedure that automatically proves the instances (over lists and trees, for example) of the more general "theorem".

Using *pro forma* theorems: As has already been suggested, this approach involves proving suitably general theorems embodying the core of the decision procedure (often direct equivalences between formulas). These theorems can then be instantiated with specific problems, quickly implementing one or more steps of the decision procedure. The "symbolic" implementation of the Omega Test (described below) uses this technique.

One problem with this technique arises when the theorem in question relates its LHS to some new formula on the right that is a function of the actual form of the LHS. Theorems 1 and 2 demonstrate this problem: Cooper's theorem requires the construction of the new $P_{-\infty}$ and $P_{+\infty}$ formulas; Pugh's theorem requires the generation of the pair-wise product of a formula's upper and lower-bound constraints. The example of the propositional rewrite above $((P \Rightarrow Q \Rightarrow R) \equiv (P \wedge Q \Rightarrow R))$ doesn't have this problem because the equivalence doesn't require any action on the formulas instantiated for P, Q and R.

If, for example, P is a predicate on $\mathbb{Z}$, with HOL type `int -> bool`, it is difficult to directly define a function to calculate $P_{-\infty}$.[5] Instead, Harrison's "shadow syntax" approach can be used [6]: a concrete type is used to implement a syntax for the formula, and an interpretation function relates this new syntax back to the original domain. Thus, in his implementation of Kreisel and Krivine's quantifier elimination algorithm for the elementary first order theory of $\mathbb{R}$, Harrison uses a constant `poly` with defining equations[6]

```
poly x [] = 0
poly x (h::t) = h + x * poly x t
```

In this way, a polynomial on variable x can be reduced to `poly` x followed by a list of the coefficients of the powers of x. Similarly, conjunctions and disjunctions of relations on polynomials are represented as lists of polynomials, interpreted by appropriate functions. Harrison proves the theorems that form the basis for the algorithm, with those theorems' manipulations of the syntax of the formulas represented by manipulations of the various lists that make up the shadow syntax.

One further advantage of the use of *pro forma* theorems is that they can provide an elegant packaging of an algorithm's fundamentals as data (the theorems themselves), rather than as the code necessary in the re-proof technique above.

External proof discovery: This technique is appropriate in applications where a decision procedure does most of its work finding a proof, and where the proof itself, however construed, is relatively small. The core idea is to do proof discovery outside

---

[5] One issue is that the size of the domain is uncountable, but the desired function only operates over the countable subset corresponding to syntactically expressible formulas.

[6] A note on HOL syntax: `[]` is the empty list; `h::t` is the list consisting of element `h` "cons"-ed onto the list `t`.

of the logical kernel, so that the kernel's general-purpose machinery can be replaced with special-purpose code tuned to the particular application. It is only when the proof is found that the kernel becomes involved; it executes the proof itself and confirms that the special-purpose code was correct.[7]

This technique is clearly applicable in deciding first order logic. There, proofs are typically very short in comparison to the work done in exploring all of the possible paths to a negated goal's refutation. This approach is exemplified by Hurd's linking of HOL to the Gandalf resolution prover [7]. There the external tool is external not just to the logical kernel, but to HOL itself. On proving a goal, Gandalf provides a log of the successful resolution and modulation steps required, and Hurd's HOL code then interprets this proof-log "back into" the logical kernel.

Another example of the technique is Boulton's implementation of his procedure for universal Presburger arithmetic on $\mathbb{N}$ [2]. On this domain, Fourier-Motzkin variable elimination can be seen as a refutation procedure. Boulton translates the negated goal into a special data structure representing the set of known constraints. When new consequences are inferred, each is accompanied by a closure that, when run, would prove that consequence.[8] If false is inferred, then just those inferences leading to that conclusion need to be replayed in the logical kernel. This implementation inspired the "no alternating quantifiers" part of the Omega Test.

4.1   Implementing Cooper's Algorithm

The implementation of Cooper's algorithm uses the theorem instance re-proof technique. Though it uses some pre-proved theorems (the various lemmas about $\mathbb{Z}$ mentioned in the course of the proof, for example), the bulk of the proof is replayed for every proof instance. The calculation of the RHS of Theorem 1, particularly the predicate $P_{-\infty}$ (or $P_{+\infty}$ depending on the choice of equivalence), can be done extra-logically, but the required properties of the new formulas on the right must still be proved.

Although the presented proof involves an induction over the structure of the general formula P, the implementation only ever proves a concrete instance (P is given as an input), so there is no induction. Instead, the procedure for proving the instance is written recursively. The procedure starts with the theorem $P(x) \vdash P(x)$. If the conclusion is of the form $P_1(x) \wedge P_2(x)$, the procedure makes recursive calls on $P(x) \vdash P_1(x)$ and $P(x) \vdash P_2(x)$ to prove $P(x) \vdash P_1(x - \delta)$ and $P(x) \vdash P_2(x - \delta)$ (assuming the B-set is being used). It is easy to then combine these theorems to generate

$$P(x) \vdash P_1(x - \delta) \wedge P_2(x - \delta)$$

Disjunctions are handled similarly. At the top-level the required implication is generated by discharging the assumption. The use of $P(x)$ as an unchanging assumption throughout the recursion models the use of the predicate Q in the earlier proof of Theorem 1.

I also implemented a version of the algorithm using a *pro forma* theorem. This required the proof in HOL of the general statement of the theorem. The shadow syntax was defined in the logic as a free algebra, with constructors such as Conjn, Disjn and

---

[7] This technique can also be seen as certificate checking; see [6, §6] for an extended discussion.

[8] The use of closures in this case is a specific instance of Boulton's general idea of *lazy theorems*.

xLT. This type provided concrete syntax for predicates over integers. The function for evaluating shadow syntax was `eval_form`, taking a formula in this concrete form and a value to evaluate with respect to it. Thus, `eval_form` can be seen as an implementation of the action of applying a predicate to an argument. Its definition was

```
eval_form (Conjn f1 f2) x = eval_form f1 x ∧ eval_form f2 x
eval_form (Disjn f1 f2) x = eval_form f1 x ∨ eval_form f2 x
eval_form (Negn f) x = ¬eval_form f x
eval_form (UnrelatedBool b) x = b
eval_form (xLT i) x = x < i
eval_form (LTx i) x = i < x
eval_form (xEQ i) x = (x = i)
eval_form (xDivided i1 i2) x = i1 int_divides x + i2
```

The final theorem proved in HOL was of the form

$$\langle \text{side conditions} \rangle \Rightarrow ((\exists\texttt{x. eval\_form f x}) \equiv \ldots)$$

This "shadow syntax" implementation of the core part of the algorithm, coded as a complete replacement for the theorem instance re-proof component, performed slightly worse than the original (though only on a small regression test-suite, see below). With the *pro forma* approach, the final step of instantiating the core theorem is constant time, but this must be preceded by an $O(n)$ translation of the formula into its shadow syntax, and a similar translation back out afterwards. Both approaches should thus have the same asymptotic complexity, and determining which to use in practice requires experimentation.

The HOL implementation also includes most of Cooper's other suggested improvements to his algorithm, including those designed to prevent or ameliorate the "δ-expansion". Though it seems impossible to prevent the introduction of new disjunctions over elements of the A or B-sets, one can delay having to expand the disjunctions over the $j \in 1 \ldots \delta$ until all of the quantifiers have been eliminated. If the final formula then includes divisibility constraints on the variables j, then the range of these constraints can be reduced, resulting in fewer disjuncts to check.

4.2   Implementing the Omega Test

The implementation of the Omega Test consists of two loosely coupled components. One uses external proof discovery, and finds refutations or satisfying assignments for existential goals. The other, "symbolic" sub-system uses *pro forma* theorems to perform quantifier elimination on formulas with alternating quantifiers, and also on existential formulas that produce "splinters".

After an input formula is normalised, it is passed to the appropriate sub-system. Both can result in the other being called. If an existential goal is not exact, is not refuted by its real shadow, and has no satisfying assignment found in its dark shadow, then it is passed to the symbolic sub-system, which will eliminate one quantifier. When the symbolic sub-system eliminates a quantifier, the resulting formula may be purely universal or existential. If so, it is passed to the external proof discovery sub-system.

The external proof discovery sub-system is inspired by Boulton's existing code for $\mathbb{N}$ in HOL. There are two interesting differences between that implementation and mine. Where his code uses closures to represent possible proofs, I use an explicit, concrete ML data structure. Its declaration is

```
datatype 'a derivation =
  ASM of 'a
| REAL_COMBIN of int * 'a derivation * 'a derivation
| GCD_CHECK of 'a derivation
| DIRECT_CONTR of 'a derivation * 'a derivation
```

A derivation represents the proof of a formula

$$0 \leq c_1 v_1 + \ldots + c_n v_n + c$$

where the v_i are the existentially bound variables. The four constructors in the type correspond to making an assumption, combining a lower and upper bound at variable i, reducing a constraint because all of its variable coefficients have a common divisor, and finding a direct contradiction, where one constraint is of the form $0 \leq X + c$, the other is $0 \leq {}^-X + d$ and where ${}^-c \not\leq d$. (X can be the sum of any number of $c_i v_i$ pairs, allowing a refutation to be found before all variables are eliminated.)

In practice, the polymorphic 'a parameter of the derivation type is instantiated to term, the type of HOL terms. Nonetheless, the implementation of the external proof discovery analysis doesn't require any connection with the HOL kernel and has been used independently by others. This is in contrast with Boulton's code, which is tied to the HOL kernel because its closures are of pending calls to the kernel's rules of inference.

More significantly, Boulton's code only finds refutations. (An implementation of SUP-INF is used separately to find witnesses for existential goals.) This is because a goal is not necessarily satisfiable if its real shadow does not refute it. On the other hand, the Omega Test implementation can find satisfying assignments when it reduces an exact or dark shadow to a formula of just one variable. Such a formula has at most two constraints, a lower and upper bound. A coefficient that isn't 1 or $^-1$ can be divided out, and one of $0 \leq cx + c_1$ and $0 \leq cx + c_2$ will imply the other, because c_1 and c_2 are constants.[9] If the constraints aren't contradictory, then either bound will satisfy the formula. Recursively unwinding the computation of the shadow, satisfying assignments can be found for other variables. The original goal can then be proved as a HOL theorem using the provided witnesses.

The "symbolic" sub-system is based on constants evallower and evalupper, which are used to interpret lists of pairs of numbers as lower and upper-bound constraints on a provided value. The defining equations for evallower are

```
evallower x [] = ⊤
evallower x ((c,lb)::cs) = lb <= &c * x ∧ evallower x cs
```

---

[9] Following [14], my implementation uses a hash-table to efficiently eliminate redundant constraints.

(The first number of each pair is a natural number, ensuring that the bound really is a lower-bound, so the & function is used to inject from $\mathbb{N}$ to $\mathbb{Z}$. The evalupper function is defined similarly.)

The theorem representing exact shadow elimination is simple to state:

```
EVERY fst_nzero uppers ∧ EVERY fst_nzero lowers ⇒
EVERY fst1 uppers ∨ EVERY fst1 lowers ⇒
((∃x. evalupper x uppers ∧ evallower x lowers) ≡
 real_shadow uppers lowers)
```

The side-conditions require that the coefficients are all non-zero, and that either all of the upper or lower coefficients are equal to 1. The real_shadow function constructs the new set of constraints. It is characterised thus:

```
real_shadow uppers lowers =
  ∀c d lb ub.
    MEM (c,ub) uppers ∧ MEM (d,lb) lowers ⇒
    &c * lb <= &d * ub
```

Finally, the HOL theorem corresponding to Theorem 2:

```
EVERY fst_nzero uppers ∧ EVERY fst_nzero lowers ∧
EVERY (λp. FST p <= m) uppers ⇒
((∃x. evalupper x uppers ∧ evallower x lowers) ≡
 dark_shadow uppers lowers ∨ ∃x. splinter x m uppers lowers)
```

This restatement of the theorem uses the fact that the variable m need not be the maximum of the upper bound coefficients, but needs only be at least as big as them all. The implementation always instantiates m to be the maximum, but it's simpler not to have to compute the maximum in the logic.

4.3   Comparing the Algorithms

I have not performed extensive performance analyses of the implementations of the algorithms. Both were developed and tested against the same regression test-suite, which, now that the algorithms' implementations are complete, contains 152 problems. Though a small collection of mainly small problems, it is a plausible test of the algorithms over one of the domains where they're most likely to be applied: interactive proof of goals that are usually valid. Another similar domain is the use of these algorithms as part of simplification. There, though the Presburger goals are more likely to be invalid, they are still usually small parts of larger goals.

The figures, based on one run of each algorithm over the suite, reveal that the Omega Test is 22% faster over the whole test-suite (on a dual processor 1.6GHz Athlon machine, Omega did the 152 problems in 54.7s, Cooper's algorithm in 66.8s). Omega solved the problem with the biggest absolute time difference in 5.4s, and Cooper's algorithm in 9.0s, so this one problem accounts for roughly a third of the difference between them. Cooper's algorithm is faster on 59 of the problems (on 16, the algorithms take equally long). Cooper's algorithm's best performance, in terms of absolute time elapsed, is a problem where it takes 4.2s, and the Omega Test takes 5.8s.

These figures can only be used to indicate that one implementation of the Omega Test seems a little quicker than one implementation of Cooper's algorithm, and that there are input problems for each where one is slower than the other. The implementation of the Omega Test has the advantage that it can work outside the logic when solving purely existential goals. Conversely, Cooper's algorithm need not convert to DNF. It is simple to construct problems to favour one or other of these strengths.

Experiments to compare the algorithms more rigorously would need careful construction. In recent work, Janičić, Green and Bundy compared implementations of Cooper's algorithm and Hodes's method applied to universal natural number Presburger goals [9]. The tests used for this work were generated randomly, and suggested that Cooper's algorithm could perform as well as Hodes's method.

5   Extensions

After implementing the basic algorithms, it is possible to extend their "reach" by applying a variety of pre-processing steps to their input formulas. Here are descriptions of some of these:

Generalisation. Where a formula contains free variables, or other terms involving symbols outside Presburger arithmetic, attempt to prove the goal where these terms are replaced with a universally quantified variable. This enhancement is trivial, but makes a big difference to usability in an interactive setting. When the goal is as likely to be unsatisfiable as valid, such as when the procedure is embedded in a simplifier, it also makes sense to negate the input formula, generalise and then try to prove the resulting goal.

Natural numbers. Closed formulas where quantified variables range over $\mathbb{N}$ can be easily converted to equivalent formulas whose quantified variables range over $\mathbb{Z}$. This makes the one procedure universal for both domains, and their mixture. The equations used for the quantifiers are

$$(\exists x : \mathbb{N}.\ P(\&x)) \equiv (\exists x : \mathbb{Z}.\ 0 \leq x \wedge P(x))$$
$$(\forall x : \mathbb{N}.\ P(\&x)) \equiv (\forall x : \mathbb{Z}.\ 0 \leq x \Rightarrow P(x))$$

where $\&$ is the function which injects from $\mathbb{N}$ into $\mathbb{Z}$. Conversion of predicates so that they range over $\mathbb{Z}$ instead of $\mathbb{N}$ is done using equations such as

$$n <_{\mathbb{N}} m\ \equiv \&n <_{\mathbb{Z}} \&m$$
$$\&(n +_{\mathbb{N}} m) = \&n +_{\mathbb{Z}} \&m$$

Dealing with natural numbers also requires a separate phase of generalisation. For example, the valid formula $0 \leq n*m$ with $n, m \in \mathbb{N}$ must be turned into $\forall p : \mathbb{N}.\ 0 \leq p$ and then to $\forall i : \mathbb{Z}.\ 0 \leq i \Rightarrow 0 \leq i$. Omitting this first phase of generalisation will result in first, the non-Presburger $\forall i\, j : \mathbb{Z}.\ 0 \leq i * j$, and then $\forall k : \mathbb{Z}.\ 0 \leq k$, both of which are invalid.

Expansion of constants. It is a trivial matter to expand many useful constants that will likely appear in goals, replacing occurrences with their definitions or appropriate characterising theorems. For example, predicates such as ODD, the unique existence quantifier ($\exists!$) and functions such as max can all be treated directly.

It is even possible to get a treatment of integer division (as long as the divisor is a non-zero constant) by observing that

$$P(x/d) \equiv \exists q\, r.\, (x = qd + r) \wedge (0 \leq r < d \vee d < r \leq 0) \wedge P(q)$$

The same technique also provides a treatment of modulus.

6 Conclusions

I have presented detailed proofs of the correctness of two complete decision procedures for full Presburger integer arithmetic. On this foundation, I described how these procedures (and in some sense, these proofs) have been implemented in the HOL theorem-proving system. The implementations further demonstrate three important techniques with which complicated algorithms can be realised in a fully expansive setting.

As a demonstration of what is possible, this work supports the call in [9] for implementors of theorem-proving systems to provide complete methods. In particular, because the Omega Test will prove all of those universal goals that incomplete implementations of Fourier-Motzkin variable elimination prove, using the same approach, there seems little reason not to extend these implementations to also prove the other universal goals, and to then also cope with alternating quantifiers.

The sketchy testing I have performed seems to indicate that "one can never have too many decision procedures". If one encounters a goal that is not handled well by one algorithm, it is useful to have another weapon in one's armoury. This holds for interactive tool use, where the user makes the selection, and also for automatic systems that combine algorithms, perhaps by running them in parallel.

Availability. All of the source code (and the test-suite) for the implementations is part of the standard HOL distribution, available from SourceForge, at http://hol.sourceforge.net.

References

[1] B. Barras, S. Boutin, C. Cornes, J. Courant, J.C. Filliatre, E. Giménez, H. Herbelin, G. Huet, C. Muñoz, C. Murthy, C. Parent, C. Paulin, A. Saïbi, and B. Werner. The Coq Proof Assistant Reference Manual – Version V6.1. Technical Report 0203, INRIA, August 1997. See the Coq home-page at http://coq.inria.fr/.

[2] R. J. Boulton. *Efficiency in a fully-expansive theorem prover.* PhD thesis, Computer Laboratory, University of Cambridge, May 1994.

[3] D. C. Cooper. Theorem proving in arithmetic without multiplication. In *Machine Intelligence*, volume 7, pages 91–99, New York, 1972. American Elsevier.

[4] M. J. C. Gordon and T. Melham, editors. *Introduction to HOL: a theorem proving environment for higher order logic.* Cambridge University Press, 1993.

[5] M. J. C. Gordon, Robin Milner, and Christopher P. Wadsworth. *Edinburgh LCF: A Mechanised Logic of Computation.* Number 78 in Lecture Notes in Computer Science. Springer, 1979.

[6] John Harrison. *Theorem Proving with the Real Numbers.* CPHC/BCS Distinguished Dissertations. Springer, 1998.

[7] Joe Hurd. Integrating Gandalf and HOL. In Yves Bertot, Gilles Dowek, André Hirschowitz, Christine Paulin, and Laurent Théry, editors, *Theorem Proving in Higher Order Logics, 12th International Conference, TPHOLs '99*, volume 1690 of *Lecture Notes in Computer Science*, pages 311–321, Berlin, September 1999. Springer.

[8] Paul B. Jackson. *The Nuprl Proof Development System. Version 4.1 Reference Manual and User's Guide.* Cornell University, Ithaca, 1994. See the Nuprl home-page at `http://www.cs.cornell.edu/Info/Projects/NuPrl/html/NuprlSystem.html`.

[9] P. Janičić, I. Green, and A. Bundy. A comparison of decision procedures in Presburger arithmetic. In *Proceedings of LIRA'97: the 8th Conference on Logic and Computer Science*, pages 91–101. University of Novi Sad, 1997. Also available as Research Paper 872, Department of AI, University of Edinburgh.

[10] Matt Kaufmann and J Moore. An industrial strength theorem prover for a logic based on Common Lisp. *IEEE Transactions on Software Engineering*, 23(4):203–213, April 1997.

[11] Michael Norrish and Konrad Slind. A thread of HOL development. *Computer Journal*, 45(1):37–45, 2002.

[12] S. Owre, J. Rushby, and N. Shankar. PVS: A Prototype Verification System. In Deepak Kapur, editor, *11th International Conference on Automated Deduction*, volume 607 of *Lecture Notes in Artificial Intelligence*, pages 748–752. Springer-Verlag, 1992.

[13] Lawrence C. Paulson. *Isabelle: A Generic Theorem Prover*, volume 828 of *Lecture Notes in Computer Science*. Springer-Verlag, Berlin, 1994.

[14] William Pugh. The Omega Test: a fast and practical integer programming algorithm for dependence analysis. *Communications of the ACM*, 35(8):102–114, August 1992.

[15] R. E. Shostak. On the SUP-INF method for proving Presburger formulas. *Journal of the ACM*, 24(4):529–543, October 1977.

[16] R. E. Shostak. Deciding linear inequalities by computing loop residues. *Journal of the ACM*, 28(4):769–779, October 1981.

Changing Data Representation within the Coq System

Nicolas Magaud

INRIA Sophia-Antipolis, France

Abstract. In a theorem prover like Coq, mathematical concepts can be implemented in several ways. Their different representations can be either efficient for computing or well-suited to carry out proofs easily. In this paper, we present improved techniques to deal with changes of data representation within Coq. We propose a smart handling of case analysis and definitions together with some general methods to transfer recursion operators and their reduction rules from one setting to another. Once we have built a formal correspondence between two settings, we can translate automatically properties obtained in the initial setting into new properties in the target setting. We successfully experiment with changing Peano's numbers into binary numbers for the whole *Arith* library of Coq as well as with changing polymorphic lists into reversed (snoc) lists.

1   Introduction

In this paper, we present a general method to change the way we look at a data type in a proof system such as Coq [5], and to enhance proof reuse when shifting from a data type representation to another [17].

For instance, one may want to switch from Peano's encoding of natural numbers to a binary representation. This change may be motivated by efficiency reasons, computations are much faster with binary integers than with unary integers. We provide a smart mechanism to avoid proving again in the final setting properties already established in the initial setting.

Previously in [12], we presented a first experiment about changes of data type representation in type theory. This work was limited to equational reasoning. We did not propose any general way to handle structural case analysis and therefore inversion techniques [6] properly. In addition, we did not consider inductive predicates and definition unfolding for logical properties. The present work aims at removing these weaknesses. We choose to develop a practical tool usable in the Coq system. As a consequence, our experiments were restricted to the Calculus of Inductive Constructions [15] and its implementation in the Coq system. Therefore we cannot easily use techniques such as induction-recursion [9] or those proposed in [13] for instance.

Throughout this paper, we will use the example of natural numbers and consider their unary and binary representations. However, we would like to emphasize that we also experimented with changing the data representation for polymorphic lists.

D. Basin and B. Wolff (Eds.): TPHOLs 2003, LNCS 2758, pp. 87–102, 2003.

1.1 Related Work

Translating proofs from one setting to another require abstracting away most of the implementation of a mathematical concept. Viewing concrete datatypes in a more abstract way can be achieved in many different ways.

- The Coq system provides some tools to deal with proofs in some algebraic settings, for instance ring [5, Chap. 19] and field [7] structures.
- Modules and functors [4], as those introduced in the latest version of Coq make it possible to have a high-level view of mathematical concepts we manipulate. It allows the user to hide the actual implementation of a data type. Signatures (module types) can be easily instantiated with various concrete representations.
- G. Barthe and O. Pons [2] suggest to use type isomorphisms to enhance proof reuse in dependent type theory. They give a computational interpretation of some type isomorphisms using coercions. Their work allows the user to view mathematical objects from various points of view.

1.2 An Example

We consider the statement $\forall n$: nat. $n \leq O \rightarrow n = O$ as an example. It is interesting because it was not processed properly by the method proposed in [12]. It can be proved in Coq by running the following script:

```
Lemma example : (n:nat)(le n O)->n=0.
Intros n H ; Inversion H ; Auto.
Qed.
```

The proof term generated from this script is shown in figure 1. The tactic *Inversion H* builds a term which features case analysis on an instance of an inductive data type H : (le n O). In addition, it contains structural case analysis on nat, intended to discriminate the assumption H_1 : ((S m) = O). We propose new methods and tools to transfer this proof from the unary setting into the binary one. We mainly focus on handling structural case analysis in a smart manner.

1.3 Outline

In section 2, we present definitions of inductive datatypes and their associated recursion operators within Coq. In section 3, we introduce the language we consider for proof terms. In section 4, we show how to remove case constructs for proof terms. In section 5, we study the issue of definition unfolding, especially for types containing logical information. In section 6, we present the implementation of our tool and two case studies. Finally, in section 7, we give some perspectives about related and future work.

λn : nat.λH : (le n O).
   let H_0 = $\langle \lambda p$: nat.$p = $ O $\rightarrow n = $ O$\rangle$
         Cases H *of*
           le_n $\Rightarrow$ λH_0 : $n = $ O.
              (eq_ind nat O λn : nat.$n = $ O (refl_equal nat O)
                    n (sym_eq nat n O H_0))
          | (le_S m H_0) $\Rightarrow$ λH_1 : (S m) = O.
             (*let* H_2 = (eq_ind nat (S m)
                    λe : nat.$\langle$Prop$\rangle$ *Cases* e *of*
                            O $\Rightarrow$ False
                        | (S _) $\Rightarrow$ True
                      end I O H_1)
             in (False_ind (le n m) $\rightarrow n = $ O H_2) H_0)
        end
   in (H_0 (refl_equal nat O)).

Fig. 1. A term proving the lemma example

2 Context of This Work

In this section, we first present the way recursion operators are defined in the Coq system. Then we recall how we proceed to make conversions explicit in a proof term [12].

2.1 Recursion Operators in the Calculus of Constructions

From an inductive definition, e.g.

```
Inductive nat   : Set :=  O : nat | S : nat->nat
```

the Coq system automatically generates structural recursion operators (one for each sort Set, Type, Prop). For instance nat_rec has the following statement:

nat_rec : $\forall P$: nat $\rightarrow$ Set. $(P$ O$) \rightarrow (\forall n$: nat. $(P\ n) \rightarrow (P\ (S\ n))) \rightarrow \forall n$: nat. $(P\ n)$

On the other hand, the definition of an inductive predicate such as le only triggers the construction of a single recursion operator le_ind.

```
Inductive le [n : nat]   : nat->Prop :=
      le_n : (le n n) | le_S : (m:nat)(le n m)->(le n (S m))
```

    le_ind : $\forall n$: nat. $\forall P$: nat $\rightarrow$ Prop.
        $(P\ n) \rightarrow (\forall m$: nat. (le n m) $\rightarrow (P\ m) \rightarrow (P\ (S\ m))) \rightarrow$
        $\forall n0$: nat. (le n $n0$) $\rightarrow (P\ n0)$

Indeed, elimination rules do not allow building elements of sorts Type or Set by case analysis on an element of sort Prop.

Dependent vs. Non-dependent Recursion Operators. The Coq system allows the definition of two kinds of induction principles: dependent (also called maximal) and non-dependent (minimal) ones [3].

As an example, in addition to the dependent recursion operator for nat, we give the non-dependent one. It corresponds to the recursion operator of Gödel's system T. nat_min_rec states that:

$$\forall P : \mathsf{Set}.\ P \to (\mathsf{nat} \to P \to P) \to \mathsf{nat} \to P \tag{1}$$

Such a recursor can be used to define basic operations such as plus easily:

plus' $= \lambda n : \mathsf{nat}.(\mathsf{nat\_min\_rec}\ \mathsf{nat} \to \mathsf{nat}$
$\qquad\quad \lambda m : \mathsf{nat}.m$
$\qquad\quad \lambda_- : \mathsf{nat}.\lambda vr : \mathsf{nat} \to \mathsf{nat}.\lambda m : \mathsf{nat}.(\mathsf{S}\ (vr\ m))$
$\qquad\quad n)$

In figure 2, we give the characteristics of the recursion operators automatically inferred after the definition of an inductive type T. The Coq proof assistant defines different recursion operators to build objects of sorts Set, Type, Prop. Columns of this array represent the sort of the element which is applied to the recursion operator and rows the sort of the element it builds.

	$T : \mathsf{Set}$ or $T : \mathsf{Type}$	$T : \mathsf{Prop}$
$P : T \to \mathsf{Set}$ or $P : T \to \mathsf{Type}$	dependent	not allowed
$P : T \to \mathsf{Prop}$	dependent	non dependent

Fig. 2. Allowed eliminations

To sum up, the definition of nat whose sort is Set triggers the automatic definition of three dependent elimination principles nat_rec, nat_ind and nat_rect. On the other hand, the definition of le triggers the definition of a single elimination principle le_ind which is a non dependent one.

Anyway, in both cases, non-dependent (resp. dependent) principles can also be defined in addition to their dependent (resp. non-dependent) counterparts using the Scheme command:

Scheme $T_{(\mathsf{ind}|\mathsf{rec}|\mathsf{rect})} :=$ (Induction | Minimality) for T Sort (Prop | Set | Type).

For instance, the non-dependent induction principle (1) for nat can be generated by the command: `Scheme nat_min_rec := Minimality for nat Sort Set.`

Recursion Operators and Their Reduction Rules. All these recursion operators are defined using fix-point and case analysis constructs. Dependent and non-dependent operators are defined in the same manner. For instance nat_rec is defined as follows:

```
nat_rec = [P:(nat->Set); f:(P (O)); f0:((n:nat)(P n)->(P (S n)))]
  Fix F {F [n:nat] : (P n) :=
          <P>Cases n of (O) => f
                      | (S n0) => (f0 n0 (F n0))
          end}
```

As a consequence of their definitions, recursion operators have a computational behavior. For nat_rec, it can be expressed by these two reduction rules:

$$\text{nat\_rec } P \ v0 \ vr \ O \xrightarrow{\iota} v0$$
$$\text{nat\_rec } P \ v0 \ vr \ (S \ n) \xrightarrow{\iota} vr \ n \ (\text{nat\_rec } P \ v0 \ vr \ n)$$

2.2 Convertibility Issues

In this section, we sum up the main results of the work presented in [12]. The aim of this work was to exhibit implicit proof steps inside proof terms. The algorithm we proposed at the time did not provide any support for handling structural case analysis.

Making Conversions Explicit. We consider the theorem plus_n_O and show how it is processed by the algorithm (see [12] for details). This theorem states that:

$$\forall n \in \text{nat}. \quad n = (\text{plus } n \ O) \tag{2}$$

A proof (as a λ-term) of this property is :

$$\lambda n : \text{nat.}(\text{nat\_ind } (\lambda n0 : \text{nat.} n0 = (\text{plus } n0 \ O))$$
$$(\text{refl\_equal nat } O)$$
$$\lambda n0 : \text{nat}; H : (n0 = (\text{plus } n0 \ O)).$$
$$(\text{f\_equal nat nat S } n0 \ (\text{plus } n0 \ O) \ H) \ n)$$

It proceeds by induction on n, using the principle nat_ind. The base case requires proving that $O = (\text{plus } O \ O)$. The step case requires proving that

$$\forall n0 : \text{nat} \quad n0 = (\text{plus } n0 \ O) \Rightarrow (S \ n0) = (\text{plus } (S \ n0) \ O).$$

The term (refl_equal nat O) is a proof of the base case. However, the inferred (or proposed) type for this term is $O = O$, whereas its expected type is $O = (\text{plus } O \ O)$. These two types are convertible thanks to the computational rules derived from the definition of plus, but they are not syntactically equal.

In our example, steps which are made explicit by the algorithm are formalized by the conjectures Ha and Hb whose statements are:

$$Ha : O = O \Rightarrow O = (\text{plus } O \ O)$$
$$Hb : \forall n : \text{nat.} (S \ n) = (S \ (\text{plus } n \ O)) \Rightarrow (S \ n) = (\text{plus } (S \ n) \ O)$$

These conjectures aim at connecting expected and proposed types in the branches of the induction principle. We see they can be proven easily, by first introducing the premises and then using the reflexivity of Leibniz's equality. This works because the terms on both sides of the equality are convertible modulo $\beta\delta\iota$-reduction. Eventually, the algorithm returns the following proof term:

$\lambda n : \mathsf{nat.(nat\_ind}$
$\qquad (\lambda n0 : \mathsf{nat}.n0 = (\mathsf{plus}\ n0\ \mathsf{O}))$
$\qquad (H a\ (\mathsf{refl\_equal}\ \mathsf{nat}\ \mathsf{O}))$
$\qquad \lambda n0 : \mathsf{nat};\ H : (n0 = (\mathsf{plus}\ n0\ \mathsf{O})).$
$\qquad\quad (H b\ n0\ (\mathsf{f\_equal}\ \mathsf{nat}\ \mathsf{nat}\ \mathsf{S}\ n0\ (\mathsf{plus}\ n0\ \mathsf{O})\ H))\ n)$

Representing Functions. In the target setting of our proof transformation process, addition may have different reduction rules compared to the ones it has in the Peano's setting. As a consequence, we have to make these computations explicit. We express them as equations. Let us consider the example of plus.

```
Fixpoint plus[n:nat] : nat -> nat :=
  Cases n of O => [m:nat] m | (S p) => [m:nat](S (plus p m)) end.
```

plus has the following reduction rules:

$$\mathsf{plus}\ \mathsf{O}\ m\ \xrightarrow{\iota}\ m \qquad\qquad \mathsf{plus}\ (\mathsf{S}\ p)\ m\ \xrightarrow{\iota}\ \mathsf{S}\ (\mathsf{plus}\ p\ m)$$

They are formalized as equations that would be translated and proved in the new setting:

$$\forall m : \mathsf{nat}.\ (\mathsf{plus}\ \mathsf{O}\ m) = m$$
$$\forall p, m : \mathsf{nat}.\ (\mathsf{plus}\ (\mathsf{S}\ p)\ m) = (\mathsf{S}\ (\mathsf{plus}\ p\ m))$$

Conjectures Ha and Hb can be proved by rewriting using these two equations. We postpone the actual translation of a proof term into the binary setting until section 4.4. In this section, we have shown how to proceed when terms do not contain case analysis constructs. In the forthcoming sections, we study how to transform a term with case constructs into a term without any. After defining formally the terms we consider, we will show how to proceed in section 4.

3   Terms

As usual in type theory, we consider a set of sorts $\mathcal{S}$ which contains Prop, Set and Type. A *term* is an element of the language $\mathcal{T}$ defined as follows:

$$\mathcal{T} ::= \lambda x : \mathcal{T}.\mathcal{T} \mid (\mathcal{T}\ \mathcal{T}) \mid \forall x : \mathcal{T}.\ \mathcal{T} \mid \mathcal{S} \mid x \mid \mathcal{C} \mid \mathcal{I} \mid \mathcal{CI}$$
$$\mid \mathsf{let}\ x\ =\ \mathcal{T} : \mathcal{T}\ \mathsf{in}\ \mathcal{T}$$
$$\mid \langle \mathcal{T} \rangle \mathsf{case}\ \mathcal{T}\ \mathsf{of}\ \{\mathcal{T}\}$$

$\mathcal{C}$ denotes the set of constants, $\mathcal{I}$ the set of inductive datatypes and $\mathcal{CI}$ the set of constructors for these inductive datatypes. This corresponds to the usual set of terms that occur in proof terms. We treat recursion as it usually appears in proof terms, i.e. hidden in a constant definition such as nat_ind. Therefore we assume that fix-point constructs do not occur explicitly in proof terms.

The process to transform a proof term is divided into two steps. We first remove all occurrences of case (see section 4); we then extract the conversion steps from the generated proof term by using the approach presented in section 2.2.

4   Removing Structural Case Analysis from Proof Terms

Case expressions can occur in proof terms because the proof script explicitly contains an occurrence of the Case tactic or because an inversion was performed. Inversion gives rise to case analysis whose result type has sort Set or Type. In this setting, reduction rules are necessary, thus it is relevant to translate them.

Structural case analysis is replaced by using a *defined* case analysis operator and its associated reduction rules (if needed). As stated previously for recursion operators, we emphasize that case analysis from Prop to Set or Type is not allowed. The only exception is inductive datatypes with a single constructor e.g. Leibnitz's equality eq.

We assume we have the following inductive definition:

$$
\begin{aligned}
\mathsf{Inductive}\ T\ :\ \mathsf{S}\ :=\ & |\ c1 : \forall t_{1,1} : T_{1,1} \ldots \forall t_{1,i_1} : T_{1,i_1}.\ T \\
& |\ \ldots \\
& |\ c_k : \forall t_{k,1} : T_{k,1} \ldots \forall t_{k,i_k} : T_{k,i_k}.\ T \\
& |\ \ldots \\
& |\ c_n : \forall t_{n,1} : T_{n,1} \ldots \forall t_{n,i_n} : T_{n,i_n}.\ T.
\end{aligned}
$$

4.1   Algorithm

We consider a proof p of an arbitrary property on the elements of T. The algorithm performs a recursive structural analysis of the term p. For most of the terms, it merely calls itself recursively on their sub-terms if they have any; otherwise it simply returns the term. The only interesting part is how case analysis is handled. In figure 3, we give an example of a case expression on t of type T. The left-hand side corresponds to the actual notation for case analysis whereas the right-hand side notation is closer to the actual implementation of case analysis in Coq. In presence of a case expression, the algorithm acts as follows:

1. It computes the type of t. Let us assume $t : T$. As seen in section 2.1, we have at most six recursion operators available for T: three dependent ones, namely T_rec, T_ind and T_rect and three non-dependent ones T_min_rec, T_min_ind and T_min_rect.

$$\langle P \rangle \; \mathsf{Cases} \; t \; \mathsf{of} \qquad\qquad\qquad \langle P \rangle \; \mathsf{Case} \; t \; \mathsf{of}$$
$$| \; (c_1 \; t_{1,1} \ldots \; t_{1,i_1}) \Rightarrow r_1 \qquad\qquad \lambda t_{1,1} : T_{1,1} \ldots \; \lambda t_{1,i_1} : T_{1,i_1}.r_1$$
$$| \ldots \qquad\qquad\qquad \ldots$$
$$| \; (c_k \; t_{k,1} \ldots \; t_{k,i_k}) \Rightarrow r_k \quad \equiv \qquad \lambda t_{k,1} : T_{k,1} \ldots \; \lambda t_{k,i_k} : T_{k,i_k}.r_k$$
$$| \ldots \qquad\qquad\qquad \ldots$$
$$| \; (c_n \; t_{n,1} \ldots \; t_{n,i_n}) \Rightarrow r_n \qquad\qquad \lambda t_{n,1} : T_{n,1} \ldots \; \lambda t_{n,i_n} : T_{n,i_n}.r_n$$
$$\mathsf{end} \qquad\qquad\qquad\qquad \mathsf{end}$$

Fig. 3. A case expression to be processed by our algorithm

2. As shown in figure 3, P is the elimination predicate associated to a case construct [5, Chap. 14]. Types of the branches of the case construct are instances of this elimination predicate. The shape of P allows us to determine whether we face dependent case analysis or not. If P is a λ-abstraction, we face a dependent case. If not, we face a non-dependent case. It remains to determine the sort of the objects we build. To do so, we compute the type of the value returned by P. For instance, if $P \equiv \lambda n : \mathsf{nat}.(\mathsf{le} \; \mathsf{O} \; n) \to n = \mathsf{O}$ then the type of the returned value is Prop.

3. Once we have the shape and the name of the right recursion operator, (let us call it induction_for_T), we build an instance of the corresponding case analysis operator, say case_for_T. For example, nat_rec is transformed into a (non-recursive) case analysis operator nat_case_rec whose type is:

$$\forall P : \mathsf{nat} \to \mathsf{Set}. \; (P \; \mathsf{O}) \to (\forall n : \mathsf{nat}. \; (P \; (\mathsf{S} \; n))) \to \forall n : \mathsf{nat}. \; (P \; n).$$

4. The algorithm recursively computes new terms $r'_1, \ldots, r'_n$ (with no more structural case expressions) for all sub-terms $r_1, \ldots, r_n$ of the case expression.

5. It remains to build an application whose head is case_for_T and that mimics structural case analysis via application of the *defined* case analysis operator. Eventually, the algorithm returns the following term instead of the case expression.

$$(\mathsf{case\_for\_T} \; P \;\; \lambda t_{1,1} : T_{1,1} \ldots \; \lambda t_{1,i_1} : T_{1,i_1}.r'_1$$
$$\ldots$$
$$\lambda t_{n,1} : T_{n,1} \ldots \; \lambda t_{n,i_n} : T_{n,i_n}.r'_n$$
$$t)$$

This transformation removes explicit structural case analysis and hides it in the application of a defined case analysis operator. It provides us with a way to reason by case analysis without knowing anything about the actual inductive representation of the data type.

4.2   What Happens to Our Example ?

If we consider the example shown in figure 1, *Cases H of* ... has been replaced by the application of the case analysis principle le_case_ind. In addition,

Cases e of ... has been replaced by the application of the non-dependent operator nat_case_rect_min whose type is $\forall P :$ Type. $P \rightarrow ($nat$ \rightarrow P) \rightarrow nat \rightarrow P$.

$\lambda n :$ nat.$\lambda H :$ (le n O).

  let H_0 = (le_case_ind n $\lambda p :$ nat.p = O $\rightarrow n$ = O

          $\lambda H_0 : n$ = O.

            (eq_ind nat O $\lambda n :$ nat.n = O (refl_equal nat O)

                  n (sym_eq nat n O H_0))

          $\lambda m :$ nat.$\lambda H_0 :$ (le n m).$\lambda H_1 :$ (S m) = O.

            (let H_2 = (eq_ind nat (S m)

                    $\lambda e :$ nat.

                    (nat_case_rect_min Prop False λ_ : nat.True e)

                    I O H_1)

              in (False_ind (le n m) $\rightarrow n$ = O H_2) H_0)

        O H)

  in (H_0 (refl_equal nat O)).

4.3 Actual Translation into a New Representation

Once we have replaced a case expression by the application of a function, we need to translate this function into the target setting. In this section, we present a binary representation of natural numbers and show how to transfer recursion operators from the Peano setting into the binary one.

Binary Representation of Natural Numbers

```
Inductive pos : Set := one: pos              (* 1 *)
                     | pI :pos -> pos        (* 2x+1, x>0 *)
                     | p0: pos -> pos.       (* 2x, x>0 *)
Inductive bin : Set := b0: bin | bp: pos -> bin.
```

From these inductive types, we define counterparts of O and S, namely b0 and bS, as well as translation functions from nat to bin (n2b) and vice-versa (b2n). These definitions are taken from [12, pp. 189-190].

Recursion Operators in the New Setting. We can prove non-dependent recursion operators and their associated reduction rules as equations via the isomorphism connecting nat and bin. We use the equation $\forall n :$ bin. (n2b (b2n n)) = n and the recursion principle for nat nat_rec_min to define the recursion operator new_bin_rec_min : $\forall P$: Set. $P \rightarrow ($bin$ \rightarrow P \rightarrow P) \rightarrow bin \rightarrow P$ and prove its properties:

$$(\text{new\_bin\_rec\_min } T \; v0 \; vr \; b0) = v0$$
$$\forall p : \text{bin. } (\text{new\_bin\_rec\_min } T \; v0 \; vr \; (\text{bS } p)) = (vr \; p \; (\text{new\_bin\_rec\_min } T \; v0 \; vr \; p))$$

However, as far as dependent recursion principles are concerned, rewriting gets stuck when trying to prove the reduction rules as equations. Therefore we choose to define the dependent recursion operators by well founded induction over binary integers. We establish their reduction rules as a fix-point equation following the technique proposed by A. Balaa and Y. Bertot in [1].

Building the Dependent Recursion Operator

1. First of all, we derive the order on binary integers from the one on Peano's numbers: $(\mathsf{Lt}\ x\ y) \equiv (\mathsf{lt}\ (\mathsf{b2n}\ x)\ (\mathsf{b2n}\ y))$. We show using the standard library of Coq that Lt is well-founded. From now on, this theorem will be named wf_Lt.

2. We then show that a binary integer p is either b0 or $(\mathsf{bS}\ q)$ for some q. This property can be stated with the following dependent inductive definition:

```
Inductive Pred_spec: bin ->Set :=
     is_zero: (Pred_spec b0)
   | is_S: (y:bin)(Pred_spec (bS y)).
```

3. The next step consists in defining a function Pred. Given a binary integer n, it computes an element of type $(\mathsf{Pred\_spec}\ n)$ which contains the predecessor of n, when n is not equal to b0. Pred is defined using a proof mode style. It makes it easier to treat dependent case analysis.

```
Definition Pred: (x:bin)(Pred_spec x).
```

4. Once the Pred function is defined, we build a higher-order function F. It takes as input a binary integer n and a function $f : \forall m \in \mathsf{bin}.\ m\ <\ n \to (P\ m)$ and computes an element of type $(P\ n)$. This function performs structural case analysis on $(\mathsf{Pred}\ n)$ and uses the hypotheses $\mathsf{h_0} : (P\ \mathsf{b0})$ and $\mathsf{h_r} : \forall n \in \mathsf{bin}.\ (P\ n) \to (P\ (\mathsf{bS}\ n))$ which correspond to the premises of the recursion operator for Peano's numbers.

```
Definition F: (n:bin) ((m:bin)(Lt m n)->(P m)) ->(P n) :=
  [n:bin]
    <[n:bin] [p:(Pred_spec n)] ((m:bin)(Lt m n)->(P m)) ->(P n)>
      Cases (Pred n) of
        is_zero => [f:(m:bin)(Lt m b0)->(P m)]h0
      | (is_S p) =>
        [f:(m:bin)(Lt m (bS p))->(P m)](hr p (f p (S_and_Lt p)))
    end.
```

S_and_Lt is a proof that $\forall p$: bin. $(\mathsf{Lt}\ p\ (\mathsf{bS}\ p))$.

5. Finally, we get our expected recursion operator by the following definition:

```
Definition new_bin_rec :=
              (well_founded_induction bin Lt wf_Lt P F).
```

unary setting	binary setting	unary setting	binary setting
nat	bin	O	b0
plus	bplus	S	bS
nat_ind	new_bin_ind	nat_case_ind	new_bin_case_ind
nat_rect_min	new_bin_rect_min	nat_case_rect_min	new_bin_case_rect_min
le	ble	lt	blt
le_ind	ble_ind	le_case_ind	ble_case_ind

Fig. 4. Bookkeeping

Reduction Rules for the Dependent Recursion Operator. Recursion operators should be considered as common functions. As for plus in section 2.2, we have to state and prove their reduction rules as equations. To do so, we build an instance of the so-called *step hypothesis* of the *transfer theorem* as presented in [1, page 5].

$\forall x : \mathsf{bin}.$
$\forall f' : \forall y : \mathsf{bin}. (P\ y).$
$\forall g : \forall y : \mathsf{bin}. (\mathsf{Lt}\ y\ x) \rightarrow (P\ y).$
$(\forall y : \mathsf{bin}.\ \forall h : (\mathsf{Lt}\ y\ x).\ (g\ y\ h) =_{(P\ y)} (f'\ y)) \rightarrow$
$(\mathsf{F}\ x\ \lambda y : bin.\lambda h : (\mathsf{Lt}\ y\ x).(g\ y\ h)) =_{(P\ x)} (\mathsf{F}\ x\ \lambda y : bin.\lambda_- : (\mathsf{Lt}\ y\ x).(f'\ y)).$

The proof is carried out by case analysis on $(\mathsf{Pred}\ \mathsf{x})$. The application of the *transfer theorem* leads to the general fix-point equation step_rec:

$$\forall n : \mathsf{bin}\ .(\mathsf{new\_bin\_rec}\ n) = (\mathsf{F}\ n\ \lambda m : \mathsf{bin}.\lambda h : (\mathsf{Lt}\ m\ n).(\mathsf{new\_bin\_rec}\ m))$$

To get the simplified form of the fix-point equation, we need to prove the following lemmas:

$$\forall v : (\mathsf{Pred\_spec}\ b0).\ v = \mathsf{is\_zero}$$
$$\forall n : \mathsf{bin}.\ \forall v : (\mathsf{Pred\_spec}\ (\mathsf{bS}\ n)).\ v = (\mathsf{is\_S}\ n)$$

The first one is trivial whereas the second one requires the use of a dependent equality and dependent inversion techniques. Once P, h_0 and h_r have been discharged, the resulting equations are:

$(\mathsf{new\_bin\_rec}\ P\ h_0\ h_r\ b0) = h_0$
$\forall n : \mathsf{bin}. (\mathsf{new\_bin\_rec}\ P\ h_0\ h_r\ (\mathsf{bS}\ n)) = (h_r\ n\ (\mathsf{new\_bin\_rec}\ P\ h_0\ h_r\ n))$

4.4   Back to Our Example

After extracting conversion steps (see section 2.2), and syntactically replacing all objects in the unary setting by their counterparts in the binary one (see figure 4), we get the following proof term:

λn : bin.λH : (ble n b0).
   let H_0 = (ble_case_ind n λp : bin.p = b0 → n = b0
          λH_0 : n = b0.
            (eq_ind bin b0 λn : bin.n = b0 (refl_equal bin b0)
                 n (sym_eq bin n b0 H_0))
          λm : bin.λH_0 : (ble n m).λH_1 : (S m) = b0.
            (let H_2 = (**example_rr2** (eq_ind bin (bS m)
                    λe : bin.
                    (new_bin_case_rect_min Prop False λ_ : bin.True e)
                    (**example_rr1** m l) b0 H_1))
             in (False_ind (ble n m) → n = b0 H_2) H_0)
         b0 H)
  in (H_0 (refl_equal bin b0)).

Its type is $\forall n$: bin. (ble n b0) → n = b0. The conjectures example_rr1 and example_rr2 are generated automatically to connect expected and proposed terms for sub-expressions of this proof term. The term example_rr1 is a proof of

$$\forall m : \text{bin. True} \to (\text{new\_bin\_case\_rect\_min Prop False } \lambda\_ : \text{bin.True (bS } m)) \quad (3)$$

and example_rr2 a proof of

$$(\text{new\_bin\_case\_rect\_min Prop False } \lambda\_ : \text{bin.True b0}) \to \text{False} \quad (4)$$

The statements (3) and (4) are proven by rewriting with the fix-point equations for new_bin_case_rect_min corresponding to reduction rules for nat_case_rect_min in the binary setting.

5   Constants Unfolding and Changes of Representations

5.1   A Basic Example

Operations in the binary setting are designed to be as efficient as possible. Therefore definitions of operations on binary integers are not straightforward translations of the ones in Peano's arithmetics.

In order to be able to reuse the proofs, we need to connect the new definition to the previous one. As an example, we consider the function which computes the double of a number.

$$\text{double} = \lambda n : \text{nat.(plus } n \text{ } n)$$

Let us suppose we already proved and want to translate the following theorem:

$$\forall n, m : \text{nat. (double (plus } n \text{ } m)) = (\text{plus (double } n) \text{ (double } m)) \quad (5)$$

In the binary setting bdouble is defined as follows:

$$\text{bdouble} = \lambda n : \text{bin.}Cases \text{ } n \text{ } of \text{ b0} \Rightarrow b0 \mid (\text{bp } p) \Rightarrow (\text{bp (pO } p)) \text{ } end$$

A proof of (5) may rely on the property that (double n) and (plus n n) are δ-convertible. This convertibility rule can be mimicked by the following equation:

$$\forall n : \mathsf{bin}.\ (\mathsf{bdouble}\ n) = (\mathsf{bplus}\ n\ n)$$

Such an equation will be useful to prove by rewriting the conjectures generated when making conversions explicit (see section 2.2).

5.2   A More Tedious Example

We now consider the definition of the relation lt:

$$\mathsf{lt} = \lambda n, m : \mathsf{nat}.(\mathsf{le}\ (\mathsf{S}\ n)\ m)$$

As a consequence of the definitions of le and lt, (le (S n) m) and (lt n m) are convertible whereas there is no reason for lt to be defined in terms of le. This becomes an issue because blt will not necessarily be defined in terms of ble in the binary setting, therefore this implicit equality will be lost. Our first idea was to proceed in the same way as above. But a problem arises. In the binary setting, we can not prove

$$\forall n, m : \mathsf{bin}.\ (\mathsf{ble}\ (\mathsf{bS}\ n)\ m) == (\mathsf{blt}\ n\ m) \tag{6}$$

where $==$ denotes Leibnitz's equality in Type [1]. Trying to prove this statement, we got into a red herring. Because the definitions of blt and ble use Leibnitz's equality, we have to prove something like (true=true)==($\neg$false=true). This happens to be unprovable in the Coq system.
However we can easily establish the equivalence property:

$$\forall n, m : \mathsf{bin}.\ (\mathsf{ble}\ (\mathsf{bS}\ n)\ m) \leftrightarrow (\mathsf{blt}\ n\ m) \tag{7}$$

where $\leftrightarrow$ is defined as $A \leftrightarrow B \equiv (A \to B) \wedge (B \to A)$. Unfortunately, one can not use this property easily. Indeed, we want to be able to substitute (ble (bS n) m) and (blt n m) and one can not directly rewrite using the equivalence relation.
In the rest of this section, we consider two options to handle this question. First, we assume the axiom $\forall P, Q : \mathsf{Prop}.\ (P \leftrightarrow Q) \to P == Q$ is valid in the calculus of constructions. Therefore the first equation (6) holds and we can perform rewriting easily. The second option is to consider the Setoid (Prop,$\leftrightarrow$) and perform setoid-rewriting.

5.3   Handling Propositional Equivalence as Leibnitz's Equality

It is safe [14] to add the following axiom in the Coq system.

$$\mathsf{Axiom\ iff\_implies\_equiv}\ :\ \forall P, Q : \mathsf{Prop}.\ (P \leftrightarrow Q) \to P == Q$$

However, in this work, we always use a definitional approach without any parameter or axiom. In addition, all translated proofs are checked by the Coq kernel before being accepted. Therefore we preferred not to use an axiom and we used Setoid rewriting with (Prop,$\leftrightarrow$), thus keeping a definitional approach.

---

[1] `Inductive eqT [A : Type; x : A] : A->Prop := refl_eqT : x==x.`

5.4   Rewriting with Setoids

Coq provides a tactic Setoid_rewrite [5, Chap. 20] which is intended to perform rewriting with an equivalence relation. We consider the setoid (Prop,↔)
and experiment how to use it to substitute (blt n m) with (ble (bS n) m).
Setoid-rewriting is not immediate. For instance rewriting (blt n m) ∧ A into
(ble (bS n) m) ∧ A for some A requires to have proved that

$$\forall A, B, C, D : \text{Prop.} \ (A \leftrightarrow C) \rightarrow (B \leftrightarrow D) \rightarrow A \wedge B \rightarrow C \wedge D.$$

Such properties can be easily established as far as logical connectives are concerned. We need to be a bit smarter if we consider inductive data type such as
sumbool[2]. We state a new theorem

$$\forall A, B, C, D : \text{Prop.} \ (A \leftrightarrow C) \rightarrow (B \leftrightarrow D) \rightarrow \{A\} + \{B\} \rightarrow \{C\} + \{D\}.$$

and use it to prove the conjectures produced by the algorithm presented in
section 2.2. It leads to slightly more complicated proofs but enables us to avoid
using an axiom in our proof development.

6   Implementation

6.1   Our Tool

We developed a prototype tool. It consists in a ML module which can be plugged
into the Coq proof assistant. With this tool, one can build a formal correspondence between two theories. Once data structures and functions in the two settings are defined and once the correspondence between them is formally established, one can automatically translate statements and proof terms to the new
representation. The tool, as well as the whole development we carried out, are
available online: http://www-sop.inria.fr/lemme/Nicolas.Magaud/Changes/.

6.2   Case Studies

We present the main results of two case studies we carried out. In addition to
changing representation for natural numbers, we also experiment with changing
representation for polymorphic lists.

Peano's Numbers into Binary Numbers. Natural numbers are our basic
example for changes of data structures. The tool we develop allows us to translate
the whole library *Arith* of the standard Coq distribution. We first define counterparts of all basic operations (plus, minus, mult. . .) and relations (le, lt. . .) on
the binary representation of natural numbers by hand. In particular, we prove
the dependent recursion operators for nat and their reduction rules as equations.

---

[2] `Inductive sumbool [A : Prop; B : Prop] : Set :=`
   `left : A->A+B | right : B->A+B.`

In addition, we transfer the induction principle for le into the binary setting. Once this part is achieved by the user (i.e reduction rules (ι or δ-reduction) for the newly defined operations are proven as equations), it is straightforward to translate automatically all statements and their proof terms from the unary representation to the binary representation of integers.

It makes it possible to prove all properties required to show the data type bin has the properties of a semi-ring. Therefore we can extend the *Ring* tactic to prove equations in the binary setting directly.

Lists into Reversed Lists. We also study the library *PolyList* of Coq. We transform polymorphic lists into polymorphic reverse lists, defined as an inductive data type rlist. We define counterparts of the functions append, head, tail, and length on reverse lists and proved their properties. In addition, we translated the inductive principle list_ind into an equivalent principle for the reverse lists; we also proved the translated counterparts of the minimal recursion operators for lists as well as their associated reduction rules as equations.

7   Discussion

In this paper, we presented some new techniques to enhance proof reuse when changing data representation in the Coq proof assistant. We improve the approach presented in [12]. It leads to a new tool that appears to be efficient and generic. Indeed, it was usable to translate the whole *Arith* library of Coq. In addition, we manage to reuse it successfully for translating polymorphic lists into reverse polymorphic lists.

Among future research directions, we can quote changing the representation of the index type of an inductive family [8]. For instance, one can imagine to translate dependent lists indexed by nat into dependent lists indexed by bin.

```
Inductive vect [A : Set]   : nat->Set  :=
      vnil : (vect A (0))
   | vcons :  (n:nat)A->(vect A n)->(vect A (S n))
```

As (pred (S n)) and n are convertible in nat, this statement is well-formed:

$$\forall v : (\text{vect } A \ n). \ \forall v' : (\text{vect } A \ (\text{pred } (S \ n))). \ v =_{(\text{vect } A \ n)} v'$$

However in the binary setting, (pred (S n)) and n will not necessarily be convertible. Consequently, two terms that were propositionally equal in the initial setting do not even live in the same type after the transformation.

A solution (out of scope within the Coq system) would be to identify judgemental (conversion) and propositional equalities, as described in [10]. Another approach may consist in connecting together the two instances of the dependent family via some coercions [16]. Z. Luo and S. Soloviev proposed in [11] some mechanisms to add coercions between a type (e.g. lists) and a family of types (e.g. vectors of length n).

Another direction is to study changes of data type where input and output types are not isomorphic. For instance, one may want to translate lists into trees. Trees would be a more efficient data structure for computing, but different trees can have the same representation as lists. Therefore connecting these two representations may not be so obvious.

References

1. A. Balaa and Y. Bertot. Fix-point Equations for Well-Founded Recursion in Type Theory. In *Theorem Proving in Higher Order Logics: TPHOLs 2000*, volume 1869 of *LNCS*, pages 1–16. Springer-Verlag, 2000.
2. G. Barthe and O. Pons. Type Isomorphisms and Proof Reuse in Dependent Type Theory. In F. Honsell and M. Miculan, editors, *FOSSACS'01*, volume 2030, pages 57–71. LNCS, Springer-Verlag, 2001.
3. Y. Bertot and P. Casteran. *Le Coq'Art*. To appear, 2003.
4. J. Chrzaszcz. Implementation of Modules in the Coq System. Draft, February 2003.
5. Coq development team, INRIA and LRI. *The Coq Proof Assistant Reference Manual*, May 2002. Version 7.3.
6. C. Cornes and D. Terrasse. Automatizing Inversion of Inductive Predicates in Coq. In *TYPES'95*, volume 1158. LNCS, Springer-Verlag, 1995.
7. D. Delahaye and M. Mayero. **Field**: une procédure de décision pour les nombres réels en **Coq**. In P. Castéran, editor, *Journées Francophones des Langages Applicatifs, Pontarlier*. INRIA, Janvier 2001.
8. P. Dybjer. Inductive Families. *Formal Aspects of Computing*, 6(4):440–465, 1994.
9. P. Dybjer. A General Formulation of Simultaneous Inductive-Recursive Definitions in Type Theory. *Journal of Symbolic Logic*, 65(2), 2000.
10. M. Hofmann. Conservativity of Equality Reflection over Intensional Type Theory. In *BRA Workshop on Types for Proofs and Programs (TYPES'95)*, volume 1158, pages 153–165. Springer-Verlag LNCS, 1996.
11. Z. Luo and S. Soloviev. Dependent Coercions. In *8th Inter. Conf. on Category Theory in Computer Science (CTCS'99)*, volume 29 of *ENTCS*, pages 23–34, Edinburgh, Scotland, 1999. Elsevier.
12. N. Magaud and Y. Bertot. Changing Data Structures in Type Theory:A Study of Natural Numbers. In *International Workshop on Types for Proofs and Programs*, volume 2277 of *LNCS*, pages 181–196. Springer-Verlag, 2000.
13. C. McBride and J. McKinna. The View from the Left. *Journal of Functional Programming*, Special Issue: Dependent Type Theory meets Programming Practice, 2002. submitted.
14. A. Miquel. Axiom $\forall P, Q : Prop.$ (P $\leftrightarrow$ Q)$\rightarrow$(P==Q) is safe. Communication in the coq-club list, November 2002.
15. C. Paulin-Mohring. Inductive Definitions in the System Coq - Rules and Properties. In M. Bezem and J.-F. Groote, editors, *Typed Lambda Calculi and Applications*, volume 664 of *LNCS*, 1993. LIP research report 92–49.
16. A. Saïbi. Typing Algorithm in Type Theory with Inheritance. In *POPL'97*. ACM, 1997.
17. P. Wadler. Views: A Way for Pattern Matching to Cohabit with Data Abstraction. In *POPL'87*. ACM, 1987.

Applications of Polytypism in Theorem Proving

Konrad Slind[1] and Joe Hurd[2]

[1] School of Computing, University of Utah
[2] Computer Laboratory, University of Cambridge

Abstract. Polytypic functions have mainly been studied in the context of functional programming languages. In that setting, applications of polytypism include elegant treatments of polymorphic equality, prettyprinting, and the encoding and decoding of high-level datatypes to and from low-level binary formats. In this paper, we discuss how polytypism supports some aspects of theorem proving: automated termination proofs of recursive functions, incorporation of the results of metalanguage evaluation, and equivalence-preserving translation to a low-level format suitable for propositional methods. The approach is based on an interpretation of higher order logic types as terms, and easily deals with mutual and nested recursive types.

1 Introduction

When a new datatype is declared in a functional language, or a higher order logic proof system, many functions on that type can be automatically defined. Prime examples of this are maps and folds, of course, but there are also many others: if we think of a datatype declaration facility as a way of introducing a particular shape of tree, common tree operations become immediately definable once such a shape is introduced. Examples include computing the number of nodes in a tree, substitution, hashing, marshalling, *etc.* Such a function is said to be *polytypic*, since its algorithm is the same, modulo the shape of the tree.

We discuss three applications of polytypism to theorem proving:

1. Size functions, which support automated termination proofs.
2. Functions for transporting values from meta-language to object-language.
3. Encoding and decoding functions, which support automated translation from high-level HOL formulas to equivalent boolean formulas.

Our approach is based on an interpretation $[\![\_]\!]_{\Theta,\Gamma}$ of higher order logic types into terms. The interpretation is parameterized by two maps: Θ, which maps type variables; and Γ, which maps type operators.

$$[\![v]\!]_{\Theta,\Gamma} = \Theta(v), \qquad\qquad\qquad \text{if } v \text{ is a type variable}$$
$$[\![(\tau_1, ..., \tau_n)c]\!]_{\Theta,\Gamma} = \Gamma(c) \ [\![\tau_1]\!]_{\Theta,\Gamma} \ \cdots \ [\![\tau_n]\!]_{\Theta,\Gamma}, \qquad \text{otherwise}$$

This interpretation is similar to the semantics of HOL types given by Pitts [15]. Although the interpretation is not itself expressible in the HOL logic, it is expressible in the meta-language (which for us is ML), and uses definitions made in the object logic each time a datatype is defined.

D. Basin and B. Wolff (Eds.): TPHOLs 2003, LNCS 2758, pp. 103–119, 2003.
© Springer-Verlag Berlin Heidelberg 2003

2   Notation and Background Definitions

We use the HOL logic [15] to develop our ideas. The syntax of HOL is based on signatures for types and terms. The type signature Ω assigns arities to type operators. The set of HOL types is the least set closed under the following rules:

type variable. There is a countable set of type variables. Greek letters, *e.g.*, α, β, *etc.* will be used to stand for type variables.

compound type. If c in Ω has arity n, and each of $\tau_1, \ldots \tau_n$ is a type, then $(\tau_1, \ldots, \tau_n)c$ is a type.

A type constant is represented by a 0-ary compound type. The initial types found in Ω: truth values (bool), function space (written $\alpha \to \beta$), and ind, an infinite set of individuals, can be used to definitionally construct a large collection of types. Readers interested in the details of the definition principle used to extend Ω may can consult [15].

Datatypes. A inductive datatype τ declared as an instance of the scheme

$$(\alpha_1, \ldots, \alpha_m)\tau \equiv C_1\ ty_{11}\ \ldots\ ty_{1k_1}\ |\ldots|\ C_n\ ty_{n1}\ \ldots\ ty_{nk_n},$$

where all the type variables in $ty_{11} \ldots ty_{nk_n}$ are in $\{\alpha_1, \ldots, \alpha_m\}$, denotes the set of all values that can be finitely built up by application of the constructors $C_1, \ldots, C_n$. Constructors are injective, and applications of different constructors always yield different values. The type is recursive if any ty_{ij} in the type declaration is $(\alpha_1, \ldots, \alpha_m)\tau$. A characterizing theorem of the following form can be derived for inductive types [21]:

$$\forall f_1 \ldots f_n.\ \exists! \mathcal{H} : (\alpha_1, \ldots, \alpha_m)\tau \to \beta.$$
$$\forall x_{11} \ldots x_{1k_1}.\ \mathcal{H}(C_1\ x_{11} \ldots x_{1k_1})\ = f_1(\mathcal{H}\ x_{11}) \ldots (\mathcal{H}\ x_{1k_1})\ x_{11} \ldots x_{1k_1}\ \wedge$$
$$\vdots \qquad\qquad\qquad\qquad\qquad\qquad \wedge$$
$$\forall x_{n1} \ldots x_{nk_n}.\ \mathcal{H}(C_n\ x_{n1} \ldots x_{nk_n}) = f_n(\mathcal{H}\ x_{n1}) \ldots (\mathcal{H}\ x_{nk_n})\ x_{n1} \ldots x_{nk_n}.$$

This theorem embodies the primitive recursion principle for functions over the specified type. More complex datatypes, featuring mutual and nested recursion, allow similar theorems to be proved for them [17,18,5]. We will make use of the following types (given in SML syntax):

```
1.    datatype 'a option = NONE | SOME of 'a
2.    datatype 'a list = [] | :: of 'a * 'a list
3.    datatype 'a tree = Node of 'a * 'a tree list
4.    datatype ('a,'b)exp = Var of 'a
                          | Cond of ('a,'b)bexp * ('a,'b)exp * ('a,'b)exp
                          | App of 'b * ('a,'b)exp list
      and      ('a,'b)bexp = Less of ('a,'b)exp * ('a,'b)exp
                          | And of ('a,'b)bexp * ('a,'b)bexp
                          | Not of ('a,'b)bexp
```

The first two declaration are for the well-known types of options and polymorphic lists, the third is a type of finitely branching trees, and the fourth is a mutually recursive type of expressions and boolean expressions.

Miscellaneous definitions. The K combinator is defined $\mathsf{K} \equiv \lambda xy.x$. The first and second components of a pair are selected by $\mathsf{fst}(x, y) \equiv x$ and $\mathsf{snd}(x, y) \equiv y$ respectively; and the $(\mathsf{SOME}\ x) \equiv x$ returns the element from an option. The function $\mathcal{I}$ applies an interpretation to a term:

$$\mathcal{I}_{\Theta, \Gamma}(M : \tau) = [\![\tau]\!]_{\Theta, \Gamma}(M) \ .$$

Note. Although constructors in ML take a single argument tuple, by default constructors in HOL are curried.

3   Wellfounded Relations for Datatypes

In a logic of total functions such as HOL, the termination of recursive function definitions must be proved. A simple and yet effective approach is to show that the arguments of all recursive calls decrease in size. Therefore, it is common practice to define *size measures* on datatypes. The following formal definitions and theorems provide justification (where $\mathsf{WF} : (\alpha \rightarrow \alpha \rightarrow \mathsf{bool}) \rightarrow \mathsf{bool}$ is a predicate that singles out the *wellfounded* relations):

inv_image $R\ f \equiv \lambda x\ y.\ R\ (f\ x)\ (f\ y)$ $\vdash \mathsf{WF}(R) \supset \mathsf{WF}\ (\mathsf{inv\_image}\ R\ f)$
measure $\equiv$ inv_image $(<)$ $\vdash \forall f : \alpha \rightarrow \mathsf{num}.\ \mathsf{WF}\ (\mathsf{measure}\ f)$

Thus termination of a recursive function over a type τ may be proved by showing that the recursive calls are in the relation $\mathsf{measure}(size_\tau)$. Thinking of an element of a datatype as a tree, it is standard to define its size as one plus the sum of the sizes of the subtrees (leaves are assigned a size of zero).[1] We now encounter a problem: how to define size for *polymorphic* datatypes? For example, it would be easy, natural, and unsatisfactory—for our notion of size, which is the number of internal nodes in a tree—to define the size of a list as its length: length does not capture the size of a list of numbers, or a list of lists. Moreover, how are we to capture, in a single definition, the sizes of lists of elements of types not yet defined? It seems that the notion of size for a polymorphic type would have to know about all types that have been defined in the past, and also all types that could be defined in the future!

We solve this polymorphic quandary by mapping each type variable in the type to a term variable representing a size function. Thus, we intend to define the size of elements of datatype $(\alpha_1, \ldots, \alpha_n)\tau$ as a higher order function parameterized by n size functions, one for each type variable:

$$\tau\text{-size}\ (f_1 : \alpha_1 \rightarrow \mathsf{num}) \ldots (f_n : \alpha_n \rightarrow \mathsf{num})\ (x : (\alpha_1, \ldots, \alpha_n)\tau) \equiv \ldots$$

A general way to construct such definitions uses $[\![\_]\!]_{\Theta, \Gamma}$. The idea is to traverse the type, and build a term by replacing type operators by size functions (by use of Γ), and type variables by parameters (by use of Θ). Thus Γ maps previously defined type operators to their associated size functions, and Θ maps $\alpha_1, \ldots, \alpha_n$ to $f_1, \ldots, f_n$.

---

[1] This seems to be motivated by the desire to have the size of Peano numerals be the identity function.

Definition 1 (Datatype size).

Suppose datatype $(\alpha_1, \ldots, \alpha_n)\tau$ has been defined, with constructors $C_1, \ldots, C_k$ in size context Γ. Create function variables $(f_1 : \alpha_1 \to \text{num}), \ldots, (f_n : \alpha_n \to \text{num})$, and let Θ be $\{\alpha_1 \mapsto f_1, \ldots, \alpha_n \mapsto f_n\}$. Extend Γ with a binding for size_τ:

$$\Delta = \lambda tyop. \; if \; tyop = \tau \; then \; \text{size}\_\tau \; else \; \Gamma(tyop).$$

Then define

$$
\begin{aligned}
\text{size}\_\tau \; f_1 \ldots f_n \; C_i &\equiv 0, \quad if \; C_i \; is \; nullary; \; otherwise, \\
\text{size}\_\tau \; f_1 \ldots f_n \; (C_i \; x_1 \ldots x_m) &\equiv 1 + \sum_{i=1}^{m} \mathcal{I}_{\Theta,\Delta}(x_i)
\end{aligned}
$$

$\square$

Example 1. Size definitions for our example types:

– Lists:

$$
\begin{aligned}
\text{list\_size} \; f \; [] &= 0 \\
\text{list\_size} \; f \; (h :: t) &= 1 + f \; h + \text{list\_size} \; f \; t.
\end{aligned}
$$

– Trees:

$$\text{tree\_size} \; f \; (\text{Node} \; x \; tlist) = 1 + fx + \text{list\_size} \; (\text{tree\_size} \; f) \; tlist.$$

– Expressions, boolean expressions, and expression lists:

$\text{esize} \; f \; g \; (\text{Var} \; a)$	$= 1 + f \; a$	
$\text{esize} \; f \; g \; (\text{Cond} \; b \; e_1 \; e_2)$	$= 1 + \text{bsize} \; f \; g \; b + \text{esize} \; f \; g \; e_1 + \text{esize} \; f \; g \; e_2$	
$\text{esize} \; f \; g \; (\text{App} \; fn \; \ell)$	$= 1 + g \; fn + \text{elsize} \; f \; g \; \ell$	
$\text{bsize} \; f \; g \; (\text{Less} \; e_1 \; e_2)$	$= 1 + \text{esize} \; f \; g \; e_1 + \text{esize} \; f \; g \; e_2$	
$\text{bsize} \; f \; g \; (\text{And} \; e_1 \; e_2)$	$= 1 + \text{bsize} \; f \; g \; e_1 + \text{bsize} \; f \; g \; e_2$	
$\text{bsize} \; f \; g \; (\text{Not} \; b)$	$= 1 + \text{bsize} \; f \; g \; b$	
$\text{elsize} \; f \; g \; []$	$= 0$	
$\text{elsize} \; f \; g \; (h :: t)$	$= 1 + \text{esize} \; f \; g \; h + \text{elsize} \; f \; g \; t$	

This approach to defining the size of datatype elements becomes particularly useful when dealing with functions defined over instances of polymorphic datatypes.

Example 2. Consider a polymorphic function flat : α list list $\to$ α list for removing a level of bracketing from a list:

$$
\begin{aligned}
\text{flat} \; [] &\equiv [] \\
\text{flat} \; ([] :: \ell) &\equiv \text{flat} \; \ell \\
\text{flat} \; ((h :: t) :: \ell) &\equiv h :: \text{flat} \; (t :: \ell).
\end{aligned}
$$

Note that simply measuring the length of the argument will not prove termination. To show that flat terminates, we first ensure that Γ contains list $\mapsto$ list_size, and that $\Theta \equiv \{\alpha \mapsto K \; 0\}$. Then

$$[\![\alpha \; \text{list list}]\!]_{\Theta,\Gamma} = \text{list\_size} \; (\text{list\_size} \; (K \; 0)),$$

and proving termination of flat can be done by showing that the recursive calls of flat lie in the relation measure $(\mathsf{list\_size}\ (\mathsf{list\_size}\ (\mathsf{K}\ 0)))$, *i.e.*, making the informal abbreviation $\mathcal{M} \equiv \mathsf{list\_size}\ (\mathsf{K}\ 0)$, by showing

$$
\begin{aligned}
1.\ \mathsf{list\_size}\ \mathcal{M}\ \ell\ \ &<\ \mathsf{list\_size}\ \mathcal{M}\ ([]\ ::\ \ell)\\
&=\ 1 + \mathcal{M}\ [] + \mathsf{list\_size}\ \mathcal{M}\ \ell
\end{aligned}
$$

$$
\begin{aligned}
2.\ \mathsf{list\_size}\ \mathcal{M}\ (t\ ::\ \ell) &= 1 + \mathcal{M}\ t + \mathsf{list\_size}\ \mathcal{M}\ \ell\\
&< \mathsf{list\_size}\ \mathcal{M}\ ((h\ ::\ t)\ ::\ \ell)\\
&= 1 + \mathcal{M}\ (h\ ::\ t) + \mathsf{list\_size}\ \mathcal{M}\ \ell\\
&= 1 + (1 + (\mathsf{K}\ 0)\ h + \mathcal{M}\ t) + \mathsf{list\_size}\ \mathcal{M}\ \ell\\
&= 1 + (1 + \mathcal{M}\ t) + \mathsf{list\_size}\ \mathcal{M}\ \ell
\end{aligned}
$$

This kind of derivation is straightforward to automate: $[\![-]\!]$ is used to construct a measure on the sizes of recursive calls and then the resulting problem is reduced via rewriting to a problem in linear arithmetic. This has been implemented for several years in the HOL-4 system. Such termination proofs fail either because the termination relation is wrong or because the automated termination condition prover is too weak. For example, termination of the following 'higher order recursion' fails to be proved automatically: the size measure is correct but the termination prover is currently too weak, since it doesn't attempt induction.

Example 3. Consider a function for accumulating the node elements of a tree into a set (using 'foldl', a fold on lists):

$$\mathsf{Nodeset}\ (\mathsf{Node}\ v\ \ell) = \mathsf{foldl}\ (\boldsymbol{\lambda}acc\ t.\ acc \cup \mathsf{Nodeset}\ t)\ \{v\}\ \ell$$

The size measure for this definition is measure $(\mathsf{tree\_size}\ (\mathsf{K}\ 0))$, and the synthesized termination requirement [25, pages 131-133] is

$$\exists R.\ \mathsf{WF}\ R \wedge \forall v\ \ell\ t.\ \mathsf{mem}\ t\ \ell \supset R\ t\ (\mathsf{Node}\ v\ \ell).$$

Using the size measure as a witness results in a goal

$$\forall \ell\ t.\ \mathsf{mem}\ t\ \ell \supset \mathsf{tree\_size}(\mathsf{K}\ 0)\ t < \mathsf{list\_size}\ (\mathsf{tree\_size}\ (\mathsf{K}\ 0))\ \ell + 1$$

which is provable by induction on ℓ.   □

A typical Γ would include at least the following:

type	size definition
$\tau_1 * \tau_2$	**prod_size** $f\ g\ (x, y) \equiv f\ x + g\ y$
$\tau_1 + \tau_2$	**sum_size** $f\ g\ (\mathsf{INL}\ x) \equiv f\ x$
	sum_size $f\ g\ (\mathsf{INR}\ y) \equiv g\ y$
bool	**bool_size** $x \equiv 0$
num	**num_size** $x \equiv x$
option	**option_size** $f\ \mathsf{NONE} \equiv 0$
	option_size $f\ (\mathsf{SOME}\ x) \equiv 1 + (f\ x)$

Remarks. The size of a pair is just the sum of the sizes of the two projections: since pairs are not recursive, it is not useful (for the purposes of termination proofs) to add one to the sum. The size of an element of a sum type is just the size of the injected item: since sum constructors are used as discriminatory tags, any nesting of INL and INR should be ignored in the computation of an object's size. We have found this to be a useful approach when proving termination of mutually recursive functions, which are modelled using sum types [6]. As a map, Γ is partial: if a type constructor is not in Γ, then all elements of that type are deemed to be of a fixed size. For example, functions have a fixed size (zero).

Summary. In this section we have examined a way to automatically generate size measures for datatypes, and sketched a method for automated termination proofs of recursive functions. The approach is naive, especially compared to the work in [11,12]. However, our size measures automatically prove termination for a relatively large class of functions and can be used as the base relation in more powerful relations (multiset, rpo, *etc*), so our work is of general utility.

4   Lifting of Metalanguage Values

Although evaluation by means of deductive steps can be implemented in HOL in an asymptotically efficient way [2], it is still very attractive to be able to execute ground terms—when possible—with a more efficient engine, such as the ML implementation underlying HOL. A recent example of this is [4], in which ML is used to evaluate recursive functions and (some) inductive relations defined in Isabelle/HOL. Other systems that exploit the speed of evaluation in the implementation language are ACL2 and PVS [22,24]. These two systems are based in LISP, the reflective capabilities of which make for a smooth passage back and forth between meta- and object- languages.

However, current logic implementations with an ML-evaluation feature have the drawback that answers computed at the ML level are not automatically lifted back into object-language terms. This is somewhat unsatisfying since we'd like to make use of the following diagram:

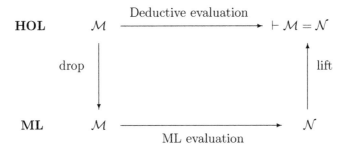

Such a system—mapping HOL terms to ML expressions, performing ML evaluation, and lifting the result back to HOL—is useful with large formalizations. For example, in a recent model of the ARM [9,10], deductive evaluation of ARM assembly programs achieves a speed of a few tens of instructions per second.

In contrast, much higher execution speeds for hardware models have been reported with ACL2, which compiles and evaluates formal definitions directly in the underlying LISP implementation. We would like to attain similar speeds in HOL.

It is relatively easy to drop HOL terms—it is just a matter of prettyprinting to ML syntax—but lifting is more difficult, because the lifter depends on the type of the data to be lifted and so can't be written once and forall as an ML function. Of course, if the results of ML execution aren't needed in the object logic, the lifting step can be dispensed with. However, it may be that results computed in ML can find other application, *e.g.*, existential witnesses or counterexamples may be found by external tools, and then lifted to terms in proofs.

Our approach is to interpret a HOL type[2] $\ulcorner\tau\urcorner$ into an ML program which will lift an ML value $M : \tau$ to a HOL term $\ulcorner M : \tau\urcorner$. We will have to modify our interpretation so that it explicitly passes the type. This allows, for example, the lifting of [] : **num list**.

$$[\![\tau]\!]_{\Theta,\Gamma} = \Theta(\tau), \qquad\qquad \text{if } \tau \text{ is a type variable}$$
$$[\![\tau]\!]_{\Theta,\Gamma} = \Gamma(c)\ \tau\ [\![\tau_1]\!]_{\Theta,\Gamma} \cdots [\![\tau_n]\!]_{\Theta,\Gamma} \qquad \text{where } \tau = (\tau_1, ..., \tau_n)c$$

This is analogous to the difference between primitive recursion and iteration, an issue explored in a slightly different context by Weirich [26].

Definition 2 (Datatype lifting). *Suppose datatype* $(\alpha_1, \ldots, \alpha_n)\tau$ *has been defined in HOL, with constructors* $C_1, \ldots, C_k$ *in lifter context* Γ. *Also assume that the same datatype has been declared in ML. Create ML function variables* $(f_1 : \alpha_1 \to \mathsf{term}), \ldots, (f_n : \alpha_n \to \mathsf{term})$, *and let* Θ *be* $\{\alpha_1 \mapsto f_1, \ldots, \alpha_n \mapsto f_n\}$. *Extend* Γ *with a binding for* lift_τ:

$$\Delta = \boldsymbol{\lambda} tyop.\ \mathit{if}\ tyop = \tau\ \mathit{then}\ \mathit{lift}\_\tau\ \mathit{else}\ \Gamma(tyop).$$

Then define the ML function

$$\mathsf{lift}\_\tau\ \tau\ f_1 \ldots f_n\ (C_i\ (x_1, \ldots, x_m)) \equiv \ulcorner C_i\ (\mathcal{I}_{\Theta,\Delta}(x_1)) \ldots (\mathcal{I}_{\Theta,\Delta}(x_m))\ :\ \tau \urcorner.$$

$\square$

Example 4. The lifter $\mathsf{lift\_list} : \mathsf{hol\_type} \to (\alpha \to \mathsf{term}) \to \alpha\ \mathsf{list} \to \mathsf{term}$ for the datatype of lists is :

$$\mathsf{lift\_list}\ ty\ f\ [] \equiv \ulcorner [] : ty \urcorner$$
$$\mathsf{lift\_list}\ ty\ f\ (h :: t) \equiv \ulcorner f\ h :: \mathsf{lift\_list}\ ty\ f\ t \urcorner.$$

The actual definition made in our implementation is more contorted, mainly in order to avoid type instantiations at each node in the list. $\square$

An inference rule **ML_EVAL** that reduces ground HOL terms by ML evaluation can be easily implemented by dropping the given term $M : \tau$, evaluating M in

---

[2] The notation $\ulcorner-\urcorner$ is used to distinguish HOL types and terms from ML types and expressions.

ML, and then using τ to synthesize and apply a lifter to the result, yielding a HOL term N. The result is then asserted as an *oracle* theorem $\vdash M = N$ having an attached tag that attests to the ML excursion [23]. Thus theorems generated by ML_EVAL are *weakened* by the meta-language excursion, but the speed-up may be worth it in some cases.

Example 5. The improvement of execution speed for ground formulas is as expected: deductively evaluating (with EVAL) the standard factorial function over the first twenty-one numbers takes 3.6 seconds and 123,520 primitive inference steps.

```
- Count.apply EVAL (Term 'Map Fact (iota 0 20)');
runtime: 3.625s,      gctime: 0.331s,      systime: 3.625s.
HOL primitive inference steps: 123520.
> val it = |- Map Fact (iota 0 20) =
    [1; 1; 2; 6; 24; 120; 720; 5040; 40320; 362880; 3628800; 39916800;
    479001600; 6227020800; 87178291200; 1307674368000; 20922789888000;
    355687428096000; 6402373705728000; 121645100408832000;
    2432902008176640000] : thm
```

In contrast, the expression sent to ML by ML_EVAL

lift_list ⌜: num list⌝ (lift_num ⌜: num⌝)
(Map Fact (iota (numML.fromString"0")(numML.fromString"20")))

wraps the lifter generated from the type num list around the ML expression generated from the HOL term Map Fact (iota 0 20) and takes 0.03 seconds and one inference step.   □

5   Encoding and Decoding

It is common in computer science to create operations that package up high-level data as flat strings of bits, and corresponding operations to unpack strings of bits and recover the high-level data. When this is done to send data over a communication network, it is called marshalling/unmarshalling, but we will use the general terminology *encoding/decoding* or just *coding*. An advantage of encoding high-level data as strings of bits is that operations such as encryption or compression can be uniformly applied to any kind of data. An interesting application of coding in HOL is the mapping of high-level formulas into equivalent quantified boolean formulas suitable for input to the powerful SAT implementations that have recently become popular.

5.1   Encoders

Intuitively, an encoding function can be thought of simply as an injective function $\tau \to$ bool list mapping elements of type τ to lists of booleans. The injectivity condition prevents two elements of τ being encoded as the same list of booleans, and so guarantees that if a list can be decoded then the decoding will be unique.

Encoding functions can be automatically defined when a new datatype is declared, in exactly the same way as the size functions of Section 3.

Definition 3 (Datatype encoding).

Suppose datatype $(\alpha_1, \ldots, \alpha_n)\tau$ has been defined, with k constructors $C_1, \ldots, C_k$ in encoding context Γ. Create function variables $(f_1 : \alpha_1 \rightarrow$ bool list$), \ldots, (f_n : \alpha_n \rightarrow$ bool list$)$, and let Θ be $\{\alpha_1 \mapsto f_1, \ldots, \alpha_n \mapsto f_n\}$. Extend Γ with a binding for encode_τ:

$$\Delta = \lambda tyop. \; if \; tyop = \tau \; then \; \text{encode\_}\tau \; else \; \Gamma(tyop).$$

Then define

$$\text{encode\_}\tau \; f_1 \ldots f_n \; (C_i \; (x_1 : \tau_1) \ldots (x_m : \tau_m))$$
$$\equiv \; \text{marker} \; k \; i \; @ \; (\mathcal{I}_{\Theta, \Delta}(x_1)) \; @ \; \cdots \; @ \; (\mathcal{I}_{\Theta, \Delta}(x_m))$$

where @ represent the list append function, and marker k i *is the ith boolean list of length N (N is the smallest natural number satisfying $k \leq 2^N$.)* □

Example 6. The encoding function for the datatype of lists:

$$\text{encode\_list} \; f \; [] \equiv [\bot] \; \wedge$$
$$\text{encode\_list} \; f \; (h :: t) \equiv \top :: f \; h \; @ \; \text{encode\_list} \; f \; t$$

Lists have two constructors, which are distinguished in each case of encode_list by the prepending of marker $2 \; 0 = [\bot]$ and marker $2 \; 1 = [\top]$. □

The marker lists are designed to be just long enough to be able to distinguish between the datatype constructors. Lists have two constructors, and so the marker lists have length one. A datatype with eight constructors would need marker lists of length three. As the next example shows, nothing needs to be altered in the special case of a datatype with a single constructor.

Example 7. The encoding function for the datatype of trees:

$$\text{encode\_tree} \; e \; (\text{Node} \; a \; b) \equiv e \; a \; @ \; \text{encode\_list} \; (\text{encode\_tree} \; e) \; b$$

Since the tree datatype has only one constructor, the encoding function prepends marker $1 \; 0 = []$ to the result (and this gets simplified away). □

The final example we present shows the definition of a custom encoder. Although encoders are automatically defined for every datatype declared, the user may wish to override the automatic definition with an alternative version, or to provide an encoder for a non-datatype.

Example 8. The encoding function for the type num of natural numbers:

$$\text{encode\_num} \; n \equiv \text{if} \; n = 0 \; \text{then} \; [\top; \top]$$
$$\text{else if even} \; n \; \text{then} \; \bot :: \text{encode\_num} \; ((n - 2) \; \text{div} \; 2)$$
$$\text{else} \; \top :: \bot :: \text{encode\_num} \; ((n - 1) \; \text{div} \; 2)$$

Note that in the even case, recursing with $(n - 2)$ div 2 instead of n div 2 leads to a more compact encoding. □

A typical environment Γ for encoding functions would include at least:

type	encoder	
$\tau_1 * \tau_2$	encode_prod f g $(x, y) \equiv f\ x \mathbin{@} g\ y$	
$\tau_1 + \tau_2$	encode_sum f g (INL x) $\equiv \bot :: f\ x$	
	encode_sum f g (INR y) $\equiv \top :: g\ y$	
bool	encode_bool $x \equiv [x]$	
option	encode_option f NONE $\equiv [\bot]$	
	encode_option f (SOME x) $\equiv \top :: f\ x$	
num	encode_num	(defined above)
τ list	encode_list	(defined above)

As can be seen, function spaces are omitted completely from this list; we cannot simply return a default value (as we did for size functions) because we require that all encoders are injective functions. On the other hand, we include the list type because lists play such a fundamental role in encoding.

5.2 Decoders: Existence

A decoder for type τ is an algorithm that takes as input a list of booleans and returns an element of type τ. The strategy we will present makes it possible to build decoders in a type-directed way. The key is to think of a decoder for type τ as a function

$$\text{decode\_}\tau : \text{bool list} \to (\tau \times \text{bool list}) \text{ option}$$

This function tries to 'parse' an input list of booleans into an element of type τ, and if it succeeds then it returns the element of τ *together with the list of booleans that were left over*. If it fails to parse the input list, it signals this by returning NONE. A standard decoding function of type bool list $\to \tau$ can be recovered from decode_τ using the function $\langle \cdot \rangle$, defined as $\langle \text{decode\_}\tau \rangle \equiv \text{fst} \circ \text{the} \circ \text{decode\_}\tau$.

Given some datatype $(\alpha_1, \ldots, \alpha_n)\tau$, we would like to specify decode_τ as the inverse of encode_τ. For a given domain predicate P, the coder P e d property requires that the encoder e and decoder d are mutually inverse:

$$\text{coder } P\ e\ d \equiv \forall l, x, t.\ P\ x \supset ((l = e\ x \mathbin{@} t) \iff (d\ l = \text{SOME }(x, t)))$$

This allows us to use encode_τ to define the specification of decode_τ:

$$\text{coder } P_1\ e_1\ d_1 \wedge \cdots \wedge \text{coder } P_n\ e_n\ d_n \supset$$
$$\text{coder } (\text{all\_}\tau\ P_1 \ldots P_n)\ (\text{encode\_}\tau\ e_1 \ldots e_n)\ (\text{decode\_}\tau\ d_1 \ldots d_n)$$

The function all_τ lifts the predicates $P_i : \alpha_i \to \text{bool}$ to a predicate of the datatype $(\alpha_1, \ldots, \alpha_n)\tau$, and has type

$$\text{all\_}\tau : (\alpha_1 \to \text{bool}) \to \cdots \to (\alpha_n \to \text{bool}) \to (\alpha_1, \ldots, \alpha_n)\tau \to \text{bool}$$

Similarly to size_τ and encode_τ functions, we can use polytypism to define an all_τ function whenever a new datatype is declared.

It turns out that there exists a decode_τ satisfying the above specification precisely when encode_τ is prefix-free on domain all_τ $P_1 \ldots P_n$, where

$$\text{prefixfree } P\ e \;\equiv\; \forall x, y.\ P\ x \wedge P\ y \wedge \text{is\_prefix } (e\ x)\ (e\ y) \supset x = y$$

Since every list l satisfies is_prefix $l\ l$, being prefix-free is a stronger property on encode_τ than being an injective function. Therefore, the following theorem is all we need to show the existence of a decode_τ satisfying the above specification:

$$\text{prefixfree } P_1\ e_1 \wedge \cdots \wedge \text{prefixfree } P_n\ e_n \supset$$
$$\text{prefixfree } (\text{all\_}\tau\ P_1 \ldots P_n)\ (\text{encode\_}\tau\ e_1 \ldots e_n)$$

Our scheme of defining encoders using marker lists means that it would not be difficult to provide a polytypic tactic that proves this theorem automatically for every new datatype.

Once we have proved the existence of decoder functions satisfying the above specification, the final step is to pick an arbitrary one (using the axiom of choice) to define a new constant called decode_τ.

5.3 Decoders: Recursion Equations

Given a new datatype $(\alpha_1, \ldots, \alpha_n)\tau$, we have shown how to use polytypism to define decode_τ as the inverse of encode_τ. This is a useful sanity check, demonstrating that it is always possible to uniquely decode an element of τ that was previously encoded as a boolean list.

Unfortunately, the specification of decode_τ is not in a form that allows us to directly execute it on a boolean list. However, using polytypism once again we can write down a set of recursion equations for decode_τ, and then use logical inferences to show that they follow from the specification.

Example 9. The recursion equations for decode_bool:

$$\text{decode\_bool } [] \equiv \text{NONE } \wedge$$
$$\text{decode\_bool } (h :: t) \equiv \text{SOME } (h, t)$$

In other words, the only time we fail to decode an element of type bool is when we are given the empty list.   □

Deriving the recursion equations for a decoder proceeds by case analysis on the input list, followed by application of the decoder specification and the definition of the corresponding encoder. This proof strategy also works when the recursion equations for a decoder are recursive, as is the case for the list type.

Example 10. The recursion equations for decode_list:

$$\begin{aligned}
&\text{reducing } d \;\supset \\
&\quad \text{decode\_list } d\ [] \;\equiv\; \text{NONE } \wedge \\
&\quad \text{decode\_list } d\ (\bot :: l) \;\equiv\; \text{SOME } ([], l) \wedge \\
&\quad \text{decode\_list } d\ (\top :: l) \equiv \\
&\qquad \text{case } d\ l \text{ of NONE } \rightarrow \text{ NONE} \\
&\qquad \mid \text{SOME } (h, l') \;\rightarrow\; \text{case decode\_list } d\ l' \text{ of NONE } \rightarrow \text{ NONE} \\
&\qquad\qquad\qquad\qquad\qquad\quad \mid \text{SOME } (t, l'') \;\rightarrow\; \text{SOME } (h :: t, l'')
\end{aligned}$$

Termination of the recursion equations is ensured by the reducing d side-condition, which requires that the boolean list returned by d is always a sublist of its input (all decoders will satisfy this property). ☐

From the previous example we can see that in general the recursion equations for decode_τ will be co-recursive and have side-conditions requiring the sub-decoders $d_1, \ldots, d_n$ to satisfy reducing. Such definitions combined with higher-order recursion can produce some entertaining problems, and we finish with a particularly tricky example.

Example 11. The recursion equations for decode_tree:

reducing d ⊃
  decode_tree d l ≡
    case d l of NONE → NONE
    | SOME (a, l') → case decode_list (decode_tree d) l' of NONE → NONE
                                   | SOME (b, l'') → SOME (Node a b, l'')

Because we defined decode_tree as the inverse of encode_tree, we can first prove that reducing (decode_tree d) holds, and then make use of the decode_list recursion equations to derive the decode_tree recursion theorems. However, without such a back door it appears to be difficult to define this kind of function in HOL, and we present decode_tree as a challenge example for termination proving. ☐

Example 12. Executing an encoder followed by a decoder.

encode_list encode_num $[1; 2]$ = $[\top; \top; \bot; \top; \top; \top; \bot; \top; \top; \bot]$
decode_list decode_num $[\top; \top; \bot; \top; \top; \top; \bot; \top; \top; \bot]$ = SOME $([1; 2], [])$

5.4   Converting Formulas to Boolean Form

Up to this point we have only applied encoders to ground datatype terms, but to create versions of problems suitable for SAT solvers or model checkers we need to convert whole formulas to boolean form, in particular handling variables properly. Our translation methodology has much in common with that used in bounded model checking to map temporal logic formulas to propositional logic [1]. We first define the *boolean propagation theorems* which we use to replace the functions and predicates in the formula with boolean versions.

Definition 4 (Boolean propagation theorems). *For every function*

$$f : \tau_1 \to \cdots \to \tau_n \to \tau$$

of arity n that occurs in formulas to be converted to boolean form, we must define a version

$$\hat{f} : \text{bool list} \to \cdots \to \text{bool list} \to \text{bool list}$$

that operates on boolean lists. The boolean propagation theorem for f is

$$f\,(\langle \text{decode\_}\tau_1 \rangle\, x_1) \ldots (\langle \text{decode\_}\tau_n \rangle\, x_n) = \langle \text{decode\_}\tau \rangle\, (\hat{f}\, x_1 \ldots x_n).$$

Similarly, for each predicate $P : \tau_1 \to \cdots \to \tau_n \to$ bool,
we define a boolean version $\hat{P} :$ bool list $\to \cdots \to$ bool list $\to$ bool
and prove the theorem $\qquad P(\langle \text{decode}\_\tau_1 \rangle\, x_1) \ldots (\langle \text{decode}\_\tau_n \rangle\, x_n) = \hat{P}\, x_1 \ldots x_n.$

□

Secondly, we show how to convert quantifiers over high-level datatypes to quantifiers over boolean variables.

Definition 5 (Boolean variable introduction). *We define two predicates: the first selects elements of a type τ that encode to a particular length of boolean list, and the second selects boolean lists that are decodable.*

$$\text{width } d\, n\, x \equiv \exists l.\ (\text{length } l = n) \wedge (d\, l = \text{SOME } (x, []))$$
$$\text{decodable } d\, l \equiv \exists x.\ d\, l = \text{SOME } (x, [])$$

Now we can prove the following quantifier conversion theorems:

$$(\forall x.\ \text{width } d\, n\, x \supset P\, x) \equiv \forall l.\ (\text{length } l = n) \wedge \text{decodable } d\, l \supset P\, (\langle d \rangle\, l)$$
$$(\exists x.\ \text{width } d\, n\, x \wedge P\, x) \equiv \exists l.\ (\text{length } l = n) \wedge \text{decodable } d\, l \wedge P\, (\langle d \rangle\, l)$$

We assume that all quantifiers over type τ are restricted by a width decode$\_\tau$ n predicate where n is a concrete natural number. □

By repeatedly applying boolean variable introduction and the boolean propagation theorems throughout a formula over high-level datatypes, it will be converted into a formula over boolean lists. Only the subformulas containing free variables will be left in their original form. The final step is to reduce the quantifiers over boolean lists to quantifiers over boolean variables, and we do this with the following rewrites:

$$(\forall l.\ \text{length } l = 0 \qquad \supset P\, l) \equiv P\, []$$
$$(\forall l.\ \text{length } l = \text{suc } n \supset P\, l) \equiv \forall l.\ \text{length } l = n \supset \forall b.\ P\, (b :: l)$$
$$(\exists l.\ \text{length } l = 0 \qquad \wedge P\, l) \equiv P\, []$$
$$(\exists l.\ \text{length } l = \text{suc } n \wedge P\, l) \equiv \exists l.\ \text{length } l = n \wedge \exists b.\ P\, (b :: l)$$

5.5   Example: Missionaries and Cannibals

We end our discussion of encoding and decoding with a classic example: three missionaries and three cannibals initially stand on the left bank of a river, and there is a boat available that can carry two people. The aim is get the whole party to the right bank of the river, without ever getting in the situation where the cannibals outnumber the missionaries on either bank. Gordon [13] solved a generalized version of this problem using an embedding of a BDD package into HOL-4. Here we show how to convert the transition relation of the standard problem into boolean form. Following Gordon, we will represent the state as a triple (m, c, b) where $m \le 3$ is the number of missionaries on the left bank, $c \le 3$ is the number of cannibals on the left bank, and b is a boolean that is true whenever the boat is on the left bank. A transition is possible between states s and s' whenever the following formula holds:[3]

$$\exists m.\ m \leq 3 \wedge \exists c.\ c \leq 3 \wedge \exists b.\ \exists m'.\ m' \leq 3 \wedge \exists c'.\ c' \leq 3 \wedge \exists b'.$$

$$\begin{array}{ll}
(s = (m,c,b)) \wedge (s' = (m',c',b')) \wedge & \text{[the states are well-formed]} \\
b' = \neg b \wedge & \text{[the boat switches banks]} \\
(m' = 0 \vee c' \leq m') \wedge & \text{[left bank not outnumbered]} \\
(m' = 3 \vee m' \leq c') \wedge & \text{[right bank not outnumbered]} \\
\text{if } b \text{ then} & \left[\begin{array}{l}\text{if the boat starts on} \\ \text{the left, 1 or 2 people} \\ \text{travel from left to right}\end{array}\right] \\
\quad m' \leq m \wedge c' \leq c \wedge & \\
\quad m' + c' + 1 \leq m + c \leq m' + c' + 2 & \\
\text{else} & \left[\begin{array}{l}\text{else if the boat starts on} \\ \text{the right, 1 or 2 people} \\ \text{travel from right to left}\end{array}\right] \\
\quad m \leq m' \wedge c \leq c' \wedge & \\
\quad m + c + 1 \leq m' + c' \leq m + c + 2 &
\end{array}$$

To convert this formula to boolean form, we fix an encoding bnum of numbers as fixed-length bitstrings, and for concrete numbers n permit $\exists x.\ x \leq n \wedge p\ x$ as syntactic sugar for $\exists x.\ \text{width}\ (\text{decode\_bnum}\ k)\ k\ x \wedge p\ x$, where k is the smallest number satisfying $n < 2^k$. Then we apply our conversion algorithm to obtain

$$\exists m_0, m_1.\ [m_0;\ m_1] \mathrel{\hat{\leq}} [\top;\ \top]\ \wedge\ \exists c_0, c_1.\ [c_0;\ c_1] \mathrel{\hat{\leq}} [\top;\ \top]\ \wedge$$
$$\exists m'_0, m'_1.\ [m'_0;\ m'_1] \mathrel{\hat{\leq}} [\top;\ \top]\ \wedge\ \exists c'_0, c'_1.\ [c'_0;\ c'_1] \mathrel{\hat{\leq}} [\top;\ \top]\ \wedge\ \exists b'.$$
$$s = (\langle\text{decode\_bnum}\rangle\ [m_0;\ m_1], \langle\text{decode\_bnum}\rangle\ [c_0;\ c_1], \neg b') \wedge$$
$$s' = (\langle\text{decode\_bnum}\rangle\ [m'_0;\ m'_1], \langle\text{decode\_bnum}\rangle\ [c'_0;\ c'_1], b') \wedge$$
$$([m'_0;\ m'_1] \mathrel{\hat{=}} []\ \vee\ [c'_0;\ c'_1] \mathrel{\hat{\leq}} [m'_0;\ m'_1])\ \wedge$$
$$([m'_0;\ m'_1] \mathrel{\hat{=}} [\top;\ \top]\ \vee\ [m'_0;\ m'_1] \mathrel{\hat{\leq}} [c'_0;\ c'_1])\ \wedge$$
$$\text{if } \neg b' \text{ then}$$
$$\quad [m'_0;\ m'_1] \mathrel{\hat{\leq}} [m_0;\ m_1]\ \wedge\ [c'_0;\ c'_1] \mathrel{\hat{\leq}} [c_0;\ c_1]\ \wedge$$
$$\quad [m'_0;\ m'_1] \mathrel{\hat{+}} [c'_0;\ c'_1] \mathrel{\hat{<}} [m_0;\ m_1] \mathrel{\hat{+}} [c_0;\ c_1]\ \wedge$$
$$\quad [m_0;\ m_1] \mathrel{\hat{+}} [c_0;\ c_1] \mathrel{\hat{\leq}} [m'_0;\ m'_1] \mathrel{\hat{+}} [c'_0;\ c'_1] \mathrel{\hat{+}} [\bot;\ \top]$$
$$\text{else}$$
$$\quad [m_0;\ m_1] \mathrel{\hat{\leq}} [m'_0;\ m'_1]\ \wedge\ [c_0;\ c_1] \mathrel{\hat{\leq}} [c'_0;\ c'_1]\ \wedge$$
$$\quad [m_0;\ m_1] \mathrel{\hat{+}} [c_0;\ c_1] \mathrel{\hat{<}} [m'_0;\ m'_1] \mathrel{\hat{+}} [c'_0;\ c'_1]\ \wedge$$
$$\quad [m'_0;\ m'_1] \mathrel{\hat{+}} [c'_0;\ c'_1] \mathrel{\hat{\leq}} [m_0;\ m_1] \mathrel{\hat{+}} [c_0;\ c_1] \mathrel{\hat{+}} [\bot;\ \top]$$

The only non-boolean parts are the subformulas containing the free s, s' variables. The variable b is no longer present, since it was simplified away to $\neg b'$ during the boolean conversion. If we wanted to take this formula a step further, then we could use Gordon's HolBddLib to symbolically execute these boolean versions of the arithmetic operations, and end up with a BDD representing the transition relation as a pure propositional formula.

6   Related Work

Polytypism has been investigated in the functional programming world for about a decade, in various guises. Hinze [20] gives a nice introduction of an approach

---

[3] We use the convention that primed variables refer to the state after the transition.

similar to ours. One thrust of research into polytypism is to provide user-level interfaces for polytypic functions; recently, also polytypic *datatypes* such as tries have been investigated [19]. Another avenue of research investigates the use of polytypism in compilation of advanced language features [26]. Our approach to size function definitions appeared in [25].

Capretta [7] showed how to encode datatypes internally in Type Theory, after which polytypic functions may be defined over the encoding. Melham's approach to datatypes [21] could also be cast in this mode: when a single 'large' type of trees is used to encode a class of 'small' types, one could hope that general functions over the large type might be customized to versions over the small types.

Our work on lifting ML values to HOL terms is similar in spirit to work on Normalization by Evaluation, initiated by Berger and Schwichtenberg [3]. This surprising work showed that functions may also be lifted (this is called *readback* in the literature). This work has been taken up by researchers in Type Directed Partial Evaluation [8]. In recent work, Grégoire and Leroy modify the OCAML interpreter so that it implements strong reduction for proof checking in Coq [16]. This relies on a readback function that doesn't follow the structure of types.

Work in model checking has stimulated much interest in automated boolean encodings of temporal logic formulas and transition relations [1]. A handcrafted propositional encoding in HOL of formulas over high-level types *e.g.*, finite sets of pairs of numbers, can be found in [14].

7   Conclusions and Future Work

We have shown how an interpretation of HOL types into terms supports some useful proof automation activities in the HOL-4 system. The interpretation is simple, easy to apply, and deals with all types definable by our datatype package. In our approach, a polytypic function is represented as a derived definition principle.

We have not as yet attempted to provide a user-level interface for defining polytypic functions. However, it seems plausible to let the user instantiate $\mathcal{G}$ in the following scheme:

$$Fn\ (\mathsf{C}_i\ (x_1, ..., x_n)) = \mathcal{G}\ \mathsf{C}_i\ [\mathcal{I}_{\Theta,\Delta}(x_1), \ldots, \mathcal{I}_{\Theta,\Delta}(x_n)]$$

Thus $\mathcal{G}$ would be an ML function expecting a constructor term and a list of terms (the result of applying the interpretation to the arguments of the constructor) and returning a term. This could be used to build each clause in a primitive recursive definition over a datatype. Unfortunately, this scheme would not be general enough to automatically define encoders, which need to know how many constructors a type has.

Acknowledgements. Thanks to Mike Gordon for comments on an intermediate draft. Hurd is supported by EPSRC project GR/R27105/01.

References

1. A.Biere, A. Cimatti, E. Clarke, O. Strichman, and Y. Zhu, *Bounded model checking*, To appear in Advances in Computers, Number 58.

2. Bruno Barras, *Proving and computing in HOL*, Theorem Proving in Higher Order Logics, 13th International Conference, TPHOLs 2000, Portland, Oregon, USA, August 14-18, 2000, Proceedings (Mark Aagaard and John Harrison, eds.), Lecture Notes in Computer Science, vol. 1869, Springer, 2000, pp. 17–37.

3. U. Berger and H. Schwichtenberg, *An inverse of the evaluation functional for typed λ-calculus*, Proceedings of the Sixth Annual IEEE Symposium on Logic in Computer Science LICS'91 (Amsterdam), IEEE Computer Society Press, July 1991, pp. 203–211.

4. Stefan Berghofer and Tobias Nipkow, *Executing higher order logic*, Types for Proofs and Programs (TYPES 2000) (P. Callaghan, Z. Luo, J. McKinna, and R. Pollack, eds.), Lecture Notes in Computer Science, vol. 2277, Springer Verlag, 2002, pp. 24–40.

5. Stefan Berghofer and Markus Wenzel, *Inductive datatypes in HOL - lessons learned in Formal-Logic Engineering*, Proceedings of the 12th International Conference on Theorem Proving in Higher Order Logics (TPHOLs'99) (Nice) (Y. Bertot, G. Dowek, A. Hirschowitz, C. Paulin, and L. Thery, eds.), LNCS, no. 1690, Springer-Verlag, 1999.

6. Richard Boulton and Konrad Slind, *Automatic derivation and application of induction schemes for mutually recursive functions*, Proceedings of the First International Conference on Computational Logic (CL2000) (London, UK), July 2000.

7. Venanzio Capretta, *Recursive families of inductive types*, Theorem Proving in Higher Order Logics: 13th International Conference, TPHOLs 2000 (J. Harrison and M. Aagaard, eds.), Lecture Notes in Computer Science, vol. 1869, Springer-Verlag, 2000, pp. 73–89.

8. A. Filinski, *Normalization by evaluation for the computational lambda calculus*, Typed Lambda Calculi and Applications 5th International Conference, TLCA 2001 (Krakow, Poland) (S. Abramsky, ed.), LNCS, vol. 2044, Springer Verlag, May 2001.

9. A. Fox, *A HOL specification of the ARM instruction set architecture*, Tech. Report 545, University of Cambridge Computer Laboratory, June 2001.

10. ———, *Formal verification of the ARM6 micro-architecture*, Tech. Report 548, University of Cambridge Computer Laboratory, November 2002.

11. Juergen Giesl, *Termination analysis for functional programs using term orderings*, Proceedings of the 2nd International Static Analysis Symposium (Glasgow, Scotland), Springer-Verlag, 1995.

12. Jürgen Giesl, *Automatisierung von terminierungsbeweisen für rekursiv definiierte algorithmen*, Ph.D. thesis, Technische Hochshule Darmstadt, 1995.

13. Michael J. C. Gordon, *Programming combinations of deduction and BDD-based symbolic calculation*, LMS Journal of Computation and Mathematics **5** (2002), 56–76.

14. Mike Gordon, *PuzzleTool: an example of programming computation and deduction*, Theorem Proving in Higher Order Logics, 15th International Conference, TPHOLs 2002, Hampton, Virginia, USA, August 2002, Proceedings (V. A Carreno, C. A. Munoz, and S. Tahar, eds.), Lecture Notes in Computer Science, vol. 2410, Springer, 2002, pp. 214–229.

15. Mike Gordon and Tom Melham, *Introduction to HOL, a theorem proving environment for higher order logic*, Cambridge University Press, 1993.

16. Benjamin Grégoire and Xavier Leroy, *A compiled implementation of strong reduction*, International Conference on Functional Programming 2002, ACM Press, 2002.

17. E. L. Gunter, *A broader class of trees for recursive type definitions for HOL*, Higher Order Logic Theorem Proving and its Applications: 6th International Workshop (HUG'93) (J. J. Joyce and C.-J. H. Seger, eds.), Lecture Notes in Computer Science, no. 780, Springer-Verlag, Vancouver, B.C., August 11-13 1994, pp. 141–154.

18. John Harrison, *Inductive definitions: automation and application*, Proceedings of the 1995 International Workshop on Higher Order Logic theorem proving and its applications (Aspen Grove, Utah) (E. Thomas Schubert, Phillip J. Windley, and James Alves-Foss, eds.), LNCS, no. 971, Springer-Verlag, 1995, pp. 200–213.

19. R. Hinze, J. Jeuring, and A. Loeh, *Type-indexed data types*, Mathematics of Program Construction 6th International Conference, MPC 2002 Proceedings (Dagstuhl Castle, Germany) (E.A. Boiten and B. Moeller, eds.), LNCS, no. 2386, Springer Verlag, July 2002, pp. 98–114.

20. Ralf Hinze, *A new approach to generic functional programming*, 27th ACM SIGPLAN-SIGACT Symposium on Principles of Programming Languages (POPL'00) (Boston, Massachusetts), ACM Press, 2000.

21. Tom Melham, *Automating recursive type definitions in higher order logic*, Current Trends in Hardware Verification and Automated Theorem Proving (Graham Birtwistle and P.A. Subrahmanyam, eds.), Springer-Verlag, 1989, pp. 341–386.

22. J Moore, *Symbolic simulation: An ACL2 approach*, Proceedings of the Second International Conference on Formal Methods in Computer-Aided Design (FM-CAD'98) (G. Gopalakrishnan and P. Windley, eds.), vol. LNCS 1522, Springer-Verlag, November 1998, pp. 334–350.

23. M. Norrish and K. Slind, *A thread of HOL development*, The Computer Journal **45** (2002), no. 1, 37–45.

24. N. Shankar, *Static analysis for safe destructive updates in a functional language*, Logic Based Program Synthesis and Transformation, 11th International Workshop, LOPSTR 2001, Paphos, Cyprus, November 28-30, 2001, Selected Papers (Alberto Pettorossi, ed.), Lecture Notes in Computer Science, vol. 2372, Springer Verlag, 2001, pp. 1–24.

25. Konrad Slind, *Reasoning about terminating functional programs*, Ph.D. thesis, Institut für Informatik, Technische Universität München, 1999, http://tumb1.biblio.tu-muenchen.de/publ/diss/in/1999/slind.html.

26. Stephanie Weirich, *Higher-order intensional type analysis*, Programming Languages and Systems: 11th European Symposium on Programming, ESOP 2002 Held as Part of the Joint European Conferences on Theory and Practice of Software, ETAPS 2002 Grenoble, France, April 8-12, 2002 (Daniel Le Métayer, ed.), 2002, pp. 98–114.

A Coverage Checking Algorithm for LF

Carsten Schürmann[1] and Frank Pfenning[2*]

[1] Yale University
New Haven, CT, USA,
carsten@cs.yale.edu
[2] Carnegie Mellon University
Pittsburgh, PA, USA,
fp@cs.cmu.edu

Abstract. Coverage checking is the problem of deciding whether any closed term of a given type is an instance of at least one of a given set of patterns. It can be used to verify if a function defined by pattern matching covers all possible cases. This problem has a straightforward solution for the first-order, simply-typed case, but is in general undecidable in the presence of dependent types. In this paper we present a terminating algorithm for verifying coverage of higher-order, dependently typed patterns. It either succeeds or presents a set of counterexamples with free variables, some of which may not have closed instances (a question which is undecidable). Our algorithm, together with strictness and termination checking, can be used to certify the correctness of numerous proofs of properties of deductive systems encoded in a system for reasoning about LF signatures.

1 Introduction

Coverage checking is the problem of deciding whether any closed term of a given type is an instance of at least one of a given set of patterns. This has a number of applications: in functional programming, it is used to decide if a given set of cases defining a function is exhaustive or not. In proof assistants it is used to verify if a purported proof covers all possible cases. Depending on the application, the underlying term algebra, meta-theoretic requirements, and efficiency considerations, a variety of algorithms that implement or decide properties about pattern matching emerge. In this paper we discuss one algorithm for coverage checking in the logical framework LF [8].

The choice of the underlying term algebra is essential. In traditional functional programming languages, for example, we have only simple types and possibly prefix polymorphism, and the structure of functions is not observable by pattern matching. This makes coverage checking straightforward, both in theory practice. In LF, on the other hand, we have dependent types and functions are intensional: their structure can be observed by pattern matching. This makes

---

* This work was supported in part by the National Science Foundation under grants CCR-0133502 and CCR-9988281.

D. Basin and B. Wolff (Eds.): TPHOLs 2003, LNCS 2758, pp. 120–135, 2003.
© Springer-Verlag Berlin Heidelberg 2003

coverage checking undecidable since, for example, *any* set of patterns will cover all terms of an empty type and emptiness is undecidable.

Nonetheless, coverage checking has many applications in logical frameworks. Coquand's seminal paper [2] is concerned with the natural expression of proofs in a proof checker. Moreover, in certain dependent type theories, functions defined by pattern matching are strictly more expressive than schemata of primitive recursion [9]. In addition to coverage checking, proof verification requires termination analysis which we do not consider here, but has previously been treated [19,17]. Related is the work on Delphin [22] where functions may be defined by pattern matching over LF terms in their full generality. Verifying that such functions represent correct proofs requires coverage checking. In the context of the Twelf system [16], coverage checking is used to verify that a given logic program covers all cases for its input arguments. Besides checking the exhaustiveness of definitions, coverage checking is used to verify the correctness of meta-theoretic proofs represented as relations. Numerous case studies of this style of verification have been carried out, including cut-elimination for classical and intuitionistic logics, the Church-Rosser theorem for the untyped λ-calculus, and various translations between logical systems (see [14] for an introduction and survey). The running example in this paper is the correctness of bracket abstraction, which is a critical step in the translation from natural deduction to derivations from Hilbert's axioms.

As mentioned above, the coverage checking problem is in general undecidable. Our approach has been to design a sound approximation that always terminates and either certifies coverage or produces a set of potential counterexamples. Sometimes, these counterexamples are in effect impossible (due to dependent types). This algorithm has been fully implemented in the Twelf system and has proved enormously useful in practice to verify the correctness of meta-theoretic proofs expressed as relations. The largest project undertaken so far is Crary's implementation of foundational typed assembly language with about 30,000 lines of Twelf code [3] with more than 1000 theorems; other examples have been mentioned above. One valuable experience gained trough these experiments is that in the case of failure with spurious counterexamples it is generally possible to make a proof more explicit in such a way that it then passes the coverage checker.

The remainder of the paper is organized as follows: In Section 2 we briefly introduce the logical framework LF, and sketch the most important concepts necessary for this paper. In Section 3 we describe the coverage problem in detail and present our coverage algorithm. We discuss some related work in Section 4 and assess results and conclude in Section 5.

2   LF

The type-theoretic foundation for this paper is the logical framework LF [8]. In addition to the standard syntactic categories of objects, types, and kinds, we will also use substitutions in a critical way throughout this paper so we briefly introduce them here (see also, for example, [1]).

$$
\begin{array}{lll}
Kinds & K ::= \text{type} \mid \Pi x{:}A.\,K \\
Atomic\ Types & B ::= a \mid B\ M \\
Types & A ::= B \mid \Pi x{:}A_1.\,A_2 \\
Objects & M ::= x \mid c \mid M_1\ M_2 \mid \lambda x{:}A.\,M \\[4pt]
Signatures & \Sigma ::= \cdot \mid \Sigma, a : K \mid \Sigma, c : A \\
Contexts & \Gamma ::= \cdot \mid \Gamma, x : A \\
Substitutions & \sigma ::= \cdot \mid \sigma, M/x
\end{array}
$$

We write a for constant type families, x or u for object-level variables, and c for constructors. A *term* may come form any of the syntactic levels. As usual, we identify α-equivalent terms. In order to state certain definitions and propositions more concisely, we write U to stand for either an object or a type and V for either a type or a kind and h for a family-level or object-level constant. We take $\beta\eta$-conversion as the notion of definitional equality [8,1], for which we write $U \equiv U'$ and $V \equiv V'$. Substitutions are capture-avoiding and written as $U[\sigma]$ or $V[\sigma]$ with the special form $U[M/x]$ and $V[M/x]$. Often, we write Δ for contexts that are interpreted existentially, and Γ for universal ones. When we write $\Gamma[\sigma]$, it is a shorthand for applying σ in left to right order to each variable type in Γ. Signatures, contexts, and substitutions may not declare a variable or constant more than once, and renaming of bound variables may be applied tacitly to ensure that condition. Besides equality, the main judgment is typing $\Gamma \vdash U : V$, suppressing the fixed signature Σ. We always assume our signatures, contexts and types to be valid.

Example 1 (Propositional Hilbert Calculus). An LF signature that encodes the Hilbert calculus in LF is given in Figure 1. Terms are captured by type i, formulas by o, and proofs in the Hilbert calculus by the type family hil : o → type. As usual we omit the leading Π-binders of variables whose types are inferable, denoted above by uppercase variable names.   □

Example 2 (Bracket abstraction). Figure 2 displays a relational representation of bracket abstraction. The type family ded relates hypothetical Hilbert derivations (hil A → hil B) with their categorical counterpart hil (A imp B). Each of the four defining cases corresponds to one of the constant declarations. Again, in the interest of space we have omitted the implicit Π-abstractions.   □

```
imp   : o → o → o.
forall : (i → o) → o.
k     : hil (imp A (imp B A)).
s     : hil (imp (imp A (imp B C)) (imp (imp A B) (imp A C))).
mp    : hil (imp A B) → hil A → hil B.
```

Fig. 1. The Propositional Hilbert Calculus

```
ded  :  (hil A → hil B)  →  hil (A imp B)  →  type.
ded_id  :  ded (λx:hil A.  x) (mp (mp s k) k).
ded_k  :  ded (λx:hil A.  k) (mp k k).
ded_s  :  ded (λx:hil A.  s) (mp k s).
ded_mp  :
    ded (λx:hil A.  H₂ x) H₂′ → ded (λx:hil A.  H₁ x) H₁′
        → ded (λx:hil A.  mp (H₁ x) (H₂ x)) (mp (mp s H₁′) H₂′).
```

Fig. 2. Bracket abstraction

Type-checking and definitional equality on well-typed terms for LF are decidable. Every term is equal to a unique β-normal η-long form which we call *canonical form*. In the remainder of the paper we assume that all terms are in canonical form, because it simplifies the presentation significantly. In the implementation this is achieved incrementally, first by an initial conversion of input terms to η-long form and later by successive weak-head normalization as terms are traversed.

Since it is perhaps not so well-known, we will give only the typing rules for substitutions, which are used pervasively in this paper.

$$\frac{}{\Gamma' \vdash \cdot : \cdot} \qquad \frac{\Gamma' \vdash \sigma : \Gamma \qquad \Gamma' \vdash M : A[\sigma]}{\Gamma' \vdash (\sigma, M/x) : (\Gamma, x{:}A)}$$

For a context $\Gamma = (x_1{:}A_1, \ldots, x_n{:}A_n)$, we define $\mathrm{id}_\Gamma = (x_1/x_1, \ldots, x_n/x_n)$ so that $\Gamma \vdash \mathrm{id}_\Gamma : \Gamma$.

Composition of substitutions is defined by $(\cdot) \circ \sigma = (\cdot)$ and $(M/x, \theta) \circ \sigma = (M[\sigma]/x, \theta \circ \sigma)$. We will only apply a substitution $\Gamma' \vdash \sigma : \Gamma$ to a term $\Gamma \vdash U : V$ or a substitution $\Gamma \vdash \theta : \Gamma''$ resulting in $\Gamma' \vdash U[\sigma] : V[\sigma]$ and $\Gamma' \vdash \theta \circ \sigma : \Gamma''$, respectively.

3   Coverage

In this section we first formally define the problem of coverage in the LF type theory in Section 3.1. This relies on *higher-order matching*, a problem whose decidability is an open question. We therefore identify an important subclass, the *strict coverage problems* (Section 3.2) which guarantee not only decidability but also uniqueness of matching substitutions. All examples we have ever encountered in practice belong to this class and we explain the reasons for this after the necessary definitions. Then we define *splitting* in Section 3.3, which is the second critical operation to be performed during coverage checking. Next we describe our basic coverage algorithm and prove it sound and terminating in Sections 3.4 and 3.5. The last component of our coverage checker is *finitary splitting*, discussed and proved correct in Section 3.6.

ded_0 : ΠA:o. ΠB:o. (hil A → hil B) → type.
$\mathsf{ded}_0\_\mathsf{id}$: ΠA:o. ded_0 A A (λx:hil A. x).
$\mathsf{ded}_0\_\mathsf{k}$: ΠA:o. ΠA_1:o. ΠA_2:o.
    ded_0 A (imp A_1 (imp A_2 A_1)) (λx:hil A. k A_1 A_2).
$\mathsf{ded}_0\_\mathsf{s}$: ΠA:o. ΠA_1:o. ΠA_2:o. ΠA_3:o.
    ded_0 A (imp (imp A_1 (imp A_2 A_3)) (imp (imp A_1 A_2) (imp A_1 A_3)))
      (λx:hil A. s A_1 A_2 A_3).
$\mathsf{ded}_0\_\mathsf{mp}$: ΠA:o. ΠA_1:o. ΠA_2: o. ΠH_1:hil A → hil (imp A_2 A_1).
    ΠH_2:hil A → hil A_2. ded_0 A A_1 (λx:hil A. mp A_2 A_1 (H_1 x) (H_2 x)).

Fig. 3. Patterns

3.1 Definition of Coverage

A coverage goal is simply a term (object or type) with some free variables. Intuitively, a coverage goal stands for all of its closed instances. In order to emphasize the interpretation of the variables as standing for closed terms, we write Δ for such contexts and denote variables in Δ by u and v rather than x and y. The distinction between Δ and Γ can be formalized (see [18]), but this is not necessary for the present purposes.

A coverage problem is given by a goal and a set of patterns. One can think of these as the patterns of a case expression in a functional program, or the input terms in the clause heads of a logic program. In the general case, a set of patterns is just a set of terms with free variables.

Example 3. Consider the type family ded from Example 2 that encodes the algorithm of bracket abstraction. To satisfy coverage, ded must provide a case covering every possible input argument upon invocation, independent of the output. Thus, in Figure 3, the type family ded_0 is a reduction of ded to set of patterns for the coverage goal

$$u : \mathsf{o}, v : \mathsf{o}, w : (\mathsf{hil}\ u \to \mathsf{hil}\ v) \vdash \mathsf{ded}_0\ u\ v\ w : \mathsf{type}. \tag{1}$$

Note that for the sake of completeness all arguments to ded_0 are explicit. □

Definition 1 (Immediate Coverage). *We say a coverage goal $\Delta \vdash U : V$ is immediately covered by a collection of patterns $\Delta_i \vdash U_i : V_i$ if there is an i and a substitution $\Delta \vdash \sigma_i : \Delta_i$ such that $\Delta \vdash U \equiv U_i[\sigma_i] : V$.*

Example 4. Let p be a propositional symbol, $A = B = \mathsf{imp}\ p\ p$ and $M = \lambda u : \mathsf{hil}\ (\mathsf{imp}\ p\ p).\, u$. The goal

$$p : \mathsf{o} \vdash \mathsf{ded}_0\ (\mathsf{imp}\ p\ p)\ (\mathsf{imp}\ p\ p)\ (\lambda u : \mathsf{hil}\ (\mathsf{imp}\ p\ p).\, u) : \mathsf{type}$$

is immediately covered by $\mathsf{ded}_0\_\mathsf{id}$.

Coverage has an infinitary definition, requiring immediate coverage of every ground instance of a goal.

Definition 2 (Coverage). *We say* $\Delta \vdash U : V$ *is* covered *by a collection of patterns* $\Delta_i \vdash U_i : V_i$ *if every ground instance* $\cdot \vdash U[\tau] : V[\tau]$ *for* $\cdot \vdash \tau : \Delta$ *is immediately covered by the collection of terms* $\Delta_i \vdash U_i : V_i$.

In this formulation the problem of coverage is very general, because the type of U and the type of the U_i's may not be the same. It turns out that the algorithm is significantly easier to describe and prove correct if we restrict U and U_i to be types, and $V = V_i = \text{type}$.

The implementation in Twelf transforms any coverage problems that arise into this type-level form. This translation is straightforward and only sketched here. Given a coverage goal $\Delta \vdash M : A'$. Assume first that $A' = a' N_1 \ldots N_k$ for $a' : \Pi x_1 : A_1 \ldots \Pi x_n : A_n.\text{type}$. In this case we declare a new type family $a : \Pi x_1 : A_1 \ldots \Pi x_n : A_n.a' x_1 \ldots x_n \to \text{type}$. The new coverage goal is now simply $\Delta \vdash a N_1 \ldots N_k M : \text{type}$. All patterns are transformed in the analogous way, using the same a to replace a'. If A' starts with some leading Π-quantifiers we carry them over from the general to the restricted form.

To summarize, without loss of generality, in the remainder of this paper we consider only coverage goals of the form $\Delta \vdash A : \text{type}$ and patterns of the form $\Delta_i \vdash A_i : \text{type}$.

3.2   Strict Patterns

To determine if a goal is immediately covered we have to solve a higher-order matching problem, instantiating the patterns A_i to match the goal A. Not incidentally, this is also the operation that is performed when matching a case subject against the patterns in each arm of a case branch, or when unifying the input arguments to a predicate with the clause head on a well-moded predicate.

In order for this pattern matching to be decidable (for the coverage algorithm) and also so that the operational semantics is well-defined (for the execution of a functional or logic program), we require the patterns to be *strict*. Strictness for a pattern $\Delta_i \vdash A_i : \text{type}$ requires that each variable in Δ_i must occur in A at least once in a rigid position [10,15].

Definition 3 (Strictness). *We say that* u *has a strict occurrence in* U *if* $\Delta; \Gamma \vdash_u U$ *as defined by the rules depicted in Figure 4. A pattern* $\Delta_i \vdash A_i : \text{type}$ *is strict if* $\Delta_i; \cdot \vdash_u A_i$ *for each variable* u *in* Δ_i.

Informally, an occurrence of u is strict if it is not below another variable in Δ and if that occurrence forms a higher-order pattern in the sense of Miller [13], that is, u is applied to distinct parameters as expressed by the judgment $\Gamma \vdash u x_1 \ldots x_n$ pat. Unlike higher-order patterns in the sense of Miller, however, other forms of occurrences of u are allowed, which is a practically highly significant generalization. All of the examples in Twelf are strict, but many higher-order examples are not patterns in the sense of Miller. Strictness is sufficient here because we are only interested in matching and not full unification.

$$\frac{\Delta; \Gamma \vdash_u A}{\Delta; \Gamma \vdash_u \lambda y : A. M} \text{ ls\_ld} \qquad \frac{\Delta; \Gamma, y : A \vdash_u M}{\Delta; \Gamma \vdash_u \lambda y : A. M} \text{ ls\_lb}$$

$$\frac{\Delta; \Gamma \vdash_u A_1}{\Delta; \Gamma \vdash_u \Pi y : A_1. A_2} \text{ ls\_pd} \qquad \frac{\Delta; \Gamma, y : A_1 \vdash_u A_2}{\Delta; \Gamma \vdash_u \Pi y : A_1. A_2} \text{ ls\_pb}$$

$$\frac{\Delta; \Gamma \vdash_u M_i}{\Delta; \Gamma \vdash_u c \, M_1 \ldots M_n} \text{ ls\_c} \quad (1 \leq i \leq n) \qquad \frac{\Delta; \Gamma \vdash_u M_i}{\Delta; \Gamma \vdash_u a \, M_1 \ldots M_n} \text{ ls\_a} \quad (1 \leq i \leq n)$$

$$\frac{y : A \in \Gamma \quad \Delta; \Gamma \vdash_u M_i}{\Delta; \Gamma \vdash_u y \, M_1 \ldots M_n} \text{ ls\_var} \quad (1 \leq i \leq n)$$

$$\frac{\Gamma \vdash u \, x_1 \ldots x_n \text{ pat}}{\Delta; \Gamma \vdash_u u \, x_1 \ldots x_n} \text{ ls\_pat} \qquad \begin{array}{l} \text{no rule for } \Delta; \Gamma \vdash_u v \, M_1 \ldots M_n \\ \text{for } u \neq v, v : A \in \Delta \end{array}$$

Fig. 4. A formal system for strictness

Theorem 1. *Given a coverage goal $\Delta \vdash A$: type and a strict pattern $\Delta_i \vdash A_i$: type. Then it is decidable if there is a substitution $\Delta \vdash \sigma : \Delta_i$ such that $A \equiv A_i[\sigma]$. Moreover, if such a substitution exists it is uniquely determined.*

Proof. See [21].

If such a σ exists then the coverage goal in question is covered by one of the patterns. On the other hand, if no such σ exist, either there exists a pattern that covers the coverage goal but does not happen to cover it immediately, or none of the patterns will ever cover it, in which case coverage should fail.

3.3 Splitting

In the case that the coverage goal is not immediately covered by a pattern, there is only one way to make progress on the coverage problem. Assuming we can recognize coverage failure easily (which we can, as discussed in Section 3.4), we can bridge the gap between coverage goal and patterns by splitting the coverage goal into a set of new coverage goals, by partially instantiating free variables in Δ. Since there may be infinitely many ground instances, we instantiate the coverage goal only partially, one layer at a time.

Definition 4 (Non-redundant complete set of substitutions).
Let $\Delta \vdash A$: type be a coverage goal. We say a finite collection $\Delta_i \vdash \tau_i : \Delta$ is a non-redundant complete set of substitutions if for every $\cdot \vdash \tau : \Delta$ there exists a unique i and a unique $\cdot \vdash \sigma_i : \Delta_i$ such that $\cdot \vdash \tau = \tau_i \circ \sigma_i$.

Splitting a coverage goal using a non-redundant complete set of substitutions is conservative with respect to the coverage property, because the original coverage goal is covered if and only if the resulting set of coverage goals is covered.

Theorem 2 (Conservativity). *Let $\Delta \vdash A$: type be a coverage goal and $\Delta_i \vdash \tau_i : \Delta$ a non-redundant complete collection of substitutions. All $\Delta_i \vdash A[\tau_i]$: type are covered by a given set of patterns if and only if $\Delta \vdash A$: type is covered.*

Proof. Coverage depends only on the set of ground instances of a coverage goal. But the collection of all ground instances of $\Delta_i \vdash A[\tau_i]$ is exactly the same as the set of ground instanced of $\Delta \vdash A$: type since the τ_i form a complete set. □

The splitting operation discussed in the remainder of this section generates a non-redundant complete set of substitutions. Its definition is inspired by a similar operation in ALF [2] which in turn has its root in the basic steps of Huet's algorithm for higher-order unification [10].

First, among all coverage goals that are not immediately covered, splitting selects coverage goal $\Delta \vdash A$: type and a declaration $u{:}A_j$ from its context Δ that is below referred to as *splitting variable*. A_j may be a function type, therefore, without loss of generality, it is of the following form

$$\Delta \vdash u : \Pi\Gamma.\, a\, M_1 \ldots M_m.$$

For the sake of conciseness, we consolidate all successive Π-binders into one context Γ. This is only an abbreviation and does not properly extend LF. We also use the following abbreviations $h\,\Gamma$ which stands for $h\,x_1 \ldots x_m$ if $\Gamma = x_1{:}A_1, \ldots, x_m{:}A_m$ where h is a constant or a parameter. Furthermore $h\,(\Delta\,\Gamma)$ is a shorthand for $h\,(u_1\,\Gamma) \ldots (u_n\,\Gamma)$ for $\Delta = u_1{:}A'_1, \ldots, u_n{:}A'_n$.

Next, splitting considers all possible top-level structures of a term M : $\Pi\Gamma.\, a\, M_1 \ldots M_m$. Because of the existence of canonical forms, each structure is determined by a constant declared in the signature or a parameter declared in the local context that occur in head position in M. Without loss of generality, the respective type of the constant or parameter his $\Pi u_1{:}A_1. \ldots \Pi u_n{:}A_n.\, B$ with an atomic type B. Each u_i is intuitively interpreted as an existential variable that can be instantiated to terms valid in Γ. To account for those local dependencies, splitting raises them therefore by Γ and turns all u_i into variables of functional type.

Definition 5 (Raising). *Let Γ be a context of local parameters, A the type of a constant c. Raising A by Γ yields a $\langle \Delta \vdash A' \rangle$, a context Δ of raised existential variables and a raised type A' (that always has the form $\Pi\Gamma.\, B$).*

$$raise\langle \Gamma \vdash A \rangle = \begin{cases} \langle \cdot \vdash \Pi\Gamma.\, A \rangle & \text{if } A \text{ is atomic} \\ \langle u : \Pi\Gamma.\, A_1, \Delta \vdash A' \rangle & \text{if } A = \Pi u{:}A_1.\, A_2 \\ & \text{and } \langle \Delta \vdash A' \rangle = raise\langle \Gamma \vdash A_2[u\,\Gamma/u] \rangle \end{cases}$$

If a constant or a parameter are valid candidates for a head position of M is decided by higher-order pattern unification that postpones unresolved unification equation as constraints [4]. Although we allow constraints to arise during the process of unification, we require that after completion all constraints have been resolved. Otherwise the specified variable cannot be split, and splitting must select another variable $u : A \in \Delta$ instead. Unfortunately, successive selections of splitting variables are not independent and it is possible that some sequences of splitting operations fail (with spurious counterexamples) while other sequences could succeed. In principle splitting could backtrack here, but this is currently not implemented.

Definition 6 (Splitting). *Let* $\Delta \vdash A :$ type *a coverage goal, and* u *in* $\Delta = \Delta_1, u : \Pi\Gamma.B_u, \Delta_2$ *a splitting variable. The splitting operation considers each constant* c *declared in the signature* Σ *and each local parameter* y *declared in* Γ *in turn, and determines a set of substitutions* σ_c, σ_y *as follows.*

1. Constants: *Let* $c : \Pi\Delta_c.B_c \in \Sigma$, *and* $\langle\Delta'_c \vdash \Pi\Gamma.B'_c\rangle = raise\langle\Gamma \vdash \Pi\Delta_c.B_c\rangle$. *Let* $\Delta' \vdash \sigma_c : \Delta, \Delta'_c$ *be the most general unifier of the higher-order unification problem*

$$\exists\Delta.\,\exists\Delta'_c.\,(\Pi\Gamma.B_u \approx \Pi\Gamma.B'_c) \wedge (u \approx \lambda\Gamma.c\,(\Delta'_c\,\Gamma)) \tag{2}$$

   if it exists.
2. Bound Variables: *Let* $y : \Pi\Delta_y.B_y \in \Gamma$, *and* $\langle\Delta'_y \vdash \Pi\Gamma.B'_y\rangle = raise\langle\Gamma \vdash \Pi\Delta_y.B_y\rangle$. *Let* $\Delta' \vdash \sigma_y : \Delta, \Delta'_y$ *be the most general unifier of the higher-order unification problem*

$$\exists\Delta.\,\exists\Delta'_y.\,(\Pi\Gamma.B_u \approx \Pi\Gamma.B'_y) \wedge (u \approx \lambda\Gamma.y\,(\Delta'_y\,\Gamma)) \tag{3}$$

   if it exists.

Since we collect all such most general unifiers, cases for which the unification problem fails[1] simply do not contribute a substitution to the result of the splitting operation.

Example 5. Recall the original coverage goal (1): $u : o, v : o, w : (\text{hil } u \to \text{hil } v) \vdash \text{ded}_0\, u\, v\, w :$ type. Splitting w results in four new coverage goals, because x, k, s, or mp are all possible head constants for functions of type hil $u \to$ hil v.

$u : o \vdash \text{ded}_0\, u\, u\, (\lambda x : \text{hil } u.\, x) :$ type
$u : o, u_1 : o, u_2 : o$
     $\vdash \text{ded}_0\, u\, (\text{imp } u_1\, (\text{imp } u_2\, u_1))\, (\lambda x : \text{hil } u.\, \text{k}\, u_1\, u_2) :$ type
$u : o, u_1 : o, u_2 : o, u_3 : o$
     $\vdash \text{ded}_0\, u\, (\text{imp } (\text{imp } u_1\, (\text{imp } u_2\, u_3))$
                    $(\text{imp } (\text{imp } u_1\, u_2)\, (\text{imp } u_1\, u_3)))\, (\lambda x : \text{hil } u.\text{s}\, u_1\, u_2\, u_3) :$ type
$u : o, u_1 : o, u_2 : o, v : \text{hil } u \to \text{hil } (\text{imp } u_2\, u_1), w : \text{hil } u \to \text{hil } u_2$
     $\vdash \text{ded}_0\, u\, u_1\, (\lambda x : \text{hil } u.\text{mp}\, (u_2\, x)\, u_1\, (v\, x)\, (w\, x)) :$ type

The main result of this section is that splitting generates always a set of substitutions that is non-redundant and complete.

Theorem 3 (Splitting is non-redundant and complete). *The set of substitutions generated by splitting is non-redundant and complete.*

Proof. From properties of complete sets of most general unifiers and lemmas about raising (see [21]). □

---

[1] but not those whose results are indeterminate because of residual equations, which are are not permitted

3.4   The Coverage Algorithm

Recall that a coverage goal $\Delta \vdash A :$ type is immediately covered by a collection of terms $\Delta_i \vdash A_i :$ type if there is an i and $\Delta \vdash \sigma_i : \Delta_i$ such that $\Delta \vdash A \equiv A_i[\sigma_i] :$ type.

Immediate coverage is central to the naive, non-deterministic coverage algorithm which we discuss next. We assume we have a set of coverage goals, all of which must be covered for the algorithm to succeed. In the first step, this is initialized with the goal $\Delta \vdash A :$ type. We pick one of the coverage goals and determine, via strict higher-order matching, if it is immediately covered by any covering type A_i. If so we remove it from the set and continue. If not, we non-deterministically select a variable in the coverage goal and split it into multiple goals, which replace it in the collection of coverage goals. This coverage algorithm is naive because it may not terminate: even if types are non-empty and coverage holds, splitting the wrong variable can lead to non-termination.

The procedure we propose in this section always terminates and either indicates that coverage holds, or outputs a set of potential counterexamples. Some of these may fail to be actual counterexamples, because we me may not be able to instantiate the remaining variables to a ground term that is not covered. If the counterexample is ground, however, it is guaranteed to be an actual counterexample. We analyze the possible forms of counterexamples in more detail at the beginning of Section 3.6.

The basic idea is to record *why* immediate coverage fails and not just *if* it does. Assume we are given a coverage goal $\Delta \vdash A :$ type and a pattern $\Delta' \vdash A' :$ type. Instead of just applying our matching algorithm, we then construct a conjunction of equations E and the symbols $\top$ (success) or $\bot$ (failure) such that $\langle \Delta, \Delta'; \cdot \vdash A < A' \rangle \Longrightarrow E$. This is accomplished by using the rules for the judgment

$$\langle \Delta; \Gamma \vdash U < U' \rangle \Longrightarrow E$$

defined in Figure 5, which reads as: *Match U against pattern U' in the parameter context Γ to obtain the residual equations E.* Δ is the disjoint union of the (existential) variables in U and U', of which only those in U may be instantiated during matching. Initially, the context Γ is always empty, and both U and U' are types. However, internally we require the context Γ of shared local parameters.

Example 6 (Rigid Matching Algorithm). The rigid matching algorithm compares the goal (1) from Example 3 to each of the four cases defining ded_0. For each case, it produces a set of residual equations (with contexts elided).

1. Case $\mathsf{ded}_0\_\mathsf{id}$. $u \equiv A \wedge v \equiv A \wedge w \equiv (\lambda x{:}\mathsf{hil}\ A.\ \ x)$
2. Case $\mathsf{ded}_0\_\mathsf{k}$. $u \equiv A \wedge v \equiv (\mathsf{imp}\ A_1\ (\mathsf{imp}\ A_2\ A_1))$
$\wedge\, w \equiv (\lambda x{:}\mathsf{hil}\ A.\ \mathsf{k}\ A_1\ A_2)$
3. Case $\mathsf{ded}_0\_\mathsf{s}$. $u \equiv A \wedge v \equiv (\mathsf{imp}\ (\mathsf{imp}\ A_1\ (\mathsf{imp}\ A_2\ A_3))$
$(\mathsf{imp}\ (\mathsf{imp}\ A_1\ A_2)\ (\mathsf{imp}\ A_1\ A_3)))$
$\wedge\, w \equiv (\lambda x{:}\mathsf{hil}\ A.\ \mathsf{s}\ A_1\ A_2\ A_3)$
4. Case $\mathsf{ded}_0\_\mathsf{mp}$. $u \equiv A \wedge v \equiv A_1$
$\wedge\, w \equiv (\lambda x{:}\mathsf{hil}\ A.\ \mathsf{mp}\ (A_2\ x)\ A_1\ (H_1\ x)\ (H_2\ x))$

$$\frac{\langle \Delta; \Gamma, x{:}A \vdash U < U' \rangle \Longrightarrow E}{\langle \Delta; \Gamma \vdash \lambda x{:}A.\, U < \lambda x{:}A.\, U' \rangle \Longrightarrow E}$$

$$\frac{\langle \Delta; \Gamma \vdash A < A' \rangle \Longrightarrow E_1 \qquad \langle \Delta; \Gamma, x{:}A' \vdash B < B' \rangle \Longrightarrow E_2}{\langle \Delta; \Gamma \vdash \Pi x{:}A.\, B < \Pi x{:}A'.\, B' \rangle \Longrightarrow E_1 \wedge E_2}$$

$$\overline{\langle \Delta; \Gamma \vdash \Pi x{:}A.\, B < a \ldots \rangle \Longrightarrow \bot} \qquad \overline{\langle \Delta; \Gamma \vdash a \ldots < \Pi x{:}A.\, B \rangle \Longrightarrow \bot}$$

$$\frac{c \neq c'}{\langle \Delta; \Gamma \vdash c \ldots < c' \ldots \rangle \Longrightarrow \bot} \qquad \frac{h{:}A \in \Sigma, \Gamma \quad \langle \Delta; \Gamma \vdash U_i < U_i' \rangle \Longrightarrow E_i \ \text{ for } 1 \leq i \leq n}{\langle \Delta; \Gamma \vdash h\, U_1 \ldots U_n < h\, U_1' \ldots U_n' \rangle \Longrightarrow E_1 \wedge \ldots \wedge E_n}$$

$$\frac{x{:}A \in \Gamma \quad h{:}A' \in \Sigma, \Gamma \quad x \neq h}{\langle \Delta; \Gamma \vdash x \ldots < h \ldots \rangle \Longrightarrow \bot}$$

$$\frac{u{:}A \in \Delta \quad h{:}A' \in \Sigma, \Gamma}{\langle \Delta; \Gamma \vdash u\, U_1 \ldots U_n < h\, U_1' \ldots U_m' \rangle \Longrightarrow \langle \Gamma \vdash u\, U_1 \ldots U_n \approx h\, U_1' \ldots U_m' \rangle}$$

$$\overline{\langle \Delta; \Gamma \vdash U < u'\, U_1' \ldots U_m' \rangle \Longrightarrow \langle \Gamma \vdash U \approx u'\, U_1' \ldots U_m' \rangle}$$

Fig. 5. Rigid Matching Algorithm

We can think of the algorithm as a rigid decomposition, which corresponds to the `simplify` function in Huet's algorithm for higher-order unification. If all residual equations can be solved (and there is no $\bot$), then matching is successful. Otherwise, we have to interpret the equations to determine candidates for splitting that will make progress (as defined below).

Note that during rigid matching, no variable assignment takes place: where the two terms disagree, we record an equation. But if matching is not possible, we might either record an equation or return $\bot$.

In order the state the lemmas in the generality required for an inductive proof, we say that for $\Delta; \Gamma \vdash U : V$ and $\Delta'; \Gamma \vdash U' : V'$ that U' *covers* U if there is a substitution $\Delta, \Gamma \vdash \sigma, \mathrm{id}_\Gamma : \Delta', \Gamma$ such that $\Delta, \Gamma \vdash U \equiv U'[\sigma, \mathrm{id}_\Gamma] : V$.

Lemma 1. *If $\Delta, \Delta'; \Gamma \vdash U < U' \Longrightarrow E$ where E contains $\bot$, then U' does not immediately cover U or any instance of U.*

Proof. By induction on the given derivation.

Because U' cannot immediately cover any instance of U, we do not generate any candidate variables for splitting in Δ' in this case.

Lemma 2. *If $\Delta, \Delta'; \Gamma \vdash U < U' \Longrightarrow E$ where E does not contain $\bot$, but contains equations of the form $u \ldots \approx c \ldots$ or $u \ldots \approx x \ldots$. Then U' does not immediately cover U (but U' could possibly cover some instance of U).*

Proof. By induction on the given derivation. In the base cases, x and c are rigid and therefore cannot be instantiated to u.

In this case, any variable u occurring in an equation of the given form is added to the set of candidate variables for splitting, since it is possible that splitting might make progress.

Lemma 3. *If* $\Delta, \Delta'; \Gamma \vdash U < U' \implies E$, *where* E *does not contain* $\bot$ *or equations for the form* $u \ldots \approx c \ldots$ *or* $u \ldots \approx x \ldots$. *Then any substitution* $\Delta \vdash \sigma : \Delta'$ *such that for each residual equation* $\langle \Gamma_i \vdash U_i \approx U'_i \rangle$ *in* E *we have* $\Gamma_i \vdash U_i \equiv U'_i[\sigma, \mathrm{id}_{\Gamma_i}]$ *is a valid match and shows that* U' *covers* U.

Proof. Again, by induction on the given derivation. The base cases are evident. The tricky part in the inductive argument is that the two matched terms do not necessarily have the same type or kind (even though the do initially) because we postpone non-rigid equations. However, as in the case of higher-order dependently typed unification [5], it is enough to maintain well-typedness modulo postponed equations if we eventually solve them from left-to-right.

This means that if we have no candidates from the first two kinds of equations, we call a strict higher-order matching algorithm [21] on the residual equations. If this succeeds then A' covers A. Otherwise, A' does not cover A and we suggest no candidate variables for splitting because it would be difficult to guarantee termination.

When considering a particular coverage goal $\Delta \vdash A :$ type, we apply the above algorithm with each pattern. If one of them immediately covers, we are done. If not, we take the union of all the suggested candidates and pick one non-deterministically. The current implementation picks the rightmost candidate in Δ, because internal dependencies might further constrain variables to its left during the splitting step. If splitting fails because higher-order unification with the algorithm in [4] can not determine a complete and non-redundant set of substitutions, then we try another candidate, and so on. If there are no remaining splitting candidate, we add the coverage goal to the set of potential counterexamples and pick another goal.

3.5   Termination

The overall structure of the algorithm is such that the splitting step replaces a coverage goal by several others. In order to show termination with respect to a simple multi-set ordering, we must show that each of the subgoals that replace a given goal are smaller according some well-founded measure.

We calculate this measure as follows. Given a coverage goal $\Delta \vdash A :$ type apply rigid matching against each pattern. Eliminate those equations that contain $\bot$. Among the remaining ones, consider only equations $u\, U_1 \ldots U_n \approx h'\, U'_1 \ldots U'_m$ where $h' = x$ or $h' = c$. Note that all candidates for splitting appear on the left-hand side of such an equation. Take the sum of the sizes of the right-hand sides as measured by the number of bound variable and constant occurrences.

When we apply splitting to any candidate variables in Δ, that is, one of the variables u that appears on the left-hand side of an equation as given above, then this measure decreases. Given a coverage goal $\Delta \vdash A$: type and a fixed set of patterns proposed to cover it. If we split the coverage goal along a variable u suggested by rigid matching, each of the resulting subgoals has a smaller measure than the original goal.

Theorem 4. *Coverage checking terminates after a finite number of steps, yielding either an indication of coverage or a finite set of potential counterexamples.*

3.6   Finitary Splitting

The failure-directed algorithm described above works well in most practical cases, within or outside the pattern fragment. There are two remaining difficulties: one are remaining constraints during splitting as discussed in Section 3.3, the other is that occasionally the generated counterexamples fail to be actual counterexamples. The latter is a common occurrence. In large part this is because meta-theoretic proofs represented as dependently typed functions or relations often have a number of cases that are impossible. Instead of explicitly proving that the cases are impossible, one usually just lists the cases that can arise if it is syntactically obvious that the others can not arise.

What are the types of spurious counterexamples that may be produced by the algorithm? The most obvious one is a coverage goal that is incompatible with all patterns, but has no ground instances. We explain below how to handle some of these case. A less obvious problem is that matching the residual equations fail because of a spurious dependency that cannot be an actual dependency because of subordination considerations. We treat this case by applying strengthening [21] to eliminate these spurious dependencies throughout the algorithm. Finally, it is possible that two distinct variables of the coverage goal fail to match, yet they must be identical because the type has only one element. Finitary splitting will often catch these cases and correctly report coverage.

In order to handle as many spurious counterexamples as possible, we extend the algorithm described above as follows. Once the algorithm terminates with a set of proposed counterexamples to coverage, we examine each such counterexample to see if we can determine if it is impossible, that is, if it quantifies over an empty type. More concretely, let $\Delta \vdash A$: type be a counterexample, that is, coverage goal that is not covered and does not produce any splitting candidates. We now attempt to split each variable $u{:}A$ in Δ in turn, leading to a new set of coverage goals $\Delta_i \vdash U_i : V_i$ for $0 \leq i < n$. If $n = 0$ we know that the case is impossible.

If $n > 0$ we could, in principle, continue the algorithm recursively to see if each of the subgoals $\Delta_i \vdash U_i : V_i$ are impossible. However, in general this would not terminate (and cannot, because inhabitation is undecidable). Instead, we only continue to split further if all of the new variables $u_k : A_k$ in Δ_i have a type that is strictly subordinate to the type A [23,21]. Otherwise, we fail and report the immediate supergoal as a potential counterexample.

Theorem 5. *Finitary splitting terminates, either with an indication that the given coverage goal has no ground instances, or failure.*

Proof. There are only a finite number of variables in a given coverage goal. During each step of splitting we either stop or obtain subgoals where a variable $u : A$ has been replaced by several variables $u_i : A_i$ each of which has a type strictly lower in the subordination hierarchy. Since this hierarchy is well-founded, finitary splitting will terminate.

This process can be very expensive. Fortunately, we have not found it to be a bottleneck in practice, because finitary splitting is applied only to remaining counterexamples. Usually, there are not many, and usually it is immediate to see that they are indeed possible because most types are actually inhabited. We do not presently try to verify if the types are actually inhabited (that is, start a theorem prover), although it may be useful for debugging purposes to distinguish between definite and potential counterexamples. However, in a future extension this could be done at the user's direction if he or she cannot easily detect the source of the failure of coverage.

4   Related Work

Coquand has considered the problem of coverage for a type theory in the style of Martin-Löf [2]. He defines coverage and splitting in much the same way we do here, except that no matching against the structure of λ-expressions is allowed. He also suggests a non-deterministic semi-decision procedure for coverage by guessing the correct sequence of variable splits. In an implementation this split can be achieved interactively.

Most closely related to ours is the work by McBride [12]. He refines Coquand's idea by suggesting an algorithm for successive splitting that is quite similar to ours in the first-order case. He also identifies the problem of empty types and suggest to recognize "obviously" empty types, which is a simpler variant of finitary splitting. Our main contribution with respect to McBride's work is that we allow matching against the structure of higher-order terms which poses significant additional challenges.

Another related development is the theory of partial inductive definitions [7], especially in its finitary form [6] and the related notion of definitional reflection [20]. This calculus contains a rule schema that, re-interpreted in our context, would allow any (finite) complete set of unifiers between a coverage goal $\Delta \vdash A : \text{type}$ and the heads of the clauses defining A. Because of the additional condition of so-called a-sufficiency for the substitutions, this was never fully automated. Also, it appears that a simple, finite complete set of unifiers was computed as in the splitting step, but that the system could not check whether an arbitrary given set of premises could be obtained as a finite complete set of unifiers.

In the Coq system [11] functions defined by patterns can be compiled to functions defined by standard primitive recursive elimination forms. Because of the requirement to compile such functions back into pure Coq and the lack of matching against functional expressions, the algorithm is rather straightforward compared to our coverage checker and does not handle variable dependencies, non-linearity, or empty types. It does, however, treat polymorphism which we have not considered.

5   Conclusion

We have presented a solution to the coverage checking problem for LF, generalizing and extending previous approaches. The central technical developments are strict patterns (which significantly generalize higher-order patterns in the sense of Miller), strict higher-order matching, splitting in the presence of full higher-order unification, and a two-phase control structure to guarantee termination of the algorithm.

Our coverage algorithm is sound and terminating, but it is necessarily incomplete. Applied to a given set of patterns, it either reports "yes", or it generates a set of potential counterexamples, which often contain the vital information about why coverage has failed. Because coverage is undecidable in the case of LF, the algorithm sometimes generates spurious counterexamples, that can sometimes be removed with a highly specialized albeit incomplete algorithm called finitary splitting and has proven tremendously useful in practice.

All algorithms and techniques described in this paper are implemented in the Twelf system, Version 1.4 (December 2002). Many examples of coverage are available in the example directories of the Twelf distribution. The current implementation is somewhat more general than what we describe here since it also accounts for regular worlds [21]. We plan to extend the rigorous treatment given here to this larger class of coverage problems in a future paper.

References

1. T. Coquand. An algorithm for testing conversion in type theory. In G. Huet and G. Plotkin, editors, *Logical Frameworks*, pages 255–279. Cambridge University Press, 1991.
2. T. Coquand. Pattern matching with dependent types. In *Proceedings of the Workshop on Types for Proofs and Programs*, pages 71–83, Båstad, Sweden, 1992.
3. K. Crary. Toward a foundational typed assembly language. In G. Morrisett, editor, *Proceedings of the 30th Annual Symposium on Principles of Programming Languages*, pages 198–212, New Orleans, Louisiana, Jan. 2003. ACM Press.
4. G. Dowek, T. Hardin, C. Kirchner, and F. Pfenning. Unification via explicit substitutions: The case of higher-order patterns. In M. Maher, editor, *Proceedings of the Joint International Conference and Symposium on Logic Programming*, pages 259–273, Bonn, Germany, Sept. 1996. MIT Press.
5. C. M. Elliott. *Extensions and Applications of Higher-Order Unification*. PhD thesis, School of Computer Science, Carnegie Mellon University, May 1990. Available as Technical Report CMU-CS-90-134.

6. L.-H. Eriksson. *Finitary Partial Inductive Definitions and General Logic*. PhD thesis, Department of Computer and System Sciences, Royal Institute of Technology, Stockholm, 1993.
7. L. Hallnäs. Partial inductive definitions. *Theoretical Computer Science*, 87(1):115–142, Sept. 1991.
8. R. Harper, F. Honsell, and G. Plotkin. A framework for defining logics. *Journal of the Association for Computing Machinery*, 40(1):143–184, Jan. 1993.
9. M. Hofmann and T. Streicher. The groupoid model refutes uniqueness of identity proofs. In *Proceedings of the 9th Annual Symposium on Logic in Computer Science (LICS'94)*, pages 208–212, Paris, France, 1994. IEEE Computer Society Press.
10. G. Huet. A unification algorithm for typed λ-calculus. *Theoretical Computer Science*, 1:27–57, 1975.
11. INRIA. *The Coq Proof Assistant*, version 7.4 edition, Feb. 2003. Reference Manual.
12. C. McBride. *Dependently Typed Functional Programs and their Proofs*. PhD thesis, University of Edinburgh, 1999. Available as Technical Report ECS-LFCS-00-419.
13. D. Miller. A logic programming language with lambda-abstraction, function variables, and simple unification. *Journal of Logic and Computation*, 1(4):497–536, 1991.
14. F. Pfenning. Logical frameworks. In A. Robinson and A. Voronkov, editors, *Handbook of Automated Reasoning*, chapter 17, pages 1063–1147. Elsevier Science and MIT Press, 2001.
15. F. Pfenning and C. Schürmann. Algorithms for equality and unification in the presence of notational definitions. In T. Altenkirch, W. Naraschewski, and B. Reus, editors, *Types for Proofs and Programs*, pages 179–193, Kloster Irsee, Germany, Mar. 1998. Springer-Verlag LNCS 1657.
16. F. Pfenning and C. Schürmann. System description: Twelf — a meta-logical framework for deductive systems. In H. Ganzinger, editor, *Proceedings of the 16th International Conference on Automated Deduction (CADE-16)*, pages 202–206, Trento, Italy, July 1999. Springer-Verlag LNAI 1632.
17. B. Pientka. Termination and reduction checking for higher-order logic programs. In *First International Joint Conference on Automated Reasoning (IJCAR)*, pages 401–415, Siena, Italy, 2001. Springer Verlag, LNCS 2083.
18. B. Pientka and F. Pfenning. Optimizing higher-order pattern unification. In F. Baader, editor, *Proceedings of the 19th Conference on Automated Deduction (CADE-19)*, Miami Beach, Florida, July 2003. Springer-Verlag LNCS. To appear.
19. E. Rohwedder and F. Pfenning. Mode and termination checking for higher-order logic programs. In H. R. Nielson, editor, *Proceedings of the European Symposium on Programming*, pages 296–310, Linköping, Sweden, Apr. 1996. Springer-Verlag LNCS 1058.
20. P. Schroeder-Heister. Rules of definitional reflection. In M. Vardi, editor, *Proceedings of the Eighth Annual IEEE Symposium on Logic in Computer Science*, pages 222–232, Montreal, Canada, June 1993.
21. C. Schürmann. *Automating the Meta Theory of Deductive Systems*. PhD thesis, Department of Computer Science, Carnegie Mellon University, Aug. 2000. Available as Technical Report CMU-CS-00-146.
22. C. Schürmann, R. Fontana, and Y. Liao. Delphin: Functional programming with deductive systems. Draft.
23. R. Virga. *Higher-Order Rewriting with Dependent Types*. PhD thesis, Department of Mathematical Sciences, Carnegie Mellon University, Sept. 1999. Available as Technical Report CMU-CS-99-167.

Automatic Generation of Generalization Lemmas for Proving Properties of Tail-Recursive Definitions*

Deepak Kapur and Nikita A. Sakhanenko

Department of Computer Science
University of New Mexico,
Albuquerque, NM, USA
{kapur,sanik}@cs.unm.edu

Abstract. Automatically proving properties of tail-recursive function definitions by induction is known to be challenging. The difficulty arises due to a property of a tail-recursive function definition typically expressed by instantiating the accumulator argument to be a constant only on one side of the property. The application of the induction hypothesis gets blocked in a proof attempt. Following an approach developed by Kapur and Subramaniam, a transformation heuristic is proposed which hypothesizes the other side of property to also have an occurrence of the same constant. Constraints on the transformation are identified which enable a generalization of the constant on both sides with the hope that the generalized conjecture is easier to prove. Conditions are generated from which intermediate lemmas necessary to make a proof attempt to succeed can be speculated. By considering structural properties of recursive definitions, it is possible to identify properties of the functions used in recursive definitions for the conjecture to be valid. The heuristic is demonstrated on well-known tail-recursive definitions on numbers as well as other recursive data structures, including finite lists, finite sequences, finite trees, where a definition is expressed using one recursive call or multiple recursive calls. In case, a given conjecture is not valid because of a possible bug in an implementation (a tail-recursive definition) or a specification (a recursive definition), the heuristic can be often used to generate a counter-example. Conditions under which the heuristic is applicable can be checked easily. The proposed heuristic is likely to be helpful for automatically generating loop invariants as well as in proofs of correctness of properties of programs with respect to their specifications.

1 Introduction

While attempting proofs of properties of recursive definitions by induction, it is often necessary to use intermediate lemmas which are not easy to generate automatically. This problem becomes especially acute with tail-recursive definitions for which conjectures are typically expressed by fixing one of its arguments

---

* This research was partially supported by an NSF ITR award CCR-0113611.

D. Basin and B. Wolff (Eds.): TPHOLs 2003, LNCS 2758, pp. 136–154, 2003.

(accumulator) to be a fixed value, whereas in the recursive definition, there is no corresponding argument [3,11,6,2]. Such asymmetry makes mechanization of proofs of inductive properties of tail-recursive definitions quite challenging as (i) the induction hypotheses generated using the recursive definition (e.g. in Boyer and Moore's approach [3], in the cover set method [12] as well as other methods based on recursion analysis [11,2]) are not applicable and (ii) intermediate lemmas generalizing the accumulator position are often needed to successfully complete proof attempts.[1]

By analyzing the recursive structure of tail-recursive and nontail-recursive definitions, structural conditions are identified in this paper, relating other **helper functions** used in the definitions such that for a given conjecture to be valid, these helper functions must have certain properties. This is done in an abstract generic setting. Recursive and tail recursive definitions are given generically using helper functions, on a recursively defined data structure generated by a finite set of basic constructors and a finite set of "recursive" constructors. A conjecture expressing the equivalence of a function defined tail-recursively to a function defined nontail-recursively is formulated and a generic proof is attempted. Since one side of the conjecture has a constant value in its accumulator position, the other side of the conjecture is **transformed** to hypothesize an occurrence of the same constant value so that the transformed conjecture can be generalized by abstracting the constant value to a variable. Following the approach proposed by Kapur and Subramaniam in [8], constraints on the transformation are identified in order to make a proof attempt of the generalized conjecture to succeed. Many of these constraints are dictated by the desire to make the induction hypothesis applicable. These constraints are then used to speculate about the nature of the transformation, namely whether the transformation can be replaced by a term expressed using already known functions.[2]

The proposed approach produces two types of constraints – *necessary* and *sufficient* constraints, on the helper functions used in expressing the definitions. Each necessary constraint must be satisfied for the original conjecture to be valid. Even if all the necessary constraints are satisfied, the original conjecture may not be valid. However, if any necessary constraint is not satisfied, then the conjecture can be declared false. Such constraints are thus a good source for generating counter-examples from false conjectures. If all sufficient constraints are satisfied, then the original conjecture is valid. However, nothing can be said about the validity of the original conjecture if a sufficient constraint is not satisfied. Each

---

[1] Since tail-recursive definitions are essentially iterative definitions, the problem of intermediate lemma generation is closely related to the problem of discovering invariants of loops. Results discussed in this paper should be useful in automatically synthesizing inductive invariants of loops.

[2] In this paper, we have focussed on the use of rewriting techniques, narrowing, and related heuristics; high-order unification could also be used for searching for a function satisfying the constraints to serve as the hypothesized transformation; see [6] where such an approach based on proof planning and higher-order unification has been investigated.

of these necessary and sufficient constraints can thus serve as a lemma useful to carry out a proof of the original conjecture.

The proposed approach is based on using (generic) schematic definitions. The proofs of related conjectures do not have to be repeated, since the definitions involved are instances of the schemes considered. Instead, proofs of the constraints constitute an attempt of a proof of the conjecture. This is in sharp contrast to other approaches proposed in the literature where for each specific conjecture being attempted, it becomes necessary to carry out all the proofs separately so as to identify intermediate lemmas for each specific conjecture.

In the next subsection, the difficulty in establishing the equivalence of a tail-recursive definition with a primitive-recursive definition is illustrated using the example of the *factorial* function defined both tail-recursively as well as in primitive-recursive style. Section 2 discusses related work. Section 3 starts with another example of a function defining wsum, which is used to illustrate the proposed approach of transforming the right side of a given conjecture so as to generalize it. The proposed approach is then discussed in detail for an arbitrary tail-recursive definition scheme and an arbitrary primitive-recursive definition with the restriction that there is exactly one recursive call. In a later section, the proposed approach is discussed for definitions with two recursive calls.

1.1   Tail-Recursive Function Definitions

Definition 1. *A recursive definition of a function on nonnegative numbers is called* tail-recursive *if it has the following form:*

$$\begin{bmatrix} \mathsf{g}(0, x_1, ..., x_k, y) \to \mathsf{h}_1(x_1, ..., x_k, y), \\ \mathsf{g}(\mathsf{s}(x), x_1, ..., x_k, y) \to \mathsf{g}(x, x_1, ..., x_k, \mathsf{h}_2(x, x_1, ..., x_k, y)). \end{bmatrix}$$

In this case, the last argument is called *accumulator* since it is used to compute the result. A tail-recursive definition of a function can be given on any recursive data structure in a similar way.

As seen above, a tail-recursive function definition returns the result of the helper function (h_1) in the basis step of the definition, on the result returned by the last recursive call.[3] Tail-recursive definitions are preferred over general recursive definitions because of the efficiency in computing them. Many compilers have optimizations and heuristics to recognize recursive definitions to tail-recursive definitions. See [9] for a formal definition of tail recursive function definitions and space efficiency analysis.

Consider the factorial function fact written in the usual recursive style and its tail-recursive representation tr_fact:

$$\begin{bmatrix} \mathsf{fact}(0) \to \mathsf{s}(0), \\ \mathsf{fact}(\mathsf{s}(n)) \to \mathsf{s}(n) * \mathsf{fact}(n), \end{bmatrix} \qquad \begin{bmatrix} \mathsf{tr\_fact}(0, y) \to y, \\ \mathsf{tr\_fact}(\mathsf{s}(n), y) \to \mathsf{tr\_fact}(n, \mathsf{s}(n) * y). \end{bmatrix}$$

---

[3] Without any loss of generality, in the above definition, the function definition is given by recursing on the first argument and accumulator is made the last argument. Any argument positions (including multiple arguments), insofar as they are disjoint, could have been used for these purposes.

In order to prove the equivalence of a recursive definition with a tail-recursive definition, a conjecture relating the recursive definition to the tail-recursive definition with the accumulator taking a fixed value must be formulated. For fact and tr_fact defined above, such a conjecture is:

$$\text{tr\_fact}(n, 1) = \text{fact}(n).\tag{1}$$

1.2   Failure of Proof Due to Inapplicability of Induction Hypothesis

During an inductive proof of (1), the basis step goes through; however, the induction step $\text{tr\_fact}(\text{s}(n), 1) = \text{fact}(\text{s}(n))$, cannot be established. Simplification of the conclusion gives $\text{tr\_fact}(n, \text{s}(n) * 1) = \text{s}(n) * \text{fact}(n)$. Term $\text{s}(n) * 1$ (or its normal form $\text{s}(n)$ assuming that the definition of $*$ simplifies it) from the conclusion does not match the constant 1 in the hypothesis, implying that the induction hypothesis does not apply and consequently, the proof attempt fails.[4]

One possible way to attempt proving (1) is to generalize the conjecture by replacing 1 in the accumulator position of tr_fact by a variable. Such a generalization is likely to be useless since 1 appears only on one side of the conjecture. To fix this problem, the conjecture can be transformed to an equivalent conjecture with 1 on both sides that can be generalized. Using the property

$$1 * y = y$$

of $*$, a new conjecture

$$\text{tr\_fact}(n, 1) = 1 * \text{fact}(n)$$

is generated which is equivalent to (1). Now both sides of the new conjecture have a common subterm 1 and a generalization is attempted to obtain

$$\text{tr\_fact}(n, y) = y * \text{fact}(n).$$

Using the properties of $*$, such as commutativity and associativity, a proof of this generalized conjecture can be automatically carried out (e.g., using RRL).

1.3   Overview of the Proposed Approach

The method starts with a tail-recursive definition and a nontail-recursive definition, and a conjecture relating them. Typically such a conjecture has a constant term in the accumulator position only on one side of the conjecture. To abstract

---

[4] For this simple example, a generalization could have been performed by abstracting $\text{s}(n)$ to y; in fact, this is what our theorem prover *Rewrite Rule Laboratory* (*RRL*) will do [7]. However, such a generalization is not obvious in most cases.

that constant, the other side of the conjecture is transformed by hypothesizing a term to include this constant as well. The goal is to generate constraints on the hypothesized term assuming the original conjecture to be valid. These constraints are then used to speculate the hypothesized term. To generate constraints, the transformed conjecture is generalized by abstracting the constant to be a variable. A proof is attempted and constraints are generated on the transformation to facilitate the applicability of the induction hypothesis in various proof steps. From these constraints, the hypothesized term is then speculated.

The proposed method often outputs whether the conjecture is *valid* or *not*; in some cases, it may output *don't know*. If not valid, the method can often exhibit an example on which the conjecture is not valid. Otherwise, it attempts to generate constraints on helper functions used in the definitions whose proofs can establish the original conjecture. If any of these intermediate conjectures is not valid, the original conjecture may not be valid depending upon whether the validity of some of the intermediate conjectures is a necessary condition for the original conjecture to hold.

2   Related Work

The idea of transforming a conjecture in order to obtain a constant subterm on both sides was proposed in Aubin's papers [1]. He called the tactic *indirect generalization* which he illustrated using lots of examples; little attempt was made to formalize the idea which consisted of (i) transforming the original conjecture using given properties of helper functions so as to have the same constant value on both sides of the conjecture, and (ii) generalizing the conjecture by abstracting the constant to be variable. The major difference between Aubin's approach and the proposed approach is in how the transformation function and its associated property are obtained. For the factorial example, Aubin assumed the property $1 * y = y$ as given; the user is supposed to provide this property before trying to prove conjecture (1). In contrast, we are interested in automatically deriving such a property.

Inspired by Aubin's approach, Castaing [4] proposed a heuristic in which all subterms responsible for the failure in matching of an induction hypothesis with the conclusion are analyzed. The user is expected to provide properties of helper functions which might be useful in processing subterms responsible for this failure, with the view that these subterms can be replaced by equivalent subterms to make the induction hypothesis applicable. As in Aubin's method, Castaing did not discuss whether these properties can be automatically generated as constraints from an unsuccessful proof attempt or how these properties are used when available.

In his thesis [5], Giesl proposed an approach to transform a conjecture about a tail-recursive function to an equivalent conjecture from which the tail-recursive function is eliminated, so as to avoid the need for generalization. In a tail-recursive definition, the *context* refers to the term structure around the accumulator position. Giesl defined three transformations: *context-moving*, *context-*

splitting, and *preprocessing* so as to enable the first two transformations. Giesl's method works based on the structure of function definitions, without taking into consideration conjectures being attempted. In this sense, Giesl's method is radically different from the other approaches.

Ireland and Bundy [6] proposed the use of *proof planning* and *rippling* for generalizing a fixed value in the accumulator position in a conjecture. Using rippling, the rewriting of the conclusion is restricted so as to preserve the matching between an induction hypothesis and conclusion. Also the strategy of the so-called *eager instantiation* in the second-order unification used by Ireland and Bundy may give rise to an over-generalization; the counter example checker is used to filter candidate instantiations. Their method seems to be more complex than the proposed method.

The proposed approach is inspired by Vadera's paper [10] but uses techniques proposed in Kapur and Subramaniam's paper [8]. We first discuss the salient features in Vadera's paper and then discuss aspects of Kapur and Subramaniam's paper most related to the proposed approach.

Vadera considered generic definition schemes and identified properties which will have to be established to show their equivalence. Some of these properties are existential in nature, i.e., formulas involving existential quantifiers where Vadera hypothesized the existence of constants and functions satisfying certain constraints. Vadera did not explain how such functions could be discovered. Similar to Vadera's approach, generic recursive and tail-recursive schemes are analyzed in this paper leading to identifying conditions/constraints on function definitions to establish equivalence of such schemes. Depending on the validity of these conditions, the original conjecture can be transformed to an equivalent one, which is easy to prove.

Kapur and Subramaniam's approach [8] is based on the assumption that for an induction proof attempt to succeed, it must be possible to use the induction hypothesis in every induction case. In order to force the application of the induction hypothesis (in case it is not applicable on a conclusion subgoal), an intermediate conjecture is hypothesized by formulating one of its sides as a term scheme with the desired characteristics. Using the intermediate conjecture, the induction hypothesis becomes applicable (particularly, if a constant or a new variable is desired in the right side of an intermediate conjecture, then the one side of the intermediate conjecture should include it). From this proof attempt, constraints on the hypothesized term scheme in the intermediate conjecture are generated. Using these constraints along with the definitions of helper functions and their properties, the hypothesized term scheme is speculated.

In the proposed approach, a more general conjecture is hypothesized as in [8]. Since conjectures relating a tail-recursive definition to a nontail-recursive definition are considered, the goal is to come up with general conditions on the function definitions and the properties of helper functions appearing in the definitions under which the equivalence can be established. This restricts the search space for speculation about term schemes as illustrated below.

3 Proposed Approach

Before discussing the proposed approach, we illustrate it using an example. We provide lots of details so as to make every step in the proposed approach clear and thus convince the reader about its mechanization. We first consider definitions in which recursive rules have a single recursive call. This example is artificially designed in such a way that one cannot apply direct generalization to it. Nonetheless, our method works for such an example where other generalization methods fail.

Given a recursive definition of the function wsum[5]

$$\left[\begin{array}{l} \mathsf{wsum}(0) \to 0, \\ \mathsf{wsum}(\mathsf{s}(x)) \to \mathsf{s}(\mathsf{s}(x)) + \mathsf{wsum}(x), \end{array}\right. \tag{2}$$

and a tail-recursive definition of wsigma,

$$\left[\begin{array}{l} \mathsf{wsigma}(0, y) \to y, \\ \mathsf{wsigma}(\mathsf{s}(x), y) \to \mathsf{wsigma}(x, y + (\mathsf{s}(\mathsf{s}(0)) + x)), \end{array}\right. \tag{3}$$

the goal is to check whether

$$\mathsf{wsigma}(x, 0) = \mathsf{wsum}(x). \tag{4}$$

(The function wsum does not compute the sum of first n numbers; that is why the name wsum is used to suggest that the function is weird.)

Much like the factorial example discussed above, a proof of the above conjecture gets stuck because of the inapplicability of the induction hypothesis. Using the ideas proposed in [8], our goal is to transform the right side of the conjecture to obtain a term which involves occurrence of 0:

$$\mathsf{wsigma}(x, 0) = T(\mathsf{wsum}(x), 0), \tag{5}$$

where T is an unknown term in which $\mathsf{wsum}(x)$ and 0 occur. Constraints on T are generated making its speculation feasible using the heuristics developed in [8]. To make the above conjecture equivalent to the original conjecture,

$$T(\mathsf{wsum}(x), 0) = \mathsf{wsum}(x). \tag{6}$$

The conjecture (5) is generalized by replacing 0 by a variable.

$$\mathsf{wsigma}(x, y) = T(\mathsf{wsum}(x), y). \tag{7}$$

To generate additional constraints on T, its proof is attempted using the *cover-set induction* method [12]; if there is a choice in selecting the cover set for generating an induction scheme, the cover set associated with the accumulator-based

---

[5] The function + on natural numbers is assumed to be defined as the terminating rewrite rules $x + 0 \to x$, $x + \mathsf{s}(y) \to \mathsf{s}(x + y)$. For illustrative purposes, no other property of + is assumed.

definition is preferred.[6] If the generalization (7) is valid, the initial conjecture being its instance is also valid.

Proving (7) by the cover-set induction method the basis step yields $\mathsf{wsigma}(0, y) = T(\mathsf{wsum}(0), y)$, which simplifies further to

$$y = T(\mathsf{wsum}(0), y). \tag{8}$$

The induction step gives $\mathsf{wsigma}(\mathsf{s}(x), y) = T(\mathsf{wsum}(\mathsf{s}(x)), y)$ assuming hypothesis $\mathsf{wsigma}(x, y+(\mathsf{s}(\mathsf{s}(0))+x)) = T(\mathsf{wsum}(x), y+(\mathsf{s}(\mathsf{s}(0))+x))$. Simplifying the conclusion and applying the induction hypothesis, we get

$$T(\mathsf{wsum}(\mathsf{s}(x)), y) = T(\mathsf{wsum}(x), y + (\mathsf{s}(\mathsf{s}(0)) + x)). \tag{9}$$

Equations (8) and (9) can be instantiated for $y = 0$ and simplified using (6). This gives a constraint that for the original conjecture (8) to be valid, $0 = T(\mathsf{wsum}(0), 0) = \mathsf{wsum}(0)$ should be valid. For this example, this constraint is trivial, but in general, this property could be nontrivial; even in the general case, it does not depend on T.

Similarly, if $T(\mathsf{wsum}(\mathsf{s}(x)), 0) = T(\mathsf{wsum}(x), 0 + (\mathsf{s}(\mathsf{s}(0)) + x))$, the instance of (9) with y being 0, is not valid, then (9) is not valid either. Using (6), this instance of (9) simplifies to: $\mathsf{s}(\mathsf{s}(x)) + \mathsf{wsum}(x) = T(\mathsf{wsum}(x), 0 + (\mathsf{s}(\mathsf{s}(0)) + x))$. If

$$\mathsf{s}(\mathsf{s}(x)) = 0 + (\mathsf{s}(\mathsf{s}(0)) + x))$$

can be proved to be valid,[7] then from,

$$\mathsf{s}(\mathsf{s}(x)) + \mathsf{wsum}(x) = T(\mathsf{wsum}(x), \mathsf{s}(\mathsf{s}(x))), \tag{10}$$

T can be speculated to be $+$ but with switched arguments. The property (6) becomes $0 + \mathsf{wsum}(x) = \mathsf{wsum}(x)$, which can be easily proved.

This leads to a successful proof of the conjecture

$$\mathsf{wsigma}(x, 0) = 0 + \mathsf{wsum}(x) \tag{11}$$

containing 0on both sides. Its generalization, $\mathsf{wsigma}(x, y) = y + \mathsf{wsum}(x)$, is proved using the associativity of $+$ and $0 + x = x$ as the intermediate lemmas.

---

[6] Inspired by Boyer and Moore's work, the cover set induction method implements well-founded induction using a well-founded ordering employed to show termination of a function definition given as a finite set of terminating rewrite rules. Each rewrite rule in the definition contributes a subgoal constructed using the substitution from its left side; the substitutions for induction hypotheses generated by the induction scheme are constructed from the recursive calls to the function in the right side of the rule. For more details, the reader can consult [12].

[7] If the commutativity property of $+$ is already established, then this equation is valid. We admit that this example is somewhat artificial and easy, but it is being used to illustrate the key ideas of the proposed approach. The properties needed for the successful proof attempts can be discovered during the procedure.

3.1   Identifying Constraints on a Generic Transformation Function

Consider the following two recursive definition schemes – nontail-recursive and tail-recursive, each defined on a generic recursive data structure. The values of the recursive data structure are constructed by a finite set of basis constructors $C_i{}^8$, "recursive" constructors $C_j(v, x_l, x_r)$. These constructors are assumed to be *free* in the sense that for any $i \neq j$,

$$C_i(\cdots) \neq C_j(\cdots), \quad \text{and}$$

$$C_j(v_1, u_1, u_2) = C_j(v_1', u_1', u_2') \Rightarrow [v_1 = v_1' \wedge u_1 = u_1' \wedge u_2 = u_2'].$$

For simplicity, the recursive definition (12) below exhibits only one argument and the tail-recursive definition (13) has two arguments with the last argument being the accumulator. Recursive definitions with more than one argument can be handled easily; in that case also, the definitions are assumed to be given by recursing on the first argument and the accumulator being in the last argument.

$$\begin{bmatrix} f(C_i) \to m_i(C_i), \ 1 \leq i \leq k, \\ f(C_j(v, x_l, x_r)) \to m_j(f(x_l), t_j(v, x_l, x_r)), \ k+1 \leq j \leq n, \end{bmatrix} \tag{12}$$

and

$$\begin{bmatrix} g(C_i, y) \to n_i(C_i, y), \ 1 \leq i \leq k, \\ g(C_j(v, x_l, x_r), y) \to g(x_l, n_j(v, x_l, x_r, y)), \ k+1 \leq j \leq n. \end{bmatrix} \tag{13}$$

The function g has a tail-recursive definition with an accumulator in its second argument position. The functions m_i, m_j, t_j, n_i, n_j in the above definitions are *helper* functions and are assumed to be defined elsewhere. As the reader can see, the above generic schemes can consider recursive definitions on most recursive data structures including numbers (with 0 as the basis constructor and $s(x)$ as the recursive constructor), lists (with nil and $cons(a, x)$ as constructors) and binary trees (with $empty(val)$, $mktree(val, left, right)$ as constructors).

The objective is to check whether for some constant d,

$$g(x, d) = f(x). \tag{14}$$

The reader can verify that a straightforward induction proof of this conjecture fails because of the same reason we discussed above: *inability to apply the induction hypothesis on the conclusion.* Further, the constant d in the accumulator position in the conjecture cannot be abstracted as a new variable in a useful way primarily because its right side does not have this constant.

Following [8], we hypothesize that the right side of (14) can be made equivalent to a term containing d so that the transformed conjecture can be generalized.

---

[8] which could also have arguments, but for simplicity, we have assumed them to be constants without any arguments.

Let $g(x, d) = T(f(x), d)$, where the *transformation* function T is unknown; however, in order for it to be useful to prove the original conjecture, T must satisfy the first constraint:

$$T(f(x), d) = f(x). \tag{15}$$

The transformed conjecture $g(x, d) = T(f(x), d)$, is generalized by replacing d with a new variable y.

$$g(x, y) = T(f(x), y). \tag{16}$$

Following [8], we now try to find additional constraints on T by attempting to prove the above generalized conjecture (16).

There are several basis steps:

$$n_i(C_i, y) = T(f(C_i), y), \quad 1 \leq i \leq k. \tag{17}$$

In the jth induction step, the conclusion is

$$g(C_j(v, x_l, x_r), y) = T(f(C_j(v, x_l, x_r)), y),$$

with the induction hypothesis $g(x_l, n_j(v, x_l, x_r, y)) = T(f(x_l), n_j(v, x_l, x_r, y))$, for each $k + 1 \leq j \leq n$. After simplification of the left hand side of the conclusion, the induction hypothesis is applied to produce:

$$T(f(C_j(v, x_l, x_r)), y) = T(f(x_l), n_j(v, x_l, x_r, y)). \tag{18}$$

If T can be found such that (15), (17) and (18) can be proved, then the conjecture (16) is proved. However, to prove (14), it suffices to show (17) and (18) for $y = d$.

Using the property (15) in which the second argument of T is instantiated to d, we get from (17): $n_i(C_i, d) = T(f(C_i), d))$, resulting in:

$$n_i(C_i, d) = m_i(C_i) \quad 1 \leq i \leq k. \tag{19}$$

Theorem 2. *Given the above definition schema f and g, the conjecture $g(x, d) = f(x)$ does not hold if the constraint $n_i(C_i, d) = m_i(C_i)$ is not satisfied by n_i, m_i, C_i, d for at least one i, $1 \leq i \leq k$.*

Theorem 2 is particularly useful in invalidating inductive conjectures and most often, in debugging definitions.

Example 3. As an example, consider definitions of the exponentiation function 2^n, where n is a natural number. The conjecture under consideration is:

$$\text{two\_t}(x, s(0)) = \text{two}(x), \tag{20}$$

where functions two_t and two are defined as follows

$$\left[\begin{array}{l} \mathsf{two\_t}(0,y) \to y, \\ \mathsf{two\_t}(\mathsf{s}(x),y) \to \mathsf{two\_t}(x,\mathsf{s}(\mathsf{s}(0)) * y), \end{array}\right. \qquad \left[\begin{array}{l} \mathsf{two}(0) \to \mathsf{s}(\mathsf{s}(0)), \\ \mathsf{two}(\mathsf{s}(x)) \to \mathsf{s}(\mathsf{s}(0)) * \mathsf{two}(x). \end{array}\right.$$

Using Theorem 2, the property (20) is not valid because the constraint $n_1(C_1, d) = m_1(C_1)$, which in this case is $s(0) = s(s(0))$, is not valid. From this analysis, we can conclude that there is a mistake perhaps in the basis definition of two: $\mathsf{two}(0)$ should be $\mathsf{s}(0)$ instead of $\mathsf{s}(\mathsf{s}(0))$. $\qquad\square$

So far we have analyzed the constraints arising from the basis steps of an inductive proof attempt. Considering the induction steps, recall (18):

$$T(\mathsf{f}(\mathsf{C}_j(v, x_l, x_r)), y) = T(\mathsf{f}(x_l), \mathsf{n}_j(v, x_l, x_r, y)).$$

Instantiating y in the above to d gives:

$$T(\mathsf{f}(\mathsf{C}_j(v, x_l, x_r)), \mathsf{d}) = T(\mathsf{f}(x_l), \mathsf{n}_j(v, x_l, x_r, \mathsf{d})).$$

Using (15) and the definition of f, this simplifies to:

$$m_j(\mathsf{f}(x_l), \mathsf{t}_j(v, x_l, x_r)) = T(\mathsf{f}(x_l), \mathsf{n}_j(v, x_l, x_r, \mathsf{d})), \tag{21}$$

for each $k + 1 \le j \le n$.

This set of conjectures (21) provides constraints on T. Along with other properties of T, these conjectures are particularly helpful for speculating T. By making additional assumptions on subterms appearing in (21), we attempt to speculate about T.

Case 1: $\mathsf{n}_j(v, x_l, x_r, \mathsf{d}) = \mathsf{t}_j(v, x_l, x_r)$

Theorem 4. *Given the above definition schema* f *and* g, *if* $\mathsf{n}_j, \mathsf{d}, \mathsf{t}_j$ *are such that* $\mathsf{n}_j(v, x_l, x_r, \mathsf{d}) = \mathsf{t}_j(v, x_l, x_r)$ *is valid for each* $k + 1 \le j \le n$, *then* T *behaves the same as* m_j *on the subset* $\{\langle \mathsf{f}(x_l), \mathsf{t}_j(v, x_l, x_r)\rangle\}$ *of the domain of* m_j.

This requirement on $\mathsf{n}_j, \mathsf{d}, \mathsf{t}_j$ allows the subterm $\mathsf{t}_j(v, x_l, x_r)$ on both sides of (21) to be generalized to:

$$m_j(\mathsf{f}(x_l), z) = T(\mathsf{f}(x_l), z). \tag{22}$$

Typically, a data structure under consideration has only one recursive constructor, thus implying that $n = k + 1$. In that case (and also in the case when $m_p = m_q$, $k + 1 \le p, q \le n$), it can be speculated that $T = m_n$ from the conjecture (22); especially, if f is onto, then this speculation is even sound.

In that case, the following property of m_n must be established:

$$m_n(\mathsf{f}(x), \mathsf{d}) = \mathsf{f}(x).$$

Conjectures (17) and (18) on T become (after using the definition of f) as:

$$n_i(C_i, y) = m_n(m_i(C_i), y), \quad 1 \leq i \leq k, \quad \text{and}$$

$$m_n(f(C_n(v, x_l, x_r)), y) = m_n(f(x_l), n_n(v, x_l, x_r, y)),$$

which further simplifies using the definition of f to:

$$m_n(m_n(f(x_l), t_j(v, x_l, x_r)), y) = m_n(f(x_l), n_n(v, x_l, x_r, y)).$$

If these properties of m_n can be established, the initial conjecture (14) is proved. The example discussed above and the example 6 in Section 4 illustrate this case.

Case 2: $n_j(v, x_l, x_r, d) \neq t_j(v, x_l, x_r)$

The proposed methodology relies on simplifying (21) to get a nonvariable common subterm on both sides and abstract it. In the case when $n_j(v, x_l, x_r, d)$ and $t_j(v, x_l, x_r)$ are not equal, if they can be simplified to subterms sharing a common nonvariable subterm, say α, a generalization of α can be attempted.[9]
    Suppose $n_j(v, x_l, x_r, d)$ simplifies to $n_j'(\cdots \alpha \cdots)$, and similarly, $t_j(v, x_l, x_r)$ simplifies to $t_j'(\cdots \alpha \cdots)$. The simplified conjecture (21) is:

$$m_j(f(x_l), t_j'(\cdots \alpha \cdots)) = T(f(x_l), n_j'(\cdots \alpha \cdots)). \tag{23}$$

If α is generalized to a variable, yielding

$$m_j(f(x_l), t_j'(\cdots z \cdots)) = T(f(x_l), n_j'(\cdots z \cdots)).$$

A proof of the generalized conjecture can be attempted. If the proof succeeds, the original conjecture is valid; otherwise, nothing can be said. These constraints along with other constraints on T are useful in speculating T.

Example 5. This example from [10] is challenging. Define a function tail_prod to compute:

$$\text{tail\_prod}(n, 1) = \prod_{i=1}^{n} i^{2^{i-2}}.$$

For $n = 0$, tail_prod$(n, 1)$ is assumed to return 0, and $i - j = 0$ if $i < j$. In addition, the following usual definitions of $*$ and x^y are assumed

$$\left[\begin{array}{l} x * 0 \to 0, \\ x * s(y) \to x + (x * y), \end{array} \right. \qquad \left[\begin{array}{l} x^0 \to s(0), \\ x^{s(y)} \to x * (x^y). \end{array} \right.$$

---

[9] It is also possible that $n_j(v, x_l, x_r, d)$ (respectively, $t_j(v, x_l, x_r)$) can be shown to be equivalent to a proper subterm of $t_j(v, x_l, x_r)$ (respectively, a proper subterm of $n_j(v, x_l, x_r, d)$). And, there are perhaps other possibilities as well which can arise after using known properties of functions appearing in (21).

A tail-recursive definition of tail_prod is:

$$\left[\begin{array}{l} \text{tail\_prod}(0, y) \to 0, \\ \text{tail\_prod}(\text{s}(0), y) \to y, \\ \text{tail\_prod}(\text{s}(\text{s}(x)), y) \to \text{tail\_prod}(\text{s}(x), \text{s}(\text{s}(x)) * (y * y)). \end{array}\right.$$

To verify that tail_prod computes the above product, it must be proved that

$$\text{prod}(n) = \text{tail\_prod}(n, \text{s}(0)),$$

where the function prod has the following definition:

$$\left[\begin{array}{l} \text{prod}(0) \to 0, \\ \text{prod}(\text{s}(0)) \to \text{s}(0), \\ \text{prod}(\text{s}(\text{s}(x))) \to \text{s}(\text{s}(x))^{2^x} * \text{prod}(\text{s}(x)), \end{array}\right.$$

In this case, $n_j(v, x_l, x_r, \text{d})$ is $\text{s}(\text{s}(x)) * \text{s}(0)^2$ and $t_j(v, x_l, x_r)$ is $\text{s}(\text{s}(x))^{2^x}$. It is easy to see that these two terms are not equal.

There is however a common subterm $\text{s}(\text{s}(x))$ on both sides: $\text{s}(\text{s}(x)) * \text{s}(0)^2$ (after simplification, it becomes $\text{s}(\text{s}(x))$) and $\text{s}(\text{s}(x))^{2^x}$. The subterm $\text{s}(\text{s}(x))$ can be generalized to y to give:

$$T(\text{prod}(\text{s}(x)), y) = y^{2^x} * \text{prod}(\text{s}(x)).$$

The rest of the proof goes through mechanically using the associativity and commutativity properties of $*$ and $1^x = 1$.   □

3.2   Procedure

The above methodology leads to the following procedure.

Input. Conjecture $g(x, \text{d}) = f(x)$ with functions f and g defined by (12) and (13), respectively.

Output. Intermediate conjecture(s), if any, and the answer, *yes, no,* or *don't know.*

Method.

1. Check the basis constraints $n_i(C_i, \text{d}) = m_i(C_i)$ for each $1 \le i \le \text{k}$. If any of them is not valid, then return *no* to the conjecture. Use it to generate a counter-example to the conjecture as well.

2. Check if the condition $n_j(v, x_l, x_r, \text{d}) = t_j(v, x_l, x_r)$ is valid. If so, then speculate T to be m_j and prove the property (15) assuming T is m_j. If the proof goes through, then return *yes.* Generate the needed intermediate lemmas. Otherwise, return *don't know.*

3. If the condition $n_j(v, x_l, x_r, \text{d}) = t_j(v, x_l, x_r)$ does not hold, then consider conjecture (23) for speculation. See whether T can be speculated to be m_j, especially if $n'_j(\cdots \alpha \cdots) = \alpha$. In that case, do as in Step 2. Otherwise, return *don't know.*

Example 6. To prove whether $\mathsf{rev}(x) = \mathsf{rev2a}(x, \mathsf{nil})$ with the following function definitions on lists:

$$\left[\begin{array}{l} \mathsf{rev}(\mathsf{nil}) \to \mathsf{nil}, \\ \mathsf{rev}(\mathsf{cons}(a, x)) \to \mathsf{app}(\mathsf{rev}(x), \mathsf{cons}(a, \mathsf{nil})), \end{array}\right.$$

and

$$\left[\begin{array}{l} \mathsf{rev2a}(\mathsf{nil}, y) \to y, \\ \mathsf{rev2a}(\mathsf{cons}(a, x), y) \to \mathsf{rev2a}(x, \mathsf{cons}(a, y)). \end{array}\right.$$

We have: $C_1 = \mathsf{nil}, C_2 = \mathsf{cons}(a, x), m_1(x) = x, m_2 = \mathsf{app}, t_2(a, x, y) = \mathsf{cons}(a, \mathsf{nil})$, $n_1(\mathsf{nil}, y) = y, n_2(a, x, y) = \mathsf{cons}(a, y)$.

The constraint in Theorem 2, $\mathsf{nil} = \mathsf{nil}$, is trivially valid. The condition in Theorem 4 corresponds to trivial conjecture $\mathsf{cons}(a, \mathsf{nil}) = \mathsf{cons}(a, \mathsf{nil})$. The constraint $\mathsf{app}(\mathsf{rev}(x), \mathsf{nil}) = \mathsf{rev2a}(x, \mathsf{nil})$ is the intermediate lemma. This lemma can be generalized to $\mathsf{app}(\mathsf{rev}(x), y) = \mathsf{rev2a}(x, y)$, which can be proved to be valid. Similarly, the property $\mathsf{app}(\mathsf{rev}(x), \mathsf{nil}) = \mathsf{rev}(x)$ can be proved to be valid.

Based on these, the original conjecture can be declared to be valid.   □

4   Definitions with More than One Recursive Calls

The approach proposed in the above section generalizes, i.e., definitions with more than one recursive calls can be handled as discussed below[10]:

$$\left[\begin{array}{l} \mathsf{f}(C_i) \to m_i(C_i), \ 1 \le i \le \mathsf{k}, \\ \mathsf{f}(C_j(v, x_l, x_r)) \to m_j(l_j(\mathsf{f}(x_l), v), r_j(\mathsf{f}(x_r), v)), \ \mathsf{k} + 1 \le j \le \mathsf{n}, \end{array}\right. \tag{24}$$

and

$$\left[\begin{array}{l} \mathsf{g}(C_i, y) \to n_i(C_i, y), \ 1 \le i \le \mathsf{k}, \\ \mathsf{g}(C_j(v, x_l, x_r), y) \to \mathsf{g}(x_l, \mathsf{g}(x_r, n_j(v, x_l, x_r, y))), \ \mathsf{k} + 1 \le j \le \mathsf{n}. \end{array}\right. \tag{25}$$

The above definition of g is given using an accumulator; notice also that it has nested recursion. (As before, to keep the presentation simple, f is assumed to have a single argument; in the case when f has more than one arguments, it is assumed that f recurses on the first argument, keeping the remaining arguments invariant; further, the accumulator in an accumulator-based definition always appears as the last argument of the function.) The objective is to check whether

$$\mathsf{g}(x, \mathsf{d}) = \mathsf{f}(x). \tag{26}$$

A straightforward proof of the above conjecture has the same problem of the inapplicability of the induction hypotheses.

---

[10] Theses definition schemes with multiple recursive calls are a representative; other definition schemes can be handled as well.

Example 7. The following definitions satisfy the above schema[11]:

$$\left[\begin{array}{l} \mathsf{count}(\mathsf{empty}) \to 0, \\ \mathsf{count}(\mathsf{mktree}(val, left, right)) \to \mathsf{count}(left) + (\mathsf{s}(0) + \mathsf{count}(right)), \end{array}\right. \tag{27}$$

$$\left[\begin{array}{l} \mathsf{tc}(\mathsf{empty}, y) \to y. \\ \mathsf{tc}(\mathsf{mktree}(val, left, right), y) \to \mathsf{tc}(left, \mathsf{tc}(right, \mathsf{s}(y))). \end{array}\right. \tag{28}$$

□

In the above example, $k = 1, n = 2, C_1 = \mathsf{empty}, C_2 = \mathsf{mktree}(val, left, right)$ and $m_1(C_1) = 0, n_1(C_1, y) = y, m_2(u, v) = u + v, l_2(u, v) = u, r_2(u, v) = \mathsf{s}(0) + u,$ $n_2(val, left, right, y) = \mathsf{s}(y)$. We wish to check whether $\mathsf{count}(tree) = \mathsf{tc}(tree, 0)$.[12]
As before, a transformation T is hypothesized such that

$$g(x, y) = T(f(x), y) \tag{29}$$

assuming

$$T(f(x), d) = f(x). \tag{30}$$

In a proof attempt of the conjecture (29) by induction, we get:

$$n_i(C_i, y) = T(f(C_i), y), \quad 1 \le i \le k, \tag{31}$$

and

$$T(f(x_l), T(f(x_r), n_j(v, x_l, x_r, y))) = T(f(C_j(v, x_l, x_r)), y), \quad k+1 \le j \le n. \tag{32}$$

When y is instantiated to d, we get: $n_i(C_i, d) = m_i(C_i), \ 1 \le i \le k$, and

$$T(f(x_l), T(f(x_r), n_j(v, x_l, x_r, d))) = m_j(l_j(f(x_l), v), r_j(f(x_r), v)), \quad k+1 \le j \le n. \tag{33}$$

Analogous to Theorem 2 earlier, we have:

Theorem 8. *Given recursive definition schema* f *and* g *as defined above, the conjecture* $g(x, d) = f(x)$ *is not valid if the constraints* $n_i(C_i, d) = m_i(C_i)$ *is not satisfied by* n_i, m_i, C_i, d *for any* $1 \le i \le k$.
If l_j is such that

$$l_j(f(x_l), v) = f(x_l), \tag{34}$$

there are at least two subcases, both leading to the speculation that $T = m_j$.

---

[11] If the right side of the second rule defining count below is expressed as $\mathsf{s}(\mathsf{count}(left) + \mathsf{count}(right))$, then our method gets stuck. In that case, the example can be nicely handled if our method is extended to use higher-order unification to search for T.

[12] Depending upon what is known about the properties of $+$, in the above definitions, there are many possible solutions for m_2, l_2, r_2 (which can be found using unification, narrowing and rewriting). We have discussed one solution; another possible solution is $m_2(u, v) = \mathsf{s}(u + v), l_2(u, v) = u, r_2(u, v) = u$.

Case 1: $r_j(f(x_r), v) = f(x_r)$ and $n_j(v, x_l, x_r, d) = d$.

Using (34) and the above constraints, (33) simplifies to:

$$T(f(x_l), f(x_r)) = m_j(f(x_l), f(x_r)).$$

Theorem 9. *Given recursive definition schema* f *and* g *as formulated above, if* l_j, r_j, n_j, d *are such that* $l_j(f(x_l), v) = f(x_l)$, $r_j(f(x_r), v) = f(x_r)$ *and* $n_j(v, x_l, x_r, d) = d$ *are valid for* $k + 1 \le j \le n$, *then the transformation function* T *is equivalent to* m_j *on the subset* $\{\langle f(x_l), f(x_r) \rangle\}$ *of the domain of* m_j.

The transformation function T can thus be speculated by using Theorem 9 (especially if f is onto). Note that if any of the above properties of l_j, r_j, n_j, d is not valid, that does not mean that the original conjecture is false.

Case 2: One of $r_j(f(x_r), v) = f(x_r)$ and $n_j(v, x_l, x_r, d) = d$ is not valid.

If it is assumed that

$$T(f(x_r), n_j(v, x_l, x_r, d)) = r_j(f(x_r), v),$$

then (33) simplifies to: $T(f(x_l), r_j(f(x_r), v)) = m_j(f(x_l), r_j(f(x_r), v)).$

Theorem 10. *Given recursive definition schema* f *and* g *as formulated above, if* $l_j(f(x_l), v) = f(x_l)$ *is valid for* $k + 1 \le j \le n$, *then under the condition* $m_j(f(x_r), n_j(v, x_l, x_r, d)) = r_j(f(x_r), v)$, *the transformation function* T *is equivalent to* m_j *on the subset* $\{\langle f(x_l), r_j(f(x_r), v) \rangle\}$ *of the domain of* m_j

The above conjecture can be generalized on the second argument, yielding:

$$T(f(x_l), z) = m_j(f(x_l), z).$$

In this case also, speculating T to be m_j seems plausible.

Assuming $T = m_j$, we have the following constraint on m_j:

$$m_j(f(x_r), n_j(v, x_l, x_r, d)) = r_j(f(x_r), v).$$

There are additional constraints on m_j.

Heuristics similar to the ones discussed for the one recursive call case can also be attempted; we do not discuss them here because of lack of space.

4.1   Procedure

As in the previous section, we give a procedure based on the above methodology.

Input. The conjecture $g(x, d) = f(x)$ with f and g defined by (24) and (25) respectively.
Output. Lemmas about helper functions, with *yes, no,* or *don't know.*

Method.
1. Check the basis constraints $n_i(C_i, d) = m_i(C_i)$, $1 \le i \le k$. If any of the constraints is not valid, then return *no*. Again, a disproof of a basis constraint can be used to generate a counter-example to the original conjecture.
2. Check if each of the conditions $l_j(f(x_l), v) = f(x_l)$, $r_j(f(x_r), v) = f(x_r)$ and $n_j(v, x_l, x_r, d) = d$ is valid. If so, then speculate T to be m_j, verify (31) and (32) in which T is replaced by m_j. If these constraints can be proved, then return *yes* to the conjecture. Otherwise, return *don't know*.
3. If any of $l_j(f(x_l), v) = f(x_l)$, $r_j(f(x_r), v) = f(x_r)$ and $n_j(v, x_l, x_r, d) = d$ does not hold, then check whether $l_j(f(x_l), v) = f(x_l)$ and $m_j(f(x_r), n_j(v, x_l, x_r, d)) = r_j(f(x_r), v)$. If each of these is valid, then again speculate T to be m_j, and do as in the previous step. Otherwise, return *don't know*.

Example 11 (Count).
    The goal is to decide $tc(x, 0) = count(x)$ with (27) and (28) as the function definitions. In this case, $d = 0$.
1. The basis constraint, $0 = 0$, is trivially true.
2. Condition $l_j(f(x_l), v) = f(x_l)$ corresponds to $count(left) = count(left)$, which is trivially valid.
3. Condition $r_j(f(x_r), v) = f(x_r)$ is not satisfied since $s(0) + count(x_r) \ne count(x_r)$. So T cannot be speculated to be $+$ based on Theorem 9.
4. $m_j(f(x_r), n_j(v, x_l, x_r, d)) = r_j(f(x_r), v)$ corresponds to $count(x_r) + s(0) = s(0) + count(x_r)$. This property of $+$ can be easily proved. Hence, T can be speculated to be $+$.
5. The property (30) corresponds to the lemma $count(x) + 0 = count(x)$, which immediately follows from the definition of $+$.
6. The basis case (31) becomes $y = 0 + y$, which can be easily proved. The induction step (32) becomes $count(left) + (count(right) + s(y)) = (count(left) + (s(0) + count(right))) + y$, which follows from the associativity and commutativity of $+$.
    The procedure returns *yes* which indicates that the original conjecture is true using properties of $+$ such as associativity and commutativity. The generalized intermediate lemma is $tc(tree, y) = count(tree) + y$.   □

5   Conclusion

A methodology for showing the equivalence of accumulator-based definitions (including tail-recursive definitions) to their recursive counter-parts is presented, based on developing generalizations guided by the properties of the helper functions in the definitions. By analyzing the structural properties of the definitions, it can be mechanically determined whether a given conjecture is valid or not. Sufficient conditions are identified on helper functions, which can be formulated as intermediate conjectures, such that if these properties are proved, then the original conjecture is valid. The proposed approach is particularly amenable to mechanization of proving properties of tail-recursive definitions. Proofs of such properties are automatically reduced to simpler conditions which are easier to establish.

The proposed methodology can also be helpful in debugging specifications (written in recursive style) and implementations (written in accumulator-based recursive style which can be translated to efficient implementations). Counter-examples can be generated from necessary conditions on helper functions which must be satisfied for the implementation to meet the corresponding specification.

The proposed approach for automatically generating intermediate lemmas is useful in proving properties of an accumulator-based implementation. Since accumulator-based definitions are related to loops, the proposed approach may aid automatic generation of loop invariants as well.

Searching for functions which satisfy the constraints on the transformation T identified by the proposed methodology was done using rewriting in this paper. One possible way to make it more systematic is to use higher-order unification incorporating the semantics of helper functions used in definitions. This direction is worth exploring. Another direction for further research is identifying a collection of heuristics and case analyses that can lead to more intelligent speculation about the transformation T. The implementation of the proposed approach will enable more experimentation to test their effectiveness.

In the paper, we have considered simple conjectures relating an accumulator-based function definition to an arbitrary recursive definition. It appears that the proposed approach also works for more general conjectures involving accumulator-based function definitions, e.g., $\mathsf{rev2a}(x, \mathsf{rev2a}(x, \mathsf{nil})) = x$. This is worth investigating.

The proposed approach is quite sensitive to the way definitions of helper functions are formulated. For instance, if definitions of $+, *$, etc, are given by recursing on the first argument instead of the second argument (or definitions of $\mathsf{fact}, \mathsf{tr\_fact}, \mathsf{wsum}, \mathsf{wsigma}$ are given slightly differently), the procedure can get stuck unless properties of $+, *$ such as associativity and commutativity are assumed. This relationship between the structure of definitions and properties of helper functions needs further analysis.

References

1. R. Aubin. Mechanizing structural induction II: Strategies. *Theoretical Computer Science*, 9:347–361, 1979.
2. A. Bundy. The Automation of Proof by Mathematical Induction. A. Robinson and A. Voronkov (eds.), *Handbook of Automated Reasoning, Vol. 1*, pp. 845–911, 2001.
3. R. S. Boyer and J. Moore. A Computational Logic. *Academic Press*, 1979.
4. J. Castaing. How to facilitate the proof of theorems by using the induction-matching and by generalization. *Proceedings of the Ninth International Joint Conference on Artificial Intelligence*, pages 1208–1213, 1985.
5. J. Giesl. Context-Moving Transformations for Function Verification. *Proceedings of the Ninth International Workshop on Logic-based Program Synthesis and Transformation (LOPSTR '99)*, LNCS 1817, pages 293–312, 2000.
6. A. Ireland and A. Bundy. Automatic Verification of Functions with Accumulating Parameters. *Journal of Functional Programming*, 9(2):225–245, 1999.
7. D. Kapur and H. Zhang. An Overview of Rewrite Rule Laboratory (*RRL*). *Journal of Computer and Mathematics with Applications*, 29:91–114, 1995.

8. D. Kapur and M. Subramaniam. Lemma Discovery in Automating Induction. *Proc. CADE-13*, LNAI 1104, pages 538–552, 1996.

9. W.D. Klinger. Proper Tail Recursion and Space Efficiency. *Proc. ACM Programming Language Design and Implementation*, 1998.

10. S. Vadera. Generalization for Induction Mechanizing. *Technical Report UMCS-93-6-8*, 1993.

11. C. Walther. Mathematical Induction. D. M. Gabbay, C. J. Hogger, and J. A. Robinson (eds.), *Handbook of Logic in Artificial Intelligence and Logic Programming, Vol. 2*, Oxford University Press, 1994.

12. H. Zhang, D. Kapur, and M. S. Krishnamoorthy. A Mechanizable Induction Principle for Equational Specifications. *Proc. CADE-9*, LNCS 310, pages 162–181, 1988.

Embedding of Systems of Affine Recurrence Equations in Coq

David Cachera and David Pichardie

IRISA / ENS Cachan (Bretagne)
IRISA, Campus de Beaulieu
F-35042 Rennes, France
{david.cachera,david.pichardie}@irisa.fr

Abstract. Systems of affine recurrence equations (SAREs) over polyhedral domains are widely used to model computation-intensive algorithms and to derive parallel code or hardware implementations. The development of complex SAREs for real-sized applications calls for the elaboration of formal verification techniques. As the systems we consider are generic, *i.e.,* depend on parameters whose value are not statically known, we considered using theorem provers, and have implemented a translation from SAREs into the Coq system. We take advantage of the regularity of our model to automatically generate an inductive type adapted to each particular system. This allows us to automatically prove that the functional translation of equations respects the wanted fixpoint properties, and to systematically derive mutual induction schemes.

1   Introduction

Systems of recurrence equations [10] provide a foundation for designing parallel multidimensional arrays for computation intensive applications. The polyhedral model uses an extension of the formalism of recurrence equations, specifically that of Systems of Affine Recurrence Equations (SAREs) over *polyhedral domains*. The ALPHA language [17] and the MMALPHA environment [16] provide the syntax and tools to handle such recurrence equations. The MMALPHA environment implements polyhedral transformations that allow one to refine a high level specification into a synthesizable architectural description. It also enables the derivation of imperative loop nest code.

Most of the transformations implemented in MMALPHA are rewritings that preserve the semantics, thus ensuring an equivalence between the original specification and the final code. Nevertheless, there are cases where we need to formally prove certain properties that are not ensured by the refinement process. For instance, the user is allowed to introduce hand-tuned optimizations during an intermediate refinement step, and we will have to check functional equivalence between the newly introduced fragment and the previous stage. Moreover, some properties we want to prove are not expressible in the formalism of SAREs. More generally, the development of more complex systems for real sized applications calls for the elaboration of verification tools. In particular, we have to be able to perform proof by induction following complex induction schemes.

D. Basin and B. Wolff (Eds.): TPHOLs 2003, LNCS 2758, pp. 155–170, 2003.
© Springer-Verlag Berlin Heidelberg 2003

The systems we consider are generic, *i.e.*, they depend on parameters whose value is not statically known. The proof assistant Coq provides higher-order logic and abstraction that are well-suited for our purposes. On the other hand, this kind of general-purpose theorem proving tool suffer from a lack of automation. User-defined tactics may partially overcome this problem, by automatizing proof steps which share a common structure.

The major contribution in this work lies in the fact that we make use of the specific features of the polyhedral model to generate a translation from recurrences equations to Coq.

- We first generate an intermediate functional translation of recurrence equation. Due to its type-theoretical nature, this function has to carry a proof of its termination.
- We automatically derive from this translation a simpler function, by just keeping the computational part that reflects the initial equations. To that purpose, we make use of a schedule of the system of equations given by the MMALPHA environment. This allows us to derive theorems that express system variables as solutions of fixpoint equations. These theorems will be the base for further proofs.
- At the same time, we automatically generate an induction principle that is specific to the considered system. Any inductive property about this system can thus be proved by instantiating this induction scheme. This strategy automatizes the most technical part of the proof (complex mutual recursions) and relies on the user only for some properties the prover cannot deal with (for instance, arithmetic properties that are not in a decidable fragment).
- We provide additional tactics that automate the use of fixpoint theorems by simplifying rewritings during the proof process.

The paper is organized as follows. Sections 2 present the polyhedral model. We show in section 3 how we translate SAREs into Coq, and in section 4 how we generate specific induction schemes and proof tactics. Section 5 gives two simple application examples. Section 6 is devoted to related work, and we conclude in section 7.

2   The Polyhedral Model

We now present the basic definitions of systems of recurrence equations and some related notions. In the following, we denote by $\mathbb{N}$, $\mathbb{Z}$, $\mathbb{Q}$ and $\mathbb{R}$ the sets of, respectively, natural numbers, integers, rational and real numbers.

2.1   Polyhedral Domains and Recurrence Equations

Definition 1 (Polyhedral Domain). *An n-dimensional polyhedron is a subset $\mathcal{P}$ of $\mathbb{Q}^n$ bounded by a finite number of hyperplanes. We call* polyhedral domain *(or, for short,* domain*) a subset $\mathcal{D}$ of $\mathbb{Z}^n$ defined by*

$$\mathcal{D} = \mathbb{Z}^n \cap \mathcal{P}$$

where $\mathcal{P}$ is a finite union of n-dimensional polyhedra. A domain can be seen as a set of points, which will be called its indices.

Definition 2 (Variable). *An n-dimensional variable X is a function from a domain of $\mathbb{Z}^n$ into a base set (booleans, integers or reals). An* instance *of the variable X is a restriction of X to a single point z of its domain, and is denoted by $X[z]$. Constants are associated to the trivial domain $\mathbb{Z}^0$.*

Definition 3 (Recurrence Equations). *A Recurrence Equation defining a function (variable) X at all points, z, in a domain, $\mathcal{D}_X$, is an equation of the form*

$$X = \mathcal{D}_X : g(\ldots, X.d, \ldots)$$

where

- *X is an n-dimensional variable;*
- *d is a dependency function, $d : \mathbb{Z}^n \to \mathbb{Z}^n$; the value of expression $X.d$ at index i is the value of variable X at index $d(i)$;*
- *g is a strict, single-valued function; it is often written implicitly as an expression involving operands of the form $X.d$ combined with basic operators and parentheses;*
- *$\mathcal{D}_X$ is a polyhedral domain of $\mathbb{Z}^n$ and is called the domain of the equation.*

A variable may be defined by more than one equation. In this case, we use the syntax shown below:

$$X = \begin{cases} \text{case} \\ \quad \mathcal{D}_{X_1} : g_1(\ldots X.d_{i_1} \ldots) \\ \quad \vdots \\ \quad \mathcal{D}_{X_l} : g_l(\ldots X.d_{i_l} \ldots) \end{cases} \tag{1}$$

Each line is called a branch, *and the domain of X is the union of the (disjoint) domains of all the branches, $\mathcal{D}_X = \bigcup_i \mathcal{D}_{X_i}$. We also say that the dependency function, d_i holds over the (sub) domain $\mathcal{D}_{X_i}$.*

Definition 4. *A recurrence equation as defined above, is called an* Affine Recurrence Equation (ARE) *if every dependence function is of the form, $d(z) = Az + a$, where A is an integer $n \times n$ matrix and a is an integer n-vector.*

Definition 5. *A* system *of recurrence equations is a set of m such equations, defining the data variables $X_1 \ldots X_m$. Each variable, X_i is of dimension n_i, and since the equations may now be mutually recursive, the dependence functions f must now have the appropriate type.*

2.2   Dependence Graphs and Schedules

Definition 6 (Dependence Graph). *We say that an instance $X[z]$ of a variable X depends on an instance $Y[z']$ of a variable Y if there exists an equation of the form $X = g(\ldots, Y.d, \ldots)$ with $z' = d(z)$. We denote by $X[z] \to Y[z']$ this fact.*

We call dependence graph *the graph whose vertices are the variable instances, and where there is an edge between vertices x and y iff $x \to y$.*

In order to get a valid implementation from a set of recurrence equations, we need (among other things) to determine a particular order in which computations should take place. The definitions above do not specify such an order, and do not even guarantee that it may exist.

Definition 7. *A* schedule t_X *is a function such that $t_X(z)$ specifies the time instant at which $X[z]$ is computed. Typically, the range of t_X is $\mathbb{N}$, but any total order is allowed (for example $\mathbb{N}^k$ under the lexicographic order). In the following, we restrict ourselves to one-dimensional schedules. A schedule is said to be* valid *if for any instances $X[z]$ and $Y[z']$,*

$$X[z] \to Y[z'] \implies t_X(z) > t_Y(z')$$

A set of recurrence equations is said to be schedulable *if such a valid schedule exists. The problem of determining if a SARE is schedulable is undecidable in the general case [14], but much work has been devoted to develop heuristics to find schedules in specific cases.*

2.3   The ALPHA Language and the MMALPHA Environment

The combination of polyhedral domains and affine dependence functions is the basis of the so-called *polyhedral model*. This model has a rich set of formal correctness preserving transformations. The ALPHA language, originally developed for the design of regular (systolic) arrays, provides a syntax to define and manipulate SAREs. We give here an example of an ALPHA program to get an insight on this syntax (see [17] for more details). The program displayed in Figure 1 implements an auto adaptive filter [11] used in signal processing for noise cancellation or system identification. It takes an input signal x and a reference input d and updates its convolution coefficients so as the output signal res will converge towards the reference input.

In this example, expressions such as {n | N<=n<=M} denote domains, N, M, D are parameters (respectively representing the number of weights of the filter, the number of inputs and the delay), x and d are the input variables, res is the output variable and W, Y, E are local variables. Note that a program may have several output variables.

This program is written in *array notation*: for syntactic convenience, instead of writing equations like W=...W.(n,i->n-1,i)... where (n,i->n-1,i) denotes the dependence function $(n, i) \mapsto (n-1, i)$, we use the following notation:

```
system DLMS : {N,M,D | 3<=N<=(D-1,M-D-1)}
              (x : {n | 1<=n<=M} of integer;
               d : {n | N<=n<=M} of integer)
      returns (res : {n | N<=n<=M} of integer);
var
  W : {n,i | N<=n<=M; 0<=i<=N-1} of integer;
  Y : {n,i | N<=n<=M; -1<=i<=N-1} of integer;
  E : {n | N<=n<=M} of integer;
let
  W[n,i] =
      case
        { | n<=N+D-1} : 0[];
        { | N+D<=n} : W[n-1,i] + (E[n-D] * x[n-i-D]);
      esac;
  Y[n,i] =
      case
        { | i=-1} : 0[];
        { | 0<=i} : Y[n,i-1] + (W[n,i] * x[n-i]);
      esac;
  E[n] = (d[n] - res[n]);
  res[n] = Y[n,N-1];
tel;
```

Fig. 1. DLMS ALPHA system

$W[n,i]=...W[n-1,i]...$. As a consequence, constants like 0 are followed by square brackets to indicate that they can be expanded from their initial domain $\mathbb{Z}^0$ to any multidimensional domain. Moreover, as in array notation indices are given a name in the lhs of equations, names indices do not appear any more in domain definition of case branches, hence the notation (for instance) $\{|N+D<=n\}$ instead of $\{n,i|N+D<=n\}$.

The MMALPHA environment [16] implements a number of manipulations on ALPHA programs. The environment provides a set of predefined commands and functions to namely achieve the following purposes.

- Static analysis of programs, including analysis of polyhedral domains' shapes and sizes.
- Simulation, architectural description and VHDL generation.
- Transformations of ALPHA programs, based on polyhedra manipulations and including pipelining of variables, scheduling, change of basis, etc.

3   Translation of SAREs into Coq

To prove properties about a SARE, we first must translate it into the Coq system. We benefit from the equational nature of the underlying model to directly translate the constructs of our language into the formalism of Coq, instead of writing down a formalization of its semantics.

Each variable of a SARE is a partial function defined on a polyhedral domain. There are many ways of translating them to Coq. These methods reflect the semantics in a more or less precise manner. We follow an approach in two steps:

- Variables are first defined as mutually recursive functions. As we deal with a constructive logic, in addition to their indices, variables need an argument representing a proof that these indices are "accessible". This fact is explained below.
- The only information the user needs in a proof process is the set of equalities defining the system. We thus have to show that the variables previously defined are indeed a fixpoint for these equations. We will use a schedule to prove this fact by induction on time.

These steps are detailed in the next subsections.

3.1 Domains

Let us consider a variable X of domain $\mathcal{D}_X$, and of dimension n. This domain is simply represented by a predicate over $\mathbb{Z}^n$, holding a conjunction of affine constraints on domain indices. This results in the following type.

$$\mathrm{Dom}_X : \overbrace{\mathtt{Z} \texttt{ -> } \ldots \texttt{ -> } \mathtt{Z}}^{n \text{ times}} \texttt{ -> Prop}$$

3.2 Mutually Recursive Functions

Let us consider a SARE defined as follows, where each variable X_j is defined on a domain of dimension n_j and has a number l_j of case branches.

$$
X_1 = \begin{cases}
\text{case} \\
\qquad \vdots \\
\qquad \mathcal{D}_{X_{1,i}} : g_{1,i}(\ldots X_j.d_{1,i,j} \ldots) \\
\qquad \vdots
\end{cases}
$$

$$
X_p = \begin{cases}
\text{case} \\
\qquad \vdots \\
\qquad \mathcal{D}_{X_{p,i}} : g_{p,i}(\ldots X_j.d_{p,i,j} \ldots) \\
\qquad \vdots
\end{cases}
$$

We want to define these variables as mutually recursive functions. As we are in a type-theoretic framework, we must have a structurally decreasing argument in the definition of recursive functions. A well-known technique to address this point is to use an accessibility predicate [5]. The standard technique is to use a well-founded recursion principle derived from the accessibility predicate. We

Inductive $\text{Acc}_{X_1} : \text{Z} \rightarrow \cdots \rightarrow \text{Z} \rightarrow \text{Set} :=$
$\quad\quad | \;\text{Acc}_{X_{1,1}} : (i_1, \ldots, i_{n_1} : \text{Z})(\text{Dom}_{X_1} i_1 \ldots i_{n_1}) \rightarrow$
$\quad\quad\quad\quad\quad\quad\quad < \mathcal{D}_{X_{1,1}} > \rightarrow (\text{Acc}_{X_1} i_1 \ldots i_{n_1})$
$\quad\quad$/* case branch without dependencies */
$\quad\quad\quad\quad\vdots$
$\quad\quad | \;\text{Acc}_{X_{1,l_1}} : (i_1, \ldots, i_{n_1} : \text{Z})(\text{Dom}_{X_1} i_1 \ldots i_{n_1}) \rightarrow < \mathcal{D}_{X_{1,l_1}} > \rightarrow$
$\quad\quad\quad\quad\quad \cdots \rightarrow (\text{Acc}_{X_j} (d_{1,l_1,j} \; i_1 \ldots i_{n_1})) \rightarrow \cdots \rightarrow (\text{Acc}_{X_1} i_1 \ldots i_{n_1})$
$\quad\quad$/* case branch where X_1 depends on some variables X_j*/
$\quad\quad\quad\quad\vdots$
with $\text{Acc}_{X_p} : \text{Z} \rightarrow \cdots \rightarrow \text{Z} \rightarrow \text{Set} :=$
$\quad\quad\quad\quad\vdots$
$\quad\quad | \;\text{Acc}_{X_{p,i}} : (i_1, \ldots, i_{n_p} : \text{Z})(\text{Dom}_{X_p} i_1 \ldots i_{n_p}) \rightarrow < \mathcal{D}_{X_{p,i}} > \rightarrow$
$\quad\quad\quad\quad\quad \cdots \rightarrow (\text{Acc}_{X_j} (d_{p,i,j} \; i_1 \ldots i_{n_p})) \rightarrow \cdots \rightarrow (\text{Acc}_{X_p} i_1 \ldots i_{n_p})$
$\quad\quad\quad\quad\vdots$

Fig. 2. Accessibility predicate in Coq-like notation

follow Bove's more specific approach which defines a special-purpose accessibility predicate for each function: in addition to its indices, each variable carries an argument stating that these indices are accessible. In this particular case, accessibility is defined by means of the dependencies between variable instances, the base case being that of input variables whose indices are trivially accessible on their whole domain. This accessibility argument is structurally decreasing: if an instance $X[z]$ depends on an instance $Y[z']$ then the accessibility argument of $Y[z']$ is a subterm of that of $X[z]$.

We begin with the definition of an accessibility inductive type, simultaneously defined for all variables. This inductive type is displayed on Figure 2. In this inductive type definition, there is one type constructor for each branch in the definition of each variable: constructor $\text{Acc}_{X_{j,i}}$ is used for the ith branch of the jth variable. Moreover, $< \mathcal{D}_{X_{j,i}} >$ denotes the set of affine constraints involved by domain $\mathcal{D}_{X_{j,i}}$.

Using this accessibility type, we now can define the variables as mutual fixpoints. The definition uses a filtering on an accessibility "witness", that is, a term expressing the fact that the considered indices are indeed accessible (cf. Figure 3).

3.3   Using a Particular Schedule

As such, variables are already defined as a fixpoint of the equations. But using this specification in a proof process presents the major drawback of handling this accessibility term in any proof step. To simplify the proof procedure, we aim at suppressing this argument. We rely on a particularity of the polyhedral model to do this. In the following, we use a schedule of the system to make a recurrence on a variable representing time. As a consequence, our technique only applies

```
Fixpoint X₁_f : [i₁,...,in₁ : Z][acc : (AccX₁ i₁ ... in₁)] : Z :=
    Cases acc of
    | (AccX₁,₁ i₁ ... in₁ _ _) ⇒ g₁,₁
      ⋮
    | (AccX₁,l₁ i₁ ... in₁ _ _ ... depⱼ ...) ⇒ (g₁,l₁ ... (X₁_f (d₁,l₁,j i₁ ... in₁) depⱼ)...)
with X₂_f : ...
```

Fig. 3. Definition of a SARE as a mutual fixpoint

to schedulable systems. In practice, this restriction does not matter since only schedulable systems can be implemented.

Given a particular schedule, we will prove that for any variable X_j and for any indices $i_1, \ldots, i_{n_j}$, we have the following implication[1].

$$(\mathtt{Dom}_{X_j}\ i_1 \ldots i_{n_j}) \Rightarrow (\mathtt{Acc}_{X_j}\ i_1 \ldots i_{n_j})$$

The particular schedule we work with is given by MMALPHA scheduling heuristics, and is expressed as a function $\mathbb{Z}^{n_j} \to \mathbb{Z}$, denoted by $t_{X_j}[i_1, \ldots, i_{n_j}]$

The proof proceeds in two steps.

- We first prove by induction (in $\mathbb{Z}_+$) the following theorem

Theorem 1 (Accessibility w.r.t. time).

$$\forall t \geq 0\, (\forall (i_1 \ldots i_{n_1}) \in \mathcal{D}_{X_1}, \text{if } t = t_{X_1}[i_1, \ldots, i_{n_1}] \text{ then } (\mathtt{Acc}_{X_1}\ i_1 \ldots i_{n_1}))$$
$$\vdots$$
$$\wedge\, (\forall (i_1 \ldots i_{n_p}) \in \mathcal{D}_{X_p}, \text{if } t = t_{X_p}[i_1, \ldots, i_{n_p}] \text{ then } (\mathtt{Acc}_{X_1}\ i_1 \ldots i_{n_p}))$$

The proof is automatically generated by constructing a term of the corresponding type. It uses a number of intermediate lemmas stating the validity of the considered schedule w.r.t. dependencies.
- We then eliminate time in the preceding theorem, and get for each variable, a lemma stating the desired result.

We now have proved that any index in the domain of a variable is "accessible".

3.4   Proof Irrelevance

To be able to get rid of the accessibility term in the variable definition, we now must prove that the value of a variable instance does not depend on the way its indices are accessible. More precisely, we prove the following property: for any variable X_j and for any H_1 and H_2 of type $(\mathtt{Acc}_{X_j}\ i_1 \ldots i_{n_j})$ we have

$$(X_j\_f\ i_1 \ldots i_{n_j}\ H_1) = (X_j\_f\ i_1 \ldots i_{n_j}\ H_2)$$

Once more, the proof is automatically generated. It makes use of the inductive type of Section 3.2, under the form of an induction principle that is systematically generated by Coq for each inductive type.

---

[1] More precisely, we construct a term of type $(\mathtt{Acc}_{X_j}\ i_1 \ldots i_{n_j})$ under the hypothesis that $(\ i_1 \ldots i_{n_j})$ is in $\mathcal{D}_{X_j}$.

3.5   Undefined Values

The properties we have established so far allow us to handle indices that are in the domain of a variable: for these indices, we now are in position to define the corresponding variable value. For indices that are out of the considered domain, we assume the existence of a particular undefined value which will be denoted by $\perp^2$.

The "final" definition of variables is thus given by

$$(\mathtt{X}_j \ i_1 \ldots i_{n_j}) = \mathit{if} \ (i_1, \ldots, i_{n_j}) \ \in \mathcal{D}_{X_j} \ \mathit{then} \ (\mathtt{X}_j\_\mathtt{f} \ i_1 \ldots i_{n_j} \ acc) \ \mathit{else} \ \perp$$

where acc is a "proof" that $(i_1, \ldots, i_{n_j})$ is an accessible index vector knowing that (i) it is in the domain of X_j and (ii) any index in this domain is accessible.

3.6   Fixpoint Properties Extraction

We finally have to gather all preceding definitions and theorems to state the fact that a given variable is indeed a fixpoint for its defining equation. This results in a theorem that has exactly the same aspect as the initial recurrence equation.

To sum up the whole process, all the user has to do is to write the initial SARE, and provide a schedule (which is in most cases computed by the MMALPHA environment). All theorems mentioned above are then automatically generated and proved.

4   Verification Strategies

Once the system is translated, the user writes down a set of properties he wants to check. During the translation of the system, we create tactics which will facilitate the proofs of these properties and, in the best cases, automate them.

4.1   Using Fixpoint Properties

When proving a specification for an ALPHA program, the user has to replace variable instances $X[z]$ by their definitions. This is made possible by the previous fixpoint properties theorems, but the use of these theorems is a bit technical: you first have to prove that z is in the domain of X and then, if X is defined with a case expression, explore each branch of this expression. We generate three tactics to automate this work.

1. The translation program first defines a tactic which looks in the current assumptions for two affine constraints corresponding to two different branches of a case expression. If the search succeeds, a lemma about branches disjointness can end up the current goal.

---

[2] More precisely, we define a particular value for each base type: $\perp$ for boolean values will be named boolnone, etc.

2. To prove that an affine constraint is ensured, it may be useful to unfold all domain predicates in the current goal and in the assumptions. The tactic `UnfoldAllDom` makes this work. This is not done before to improve the readability during the interactive proof.
3. Although these two tactics may be called by the user, they are often indirectly called by the third tactic `RewriteX` which, for a given variable X, replaces the first instance $X[z]$ in the current goal by its definition, automatically proves that z is in the domain of X, and rejects all `case` branches which are not compatible with the current assumptions (*in fine*, this instance has been replaced only by the subexpression found in the corresponding branch).

These tactics are written in the tactic langage $\mathcal{L}_{tac}$ of Coq [7]. As constraints are *ground Presburger formulae* [8], solving them reduces to a decidable problem wich is handled by the Coq tactic `Omega`.

4.2   Induction Principle Associated to a System

Many proofs about SAREs are done by induction, due to the obvious recursive structure of such systems. In the general case, the induction principle for a given SARE relies on a quite intricate well-founded order. We directly make use of the accessibility inductive type of Section 3.2 to generate an induction scheme that exactly maps the structure of the differents proofs we may have to do on the system. When defining an inductive type in Coq, an induction principle is systematically associated to it. In our case, we simultaneously defined an inductive accessibility type for all variables. This definition yields one induction scheme for each variable. We collect together all these schemes in a general induction scheme for the whole system by using the Coq `Scheme` feature [15]. In this generated induction principle, accessibility predicates appear as arguments just like in the initial mutually recursive variable definition of Section 3.2. We finally eliminate these accessibility arguments to get a more tractable induction scheme. The final induction scheme has the general form displayed in Figure 4.

$$(\mathsf{P}_{X_1} : (\mathsf{Z}^{n_1} \to \mathsf{Prop}) \ \ldots \ \mathsf{P}_{X_p} : (\mathsf{Z}^{n_p} \to \mathsf{Prop}))$$
$$((i_1, \ldots, i_{n_1} : \mathsf{Z})(\mathsf{Dom}_{X_1} \ i_1 \ldots i_{n_1}) \ \to \ <\mathcal{D}_{X_{1,1}}> \ \to \ (\mathsf{P}_{X_1} \ i_1 \ldots i_{n_1}))$$
$$\cdots$$
$$\to ((i_1, \ldots, i_{n_1} : \mathsf{Z})(\mathsf{Dom}_{X_1} \ i_1 \ldots i_{n_1}) \ \to \ <\mathcal{D}_{X_{1,l_1}}> \ \to$$
$$\cdots \ (\mathsf{P}_{X_j} \ (d_{1,l_1,j} \ i_1 \ldots i_{n_1})) \cdots \ \to \ (\mathsf{P}_{X_1} \ i_1 \ldots i_{n_1}))$$
$$\vdots$$
$$\to ((i_1, \ldots, i_{n_p} : \mathsf{Z})(\mathsf{Dom}_{X_p} \ i_1 \ldots i_{n_p}) \ \to \ <\mathcal{D}_{X_{p,1}}> \ \to \ (\mathsf{P}_{X_p} \ i_1 \ldots i_{n_p}))$$
$$\cdots$$
$$\to ((i_1, \ldots, i_{n_p} : \mathsf{Z})(\mathsf{Dom}_{X_p} \ i_1 \ldots i_{n_p}) \ \to \ <\mathcal{D}_{X_{p,l_p}}> \ \to$$
$$\cdots \ (\mathsf{P}_{X_j} \ (d_{p,l_p,j} \ i_1 \ldots i_{n_p})) \cdots \ \to \ (\mathsf{P}_{X_p} \ i_1 \ldots i_{n_p}))$$
$$\to ((i_1, \ldots, i_{n_k} : \mathsf{Z})(\mathsf{Dom}_{X_k} \ i_1 \ldots i_{n_k}) \ \to \ (\mathsf{P}_{X_k} \ i_1 \ldots i_{n_k}))$$

Fig. 4. Generated induction scheme for variable X_k

```
(P_W,P_Y:(Z->Z->Prop); P_E,P_res,P_x,P_d:(Z->Prop))
      ((n,i:Z)(Dom_W n i)->'(-1)+[D]-n+[N] >= 0'->(P_W n i))
      ->((n,i:Z)(Dom_W n i) ->'(-[D])+n-[N] >= 0'->
            (P_W '(-1)+n' i)->(P_E '(-[D])+n')->(P_x '(-[D])-i+n')->
              (P_W n i))
      ->((n,i:Z)(Dom_Y n i)->'1+i = 0'->(P_Y n i))
      ->((n,i:Z)(Dom_Y n i)->'i >= 0'->
            (P_Y n '(-1)+i')->(P_W n i)->(P_x '(-i)+n')->(P_Y n i))
      ->((n:Z)(Dom_E n)->(P_d n)->(P_res n)->(P_E n))
      ->((n:Z)(Dom_res n)->(P_Y n '(-1)+[N]')->(P_res n))
      ->((n:Z)(Dom_x n)->(P_x n))
      ->((n:Z)(Dom_d n)->(P_d n))
      ->(n:Z)(Dom_res n)->(P_res n)
```

Fig. 5. Generated induction scheme for the DLMS filter

The particular case for the DLMS example of Section 2 is displayed in Figure 5

This scheme associates one property to each polyhedral domain, and can be seen as a "generalized invariant rule": instead of dealing with one invariant for a single loop, we have to manipulate multiple mutually dependent invariants, and the structure of the induction principle reflects the structure of the program's dependencies. In other words, the induction principle captures the "static" part of the semantics (the dependence scheme) while the invariant instantiations reflect the "dynamic" part (value computations between variable instances).

From a practical point of view, all the user has to do is to provide these invariants by instantiating each domain property.

5 Example

5.1 Binary Product

The program displayed in Figure 6 computes the binary product of two arrays A and B of W bits. Output variable X is an array of W bits corresponding to the W most significant bits of the product. We proved with Coq this functional specification. We detail here the successive verification steps.

1. First of all, we developed a Coq module handling conversions between bit vectors (represented by functions of type Z->bool) and integers. The main functions of this module are

$$\texttt{bool2Z : bool -> Z}$$

which converts one bit into an integer, and

$$\texttt{bin2Z : (Z->bool) -> Z -> Z}$$

which, given a function f of type Z->bool and a positive integer k, computes the integer n represented by the $k+1$ bits (f 0), . . . , (f k): $n = \sum_{i=0}^{k} 2^i \cdot (\text{f } i)$.

```
system Times : {W | 2<=W}
                (A : {b | 0<=b<=W-1} of boolean;
                 B : {b | 0<=b<=W-1} of boolean)
        returns (X : {b | 0<=b<=W-1} of boolean);
var
  P : {b,m | 0<=b<=W-1; 0<=m<=W-1} of boolean;
  Si : {b,m | 0<=b<=W-1; 0<=m<=W-1} of boolean;
  So : {b,m | 0<=b<=W; 0<=m<=W-1} of boolean;
  Cin : {b,m | 0<=b<=W-1; 0<=m<=W-1} of boolean;
  XF : {b,m | 0<=b<=W-1; 0<=m<=W-1} of boolean;
  CoutF : {b,m | 0<=b<=W-1; 0<=m<=W-1} of boolean;
let
  P[b,m] = A[b] and B[m];
  Cin[b,m] =
      case
        { | b=0; 0<=m<=W-1} : False[];
        { | 1<=b<=W; 0<=m<=W-1} : CoutF[b-1,m];
      esac;
  XF[b,m] = Si xor P xor Cin;
  CoutF[b,m] = Si and P or Si and Cin or P and Cin;
  So[b,m] =
      case
        { | 0<=b<=W-1; 0<=m<=W-1} : XF;
        { | b=W; 0<=m<=W-1} : CoutF[W-1,m];
      esac;
  Si[b,m] =
      case
        { | m=0} : False[];
        { | 0<=b<=W-1; 1<=m<=W} : So[b+1,m-1];
      esac;
  X[b] = So[b+1,W-1];
tel;
```

Fig. 6. ALPHA system computing binary product

2. The system is loaded in MMALPHA. The following schedule is proposed:

$$t_X[b] = 1 + 2b + 5W \qquad t_P[b,m] = 1$$
$$t_{Si}[b,m] = 1 + 2b + 5m \qquad t_{So}[b,m] = 3 + 2b + 5m$$
$$t_{Cin}[b,m] = 1 + 2b + 5m \qquad t_{XF}[b,m] = 2 + 2b + 5m$$
$$t_{CoutF}[b,m] = 2 + 2b + 5m$$

3. The translation function is called on the system and the corresponding Coq file Times.v is generated.

4. At the end of the generated Coq file we add the following theorem:

Theorem X_mult :
  '(bin2Z X (W-1))=((bin2Z A (W-1))*(bin2Z B (W-1)))/(two_p W)'.

where (two_p W) represents 2^W.

5. We introduce a number of intermediate lemmas about local variables. Some of these lemmas deal with non trivial mathematical results on euclidean division. The generated tactics allow us to focus only on the "conceptual" parts of the proof. In particular the tactics handling variable rewritings and case branches exploration save a considerable amount of tedious work. In this particular example, we didn't make use of the induction scheme, since the involved dependencies are quite simple, and most of the work is dedicated to conversions from bit vectors to integers.

The corresponding Coq file is available at [1].

5.2 DLMS

To illustrate the use of the induction principle associated to an ALPHA system, we show here how we prove a simple property of the DLMS system which requires multiple mutual induction. The theorem we want to prove is the following

Theorem 2. $(\forall n \in \mathcal{D}_d,\ (\mathtt{d}\ n) = 0) \Rightarrow (\forall n \in \mathcal{D}_{\text{res}},\ (\mathtt{res}\ n) = 0)$

According to the dependencies of the DLMS system, the proof of this theorem requires an additional lemma expressing the fact that "all instances of Y are equal to zero". But this lemma requires "all instances of X are equal to zero" to be proved, which in turn depends on "all instance of E are equal to zero". This last property itself depends on the nullity of the instances of res. This cycle in the proof process shows the technical difficulties of reasoning about mutual recursive functions.

Thanks to the induction principle generated and proved during the translation process, all these lemmas and the final theorem can be proved together. We just have to apply the induction principle with the relevant properties. This results in the following Coq proof command:

```
Apply res_induction
          with  P_W:=[n,i:Z](W n i)='0'  P_Y:=[n,i:Z](Y n i)='0'
                P_E:=[n:Z](E n)='0'      P_res:=[n:Z](res n)='0'
                P_d:=[n:Z](d n)='0'      P_x:=[n:Z]True.
```

We now have 9 subgoals to prove, the majority of them are obvious and are automatically discharged by Coq. The theorem is thus finally proved with a few 10 lines of proof commands. After closing the Coq section, the final exported version of the theorem is:

```
(Znone,N,M,D:Z; x,d:(Z->Z);
  paramsCond:('(-1)-D+M-N >= 0'/\'(-1)+D-N >= 0'/\'(-3)+N >= 0'))
  ((n:Z)([n:Z]'M-n >= 0'/\'n-N >= 0' n)->'(d n) = 0') ->
  (n:Z)([n:Z]'M-n >= 0'/\'n-N >= 0' n)
          ->'(res Znone N M D x d paramsCond n) = 0'
```

This form illustrates the assumptions we made during the Coq section, *i.e.*, the output variable res depends on the two input variables x and d, but also on the undefined value Znone, the 3 parameters N, M, D and on a proof (paramsCond) that these parameters satisfy the system constraints.

6   Related Work

When using theorem proving tools to model and verify systems or programs, one has to chose between formalizing the program's semantics or directly translating its syntactic constructs into "equivalent" ones. In the case of an imperative language, we would have to model its constructs under the form of denotational, operational or axiomatic semantics (see [13] for an example of a translation of a simple imperative language in PVS and further references, or [9] for a translation of the semantics of an imperative language in Coq). Translation of an equational language into Coq has been done with the reactive language Signal [12]. In this work, the co-inductive trace semantics of Signal is implemented as a set of Coq libraries that model the primitives of the language and provide basic lemmas and theorems. The translation of a particular system is done "by hand" using these primitives, and equations are translated as axioms.

Modelling mutual recursive functions in type theory is a difficult problem, since one has to prove function termination by using only structural recursive definitions. We may either try to prove termination via a structural ordering on value domains (see [2] for instance for this kind of approach and related work), or add to the initial function definition an argument which is known to be structurally recursive. In [5], a general method is given for the latter approach: a first definition of functions is given, which includes in its arguments a special-purpose accessibility predicate. This predicate is then proved true for all inputs. This allows for giving a simpler version of the function without accessibility predicates. In our approach we take advantage of the possible existence of a scheduling to (i) automatically generate the proof that all inputs (in our case, domain indices) are accessible and (ii) automatically generate a theorem stating that the variables are indeed a fixpoint for the initial equations. In [4], an approach based on the HOL theorem prover is used to construct induction schemes for mutually recursive functions. They develop specific algorithms for this construction. Due to the use of Coq and of its type-theoretic nature, we cannot use the same techniques. When dealing with SAREs, the use of measures would have given an easier definition of recursive functions in PVS and HOL/Isabelle. Nevertheless, most of the theorems we have to prove here would also have been necessary with this other technique. Anyway, the additional technical lemmas are fully automatically discharged.

Though many properties concerning parameterized SAREs are undecidable, recent work gives heuristics for automatically checking equivalence of two SAREs in some particular cases [3]. By using a general-purpose theorem prover, we considerably extend the possibilities of verification to complex properties. This work extends a previous similar one that had been implemented with PVS [6]. In this previous work however, induction schemes were not generated but had to be explicitly provided by the user. Moreover fixpoint equations were defined as axioms.

7   Conclusion

We have presented a tool and a method for proving properties on parameterized systems of affine recurrence equations. We proceed by translating SAREs into the specification language of the Coq theorem prover. We make an extensive use of the specific features of the polyhedral model to automatically generate Coq theorems that will be usable in a further proof process. For a given system, we take advantage of the possible existence of a particular schedule to get a functional translation of recurrence equations where accessibility predicates have been eliminated. The translation relies on the definition of a mutual inductive type, that will be used at the same time to get a functional version of recurrence equations and an induction scheme that is specific to the translated system.

We partially overcome the lack of automation by generating tactics adapted to each system's structure. These tactics implement complex induction schemes or theorem instantiations. For a given system, this allows to factorize and automate the most technical steps of the proofs.

Much work remains to be done. First, we need to extend this work to hierarchically structured systems, to be able to handle more complex systems and reuse proofs in a modular manner. We could also combine the different tactics we developed in a more general strategy that would explore a bounded-depth tree of rewritings, use of previously proved theorems and generated tactics. We also could study the specialization of the induction scheme to the problem of deciding wether two SAREs are equivalent, in order to get an automatic equivalence checker. It would finally be valuable to take advantage of a better interaction between Coq and the static polyhedral analysis performed by the MMALPHA tool, to decrease the number of calls made to the Omega library.

References

1. http://www.irisa.fr/lande/pichardie/coqalpha/.
2. A. Abel. Specification and verification of a formal system for structurally recursive functions. In *Types for Proof and Programs, International Workshop, TYPES '99*, volume 1956 of *Lecture Notes in Computer Science*, pages 1–20. Springer-Verlag, 2000.
3. D. Barthou, P. Feautrier, and X. Redon. On the equivalence of two systems of affine recurrence equations. Technical Report 4285, INRIA, 2001.
4. R. J. Boulton and K. Slind. Automatic derivation and application of induction schemes for mutually recursive functions. In *First International Conference on Computational Logic*, volume 1861 of *Lecture Notes in Artificial Intelligence*, pages 629–643, London, UK, July 2000. Springer-Verlag.
5. A. Bove. *General Recursion in Type Theory*. PhD thesis, Department of Computing Science, Chalmers University of Technology, Sweden, nov 2002.
6. D. Cachera, P. Quinton, S. Rajopadhye, and T. Risset. Proving properties of multidimensional recurrences with application to regular parallel algorithms. In *FMPPTA'01*, San Francisco, CA, April 2001.
7. D. Delahaye. A Tactic Language for the System Coq. In *Proceedings of Logic for Programming and Automated Reasoning (LPAR)*, volume 1955, pages 85–95, Reunion Island, November 2000. Springer-Verlag LNCS/LNAI.

8. J. Ferrante and C. Rackoff. A decision procedure for the first order theory of real addition with order. *SIAM Journal of Computing*, 1975.

9. J.-C. Filliâtre. *Preuve de programmes impératifs en théorie des types*. Thèse de doctorat, Université Paris-Sud, July 1999.

10. R. M. Karp, R. E. Miller, and S. Winograd. The organization of computations for uniform recurrence equations. *Journal of the ACM*, 14(3):563–590, July 1967.

11. M. Katsushige, N. Kiyoshi, and K. Hitoshi. Pipelined LMS Adaptive Filter Using a New Look-Ahead Transformation. *IEEE Transactions on Circuits and Systems*, 46:51–55, January 1999.

12. D. Nowak, J.R. Beauvais, and J.P. Talpin. Co-inductive axiomatization of a synchronous language. In *Proceedings of the 11th International Conference on Theorem Proving in Higher Order Logics (TPHOLs'98)*, volume 1479 of *Lecture Notes in Computer Science*, pages 387–399. Springer-Verlag, September 1998.

13. H. Pfeifer, A. Dold, F. W. von Henke, and H. Ruess. Mechanised semantics of simple imperative programming constructs. Technical Report UIB-96-11, Ulm University, dec 1996.

14. Y. Saouter and P. Quinton. Computability of Recurrence Equations. Technical Report 1203, IRISA, 1990.

15. LogiCal Project The Coq Development Team. *The Coq proof Assistant, Reference Manual*.

16. D. Wilde. A library for doing polyhedral operations. Technical Report 785, Irisa, Rennes, France, 1993.

17. D. K. Wilde. The Alpha language. Technical Report 999, IRISA, Rennes, France, January 1994.

Programming a Symbolic Model Checker in a Fully Expansive Theorem Prover

Hasan Amjad

University of Cambridge Computer Laboratory,
William Gates Building,
15 JJ Thomson Avenue,
Cambridge CB3 0FD, UK
Hasan.Amjad@cl.cam.ac.uk

Abstract. Model checking and theorem proving are two complementary approaches to formal verification. In this paper we show how binary decision diagram (BDD) based symbolic model checking algorithms may be embedded in a theorem prover to take advantage of the comparatively secure environment without incurring an unacceptable performance penalty.

1 Introduction

Model checking and theorem proving are two complementary approaches to formal verification. Model checking models the system as a state machine and desired properties of the system are expressed as temporal logic formulae that are true in the desired states of the system. Verification is fully automatic and can provide counter-examples for debugging but suffers from the state explosion problem when dealing with complex systems. Theorem proving models the system as a collection of definitions and desired properties are proved by formal derivations based on these definitions. It can handle complex systems but requires skilled manual guidance for verification and human insight for debugging.

An increasing amount of attention has thus been focused on combining these two approaches (see [38] for a survey). In this paper we demonstrate an approach to embedding a model checker in a theorem prover. The expectation is that this will ease combination of state-based and definitional models and the respective property checking techniques. Model checkers are typically written in tightly optimised C with an emphasis on performance. Theorem provers typically are not. Preliminary benchmarking shows that the loss in performance using our approach is within acceptable bounds.

Since our emphasis is on security (in the sense of soundness not being compromised), we have chosen the HOL theorem prover [20] for our task. HOL is based on the HOL logic [18] which is an extension of Church's simple theory of types [6], and is written in Moscow ML. Terms (of ML type `term`) in the logic can be freely constructed. Theorems (of ML type `thm`) can be constructed using the core axioms and inference rules only, i.e. by proof. This reliance on a very

D. Basin and B. Wolff (Eds.): TPHOLs 2003, LNCS 2758, pp. 171–187, 2003.

small trusted core is often named the "fully-expansive" approach and gives a high assurance of security.

Symbolic model checking [26] is a popular model checking technique. Sets of states are represented by the BDDs [3] of their characteristic functions. This representation is compact and provides an efficient[1] way to test set equality and do image computations. This is useful because evaluating temporal logic formulae almost always requires a fixed point computation that relies on image computations to compute the next approximation to the fixed point and a set equality test to determine termination. Most of the work is done by the underlying BDD engine.

By representing primitive BDD operations as inference rules added to the core of the theorem prover, we can model the execution of a model checker for a given property as a formal derivation tree rooted at the required property. These inference rules are hooked to a high performance BDD engine [4] external to the theorem prover. Thus the loss of performance is low, and the security of the theorem prover is compromised only to the extent that the BDD engine or the BDD inference rules may be unsound. Since we do almost everything within HOL and use only the most primitive BDD operations, we expect a higher assurance of security than from an implementation that is entirely in C.

2   Representing BDDs in the Theorem Prover

In order to provide a platform for programming model checking procedures from within HOL, the BuDDy [4] BDD engine has been interfaced to ML so that BDDs can be manipulated as ML values of type **bdd**. To represent BDD operations as inference rules, we use judgements of ML type **term_bdd** of the form

$$\rho\, t \mapsto b$$

where t is a HOL term (which we shall call the *term part* of the judgement) and b is a BDD (called the *BDD part* of the judgement). The only free variables of t are the boolean variables used in b (also called the *support* of b). Intuitively, if we collect these boolean variables together in a tuple s, the judgement is saying that for all assignments to the variables in s, an assignment will satisfy t if and only if it is also a satisfying assignment for b. The variable map ρ (of ML type **vm**) maps HOL variables to numbers. The map is required because BuDDy uses numbers to represent variables and for the moment its presence is only a technical requirement.

Our approach to 'proving' such a judgement is implemented analogously to the manner in which we prove theorems i.e. BDD representation judgements cannot be freely constructed but may be derived using primitive inference steps.

Table 1 presents a subset (that is relevant to our work) of the rules that form the primitive operations for BDD judgements, along with the names of ML

---

[1] The problem is NP-complete. So this efficiency is of heuristic value only.

Table 1. Primitive Operations for Representation Judgements

$(\mathsf{BddT} : \mathtt{vm} \to \mathtt{term\_bdd})$ $\rho\,\mathsf{T} \mapsto \mathtt{TRUE}$ $(\mathsf{BddF} : \mathtt{vm} \to \mathtt{term\_bdd})$ $\rho\,\mathsf{F} \mapsto \mathtt{FALSE}$

$$(\mathsf{BddVar} : \mathtt{vm} \to \mathtt{term} \to \mathtt{term\_bdd}) \quad \frac{\rho(v) = n}{\rho v \mapsto \mathtt{ithvar}n}$$

$$(\mathsf{BddNot} : \mathtt{term\_bdd} \to \mathtt{term\_bdd}) \quad \frac{\rho t \mapsto b}{\rho\,\neg t \mapsto \mathtt{NOT}\,b}$$

$$(\mathsf{BddAnd} : \mathtt{term\_bdd} * \mathtt{term\_bdd} \to \mathtt{term\_bdd}) \quad \frac{\rho\,t_1 \mapsto b_1 \quad \rho\,t_2 \mapsto b_2}{\rho\,t_1 \wedge t_2 \mapsto b_1\ \mathtt{AND}\,b_2}$$

$$(\mathsf{BddOr} : \mathtt{term\_bdd} * \mathtt{term\_bdd} \to \mathtt{term\_bdd}) \quad \frac{\rho\,t_1 \mapsto b_1 \quad \rho\,t_2 \mapsto b_2}{\rho\,t_1 \vee t_2 \mapsto b_1\ \mathtt{OR}\,b_2}$$

$(\mathsf{BddAppEx} : \mathtt{termlist} \to \mathtt{term\_bdd} * \mathtt{term\_bdd} \to \mathtt{term\_bdd})$

$$\frac{\rho(v_1) = n_1 \ \ldots \ \rho(v_p) = n_p \quad \rho\,t_1 \mapsto b_1 \quad \rho\,t_2 \mapsto b_2}{\rho\,\exists v_1 \ldots v_p.t_1\ op\,t_2 \mapsto \mathbf{appex}\,b_1\,b_2\,(n_1, \ldots, n_p)}$$

functions implementing them (in brackets). The BuDDy function `ithvar` (as interfaced to ML) simply returns the BDD of the boolean variable v. TRUE and FALSE denote the corresponding BDDs, T and F are HOL terms for truth and falsity, and NOT, AND and OR denote the eponymous BDD operations (see [17] for details).

In practice, existential quantification of conjunction (often called the relational product or image computation) occurs frequently and is an expensive operation. BuDDy provides a special operation **appex** for performing quantification of a boolean operation in one pass, and we have a BDD inference rule BddAppEx corresponding to it.

Theorem proving support is provided by two rules. The first expresses the fact that logically equivalent terms should have the same BDD (up to variable orderings).

$$(\mathsf{BddEqMp}) \quad \frac{\rho\,t_1 \mapsto b}{\rho\,t_2 \mapsto b} \vdash t_1 \Leftrightarrow t_2 \tag{1}$$

This rule enables us to use higher-order predicates in the term part of judgements to succinctly express the propositional content of the BDD part of the judgement.

The second rule is the only way to make theorems. It simply checks to see if the BDD part of the judgement is TRUE and if so, returns the term part as a theorem.

$$(\mathsf{BddOracleThm}) \quad \frac{\rho\,t \mapsto \mathtt{TRUE}}{\vdash t} \tag{2}$$

This theorem is only as good as the BDD that was produced: the soundness of it depends on the soundness of the BDD engine and of our representation judgement inference rules. By treating BDD operations as inference applications, we restrict the scope of soundness bugs to single operations which are easy to get right. This is why this approach was chosen in favour of a single powerful rule which, given a term, would return its BDD. A formal proof of the soundness of this calculus is underway.

3   Model Checking

Our general approach is independent of the choice of temporal logic. We shall apply it to the model checking procedure for the propositional μ-calculus L_μ from [24]. L_μ is very expressive and a model checker for it gives us model checkers for the popular temporal logics CTL and LTL.[2]

Formulae of L_μ describe properties of a system that can be represented as a state machine. In particular, the semantics of a formula is the set of states of the system satisfying the formula. The model checking algorithm computes this set given a formula and a system.

We need to make the notion of "system" precise. For our purposes, the system is represented by a Kripke structure. If AP is the set of atomic propositions relevant to the system we wish to model, then a Kripke structure over AP is defined as follows:

Definition 1. *A Kripke structure M over AP is a tuple (S, S_0, T, L) where*

- *S is a finite set of states.*
- *$S_0 \subseteq S$ is the set of initial states.*
- *T is the set of actions (or transitions or program letters) such that for any action $a \in T$, $a \subseteq S \times S$.*
- *$L : S \to 2^{AP}$ labels each state with the set of atomic propositions true in that state.*

We now present the syntax of L_μ, essentially as given in [8].

Definition 2. *Let VAR be the set of relational variables, $p \in AP$ be an atomic proposition and $a \in T$ be an action. Then if f and g are L_μ formulas, so are: True, False, p, $\neg f$, $f \wedge g$, $f \vee g$ (the propositional fragment); $[a]f$ and $\langle a \rangle f$ (the modal fragment); P, $\mu Q.f$ and $\nu Q.f$ (the relational or recursive fragment where $\{P, Q\} \subseteq VAR$ and all occurrences of Q in the negated normal form[3] (NNF) of f are not negated).*

---

[2] Though from a practical viewpoint, model checkers for L_μ are not as efficient as say SMV [26] or SPIN [21]. Note also that for logics that do not admit a direct syntactic embedding into L_μ, e.g. LTL, the translation into L_μ is non-trivial and a fully-expansive translation provides much needed assurance of soundness.

[3] This is a syntactic transformation that pushes all negations inwards to the atoms using the De Morgan style dualities $\neg(f \wedge g) = \neg f \vee \neg g$, $\neg(f \vee g) = \neg f \wedge \neg g$, $\neg[a]f = \langle a \rangle \neg f$, $\neg \langle a \rangle f = [a] \neg f$, $\neg \mu Q.f(Q) = \nu Q.\neg f(\neg Q)$ and $\neg \nu Q.f(Q) = \mu Q.\neg f(\neg Q)$ and the involutiveness of $\neg$.

We often use the term "variable" instead of "relational variable" or "propositional variable"; the meaning should be clear from the context. We use $p, p_0, \ldots$ to denote propositional atoms and $Q, Q_0, Q_1, \ldots$ for relational variables. In the formulas $\mu Q.f$ and $\nu Q.f$, μ and ν are considered binders on Q, and thus there is the standard notion of bound and free variables. We use $f(Q_1, Q_2, \ldots)$ to denote that $Q_1, Q_2, \ldots$ occur free in f.

The semantics of a formula f is written $[\![f]\!]_M e$, where M is a Kripke structure and the environment $e : VAR \to 2^S$ holds the state sets corresponding to the free relational variables of f. By $e[Q \leftarrow W]$ we mean the environment that has $e[Q \leftarrow W]Q = W$ but is the same as e otherwise. We now define $[\![f]\!]_M e$.

Definition 3. *The semantics of L_μ are defined recursively as follows*

- $[\![True]\!]_M e = S$ *and* $[\![False]\!]_M e = \emptyset$
- $[\![p]\!]_M e = \{s \mid p \in L(s)\}$
- $[\![Q]\!]_M e = e(Q)$
- $[\![\neg f]\!]_M e = S \backslash [\![f]\!]_M e$
- $[\![f \wedge g]\!]_M e = [\![f]\!]_M e \cap [\![g]\!]_M e$
- $[\![f \vee g]\!]_M e = [\![f]\!]_M e \cup [\![g]\!]_M e$
- $[\![\langle a \rangle f]\!]_M e = \{s \mid \exists t. s \overset{a}{\to} t \wedge t \in [\![f]\!]_M e\}$
- $[\![[a]f]\!]_M e = \{s \mid \forall t. s \overset{a}{\to} t \Rightarrow t \in [\![f]\!]_M e\}$
- $[\![\mu Q.f]\!]_M e$ *is the least fix-point of the predicate transformer* $\tau : 2^S \to 2^S$ *given by* $\tau(W) = [\![f]\!]_M e[Q \leftarrow W]$
- $[\![\nu Q.f]\!]_M e$ *is the greatest fix-point of the predicate transformer* $\tau : 2^S \to 2^S$ *given by* $\tau(W) = [\![f]\!]_M e[Q \leftarrow W]$

Environments can be given a partial ordering $\subseteq$ under component-wise subset inclusion. By Tarski's fix-point theorem [37], if

$$e[Q \leftarrow W] \subseteq e'[Q \leftarrow W'] \Rightarrow [\![f(Q)]\!]_M e[Q \leftarrow W] \subseteq [\![f(Q)]\!]_M e'[Q \leftarrow W']$$

i.e. the semantics evaluate monotonically over environments, then the existence of fix-points is guaranteed. In fact, since S is finite, monotonicity implies continuity [37], which gives

Proposition 4. $[\![\mu Q.f]\!]_M e = \bigcup_i \tau^i(\emptyset)$ *and* $[\![\nu Q.f]\!]_M e = \bigcap_i \tau^i(S)$

where $\tau^i(Q)$ is defined by $\tau^0(Q) = Q$ and $\tau^{i+1} = \tau(\tau^i(Q))$. So we can compute the fix-points by repeatedly applying τ to the result of the previous iteration, starting with $[\![False]\!]_M e$ for least fix-points and $[\![True]\!]_M e$ for greatest fix-points. Since S is finite, the computation stops at some $k \leq |S|$, so that the least fix-point is given by $\tau^k([\![False]\!]_M e)$ and the greatest fix-point by $\tau^k([\![True]\!]_M e)$. We then have that

Proposition 5. *If* $\tau^i(Q) = \tau^{i+1}(Q)$ *then* $k = i$.

Essentially, the semantics describe the model checking algorithm itself. An executable version of Proposition 5 would rely on being able to efficiently test state sets for equality. Since states are boolean tuples, we can represent state sets by the BDDs of their characteristic functions. Since the semantics are constructed using set operations, every step of the algorithm can be represented by an operation on BDDs. Hence every step can be represented by the application of a BDD representation judgement inference rule.

From Table 1, we can give a more concrete semantics for μ-formulae, this time using representation judgements.

Definition 6. *The L_μ model checking procedure $\mathcal{T}[\![-]\!]_M^\rho e$ is defined recursively over the structure of μ-formulae as follows*

- $\mathcal{T}[\![True]\!]_M^\rho e = \mathsf{BddT}\,\rho$ *and* $\mathcal{T}[\![False]\!]_M^\rho e = \mathsf{BddF}\,\rho$
- $\mathcal{T}[\![p]\!]_M^\rho e = \mathsf{BddVar}(\rho\,p)$
- $\mathcal{T}[\![\neg f]\!]_M^\rho e = \mathsf{BddNot}(\mathcal{T}[\![f]\!]_M^\rho e)$
- $\mathcal{T}[\![f \wedge g]\!]_M^\rho e = \mathsf{BddAnd}(\mathcal{T}[\![f]\!]_M^\rho e, \mathcal{T}[\![g]\!]_M^\rho e)$
- $\mathcal{T}[\![f \vee g]\!]_M^\rho e = \mathsf{BddOr}(\mathcal{T}[\![f]\!]_M^\rho e, \mathcal{T}[\![g]\!]_M^\rho e)$
- $\mathcal{T}[\![\langle a \rangle f]\!]_M^\rho e = \mathsf{BddAppEx}(\wedge, [\![M.T(a)]\!], \mathcal{T}[\![f]\!]_M^\rho e)$
  where $[\![M.T(a)]\!]$ is the BDD judgement for the action a
- $\mathcal{T}[\![[a]f]\!]_M^\rho e = \mathcal{T}[\![\neg\langle a \rangle \neg f]\!]_M^\rho e$
- $\mathcal{T}[\![\mu Q.f]\!]_M^\rho e = \bigcup_{i=0}^k \tau^i(\emptyset)$
  where $\tau = \lambda W.\mathcal{T}[\![f]\!]_M^\rho e[Q \leftarrow W]$ and $\tau^k(\emptyset) = \tau^{k+1}(\emptyset)$
- $\mathcal{T}[\![\nu Q.f]\!]_M^\rho e = \bigcap_{i=0}^k \tau^i(S)$
  where $\tau = \lambda W.\mathcal{T}[\![f]\!]_M^\rho e[Q \leftarrow W]$ and $\tau^k(S) = \tau^{k+1}(S)$

Executing the procedure in Definition 6 for some L_μ formula f with respect to a Kripke structure M and environment e will yield a judgement $\rho\,f' \mapsto b$ where ρ is the variable map, f' is the *boolean* semantic equivalent of f and b is the BDD of f'. So f' is likely to be large, unreadable and unsuitable for further manipulation by the theorem prover. Ideally, we would like f' to be some term expressing satisfiability of f in M and e i.e. we would like to obtain a judgement

$$\rho\,(s \models_M^e f) \mapsto b,$$

where the state s is a tuple of free boolean variables corresponding to the support of b. Deriving a judgement in the form above is what we shall now attempt. To do this, we must provide a definition and semantics of L_μ to the theorem prover.

4   Model Checking in the Theorem Prover

This section presents a mechanical formalisation of the theory and algorithms described above. To save space, the lengthy and theorem prover specific formal proofs are not given. Proof sketches are provided where they aid intuition.

4.1   Formalising the Theory

The formalisation goes along the lines of section 3. The propositional atoms $p \in AP$ have type β. We use α to denote the type of a state. During a model checking run α would be specialised to $(\beta \times \beta \times \ldots \times \beta)$ where the size of the product would be $|AP|$. Currently β is always specialised to the HOL boolean type bool. Kripke structures are represented by a simple record type KS, with fields $S : \alpha\, set$, $S0 : \alpha\, set$, $T : string \to (\alpha \times \alpha) \to bool$ and $L : \alpha \to \beta \to bool$ representing components so named in Definition 1.[4] Note that action names are modelled as strings.

At the time of writing HOL did not support predicate subtypes, so a well-formedness predicate on Kripke structures had to be defined separately.

Definition 7. *A Kripke structure* M *is well-formed if* $S = \mathcal{U} : (\alpha\, set)$ *where* $\mathcal{U}$ *is the universal set of all things of type* α.

The identification of S with all states is not a strict requirement. It is a technical convenience and does not result in loss of generality in the current context.

Formulas of L_μ are represented by a simple recursive datatype. The syntactic constraint on bound variables (see Definition 2) is enforced by a well-formedness predicate on μ-formulas.

Definition 8. *A well-typed* L_μ *formula* f *is well-formed,* wff f, *if and only if all subformulas of* f *are well-formed. However, if* $f \equiv \mu Q.g$ *or* $f \equiv \nu Q.g$ *then we additionally require that* $\neg Q \not\sqsubseteq NNF g$.

The subformula relation $\sqsubseteq$ is defined as expected. The definition of negated normal form (sketched earlier in the footnote to Definition 2) requires a limited form of substitution (the notation $f(\neg Q)$ abbreviates $f[\neg Q/Q]$). Since HOL has no native support for variable binding in higher order abstract syntax,[5] the definition of negated normal form has to explicitly avoid free variable capture. We shall assume that all formulas are well-formed and elide the well-formedness condition from theorem statements to avoid clutter.

The heart of the formalisation is the formal semantics, which follow Definition 3.

Definition 9. *The formal semantics of the* μ-*calculus for a Kripke structure* M *and environment* e *are defined by the mutual recursion*

---

[4] Sets in HOL are not ZF sets [32]. A set $S : \alpha set$ in HOL is a predicate of type $\alpha \to bool$. Thus set membership $x \in S$ is equivalent to the application Sx. We use both notations as appropriate.

[5] Providing automatic α-conversion is an active research area. Work done on this includes [14,15,16]

$$\mathcal{FS}[True]_M^e = S \wedge$$
$$\mathcal{FS}[False]_M^e = \emptyset \wedge$$
$$\mathcal{FS}[p]_M^e = \{s | s \in S \wedge p \in M.Ls\} \wedge$$
$$\mathcal{FS}[Q]_M^e = \{s | s \in S \wedge e\,Q\,s\} \wedge$$
$$\mathcal{FS}[\neg f]_M^e = S \backslash \mathcal{FS}[f]_M^e \wedge$$
$$\mathcal{FS}[f \vee g]_M^e = \mathcal{FS}[f]_M^e \cup \mathcal{FS}[g]_M^e \wedge$$
$$\mathcal{FS}[f \wedge g]_M^e = \mathcal{FS}[f]_M^e \cap \mathcal{FS}[g]_M^e \wedge$$
$$\mathcal{FS}[\langle a \rangle f]_M^e = \{s | \exists q.q \in S \wedge s \xrightarrow{a} q \wedge q \in \mathcal{FS}[f]_M^e\} \wedge$$
$$\mathcal{FS}[[a]f]_M^e = \{s | \forall q.q \in S \wedge s \xrightarrow{a} q \Rightarrow q \in \mathcal{FS}[f]_M^e\} \wedge$$
$$\mathcal{FS}[\nu Q.f]_M^e = \{s | \forall n.s \in FP\,f\,Q\,M\,e[Q \leftarrow S]\,n\} \wedge$$
$$\mathcal{FS}[\mu Q.f]_M^e = \{s | \exists n.s \in FP\,f\,Q\,M\,e[Q \leftarrow \emptyset]\,n\} \wedge$$
$$FP\,f\,Q\,M\,e\,0 = e\,Q \wedge$$
$$FP\,f\,Q\,M\,e\,(n+1) = \mathcal{FS}[f]_M^{e[Q \leftarrow FP\,f\,Q\,M\,e\,n]}$$

Since we need to test semantics for boolean satisfiability (Proposition 5 requires this), we need to define satisfaction of a formula in a state.

Definition 10. *A μ-calculus formula f is satisfied by a state s of a Kripke structure M under an environment e if and only if $s \in \mathcal{FS}[f]_M^e$. We denoted this by*

$$s \models_M^e f$$

For efficiency, theorems expressing satisfiability of all μ-calculus operators (see Table 2) are proved in terms of $\models$ using Definition 9, assuming the Kripke structure is well-formed.[6] This is trivial due to the simple connection between $\models$ and $\mathcal{FS}[-]$.

For fixed point computations, we require theorems that tell us when a fixed point has been reached. The first step is to prove monotonicity of the semantics of a formula with respect to the free variables i.e. the environment. We show the results for the least fixed point operator only (greatest fixed points follow by duality).

Theorem 11. *For a well-formed Kripke structure M and well-formed μ-calculus formula $\mu Q.f$, we have that*

$$\forall e\,e'\,X\,Y.$$

$$X \subseteq Y$$
$$\wedge \quad \forall Q'. \text{ if } (\neg Q' \sqsubseteq \text{NNF } f) \text{ then } e\,Q' = e'\,Q' \text{ else } e\,Q' \subseteq e'\,Q'$$
$$\Rightarrow \quad \mathcal{FS}[f]_M^{e[Q \leftarrow X]} \subseteq \mathcal{FS}[f]_M^{e'[Q \leftarrow Y]}$$

---

[6] The missing modal and fix-point operator theorems follow by duality. Fix point computations require several other satisfiability theorems discussed later.

Table 2. Satisfiability theorems for model checking based on Definition 9

$$\forall s\, M\, e. \qquad s \models^{e}_{M} True \Leftrightarrow \mathbf{T} \tag{3}$$

$$\forall s\, M\, e. \qquad s \models^{e}_{M} False \Leftrightarrow \mathbf{F} \tag{4}$$

$$\forall s\, M\, e. \qquad s \models^{e}_{M} p \Leftrightarrow p \in M.L\, s \tag{5}$$

$$\forall s\, M\, e\, f. \qquad s \models^{e}_{M} \neg f \Leftrightarrow s \not\models^{e}_{M} f \tag{6}$$

$$\forall s\, M\, e\, f\, g. \qquad s \models^{e}_{M} f \wedge g \Leftrightarrow s \models^{e}_{M} f \wedge s \models^{e}_{M} g \tag{7}$$

$$\forall s\, M\, e\, f\, g. \qquad s \models^{e}_{M} f \vee g \Leftrightarrow s \models^{e}_{M} f \vee s \models^{e}_{M} g \tag{8}$$

$$\forall s\, M\, e\, Q. \qquad s \models^{e}_{M} Q \Leftrightarrow e\, Q\, s \tag{9}$$

$$\forall s\, M\, e\, a\, f. \qquad s \models^{e}_{M} \langle a \rangle f \Leftrightarrow \exists q.(M.T\, a)(s,q) \wedge q \models^{e}_{M} f \tag{10}$$

$$\forall f\, M\, e\, Q\, s\, X\, n.\ s \models^{e[Q \leftarrow FP\, f\, Q\, M\, e[Q \leftarrow X]n]}_{M} f$$

$$\Leftrightarrow FP\, f\, Q\, M\, e[Q \leftarrow X]\,(n+1)\, s \tag{11}$$

Proof Sketch By the remarks preceding Proposition 4. Monotonicity can be shown by the observations that

1. Each of the operators except negation is monotonic.
2. Only relational variables occur negated in the NNF of a formula.
3. Bound variables occur non-negated in the NNF of a formula.
4. The negated normal form of f has the same semantics as f.

So we can effectively remove all negations from a formula without affecting the semantics. Monotonicity follows immediately. The second hypothesis in the antecedent expressing subset inclusion of environments is more complex than expected because it needs to account for the possibility of the environment having variables not occurring in the formula. This is a technical side-effect of HOL not supporting predicate subtypes. In the case of $e = e'$, this is trivial.   □

Using monotonicity, we are able to formally derive the equivalent of Proposition 5.

Theorem 12. *For a well-formed Kripke structure* M *and well-formed μ-calculus formula $\mu Q.f$, we have that*

$$\forall e\, n.$$

$$FP\, f\, Q\, M\, e[Q \leftarrow \emptyset]n = FP\, f\, Q\, M\, e[Q \leftarrow \emptyset](n+1)$$

$$\Rightarrow \mathcal{FS}[\![\mu Q.f]\!]^{e}_{M} = FP\, f\, Q\, M\, e[Q \leftarrow \emptyset]\, n$$

Proof Sketch It follows from Theorem 11 and [37] that $FP\, f\, Q\, M\, e[Q \leftarrow \emptyset]\, n$ is the least upper bound (under subset inclusion) of all $FP\, f\, Q\, M\, e[Q \leftarrow \emptyset]\, m$ for $m \leq n$, and that $FP\, f\, Q\, M\, e[Q \leftarrow \emptyset]\, n = FP\, f\, Q\, M\, e[Q \leftarrow \emptyset]\, m$ for $m \geq n$. Then

$$FP\, f\, Q\, M\, e[Q \leftarrow \emptyset]\, n$$

$$= \bigcup_{i \in \mathbb{N}} FP\, f\, Q\, M\, e[Q \leftarrow \emptyset]\, i$$

$$= \mathcal{FS}[\![\mu Q.f]\!]^{e}_{M}$$

using Definition 9.   □

4.2 Formalising the Model Checker

We wish to be able to pass a well-formed Kripke structure M, a well-formed formula f, an environment e and a variable map ρ to the model checking procedure $\mathcal{T}$ which returns a judgement of the form

$$\rho\ (s \models^e_M f) \mapsto \mathbf{b} \tag{12}$$

where the state s is a boolean tuple comprising the atomic propositions M is defined over.

Preliminaries. The first step in implementing the model checker is to prove the well-formedness of M and f. This is trivial but does require that both be HOL terms. Representing M as a HOL term throughout the model checking would be inefficient as the T component can be quite large. So we simply use M as an abbreviation for the entire structure. Additionally, evaluation of $T(a)$ directly from the term representation is $O(|T|)$. So we construct an ML binary search tree (BST) T_m which maps each action $a \in T$ to its transition relation. With T_m we can evaluate $T(a)$ in time $O(\log_2 |T|)$. Since M does not change during the model checking, we do not require write access to it. Once we have proved well-formedness, the theorems of Table 2 are specialised to f, M and s.

The environment occurs in the term part of the result and therefore also needs to be represented as a HOL term. However, environments change during every iteration of a fixed point computation. Thus they cannot be abbreviated as above without creating HOL definitions on the fly, which is messy and slow. Fortunately the term representation of environments is not large so they can be represented directly. The changing environments mean that all the satisfiability theorems we proved in Table 2 change with each iteration. The solution is to specialise them with the updated environment for each iteration. Finally, we construct an ML BST e_m which is an efficient version of e, analogous to T_m.

The Kernel. The core algorithm is based on Definition 6, i.e. by recursion over the $L_\mu$formula. Each step in the recursion consists of a one application of a BDD inference rule from Table 1 followed by an application of BddEqMp (from 1) together with the appropriate theorem (now specialised) from Table 2. Thus each step results in a judgement of the form of 12. In the end we use BddOracleThm to derive the final theorem.

As a trivial example, suppose we have a Kripke structure M over $\{p_0\}$ and an environment e that maps Q to the set $[\![\neg p_0]\!]^e_M$. Then $p_0 \vee Q$ should hold in all states. This theorem is derived (with mild notational abuse) by

$$
\cfrac{
\cfrac{
\text{BddEqMp}\cfrac{\text{BddVar}\cfrac{}{\rho\,p_0 \mapsto \texttt{ithvar}\,0}\ \rho(p_0){=}0}{\rho\,s\models p_0 \mapsto \texttt{ithvar}\,0}\vdash p_0 \Leftrightarrow s\models^e_M p_0
\qquad
\text{BddNot}\cfrac{\text{BddEqMp}\cfrac{\text{BddVar}\cfrac{}{\rho\,p_0 \mapsto \texttt{ithvar}\,0}\ \rho(p_0){=}0}{\rho\,s\models^e_M Q \mapsto [\![\neg p_0]\!]^e_M}\ \cfrac{\rho\,\neg p_0 \mapsto [\![\neg p_0]\!]^e_M}{}\vdash \neg p_0 \Leftrightarrow s\models^e_M Q}
}{
\text{BddOr}\cfrac{\text{BddEqMp}\cfrac{\rho\,s\models p_0 \vee s\models^e_M Q \mapsto \texttt{TRUE}}{\rho\,s\models_{p_0}\vee Q \mapsto \texttt{TRUE}}\vdash s\models^e_M p_0 \vee s\models^e_M Q \Leftrightarrow s\models^e_M p_0 \vee Q}{\text{BddOracleThm}\cfrac{}{\vdash s\models^e_M p_0\vee Q}}
}
$$

where the side-conditions to BddEqMp are derived from Table 2 and Defn. 3.

In the case of propositional atoms, relational variables and the modal operators, we do not have one theorem but sets of theorems AP_t, VAR_t and T_t indexed by the name of the atom, relational variable or action respectively; the appropriate theorem is picked out for passing to BddEqMp. The theorems in AP_t, VAR_t and T_t are obtained by specialising the theorems 5, 9 and 10 of Table 2. The HOL terms for the maps L and T are constructed so that a "lookup" i.e. a rewrite evaluating the application of an atom or action name to L or T respectively, has the same asymptotic cost as a lookup in a Patricia tree. All theorem sets are cached in ML BSTs for efficiency. The case for fixed point operators is more involved and is discussed in the next section.

It should be noted that the model checker derives every step from theorems proved in HOL and thus the result is provably correct (this does not apply to the BDD engine, but so far we have not *used* the BDD part of the representation judgements though of course it is updated by the inference rules). As we shall show, the performance penalty for this proof has been acceptable in regression tests. This is the justification for using representation judgements.

Computing Fixed Points. We limit our discussion to computing least fixed points and elide well-formedness predicates (for the Kripke structure and formula). If in a recursive descent $\mathcal{T}$ encounters a subformula $\mu Q.f$, we would like to derive the judgement

$$\rho \, (s \models^e_M \mu Q.f) \mapsto b$$

where, if we consider the BDD b as a set, we would like $b = \bigcup_{i=0}^{k} \tau^i(\emptyset)$ where $\tau = \lambda W.\mathcal{T}[\![f]\!]^\rho_M e[Q \leftarrow W]$ and $\tau^k(\emptyset) = \tau^{k+1}(\emptyset)$ (see Definitions 3 and 6).

Thus, by Theorem 12, if we can show that in the $(i+1)^{th}$ iteration

$$FP \, f \, Q \, M \, e[Q \leftarrow \emptyset] \, i = FP \, f \, Q \, M \, e[Q \leftarrow \emptyset] \, (i+1) \qquad (13)$$

we have the required result (using Definition 10).

To start, we require a "bootstrap" theorem.

Theorem 13.

$$\forall f \, M \, e \, Q \, s. FP \, f \, Q \, M \, e[Q \leftarrow \emptyset] \, 0 \, s = F$$

Proof Sketch Immediate from Definition 9 and the HOL definition of $\emptyset$.   □

Now we update the environment e with the mapping

$$[Q \leftarrow \rho \, (FP \, f \, Q \, M \, e[Q \leftarrow \emptyset] \, 0) \mapsto \textsf{FALSE}]$$

justified by Theorem 13 and the BddF rule from Table 1. Intuitively we can say that $\rho \, (FP \, f \, Q \, M \, e[Q \leftarrow \emptyset] \, 0) \mapsto \textsf{FALSE}$ is the mechanised version of $\tau^0(\emptyset)$.

For the iteration, we require a "substitution" theorem.

Theorem 14.

$$\forall f\, Q\, M\, e\, n\, s.s \models_M^{e[Q\leftarrow FP\,f\,Q\,M\,e\,(n+1)]} Q \Leftrightarrow s \models_M^{e[Q\leftarrow FP\,f\,Q\,M\,e\,n]} f$$

Proof Sketch Simplification with Definitions 9 and 10.   □

Then, for the ith iteration, a single call to the model checker returns the judgement[7]

$$\rho\,(s \models_M^{e[Q\leftarrow FP\,f\,Q\,M\,e[Q\leftarrow\emptyset]\,i]} f[f/Q]) \mapsto b$$

We use this and BddEqMp together with equation 11 of Table 2 and Theorem 14 to derive

$$\rho\,(FP\,f\,Q\,M\,e[Q\leftarrow\emptyset]\,(i+1)) \mapsto b$$

which is the mechanised version of $\tau^{i+1}(\emptyset)$. This is then made the new value of Q in e before calling the model checker again. At each iteration, all satisfiability theorems are recreated by specialising the theorems (or theorem sets) from Table 2 with the updated environment e. However, the theorem in VAR_t corresponding to Q has to be proved from scratch each time since the value of Q changes with every iteration.

After each call to the model checker, we check if the BDD parts of the two most recent iterations are equal. If so, we are able to derive the condition in equation 13 using BddOracleThm and stop. This is the only point where BDDs are actually used. Thus the result is guaranteed to be correct assuming the BDD representation judgement inference rules are sound (modulo the soundness of the BDD engine and HOL itself). We have already commented on the relatively high likelihood of this.

5   Empirical Results

This section presents the results of the first round of benchmarks. We compare the speed of our model checker with one we wrote in plain ML that bypasses HOL and works directly with the BDD engine. The numbers given in Table 3 are ratios normalised to the plain model checker's time. The lower the numbers, the lower the performance hit caused by the theorem proving overhead.

Our "fully-expansive" model checker's CPU time can be split into two phases: setting up the model (overhead time) and checking it. The overhead work needs to be done only once per model. The benchmarks show the amortised checking time by spreading overhead time over the various properties checked for the same model.

The model is a simple 3-stage pipelined ALU, described in [8] and earlier work. The BDD variable ordering is that recommended in [5]. We do not have space to describe the model in detail. The properties we checked use fixed point

---

[7] The substitution notation denotes that syntactic recursion occurs in the term part.

Table 3. Performance: fully-expansive to non-fully-expansive execution time ratio

Datapath/Address space	1	2	3
1	5.58	9.7	8.04
2	5.52	9.21	4.39
3	6.37	9.34	3.46
4	8.33	9.07	3.1
5	10.14	8.08	1.69
6	11.94	9.04	1.45
7	15.29	9.16	1.32
8	18.93	8.97	1.29

computations and thus thoroughly exercise both implementations. All benchmarks were conducted in the same hardware and software environment.

Both programs were run for datapaths of one to eight bits, and address spaces of one to three bits (i.e. two to eight registers). An increase in either increases the branching complexity of the model, with increases in address space having a stronger effect. Although several properties can be checked for this ALU, the results shown are for the one which represents the worst (greatest) performance difference. Overhead costs can still be amortised over this because it is a template that needs to be separately checked for each bit on the datapath.

Due to the absence of any optimisations, the system began to thrash with an address space of four bits. Nevertheless, the table shows that the difference in performance closes as the branching complexity of the system increases and becomes acceptably small for the larger examples. This is because the most expensive BDD operation, the relational product, is hit particularly hard by any increase in branching complexity, whereas the corresponding operation on the term part of the judgement is trivial. This allows the theorem proving component of the program to "catch up" with the BDD component.

These numbers should be considered preliminary because we have as yet not implemented any of the standard optimisations such as partitioning the transition relation, iterative squaring, caching or exploiting non-alternating quantifiers [13]. All these would speed up the BDD component and increase the performance difference. On the other hand, our test bed is a toy example and the expectation is that even with all these optimisations, the theorem proving component, which does not scale as badly as BDDs for larger examples, will catch up when the program is run for harder examples.

6   Related Work

The system closest in spirit to our own is the HOL-Voss system [31]. Voss has a lazy functional language FL with BDDs as a built-in datatype. In [23] Voss was interfaced to HOL and verification using a combination of deduction and symbolic trajectory evaluation (STE) was demonstrated. Later work can be found in [1]. Recent developments have been outside the public domain after the developers moved to Intel.

Local model checkers have been implemented in a purely deductive fashion. This is possible because local model checking [10,35,39] does not require external oracles like BDD engines for efficiency. Thus it is difficult to directly compare this work with our own global model checker. In [2] a local model checking algorithm is given for L_μ. However monotonicity conditions for assertions are proved on-line rather than as a general theorem (e.g. Theorem 11) that can later be specialised. A deeper treatment for the less expressive logic CTL* can be found in [33]. This work also proves the proof system sound and complete using game-theoretic analysis.

An early example of combination of theorem provers and model checkers can be seen in [25]. Here the prover is used to split the proof into various sub-goals which are small enough to be verified by a separate model checker. There is no actual integration so the translation between the languages of the theorem prover and the model checker is done manually.

Improved integrations of theorem provers with global model checkers typically enable the theorem prover to call upon the model checker as a black-box decision procedure given as an atomic proof rule [29,27]. The prover translates expressions involving values over finite domains into purely propositional expressions that can be represented by BDDs. This allows use of the result as a theorem (as in our framework) but this method does not extend readily to the fully expansive approach. It thus achieves better efficiency at the expense of higher assurance of soundness.

Theorem provers have also been used to help with abstraction refinement [19,12,30] for model checking. Decision procedures in the theorem prover are used to discharge assumptions added to refine an abstraction that turns out to be too coarse and adds too much non-determinism to the system resulting in spurious counter-examples. Decision procedures for some subsets of first order logic have been used in automatic discovery of abstraction predicates [11] and invariant generation [28]. There is no technical obstacle to implementing these frameworks in our setting.

Well-known tools that implement some of the research sketched here include [20,22,34,36].

7 Concluding Remarks

The implementation presented here does not contain non-trivial pieces of code whose soundness might be suspect: the core model checker is straight-forward. We expect this approach to pay off when we add optimisations and enhancements, particularly those that combine deductive and algorithmic verification.

The implementation itself is about 2000 lines of definitions and theorems about L_μ and sets, and about 500 lines of executable ML code. The proof of Theorem 11 is non-trivial, on account of having to do explicit α-conversion for the higher-order binders. The executable part is much easier to code, mainly because no soundness checks of the code are required: if the procedure terminates, the result is correct by construction.

Future work will focus on: providing error traces that can be manipulated in the theorem prover; leveraging the model checker for logics other than L_μ, justified by a semantics-based translation of the language into L_μ using the theorem prover; implementing more powerful versions of standard abstraction frameworks (e.g. [9,7]) using the decision procedures and simplifiers provided by HOL.

A different aspect that we have not touched on is that this approach enables us to simultaneously get a handle on both the syntax and semantics of the derivation/evaluation[8] at every step, via the representation judgement. We strongly expect that this will enable deeper investigation of methods combining proof-space search with state-space search.

References

1. M. D. Aagaard, R. B. Jones, and C-J. H. Seger. Combining theorem proving and trajectory evaluation in an industrial environment. In *Design Automation Conference (DAC)*, pages 538–541. ACM/IEEE, 1998.
2. S. Agerholm and H. Skjodt. Automating a model checker for recursive modal assertions in HOL. Technical Report 92, Aarhus University, January 1990.
3. R. E. Bryant. Symbolic boolean manipulation with ordered binary decision diagrams. *ACM Computing Surveys*, 24(3):293–318, September 1992.
4. The BuDDy ROBDD Package. http://www.itu.dk/research/buddy, 2002.
5. J. R. Burch, E. M. Clarke, and D. E. Long. Representing circuits more efficiently in symbolic model checking. In *Proceedings of the ACM Design Automation Conference*, 1991.
6. A. Church. A formulation of the simple theory of types. *Journal of Symbolic Logic*, 5(2):56–68, June 1940.
7. E. Clarke, A. Gupta, J. Kukula, and O. Strichman. SAT based abstraction-refinement using ILP and machine learning techniques. In *Proc. of Conference on Computer-Aided Verification (CAV'02)*, LNCS, 2002.
8. E. M. Clarke, O. Grumberg, and D. Peled. *Model Checking*. The MIT Press, 1999.
9. Edmund M. Clarke, Orna Grumberg, and David E. Long. Model checking and abstraction. *ACM Transactions on Programming Languages and Systems*, 16(5):1512–1542, September 1994.
10. R. Cleaveland. Tableau-based model checking in the propostional mu-calculus. Extended Abstract, 1988. Computer Science Department, University of Sussex.
11. Satyaki Das and David L. Dill. Counter-example based predicate discovery in predicate abstraction. In *Formal Methods in Computer-Aided Design*, November 2002.
12. J. Dingel and T. Filkorn. Model checking for infinite state systems using data abtraction, assumption-commitment style reasoning and theorem proving. In *Proceedings of the 1995 Workshop on Computer Aided Verification*, volume 939 of *LNCS*, pages 54–69. Springer, 1995.
13. E. A. Emerson and C-L. Lei. Efficient model checking in fragments of the propositional mu-calculus. In *1st Annual Symposium on Logic in Computer Science*, pages 267–278. IEEE Computer Society Press, 1986.

---

[8] But not in the sense of the Curry-Howard isomorphism.

14. M. P. Fiore, G. D. Plotkin, and D. Turi. Abstract syntax and variable binding. In *Proceedings of the 14th Logic in Computer Science Conference*, pages 193–202. IEEE, Computer Society Press, 1999.

15. M. J. Gabbay and A. M. Pitts. A new approach to abstract syntax with variable binding. *Formal Aspects of Computing*, 2001. Special issue in honour of Rod Burstall.

16. A. D. Gordon and T. Melham. Five axioms of alpha-conversion. In *Proceedings of the 9th International Conference on Theorem Proving in Higher Order Logics*, volume 1125 of *LNCS*. Springer, 1996.

17. M. J. C. Gordon. Programming combinations of deduction and bdd-based symbolic calculation. *LMS Journal of Computation and Mathematics*, August 2002.

18. M. J. C. Gordon and T. F. Melham. *Introduction to HOL (A theorem-proving environment for higher order logic)*. Cambridge University Press, 1993.

19. S. Graf and H. Saidi. Construction of abstract state graphs with pvs. In *Proceedings of Computer Aided Verification (CAV '97)*, volume 1254 of *Lecture Notes in Computer Science*. Springer-Verlag, 1997.

20. The HOL Proof Tool. `http://hol.sf.net`, 2003.

21. G. J. Holzmann and D. Peled. The state of spin. In *CAV'96: 8th International Conference on Computer Aided Verification*, volume 1102 of *LNCS*, pages 385–389. Springer, 1996.

22. SRI International. Prototype verification system. `http://pvs.csl.sri.com`.

23. J. Joyce and C. Seger. The HOL-Voss system : Model checking inside a general-purpose theorem prover. In *Higher Order Logic Theorem Proving and its Applications*, volume 780 of *LNCS*, pages 185–198. Springer, 1993.

24. D. Kozen. Results on the propositional mu-calculus. *Theoretical Computer Science*, 27:333–354, 1983.

25. R. P. Kurshan and L. Lamport. Verification of a multiplier: 64 bits and beyond. In C. Courcoubetis, editor, *Proceedings of the 5th Workshop on Computer Aided Verification*, pages 166–180, June 1993.

26. K. L. McMillan. *Symbolic Model Checking*. Kluwer Academic Publishers, 1993.

27. Sam Owre, S. Rajan, J. M. Rushby, N. Shankar, and M. K. Srivas. Pvs: Combining specification, proof checking, and model checking. In *CAV'96: 8th International Conference on Computer Aided Verification*, pages 411–414, 1996.

28. A. Pnueli, S. Rua, and L. Zuck. Automatic deductive verification with invisible invariants. In *Proceedings of Tools and Algorithms for the Construction and Analysis of Systems*, 2001.

29. S. Rajan, N. Shankar, and M. K. Srivas. An integration of model checking and automated proof checking. In *Proceedings of Computer Aided Verification*. Springer-Verlag, 1995.

30. H. Saidi. Model checking guided abstraction and analysis. In *Proceedings of the 7th International Static Analysis Symposium*, 2000.

31. C-J. H. Seger. Voss - a formal hardware verification system: User's guide. Technical report, The University of British Columbia, December 1993. UBC-TR-93-45.

32. T. Skolem. Some remarks on axiomatised set theory. In J. van Heijenoort, editor, *From Frege to Godel: A Source Book in Mathematical Logic, 1879-1931*, pages 290–301. Harvard University Press, 1967.

33. C. Sprenger. *Deductive Local Model Checking*. PhD thesis, Computer Networking Laboratory,Swiss Federal Institute of Technology, Lausanne, Switzerland, 2000.

34. Stanford Temporal Prover. `http://www-step.stanford.edu`.

35. C. Stirling and D. J. Walker. Local model checking in the modal mu-calculus. In Josep Díaz and Fernando Orejas, editors, *Proceedings of the Colloquium on Trees in Algebra and Programming (CAAP)*, number 1 in Lecture Notes in Computer Science. Springer, 1989. CAAP is the predecessor to ETAPS.
36. Symbolic Model Prover. `http://www.cs.cmu.edu/~modelcheck/symp.html`.
37. A. Tarski. A lattice-theoretical fixpoint theorem and its applications. *Pacific Journal of Mathematics*, 5:285–309, 1955.
38. T. E. Uribe. Combinations of model checking and theorem proving. In *Proceedings of the Third Intl. Workshop on Frontiers of Combining Systems*, volume 1794 of *LNCS*, pages 151–170. Springer-Verlag, March 2000.
39. G. Winskel. A note on model checking in the modal ν-calculus. In Giorgio Ausiello, Mariangiola Dezani-Ciancaglini, and Simona Ronchi Della Rocca, editors, *Proceedings of the International Colloquium on Automata, Languages and Programming*, volume 372 of *Lecture Notes in Computer Science*. Springer, 1989.

Combining Testing and Proving in Dependent Type Theory

P. Dybjer, Q. Haiyan, and M. Takeyama

Department of Computing Science,
Chalmers University of Technology,
412 96 Göteborg, Sweden
{peterd,qiao,makoto}@cs.chalmers.se

Abstract. We extend the proof assistant Agda/Alfa for dependent type theory with a modified version of Claessen and Hughes' tool QuickCheck for random testing of functional programs. In this way we combine testing and proving in one system. Testing is used for debugging programs and specifications before a proof is attempted. Furthermore, we demonstrate by example how testing can be used repeatedly during proof for testing suitable subgoals. Our tool uses testdata generators which are defined inside Agda/Alfa. We can therefore use the type system to prove properties about them, in particular surjectivity stating that all possible test cases can indeed be generated.

1   Introduction

A main goal of the theorem proving community is to use proof assistants for producing correct programs. However, in spite of faster type-checkers, more automatic proof-search, better interfaces, larger libraries, proving programs correct is still very time consuming, and requires great skill of the user.

Testing has often been disregarded by the theorem proving community since, as Dijkstra emphasised, testing can only show the presence of errors, not the absence of them. However, testing is of course the method used in practice!

Most research on testing has concerned imperative programs. However, an interesting tool QuickCheck for random testing of functional programs (written in the lazy functional programming language Haskell) has recently been developed by Claessen and Hughes [5]. With this tool, correctness properties of functional programs can easily be checked for randomly generated inputs. Experience shows that this is a useful method for debugging programs [6].

Nevertheless, missing rare counterexamples is unacceptable for certain applications. Furthermore, not all correctness properties have a directly testable form. Since both testing and proving have their obvious shortcomings, it would be interesting to combine testing and proving in one system. The idea is to use testing to debug programs and specifications before a proof is attempted. Furthermore, we can debug subgoals which occur during proof, and we can also balance cost and confidence by testing assumptions instead of proving. It may

D. Basin and B. Wolff (Eds.): TPHOLs 2003, LNCS 2758, pp. 188–203, 2003.

also be interesting to systematically study testing methods in the context of a full-fledged logic of functional programs.

To this end we have extended the proof assistant Agda/Alfa developed by Coquand [7] and Hallgren [13] with a testing tool similar to QuickCheck. The Agda/Alfa system is an implementation of a logical framework for Martin-Löf type theory. Intuitionistic logic is available via the Curry-Howard correspondence between propositions and types. Martin-Löf type theory is also a programming language which can be briefly described as a functional programming language with dependent types, where all programs terminate. Termination is ensured by only allowing certain recursion patterns. Originally only structural recursion over well-founded datatypes was allowed, but recent work on pattern matching with dependent types [8] and termination checking [22] has extended the class of programs accepted by the system. There is also a significant amount of work on the question of how to reason about general recursive programs in dependent type theory. For some recent contributions to this problem, see Bove [3].

As a first case study we are developing a certified library of classic data structures and algorithms. To illustrate our tool we consider the correctness of some simple search tree algorithms (search and insertion in binary search trees and AVL-trees). As Xi and Pfenning [23] have emphasized in their work on DML (Dependent ML), dependent types are useful for expressing invariants of such data structures. Our goals should be compared to those of Okasaki, who is currently developing Edison – a library of efficient functional data structures written in Haskell [18]. Okasaki uses QuickCheck to test his programs, and also includes QuickCheck test data generators to be used in applications of his data structures. We aim to build an analogous library for the Agda/Alfa system, where we can use dependent types to capture more invariants of the algorithms, and even provide full correctness proofs whenever this is feasible.

The idea of combining proving and testing is also part of the Programatica project currently under development at Oregon Graduate Centre [20]. Some early work on combining proving and testing was done by Hayashi, who used testing to debug lemmas while doing proofs in his PX-system [14]. Hayashi is currently pursuing the idea of testing proofs and theorems in his foundationally oriented project on "proof animation" [15]. AVL-insertion has been implemented and proven correct in Coq by Catherine Parent [19].

Plan. In Section 2 we introduce QuickCheck. In Section 3 we introduce the proof assistant Agda/Alfa. In Section 4 we extend Agda/Alfa with a QuickCheck-like tool. In Section 5 we discuss test case generation. In Section 6 we summarize our experiments with algorithms for insertion in AVL-trees and illustrate how testing helps during proof development. In Section 7 we briefly describe how AVL-tree insertion can be implemented by using dependent types, so that the type system ensures that the insertion preserves the AVL-tree property. Section 8 concludes with a brief discussion of further research. Appendix A contains some Haskell programs from Section 2.

Acknowledgments. We wish to thank Koen Claessen and John Hughes for many discussions.

2   QuickCheck

The basic idea of QuickCheck is to test whether a boolean property

```
p[x1, ..., xn] :: Bool
```

is `True` for random instances of the variables `x1 :: D1, ..., xn :: Dn`. (The notation `p[x1,...,xn]` means that the expression `p` may contain occurrences of the free variables `x1,...,xn`. The reader is warned not to confuse this notation with Haskell's list notation!)

For example, if we wish to test that

```
reverse (reverse xs) == xs
```

for arbitrary integer lists `xs`, we write a property definition

```
prop_RevRev xs = reverse (reverse xs) == xs
  where types = xs :: [Int]
```

Then we call QuickCheck

```
Main> quickCheck prop_RevRev
OK, passed 100 tests.
```

QuickCheck here uses a library test data generator for integer lists. It is also possible for the user to define her own test data generator.

More generally, QuickCheck can test conditional properties written

```
p[x1,...,xn] ==> q[x1,...,xn]
```

where `p[x1,...,xn]`, `q[x1,...,xn] :: Bool`. QuickCheck performs a sequence of tests as follows (at least conceptually):

1. A random instance `r1 :: D1, ..., rn :: Dn` is generated.
2. `p[r1, ..., rn]` is computed. If it is `False`, the test is discarded and a new random instance is generated. If on the other hand it is `True`, then
3. `q[r1, ..., rn]` is computed. If it is `False`, QuickCheck stops and reports the counterexample. If it is `True` the test was successful and a new test is performed.

QuickCheck repeats this procedure 100 times, by default. Only tests which are not discarded at step 2 are counted.

Another example of a QuickCheckable property is the following correctness property of a search algorithm `binSearch` for binary search trees. The property states that the algorithm correctly implements membership in binary search trees:

```
isBST lb ub t ==> binSearch t key == member t key
```

Here `t` is a binary tree of type `BT`, the type of binary trees with integers in the nodes; in Haskell:

```
data BT = Empty | Branch Int BT BT
```

isBST lb ub t holds if t is a binary search tree with elements strictly between lb and ub, (see Appendix A for the definitions in Haskell).

Before we can use QuickCheck we need a suitable test data generator. A generator for BT could be used, but is inappropriate. The reason is that most randomly generated binary trees will not be binary search trees, so most of them will be discarded. Furthermore, the probability of generating a binary search tree decreases with the size of the tree, so most of the generated trees would be small. Thus the reliability of the testing would be low. A better test case generator generates binary search trees only.

For more information about QuickCheck, see Claessen and Hughes [5] and the homepage http://www.cs.chalmers.se/~rjmh/QuickCheck/. Much of the discussion about QuickCheck, both about pragmatics and concerning possible extensions seems relevant to our context.

3   The Proof Assistant Agda/Alfa

This section briefly describes the proof assistant Agda/Alfa. The reader familiar with Agda/Alfa can skip it.

Agda [7] is the latest version of the ALF-family of proof systems for dependent type theory developed in Göteborg since 1990. Alfa [13] is a window interface for Agda. We quote from the Alfa home page [13]:

> Alfa is a successor of the proof editor ALF, i.e., an editor for direct manipulation of proof objects in a logical framework based on Per Martin-Löf's Type Theory. It allows you to, interactively and incrementally, define theories (axioms and inference rules), formulate theorems and construct proofs of the theorems. All steps in the proof construction are immediately checked by the system and no erroneous proofs can be constructed.

That "no erroneous proofs can be constructed" only means that a completed proof is indeed correct. It does not help you to avoid blind alleys.

The syntax of Agda/Alfa has been strongly influenced by the syntax of Haskell and also of Cayenne [1], a functional programming language with dependent types. In addition to the function types a -> b available in ordinary functional languages, there are dependent function types written (x :: a) -> b, where the type b may depend on x :: a.

Agda/Alfa also has dependent record types (signatures) written

```
sig {x1 :: a1; x2 :: a2; ...; xn :: an}
```

where a2 may depend on x1 :: a1 and an may depend on x1 :: a1, x2 :: a2, etc. Elements of signatures are called structures written

```
struct{x1 = e1; x2 = e2; ...; xn = en}
```

Signatures are much like iterated Σ-types Σx1 :: a1.Σx2 :: a2. ... an.
and structures are much like iterated tuples (e1, (e2, ..., en)) inhabiting
them.

Furthermore, Agda/Alfa has a type Set of sets in Martin-Löf's sense. Such
sets are built up from basic inductive data structures, using dependent function
types and signature types. A basic example is the set of natural numbers. Its
definition in Agda/Alfa is

```
data Nat = Zero | Succ (n :: Nat)
```

More generally, constructors for sets may have dependent types, see for example the definition of AVL-trees in Section 7.

Remark. The reader is warned that the dependent type theory code given here
is not accepted verbatim by the Agda/Alfa system, although it is very close to
it. To get more readable notation and avoiding having to discuss some of the
special choices of Agda/Alfa we borrow some notations from Haskell, such as
writing [a] for the set of lists of elements in a. In particular, we use Haskell-
style overloading although this feature is not present in Agda/Alfa.

Predicates on a set D are propositional functions with the type D -> Set
by the identification of propositions as sets. Decidable predicates have the type
D -> Bool. To convert from decidable to general predicates we use the function

```
T :: Bool -> Set
T True  = Truth
T False = Falsity
```

where Truth = Unit represents the trivially true proposition and Falsity is
the empty set representing the false proposition.

For a more complete account of the logical framework underlying Agda/Alfa
including record types see the paper about structured type theory [9] and for the
inductive definitions available in type theory, see Dybjer [10] and Dybjer and
Setzer [11,12].

4   A Testing Tool for Agda/Alfa

Our testing tool can test properties of the following form:

```
(x1 :: D1) -> ... -> (xn :: Dn[x1, ..., x(n-1)]) ->
T (p1[x1, ..., xn]) -> ... -> T (pm[x1, ..., xn]) ->
T ( q[x1, ..., xn])
```

Under the identification of 'propositions as types', this reads

$$\forall x_1 \in D1. \cdots \forall x_n \in Dn[x_1, \cdots, x_{n-1}].$$
$$p1[x_1, \cdots, x_n] \implies pm[x_1, \cdots, x_n] \implies$$
$$q[x_1, \cdots, x_n]$$

This is essentially the form of properties that QuickCheck can test, except that in dependent type theory the data domains Di can be dependent types.

The user chooses an option "test" in one of the menus provided by Alfa. The plug-in calls a test data generator and randomly generates a number of cases (at the moment 50) for which it checks the property.

Consider again the correctness property of binary search. It is the following Agda/Alfa type (using Nat rather than Int for simplicity):

```
(lb, ub, key :: Nat) -> (t :: BT) ->  T (isBST lb ub t) ->
  T (binSearch t key == member t key)
```

Fig. 1 shows how this property is displayed in an Alfa-window:

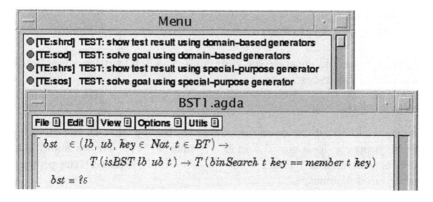

Fig. 1. Testing binary search

here *bst* is a proof object for the correctness of binary search; *bst* is yet to be defined by instantiating the highlighted question mark $?_5$. This can now be done either by proving or testing. If we choose to prove it, $?_5$ should be instantiated to a proof term which we can build interactively by pointing and clicking (see the Alfa homepage for details [13]). If we instead want to test it, we choose one of the testing options found in one of Alfa's menus (see Fig. 1). We can either use a *domain-based* or a *special purpose* test data generator. The domain-based option looks for generators for the data domains Di. The special purpose option looks for a generator for the lemma in question; it can therefore take the conditions into account. We can also choose whether we want to see the results of testing in a separate window, or just try to solve the goal, and if successful replace $?_5$ by the pseudo proof term "Tested" indicating that the goal has been successfully tested, but not proved (see Figure 2).

If testing fails, a counterexample is returned. For example, if we remove the condition T (isBST lb ub t), then the property above is not true any more, and the plug-in will report a counterexample, as in Fig. 3.

$$\begin{bmatrix} bst & \in (lb,\, ub,\, key \in Nat,\, t \in BT) \to \\ & T\,(isBST\;lb\;ub\;t) \to T\,(binSearch\;t\;key == member\;t\;key) \\ bst \equiv Tested \end{bmatrix}$$

Fig. 2. The goal is 'Tested'

$Counterexample\;where$
$key := Zero$
$t := Branch\,(Succ\;Zero)\,Empty\,(Branch\;Zero\;Empty\;Empty)$

Fig. 3. A counterexample

5   Test Data Generators

In principle we could generate test data for a type D, by writing a function which enumerates its elements:

```
enum :: Nat -> D
```

Then we could either use enum for exhaustive testing, that is, the plug-in could test the property for enum 0, enum 1, enum 2, ... Or we could generate a sequence of random natural numbers $r_0, r_1, r_2, \ldots$ and test the property for enum r_0, enum r_1, enum $r_2, \ldots$.

However, rather than starting with randomly generated natural numbers we shall start with randomly generated binary trees of natural numbers. This is a somewhat more practical way to write test data generators for a wide variety of types. For example, it is easy to get the next random seed when writing a generator.

Thus a test data generator for the type D has type

```
genD :: BT -> D
```

The Agda/Alfa system does not have a built in random number generator. So the plug-in first calls Haskell to generate a random element of the Agda/Alfa type BT. Then it applies genD to convert it to an element of D. An alternative approach would be to write test data generators for D directly in Haskell. However, using Agda/Alfa for this purpose has several advantages. The user can stay inside the language of Agda/Alfa when testing as well as when proving. Moreover, we can use Agda/Alfa for enforcing dependent type correctness of genD, and also for showing that it is a *surjective* function, expressing that every element of D can indeed be produced by the test data generator.

The drawback is efficiency: Haskell's evaluator is much more efficient than Agda/Alfa's. However, for our present experiments this is not a major problem; we expect that later versions of Agda/Alfa will be as efficient as Cayenne [1].

Let us see some generator examples.

Example 1. The following function defines a generator for [Nat]:

```
genList :: BT -> [Nat]

genList Empty                 = []
genList (Branch root lt rt) = root:genList lt
```

We can prove that the generator genList is surjective, that is

$$\forall xs \in [\text{Nat}]. \, \exists seed \in \text{BT}. \, \text{genList } seed \, = \, xs.$$

Existential quantification becomes dependent sum under the propositions as types identification, so what we prove in Agda/Alfa is Surj genList, where

```
Surj :: (g :: BT -> a) -> Set
Surj g = (x :: a) -> sig { seed :: BT; prf :: T (g seed == x) }
```

Example 2. Here is a generator for binary search trees:

```
genBST :: Nat -> Nat -> BT -> BT

genBST lb ub Empty = Empty
genBST lb ub (Branch rnd l r) =
  let newroot = lb + 1 + (rnd 'mod' (ub - lb - 1))
      lt = genBST lb newroot l
      rt = genBST newroot ub r
  in if (ub > lb + 1) (Branch newroot lt rt) Empty
```

We can now prove (or test!) that genBST only generates binary search trees:

```
(lb, ub :: Nat) -> T (lb < ub) ->
(  seed :: BT ) -> T (isBST lb ub (genBST lb ub seed))
```

We can also prove that genBST is surjective on binary search trees:

```
(lb, ub :: Nat) -> T (lb < ub) ->
(    t :: BT ) -> T (isBST lb ub t) ->
sig { seed :: BT;  prf :: T (genBST lb ub seed) == t }
```

Now we can choose "using special generator" to test the property in Fig. 1 and the result is "passed 50 successful tests" . If we choose the option "solve the goal", then the goal is filled with "Tested" (see Fig. 2).

6   Combining Testing and Proving

In this section we show some concrete examples to illustrate the following general points about how testing and proving help each other:

[a] The essence of creative user interaction is the introduction of lemmas. This is often a speculative process. If a user fails to prove a conjecture or its hypotheses, she must backtrack and try another formulation. Testing before proving is a quick and effective way to discard wrong or inapplicable conjectures.

[b] Analysis of failed tests gives useful information for proving. We call a counterexample to a conjecture *spurious* if it lies outside the intended domain of application of the conjecture. Having those at hand, the user can formulate a sharper lemma that excludes them. Genuine counterexamples on the other hand helps locating bugs in programs or in the formalisation of intended properties.

[c] A given goal may not be (efficiently) testable. When interaction with the proof assistant produces testable subgoals, it is guaranteed that testing all of them is at least as good as testing the original goal; we know that no unintended logical gaps are introduced.

[d] Interactive proving increases confidence in the coverage and rationality of testing. Suppose a program consists of various components and branches, and it passes a top-level test for a property. When we try to prove the goal, the proof assistant typically helps us derive appropriate subgoals for the different components or branches. Testing these subgoals individually reduces the risk of missed test cases in the top-level testing.

Example 3 (list reverse). Consider again the example of reversing a list twice. We proceed as follows:

1. Test the `main` goal using a domain-based generator for `[Nat]`, to check for a bug in the program or the specification ([b]).

   ```
   main       :: (xs :: [Nat]) -> T (reverse (reverse xs) == xs)
   ```

2. Start proving by induction on `xs`. The `nil_case` is trivial. The testable subgoal `cons_case` is automatically derived by Alfa.

   ```
   cons_case :: (x :: Nat) -> (xs' :: [Nat]) ->
                T (reverse (reverse xs' ++ [x]) == x:xs')
   ```

   It is testable in principle, although there is little point in doing so; most test cases for the top-level goal probably already had `cons`-form.

3. The normalization in Agda/Alfa was blocked by a non-reducing `++`. Therefore we speculate the `lemma` by changing variables:

   ```
   lemma      :: (x :: Nat) -> (ys  :: [Nat]) ->
                T (reverse (ys  ++ [x]) == x:reverse ys)
   ```

   This is a creative step not forced by logic. Therefore it is worth testing `lemma` before trying to prove it. Although a brief thought shows its equivalence to `cons_case` under the induction hypothesis, running a test is cheaper ([a]).

4. Proceed by proving `lemma` by induction on `ys`, which finishes the proof.

Example 4 (AVL-tree insertion). Recall that an AVL-tree `t` is a binary search tree which is balanced (`Bal t`): the height difference between the left and right subtrees of each node is at most 1.

```
Bal :: BT -> Bool
Bal Empty             = True
Bal (Branch n lt rt) = |#lt - #rt| <= 1 && Bal lt && Bal rt
```

where `#t` is the height of `t` and `|x|` is the absolute value of the integer `x`.

The following algorithm inserts a key in an AVL-tree and is adapted from a textbook on functional data structures [21]. We show relevant parts only:

```
insert :: BT -> Nat -> BT

insert Empty               k          = Branch  k       Empty Empty
insert (Branch n lt rt) k | k == n = Branch   n            lt     rt
                          | k <  n = insert_l n (insert lt k) rt
                          | k >  n = insert_r n lt (insert rt k)
insert_l :: Nat -> BT -> BT -> BT

insert_l n newlt@(Branch n' lt' rt') rt
  | #newlt - #rt == 2 = if #lt' > #rt' then rotateLeft t'
                        else            doubleRotateLeft t'
  | otherwise         = t'
                        where t' = Branch n newlt rt
insert_l n Empty       = Empty -- unreachable
```

where the pattern `var@pat` expresses that `var` is a name for the value being matched by `pat`.

One of the required properties of `insert` is to maintain the height balance:

```
main :: (t :: BT) -> Bal t -> (k :: Nat) -> Bal (insert t k)
```

(We omit writing T in T (`Bal t`) etc. in this section.)

We now summarize how testing interacts with proving while verifying a part of **main**. Note that our aim is not to show a well-organised development with much afterthought; rather, our point is to show how the combination cost-effectively helps in a real life 'first-try'. (Ti is here a testing step and Pi is a proving step.)

T1 Test **main** using the special purpose generator for balanced trees: A bug in
    insert or in **Bal** is likely to be discovered early.
P2 Do induction on **t**, and split the **Branch** case according to the structure of
    insert: correct subgoals are automatically generated by Alfa.

Here we take the simplest subgoal as an example. In case `t = Branch n lt rt`, `k < n`, and not `#newlt - #rt == 2` (writing `newlt` for `insert lt k`), we get

```
subgoal :: Bal t -> Bal (Branch n newlt rt)
```

When we unfold the definition of `Bal` to the right we get three conjuncts, where only `|#newlt - #rt| <= 1` is not immediate. Thus we need to prove the following:

```
subgoal' ::  |   #lt - #rt| <= 1
         ->   #newlt - #rt  /= 2
         ->  |#newlt - #rt| <= 1
```

P3 Abstracting from tree heights to plain numbers, we speculate the following

```
lemmaA :: (x,y,z :: Nat) -> |y-z| <= 1 -> x-z  /= 2 ->
                                          |x-z| <= 1
```

The intended instantiation is $(x, y, z) = (\texttt{\#newlt}, \texttt{\#lt}, \texttt{\#rt})$. The speculated preconditions here abstract away much of the relationship among those heights.

T4 Testing `lemmaA` shows a counterexample $(x, y, z) = (3, 1, 0)$.

A moment's reflection reveals that this counterexample is spurious; `newlt` contains at most one more element than `lt` and rotations do not increase height, so `#newlt` cannot increase by two from `#lt`.

P5 Therefore we add an extra hypothesis `x-y <= 1` to `lemmaA`:

```
lemmaA' :: (x,y,z :: Nat) -> |y-z| <= 1 ->   x-z  /= 2 ->
                             x-y  <= 1 -> |x-z| <= 1

lemmaB  :: (lt :: BT) -> Bal lt -> #(insert lt k) - #lt <= 1
```

`lemmaB` is needed to discharge the added hypothesis `x-y <= 1` in `lemmaA'`.

T6 Test lemmas: `lemmaB` passes the test, but `lemmaA'` fails again with $(x, y, z) = (0, 1, 2)$. This reminds us that `#newlt >= #lt` also must be used in the proof.

P7 Add yet another hypothesis to `lemmaA'`:

```
lemmaA'' :: (x,y,z :: Nat) -> |y-z| <= 1 ->   x-z  /= 2 ->
                        x >= y ->   x-y  <= 1 -> |x-z| <= 1

lemmaC  :: (lt :: BT) -> Bal lt -> #(insert lt k) >= #lt
```

T8 Test lemmas: Both now pass tests.

P9 Prove `lemmaA''`, `lemmaB`, and `lemmaC`. This finishes the proof of this particular `subgoal`.

When a proof proceeds with nested cases, the context of a subgoal may quickly become unmanageably large and essential information may be obscured. Besides the general points, this example demonstrates how testing lets us first try reckless abstractions and then recover the needed pieces of information.

7 Using Dependently Typed Data Structures

We also experimented with several ways of writing a dependently typed version
of AVL-insertion. Let `AVL h lb ub` be the set of AVL-trees with height `h` and
bounds `lb` and `ub`. The insertion function then gets the type:

```
insertAVL :: (h, lb, ub :: Nat) -> AVL h lb ub ->
             (k :: Nat) -> Between lb k ub ->
             (AVL h lb ub  +  AVL (Succ h) lb ub)
```

expressing that the height is either unchanged or increased by one. `Between lb`
`k ub` abbreviates `T (lb <= k && k < ub)`. The definition of `AVL` is as follows.

```
AVL  Zero            lb ub = T (lb <= ub)
AVL (Succ    Zero)   lb ub = data Leaf (k :: Nat)
                                       (p :: Between lb k ub)
AVL (Succ (Succ h)) lb ub =
  data LH (root :: Nat) (lt :: AVL (Succ h) lb            root)
                        (rt :: AVL  h        (Succ root) ub  )
     | EQ (root :: Nat) (lt :: AVL (Succ h) lb            root)
                        (rt :: AVL (Succ h) (Succ root) ub  )
     | RH (root :: Nat) (lt :: AVL  h        lb            root)
                        (rt :: AVL (Succ h) (Succ root) ub  )
```

Furthermore, we get informative types of the rotations. For example,

```
rotLeft :: (n, lb, ub, root :: Nat)
           -> (lt :: AVL (Succ (Succ n)) lb            root)
           -> (rt :: AVL n                (Succ root) ub  )
           ->         AVL (Succ (Succ n)) lb            ub
```

A complete version of `insertAVL` which does not deal with the search tree
condition, but only with the balance condition can be found at
`http://www.cs.chalmers.se/~qiao/papers/TestingProving/`.
It is about one page long.

When writing these programs in Alfa, we start with their dependent type.
While building the programs the type-checker ensures that we do not do anything
wrong, hence no need for testing! However, we should keep in mind that this
algorithm was written after a certain amount of experimentation with Haskell-
style algorithms, where both testing and proving helped us to gain insight into
the logical structure of the problem. Moreover, even for this dependently typed
`insertAVL`, which has a type that shows that it maintains the AVL-tree property,
testing is still useful for making sure that it satisfies the insertion axiom:

```
(m :: s) -> (x, y :: a) ->
T (member (insert m x) y == (x == y) || member m y)
```

when `s` is the set of all AVL-trees, `a = Nat`, `member` is binary search for AVL-
trees, and `insert` is implemented using `insertAVL`.

When building a library of datastructures we may go further and show that concrete datastructures, such as AVL-trees with associated operations, satisfy all properties of suitable abstract data types. We can use Agda/Alfa's dependent records (signatures and structures) for this purpose. For example, a signature for the ADT of finite sets, including both operations and axioms, can be formalized as follows:

```
AbsSet :: (a, s :: Set) -> Eq a ->
    sig  empty    :: s
         member   :: s -> a -> Bool
         insert   :: s -> a -> s
         single   :: a -> s
         union    :: s -> s -> s
         . . .
         insertAx :: (m :: s) -> (x, y :: a) ->
                       T (member (insert m x) y
                           == (x == y) || member m y)
         singleAx :: (m :: s) -> (x, y :: a) ->
                       T (member (single x) y == (x == y))
         unionAx  :: (m,m' :: s) -> (x :: a) ->
                       T (member (union m m') x
                           == member m x || member m' x)
         . . .
```

where the dots indicate that we may include all the usual set operations and their axioms, and `Eq a` specifies that the equality (==) on the set `a` is an equivalence relation:

```
Eq :: Set -> Set

Eq a = sig  (==) :: a -> a -> Bool
            ref  :: (x     :: a) -> T (x == x)
            sym  :: (x,y   :: a) -> T (x == y) -> T (y == x)
            tra  :: (x,y,z :: a) -> T (x == y) ->
                                    T (y == z) -> T (x == z)
```

Note that both `Eq a` and `AbsSet a s eq` are "testable signature" since all axioms are testable properties.

8   Discussion and Further Research

This paper is a first progress report on combining testing and proving in dependent type theory. We have built a simple tool for random testing of goals occurring during proof construction in the proof assistant Agda/Alfa. We have also carried out some case studies.

Like Hayashi, we feel that it is indeed fruitful to combine proving and testing. In formulating theorems and planning proofs, testing is helpful for avoiding false starts and wrong turns, while recovering from these is costly in traditional proof assistants.

Claessen and Hughes report three common kinds of errors discovered by testing: errors in programs, errors in specifications, and errors in test data generators which sometimes are complex programs themselves. Since our test data generators are written in Agda/Alfa, we can prove properties, such as surjectivity, about them. In this way we increase confidence in successful test runs. We can also use the dependent type system to ensure that generated test data have the expected property.

Testing encourages an experimental frame of mind. You try this and you try that. Once you have access to suitable test data generators it is easy to test different lemmas. Proving on the other hand requires that you think very clearly about the problem. It is a familiar observation that you pay a high price for lack of elegance when trying to prove a property. So you are forced to think more deeply about the reasons why a program works.

A consequence of this is that you feel inclined to improve the design of your program. Much work on program verification and derivation has been based on what seems like a too simple model of programming. First you write a specification. Then you write a program. Then you prove that the program meets the specification. Alternatively, you may try to systematically derive the program from the specification in such a way that it meets the specification. (This latter view has been popular in the type theory community.) This seems to be an unrealistic model of program development, however. What happens in practice seems to be that both the specification and the program evolve gradually. We believe that both testing and formal proof can help during this process, and it is advantageous to have a system where you can easily switch between the two.

We believe that combining testing and proving will give rise to new research problems distinct from those which arise when doing testing and proving separately. Here are some questions that we asked ourselves, while carrying our case studies:

- How often in a proof do we encounter (efficiently) testable subgoals? In the small examples in this paper testable subgoals appeared sufficiently often to make testing a useful guide for proving. But will this be the case when doing larger and more complex proofs?
- Can we automate test data generation more? At the moment test data generation has to be done manually, but the technique of generic (or polytypic) programming [2] may help us write domain-based test data generators uniformly for a large class of data types. Can even the activity of writing special purpose generators be automated to some extent? Another question is to consider alternatives to the approach of the present paper where random binary trees are first generated and then converted to appropriate data types.
- Should we consider systematic test data generation instead? Can we use the structure of the specification term q[x1, ..., xn] to generate test data with good coverage properties?

- Can we generalize the class of testable properties that our tool accepts? In a sense Martin-Löf's meaning explanations for type theory say that all judgements are testable! (A discussion of this point is outside the scope of this paper.) Can we make use of this observation?

References

1. Lennart Augustsson: Cayenne: a Language with Dependent Types. In *Proceedings of the third ACM SIGPLAN International Conference on Functional Programming (ICFP-98)*, ACM SIGPLAN Notices, 34(1), pages 239–250, 1998.
2. R. Backhouse, P. Jansson, J. Jeuring, and L. Meertens: Generic Programming – An Introduction. LNCS 1608, pages 28–115, 1999.
3. Ana Bove: General Recursion in Type Theory. PhD thesis. Chalmers University of Technology. 2002.
4. Magnus Carlsson and Thomas Hallgren: Fudgets - Purely Functional Processes with applications to Graphical User Interfaces. PhD thesis. Chalmers University of Technology. 1998.
5. Koen Claessen and John Hughes: QuickCheck: a lightweight tool for random testing of Haskell programs. In *Proceedings of the ACM Sigplan International Conference on Functional Programming (ICFP-00)* volume 35.9, pages 18–22. ACM Press, 2000.
6. Koen Claessen and John Hughes: QuickCheck: Automatic Specification-Based Testing: http://www.cs.chalmers.se/~rjmh/QuickCheck/.
7. Catarina Coquand: Agda, available from http://www.cs.chalmers.se/~catarina/agda.
8. Thierry Coquand: Pattern Matching with Dependent Types. In Bengt Nordström, Kent Petersson and Gordon Plotkin, editors, *Proceedings of The 1992 Workshop on Types for Proofs and Programs* pages 71–84. Båstad, 1992.
9. Thierry Coquand: Structured Type Theory. draft, 1999, available from http://www.cs.chalmers.se/~coquand/type.html.
10. Peter Dybjer: Inductive Families. In *Formal Aspects of Computing*, volume 6, pages 440–465, 1994.
11. Peter Dybjer and Anton Setzer: A finite axiomatization of inductive-recursive definitions. In *Typed Lambda Calculi and Applications, Lecture Notes in Computer Science* 1581, pages 129–146. 1999.
12. Peter Dybjer and Anton Setzer: Indexed Induction-Recursion. In *Proof Theory in Computer Science, LNCS* 2183, pages 93–113, 2001.
13. Thomas Hallgren: Alfa, available from http://www.cs.chalmers.se/~hallgren/Alfa.
14. Susumu Hayashi and Hiroshi Nakano: PX, a Computational Logic. The MIT Press. 1988.
15. Susumu Hayashi, Ryosuke Sumitomo and Ken-ichiro Shii: Towards Animation of Proofs - testing proofs by examples. In *Theoretical Computer Science*, volume 272, pages 177–195, 2002.
16. Per Martin-Löf: Constructive Mathematics and Computer Programming. In *Logic, Methodology and Philosophy of Science, VI, 1979*, pages 153–175. North-Holland, 1982.
17. Per Martin-Löf: Intuitionistic Type Theory. Bibliopolis, 1984.
18. Chris Okasaki: An Overview of Edison. In *Haskell Workshop*, pages 34–54, September 2000.

19. Catherine Parent: A collection of examples using the Program tactic. available from http://pauillac.inria.fr/coq/contribs-eng.html.
20. Programatica: Integrating Programming, Properties, and Validation. http://www.cse.ogi.edu/PacSoft/projects/programatica/.
21. F.A. Rabhi and G. Lapalme: Algorithms: a functional programming approach. Addison-Wesley Press, 1999.
22. David Wahlstedt: Detecting termination using size-change in parameter values. Master thesis. Chalmers University of Technology, 2000.
23. Hongwei Xi and Frank Pfenning: Dependent types in practical programming. In *Proceedings of the 26th ACM SIGPLAN-SIGACT on Principles of programming languages*, pages 214–227, ACM Press, 1999.

A   Haskell Programs in Section 2

```
isBST :: Int -> Int -> BT -> Bool
isBST lb ub Empty = lb < ub
isBST lb ub (Branch root left rt) = lb < root && root < ub
             && isBST lb root left && isBST root ub rt
```

The membership algorithm for general binary trees is

```
member :: BT -> Int -> Bool
member Empty               key = False
member (Branch root lt rt) key = key == root
                               || member lt key || member rt key
```

The binary search algorithm is

```
binSearch :: BT -> Int -> Bool
binSearch Empty                key = False
binSearch (Branch root lt rt)  key
          | key < root  = binSearch lt key
          | key == root = True
          | key > root  = binSearch rt key
```

Reasoning about Proof Search Specifications: An Abstract

Dale Miller

INRIA/Futurs/Saclay & École polytechnique

Formally proving the correctness of computation systems has traditionally been divided into two high-level steps: first implement a framework for mathematics and then encode computation systems into the resulting mathematical formalism. The first step generally involves typed λ-calculus, set theory, or higher-order intuitionistic or classical logic; the second step generally involves encoding a model theoretic semantics of the computation system. Such frameworks have been successful in a number of ways and they continue to attract researchers and system developers.

Despite the success of such systems, there is a growing collection of specifications of computational systems where factoring correctness issues via conventional mathematical structures and techniques seems to hinder formal approaches to correctness. These specifications are based on proof search (logic programming) in rich logics such as higher-order and linear logics, and provide declarative and elegant encodings of operational semantics, π-calculus, security protocols, sequent calculus, etc. These logics are highly intensional in nature: for example, linear logic is sensitive to resources and higher-order logics exist in which λ-abstractions denoting expressions instead of functions (a feature used to encode higher-order abstract syntax). The model theoretic semantics of such logics is either unknown or involves complicated constructions. As a result, if the first step to reasoning about such specifications involves encoding such model theoretical semantics in a mathematical framework, reasoning with these specifications can prove daunting.

None-the-less, reasoning with such proof search specifications can often be done directly and succinctly using proof theory techniques. We shall outline a current research project that attempts to formalize how proof theory techniques can be used to reasoning about proof search specifications, thus avoiding the need to first encode a model theoretic semantics.

D. Basin and B. Wolff (Eds.): TPHOLs 2003, LNCS 2758, p. 204, 2003.

Program Extraction from Large Proof Developments

Luís Cruz-Filipe[1,2] and Bas Spitters[1]

[1] University of Nijmegen, The Netherlands
[2] Center for Logic and Computation, Portugal
{lcf,spitters}@cs.kun.nl

Abstract. It is well known that mathematical proofs often contain (abstract) algorithms, but although these algorithms can be understood by a human, it still takes a lot of time and effort to implement these algorithms on a computer; moreover, one runs the risk of making mistakes in the process.

From a fully formalized constructive proof one can automatically obtain a computer implementation of such an algorithm together with a proof that the program is correct. As an example we consider the fundamental theorem of algebra which states that every non-constant polynomial has a root. This theorem has been fully formalized in the Coq proof assistant. Unfortunately, when we first tried to extract a program, the computer ran out of resources. We will discuss how we used logical techniques to make it possible to extract a feasible program. This example is used as a motivation for a broader perspective on how the formalization of mathematics should be done with program extraction in mind.

Keywords: Program extraction, Constructive mathematics, Formalized mathematics, Type Theory.

1 Introduction

It has long been realized that constructive mathematics has computational content in the sense that proofs of existential statements actually correspond to algorithms to compute a witness, see [3,14].

Also intuitionistic logic, which describes the reasoning in constructive mathematics, is the natural language for type-theory based proof-assistants. Among these, Coq currently provides a tool that translates proofs of mathematical statements into functional programs which are guaranteed to be correct. This mechanism, described in detail in [13], works by assigning different types to terms which represent data and terms which represent properties of the data. The latter are assumed to be *computationally irrelevant* in the sense that they can not be used to define data; they can, however, be used to prove properties of functions (termination, correctness, etc.) which operate on this data, and therefore need never be extracted. Throughout this paper, we will refer to this mechanism as *program extraction*. For a short overview of this, see Section 2.

D. Basin and B. Wolff (Eds.): TPHOLs 2003, LNCS 2758, pp. 205–220, 2003.

The FTA-project in Nijmegen [10] was the first attempt to formalize a large piece of constructive mathematics, namely the Fundamental Theorem of Algebra, in Coq; therefore it was a natural testing ground for the program extraction mechanism. However, a problem soon arose regarding what, in the formalization, should be considered as "properties". The intuitive approach that all predicates are properties does not work. As an example, consider the logarithm function; a possible way to formalize it is as a function taking a real argument x and a proof that x is positive. According to this approach, this proof is a property of the data which the algorithm itself never needs to examine; but there is actually no algorithm which satisfies this criterion.

This is just an instance of the fact that constructively, proof terms are computationally important and analysis of these can be used to define objects, e.g. functions. Therefore it is necessary to keep the proof-objects, which means that all predicates should be regarded as data. This implies that all proof terms get extracted, which increases the program size enough to make extraction unfeasible.

In Section 3 we describe how the Coq type theory was used to explicitly distinguish between computationally relevant and irrelevant mathematical statements in order to make program extraction possible for this example. Although this is not a new idea, our approach does differ from others in that we focus on the development of mathematics (including logic) as opposed to the precise implementation of the extraction procedure. This is in some sense an orthogonal approach which, we expect, can be combined with the various existing extraction mechanisms.

In Section 4 we examine the more subtle problems that could be discovered once a program could be extracted for the first time, and present solutions that allow to reduce this program to reasonable size; in Section 5 we also show some of the current limitations of the Coq type theory and refer to the work in progress that suggests that these might be overcome in the near future.

In Section 6, we generalize from our experience and analyze how the formalization of constructive mathematics can be done so that program extraction automatically succeeds. To make the development of both constructive and classical mathematics go more smoothly, we propose and discuss some changes to the Coq type theory.

2   An Overview of Extraction

Computer implementations of program extraction have been around for about two decades now. Among these, Paulin [16] was the first to provide an extraction mechanism for Coq.

There are several approaches to the issue, and several different ways to formalize it; for more detailed information, the reader is advised to check the cited works and their references. For a more detailed overview, although in a slightly different setting, see [19].

In all approaches, however, the basic outline is the same: through the Curry-Howard isomorphism, proofs are identified with programs in a given programming language. However, the resulting programs contain much irrelevant information (from the computational point of view), therefore some mechanism is devised to identify this irrelevant parts and remove them from the final program.

One approach, studied in the context of Coq by Prost [18], is to look at the proof term and recursively mark its subterms according to whether they contribute to the final output of the program or not; this marking is done in a way that is coherent with type checking, so that removing the marked parts will still return a correct λ-term. This *a posteriori* approach, also known as *pruning*, has the advantage of typically yielding smaller and more efficient programs, as it is actually an algorithm for dead code removal, but its time cost is exponential, as it invokes the type checking algorithm.

A different approach, which is taken in the Coq proof assistant [20,13], is to define *a priori* a type for data (e.g. propositions) which will never be extracted. The underlying type system then ensures that terms of this type will never be allowed to have computational significance, so that simply removing them yields a correct program. This method itself is naturally faster than the previous approach, but it has the disadvantage that the terms which are not to be extracted have to be specified in advance; therefore the extraction process cannot recognize and eliminate e.g. dummy arguments. It has actually been shown in [18] that the *a posteriori* method of Prost can simulate the *a priori* method of Paulin of which Letouzey's is a generalization.

The most significant drawback of this approach is that propositions are always assumed to be irrelevant for the extraction. This is not true, however, when we are dealing with constructive formalizations where case analysis on proof terms can be (and is) used to define functions. Therefore, we sought a way to combine the time-efficiency advantages of the *a priori* approach with the flexibility of the *a posteriori* approach while maintaining a syntactic distinction between data and propositions. In the example we will focus on, *a posteriori* methods seem to be unusable, as they require too much computer time and resources. Moreover, it seems to be difficult to combine *a posteriori* methods with a module system, which we will later on argue to be desirable, since modules behave as black boxes.

The second issue is where the extracted program will live. Traditionally, efficiency criteria strongly suggested an *external* extraction, in the sense that the proof term is translated from the proof language into a program in a (different) programming language; this also has some other advantages, as programming languages are usually less restrictive and allow among others for potentially non-terminating loops and partial functions. Also, existing technology such as compilers and interfaces can be reused.

Internal extraction (which is a *contradictio in terminis*) has the advantage that the original and final type-systems are the same. This allows a simple implementation as additional reduction rules inside the type theory, such that the proof terms simply reduce to the appropriate programs [8]. Moreover, realizability (extraction) can be used to strengthen results. For instance, the realizability interpretation validates both the axiom of choice and the independence of premise [22,21], so these principles do not have to be assumed as axioms, but can be derived for each particular instance. Finally, in the specific case of Coq, the new version will incorporate a Coq compiler [12]; therefore the speed of the program does not seem to be a real issue anymore.

Our Approach

We chose to work with the Coq extraction mechanism to ML, which is an external *a priori* extraction. The main reason for this is simply that the formalization we focused on was already present and had been developed in Coq. It should be pointed out, however, that we expect our work to be quite straightforwardly applicable to the other theories of extraction based on type theory. Also, in our opinion, there is no best method; rather an intelligent combination of *a priori* and *a posteriori* approaches will likely yield the most efficient program.

The reader may wonder why we only focus on the size of the extracted program and not on its efficiency. There are three main reasons for this. First, as we pointed out, size is the main obstacle in the actual extraction. Second, size is an important issue, as it is reasonable to want the extracted programs to be readable; and if two different programs implement the same algorithm in essentially the same way, it sounds reasonable to argue that the shorter one is better. Finally, in the FTA-project the real numbers were formalized as arbitrary Cauchy-sequences, which is computationally very inefficient; therefore analyzing the efficiency of the extracted program seemed uninteresting. These reasons also justify that we do not compare our extracted program with the algorithm which one might directly implement.

The algorithm implicitly present in the Kneser proof is actually as efficient as the well known Newton-Raphson method, as was shown in [11]; unfortunately, the presently inefficient formalization of the real numbers actually prevents the computation of zeros of a polynomial using the proof of the FTA. Fortunately, two efficient formalizations of the reals [6,15] are almost completed.

3   Positive and Negative Statements

The Coq type theory, based on the Calculus of Inductive Constructions [20], contains two kinds of sorts. On the one hand, there are sorts Set and Prop, representing respectively data types and types of properties; these correspond both to what is usually represented by $*$ in Pure Type System (PTS) [1]. On the other side, there is a family $(\mathsf{Type}_i)_{i \in \mathbb{N}}$ of sorts (corresponding to $\square$ in the PTS approach) which, among other things, rules how higher types are formed.[1] Also the typing statements $\mathsf{Set} : \mathsf{Type}_0$ and $\mathsf{Prop} : \mathsf{Type}_0$ hold.

The Calculus of Inductive Constructions also provides mechanisms which allow to define inductive types. We will not go into details on how this is done,

---

[1] Herman Geuvers argued (in private communication) that the datatypes should have sort Type; we will return to this question.

but it is important to point out that the way they deal with inductive types is actually where Set and Prop mostly differ: Set allows stronger elimination rules for inductive types than Prop (for more details, refer to [20]). The reasons for this have to do precisely with not wanting to allow data to depend on properties of other data.

In order to take advantage of this distinction, we classify properties in positive and negative statements, that is, with and without computational content. The former need to be extracted, the latter should not be extracted. This is achieved by representing the first ones by objects of type Set and the latter ones by objects of type Prop.

In fact, we would like to have some overloading which would allow us to treat all propositions (whether typed in Set or in Prop) uniformly; unfortunately, this is not possible in the present version of Coq.

However, the situation is not as bad as it might seem at first glance. Suppose for a moment that we have decided which types the primitive statements have; then, the types of compound statements can be automatically derived as we now explain. We use s, s_1 and s_2 to denote either Set or Prop.

The computational content of the implication is determined by its second argument; this can be seen by taking into account that implication is actually represented (through the Curry-Howard isomorphism) by non-dependent functional abstraction. Therefore, $\rightarrow: s_1 \rightarrow s_2 \rightarrow s_2$.

The negation of a statement does not have computational content, as it simply means that a certain case does not occur. So $\neg : s \rightarrow$ Prop. This is also consistent with the fact that $\neg A$ is usually defined as $A \rightarrow \bot$, which according to the previous rule always has type Prop.

For a disjunction we want to keep track of which option is relevant, in order to define functions by cases. Therefore, $\vee : s_1 \rightarrow s_2 \rightarrow$ Set.

The type of the conjunction is determined by the types of the conjuncts. In case they both have type Prop, neither of them has computational content, and therefore neither does their conjunction; otherwise, the conjunction must have type Set.

Notice that all these maps are already present in the Coq standard library, except for some variants of $\wedge$ and $\neg$. These are straightforward to define.

In summary, the types of logical connectives are:

$$\neg : s \rightarrow \text{Prop}$$
$$\rightarrow : s_1 \rightarrow s_2 \rightarrow s_2$$
$$\vee : s_1 \rightarrow s_2 \rightarrow \text{Set}$$
$$\wedge : s_1 \rightarrow s_2 \rightarrow \begin{cases} \text{Prop} & s_1 = s_2 = \text{Prop} \\ \text{Set} & \text{otherwise} \end{cases}$$

Unfortunately, Coq does not allow overloading, it is not possible to use the standard notations for the new connectives. Therefore, we defined some abbreviations. Conjunction and disjunction are represented respectively by * and +, with arguments from Prop enclosed in braces. (This notation for disjunction is already defined.) The proposition $\neg A$ is represented by (Not A), while implication is written as usual: A->B for $A \to B$.

Finally, we use the quantifiers already defined in Coq. Universal quantification behaves similarly to implication, so $\forall : \Pi(A : s_1).(A \to s_2) \to s_2$. In Coq, (x:A)(P x) stands for $\forall_{x:A}(Px)$.

As regards existential quantification, we always need to keep track of its witness, so $\exists : \Pi(A : \mathsf{Set}).(A \to s) \to \mathsf{Set}$. We represent $\exists_{x:A}(Px)$ in Coq by either {x:A & (P x)}, if $P : A \to \mathsf{Set}$, or {x:A | (P x)}, if $P : A \to \mathsf{Prop}$.

The Coq system also provides a Prop-valued existential quantifier, but we never had occasion to use it in our example.

3.1   Primitive Formulas

The only thing now missing is to describe how to type the primitive formulas. Our development is based on the notion of a *setoid*, that is a set together with an apartness relation.[2] An apartness relation is a relation # such that for all x, y and z:

1. $\neg x \# x$;
2. $x \# y \to y \# x$;
3. $x \# y \to x \# z \lor y \# z$.

Usually, for instance in the case of the real numbers, the apartness is computationally meaningful, so apartness has type Set. This can easily be seen from the third axiom where the conclusion is a disjunction; its computational content can only be realizable if the apartness is in Set. This is consistent with what was said above: in the Cauchy model of the real numbers, for example, apartness is defined by means of an existential statement which must be typed in Set.

Our setoids all have a *stable* equality, that is $x = y$ iff $\neg\neg x = y$. So the equality does not have computational content, and should be placed in Prop.

Another way to look at it is to see that the equality can be characterized as the negation of the apartness: $x = y \iff \neg x \# y$, and as such should go to Prop. This is actually a stronger condition than the previous one, as it then follows that

$$x = y \iff \neg x \# y \iff \neg\neg\neg x \# y \iff \neg\neg x = y.$$

Finally, we have an abstract model of the real numbers, in which $<$ is a primitive relation. This relation is computationally meaningful; for instance, in the model of the Cauchy sequences it is defined as an existentially quantified proposition. In abstract, this meaningfulness can be easily seen from the fact that $x < y$ should be equivalent to $x \# y \land \neg(y < x)$, and the latter has type Set.

The relation $\geq$ is defined as the negation of $<$, so $\geq$ is of type Prop. (Remark that constructively the relation $x \geq y$ is not the same as either $x = y$ or $x > y$ but weaker, as the latter would give us a way to decide which of the two options is the case.)

---

[2] These are actually known as setoids *with apartness*, or *constructive setoids*, but we will simply call them setoids as they are the only ones we will refer to.

All other relations are defined from these primitives, so we can easily derive their type. The situation here is reminiscent to model theory, where we study abstract signatures and define more complicated functions and predicates defined from these primitives, but we will not pursue this line of thought.

Using this approach, we found that much more than 90% (!) of the proof terms in the formalization were then assigned the type Prop, which meant that a significant proportion of the formalization would be ignored by the extraction mechanism. Thus, we managed for the first time to extract a program, although still quite large: its size was still 15Mb (roughly equally divided between the construction of the real numbers and the proof of the FTA).

Unfortunately, due to known issues [13], the extracted ML program does not type check. This can be overcome by manually editing the program; in our case, this meant inserting an explicit type cast in around ten thousand places in the extracted program. We understand that this problem will be fixed in the next Coq version, but at the time this work was done it made it impossible to analyze the improvements described in the next section in terms of actual performance.

4   Optimization

Having successfully extracted a program, we got for the first time an opportunity to analyze our formalization from a new perspective and the viability of actually producing usable programs from formal mathematics. In this section we will analyze the reasons that made our extracted program so big and discuss how some apparently trivial modifications lead to impressive changes in its size.

When looking at the program code two main problems stand out:

1. much of the program consists of coercions between algebraic structures; for example, addition is an operation on semigroups, therefore if R is a ring a coercion is needed to cast it into a semigroup so that we can speak of the addition on R.
2. there is still much irrelevant information on the propositional level.

The first problem has to do with the fact that the FTA project attempted at generality, therefore building a cumulative algebraic hierarchy where new structures are built on top of existing ones. Unfortunately, the absence of a notion of subtyping in Coq implies that there must exist explicit casts between these structures instead of the inclusions one would expect. The new Coq version contains a module system; the extraction mechanism is being adapted to work with this modules. Hopefully, this will solve this problem.

The second problem is more interesting, and underlines an unexpected aspect of the formalization. Because of the way primitive predicates are typed, (mathematically) equivalent definitions can generate quite different extracted programs according to how they are typed. Consider the usual statement saying that $(x_n)_{n \in \mathbb{N}}$ is a Cauchy sequence:

$$\forall_{\varepsilon > 0} \exists_{N \in \mathbb{N}} \forall_{m,n > N} |x_m - x_n| < \varepsilon. \tag{1}$$

Because $<$ is a Set-valued predicate, the extracted proof that x is indeed a Cauchy sequence will consist of a function from the positive real numbers to the natural numbers (which computes the witness N) and a function that takes two numbers bigger than N and returns a computational proof of the desired inequality.

However, the following definition is easily seen to be equivalent:

$$\forall_{\varepsilon>0}\exists_{N\in\mathbb{N}}\forall_{m,n>N}\,|x_m \quad x_n| \leq \varepsilon. \tag{2}$$

(Equation (1) trivially implies (2); for the reciprocal, just take $\varepsilon > 0$ and apply (2) with $\frac{\varepsilon}{2}$.)

Now, the computational part of a proof that x satisfies condition (2) consists simply of an algorithm to extract the witness. This is intuitively more efficient, as it involves less computation, and is just as informative as we argued above.

Even if one is not interested in program extraction, there are good mathematical reasons for preferring to use $\leq$ instead of $<$ whenever possible. This is simply because $\leq$, being a negative predicate, allows constructive proofs by contradiction. It should also be noted that Bishop [2] very carefully uses the latter in all ε-δ-definitions and -proofs for this reason.[3]

In summary, there are two good reasons to work with negative statements: not only do the programs become shorter, but also proving is made easier.

As our construction of the real numbers was based on the model of Cauchy sequences of rationals, changing this definition (which by the way did not require changing too much of the formalization) reduced the size of the extracted reals by 80% and the whole ML program to around 8Mb.

4.1   Proof Optimization

Examining the extracted program, we realized that in fact there was still too much unnecessary or redundant information. Specifically, the proof of the Kneser lemma [11], which basically consists of several long chains of inequalities, seemed a good candidate for size reduction, and so we decided to focus on it.

The formalization of the FTA contains several results dealing with order. Among those, there are several transitivity rules for $<$ and $\leq$ and results dealing with preservation through algebraic operations.

The previous experience with the Cauchy sequences suggested that a clever use of the $\leq$ relation could significantly improve the size of the extracted program. To understand this in more detail, we will look at two examples, both of which deal with the use of transitivity.

There are four main transitivity rules with the following types (all depending on an ordered field F and variables $x, y, z : F$):

---

[3] We actually realized that this was happening when we compared the size of the FTA program with the sizes of extracted programs for Rolle's theorem or Taylor's theorem; these were around 100 times smaller, and one of the main reasons for this was in fact that all ε-δ concepts such as continuity and derivative were defined with $\leq$, following Bishop.

```
less_transitive  :  (x[<]y)->(y[<]z)->(x[<]z)
less_leEq_trans  :  (x[<]y)->(y[<=]z)->(x[<]z)
leEq_less_trans  :  (x[<=]y)->(y[<]z)->(x[<]z)
leEq_transitive  :  (x[<=]y)->(y[<=]z)->(x[<=]z)
```

The first three are extracted to ML as functions with following types:

```
less_transitive  :  (x[<]y)->(y[<]z)->(x[<]z)
less_leEq_trans  :  (x[<]y)->(x[<]z)
leEq_less_trans  :  (y[<]z)->(x[<]z)
```

(The fact that some conditions disappear does not compromise the correctness of the program, as the extraction mechanism guarantees that they will hold whenever these functions are applied in the extracted program.)

It then becomes clear that the last two lemmas will generate smaller programs, significantly smaller when you take into account that each proof of $a < b$ is typically long. By trying to cut out the bigger branches, significant improvement in the size of the program (and, one would hope, indirectly on its efficiency) can be made.

But we can even do better. Suppose that a statement of the form $a < b$ is proved through the chain of inequalities

$$a < x_1 < x_2 < x_3 < b.$$

A naive proof-term of type $a[<]b$ would then be

```
(less_transitive a x1 b H_a_x1
  (less_transitive x1 x2 b H_x1_x2
  (less_transitive x2 x3 b H_x2_x3 H_x3_b)))
```

where $H\_a\_x1 : a[<]x1$ and analogously for the other terms (which in general will be quite large).

Now, because every subterm of this proof has type Set, the extracted program will have exactly the same structure. However, we could also justify the same inequality by stating first that $a \leq x_3$ and then that $x_3 < b$. The corresponding proof term could then be (leEq_less_trans a x3 b H_a_x3 H_x3_b).

Furthermore, H_a_x3 (which will include most of the terms in the previous proof) has type Prop; therefore, the extracted program is simply

```
(leEq_less_trans a x3 b H_x3_b)
```

Notice that we gain not only by omitting H_a_x1, H_x1_x2 and H_x2_x3, but also in not having to mention x_1 and x_2; analysis of the extracted program shows that (e. g. in the Kneser proof) this is also very relevant, as these can also be quite long expressions.

This optimization of the proof of the Kneser lemma reduced the size of the extracted program by 1.5Mb, corresponding to roughly 30% of the size of the proof of the Kneser lemma.

In the next step, we decided to experiment with the known distinction between subsets as propositional functions or as subsetoids [4,5]. We found that when using propositional functions, not only do proofs become easier to write, but also the extracted program greatly reduces in size. It also increases the internal coherence of the formalization, as using this approach we can treat division simply as a partial function and apply to it the general (formalized) theory of partial functions.

This turned out to be a significant improvement; although the extracted real numbers do not change much (which is actually to be expected, as division plays no important role in their formalization), the FTA part is reduced by 60%. More significantly, there is essentially no change in the actual program due to the fact, explained in [5], that we are basically performing explicit $\beta\delta$-reduction on the proof terms (and corresponding extracted programs).

The program size was finally brought down to 3Mb by some minor changes in the proofs, which are too specific to be interesting to describe here.

We summarize these results in a table:

Change	Reals (Mb)	FTA (Mb)	Total (Mb)	$\Delta(\%)$
Original	7.5	7.5	15	
New Cauchy seq.	1.5	6.5	8	47
New Kneser proof	1.5	5.0	6.5	19
New Division	1.4	2.0	3.4	48
Various	1.4	1.6	3.0	12

It should be pointed out that the *ratios* between the sizes of the different versions are actually more relevant than the actual sizes: we can safely assume that if the changes had been done in a different order, these ratios would be similar whereas the differences in size would not.

5   Future Optimization

Throughout this section we will only consider the FTA-part of the extracted program.

Although reduced to 20% of its original size, the extracted program is still considered quite large (1, 6Mb) when one considers that the algorithm which it implements is not so complex. Therefore, we decided that we should carefully look at the program to understand precisely what was taking up so much space.

One of the first things we noticed was that even though the formalization included a constant CC, representing the type of complex numbers, this constant was nowhere to be found in the extracted program. This is a bit surprising, as we are after all extracting a function that operates on complex numbers.

As it turned out, in fact, the definition had been fully expanded every time it occurred in the proof term! Considering that the type of complex numbers is explicitly mentioned around 130 times, and that the definition is around 5000 characters long, this fact alone accounts for nearly half of the program code.

The ring of polynomials is another construction which was fully spelled out each time. Although a bit smaller than the previous one, it is still mentioned more than sixty times. Manually replacing these occurrences by a defined constant therefore reduced the program to a mere 300kb, and allowed us also to see that in fact not much more simplification was likely to be possible, as most of the functions now became quite short.[4]

At this point, the need to explicitly insert coercions is the main reason for the size of the program. A good module or subtyping system for Coq would at this stage be very useful. Our experiments suggest that this would allow the extracted program to be as small as 100kb—a factor of 75 when compared with the size of the original extracted program.

A module system also seems to be useful for the following reason: for certain datatypes we will want to have several implementations, each one tailored for a certain goal, be it a specific kind of computation or a convenient way of proving theorems. If we have an adequate module system, these different implementations can be used in harmony. Work in this area is being done [7] and will probably be included in the next Coq version.

In summary, the extracted program consists of:

Description	Size (kb)	% of total
"Relevant" code	110	6.5
Unfolding of $\mathbb{C}$	1050	62.5
Unfolding of polynomials ($R[x]$)	330	19.5
Coercions	190	11.5
Total	1680	100

As before, the relative sizes are more important than the absolute values; that is, in the earlier versions of the extracted program the relative amount of wrongly unfolded definitions and the relative amount of coercions were roughly the same as in the final version.

6   A More Abstract View

Above we explained how to use the sorts Set and Prop for the propositions. To do this we only need to decide where to place the primitive relations, the proper place for composed relations can then be derived.

However, the use of Set is a bit unsatisfactory. For example, it is not possible just by looking at the type of an object to know whether it represents data or a proposition; this is felt as a limitation, as it makes the task harder for automatic tools to interpret the contents of the library.[5] We have tried to hide this ambiguity by defining a new constant CProp (Contentful Propositions) as an alias

---

[4] This turned out to be a bug in the extraction mechanism. After mentioning it to Pierre Letouzey, he was able to identify and fix the problem, thereby reducing the size of all extracted programs by around 80%.

[5] This was quite actively discussed on the MoWGLI mailing list.

for Set, and then explicitly typing all propositional statements in CProp. However, this approach is only partially successful for two reasons: on the one hand, in some instances Coq actually requires a *sort* to be used, and CProp, though δ-convertible to a sort, is not one; this is a secondary issue that is expected to be solved in the next version of Coq. The second problem, which is more basic, is that the distinction between data types and propositions strongly depends on the user's discipline: because Set and CProp are δ-equivalent, they can be interchanged from the type theory point of view, therefore reinstating the ambiguity which we aimed at removing.

The use of Set also has serious limitations from the logical point of view. We would like to allow the addition of e.g. the axiom of the excluded middle to our formalization and build classical mathematics on that, but this is not possible for several reasons. First, it is not clear how the principle of excluded middle should (or even could) be written: because of the fact that propositions do not all have the same type there are at least four different (and not equivalent) ways to write it. Moreover, the axiom $\Pi_{A:\mathsf{Set}} A \lor \neg A$ leads to an inconsistent theory, as noted in [9,17].

With these issues in mind, we now propose a slightly modified version of the Coq type system where these problems do not arise.

Our previous discussion of the difference between positive and negative statements suggests that there should be two basic sorts for propositions. We will denote these by Prop^+ and Prop^-, with the obvious meaning. Prop is then defined to be the disjoint union of these two sorts: $\mathsf{Prop} := \mathsf{Prop}^+ \oplus \mathsf{Prop}^-$. In Figure 1 we represent the current and the proposed version of the Coq type hierarchy.[6]

Fig. 1. Type hierarchy in Coq: present (left) and proposed (right)

In order to do classical mathematics, Prop^+ also needs to be predicative.[7] On the other hand, Prop^- should enjoy proof irrelevance, which is a natural consequence of the non-informativeness of the proofs—this is actually in line with the plans of the Coq team [7].

---

[6] Herman Geuvers argued (on the MoWGLI mailing list) that the datatypes should have sort Type. This has the advantage that the logic one obtains is very similar to higher order logic, which has been thoroughly studied and is by now well-understood. In this approach, the sort Set is no longer needed; however, some additional complications arise, so we will not discuss this approach.

[7] This is the main reason why one cannot simply work within Set.

Intuitively, Prop^+ and Prop^- behave respectively as Set and Prop in the Coq type theory, the main differences residing in the predicativeness of Prop^+ and the proof irrelevance in Prop^-. With this in mind, it is then natural to define connectives in Prop following what was said in section 3:

$$\rightarrow\ :\ \mathsf{Prop} \rightarrow s \rightarrow s \qquad\qquad \forall\ :\ \Pi(A:t_\forall).(A \rightarrow s) \rightarrow s$$
$$\vee\ :\ \mathsf{Prop} \rightarrow \mathsf{Prop} \rightarrow \mathsf{Prop}^+ \qquad \exists\ :\ \Pi(A:t_\exists).(A \rightarrow \mathsf{Prop}) \rightarrow \mathsf{Prop}^+$$
$$\underline{\vee}\ :\ \mathsf{Prop} \rightarrow \mathsf{Prop} \rightarrow \mathsf{Prop}^- \qquad \underline{\exists}\ :\ \Pi(A:t_\exists).(A \rightarrow \mathsf{Prop}) \rightarrow \mathsf{Prop}^-$$
$$\wedge\ :\ s_1 \rightarrow s_2 \rightarrow \begin{cases} \mathsf{Prop}^-\ s_1 = s_2 = \mathsf{Prop}^- \\ \mathsf{Prop}^+\ \text{otherwise} \end{cases} \qquad \neg\ :\ \mathsf{Prop} \rightarrow \mathsf{Prop}^-$$

where $\{s, s_1, s_2\}$ denote either Prop^+ or Prop^-. As regards quantifiers, $t_\forall$ can be a type of propositions or a datatype, and $t_\exists$ is a generic datatype.

Notice the existence of two disjunctions and two existential quantifiers. The connectives $\vee$ and $\exists$ are the informative connectives previously described, whereas their underlined versions are non-informative. These connectives are all present in the current Coq implementation, and we will soon discuss how $\underline{\vee}$ and $\underline{\exists}$ can be used.

Also observe that from the user point of view all these connectives return objects of type Prop; that is, we achieve uniformity in the types of propositions as desired.

As regards classical reasoning, there are two versions of the Principle of Excluded Middle (PEM) which can safely be added—corresponding to the two available disjunctions.

The weaker version is the axiom

$$\Pi_{A:\mathsf{Prop}} A \underline{\vee} (\neg A) : \mathsf{Prop}.$$

This is a *non-informative* version of the PEM, which allows classical reasoning over the domain but not e.g. defining functions according to whether a given predicate holds. With this axiom it is possible to prove classically valid properties of constructive formalizations, while keeping the possibility of program extraction. At this stage the connective $\underline{\exists}$ might come in handy, as it allows us to construct non-informative existential proofs by reasoning classically.

An alternative way to achieve the same effect is to *define* the weak disjunction and existential as follows: $A\underline{\vee}B := \neg(\neg A \wedge \neg B)$ and $\underline{\exists}x : A.Px := \neg(\forall x : A.\neg(Px))$. Then the above axiom is constructively provable.

To obtain full classical mathematics, in which we can define functions by case distinction, the stronger axiom

$$\Pi_{A:\mathsf{Prop}} A \vee (\neg A)$$

is needed. However, this poses a more subtle typing issue. Because of the predicativity of Prop^+, it cannot have type Prop^+; however, it can safely be typed in a higher type (like the Coq Type type). Although this may at first look somewhat strange, it can be regarded as a natural consequence of the fact that it represents a scheme of axioms rather than a single axiom. Given any $A : \mathsf{Prop}$, we can then prove $A \vee (\neg A) : \mathsf{Prop}$. However, adding this axiom obviously destroys program extraction.

6.1 Properties of Prop^+ and Prop^-

The approach just described has many similarities with the marked types of [18]. However, there is one very important distinction, namely that propositions are assigned types *a priori* and these propagate outwards through the formalization, whereas in [18] the markings propagate inwards from the type of the final term. This means that our approach requires no extra analysis of the proof term at extraction time.

Another issue is the relation between Prop^+ and Prop^-. It is natural to define maps between these types in both directions, with the following motivations:

- $(\cdot)^+$: $\mathsf{Prop}^- \to \mathsf{Prop}^+$ represents the intuitive notion that any non-informative proposition can be viewed as informative with empty content (e.g., as a constant);
- $(\cdot)^-$: $\mathsf{Prop}^+ \to \mathsf{Prop}^-$ is a forgetful map that forgets all information associated with the proof.

These maps can be (and have been) implemented as inductive types, meaning that the only way to get a proof of P^+ (respectively P^-) is as the image of a proof of P.

These functions are important to allow uniform treatment of propositional concepts. Consider for example the formalization of partial function on a datatype A as a pair $\langle P, f \rangle$, where $P : A \to \mathsf{Prop}^+$ and $f : \Pi_{x:A}(Px) \to A$; that is, P is a computationally relevant predicate on A and f is defined on elements of A that satisfy P (and its output can eventually depend on the proof term). We would also like the situation where P is non-informative to fit into this definition; this can be achieved by using P^+ instead of P (and hopefully the system can be induced to insert $(\cdot)^+$ automatically by means e.g. of a coercion mechanism).

On the other hand, $(\cdot)^-$ can be used to mark informative terms as irrelevant in specific situations. Suppose that one wants to define a function (to be extracted) whose specification is a positive predicate P, but the function will actually never be used in subsequent work. Then it is natural to specify it using P^- instead of P, as the extracted result will be smaller.

This map also has the important property of being preserved through connectives; that is, it can be proved uniformly on A and B that e.g. $(A \wedge B)^- \to (A^- \wedge B^-)$ and similarly for the other connectives (replacing $\vee$ and $\exists$ by their weaker counterparts $\underline{\vee}$ and $\underline{\exists}$). This is trivially not true of $(\cdot)^+$, because of the lack of information in Prop^-.[8]

The map $(\cdot)^-$ has already been proposed by [18], although in a slightly different setting, and its main properties analyzed and discussed.

---

[8] This difference comes from the unavailability of some elimination rules for inductive types.

7   Conclusions

We have pointed out how to greatly reduce the size of extracted programs and presented a general guideline for developing constructive proofs in order to make extraction possible. We have also proposed some modifications to the Coq type theory that we feel will make constructive formalizations somewhat easier; at the same time, we show how these modifications make it possible to safely add the principle of the excluded middle to constructive formalizations.

Some of these ideas have been discussed with the Coq team, and have helped to improve the Coq extraction mechanism, which is still under development. As a side remark, we would like to mention that after the correction of the bug described in Section 5, it became possible to extract a program from the *original* formalization of the FTA; this program turned out to be around 20 times larger than the one originally obtained using the Set/Prop distinction we described, thus confirming our claim that this distinction allowed around 90% of the code to be removed. We would also like to note that the huge resources needed to extract this program (around 2Gb RAM memory) make the use of a method such as ours not only convenient, but indeed necessary for large program developments. Finally, we hope that it will be possible to change the Coq type theory in the near future in a way similar to what we have described.

The final version of the formalization we discussed, together with the extracted program, can be found on C-CoRN repository[9] together with a short file which only contains the basic material needed for the development of other formalizations along the lines we described.

After this paper was submitted considerable progress was made on the work we described; as this is too extensive to include here, we will report on it in due time.

Acknowledgments. Support for the work of first author was provided by the Portuguese Fundação para a Ciência e Tecnologia, under grant SFRH / BD / 4926 / 2001 and by the FCT and FEDER via CLC.

The authors wish to thank Jean-Christophe Filliâtre and Pierre Letouzey for discussions on the Coq extraction mechanism; and Henk Barendregt, Herman Geuvers, Dan Synek and Freek Wiedijk for their suggestions, ideas and comments.

References

1. H. P. Barendregt. Lambda calculi with types. In *Handbook of logic in computer science, Vol. 2*, pages 117–309. Oxford Univ. Press, New York, 1992.
2. Errett Bishop. *Foundations of Constructive Analysis*. McGraw-Hill Book Company, 1967.

---

[9] http://www.cs.kun.nl/fnds/ccorn.html

3. Errett Bishop. Mathematics as a numerical language. In *Intuitionism and Proof Theory (Proceedings of the summer Conference at Buffalo, N.Y., 1968)*, pages 53–71. North-Holland, Amsterdam, 1970.
4. Venanzio Capretta. *Abstraction and Computation*. PhD thesis, University of Nijmegen, 2002.
5. Jesper Carlström. Subsets, quotients and partial functions in martin-löf's type theory. In *Proceedings of the TYPES Conference 2002, to appear*, LNCS. Springer-Verlag, 2003.
6. Alberto Ciaffaglione and Pietro Di Gianantonio. *A co-inductive approach to real numbers*, volume 1956 of *LNCS*. Springer-Verlag, 2000.
7. Judicaël Courant. MC2: A module calculus for pure type systems. Technical Report 1292, LRI, September 2001.
8. Maribel Fernández, Ian Mackie, Paula Severi, and Nora Szasz. A uniform approach to program extraction: Pure type systems with ultra σ-types.
   http://www.cmat.edu.uy/~severi/publications.html
9. Herman Geuvers. Inconsistency of classical logic in type theory.
   http://www.cs.kun.nl/~herman/note.ps.gz
10. Herman Geuvers, Randy Pollack, Freek Wiedijk, and Jan Zwanenburg. The algebraic hierarchy of the FTA Project. In Sebasitani S. Linton, editor, *Journal of Symbolic Computation, Special Issue on the Integration of Automated Reasoning and Computer Algebra Systems*, pages 271–286. Elsevier, 2002.
11. Herman Geuvers, Freek Wiedijk, and Jan Zwanenburg. A constructive proof of the Fundamental Theorem of Algebra without using the rationals. In Paul Callaghan, Zhaohui Luo, James McKinna, and Robert Pollack, editors, *Types for Proofs and Programs, Proceedings of the International Workshop, TYPES 2000*, volume 2277 of *LNCS*, pages 96–111. Springer, 2001.
12. B. Grégoire and X. Leroy. A compiled implementation of strong reduction. In *Proceedings ICFP'02*.
13. Pierre Letouzey. A new extraction for Coq. In *Proceedings of the TYPES Conference 2002, to appear*, LNCS. Springer-Verlag, 2003.
14. Per Martin-Löf. Constructive mathematics and computer science. In *Logic, Methodology and the Philosophy of Science VI*, pages 153–175. North-Holland, 1982.
15. Milad Niqui. Exact arithmetic on Stern-Brocot tree. 2003. submitted.
16. C. Paulin-Mohring. Extracting F_ω's programs from proofs in the Calulus of Constructions. In *Sixteenth Annual ACM Symposium on Principles of Programming Languages*, Austin, 1989. ACM.
17. Loïc Pottier. Quotients dans le CCI. Technical Report RR-4053, INRIA, November 2000. http://www-sop.inria.fr/rapports/sophia/RR-4053.html.
18. Frédéric Prost. Marking techniques for extraction. Technical Report 95-47, Laboratoire de l'informatique du Parallélisme, Ecole Normale Supérieure de Lyon, 1995.
19. H. Schwichtenberg. Minimal logic for computable functionals. Technical report, Mathematisches Institut der Universität München, 2002.
20. The Coq Development Team. *The Coq Proof Assistant Reference Manual Version 7.3*. INRIA-Rocquencourt, 2002.
21. A.S. Troelstra. *Realizability*, volume Handbook of Proof Theory, pages 407–473. North-Holland, 1998.
22. A.S. Troelstra and D. van Dalen. *Constructivism in mathematics. An introduction*. Number 123 in Studies in Logic and the Foundations of Mathematics. North-Holland, 1988.

First Order Logic with Domain Conditions

F. Wiedijk and J. Zwanenburg

Department of Computer Science, University of Nijmegen
Toernooiveld 1, 6525 ED Nijmegen, The Netherlands

Abstract. This paper addresses the crucial issue in the design of a proof development system of how to deal with *partial functions* and the related question of how to treat *undefined terms*. Often the problem is avoided by artificially making all functions total. However, that does not correspond to the practice of everyday mathematics.

In type theory partial functions are modeled by giving functions extra arguments which are *proof objects*. In that case it will not be possible to apply functions outside their domain. However, having proofs as first class objects has the disadvantage that it will be unfamiliar to most mathematicians. Also many proof tools (like the theorem prover Otter) will not be usable for such a logic. Finally expressions get difficult to read because of these proof objects.

The PVS system solves the problem of partial functions differently. PVS generates *type-correctness conditions* (TCCs) for statements in its language. These are proof obligations that have to be satisfied 'on the side' to show that statements are well-formed.

We propose a TCC-like approach for the treatment of partial functions in type theory. We add *domain conditions* (DCs) to classical first-order logic and show the equivalence with a first order system that treats partial functions in the style of type theory.

1 Introduction

1.1 Problem

Until a few decades ago mathematics was something that was done in human heads, on the blackboard or on paper. Only since the seventies have systems been developed that verify mathematics with the computer. The first of these was the Automath system from the Netherlands. Other early systems of this kind were the Mizar system [10] from Poland and the LCF system from the UK. Recently this kind of system has become widely used (mostly because of applications in computer science). Currently the most popular is the PVS system [13] from a US company called SRI International. Other contemporary systems of this kind are ACL2 [8], IMPS [6] and NuPRL [2] from the US, HOL [5] and Isabelle [12] from the UK and Germany, and the Coq system [16] from France. This last system is an implementation of an approach to formalizing mathematics called *type theory*.

This paper addresses the question of how to treat partial functions in formal mathematics. The prototypical example of a partial function is division: the

D. Basin and B. Wolff (Eds.): TPHOLs 2003, LNCS 2758, pp. 221–237, 2003.

quotient $1/0$ is problematic because 0 is outside the domain of the division function. Formal systems have to take a position on how to deal with this kind of expression.

A traditional way to model partial functions in logic is by using *relations*. A statement about division is then interpreted as a statement about a ternary predicate div_eq, that satisfies the equivalence:

$$\mathsf{div\_eq}(x, y, z) \iff y \neq 0 \wedge x/y = z$$

However when translating statements this way, they become an order of magnitude larger than the original. Therefore, for actual implementations of formal systems it is not attractive.

In [7], John Harrison enumerated the four main approaches to partial functions that one actually encounters in proof checkers:

1. *Resolutely give each partial function a convenient value on points outside its domain.*
2. *Give each partial function some arbitrary value outside its domain.*
3. *Encode the domain of the partial function in its type and make its application to arguments outside that domain a type error.*
4. *Have a true logic of partial terms.*

In the first case one would define $1/0 = 0$, in the second case $1/0$ would be some real number but one would not be able to prove which one it is, in the third case $1/0$ would be a type error, and in the last case $1/0$ would be an allowed expression but it would not denote anything (and one would be able to prove so).

In the systems listed above, ACL2 uses the first approach, HOL, Isabelle and Mizar use a mixture of the first and second approaches, Coq, NuPRL and PVS use the third approach, and IMPS uses the fourth approach.

In this paper we explore a variant of Harrison's approach number 3. Although we do present a system of our own, it is not a 'logic of partial terms'. It does not allow one to write $1/0$ or any other undefined term and there is no way to state whether a term is defined (because it always is).

The approach that we present here is inspired by type theory, but our logic actually is one-sorted, so the variables of our logic all have the same 'type'. It is easy to generalize our approach to a many-sorted logic. We restricted ourselves to the one-sorted case for simplicity.

The problem that we address in this paper is how to be able to follow approach number 3, while still doing the proofs in the ordinary first order predicate logic with total functions.

There are two reasons why it is worthwhile not to have to give up first order logic:

- First order logic is the best known logic. Users of a proof checker will understand the system better if the logic is ordinary first order logic.

– There is much technology for first order logic. For instance there are many theorem provers for it. The best known of these is Otter [18], but there are many more. They even compete in first order theorem prover competitions like the CADE system competition. It is valuable to be able to use this technology in a proof checker.

1.2   Approach

We will introduce three logical systems, called system T, system D and system P. The names of those systems are abbreviations of 'total', 'domain' and 'partial'. These systems are:

System T. Ordinary first order logic with total functions.
System D. Exactly the same logic as system T, but in this system undefined expressions are not allowed. This means that all functions have to have the arguments inside their domain.
System P. A system in type theoretical style. Extra arguments which are proof objects ensure that it is not possible to write an undefined term.

Systems T and D have exactly the same set of expressions: only the derivations of both systems differ. System P has a different set of expressions, because it also has expressions for proof terms.

(For technical reasons we have an 'if-then-else' construction in all three systems. Therefore system T is not *really* ordinary first order logic, because it has something extra. However this if-then-else should not be considered to be an essential extension to the system. It should be considered 'syntactic sugar'. We do not treat the relation between the systems with and without the if-then-else in this paper. However we expect it to be unproblematic.)

Then for system T we introduce a notion of *domain conditions*. This is a set of proof obligations that has to be satisfied to ensure that functions are not applied outside their domain. For example the domain conditions of division are such that:

$$\mathcal{DC}(\frac{1}{x-1} - \frac{1}{x+1} = \frac{2}{x^2-1}) = \{\vdash x - 1 \neq 0, \ \vdash x + 1 \neq 0, \ \vdash x^2 - 1 \neq 0\}$$

Now the main theorem that we prove consists of Propositions 9 and 18 below. Together these state that:

A statement together with its domain conditions are provable in system T *iff that statement is provable in system* P.

This means that we can morally imagine ourselves as being in system P, while doing our proofs and the presentation of the statements in system T, as long as we also prove the domain conditions.

The relation between the three systems is outlined in the following diagram:

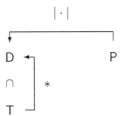

The $|\cdot|$ operation is called *erasure* (it is defined in Section 8). It erases all proof terms from the expressions. The $*$ operation is an auxiliary operation (as defined in Section 9) involved in the proof of the main theorem. It lifts a T proof to a D analogue.

1.3   Related Work

There are many logics of partial terms, like Scott's E-logic [14,17] and Beeson's LPT [1]. See [9] for an overview of the field. However our approach is not a logic of partial terms because we do not allow undefined terms. We think that $1/0$ should be *illegal*, and not just an undefined but legal expression.

Our paper integrates the type theoretical way to model partial functions with the PVS approach of having correctness conditions on the side. The type theoretical approach of having proof terms as an argument to model partial functions already dates from the Automath project (see [11] page 710). For a discussion of type-correctness conditions in PVS, see [15].

The approach that we propose here is similar to the one implemented in the LAMBDA system of Fourman [3], where each function f has an associated domain predicate DOM'f. However there is a difference in spirit: the LAMBDA system follows approach number 2 from the list on page 222,[1] while we follow approach number 3. This is also apparent from the fact that in [3] the $\mathcal{DC}$ operation (called $\ll\gg$ there) only appears in axioms corresponding to function definitions, while in our approach it takes a much more central position.

2   Examples

We will now list some examples of partial functions and show how they are treated in the systems T and P. Some of these functions occur in a proof of the fundamental theorem of algebra in the Coq system [4]. The experiences we had in this 'FTA project' was one of the motivations to write this paper.

- *Division*. In system T the division operator x/y gets a domain condition that has to be proved to show that the expression is well-formed:

$$\mathcal{DC}(x/y) = \{\vdash y \neq 0\}$$

---

[1] [3], p. 86: 'we regard a function application $f(x)$ as *always defined*, but if x is outside the intended domain of f, we will not be able to prove anything about its value.'

In system P division becomes a ternary function:

$$\mathsf{div}(x, y, \alpha)$$

having three arguments x, y and α, where α is a proof that $y \neq 0$.

This is an example of the general pattern. In system P all partial functions get one extra 'domain' argument. Therefore, in system P a function application $f(x_1, \ldots, x_n)$ becomes $f(x_1, \ldots, x_n, \alpha)$, where α is a proof of $D_f(x_1, \ldots, x_n)$ with the predicate D_f representing the *domain* of the function f.

- *Square root.* The domain condition of the real square root in system T is $\mathcal{DC}(\sqrt{x}) = \{\vdash x \geq 0\}$. Again, in system P the square root function $\mathsf{sqrt}(x, \alpha)$ has an extra argument, where α is a proof of $x \geq 0$.
- *Limit of a sequence.* The domain conditions of the limit operation are in system T:

$$DC\big(\lim_{n \to \infty} a_n\big) = \{\vdash \text{the sequence } (a_n) \text{ converges}\}$$

In system P the limit operation becomes $\lim(a, \alpha)$ where a is a sequence and where α is a proof that that sequence converges.

The natural way to express the limit operation in type theory is not first order, because the a argument is a function. But the theory we present here is first order. This means that this example should be considered in the context of set theory (like in the Mizar system) where one can talk about functions using a first order language.

- *Function application in set theory.* Set theory is untyped. When one defines function application in it, it becomes a partial operation. In set theory in the style of system T, function application would get the domain condition:

$$\mathcal{DC}(f(a)) = \{\vdash f \text{ is a function} \wedge a \in \mathsf{dom}\, f\}$$

Note that the dom function that occurs in this condition has a domain condition as well:

$$\mathcal{DC}(\mathsf{dom}\, f) = \{\vdash f \text{ is a relation}\}$$

In system P function application becomes ternary, $\mathsf{apply}(f, a, \alpha)$, where α is a proof of 'f is a function $\wedge\, a \in \mathsf{dom}\, f$'.

3   System T

We will now define the first of our three systems, namely first order predicate logic extended with an if-then-else operation.

To define our systems we fix a signature with finitely many constant, function and predicate symbols:

- constant symbols $c_1, \ldots, c_k$
- function symbols $f_1, \ldots, f_n$ with arities $a_1, \ldots, a_n$
- predicate symbols $P_1, \ldots, P_m$ with arities $r_1, \ldots, r_m$

We also have variables:

- term variables $x_0, x_1, x_2, \ldots$
- proof variables $h_0, h_1, h_2, \ldots$

(System T and D will only use term variables, but system P will also need proof variables.)

For each function symbol f of arity a there is a designated predicate symbol D_f (which is one of the P_i's) that also has arity a. D_f is the predicate that represents the *domain* of the function f. Note that this D_f is not an extra-logical abbreviation of a formula: it is a predicate *symbol*.

Constants could have been avoided by considering them to be nullary functions. However in that case our main result (Proposition 18 on page 235) would not have been true.[2]

System T has four kinds of expressions: terms, formulas, contexts and judgments. These expressions are defined inductively as the smallest sets $\mathcal{T}$, $\mathcal{F}$, $\mathcal{C}$ and $\mathcal{J}$ satisfying:

$$\mathcal{T} ::= x_i \mid c_i \mid f_i(\mathcal{T}, \ldots, \mathcal{T}) \mid (\text{if } \mathcal{F} \text{ then } \mathcal{T} \text{ else } \mathcal{T})$$
$$\mathcal{F} ::= \bot \mid P_i(\mathcal{T}, \ldots, \mathcal{T}) \mid \mathcal{T} = \mathcal{T} \mid (\mathcal{F} \to \mathcal{F}) \mid (\forall x_i . \mathcal{F})$$
$$\mathcal{C} ::= \epsilon \mid \mathcal{C}, x_i \mid \mathcal{C}, \mathcal{F}$$
$$\mathcal{J} ::= \mathcal{C} \vdash wf \mid \mathcal{C} \vdash \mathcal{T} \; wf \mid \mathcal{C} \vdash \mathcal{F} \; wf \mid \mathcal{C} \vdash \mathcal{F}$$

The four kinds of judgments mean respectively that the context is well-formed, that a term is well-formed, that a formula is well-formed and that a formula is provable.

Finally, system T has the following set of derivation rules:

$\mathcal{C}$: $(\epsilon\text{-}wf) \; \dfrac{}{\epsilon \vdash wf}$ $(decl\text{-}wf) \; \dfrac{\Gamma \vdash wf}{\Gamma, x_i \vdash wf}$ $(assum\text{-}wf) \; \dfrac{\Gamma \vdash \varphi \; wf}{\Gamma, \varphi \vdash wf}$

$\mathcal{T}$: $(var\text{-}wf) \; \dfrac{\Gamma \vdash wf}{\Gamma \vdash x_i \; wf} \; x_i \in \Gamma$ $(const\text{-}wf) \; \dfrac{\Gamma \vdash wf}{\Gamma \vdash c_i \; wf}$

$(fun\text{-}wf) \; \dfrac{\Gamma \vdash t_1 \; wf \quad \cdots \quad \Gamma \vdash t_{a_i} \; wf \quad \Gamma \vdash wf}{\Gamma \vdash f_i(t_1, \ldots, t_{a_i}) \; wf}$

$(if\text{-}wf) \; \dfrac{\Gamma \vdash \varphi \; wf \quad \Gamma \vdash t \; wf \quad \Gamma \vdash u \; wf}{\Gamma \vdash (\text{if } \varphi \text{ then } t \text{ else } u) \; wf}$

$\mathcal{F}$: $(\bot\text{-}wf) \; \dfrac{\Gamma \vdash wf}{\Gamma \vdash \bot \; wf}$ $(pred\text{-}wf) \; \dfrac{\Gamma \vdash t_1 \; wf \quad \cdots \quad \Gamma \vdash t_{r_i} \; wf \quad \Gamma \vdash wf}{\Gamma \vdash P_i(t_1, \ldots, t_{r_i}) \; wf}$

---

[2] This is shown by the following (pathological) case: one function symbol f of arity 0 with $D_f() \leftrightarrow \bot$ and $\varphi \equiv \exists x. \top$. This φ can be derived in the T system using witness $f()$, but it cannot be derived in the P system. This shows that it is essential for our theory to have constants c_i without domain conditions.

$\mathcal{P}$:

$$(\rightarrow\text{-}wf)\ \frac{\Gamma \vdash \varphi\ wf \quad \Gamma \vdash \psi\ wf}{\Gamma \vdash (\varphi \rightarrow \psi)\ wf} \qquad (\forall\text{-}wf)\ \frac{\Gamma, x_i \vdash \varphi\ wf}{\Gamma \vdash (\forall x_i.\,\varphi)\ wf}$$

$$(assum)\ \frac{\Gamma \vdash wf}{\Gamma \vdash \varphi}\ \varphi \in \Gamma \qquad (raa)\ \frac{\Gamma \vdash \neg\neg\varphi}{\Gamma \vdash \varphi}$$

$$(\rightarrow\text{-}I)\ \frac{\Gamma, \varphi \vdash \psi}{\Gamma \vdash (\varphi \rightarrow \psi)} \qquad (\rightarrow\text{-}E)\ \frac{\Gamma \vdash (\varphi \rightarrow \psi) \quad \Gamma \vdash \varphi}{\Gamma \vdash \psi}$$

$$(\forall\text{-}I)\ \frac{\Gamma, x_i \vdash \varphi}{\Gamma \vdash (\forall x_i.\,\varphi)} \qquad (\forall\text{-}E)\ \frac{\Gamma \vdash (\forall x_i.\,\varphi) \quad \Gamma \vdash t\ wf}{\Gamma \vdash \varphi[x_i := t]}$$

$$(refl)\ \frac{\Gamma \vdash t\ wf}{\Gamma \vdash t = t} \qquad (sym)\ \frac{\Gamma \vdash t = u}{\Gamma \vdash u = t} \qquad (trans)\ \frac{\Gamma \vdash t = u \quad \Gamma \vdash u = v}{\Gamma \vdash t = v}$$

$$(=\text{-}fun)\ \frac{\Gamma \vdash t_1 = t'_1 \quad \cdots \quad \Gamma \vdash t_{a_i} = t'_{a_i} \quad \Gamma \vdash wf}{\Gamma \vdash f_i(t_1, \ldots, t_{a_i}) = f_i(t'_1, \ldots, t'_{a_i})}$$

$$(=\text{-}pred)\ \frac{\Gamma \vdash t_1 = t'_1 \quad \cdots \quad \Gamma \vdash t_{r_i} = t'_{r_i} \quad \Gamma \vdash wf}{\Gamma \vdash P_i(t_1, \ldots, t_{r_i}) \rightarrow P_i(t'_1, \ldots, t'_{r_i})}$$

$$(=\text{-}if\text{-}true)\ \frac{\Gamma \vdash \varphi \quad \Gamma \vdash t\ wf \quad \Gamma \vdash u\ wf}{\Gamma \vdash (\text{if } \varphi \text{ then } t \text{ else } u) = t}$$

$$(=\text{-}if\text{-}false)\ \frac{\Gamma \vdash \neg\varphi \quad \Gamma \vdash t\ wf \quad \Gamma \vdash u\ wf}{\Gamma \vdash (\text{if } \varphi \text{ then } t \text{ else } u) = u}$$

We identify expressions that are α-equivalent. Therefore we assume in these rules the Barendregt convention: all variable names are as different as possible.

Logical operations have to be read as abbreviations from $\bot$, $\rightarrow$ and $\forall$:

$$\neg\varphi \equiv \varphi \rightarrow \bot$$
$$\varphi \vee \psi \equiv \neg\varphi \rightarrow \psi$$
$$\varphi \wedge \psi \equiv \neg(\varphi \rightarrow \neg\psi)$$
$$\varphi \leftrightarrow \psi \equiv (\varphi \rightarrow \psi) \wedge (\psi \rightarrow \varphi)$$

Some remarks about system T:

- Our presentation of first order logic is slightly non-standard in that we have variables in the contexts that bind the free variables in the terms and formulas. Instead of '$x \neq 0 \vdash 1/x \neq 0$' we write '$x, x \neq 0 \vdash 1/x \neq 0$'. We do this for aesthetic reasons. It causes many well-formedness rules, but these are all trivial. In system T well-formedness just means that all free variables occur in the context.
- The condition $\Gamma \vdash wf$ in the rules *fun-wf*, *pred-wf*, *=-fun* and *=-pred* is needed for the case that $a_i = 0$ or $r_i = 0$.
- By symmetry of equality we can derive from rule *=-pred* the analogue rule with equivalence instead of implication:

$$(=\text{-}pred\text{-}iff)\ \frac{\Gamma \vdash t_1 = t'_1 \quad \cdots \quad \Gamma \vdash t_{r_i} = t'_{r_i} \quad \Gamma \vdash wf}{\Gamma \vdash P_i(t_1, \ldots, t_{r_i}) \leftrightarrow P_i(t'_1, \ldots, t'_{r_i})}$$

- It is possible to replace the rules *sym*, *trans*, *=-fun* and *=-pred* by just one *substitution* rule:

$$(=\text{-}subst) \frac{\Gamma \vdash t = u \quad \Gamma \vdash \varphi[x := t]}{\Gamma \vdash \varphi[x := u]}$$

However this rule does not generalize to systems D and P. The term t might satisfy domain conditions that u does not.

Our systems are non-standard because they have an if-then-else construction, which corresponds to the mathematical practice of definition by cases. For example one can write 'if $x \neq 0$ then $1/x$ else 0' as an expression. The if-then-else operator occurs in all three systems, T, D and P.

We would have preferred not to have this construction in our systems. In that case system T would really have been ordinary first order logic. However we need to have this construction to keep our definitions and proofs manageable. We have tried to develop the theory without it, but it became too complex.

We believe that the if-then-else is not essential to the systems. The theorem to be proved for this is conservativity of the extended system over the basic system:

If a judgment $\Gamma \vdash \varphi$ does not contain any if-then-elses, then it is provable in the system with if-then-else iff it is provable in the system without if-then-else.

However we will not prove this theorem in this paper.

The if-then-elses can be eliminated systematically from a formula by replacing $P[(\text{if } \varphi \text{ then } t \text{ else } u)]$ by $(\varphi \rightarrow P[t]) \wedge (\neg \varphi \rightarrow P[u])$. As an example (if $x \neq 0$ then $1/x$ else 0) $\cdot x = 1$ then becomes $(x \neq 0 \rightarrow (1/x) \cdot x = 1) \wedge (x = 0 \rightarrow 0 \cdot x = 1)$.

4   System D

The expressions of system D are exactly the same as the expressions of system T. Only the set of rules is different. We show the rules that differ from the corresponding rules in system T:

$\mathcal{T}:$ $(fun\text{-}wf) \dfrac{\Gamma \vdash D_{f_i}(t_1, \ldots, t_{a_i})}{\Gamma \vdash f_i(t_1, \ldots, t_{a_i}) \ wf}$ $(if\text{-}wf) \dfrac{\Gamma, \varphi \vdash t \ wf \quad \Gamma, \neg\varphi \vdash u \ wf}{\Gamma \vdash (\text{if } \varphi \text{ then } t \text{ else } u) \ wf}$

$\mathcal{F}:$ $(\rightarrow\text{-}wf) \dfrac{\Gamma, \varphi \vdash \psi \ wf}{\Gamma \vdash (\varphi \rightarrow \psi) \ wf}$

$\mathcal{P}:$ $(=\text{-}fun) \dfrac{\Gamma \vdash t_1 = t_1' \quad \cdots \quad \Gamma \vdash t_{a_i} = t_{a_i}' \quad \Gamma \vdash D_{f_i}(t_1, \ldots, t_{a_i}) \quad \Gamma \vdash D_{f_i}(t_1', \ldots, t_{a_i}')}{\Gamma \vdash f_i(t_1, \ldots, t_{a_i}) = f_i(t_1', \ldots, t_{a_i}')}$

$$(=\text{-}if\text{-}true) \quad \frac{\Gamma \vdash \varphi \quad \Gamma, \varphi \vdash t \; wf \quad \Gamma, \neg\varphi \vdash u \; wf}{\Gamma \vdash (\text{if } \varphi \text{ then } t \text{ else } u) = t}$$

$$(=\text{-}if\text{-}false) \quad \frac{\Gamma \vdash \neg\varphi \quad \Gamma, \varphi \vdash t \; wf \quad \Gamma, \neg\varphi \vdash u \; wf}{\Gamma \vdash (\text{if } \varphi \text{ then } t \text{ else } u) = u}$$

The essential differences between systems T and D are the rules *fun-wf* and *=-fun*. In system D you are only allowed to apply a function if you can prove that the arguments are in its domain.

The other differences are not essential: rules *if-wf*, *→-wf*, *=-if-true* and *=-if-false* in system T could have been the same as in system D. (But not the other way around: in system D these rules have to be the way they are.) However we have chosen to use in system T the simpler variants of those rules. The slight differences between systems T and D in this respect do not cause any problems in the proofs below.

5   System P

The expressions of system P follow the same basic structure as the expressions of system T and D. However there is an extra kind of expression $\mathcal{P}$, for proof terms.

$$\mathcal{T} ::= x_i \mid c_i \mid f_i(\mathcal{T}, \ldots, \mathcal{T}, \mathcal{P}) \mid (\text{if } \mathcal{F} \text{ then } \lambda h_i. \mathcal{T} \text{ else } \lambda h_j. \mathcal{T})$$
$$\mathcal{F} ::= \bot \mid P_i(\mathcal{T}, \ldots, \mathcal{T}) \mid \mathcal{T} = \mathcal{T} \mid (\Pi h_i : \mathcal{F}. \mathcal{F}) \mid (\forall x_i. \mathcal{F})$$
$$\mathcal{P} ::= (\lambda h_i : \mathcal{F}. \mathcal{P}) \mid (\mathcal{P}\mathcal{P}) \mid (\lambda x_i. \mathcal{P}) \mid (\mathcal{P}\mathcal{T})$$
$$\quad \mid \mathsf{raa}(\mathcal{P}) \mid \mathsf{refl}(\mathcal{T}) \mid \mathsf{sym}(\mathcal{P}) \mid \mathsf{trans}(\mathcal{P}, \mathcal{P})$$
$$\quad \mid \mathsf{eqfun}(\mathcal{P}, \ldots \mathcal{P}, \mathcal{P}, \mathcal{P}) \mid \mathsf{eqpred}(i, \mathcal{P}, \ldots \mathcal{P})$$
$$\quad \mid \mathsf{iftrue}(\mathcal{P}, \lambda h_i. \mathcal{T}, \lambda h_j. \mathcal{T}) \mid \mathsf{iffalse}(\mathcal{P}, \lambda h_i. \mathcal{T}, \lambda h_j. \mathcal{T})$$
$$\mathcal{C} ::= \epsilon \mid \mathcal{C}, x_i \mid \mathcal{C}, h_i : \mathcal{F}$$
$$\mathcal{J} ::= \mathcal{C} \vdash wf \mid \mathcal{C} \vdash \mathcal{T} \; wf \mid \mathcal{C} \vdash \mathcal{F} \; wf \mid \mathcal{C} \vdash \mathcal{P} : \mathcal{F}$$

Here are the rules for system P. They exactly parallel the rules for system D.

$\mathcal{C}$:

$$(\epsilon\text{-}wf) \; \frac{}{\epsilon \vdash wf} \quad (decl\text{-}wf) \; \frac{\Gamma \vdash wf}{\Gamma, x_i \vdash wf} \quad (assum\text{-}wf) \; \frac{\Gamma \vdash \varphi \; wf}{\Gamma, h_i : \varphi \vdash wf}$$

$\mathcal{T}$:

$$(var\text{-}wf) \; \frac{\Gamma \vdash wf}{\Gamma \vdash x_i \; wf} \; x_i \in \Gamma \quad (const\text{-}wf) \; \frac{\Gamma \vdash wf}{\Gamma \vdash c_i \; wf}$$

$$(fun\text{-}wf) \; \frac{\Gamma \vdash \alpha : D_{f_i}(t_1, \ldots, t_{a_i})}{\Gamma \vdash f_i(t_1, \ldots, t_{a_i}, \alpha) \; wf} \quad (if\text{-}wf) \; \frac{\Gamma, h_i : \varphi \vdash t \; wf \quad \Gamma, h_j : \neg\varphi \vdash u \; wf}{\Gamma \vdash (\text{if } \varphi \text{ then } \lambda h_i. t \text{ else } \lambda h_j. u) \; wf}$$

$\mathcal{F}$:

$$(\bot\text{-}wf) \; \frac{\Gamma \vdash wf}{\Gamma \vdash \bot \; wf} \quad (pred\text{-}wf) \; \frac{\Gamma \vdash t_1 \; wf \quad \cdots \quad \Gamma \vdash t_{r_i} \; wf \quad \Gamma \vdash wf}{\Gamma \vdash P_i(t_1, \ldots, t_{r_i}) \; wf}$$

$$(\Pi\text{-}wf)\ \frac{\Gamma, h_i : \varphi \vdash \psi\ wf}{\Gamma \vdash (\Pi h_i : \varphi. \psi)\ wf}\qquad (\forall\text{-}wf)\ \frac{\Gamma, x_i \vdash \varphi\ wf}{\Gamma \vdash (\forall x_i. \varphi)\ wf}$$

$\mathcal{P}:$

$$(assum)\ \frac{\Gamma \vdash wf}{\Gamma \vdash h_i : \varphi}\ h_i : \varphi \in \Gamma\qquad (raa)\ \frac{\Gamma \vdash \alpha : \neg\neg\varphi}{\Gamma \vdash \mathsf{raa}(\alpha) : \varphi}$$

$$(\Pi\text{-}I)\ \frac{\Gamma, h_i : \varphi \vdash \alpha : \psi}{\Gamma \vdash (\lambda h_i : \varphi. \alpha) : (\Pi h_i : \varphi. \psi)}\qquad (\Pi\text{-}E)\ \frac{\Gamma \vdash \alpha : (\Pi h_i : \varphi. \psi)\quad \Gamma \vdash \beta : \varphi}{\Gamma \vdash (\alpha\beta) : \psi[h_i := \beta]}$$

$$(\forall\text{-}I)\ \frac{\Gamma, x_i \vdash \alpha : \varphi}{\Gamma \vdash (\lambda x_i. \alpha) : (\forall x_i. \varphi)}\qquad (\forall\text{-}E)\ \frac{\Gamma \vdash \alpha : (\forall x_i. \varphi)\quad \Gamma \vdash t\ wf}{\Gamma \vdash (\alpha t) : \varphi[x_i := t]}$$

$$(refl)\ \frac{\Gamma \vdash t\ wf}{\Gamma \vdash \mathsf{refl}(t) : t = t}\qquad (sym)\ \frac{\Gamma \vdash \alpha : t = u}{\Gamma \vdash \mathsf{sym}(\alpha) : u = t}$$

$$(trans)\ \frac{\Gamma \vdash \alpha : t = u\quad \Gamma \vdash \beta : u = v}{\Gamma \vdash \mathsf{trans}(\alpha, \beta) : t = v}$$

$$(=\text{-}fun)\ \frac{\Gamma \vdash \alpha_1 : t_1 = t'_1\quad \cdots \quad \Gamma \vdash \alpha_{a_i} : t_{a_i} = t'_{a_i}\quad \Gamma \vdash \beta : D_{f_i}(t_1, \ldots, t_{a_i})\quad \Gamma \vdash \beta' : D_{f_i}(t'_1, \ldots, t'_{a_i})}{\Gamma \vdash \mathsf{eqfun}(\alpha_1, \ldots \alpha_{a_i}, \beta, \beta') : f_i(t_1, \ldots, t_{a_i}, \beta) = f_i(t'_1, \ldots, t'_{a_i}, \beta')}$$

$$(=\text{-}pred)\ \frac{\Gamma \vdash \alpha_1 : t_1 = t'_1\quad \cdots \quad \Gamma \vdash \alpha_{r_i} : t_{r_i} = t'_{r_i}\quad \Gamma \vdash wf}{\Gamma \vdash \mathsf{eqpred}(i, \alpha_1, \ldots \alpha_{r_i}) : P_i(t_1, \ldots, t_{r_i}) \to P_i(t'_1, \ldots, t'_{r_i})}$$

$$(=\text{-}if\text{-}true)\ \frac{\Gamma \vdash \alpha : \varphi\quad \Gamma, h_i : \varphi \vdash t\ wf\quad \Gamma, h_j : \neg\varphi \vdash u\ wf}{\Gamma \vdash \mathsf{iftrue}(\alpha, \lambda h_i. t, \lambda h_j. u) : (\text{if } \varphi \text{ then } \lambda h_i. t \text{ else } \lambda h_j. u) = t[h_i := \alpha]}$$

$$(=\text{-}if\text{-}false)\ \frac{\Gamma \vdash \alpha : \neg\varphi\quad \Gamma, h_i : \varphi \vdash t\ wf\quad \Gamma, h_j : \neg\varphi \vdash u\ wf}{\Gamma \vdash \mathsf{iffalse}(\alpha, \lambda h_i. t, \lambda h_j. u) : (\text{if } \varphi \text{ then } \lambda h_i. t \text{ else } \lambda h_j. u) = u[h_j := \alpha]}$$

We will write $\Gamma \vdash \varphi$ if for some α we can derive that $\Gamma \vdash \alpha : \varphi$. If h_i does not occur in ψ we write $\varphi \to \psi$ for $\Pi h_i : \varphi. \psi$ like before.

The expressions for the if-then-else bind two proof variables: one for the then branch and one for the else branch. This is indicated by putting λs in the if-then-else, iffalse and iftrue expressions. These λs should not be confused with the λ-expressions that occur in the proof terms of an implication or universally quantified formula, which are introduced by the Π-I and $\forall$-I rules.

System P does not have a conversion rule. Without a conversion rule the system does not satisfy the property of subject reduction. We do not think a conversion rule is relevant for our application. We expect that adding a conversion rule will not affect the results from this paper.

Proof terms only occur as the final arguments of functions.

6   Some Properties of Derivations

The systems T, D and P are well behaved. All three systems satisfy the following four propositions (where $\mathcal{X}$ is anything that can occur after a $\vdash$):

Proposition 1. $\Gamma, \Gamma' \vdash \mathcal{X}$ then with a shorter derivation $\Gamma \vdash wf$

Proposition 2. $\Gamma, \varphi, \Gamma' \vdash \mathcal{X}$ *then with a shorter derivation* $\Gamma \vdash \varphi$ *wf*

Proposition 3. $\Gamma \vdash \varphi$ *implies* $\Gamma \vdash \varphi$ *wf.*

Proposition 4 (weakening). $\Gamma \vdash \mathcal{X}$ *and* $\Gamma, \Gamma' \vdash$ *wf imply* $\Gamma, \Gamma' \vdash \mathcal{X}$.

7   The Domain Conditions

We now define the domain conditions of an expression. For each system T expression (term, formula, judgment), its domain conditions are a set of judgments that state that in the expression no function is applied outside its domain.

Domain conditions are defined relative to a context Γ which we put as a subscript to the $\mathcal{DC}$ symbol.

$$\mathcal{DC}_\Gamma : \mathcal{T}^\mathsf{T} \to \mathcal{P}(\mathcal{J}^\mathsf{T})$$
$$\mathcal{DC}_\Gamma(x_i) = \mathcal{DC}_\Gamma(c_i) = \emptyset$$
$$\mathcal{DC}_\Gamma(f_i(t_1, \ldots, t_{a_i})) = \mathcal{DC}_\Gamma(t_1) \cup \ldots \cup \mathcal{DC}_\Gamma(t_{a_i}) \cup \{\Gamma \vdash^\mathsf{T} D_{f_i}(t_1, \ldots, t_{a_i})\}$$
$$\mathcal{DC}_\Gamma(\text{if } \varphi \text{ then } t \text{ else } u) = \mathcal{DC}_\Gamma(\varphi) \cup \mathcal{DC}_{\Gamma,\varphi}(t) \cup \mathcal{DC}_{\Gamma,\neg\varphi}(u)$$
$$\mathcal{DC}_\Gamma : \mathcal{F}^\mathsf{T} \to \mathcal{P}(\mathcal{J}^\mathsf{T})$$
$$\mathcal{DC}_\Gamma(\bot) = \emptyset$$
$$\mathcal{DC}_\Gamma(P_i(t_1, \ldots, t_{r_i})) = \mathcal{DC}_\Gamma(t_1) \cup \ldots \cup \mathcal{DC}_\Gamma(t_{r_i})$$
$$\mathcal{DC}_\Gamma(t = u) = \mathcal{DC}(t) \cup \mathcal{DC}(u)$$
$$\mathcal{DC}_\Gamma(\varphi \to \psi) = \mathcal{DC}_\Gamma(\varphi) \cup \mathcal{DC}_{\Gamma,\varphi}(\psi)$$
$$\mathcal{DC}_\Gamma(\forall x_i. \varphi) = \mathcal{DC}_{\Gamma,x_i}(\varphi)$$
$$\mathcal{DC} : \mathcal{C}^\mathsf{T} \to \mathcal{P}(\mathcal{J}^\mathsf{T})$$
$$\mathcal{DC}(\epsilon) = \emptyset$$
$$\mathcal{DC}(\Gamma, x_i) = \mathcal{DC}(\Gamma)$$
$$\mathcal{DC}(\Gamma, \varphi) = \mathcal{DC}(\Gamma) \cup \mathcal{DC}_\Gamma(\varphi)$$

Domain conditions are asymmetric in some of the propositional connectives. Therefore, although system T is just first order logic, the domain conditions do not respect logical equivalence. For instance:

$$\mathcal{DC}(\varphi \wedge \psi) \neq \mathcal{DC}(\psi \wedge \varphi)$$

In the first case $\varphi \wedge \psi \equiv \neg(\varphi \to \neg\psi)$ and we can use φ for proving the domain conditions of ψ, while in the second case $\psi \wedge \varphi \equiv \neg(\psi \to \neg\varphi)$ so in that case we can *not* use φ for the domain conditions of ψ. As an example the domain conditions of $(x \neq 0) \wedge P[1/x]$ might be provable because we can use $x \neq 0$ to prove the domain conditions of $P[1/x]$, but the domain conditions of $P[1/x] \wedge (x \neq 0)$ might not be provable because in that case we have to prove the domain conditions of $P[1/x]$ without the benefit of $x \neq 0$. In this sense the $\wedge$ connective in system T behaves like the **&&** operator of the C programming language.

The predicate symbol D_f is a *symbol* that *represents* the domain of the function f. To give this symbol a meaning we have to have an equivalence in the context.

For instance $D_/(x, y)$ is the definedness predicate of the division. It should be equivalent to $y \neq 0$. This means that we have to imagine that we are reasoning in a context:

$$\Gamma \equiv \ldots, \text{ theory of division including } \forall x, y. \, (D_/(x, y) \leftrightarrow y \neq 0), \, \ldots$$

The domain condition for division is: $\mathcal{DC}(x/y) = \{\vdash D_/(x, y)\}$. This domain condition is equivalent to $y \neq 0$ in the proper context but it is not identical to it. (So actually in the examples on pages 223–225 we were not completely correct. We 'cheated' there for the sake of the presentation.)

8   The Erasure: From P to T

The erasure operation $|\cdot|$ erases all proof terms from expressions. It maps system P expressions to system T. In such an erased expression all domain conditions hold. This is the easy direction of our main result.

$$|\cdot| : \mathcal{T}^{\mathsf{P}} \to \mathcal{T}^{\mathsf{T}}$$
$$|x_i| = x_i \quad |c_i| = c_i$$
$$|f_i(t_1, \ldots, t_{a_i}, \alpha)| = f_i(|t_1|, \ldots, |t_{a_i}|)$$
$$|(\text{if } \varphi \text{ then } \lambda h_i. \, t \text{ else } \lambda h_j. \, u)| = (\text{if } |\varphi| \text{ then } |t| \text{ else } |u|)$$
$$|\cdot| : \mathcal{F}^{\mathsf{P}} \to \mathcal{F}^{\mathsf{T}}$$
$$|\bot| = \bot$$
$$|P_i(t_1, \ldots, t_{r_i})| = P_i(|t_1|, \ldots, |t_{r_i}|)$$
$$|t = u| = |t| = |u|$$
$$|(\Pi h_i : \varphi. \, \psi)| = (|\varphi| \to |\psi|)$$
$$|(\forall x_i. \, \varphi)| = (\forall x_i. \, |\varphi|)$$
$$|\cdot| : \mathcal{C}^{\mathsf{P}} \to \mathcal{C}^{\mathsf{T}}$$
$$|\epsilon| = \epsilon$$
$$|\Gamma, x_i| = |\Gamma|, x_i$$
$$|\Gamma, h_i : \varphi| = |\Gamma|, |\varphi|$$

Proposition 5.

$$|t[x_i := u]| \equiv |t|[x_i := |u|].$$
$$|\varphi[x_i := u]| \equiv |\varphi|[x_i := |u|].$$
$$|t[h_i := \alpha]| \equiv |t|.$$
$$|\varphi[h_i := \alpha]| \equiv |\varphi|.$$

Proof. Simultaneous induction on the structure of t and φ.

Proposition 6 (from P to D).

$$\Gamma \vdash^{\mathsf{P}} wf \text{ implies } |\Gamma| \vdash^{\mathsf{D}} wf.$$
$$\Gamma \vdash^{\mathsf{P}} t \; wf \text{ implies } |\Gamma| \vdash^{\mathsf{D}} |t| \; wf.$$
$$\Gamma \vdash^{\mathsf{P}} \varphi \; wf \text{ implies } |\Gamma| \vdash^{\mathsf{D}} |\varphi| \; wf.$$

$\Gamma \vdash^P \varphi$ *implies* $|\Gamma| \vdash^D |\varphi|$.

Proof. Simultaneous induction on the size of the derivation in system P.

Proposition 7.

$\Gamma, \varphi \vdash^T t$ *wf implies* $\Gamma \vdash^T t$ *wf.*
$\Gamma, \varphi \vdash^T \psi$ *wf implies* $\Gamma \vdash^T \psi$ *wf.*

Proof. Well-formedness in system T just checks whether all free variables are in the context. Removing assumptions from the context does not affect that.

Proposition 8 (from D to T).

$\Gamma \vdash^D$ *wf implies* $\Gamma \vdash^T$ *wf and* $\mathcal{DC}(\Gamma)$.
$\Gamma \vdash^D t$ *wf implies* $\Gamma \vdash^T t$ *wf and* $\mathcal{DC}(\Gamma)$ *and* $\mathcal{DC}_\Gamma(t)$.
$\Gamma \vdash^D \varphi$ *wf implies* $\Gamma \vdash^T \varphi$ *wf and* $\mathcal{DC}(\Gamma)$ *and* $\mathcal{DC}_\Gamma(\varphi)$.
$\Gamma \vdash^D \varphi$ *implies* $\Gamma \vdash^T \varphi$ *and* $\mathcal{DC}(\Gamma)$ *and* $\mathcal{DC}_\Gamma(\varphi)$.

Proof. Simultaneous induction on the size of the derivation in system D using Proposition 7 for the →-*wf*, *if-wf*, =-*if-true* and =-*if-false* rules.

Proposition 9 (main correspondence theorem from P to T). $\Gamma \vdash^P \varphi$ *implies* $|\Gamma| \vdash^T |\varphi|$ *and* $\mathcal{DC}(|\Gamma|)$ *and* $\mathcal{DC}_{|\Gamma|}(|\varphi|)$.

Proof. Propositions 6 and 8 combined.

9   The * Operation: From T to D

Consider a statement for which the domain conditions hold. A system T proof of this statement and a system D proof of the same statement are different things. In the first case, although the domain conditions of the statement are satisfied, the *proof* might violate some domain conditions (for instance, it might reason about $1/0$ as a number). But in the second case the domain conditions have to hold *in all steps* of the proof. We will show that despite this difference these two kinds of provability are equivalent (this is Proposition 15 below). For this we will use the * operation.

The * operation maps system T to system D. It makes the partial functions total by setting them to the constant c_1 outside their domain. Then system T proofs are interpreted in system D as talking about these 'extended' functions.

$$.^* : \mathcal{T}^T \to \mathcal{T}^D$$
$$x_i{}^* = x_i \quad c_i{}^* = c_i$$
$$f_i(t_1, \ldots, t_{a_i})^* = (\text{if } D_{f_i}(t_1{}^*, \ldots, t_{a_i}{}^*) \text{ then } f_i(t_1{}^*, \ldots, t_{a_i}{}^*) \text{ else } c_1)$$
$$(\text{if } \varphi \text{ then } t \text{ else } u)^* = (\text{if } \varphi^* \text{ then } t^* \text{ else } u^*)$$
$$.^* : \mathcal{F}^T \to \mathcal{F}^D$$

$$\bot^* = \bot$$
$$P_i(t_1, \ldots, t_{r_i})^* = P_i(t_1^*, \ldots, t_{r_i}^*)$$
$$(t = u)^* = t^* = u^*$$
$$(\varphi \to \psi)^* = (\varphi^* \to \psi^*)$$
$$(\forall x_i. \varphi)^* = (\forall x_i. \varphi^*)$$
$$.^* : C^\mathsf{T} \to C^\mathsf{D}$$
$$\epsilon^* = \epsilon$$
$$(\Gamma, x_i)^* = \Gamma^*, x_i$$
$$(\Gamma, \varphi)^* = \Gamma^*, \varphi^*$$

Proposition 10.

> $\Gamma \vdash^\mathsf{D} t \ wf \ implies \ \Gamma \vdash^\mathsf{D} t = t^*$.
> $\Gamma \vdash^\mathsf{D} \varphi \ wf \ implies \ \Gamma \vdash^\mathsf{D} \varphi \leftrightarrow \varphi^*$.

Proof. Simultaneous induction on the structure of t and φ.

Proposition 11. $\Gamma \vdash^\mathsf{D} wf \ implies \ that \ \Gamma \vdash^\mathsf{D} \varphi \ iff \ \Gamma^* \vdash^\mathsf{D} \varphi$.

Proof. Induction on the structure of Γ using the second part of Proposition 10.

Proposition 12.

> $\Gamma \vdash^\mathsf{T} wf \ implies \ \Gamma^* \vdash^\mathsf{D} wf$.
> $\Gamma \vdash^\mathsf{T} t \ wf \ implies \ \Gamma^* \vdash^\mathsf{D} t^* \ wf$.
> $\Gamma \vdash^\mathsf{T} \varphi \ wf \ implies \ \Gamma^* \vdash^\mathsf{D} \varphi^* \ wf$.
> $\Gamma \vdash^\mathsf{T} \varphi \ implies \ \Gamma^* \vdash^\mathsf{D} \varphi^*$.

Proof. Simultaneous induction on the size of the derivation in system T using the previous two propositions.

Proposition 13.

> $\Gamma \vdash^\mathsf{D} wf \ and \ \mathcal{DC}_\Gamma(t) \ imply \ \Gamma \vdash^\mathsf{D} t = t^*$.
> $\Gamma \vdash^\mathsf{D} wf \ and \ \mathcal{DC}_\Gamma(\varphi) \ imply \ \Gamma \vdash^\mathsf{D} \varphi \leftrightarrow \varphi^*$.

Proof. Simultaneous induction on the structure of t and φ.

Proposition 14. $\mathcal{DC}(\Gamma) \ implies \ that \ \Gamma \vdash^\mathsf{D} \varphi \ iff \ \Gamma^* \vdash^\mathsf{D} \varphi$.

Proof. Induction on the structure of Γ using the second part of Proposition 13.

Proposition 15. $\mathcal{DC}(\Gamma) \ and \ \mathcal{DC}_\Gamma(\varphi) \ and \ \Gamma \vdash^\mathsf{T} \varphi \ imply \ \Gamma \vdash^\mathsf{D} \varphi$.

Proof. Assume $\mathcal{DC}(\Gamma)$, $\mathcal{DC}_\Gamma(\varphi)$ and $\Gamma \vdash^\mathsf{T} \varphi$. Then $\Gamma^* \vdash^\mathsf{D} \varphi^*$ by Proposition 12 and then $\Gamma \vdash^\mathsf{D} \varphi^*$ by Proposition 14 and therefore $\Gamma \vdash^\mathsf{D} \varphi$ by the second part of Proposition 13.

10   From D to P

In the previous section we got from T to D. Now we show how to get from D to P. To 'fill in' the proof objects in a system D proof we need a property called *proof irrelevance*. It says that a P expression does not change its meaning if we replace proof terms in it with different proofs of the same statements. This is stated 'locally' in the $=$-*fun* rule of system P:

$$\frac{\Gamma \vdash t_1 = t_1' \quad \cdots \quad \Gamma \vdash t_{a_i} = t_{a_i}' \qquad \Gamma \vdash \beta : D_{f_i}(t_1, \ldots, t_{a_i}) \quad \Gamma \vdash \beta' : D_{f_i}(t_1', \ldots, t_{a_i}')}{\Gamma \vdash f_i(t_1, \ldots, t_{a_i}, \beta) = f_i(t_1', \ldots, t_{a_i}', \beta')}$$

The two terms are equal despite the proof terms β and β' being different. But the property of proof irrelevance is also true 'globally':

Proposition 16 (proof irrelevance).

$\Gamma \vdash^{\mathsf{P}} t$ *wf and* $\Gamma \vdash^{\mathsf{P}} t'$ *wf and* $|t| \equiv |t'|$ *imply* $\Gamma \vdash^{\mathsf{P}} t = t'$.
$\Gamma \vdash^{\mathsf{P}} \varphi$ *wf and* $\Gamma \vdash^{\mathsf{P}} \varphi'$ *wf and* $|\varphi| \equiv |\varphi'|$ *imply* $\Gamma \vdash^{\mathsf{P}} \varphi \leftrightarrow \varphi'$.

Proof. Simultaneous induction on the size of $|t|$ and $|\varphi|$ using Proposition 5 and the $=$-*fun*, $=$-*pred*, $=$-*if-true* and $=$-*if-false* rules.

Once we have proof irrelevance, getting a system P derivation from a system D derivation is straightforward. Together with the earlier propositions this then allows us to prove the main result of this paper.

Proposition 17. *If* $\Gamma \vdash^{\mathsf{P}}$ *wf then:*

$|\Gamma| \vdash^{\mathsf{D}} t'$ *wf imply that there exists a t with* $|t| \equiv t'$ *such that* $\Gamma \vdash^{\mathsf{P}} t$ *wf*.
$|\Gamma| \vdash^{\mathsf{D}} \varphi'$ *wf imply that there exists a φ with* $|\varphi| \equiv \varphi'$ *such that* $\Gamma \vdash^{\mathsf{P}} \varphi$ *wf*.
$|\Gamma| \vdash^{\mathsf{D}} \varphi'$ *imply that there exists a φ with* $|\varphi| \equiv \varphi'$ *such that* $\Gamma \vdash^{\mathsf{P}} \varphi$.

Proof. Simultaneous induction on the size of the derivation in system D using Propositions 5 and 16.

Proposition 18 (main correspondence theorem from T to P). $\Gamma \vdash^{\mathsf{P}}$ *wf and* $|\Gamma| \vdash^{\mathsf{T}} \varphi'$ *and* $\mathcal{DC}_{|\Gamma|}(\varphi')$ *imply that there exists a φ with* $|\varphi| \equiv \varphi'$ *such that* $\Gamma \vdash^{\mathsf{P}} \varphi$.

Proof. Assume $\Gamma \vdash^{\mathsf{P}}$ *wf*, $|\Gamma| \vdash^{\mathsf{T}} \varphi'$ and $\mathcal{DC}_{|\Gamma|}(\varphi')$. Then $\mathcal{DC}(|\Gamma|)$ by Proposition 9 and then $|\Gamma| \vdash^{\mathsf{D}} \varphi'$ by Proposition 15 and therefore there exists a suitable φ by Proposition 17.

Proposition 19 (corollary). $\Gamma' \vdash^{\mathsf{T}} \varphi'$ *and* $\mathcal{DC}(\Gamma')$ *and* $\mathcal{DC}_{\Gamma'}(\varphi')$ *imply that there exist Γ and φ with* $|\Gamma| \equiv \Gamma'$ *and* $|\varphi| \equiv \varphi'$ *such that* $\Gamma \vdash^{\mathsf{P}} \varphi$.

Proof. $\Gamma' \vdash^{\mathsf{D}} \varphi'$ by Proposition 15, from which $\Gamma' \vdash^{\mathsf{D}}$ *wf*. Then $\Gamma' \vdash^{\mathsf{D}}$ *wf* implies that there exists a Γ with $|\Gamma| \equiv \Gamma'$ such that $\Gamma \vdash^{\mathsf{P}}$ *wf*, by induction on the structure of Γ' using Proposition 17. Finally we get φ from Proposition 18.

11   Conclusion

The main things left to be done are:

1. Prove the systems with if-then-else conservative over the same systems without this construction.
2. Build a proof assistant that implements the approach of reasoning in system T with domain conditions, to study how well it works in practice.
3. Investigate whether the theory from this paper extends to higher order logic.

Acknowledgments. Thanks to Herman Geuvers, Paula Severi and Venanzio Capretta for stimulating discussions. Thanks to Gilles Barthe for the idea of how to fit this paper in 16 pages. Thanks to the anonymous referees for valuable comments.

References

1. M.J. Beeson. *Foundations of constructive mathematics*. Springer-Verlag, 1985.
2. Robert L. Constable, Stuart F. Allen, H.M. Bromley, W.R. Cleaveland, J.F. Cremer, R.W. Harper, Douglas J. Howe, T.B. Knoblock, N.P. Mendler, P. Panangaden, James T. Sasaki, and Scott F. Smith. *Implementing Mathematics with the Nuprl Development System*. Prentice-Hall, NJ, 1986.
3. Simon Finn, Michael Fourman, and John Longley. Partial Functions in a Total Setting. *Journal of Automated Reasoning*, 18:85–104, 1997.
4. H. Geuvers, F. Wiedijk, and J. Zwanenburg. Equational Reasoning via Partial Reflection. In *Theorem Proving in Higher Order Logics, 13th International Conference, TPHOLs 2000*, volume 1869 of *LNCS*, pages 162–178, Berlin, Heidelberg, New York, 2000. Springer Verlag.
5. M.J.C. Gordon and T.F. Melham, editors. *Introduction to HOL*. Cambridge University Press, Cambridge, 1993.
6. J.D. Guttman and F.J. Thayer. IMPS: An Interactive Mathematical Proof System. *Journal of Automated Reasoning*, 11:213–248, 1993.
7. John Harrison. Re: Undefined terms. Message <`"swan.cl.cam.:266770:950519095422"@cl.cam.ac.uk`> as sent to the QED mailing list, <`http://www.ftp.cl.cam.ac.uk/ftp/hvg/qed-project-archive/03xx/0380`>, 1995.
8. Matt Kaufmann, Panagiotis Manolios, and J. Strother Moore. *Computer-Aided Reasoning: An Approach*. Kluwer Academic Publishers, Boston, 2000.
9. J. Kuper. *Partiality in Logic and Computation – Aspects of Undefinedness*. PhD thesis, University of Twente, Dept INF, Enschede, The Netherlands, 1994.
10. M. Muzalewski. *An Outline of PC Mizar*. Fondation Philippe le Hodey, Brussels, 1993. <`http://www.cs.kun.nl/~freek/mizar/mizarmanual.ps.gz`>.
11. R.P. Nederpelt, J.H. Geuvers, and R.C. de Vrijer. *Selected Papers on Automath*, volume 133 of *Studies in Logic and the Foundations of Mathematics*. Elsevier Science, Amsterdam, 1994.
12. T. Nipkow, L.C. Paulson, and M. Wenzel. *Isabelle/HOL – A Proof Assistant for Higher-Order Logic*, volume 2283 of *LNCS*. Springer, 2002.

13. S. Owre, J. Rushby, and N. Shankar. PVS: A prototype verification system. In D. Kapur, editor, *11th International Conference on Automated Deduction (CADE)*, volume 607 of *LNAI*, pages 748–752, Berlin, Heidelberg, New York, 1992. Springer-Verlag.

14. D.S. Scott. Identity and existence in intuitionistic logic. In M.P. Fourman, C.J. Mulvey, and D.S. Scott, editors, *Applications of Sheaves*, volume 753 of *Lecture Notes in Mathematics*, pages 660–696, Berlin, 1979. Springer-Verlag.

15. Natarajan Shankar and Sam Owre. Principles and Pragmatics of Subtyping in PVS. In Didier Bert, Christine Choppy, and Peter Mosses, editors, *Recent Trends in Algebraic Development Techniques, WADT '99*, volume 1827 of *LNCS*, pages 37–52, Toulouse, France, September 1999. Springer-Verlag.

16. The Coq Development Team. *The Coq Proof Assistant Reference Manual*, 2002. `<ftp://ftp.inria.fr/INRIA/coq/current/doc/Reference-Manual-all.ps.gz>`.

17. A. Troelstra and D. van Dalen. *Constructivism in Mathematics, an Introduction, Vols. 1-2*, volume 121 and 123 of *Studies in Logic and The Foundations of Mathematics*. North-Holland, 1988.

18. L. Wos. *The Automation of Reasoning: An Experimenter's Notebook with Otter Tutorial*. Academic Press, New York, 1996.

Extending Higher-Order Unification to Support Proof Irrelevance*

Jason Reed

Carnegie Mellon University,
Pittsburgh, PA 15213, USA
jcreed@cs.cmu.edu

Abstract. As theories and proofs in logical frameworks become larger, careful control over what information within them can safely be omitted or erased becomes useful for efficient implementation. The notion of proof irrelevance provides exactly this control, but requires existing algorithms used in logical frameworks, in particular higher-order pattern unification, to be extended to accommodate the richer type theory. We describe this extended algorithm, whose presentation is simplified by making use of recent developments in explaining unification metavariables as modal variables, which obviates the need for full explicit substitutions.

1   Introduction

1.1   Proof Irrelevance

Proof irrelevance is the treatment of all proofs of the same proposition as equal. The type system introduced by Pfenning [7] defines (in addition to an intentional equality, with which we are not concerned here) *irrelevant* versions of the ordinary typing and equality judgments. A characteristic feature of both these judgments is that they are allowed to make use of *irrelevant hypotheses* in the context, which are intuitively assumptions that some proof of a proposition (i.e. term at a type) exists that are provided only under a promise that the consumer of the assumption does not care *which* proof it is. The irrelevant version of the equality judgment is distinguished by being trivial, holding if merely the terms being compared are both well-typed. Since there is a new kind of hypothesis in the definition of contexts, there is a new function type as well, one with an irrelevant domain.

As an example of the expressivity of these functions, suppose we want to represent a lambda calculus which has a binder $\lambda^{\geq 1}$ which requires the variable

---

* This work has been partially supported by NSF Grant CCR-9988281 *"Logical and Meta-Logical Frameworks"*. Thanks are owed to Frank Pfenning, Brigitte Pientka, Kaustuv Chaudhuri, and the anonymous reviewers for many useful comments and corrections.

D. Basin and B. Wolff (Eds.): TPHOLs 2003, LNCS 2758, pp. 238–252, 2003.

it binds to occur at least once. We could try doing this by beginning with the usual higher-order abstract syntax [8] encoding of the untyped lambda calculus

$$\mathsf{tm : type}$$
$$\mathsf{app : tm \to (tm \to tm)}$$
$$\mathsf{lam : (tm \to tm) \to tm}$$

defining a predicate $occurs : (\mathsf{tm \to tm}) \to \mathsf{type}$ which is inhabited by proofs that a term closed except for one free variable actually uses it, and declaring a constant

$$olam : \mathit{\Pi} t\mathord:(\mathsf{tm \to tm}).\, occurs\, t \to \mathsf{tm}$$

to represent the binder $\lambda^{\geq 1}$. This encoding, however, is not adequate, in the sense that there are generally multiple representation-language terms which represent an object-language term. This is because, in any natural specification implementing the predicate $occurs$, each particular occurrence of the variable acts as a different witness of the fact that it occurs at least once, and so there are potentially many proofs of $occurs\, t$.

We want, however, to equate all terms constructed using $olam$ that differ only in which proof they use, for the proof ought to have no effect on the equational theory of terms — it only matters *that* the proofs exist. That is, we want an irrelevant function arrow $\to^i$, and we should declare[1] instead

$$olam : \mathit{\Pi} t\mathord:(\mathsf{tm \to tm}).\, occurs\, t \to^i \mathsf{tm}$$

and the encoding would then be adequate.

Moreover, recent work with large safety proofs in a metalogical style arising from grid computing applications [2] suggests that significant space and time savings (as alluded to in [7]) stand to be made in them without sacrificing soundness if only this sort of function type were available in the implementation of the logical framework used. These would allow many intermediate proof objects to be 'forgotten' during checking, because the type system guarantees that their exact identity is not necessary after their existence has been verified. The metalogical approach — by which is meant proving metatheorems about an object logic by writing terminating, total logic programs that compute witnesses to the objects which the metatheorem claims to exist — relies heavily, however, on the logic programming interpretation of type family declarations, which in turn relies on algorithms for unification, as well as mode checking and totality checking [12]. Revised algorithms are therefore necessary for the revised underlying type theory. We focus on the first of these algorithms as an initial step along this path, the revision of higher-order pattern unification in a dependent type theory similar to LF [5].

---

[1] This notation is merely suggestive. The syntax is made precise in the next section.

1.2   Higher-Order Pattern Unification

Using explicit substitutions [1], higher-order unification can be reduced to a
first-order equational unification problem [3]. Though higher-order unification
is in fact undecidable in general, it is decidable for the pattern subset [4]. This
decidable subset can be also solved dynamically, putting off equations that do
not fit in the pattern frament in the hope that later instantiations will turn
them into equations that do. This constraint simplification algorithm turns to
be quite useful in practice, solving many systems of equations which do not
initially consist of only patterns.

We had previously tried [10] to start with the algorithm as presented by
Dowek et al. but it is not clear how to achieve right marriage of proof irrelevance
and explicit substitutions. Either additional equations or additional rewrite rules
are necessary to establish the triviality of equality 'at irrelevant types,' but
achieving and working out the desired confluence and termination properties
seems less than trivial.

Fortunately, these difficulties can be sidestepped entirely. The use of substitutions as full first-class citizens in the language can be eliminated in favor of
limiting their role to only occurring applied to metavariables open to instantiation, and conversely requiring metavariables to only occur immediately under a
substitution. This approach [9] involves a typing discipline derived from a modal
logic of (relative) validity, and reflects faithfully aspects of the actual implementation of unification variables.

2   Language

2.1   Syntax

We work throughout with a deBruijn-index style version of LF, augmented with
proof irrelevance [7], and relative validity variables [9] as described above. While
the use of deBruijn indices is at a lower level of description than is strictly
necessary, the precision which they provide is useful for concisely defining and
reasoning about the auxiliary notions necessary for the algorithm presented below. It also has the useful side effect of highlighting the distinction between
ordinary variables (represented as indices) and unification variables (described
in terms of modal variables).

The syntax is given by

$$
\begin{aligned}
\text{Status } \mu &::= \mathsf{r} \mid \mathsf{i} \\
\text{Kinds } K &::= \mathsf{type} \mid \Pi_A^\mu K \\
\text{Families } A, B &::= a \mid A \diamond^\mu M \mid \Pi_A^\mu B \\
\text{Objects } M, N &::= c \mid M \diamond^\mu N \mid \lambda_A^\mu M \mid \mathsf{n} \mid u[\sigma] \\
\text{Substitutions } \sigma &::= \cdot \mid M \cdot^\mu \sigma \\
\text{Contexts } \Gamma, \Psi &::= \cdot \mid \Gamma \cdot^\mu A \\
\text{Modal Contexts } \Delta &::= \cdot \mid \Delta, u :: (\Psi \vdash A)
\end{aligned}
$$

Constant families are typically written a, b, constant objects c, modal variables u, v, and deBruijn indices n.

For uniformity of notation, we use superscript annotations (generally μ) on various pieces of syntax indicating whether they are relevant (r) or irrelevant (i) versions. On binders (λ_A^μ, Π_A^μ) the μ indicates whether the bound variable is 'relevantly' or 'irrelevantly' at the appropriate type, that is, whether the function or function type respectively can or cannot distinguish between different arguments passed to it. Function application ($M \diamond^\mu N$, $A \diamond^\mu M$) is written with the non-blank symbol $\diamond$ so that it can carry an annotation μ, to bring the elimination forms for function types in correspondence with the introduction forms. That is, for $M \diamond^r N$ to be well-typed, M should have type $\Pi_A^r.B$ for some A, B, and for $M \diamond^i N$ to be well-typed, M should have a type of the shape $\Pi_A^i.B$. Conses $\Gamma \cdot^\mu A$ of a variable at type A onto a context Γ have a μ to indicate whether the variable is a relevant or irrelevant hypothesis. Contexts are written left-to-right (that is, the deBruijn index 1 refers to a variable at the rightmost type in the context) so that, as customary, types only depend on other types on their left. Conses $M \cdot^\mu \sigma$ of terms M onto substitutions σ carry a μ to indicate whether the M should be typed (and dealt with respect to equality) relevantly or irrelevantly.

The 'irrelevant arrow' used in the example in the introduction becomes a Π by defining the syntactic sugar $A \to^\mu B = \Pi_A^\mu.B$ where B does not actually depend on A, a simple extension of that typically made for $\to$ in dependent type theories. The full typing of $olam$ from the example in the introduction, in the syntax developed thus far, is

$$olam : \Pi_{\Pi_{tm}^r \, tm}^r \Pi_{Occurs \diamond^r 1}^i \, tm$$

The syntax $u :: (\Psi \vdash A)$ [9] indicates a *modal variable* u which stands in place of a term which has type A in the context Ψ. The variable u is 'relatively closed' (logically, represents a hypothesis of the 'relative validity' of A relative to Ψ) in that it cannot refer to any variables in any context but Ψ.

2.2   Definitions

Since the presentation is nameless, we sketch the definition of shifting and substitution, only for the object level. The definitions given should not be surprising, as they are essentially the same as they would be if irrelevance were absent, except that all annotations μ are simply preserved. The definitions at the family and kind levels are straightforward.

The operation $\uparrow_m$ increments all indices $\geq m$. Note that this is merely an operation on terms, not a full-fledged substitution. It is defined by

$$\uparrow_m c = c \qquad \uparrow_m (M \diamond^\mu N) = \uparrow_m M \diamond^\mu \uparrow_m N \qquad \uparrow_m (\lambda_A^\mu M) = \lambda_{\uparrow_m A}^\mu (\uparrow_{m+1} M)$$

$$\uparrow_m n = \begin{cases} n+1 & \text{if } n \geq m; \\ n & \text{otherwise.} \end{cases} \qquad \uparrow_m (u[\sigma]) = u[\uparrow_m \sigma]$$

$$\uparrow_m (\cdot) = \cdot \qquad \uparrow_m (M \cdot^\mu \sigma) = \uparrow_m M \cdot^\mu \uparrow_m \sigma$$

We abbreviate $\uparrow_1$ by just $\uparrow$. Ordinary substitution $[\sigma]M$ (again merely an operation on terms) is defined by

$$[\sigma]c = c \qquad [\sigma](M \diamond^\mu N) = [\sigma]M \diamond^\mu [\sigma]N \qquad [\sigma]\lambda^\mu_A M = \lambda^\mu_{[\sigma]A}[1 \cdot^\mu \uparrow\sigma]M$$

$$[M \cdot^\mu \sigma]1 = M \qquad [M \cdot^\mu \sigma]n + 1 = [\sigma]n \qquad [\sigma](u[\tau]) = u[[\sigma]\tau]$$

$$[\sigma](\cdot) = \cdot \qquad [\sigma](M \cdot^\mu \tau) = [\sigma]M \cdot^\mu [\sigma]\tau$$

Following [9], the *operation* of substitution is written as a prefix operator to distinguish the substitution attached to occurrences of modal variables $u[\sigma]$, which is written postfix.

The introduction of modal variables carries with it a novel substitution principle. The substitution operation $[\![P/u]\!]$ of a (closed, relative to the context Ψ) term P for the modal variable $u :: (\Psi \vdash A)$ for some context Ψ and type A, is defined by

$$[\![P/u]\!]c = c \qquad [\![P/u]\!](M \diamond^\mu N) = [\![P/u]\!]M \diamond^\mu [\![P/u]\!]N$$

$$[\![P/u]\!]\lambda^\mu_A M = \lambda^\mu_{[\![P/u]\!]A}[\![P/u]\!]M \qquad [\![P/u]\!]n = n$$

$$[\![P/u]\!](u[\tau]) = [[\![P/u]\!]\tau]P$$

$$[\![P/u]\!](v[\tau]) = v[[\![P/u]\!]\tau] \qquad (\text{for } u \neq v)$$

$$[\![P/u]\!](\cdot) = \cdot \qquad [\![P/u]\!](M \cdot^\mu \tau) = [\![P/u]\!]M \cdot^\mu [\![P/u]\!]\tau$$

Since P can only refer to variables in the context Ψ, variable capture is impossible, and this substitution can be (and in practice is) carried out in the implementation by simple in-place update.

We use θ for simultaneous modal substitutions $P_1/u_1, P_2/u_2, \ldots, P_n/u_n$. We say $\Delta' \vdash \theta : \Delta$ if θ is a substitution for the variables $u_i :: (\Psi_i \vdash A_i)$ in Δ and $\Delta'; \Psi_i \vdash P_i : A_i$ for all i. The relevant substitution property is

Lemma 1. *If* $\Delta; \Gamma \vdash M : A$ *and* $\Delta' \vdash \theta : \Delta$, *then* $\Delta'; [\![\theta]\!]\Gamma \vdash [\![\theta]\!]M : [\![\theta]\!]A$.

which is easily established by induction. The identity substitution is defined by

$$\mathsf{id.} = \cdot \qquad \mathsf{id}_{\Gamma \cdot^\mu A} = 1 \cdot^\mu \uparrow(\mathsf{id}_\Gamma)$$

We often omit the subscript when it is clear from context.

The typing rules require a context promotion operation $\mathbin{-^\oplus}$, defined by

$$\cdot^\oplus = \cdot \qquad (\Gamma \cdot^\mu A)^\oplus = (\Gamma^\oplus \cdot^r A)$$

which promotes all irrelevant assumptions to relevant.

2.3 Judgments

The central judgments are

$$
\begin{array}{ll}
\vdash \Delta\,\mathsf{mctx} & \Delta \text{ is a valid modal context} \\
\Delta \vdash \Gamma\,\mathsf{ctx} & \Gamma \text{ is a valid context} \\
\Delta; \Gamma \vdash M = N :^{\mu} A & M \text{ and } N \text{ are equal at type } A \\
\Delta; \Gamma \vdash M :^{\mu} A & M \text{ has type } A \\
\Delta; \Gamma \vdash \sigma : \Psi & \sigma \text{ has type } \Psi
\end{array}
$$

We abbreviate $:^{r}$ by $:$ and $:^{i}$ by $\div$ to match the notation of [7].

There are a handful of other, analogous judgments at the family and kind level, which we again omit for brevity.

The judgments $\Delta\,\mathsf{mctx}$ and $\vdash \Gamma\,\mathsf{ctx}$, as common for dependent type theories, insure that every type in the context Γ (resp. modal context Δ) is actually constructed correctly from previous context variables. We omit the exact rules defining them.

The equality and typing judgments each have a μ annotation to indicate whether the equality or typing, respectively, takes place in a relevant or irrelevant way. The following sections detail their effect.

2.4 Object Typing

The critical rule for proof irrelevance is the sole rule which has an irrelevant typing judgment as its conclusion:

$$
\frac{\Delta; \Gamma^{\oplus} \vdash M : A \qquad \Delta; \Gamma \vdash A : \mathsf{type}}{\Delta; \Gamma \vdash M \div A}
$$

which allows (via the promotion operation defined above) irrelevant assumptions in Γ to be used to show that $M \div A$, as long as A is a valid type in Γ unpromoted. ([11] treats why this second premise is necessary)

The other typing rules are mostly straightforward:

$$
\frac{\Delta; \Gamma \vdash M : \Pi_{A}^{\mu} B \qquad \Delta; \Gamma \vdash N :^{\mu} A}{\Delta; \Gamma \vdash M \diamond^{\mu} N : [N \cdot^{\mu} \mathsf{id}_{\Gamma}] B} \qquad \frac{\Delta; \Gamma \cdot^{\mu} A \vdash M : B}{\Delta; \Gamma \vdash \lambda_{A}^{\mu} M : \Pi_{A}^{\mu} B}
$$

$$
\frac{}{\Delta; \Gamma \cdot^{r} A \vdash 1 : A} \qquad \frac{\Delta; \Gamma \vdash \mathsf{n} : B}{\Delta; \Gamma \cdot^{\mu} A \vdash \mathsf{n}+1 : \uparrow B}
$$

$$
\frac{\Delta; \Gamma \vdash M : A \qquad \Delta; \Gamma \vdash A = B : \mathsf{type}}{\Delta; \Gamma \vdash M : B}
$$

The rule for typing uses of modal variables $u :: (\Psi \vdash A)$ is

$$
\frac{\Delta, u :: (\Psi \vdash A), \Delta'; \Gamma \vdash \sigma : \Psi}{\Delta, u :: (\Psi \vdash A), \Delta'; \Gamma \vdash u[\sigma] : [\sigma] A}
$$

Intuitively, it expresses the fact that u requires (and requires no more than) a justification of Ψ to be usable; if a substitution for the variables of Ψ valid in the contexts $\Delta, u :: (\Psi \vdash A), \Delta', \Gamma$ can be found, it can be attached to u to form an object of type $[\sigma]A$.

Substitutions themselves are typed by

$$\overline{\Delta; \Gamma \vdash \cdot : \cdot}$$

$$\frac{\Delta; \Gamma \vdash M :^\mu [\sigma]A \qquad \Delta; \Gamma \vdash \sigma : \Psi}{\Delta; \Gamma \vdash M \cdot^\mu \sigma : \Psi \cdot^\mu A}$$

2.5   Object Equality

For brevity we only mention a few equality rules relevant to proof irrelevance. The others are largely similar to those in the original definition of LF.

The first is

$$\frac{\Delta; \Gamma^\oplus \vdash M : A \qquad \Delta; \Gamma^\oplus \vdash M' : A \qquad \Delta; \Gamma \vdash A : \text{type}}{\Delta; \Gamma \vdash M = M' \div A}$$

which gives the meaning of proof irrelevance: M and M' are equal at $\div A$ if they are both merely well-typed.

This 'irrelevant equality' is made use of in the rule

$$\frac{\Delta; \Gamma \vdash M = M' : \Pi_A^\mu B \qquad \Delta; \Gamma \vdash N = N' :^\mu A}{\Delta; \Gamma \vdash M \diamond^\mu N = M' \diamond^\mu N' : [N \cdot^\mu \text{id}_\Gamma]B}$$

which means in particular that $M \diamond^i N = M \diamond^i N'$, even if $N \neq N'$, as long as both N and N' are well-typed.

Continuing with the example from the introduction, suppose we have some object $t : \Pi_{\text{tm}}^r \text{tm}$ (representing an object-language term with one free variable) and two different proofs $p_1, p_2 : occurs \diamond^r t$. Now we should have

$$\Delta; \Gamma \vdash olam \diamond^r t \diamond^i p_1 = olam \diamond^r t \diamond^i p_2 : \text{tm}$$

and indeed we do; to derive this judgment we must show

$$\Delta; \Gamma \vdash olam \diamond^r t = olam \diamond^r t : \Pi_{occurs \diamond^r t}^r \text{tm}$$

which follows by a reflexivity lemma, and

$$\Delta; \Gamma \vdash p_1 = p_2 \div occurs \diamond^r t$$

which holds precisely because of the former equality rule above.

Substitution equality (required for equality of modal variable uses $u[\sigma]$) is defined by

$$\overline{\Delta; \Gamma \vdash \cdot = \cdot : \cdot}$$

$$\frac{\Delta; \Gamma \vdash M = M' :^\mu [\sigma]A \qquad \Delta; \Gamma \vdash \sigma = \sigma' : \Psi}{\Delta; \Gamma \vdash M \cdot^\mu \sigma = M' \cdot^\mu \sigma' : \Psi \cdot^\mu A}$$

Notice that in the case of $\mu = \mathsf{i}$, at irrelevant conses $\cdot^{\mathsf{i}}$ the consed terms M, M' are only required to be irrelevantly equal ($\Delta; \Gamma \vdash M = M' \div [\sigma]A$), that is, merely both well-typed.

3   Unification

3.1   Pattern Substitutions

Pattern substitutions [6,4], ordinarily substitutions consisting of only distinct bound variables, are distinguished by being injective, that is, there is at most one P such that $[\sigma]P = M$ if σ is pattern. This property makes decidable the subset of unification problems where all terms being unified are *higher-order patterns*, that is, terms where all metavariables occur under pattern substitutions.

We define the judgment $I \vdash \sigma\,\mathsf{pat}$ ("σ is a pattern substitution using variables I") for I a list of natural numbers and σ a substitution. This is a simple generalization of the ordinary definition of pattern substitution. The difference is that here we allow arbitrary terms to occur at irrelevant positions.

$$\frac{}{\vdash \cdot\,\mathsf{pat}}$$

$$\frac{I \vdash \sigma\,\mathsf{pat}}{I \vdash M \cdot^{\mathsf{i}} \sigma\,\mathsf{pat}} \qquad \frac{I \vdash \sigma\,\mathsf{pat} \qquad \mathsf{n} \notin I}{I, \mathsf{n} \vdash \mathsf{n} \cdot^{\mathsf{r}} \sigma\,\mathsf{pat}}$$

A term in context $\Delta; \Gamma \vdash M : A$ is said to be an *atomic pattern* if every subterm of M of the form $u[\sigma]$ is such that $u :: (\Psi \vdash B) \in \Delta$ with B an atomic (that is, not a function) type, and $I \vdash \sigma\,\mathsf{pat}$ for some I. Assuming all modal variables are atomic incurs no loss, however. The process of *lowering* unification variables present in the given problem to atomic type and *raising* them again before presenting the answer to the user is well-known, and in fact is concisely justified by the modal variable framework [9].

3.2   Inversion

The fact that pattern substitutions are injective has a constructive proof, namely an algorithm (see Figure 1) for computing the inverse when it exists. It is mutually recursive with the definition of the restriction substitution $\xi \mid \sigma$.

The correctness of inversion amounts to the two lemmas stated below. Since inversion is computed in the process of unification, however, it can generate new equations as necessary. There is, therefore, also a sort of conceptual mutual recursion going on with the definition of the unification algorithm itself. The statement and style of proof of these lemmas could be separated from the language of unification, but not without some complication. We therefore assume familiarity with typical reasoning about equation-rewriting unification algorithms and speak of terms being known or being shown to be equal 'modulo' the other equations in the system or being newly introduced.

That is, running the inversion algorithm on a term potentially introduces as a side-effect

- new equations into the ambient unification problem
- new variables into Δ_B, the context of modal variables existentially bound in the unification problem.

The statement that "X holds modulo the generated equations" can be read as "for all instantiations of all the modal variables that satisfy the generated equations, X holds." See the following section for more details.

C	$[\sigma]^{-1}c = c$	
NI	$[M \cdot^i \sigma]^{-1}n = \uparrow([\sigma]^{-1}n)$	
N$\neq$	$[m \cdot^r \sigma]^{-1}n = \uparrow([\sigma]^{-1}n)$	if $m \neq n$
N=	$[n \cdot^r \sigma]^{-1}n = 1$	
E	$[\cdot]^{-1}n$	fails
L	$[\sigma]^{-1}(\lambda^\mu_A M) = \lambda^\mu_{[\sigma]^{-1}A}[1 \cdot^\mu \uparrow\sigma]^{-1}M$	
A	$[\sigma]^{-1}(M \diamond^r N) = [\sigma]^{-1}M \diamond^r [\sigma]^{-1}N$	
A+	$[\sigma]^{-1}(M \diamond^i N) = [\sigma]^{-1}M \diamond^i [\sigma]^{-1}N$	if $[\sigma]^{-1}N$ exists
A$-$	$[\sigma]^{-1}(M \diamond^i N) = [\sigma]^{-1}M \diamond^i v[\mathrm{id}]$	if not, for v added to Δ_B
V+	$[\sigma]^{-1}(u[\xi]) = u[[\sigma]^{-1}\xi]$	if $[\sigma]^{-1}\xi$ exists
V$-$	$[\sigma]^{-1}(u[\xi]) = u'[[\sigma]^{-1}([\xi]\xi')]$	if not, adding the equation that $u[\mathrm{id}] = u'[\xi']$ where $\xi' = \xi \mid \sigma$, for u' added to Δ_B
SN	$[\sigma]^{-1}(\cdot) = \cdot$	
SC	$[\sigma]^{-1}(M \cdot^\mu \xi) = [\sigma]^{-1}M \cdot^\mu [\sigma]^{-1}\xi$	
R+	$(M \cdot^\mu \xi) \mid \sigma = 1 \cdot^\mu (\uparrow(\xi \mid \sigma))$	if $[\sigma]^{-1}M$ exists
R$-$	$(M \cdot^\mu \xi) \mid \sigma = (\uparrow(\xi \mid \sigma))$	if not
RN	$\cdot \mid \sigma = \cdot$	

Fig. 1. Inversion and Restriction

Lemma 2.

1. *Suppose $\Delta; \Gamma \vdash M : A$, $\Delta; \Gamma' \vdash \sigma : \Gamma$, and $I \vdash \sigma$ pat for some $\Delta, \Gamma, \Gamma', A, I$. If $[\sigma]^{-1}M$ exists, then $[\sigma][\sigma]^{-1}M = M$, modulo the additional equations generated, if any.*
2. *Suppose $\Delta; \Gamma \vdash \xi : \Gamma''$, $\Delta; \Gamma' \vdash \sigma : \Gamma$, and $I \vdash \sigma$ pat for some $\Delta, \Gamma, \Gamma', \Gamma'', I$. If $[\sigma]^{-1}\xi$ exists, then $[\sigma][\sigma]^{-1}\xi = \xi$, modulo the additional equations generated, if any.*

Proof. By induction on the structure of M, ξ and σ. That is, either we

- reduce M,
- pass from one case to the other with a reduction in size from M to ξ or vice versa, or
- fix M and reduce σ.

We show just a few representative cases.

For **NI**, we must show $n = [M \cdot^i \sigma](\uparrow([\sigma]^{-1}n))$. but it can be shown that $[M \cdot^\mu \sigma](\uparrow N) = [\sigma]N$ for any M, N, μ, σ, (cf. the $\lambda\sigma$ [1] rewrite rule **ShiftCons**) so we apply the induction hypothesis to $[\sigma][\sigma]^{-1}n$.

For **A−**, use induction hypothesis and the fact that $M \diamond^i N = M \diamond^i v[\mathrm{id}]$.

In the case of **V−** we must apply the induction hypothesis to $[\xi]\xi'$, but by inspection of the rules defining the restriction operation, it can be seen that $[\xi](\xi \,|\, \sigma)$ is just a substitution consisting of a subsequence of the terms in ξ, and so is no bigger than ξ. So we have $[\sigma](u'[[\sigma]^{-1}([\xi]\xi')]) = u'[[\sigma][\sigma]^{-1}([\xi]\xi')]$, which by the induction hypothesis is equal to $u'[[\xi]\xi'] = [\xi](u'[\xi']) = [\xi](u[\mathrm{id}]) = u[\xi]$. It is also easy to show that $[\xi](\xi \,|\, \sigma)$ always exists, by the definition of restriction.

∎

Lemma 3. *If there exists I, θ and N such that*

- $I \vdash \sigma$ pat
- $\Delta' \vdash \theta : \Delta,$
- $\Delta; \Psi \vdash N : A$
- $\Delta; \Gamma \vdash \sigma : \Psi$
- $\Delta; \Gamma \vdash M : [\sigma]A$

and $\Delta'; [\![\theta]\!]\Gamma \vdash [\![\theta]\!][\sigma]N = [\![\theta]\!]M : [\![\theta]\!][\sigma]A$, then $[\sigma]^{-1}M$ exists and is equal to N, modulo the additional equations generated, if any.

Proof. Without loss of generality, assume N and M are in η-long β-normal form. We can then proceed by induction on the structure of M and σ.

The case for the new rule **NI** requires showing that if $\Delta; [\![\theta]\!]\Gamma \vdash [\![\theta]\!][M \cdot^i \sigma]N = n$, then $[\sigma]^{-1}n$ exists and is equal to N. For N under a substitution to be equal to a deBruijn index, it must be itself a deBruijn index, and it can't be 1, since that would not be well-typed: it accesses M from $M \cdot^i \sigma$, violating the implicit contract that a legitimate, relevant term cannot use irrelevant assumptions from the context (respectively, irrelevantly cons-ed terms from a substitution) except under irrelevant application. Therefore there exists a deBruijn index m such that $N = \uparrow m$. What we know by assumption becomes $\Delta; \Gamma \vdash [\![\theta]\!][M \cdot^i \sigma]\uparrow m = n$, and **ShiftCons**-like reasoning again gives $[\sigma]m = n$. Now the induction hypothesis applies, giving $m = [\sigma]^{-1}n$, which implies $N = \uparrow([\sigma]^{-1}n)$, as required.

For **A+**, we have that $[\![\theta]\!][\sigma](N_1 \diamond^i N_2) = [\![\theta]\!](M_1 \diamond^i M_2)$, but we can only apply the induction hypothesis to M_1, N_1, because we have no guarantee of equality under the irrelevant application. However, if M_2 under the inverse of σ does not exist, then **A−** applies, and we still get the required definitional equality.

If $M = u[\xi]$ and $\mathbf{V}-$ applies, then suppose that $P/u, P'/u' \in \theta$. Then we know $[\![\theta]\!][\sigma]N = [\![\theta]\!]\xi]P$. So the new equation $u[\mathrm{id}] = u'[\xi \mid \sigma]$ means $P = [\![\theta]\!](\xi \mid \sigma)]P'$. Thus $[\![\theta]\!]\xi]P = [\![\theta]\!]([\xi](\xi \mid \sigma))]P' = [\![\theta]\!](u'[[\xi](\xi \mid \sigma)])$. By the induction hypothesis, (the new term can be construed as smaller because the substitution applied to the modal variable is now guaranteed to be in the domain of $[\sigma]^{-1}$ by the definition operation) $u'[[\sigma]^{-1}[\xi](\xi \mid \sigma)]$ exists and is equal to N, but this is the definition of $[\sigma]^{-1}M$.   ∎

The restriction operation $\xi \mid \sigma$ serves to take ξ and produce a substitution such that $[\xi](\xi \mid \sigma)$ is just like ξ only leaving out those terms that are not in the domain of $[\sigma]^{-1}$. The rule $\mathbf{R}+$ in fact needs not pass along even those irrelevant terms that do fall in the domain of $[\sigma]^{-1}$, however. We could have written instead of $\mathbf{R}+$ the two rules

$$\mathbf{RR}+ \qquad (M \cdot^r \xi) \mid \sigma = 1 \cdot^r (\uparrow(\xi \mid \sigma)) \qquad \text{if } [\sigma]^{-1}M \text{ exists}$$

$$\mathbf{RI}+ \qquad (M \cdot^i \xi) \mid \sigma = \uparrow(\xi \mid \sigma) \qquad \text{if } [\sigma]^{-1}M \text{ exists}$$

without sacrificing correctness. The reason for this is that we never strictly need, during unification, to preserve irrelevantly used terms (i.e. N in $M \diamond^i N$ or M in $M \cdot^i \sigma$) since the equational theory permits them to be replaced by fresh modal variables of the appropriate type. The restriction rules are written as they are, since preserving the terms seems desirable even if not necessary. This issue is treated in some more detail in the next section.

3.3   Unification Transformations

A unification problem $\mathcal{U}$ is given by

$$\Delta_F; \exists \Delta_B. \bigwedge_{i \in I} \Gamma_i \vdash M_i \overset{?}{=} N_i : A_i$$

for modal contexts Δ_F of *free* variables and Δ_B of *bound* variables. These two modal contexts are used to separate the two roles played by modal variables in the unification algorithm. Δ_F is initially populated by those variables for which we seek instantiations, and Δ_B contains variables for which instantiations need to exist for an instantiation of Δ_F to be a unifier. When new variables are added, (for instance, when a flex-flex equation $u[\sigma] = u[\sigma']$ is transformed to $u'[\sigma \cap \sigma']$ to enforce that u is instantiated with some term that behaves the same under σ and σ') they are added to Δ_B, since the instantiations of these new variables is not important to answer the original problem posed.

Therefore formally we say a unification problem is *unified* by a modal substitution $\Delta' \vdash \theta_F : \Delta_F$ if there exists a substitution $\Delta'' \vdash \theta_B : \Delta_B$ for Δ'' extending Δ' such that if

$$\Delta''; [\![\theta_F, \theta_B]\!]\Gamma_i \vdash [\![\theta_F, \theta_B]\!]M_i = [\![\theta_F, \theta_B]\!]N_i : [\![\theta_F, \theta_B]\!]A_i$$

for all i. We write $\theta_F(\mathcal{U})$ for the set of unifiers of $\mathcal{U}$.

Since a unifier is only required to make the terms under substitution equal up to definitional equality, we could at the outset replace every term $M \diamond^i N$ in a problem with $M \diamond^i v[\cdot]$ for a fresh modal variable v of the appropriate type. The fact that we *can* safely effect this kind of replacement is extremely important for solving problems such as

$$\lambda_A^r(c \diamond^i 1) \stackrel{?}{=} \lambda_A^r u[\cdot]$$

No modal substitution for u results in $u[\cdot]$ becoming $c \diamond^i 1$, since the argument to the function is not made available to u, but we can produce a substitution $c \diamond^i v[\cdot]/u$, which produces the equation

$$\lambda_A^r(c \diamond^i 1) \stackrel{?}{=} \lambda_A^r(c \diamond^i v[\cdot])$$

which does hold, by virtue of how equality is defined for $\diamond^i$. Note that with regard to the the problem for finding *closed* substitutions (i.e., containing no modal variables) for all the modal variables, we have merely deferred to the problem of determining whether there indeed exist closed terms at the type A.

So, as stated, it would be possible to replace at the outset all irrelevant arguments with fresh modal variables. This would in no way compromise the correctness of the algorithm, since up to definitional equality, we are changing nothing. Why not do exactly this? It is because we aim to make as easy as possible the problem of finding closed solutions, which may, because of the presence of proof irrelevance, require solving (generally undecidable) inhabitation problems. Therefore throughout the algorithm below we take care to preserve, whenever possible, the structure of irrelevant arguments, in the hope that they might later prove useful as witnesses of inhabitation.

The unification algorithm proceeds by rewriting equations in a way that maintains the same set of unifiers, towards the goal of a *solved form*

$$\Delta_F; \exists \Delta_B'. \bigwedge_{i \in J} \Psi_j \vdash u_j[\mathrm{id}_{\Psi_j}] \stackrel{?}{=} P_j : A_j$$

(where no modal variables occur in P_i) which witnesses that the mgu of the original system is $P_1/u_1, \ldots, P_m/u_m$. It is very close to the "practical transformations" in the algorithm of Dowek et al. [4] except that we need not cover cases for inverted substitutions applied to still other substitutions, because the presentation does not use full explicit substitutions. We maintain the invariant that terms in equations are weak head normal, and use the notation $\langle M \rangle$ to denote the weak head normal form of M. We omit several rules which are merely symmetric versions of rules listed, or are straightforward analyses of equations involving constants. We also omit the ordinary contexts Γ, since their role is easily inferred. For instance, **LL** written out fully is $\Gamma \vdash \lambda_A^\mu M \stackrel{?}{=} \lambda_A^\mu N \rightarrow \Gamma \cdot^\mu A \vdash \langle M \rangle \stackrel{?}{=} \langle N \rangle$.

The intersection $\sigma \cap \xi$ of two substitutions as in **VV** is defined by

$$(\mathsf{n} \cdot^r \sigma) \cap (\mathsf{n} \cdot^r \sigma') = \mathsf{n} \cdot^r (\sigma \cap \sigma')$$
$$(\mathsf{n} \cdot^r \sigma) \cap (\mathsf{m} \cdot^r \sigma') = \sigma \cap \sigma' \qquad \text{if } n \neq m$$
$$(M \cdot^i \sigma) \cap (M' \cdot^i \sigma') = M \cdot^i (\sigma \cap \sigma')$$

$$\begin{array}{lll}
\textbf{AA} & M_1 \diamond^r M_2 \stackrel{?}{=} N_1 \diamond^r N_2 \rightarrow M_1 \stackrel{?}{=} N_1 \wedge \langle M_2 \rangle \stackrel{?}{=} \langle N_2 \rangle & \\
\textbf{AAI} & M_1 \diamond^i M_2 \stackrel{?}{=} N_1 \diamond^i N_2 \rightarrow M_1 \stackrel{?}{=} N_1 & \\
\textbf{LL} & \lambda_A^\mu M \stackrel{?}{=} \lambda_A^\mu N \rightarrow \langle M \rangle \stackrel{?}{=} \langle N \rangle & \\
\textbf{TL} & N \stackrel{?}{=} \lambda_A^\mu M \rightarrow \langle M \rangle \stackrel{?}{=} \langle (\uparrow N) \diamond^\mu 1 \rangle & \text{if } \textbf{LL} \text{ can't apply} \\
\textbf{N=} & \mathsf{n} \stackrel{?}{=} \mathsf{n} \rightarrow \mathbb{T} & \\
\textbf{N} \neq & \mathsf{n} \stackrel{?}{=} \mathsf{m} \rightarrow \mathbb{F} & \text{if } m \neq n \\
\textbf{NA} & \mathsf{n} \stackrel{?}{=} M_1 \diamond^\mu M_2 \rightarrow \mathbb{F} & \\
\textbf{VV} & u[\sigma] \stackrel{?}{=} u[\xi] \rightarrow u'[\sigma \cap \xi] & {}^{1} \\
\textbf{VT} & u[\sigma] \stackrel{?}{=} M \rightarrow u[\mathsf{id}] \stackrel{?}{=} [\sigma]^{-1} M & {}^{2} \\
\textbf{OCI} & u[\sigma] \stackrel{?}{=} M \rightarrow u[\sigma] \stackrel{?}{=} [\![v[\mathsf{id}]/u]\!] M & {}^{3} \\
\textbf{OC} & u[\sigma] \stackrel{?}{=} M \rightarrow \mathbb{F} & {}^{4}
\end{array}$$

[1] for u' a fresh variable added to Δ_B
[2] if $\textbf{VV}$ does not apply, $[\sigma]^{-1} M$ exists, and u does not occur in M
[3] if $\textbf{VV}$ does not apply and u only occurs under the argument side of $\diamond^i$ in M, for v a fresh variable of the same type as u added to Δ_B
[4] if none of $\textbf{VV}$, $\textbf{VT}$, $\textbf{OCI}$ applies.

Fig. 2. Unification Transformations

3.4 Correctness

As usual for the rewriting presentation, correctness of the algorithm amounts to the preservation of the set of unifiers at every step:

Lemma 4 (Soundness). *If* $\mathcal{U} \rightarrow \mathcal{U}'$, *then* $\theta_F(\mathcal{U}) \subseteq \theta_F(\mathcal{U})$.

Lemma 5 (Completeness). *If* $\mathcal{U} \rightarrow \mathcal{U}'$, *then* $\theta_F(\mathcal{U}) \supseteq \theta_F(\mathcal{U})$.

We do not provide a full proof, because the bulk of it is already accomplished in [3,4], and instead we sketch the argument required for what is new.

The presence of proof irrelevance in the type system forces several novelties into the algorithm. The rule $\textbf{AAI}$ handles comparison of two irrelevant applications. We can neglect trying to solve the equation of the arguments, since we know that $M_1 \diamond^i N_1 = M_2 \diamond^i N_2$ if (and only if) merely $M_1 = M_2$.

The occurs-check need not (and in fact must not, to have completeness) reject equations $u[\mathsf{id}] = M$ where u occurs in M, if it occurs only "irrelevantly", that is, somewhere inside the arguments of irrelevant applications. For if it does, we can swap in (this is exactly the content of rule $\textbf{OCI}$) a new modal variable v of the same type, keeping the whole term invariant up to definitional equality.

Rules $\textbf{VV}$, $\textbf{VT}$, and $\textbf{OCI}$ use the new definitions of substitution, intersection, and inversion. To verify the correctness of $\textbf{VV}$, we must show that $[\sigma]P = [\xi]P$

if and only if there exists P' such that $P = [\sigma \cap \xi]P'$.[2] But this is established by an easy inductive argument. The correctness of the other two rules can be shown using the properties of inversion already proved.

4   Conclusions

With some modifications, an established algorithm for higher-order pattern unification can be made to perform correctly in the presence of proof irrelevance. It is hoped that future work can do the same for mode, termination, and coverage checking, so that logic programs can be written in a style conscious of which arguments are safe to discard during execution, realizing space and time savings in the distribution and checking of proof terms.

References

1. Martín Abadi, Luca Cardelli, Pierre-Louis Curien, and Jean-Jacques Lèvy. Explicit substitutions. In *Conference Record of the Seventeenth Annual ACM Symposium on Principles of Programming Languages, San Francisco, California*, pages 31–46. ACM, 1990.
2. Karl Crary and Susmit Sarkar. A metalogical approach to foundational certified code. Technical Report CMU-CS-03-108, Carnegie Mellon University, January 2003.
3. Gilles Dowek, Thérèse Hardin, and Claude Kirchner. Higher-order unification via explicit substitutions. In D. Kozen, editor, *Proceedings of the Tenth Annual Symposium on Logic in Computer Science*, pages 366–374, San Diego, California, June 1995. IEEE Computer Society Press.
4. Gilles Dowek, Thérèse Hardin, Claude Kirchner, and Frank Pfenning. Unification via explicit substitutions: The case of higher-order patterns. In M. Maher, editor, *Proceedings of the Joint International Conference and Symposium on Logic Programming*, pages 259–273, Bonn, Germany, September 1996. MIT Press.
5. Robert Harper, Furio Honsell, and Gordon Plotkin. A framework for defining logics. *Journal of the Association for Computing Machinery*, 40(1):143–184, January 1993.
6. Dale Miller. A logic programming language with lambda-abstraction, function variables, and simple unification. *Journal of Logic and Computation*, 1(4):497–536, 1991.
7. Frank Pfenning. Intensionality, extensionality, and proof irrelevance in modal type theory. In J. Halpern, editor, *Proceedings of the 16th Annual Symposium on Logic in Computer Science (LICS'01)*, pages 221–230, Boston, Massachusetts, June 2001. IEEE Computer Society Press.
8. Frank Pfenning and Conal Elliott. Higher-order abstract syntax. In *Proceedings of the ACM SIGPLAN '88 Symposium on Language Design and Implementation*, pages 199–208, Atlanta, Georgia, June 1998.

---

[2] We need not consider the possibility that σ and ξ in the left-hand side of **VV** contain occurrences of u, because if u does occur in them, it only occurs under an irrelevant cons because σ, ξ are pattern, so we can, as above, swap in a fresh modal variable in place of u without loss.

9. Brigitte Pientka and Frank Pfenning. Optimizing higher-order pattern unification. In F. Baader, editor, *Proceedings of the 19th Conference on Automated Deduction (CADE-19)*, Miami Beach, Florida, July 2003. Springer-Verlag LNCS. To appear.

10. Jason Reed. Higher-order pattern unification and proof irrelevance. Appears in TPHOLs 2002 Track B proceedings, NASA tech report CP-2002-211736, 2002.

11. Jason Reed. Proof irrelevance and strict definitions in a logical framework. Technical Report CMU-CS-02-153, Carnegie Mellon University, 2002.

12. Ekkehard Rohwedder and Frank Pfenning. Mode and termination checking for higher-order logic programs. In Hanne Riis Nielson, editor, *Proceedings of the European Symposium on Programming*, pages 296–310, Linköping, Sweden, April 1996. Springer-Verlag LNCS 1058.

Inductive Invariants for Nested Recursion[*]

Sava Krstić and John Matthews

OGI School of Science & Engineering at Oregon Health & Sciences University

Abstract. We show that certain input-output relations, termed *inductive invariants* are of central importance for termination proofs of algorithms defined by nested recursion. Inductive invariants can be used to enhance recursive function definition packages in higher-order logic mechanizations. We demonstrate the usefulness of inductive invariants on a large example of the BDD algorithm APPLY. Finally, we introduce a related concept of *inductive fixpoints* with the property that for every functional in higher-order logic there exists a largest partial function that is such a fixpoint.

1 Introduction

To prove termination of a recursively defined program, we usually argue that its execution on any given input x will make recursive calls only to arguments smaller than x, where "smaller" is specified by some wellfounded relation. When the pattern of recursive calls is simple enough, we can derive from the program text a finite set of inequalities sufficient to guarantee termination.

This simple scheme has a difficulty with nested recursion—the occurrence of recursive calls within recursive calls, as in the following simple program (of type nat $\Rightarrow$ nat) taken from [17].

$$g\,x \equiv \textbf{if } x = 0 \textbf{ then } 0 \textbf{ else } g\,(g\,(x-1)) \tag{1}$$

Even though this program clearly terminates for all inputs, the reason for it is not just a couple of easy inequalities. The simplest rigorous explanation would probably be proving by strong induction that "for all x, the algorithm terminates with input x and returns the value 0". This pattern of reasoning requires knowing something in advance about the function being defined, and proving that fact simultaneously with termination. Proving termination of functions defined by nested recursion can thus be a challenge for a human prover, not to mention automated tools.

A recursive declaration for a function $f\colon A \Rightarrow B$ is naturally represented by a functional $F\colon (A \Rightarrow B) \Rightarrow (A \Rightarrow B)$, so that defining f amounts—more or less—to showing that F has a unique fixpoint. The inductive invariants we introduce in this paper are specific invariants of the functional. They are predicates on

---

[*] The research reported in this paper was supported by the National Science Foundation Grants EIA-0072761 and CDA-9703218, Hewlett-Packard Corporation, and Intel Corporation.

$A \Rightarrow B$ that are defined by input-output relations (predicates on $A \times B$). We have found that "the extra information about the function being defined that needs to be known in order to prove termination" is invariably in the form of an invariant relation. That is, there is an inductive invariant playing an essential part in every (nested) termination proof that we have seen. It is as important a part of the termination proof as is the wellfounded relation that captures the dependency pattern of recursive calls. The inductive invariant is sometimes easy to guess, but ultimately it is the user's responsibility to come up with, just as is the wellfounded relation.

The main contribution of the paper is perhaps the discovery of this role of inductive invariants for structuring termination proofs for nested recursive definitions. While there have been attempts in the literature to formulate general principles behind such termination proofs [4,6,19], the methodology of inductive invariants appears not to have been observed as yet.

The paper is organized as follows. In Section 2, we give an overview of the state-of-the-art recursion package *recdef* by Konrad Slind [15,18]. This puts us in the framework of higher-order logic and in the context of Slind's work on nested recursion. In Section 3, we introduce inductive invariants and prove Theorem 1, which opens the way to incorporating them into *recdef*. We also demonstrate inductive invariants in a few standard small examples.

Section 4 presents a small theory of recursive definitions in HOL. We introduce the notion of *inductive fixpoints* of functionals that is arguably the closest natural concept in HOL to "terminating functional program". We also discuss *contraction conditions* as an abstraction of *recdef*'s proof obligations when presented with a non-nested recursive definition. We then extend the notion of contraction condition with an inductive invariant parameter. In Theorem 2 we show that a functional satisfying a contraction condition necessarily has an inductive fixpoint. Theorem 2 is independent of *recdef* and can be used as an alternative in situations when *recdef* is difficult to apply. This development leads naturally to general notion of a fixpoint operator in higher-order logic that given any functional produces its largest (in an appropriate sense) inductive fixpoint. Existence of such a fixpoint is stated as Theorem 3.

In Section 5 we apply the theory of Section 4 to a large and difficult example of the imperative program APPLY that is a key component of any efficient BDD (Boolean decision diagram) package. This example also reveals that nested recursion is not a rarity: it occurs in disguise—because of the hidden state variable—in every recursively defined imperative program in which there is a sequence of commands containing two recursive calls. Another example of nested recursion that occurs when modeling imperative programs is given in [3].

Section 6 draws some conclusions and comparisons with related work.

2   A Summary of *Recdef*

In this section we give a quick description of the theory underlying *recdef*, a powerful recursive function definition package designed by Slind [15,17,18,19].

Given as input a recursive declaration of the form

$$f\,x = M, \tag{2}$$

where M is some term that contains no free variables other than f and x, *recdef* attempts to produce a valid HOL definition of a function f that satisfies equation (2) for every x. It is convenient to abstract the variables in M and use the associated functional $F = \lambda f\,x.\,M\colon (A \Rightarrow B) \Rightarrow (A \Rightarrow B)$ as the input. Thus equation (2) translates into the *fixpoint equation* (or *recursion equation*)

$$\forall x.\, f\,x = F\,f\,x. \tag{3}$$

2.1 Partiality and WFREC

We will use the notation $f \restriction D$ for the restriction of a function $f\colon A \Rightarrow B$ on a subset D of A; this partial function is represented in HOL as a total function, and is defined by

$$(f \restriction D)\,x \equiv \text{if } x \in D \text{ then } f\,x \text{ else Arb},$$

where $\text{Arb} \equiv \varepsilon z.\text{True}$ is an arbitrary element of the domain of f. We will write $f =_D g$ as an abbreviation for $f \restriction D = g \restriction D$, which is equivalent to $\forall y \in D.\, f\,y = g\,y$. We will also write $\rho^{-1}x$ as an abbreviation for the set $\{y \mid \rho\,y\,x\}$, where ρ is a binary relation. This notation will be used throughout the paper.

The principle of definition by wellfounded recursion (e.g., [22], Theorem 10.19) can be expressed as follows: Given a functional $F\colon (A \Rightarrow B) \Rightarrow (A \Rightarrow B)$ and a wellfounded relation ρ on A, there exists a unique function $f\colon A \Rightarrow B$ satisfying

$$\forall x.\, f\,x = F\,(f \restriction \rho^{-1}x)\,x. \tag{4}$$

Nipkow has given an elegant formalization of this principle in HOL [17]. The theory defines a "controlled fixpoint operator" WFREC, and contains the theorem

$$\mathsf{WF}\,\rho \longrightarrow \forall x.\, \phi\,x = F\,(\phi \restriction \rho^{-1}x)\,x, \tag{5}$$

where $\phi = \mathsf{WFREC}\,\rho\,F$ and WF is the wellfoundedness predicate.

We do not need to know the exact definition of the function WFREC. The upshot is that, for any given wellfounded relation ρ, the function $\phi = \mathsf{WFREC}\,\rho\,F$ satisfies (4). Given a recursive declaration (2), we can start by introducing the function ϕ as a newly defined constant (for a suitable ρ), obtain equation (4) for free, and then work to transform that equation into the desired form of (3).

2.2 Termination Conditions

The *recdef* algorithm begins with theorem (5) in the form

$$(f = \mathsf{WFREC}\,\rho\,F) \wedge (\mathsf{WF}\,\rho) \longrightarrow \forall x.\, f\,x = F\,(f \restriction \rho^{-1}x)\,x, \tag{6}$$

leaving ρ unspecified at the beginning, and analyzes the structure of the term M (recall that $F = \lambda f\, x.\, M$) in order to find occurrences $f\, t_1, \ldots, f\, t_m$ of recursive calls as subterms of M. For simplicity, let us assume that every occurrence of f in M is applied to some argument. For each of the m calling sites, *recdef* also gathers the conjunction of conditionals Γ_i controlling it, and extracts the *termination condition* $TC_i \equiv \Gamma_i \longrightarrow \rho\, t_i\, x$. For example, the declaration (1) produces two termination conditions (where we write $<$ in place of ρ):

$$x \neq 0 \longrightarrow x - 1 < x \quad \text{and} \quad x \neq 0 \longrightarrow g\,(x - 1) < x. \tag{7}$$

By definition of function restriction, we have

$$\rho\, t_i\, x \longrightarrow (f \upharpoonright \rho^{-1} x)\, t_i = f\, t_i.$$

Thus, it is possible by a bottom-up traversal of the term M to transform theorem (6) into one where all occurrences of $f \upharpoonright \rho^{-1} x$ are replaced with f, at the price of adding termination conditions as assumptions:

$$(f = \mathsf{WFREC}\, \rho\, F) \wedge (\mathsf{WF}\, \rho) \wedge TC_1 \wedge \cdots \wedge TC_m \longrightarrow f\, x = F\, f\, x. \tag{8}$$

The desired recursion theorem for $\phi = \mathsf{WFREC}\, \rho\, F$ is now in sight: it only remains to eliminate the antecedent of implication (8), which amounts to proving the termination conditions TC_i for a suitably instantiated wellfounded relation ρ. Assuming ρ has been instantiated, the system can try to prove each termination condition $\forall x.\, TC_i$, or pass this obligation to the user. However, if the original recursive declaration is nested, then there will be occurrences of f in the termination conditions, and it is not clear at all how to systematically discharge them. So after disposing of immediately provable termination conditions, we are left with a theorem of the form

$$TC \longrightarrow \phi\, x = F\, \phi\, x, \tag{9}$$

where TC is a formula that may contain occurrences of ϕ.

2.3   Slind's Method for Nested Recursion

Normally, to prove a property of a recursively defined function f, one would use the recursion equation (3) as the main auxiliary result. Unfortunately, we are now in a position that we need to prove TC in order to derive (3). But note that there is no genuine circularity here: the function has already been defined (as $\mathsf{WFREC}\, \rho\, F$), and it may well be possible to prove that it satisfies the property TC before one proves that it satisfies (3). Slind discovered that the constrained recursion equation (9) that we have at our disposal can sometimes be used to prove the termination condition TC by induction. The induction principle he uses is not standard, however. It is given by a *provisional induction theorem* that can be automatically generated at the same time the constrained equation (9) is derived [18,19].

Space does not permit us to go into a description of provisional induction theorems. The reader is referred to the cited Slind's work for details and case studies. They include termination proofs for nested recursive definitions as complex as the first order unification algorithm.

The exact scope of Slind's method is difficult to characterize. Just for illustration, the method deals easily with the simple function given by equation (1), but not so with the following, just slightly changed equation:

$$g\,x \equiv \textbf{if } x = 0 \textbf{ then } 0 \textbf{ else } g\,(x-1) + g\,(g\,(x-1)) \tag{10}$$

3   Inductive Invariants

In both examples, given by recursive equations (1) and (10), the nested termination condition is $x \neq 0 \longrightarrow g\,(x-1) < x$. What makes it provable by Slind's method in one case, but not in the other, is the fact that this condition expresses an *inductive invariant* for the first equation, but not for the second.

Definition 1. *A predicate $S\colon A \Rightarrow B \Rightarrow$ bool is an* inductive invariant *of the functional $F\colon (A \Rightarrow B) \Rightarrow (A \Rightarrow B)$ with respect to the wellfounded relation ρ iff the following condition is satisfied:*

$$\forall f\,x.\ (\forall y.\ \rho\,y\,x \longrightarrow S\,y\,(f\,y)) \longrightarrow S\,x\,(F\,f\,x) \tag{11}$$

Predicates of the form $S\colon A \Rightarrow B \Rightarrow$ bool express input-output relations for functions $f\colon A \Rightarrow B$. We will say that f *satisfies* S if $S\,x\,(f\,x) = $ True holds for all $x \in A$. Thus, if f satisfies an inductive invariant S, it follows from (11) that $F\,f$ satisfies S as well. In this sense, inductive invariants are invariants of their associated functionals.

Checking inductive invariance is an inductive method of proving properties of WFREC $\rho\,F$, as the following key result shows.

Theorem 1. *If ρ is wellfounded and S is an inductive invariant of F with respect to ρ, then* WFREC $\rho\,F$ *satisfies S.*

Proof. Denote $\phi = $ WFREC $\rho\,F$. By instantiating f in (11) with $\phi \restriction \rho^{-1}x$, we get

$$\forall x.\ (\forall y.\ \rho\,y\,x \longrightarrow S\,y\,((\phi \restriction \rho^{-1}x)\,y)) \longrightarrow S\,x\,(F\,(\phi \restriction \rho^{-1}x)\,x).$$

This is equivalent to

$$\forall x.\ (\forall y.\ \rho\,y\,x \longrightarrow S\,y\,(\phi\,y)) \longrightarrow S\,x\,(\phi\,x) \tag{12}$$

because $(\phi \restriction \rho^{-1}x)\,y = \phi\,y$ is clearly true when $\rho\,y\,x$, and $F\,(\phi \restriction \rho^{-1}x)\,x = \phi\,x$ holds from equation (5). The formula (12) is exactly what is needed for a wellfounded-inductive proof of the formula $\forall x.\ S\,x\,(\phi\,x)$ saying that ϕ satisfies S.   □

Theorem 1 suggests the possibility of treating nested recursive definitions automatically with an extension of *recdef*: Use *recdef* to generate termination conditions, then check if they can be expressed as input-output relations, and if so then prove their inductive invariance.

We conjecture that termination proofs of most functions defined by nested recursion can be naturally based on some inductive invariant property. Termination conditions themselves are not necessarily inductive invariants, or not the most convenient ones. Rather, there exists some inductive invariant that *implies* the termination conditions. Coming up with such an invariant in every concrete nested recursive definition seems as fundamental for understanding its termination as coming up with an appropriate wellfounded relation. So just like the user-supplied wellfounded relations are essential for *recdef*, a user-supplied input-output relation (inductive invariant) could be essential for an extension of *recdef* that will treat nested cases successfully.

3.1   Examples

We give several small examples to demonstrate ubiquity of inductive invariants. In Section 5, we will give a more substantial example. The interested reader can find yet another example at the beginning of the termination proof of the unification algorithm given in [19].[1]

Nested Zero. The functional

$$G \, g \, x \equiv \textbf{if } x = 0 \textbf{ then } 0 \textbf{ else } g\left(g\left(x-1\right)\right) \tag{13}$$

corresponds to the example in equation (1). The termination condition can be written as $g\,x < x + 1$, and it is an inductive invariant. (More precisely, the inductive invariant is defined by: $S\,x\,y$ iff $y < x + 1$.) Indeed, one needs to check

$$\forall g\,x.\ (\forall y < x.\ g\,y < y + 1) \longrightarrow G\,g\,x < x + 1.$$

This is clearly true for $x = 0$, while for $x > 0$ it reads as

$$\forall g.\ (\forall y < x.\ g\,y < y + 1) \longrightarrow g\left(g\left(x-1\right)\right) < x + 1$$

and the conclusion of this formula follows by using the assumption twice.

The slightly different functional

$$G' \, g \, x \equiv \textbf{if } x = 0 \textbf{ then } 0 \textbf{ else } g\left(x-1\right) + g\left(g\left(x-1\right)\right)$$

corresponding to the equation (10) has the same termination condition $g\,x < x + 1$, but now this condition is not an inductive invariant. We leave checking this fact to interested readers.

Note also that $g\,x = 0$ is an inductive invariant for both G and G'.

---

[1] The proof is due to Manna and Waldinger; its first mechanized version is due to Paulson. See [19] for history and references.

McCarthy's Ninety-One Function. This classic example is a recursive definition of a function of type nat $\Rightarrow$ nat, given by the functional

$$F \, f \, x \equiv \textbf{if } x > 100 \textbf{ then } x - 10 \textbf{ else } f(f(x + 11))$$

The termination conditions for F are

$$x \le 100 \longrightarrow x + 11 \prec x \quad \text{and} \quad x \le 100 \longrightarrow f(x + 11) \prec x,$$

for a suitable wellfounded relation $\prec$. A relation that works is the ordering defined by $1 \succ 2 \succ 3 \succ \cdots \succ 99 \succ 100$ and $100 \succ 100 + i$ for all $i \ge 1$. This ordering discharges the first termination condition, while the second termination condition can be rewritten as

$$11 \le x \le 111 \longrightarrow x < f(x) + 11.$$

This expresses an obvious input-output relation and one can check that the relation is in fact an inductive invariant. We will check that an even stronger (but simpler) relation, namely

$$S \, x \, y \equiv x < y + 11 \tag{14}$$

is an inductive invariant for F. Thus, we need to prove

$$z < (F \, f \, z) + 11 \tag{15}$$

assuming

$$x < f(x) + 11 \tag{16}$$

holds for all $x \prec z$. For $z > 100$, the relation (15) reduces to $z < (z - 10) + 11$, which is true. In the remaining case $z \le 100$, the relation (15) rewrites as

$$z < f \, (f \, (z + 11)) + 11. \tag{17}$$

Now we can assume that (16) holds for all $x > z$, since $x \prec z$ and $x > z$ are equivalent when $z \le 100$. In particular, $z + 11 < f \, (z+11) + 11$ must hold, giving us $z < f \, (z + 11)$. Instantiating x with $f \, (z + 11)$ in (16) is now legitimate and gives us $f \, (z + 11) < f \, (f \, (z + 11)) + 11$, so (17) follows by transitivity of $<$.

HOL Version of the While Combinator. This example illustrates the utility of inductive invariants even for non-nested recursion. In *Isabelle/HOL* [15], the function while $b \, c \colon A \Rightarrow A$ is defined for any predicate $b \colon A \Rightarrow$ bool and function $c \colon A \Rightarrow A$, and it is a fixpoint of the functional

$$W \, f \, x \equiv \textbf{if } b \, x \textbf{ then } f \, (c \, x) \textbf{ else } x \tag{18}$$

One can check that, given any two predicates $P\colon A \Rightarrow$ bool and $Q\colon A \Rightarrow$ bool, the following relation S is an inductive invariant for W:

$$
\begin{aligned}
S\,x\,y \;\equiv\; & P\,x \\
& \wedge \;\; (\forall z.\; P\,z \wedge b\,z \longrightarrow P\,(c\,z) \wedge c\,z \prec z) \\
& \wedge \;\; (\forall z.\; P\,z \wedge \neg(b\,z) \longrightarrow Q\,z) \\
& \longrightarrow Q\,y
\end{aligned}
$$

The theorem while_rule supplied with *Isabelle/HOL* says precisely that while $b\,c$ satisfies every relation S of this form, provided the parameter $\prec$ is a wellfounded relation. Thus, while_rule is essentially an instance of Theorem 1.

4 Fixpoint Operators in HOL

When we use *recdef* to prove termination of an algorithm, we represent the algorithm as a functional $F\colon (A \Rightarrow B) \Rightarrow (A \Rightarrow B)$, find a wellfounded relation ρ, and then prove that the function $f \;=\; \mathsf{WFREC}\,\rho\,F$ satisfies the recursion equation

$$\forall x.\; f\,x = F\,f\,x.$$

Simple examples like $F\,f\,x \;\equiv\; f\,(x-1)$, where every constant function is a fixpoint, and $\mathsf{WFREC}\,(<)\,F$ is just one of them, show that the truth of the recursion equation does not quite correspond to termination.However, in situations when *recdef* succeeds (at least in the non-nested cases), the fixpoint is unique, and even more is true. In this section we define a simple HOL concept of *inductive fixpoints* that is related to *recdef* and that corresponds more closely to termination.

4.1 Inductive Fixpoints

The graph S_h of a function h is an input-output predicate that only h satisfies: $S_h\,x\,y$ iff $y = h\,x$. Condition (11) with S_h in place of S is equivalent to

$$\forall f\,x.\; f =_{\rho^{-1}x} h \longrightarrow F\,f\,x = h\,x. \tag{19}$$

Definition 2. *We say that h is an* inductive fixpoint *of F if S_h is an inductive invariant of F for some ρ (equivalently: if equation (19) holds).*

Lemma 1. *If h is an inductive fixpoint of F, then*

(a) h is the unique fixpoint of F;
(b) $h = \mathsf{WFREC}\,\rho\,F$ for some wellfounded relation ρ.

Proof. (a) If h' is another fixpoint of F, then we can prove $\forall x.\; h'\,x = h\,x$ by wellfounded induction using (19) with f instantiated with h'.

(b) Suppose ρ is such that (19) holds and let $\phi = \mathsf{WFREC}\,\rho\,F$. Instantiating f with $\phi \restriction \rho^{-1}x$ in (19), we get

$$\forall x.\ (\phi \restriction \rho^{-1}x) =_{\rho^{-1}x} h \longrightarrow F\,(\phi \restriction \rho^{-1}x)\,x = h\,x.$$

The antecedent here is clearly equvalent to $\phi =_{\rho^{-1}x} h$, while the consequent is, in view of the WFREC recursion equation (5), equivalent to $\phi\,x = h\,x$. Now $\phi = h$ follows by wellfounded induction. $\square$

Consider the example

$$F\,f\,x \equiv \mathbf{if}\ x = 0\ \mathbf{then}\ f(1) - f(0)\ \mathbf{else}\ f(x - 1).$$

The constant zero function is equal to $\mathsf{WFREC}\,(<)\,F$ and it is also the only fixpoint of the functional F. Yet, the constant zero function is not an inductive fixpoint of F. The example demonstrates that $\mathsf{WFREC}\,\rho\,F$ is not necessarily an inductive fixpoint even when it is a unique fixpoint.

4.2   Contraction Conditions

The (unrestricted) *contraction condition* for the functional F with respect to the wellfounded relation ρ is

$$\forall f\,g\,x.\ f =_{\rho^{-1}x} g \longrightarrow F\,f\,x = F\,g\,x. \tag{20}$$

Harrison proved in [7] that the contraction condition implies the unique existence of a fixpoint of F. In Theorem 2 below, we show that this condition actually implies that $\mathsf{WFREC}\,\rho\,F$ is an inductive fixpoint of F. For now we check that in the case of non-nested recursive declarations the contraction condition follows from the conjunction of termination conditions generated by *recdef*. Indeed, assuming a wellfounded relation ρ is fixed, we can think of *recdef* as transforming the theorem

$$f\,x = F\,(f \restriction \rho^{-1}x)\,x \tag{21}$$

into the theorem

$$TC_1 \wedge \cdots \wedge TC_m \longrightarrow f\,x = F\,f\,x. \tag{22}$$

It is true that f in these equations is the constant $\mathsf{WFREC}\,\rho\,F$, but that fact is never used in the sequence of steps (transforming the right-hand side progressively, while keeping the left-hand side fixed) that lead from (21) to (22). Consequently, the same sequence of steps would transform the trivial theorem

$$F\,(f \restriction \rho^{-1}x)\,x = F\,(f \restriction \rho^{-1}x)\,x,$$

in which f is free, into the theorem

$$TC_1 \wedge \cdots \wedge TC_m \longrightarrow F\,(f \restriction \rho^{-1}x)\,x = F\,f\,x.$$

Thus, if the (universally quantified) termination conditions are true, then

$$\forall f\,x.\ F\,(f \restriction \rho^{-1}x)\,x = F\,f\,x$$

is true as well. It is easy to see that this last equation is equivalent to saying that F satisfies the contraction condition with respect to ρ.

The contraction condition does not hold for even the simplest nested cases, like the one in (13). However, a weaker form of it that uses an inductive invariant to restrict one of the arguments may still be provable, and still be strong enough to guarantee the existence of an inductive fixpoint. We define the *restricted contraction condition* for the functional F with respect to a wellfounded relation ρ and an inductive invariant S to be the formula

$$\forall f\, g\, x.\ f =_{\rho^{-1}x} g \wedge (\forall y.\ S\, y\, (g\, y)) \longrightarrow F\, f\, x = F\, g\, x. \tag{23}$$

Note that the contraction condition (20) is a special case of (23) corresponding to the trivial (constantly true) inductive invariant S.

Theorem 2. *Suppose the restricted contraction condition (23) is satisfied and S is an inductive invariant of F associated with ρ. Then* WFREC $\rho\, F$ *is an inductive fixpoint of F.*

Proof. Instantiate (23) with $g = $ WFREC $\rho\, F$. The second conjunct is true by Theorem 1, so we obtain

$$\forall f\, x.\ f =_{\rho^{-1}x} g \longrightarrow F\, f\, x = F\, g\, x. \tag{24}$$

Instantiating f here with $g \mid \rho^{-1}x$ we obtain $F\,(g \mid \rho^{-1}x)\, x = F\, g\, x$, and then $g\, x = F\, g\, x$ by combining with the constrained recursion equation (4). Now (24) can be rewritten as

$$\forall f\, x.\ f =_{\rho^{-1}x} g \longrightarrow F\, f\, x = g\, x,$$

finishing the proof.   □

4.3   Partial Inductive Fixpoints

The techniques described in these sections readily generalize to allow termination proofs for recursive algorithms that terminate only on a specific subset of their input type. We just summarize the main definitions and results. The proofs are straightforward modifications of those already seen, as is their formalization in *Isabelle/HOL*.

Given a functional $F \colon (A \Rightarrow B) \Rightarrow (A \Rightarrow B)$ and a subset D of A, we say that h is an *inductive fixpoint of F on D*, if there exists a wellfounded relation ρ such that

$$\forall f\, x.\ x \in D \wedge f =_{D \cap (\rho^{-1}x)} h \longrightarrow F\, f\, x = h\, x. \tag{25}$$

The generalized Lemma 1 asserts that such an inductive fixpoint satisfies the guarded recursive equation

$$\forall x.\ x \in D \longrightarrow h\, x = F\, h\, x, \tag{26}$$

that $h =_D$ WFREC $\rho\, F$ for some wellfounded relation ρ, and that h is unique in the sense that $h =_D h'$ holds for any other function h' satisfying (25).

The definition of an *inductive invariant for F on D* is given by the same equation (11), except that the variables x, y need to be restricted to D. Theorem 1 generalizes to say that every such inductive invariant is satisfied by WFREC $\rho\, F$ for every input in D.

The *restricted contraction condition for F with respect to ρ, S, and D* is

$$\forall f\, g.\ \forall x \in D.\ f =_{D \cap (\rho^{-1}x)} g \wedge (\forall y \in D.\ S\, y\, (g\, y)) \longrightarrow F\, f\, x = F\, g\, x. \quad (27)$$

The generalized Theorem 2 states that when this contraction condition is satisfied and S is an inductive invariant for F on D, then WFREC $\rho\, F$ is an inductive fixpoint of F on D.

4.4 HOL Fixpoints

If h and h' are inductive fixpoints of F on D and D' respectively, let us say that *h' extends h* if $D \subseteq D'$ and $h =_D h'$.

Theorem 3. *For any functional $F \colon (A \Rightarrow B) \Rightarrow (A \Rightarrow B)$ there exists an inductive fixpoint h (defined on some domain $D \subseteq A$) that extends all other inductive fixpoints of F.*

We omit the proof for space reasons. It is more involved than the others in this paper, and we have not yet mechanized it.

Theorem 3 shows that there is a natural fixpoint operator that associates a partial function to every recursive declaration in HOL. The properties and usefulness of this fixpoint operator are left for future research.

5   Case Study: The BDD **Apply** Function

In this section we survey the proof of termination of the imperative BDD program APPLY. This proof has been verified in *Isabelle/HOL* and reported on in [9]. Our *HOL* proof did not use the *recdef* mechanism, but is instead based on the techniques described in the previous section.

Binary decision diagrams (BDDs) are a widely used representation of Boolean functions. Intuitively, a BDD is a finite rooted directed acyclic graph in which every node except the special nodes *TrueNode* and *FalseNode* is labeled by a *variable* and has two children: *low* and *high*. Special nodes represent the constant Boolean functions, and the function f_u represented by any other node u is defined recursively by $f_u =$ **if** x **then** f_l **else** f_h, where x is the variable associated with u, and l, h are its left and right children respectively. Bryant [5] originally proved that every function is represented by a unique reduced ordered BDD, where *reduced* means that no two nodes represent the same function, and *ordered* means that variable names are totally ordered and that every node's variable name precedes the variable names of its children. Efficient BDD packages implement reduced ordered BDDs. An abstract, but detailed presentation of such a package of programs is given in [1]. Our work [9] contains a *HOL* model of a significant part of the package. Referring to these papers for more detail, we will now describe just the minimum required to define the APPLY program.

The global state used by any BDD package contains a pool of BDD nodes. We assume there is an abstract type Node representing node addresses, and a type Var of variables. A primitive procedure $active$: Node $\Rightarrow$ bool indicates the presence of a node in the current state, and the accessor functions $var, low, high$ take a node as an argument and return the associated variable and children. What these functions return if the argument is not an active node is left unspecified. For simplicity we will assume that Var is the type of natural numbers whose natural ordering corresponds to the ordering of variables needed to implement the concept of ordered BDDs.

The BDD routine MK takes a variable x and two nodes l, h as inputs and returns a node u such that $var(u) = x$, $low(u) = l$, and $high(u) = h$. If a node with these three attributes already exists in the state, the state is left unchanged; otherwise MK adds u to the state. We gloss over the details how MK tests whether it needs to add a node to the existing state and the possibility that MK can raise an out-of-memory exception.

The crucial routine APPLY takes a binary operation op: bool $\times$ bool $\Rightarrow$ bool and two nodes u and v, and returns a node w which represents the Boolean function f_w specified by

$$\forall x.\ f_w\, x = op(f_u\, x, f_v\, x). \tag{28}$$

A recursive declaration of APPLY is given in pseudocode in Figure 1.

```
1    APPPLY[T](op, u, v) =
2    if u, v ∈ {TrueNode, FalseNode} then op(u, v)
3    else  if var(u) = var(v) then
4        w ⟵ MK(var(u), APPLY(op, low(u), low(v)), APPLY(op, high(u), high(v)))
5    else  if var(u) < var(v) then
6        w ⟵ MK(var(u), APPLY(op, low(u), v), APPLY(op, high(u), v))
7    else
8        w ⟵ MK(var(v), APPLY(op, u, low(v)), APPLY(op, u, high(v)))
9    return  w
```

Fig. 1. The program APPLY, as in [1], omitting the memoization part, inessential for the purpose of proving termination. The global variable T is the table of BDD nodes. The var accessor function is assumed to return 0 only for $TrueNode$ and $FalseNode$.

Clearly, the variable op is of little significance for proving the termination of APPLY. Assuming op is constant, we can think of APPLY as being a function of type Node $\times$ Node $\times$ State $\Rightarrow$ State $\times$ Node.[2] Recursion makes APPLY one of the most complicated programs in the package. Pondering the algorithm in Figure 1,

---

[2] In [9], we show how to use monadic interpretation to hide "state threading" and translate imperative programs to visibly equivalent *HOL* counterparts.

one realizes that even a hand proof of termination requires effort. The ultimate reason for termination is clear: in an ordered BDD (and these are the only ones we would like to consider), the level (that is, the *var* value) decreases when passing to child nodes, so in all recursive calls of APPLY the level decreases either for both node arguments, or decreases for the "higher", while the other stays the same. Thus, in order to prove that the arguments decrease in recursive calls, it is necessary to work with a restricted set of states, described by a predicate goodSt that needs to be preserved by APPLY. A workable invariant goodSt asserts that the associated *BDD* to each active node is ordered and reduced. Clearly, we cannot expect termination for all input-"good state" pairs. We need to add at least the restriction that the two input nodes be active in the input state. These restrictions define a subset D of Node × Node × State on which we can reasonably expect termination by means of the wellfounded relation defined by the measure that associates to an input-state triple (u, v, T) the maximum of the values $var(u)$, $var(v)$ in T.

Next we need to deal with nesting. Nesting is not immediately seen in Figure 1 because the state is not explicitly mentioned in the program text, being thus an extra hidden argument. Consider line 6; in expanded form, this piece of code could read like this:

$$6_1 \quad l_u \longleftarrow low(u)$$
$$6_2 \quad h_u \longleftarrow high(u)$$
$$6_3 \quad x \longleftarrow var(u)$$
$$6_4 \quad l \longleftarrow \text{APPLY}(op, l_u, v)$$
$$6_5 \quad h \longleftarrow \text{APPLY}(op, h_u, v)$$
$$6_6 \quad w \longleftarrow \text{MK}(x, l, h)$$

If we made the state explicit, these lines would look as follows, with primes denoting the appropriate modifications of functions representing programs:

$$6_1 \quad (l_u, T_1) \longleftarrow low'(u, T)$$
$$6_2 \quad (h_u, T_2) \longleftarrow high'(u, T_1)$$
$$6_3 \quad (x, T_3) \longleftarrow var'(u, T_2)$$
$$6_4 \quad (l, T_4) \longleftarrow \text{APPLY}'(op, l_u, v, T_3)$$
$$6_5 \quad (h, T_5) \longleftarrow \text{APPLY}'(op, h_u, v, T_4)$$
$$6_6 \quad (w, T_6) \longleftarrow \text{MK}'(x, l, h, T_5)$$

Lines 6_4 and 6_5 expose the nesting in the definition of h. Desugaring the pattern-matching of tuples, we see h is defined as

$$h = \mathsf{fst}(\text{APPLY}'(op, h_u, v, \mathsf{snd}(\text{APPLY}'(op, l_u, v, T_3)))).$$

To prove termination, we need to find input-output properties of APPLY that are sufficient to show that the measure decreases in each recursive call, and then prove that these properties are inductive invariants of the functional defining APPLY. It turns out that the input-output predicate S defined by

$$S(u, v, T)(w, T') \equiv \text{active nodes in } T \text{ are active in } T'$$
$$\wedge \; w \text{ is active in } T' \tag{29}$$
$$\wedge \; var'(w, T') \leq var'(u, T), var'(v, T)$$

is such an inductive invariant. We have carried out the proof of inductive invariance and the proof of the corresponding restricted contraction condition in *Isabelle/HOL* [9]. Other formalizations of BDD algorithms are reported in [8,20, 21].

6   Conclusion and Related Work

We have described a simple method for proving termination of functions defined by nested recursion. For a given functional F representing the recursive declaration, the user is required to supply a wellfounded relation ρ and an inductive invariant S. The user then has two possibilities to complete the definition.

(A) Generate termination conditions associated with F and ρ (e.g., using the *recdef* definition package) and prove that these conditions are true for all functions satisfying S.

(B) Prove that the restricted contraction condition (23) holds for F, ρ, S.

The challenge of justifying nested recursive definitions has attracted a great deal of attention and [4,6,12,16,19] are but a few examples of interesting case studies and general methods. They are presented in various formal system, but are all related to our work for the simple reason that inductive invariants (even if not recognized as such) are at the core of most of the known termination proofs of nested recursion.

Our work builds on Slind's [19]. Slind has discovered a method of proving termination conditions based on a specific induction theorem and a constrained recursion theorem. This method can be seen as a variation of the alternative (A) above; instead of proving that a certain property is an inductive invariant, it attempts to prove directly that the property is satisfied by WFREC ρF. Our method seems to be at least of comparable power, but is conceptually much simpler.

Alternative (B) is a general mathematical method. It can be used for termination proofs done by hand, but since the underlying theory has been formalized, (B) can be used in formal proofs as well, as we demonstrated in Section 5. Note, however, that since *recdef* normally automatically performs the task that amounts to checking the contraction condition, alternative (B) should be used only if one has difficulties with *recdef*. Such difficulties may arise because *recdef*'s working depends heavily on the requisite simplifiers of the theorem prover, and in particular on an adequate supply of *congruence rules*. There are also cases where not all occurrences of f in the recursive declaration (2) are applied; for example, f may rather occur as an argument to some higher-order function.[3] In

---

[3] A simple example: formalization of the common definition of Catalan numbers $C_{n+1} = \sum_{k=0}^{n} C_k C_{n-k}$ would require a congruence rule for the higher-order function $sum \, n \, f \equiv (f \, 0) + (f \, 1) + \cdots + (f \, n)$.

such cases, if it is not clear what congruence theorems are needed by *recdef*, it may be advantageous to go directly to the proof of the contraction condition.

While the search for an inductive invariant can be the most demanding part of a termination proof, often in this search one does not need to go further than the termination conditions themselves. The method described by Giesl [6] follows a similar route: heuristic generation of "induction lemmas" that correspond to nested termination conditions, then proving their "partial correctness", which amounts to inductive invariance. A high level of automation, which is the main virtue of Giesl's method, is also its limitation; in complex cases like the one discussed in Section 5 a human-supplied inductive invariant may be necessary. Compared with Giesl's method, ours is more general, and our proofs are considerably simpler than those in [6].

Giesl and Slind [6,19] make the point that contrary to common wisdom it is generally possible to prove termination of functions defined by nested recursion without simultaneously proving their correctness/specification. Our work corroborates this point, but note that the notions of correctness and specification are vague. The fact is that *some form* of specification is invariably being used, namely the inductive invariant! As for the full specification, it may even be totally unusable for the termination proof. An example is the APPLY algorithm specified by equation (28). The full specification uses an interpretation function associating Boolean functions to BDD nodes, but what is needed for the termination proof of APPLY is inductive invariance of the much simpler predicate given in (29).

Contraction conditions are a standard way of proving fixpoint theorems (*à la* Banach) in various contexts involving a metric. Contraction conditions along a wellfounded relation were introduced by Harrison [7] and called *admissibility conditions*. A more general version is introduced by Matthews in [11] to support recursive function definitions over types with coinductive structure.

Modeling partiality and program termination in HOL can be done in several ways, surveyed by Müller and Slind in [14]. The most accurate representation can be achieved in HOLCF [13], the HOL version of domain theory. Following *recdef*, we have adopted the simplest approach where partial functions are modeled as total functions taking an arbitrary value on arguments outside the specified domain of definition. A limitation of this approach is the difficulty in giving unique interpretations (as partial functions) of recursively specified algorithms. We offer a solution with the concept of inductive fixpoints introduced in Section 4.4. The topic seems to deserve further study. For a related concept of *optimal fixpoints*, see [10]. For recent related work in type theory, see [2,4].

Acknowledgment. We would like to thank the anonymous referees for their detailed and useful comments.

References

1. H. R. Andersen. An Introduction to Binary Decision Diagrams (Lecture Notes). www.itu.dk/people/hra/bdd97.ps.gz, October 1997.
2. A. Balaa and Y. Bertot. Fonctions récursives générales par itération en théorie des types. In *Journées francophones des langages applicatifs, JFLA'02*. INRIA, 2002.
3. Y. Bertot, V. Capretta, and K. D. Barman. Type-theoretic functional semantics. In V. A Carreno, C. A. Munoz, and S. Tahar, editors, *Theorem Proving in Higher Order Logics (TPHOLS 2002)*, volume 2410 of *LNCS*, pages 83–98. Springer, 2002.
4. A. Bove and V. Capretta. Nested general recursion and partiality in type theory. In R. J. Boulton and P. B. Jackson, editors, *Theorem Proving in Higher Order Logics (TPHOLS 2001)*, volume 2152 of *LNCS*, pages 121–135. Springer, 2001.
5. R. E. Bryant. Graph-based algorithms for Boolean function manipulation. *IEEE Transactions on Computers*, C-35(8):677–691, 1986.
6. J. Giesl. Termination of nested and mutually recursive algorithms. *Journal of Automated Reasoning*, 19(1):1–29, 1997.
7. J. Harrison. Inductive definitions: Automation and application. In E. T. Schubert, P. J. Windley, and J. Alves-Foss, editors, *Higher Order Logic Theorem Proving and Its Applications*, pages 200–213. Springer, Berlin,, 1995.
8. F. W. von Henke et al. Case Studies in Meta-Level Theorem Proving. In J. Grundy and M. Newey, editors, *Theorem Proving in Higher Order Logics (TPHOLS 1998)*, volume 1749 of *LNCS*, pages 461–478. Springer, 1998.
9. S. Krstić and J. Matthews. Verifying BDD algorithms through monadic interpretation. In A. Cortesi, editor, *Verification, Model Checking, and Abstract Interpretation (VMCAI 2002)*, volume 2294 of *LNCS*, pages 182–195. Springer, 2002.
10. Z. Manna and A. Shamir. The optimal approach to recursive programs. *Communications of the ACM*, 20(11):824–831, 1977.
11. J. Matthews. Recursive function definition over coinductive types. In Y. Bertot et al., editor, *Theorem Proving in Higher Order Logics (TPHOLS 1999)*, volume 1690 of *LNCS*, pages 73–90. Springer, 1999.
12. J. S. Moore. A mechanical proof of the termination of Takeuchi's function. *Information Processing Letters*, 9:176–181, 1979.
13. O. Müller, T. Nipkow, D. von Oheimb, and O. Slotosch. HOLCF = HOL + LCF. *Journal of Functional Programming*, 9:191–223, 1999.
14. O. Müller and K. Slind. Treating partiality in a logic of total functions. *The Computer Journal*, 40(10), 1997.
15. T. Nipkow, L. C. Paulson, and M. Wenzel. *Isabelle/HOL — A Proof Assistant for Higher-Order Logic*, volume 2283 of *LNCS*. Springer, 2002.
16. L. C. Paulson. Proving termination of normalization functions for conditional expressions. *Journal of Automated Reasoning*, 2(1):63–74, 1986.
17. K. Slind. Function definition in higher order logic. In J. von Wright et al., editor, *Theorem Proving in Higher Order Logics (TPHOLS 1996)*, volume 1125 of *LNCS*, pages 381–397. Springer, 1996.
18. K. Slind. *Reasoning about Terminating Functional Programs*. PhD thesis, Institut für Informatik, Technische Universität München, 1999.
19. K. Slind. Another look at nested recursion. In M. Aagaard and J. Harrison, editors, *Theorem Proving in Higher Order Logics (TPHOLS 2000)*, volume 1869 of *LNCS*, pages 498–518. Springer, 2000.
20. R. Sumners. Correctness proof of a BDD manager in the context of satisfiability checking. Technical Report TR-00-29, The University of Texas at Austin, Department of Computer Sciences, 2000.

21. K. N. Verma et al. Reflecting BDDs in Coq. In J. He and M. Sato, editors, *Proc. 6th Asian Computing Science Conference (ASIAN)*, volume 1961 of *LNCS*, pages 162–181. Springer, 2000.
22. G. Winskel. *The Formal Semantics of Programming Languages: an Introduction.* MIT Press, 1993.

Implementing Modules in the Coq System

Jacek Chrząszcz*

Institute of Informatics, Warsaw University
ul. Banacha 2, 02-097 Warszawa, Poland
chrzaszcz@mimuw.edu.pl

Abstract. The paper describes the implementation of interactive ML-style modules in the recent version 7.4 of Coq proof assistant. Modules (especially higher-order) provide a very convenient tool for parametrized theories which was lacking in Coq for years. Their interactive character extends naturally the interactive environment provided by the proof assistant. The implementation follows the paradigm of recent versions of Coq to separate the correctness-critical code from the rest of the system, using abstraction barriers.

1 Introduction

Computer aided theorem proving has become an important part of modern theoretical computer science. Various proof assistants gain more and more popularity and industrial size problems begin to be addressed. To become applicable in the industry, such systems must provide a high degree of automation and ways to structure large developments. From a long time ago, large developments in the Coq system [Coq] can be split across many files and a structure of one file can be nicely presented using sections. Moreover, sections provide a mechanism of abstracting individual definitions and theorems. However, what was lacking in Coq, was the possibility to conveniently define parametrized theories or parametrized certified data structures, easy to use in other developments.

If we were to implement such data structures in a functional programming language from the ML family, we would use modules. First, modules provide a means of bundling together related types and definitions into a structure. Second, the structure can be given an interface (signature), specifying what elements are to be used by the exterior of that structure and hiding its implementation details. Third, higher order modules (functors) provide a way of abstracting a structure over a module verifying a given interface. The abstracted module can later be conveniently applied to actual parameters. These three mechanisms are extended with nested modules, functor types and higher order functors, so that the module system resembles a typed lambda calculus with records, record types and monotone record subtyping.

All of this is now available in version 7.4 of Coq. First developments realized with modules prove that extension very promising and useful [MPMU03]. In this

---

* Partly supported by KBN Grant 7 T11C 028 20

D. Basin and B. Wolff (Eds.): TPHOLs 2003, LNCS 2758, pp. 270–286, 2003.

paper we present modules from the implementation point of view. We show that our implementation follows the paradigm of the recent versions of Coq (from V7.0 on) according to which correctness-critical code should be separated by abstraction barriers from the rest of the system, responsible for user interface, interactive proof development, etc. [Fil00]. We discuss implementation choices and important modifications in Coq mechanisms.

From the theoretical point of view, a version of ML-style module system suitable for type theory has been proposed by Judicaël Courant in [Cou97,Cou98]. In his work, an arbitrary pure type system is extended with a calculus of anonymous modules. Courant shows the conservativity of the resulting system over the base PTS and termination and confluence of module reductions.

Unfortunately his calculus is too complicated for direct implementation in a proof assistant, which not only provides the type-checker of a suitable calculus but also contains various extra-logical elements, like grammar and pretty-printing rules, implicit arguments declarations, tactic definitions etc.

Therefore we decided to implement a module system with some simplifying restrictions, similar to those described in [Ler94]. First, every module expression that can be used in a term must be a name (or more exactly, an access path). Second, since complex module expressions cannot appear in terms, there are no reductions on modules and the module equality is restricted to equality of names. The exact set of typing rules and formal analysis of the implemented module system can be found in [Chr03].

Many other proof assistants provide a means to structure proofs. For example PVS theories and parametric theories [OS97] roughly correspond to our structures and first order functors respectively. Isabelle locales [Kam00] are rather concerned with convenient management of assumptions than with general structuring of big proof developments. They correspond to Coq sections with much extended functionnality. It is for example possible to reopen an already closed locale, have several open locales at the same time or interactively decide to abstract a given theorem a given number of levels.

The module system that is closest to ours appears to be the one implemented in Maude [DM98]. The main difference however is the lack of implicit module subtyping forcing users to write explicit coercions, called *views*, which are absent in our system.

The rest of the paper is organized as follows. We start by giving a general overview of Coq and its architecture and an overview of the module system. Then we present module related modifications in the Coq kernel and in the management of extra-logical features. The reader interested in the implementation details is kindly invited to consult the enhanced version of this paper available at `http://www.mimuw.edu.pl/~{}chrzaszc/papers/` or the Coq sources.

2   The Coq System

Coq is a proof assistant implementing the calculus of inductive constructions [CPM90]. It is based on the so-called Curry-Howard isomorphism, which relates formulas to types and proofs to terms. Giving a proof of a theorem amounts to constructing a term of the type corresponding to the theorem. Coq provides a set of tactics to help the user interactively construct their proof-terms. One can also abbreviate complex terms by names (using definitions) and define inductive types.

Coq is entirely written in Objective Caml, the full system has about 120 000 lines of code in almost 500 files. The source tree is divided into the following directories, corresponding to implemented functionality:

kernel — the type-checker of the calculus of inductive constructions,
library — the backtracking mechanism, management of theory files and direc-
    tories,
parsing — abstract syntax trees and management of standard and user defined
    parsing and pretty-printing rules,
interp — translation from the syntax-tree to untyped terms,
pretyping — analysis of untyped terms (generation of implicit arguments, etc.),
proofs — the structure and management of an interactive proof,
tactics — predefined tactics and the tactic language,
toplevel — interactive loop.

The kernel (about 10% of the code) is the only critical part of the system. Bugs in other parts of Coq cannot compromise the mathematical correctness of the theorem prover state [Fil00].

The implementation of modules follows closely this practice. Module type-checking has been added to the kernel, while the management of extra-logical module features is implemented outside, in the **library** directory.

3   Overview of the Module System

The goal of this section is to briefly describe the module system that we imple-mented and to show most typing rules concerning modules. The complete set of rules may be found in [Chr03].

The basic module expressions are structures, which represent sequences of toplevel Coq entries. For the sake of brevity of module typing rules, we ignore inductive definitions in this presentation and adopt the convention from [Cou97, Cou98] to represent the toplevel entries as triples: a name, a specification and an implementation. The specification is used for typing subsequent entries, and the implementation is provided only as a witness of the validity of the speci-fication. According to this convention `Definition` $v_1 : e_1 := e_1'$ is represented as $v_1 : \mathsf{Ty}(e_1)\mathsf{Eq}(e_1') := e_1'$, and `Lemma` $v_2 : e_2$ with proof e_2' as $v_2 : \mathsf{Ty}(e_2) := e_2'$. The manifest specification $\mathsf{Ty}(e_1)\mathsf{Eq}(e_1')$ of v_1 indicates that the equality $v_1 \approx e_1'$ may be used in the conversion relation for typing subsequent entries. On the other hand, the abstract specification $\mathsf{Ty}(e_2)$ of v_2 does not export the equality $v_2 \approx e_2'$ and therefore it cannot be used in the conversion.

The basic module types used to type structures are signatures. They contain only the information relevant for typing, i.e. names v_i's and specifications t_i's. The typing rule for structures is the following:

(STRUCT)
$$\frac{E; v_1 : t_1 \ldots v_{i-1} : t_{i-1} \vdash q_i : t_i \quad \text{for all } i = 1 \ldots n}{E \ \vdash \ \text{Struct } v_1 : t_1 := q_1 \ldots v_n : t_n := q_n \ \text{End} \ : \ \text{Sig } v_1 : t_1 \ldots v_n : t_n \ \text{End}}$$

which shows that implementations q_i's are not used for typing indeed. Note that the signature assigned to a structure by this rule reflects all manifest specifications of the structure components.

Since structures can possibly be nested (i.e. contain module components), a triple $v : t := q$ may as well denote a module definition of the form $v : S := m$, where S is a module type and m a module expression.

In our system, the only way a module may be used in a term is when it is named. To access components of modules one uses the dot notation, and since modules can be nested, the module expressions allowed in terms are access paths (given by the grammar on the left). The specification of a variable v can simply be looked up in the environment and the specification of a longer access path $p.v$ can be inferred by the following typing rule (on the right):

(ACCESS)

$$p ::= v \mid p.v \qquad \frac{E \ \vdash \ p \ : \ \text{Sig } v_1 : t_1 \ldots v_n : t_n \ \text{End}}{E \ \vdash \ p.v_i \ : \ t_i \{ v_j \mapsto p.v_j \}_{j<i}}$$

Note that the syntactic restriction that only access paths are allowed in terms is preserved by the substitution applied in the conclusion of the (ACCESS) rule.

A functor is a module abstracted with respect to a module verifying a given module type. Functors informally correspond to λ-abstractions and their types to dependent products. In the rules below V is a variable, S and S' module types, m a module expression, and p_1, p_2 access paths.

(FUNCTOR)   (APP)

$$\frac{E; V : S \ \vdash \ m : S'}{E \ \vdash \ \text{Functor}[V : S]m \ : \ \text{Funsig}(V : S)S'} \qquad \frac{E \vdash p_1 : \text{Funsig}(V : S)S' \quad E \vdash p_2 : S}{E \vdash p_1 \ p_2 : S'\{V \mapsto p_2\}}$$

Note that in order to apply a functor to a module expression, both elements must be named. Due to this restriction, the resulting module type is always well-formed.

The last very important element of the module typing is the subtyping relation on module types, denoted $S_1 <: S_2$. On signatures the subtyping is a monotone extension of the subtyping on specifications of components (allowing to forget manifest specifications, to reorder and to drop fields in the supertype). For example, if $S_2 <: S_2'$ then

$$\text{Sig } v_1 : \text{Ty}(e_1); \ v_2 : S_2; \ v_3 : \text{Ty}(e_3)\text{Eq}(e_3') \ \text{End} \quad <: \quad \text{Sig } v_3 : \text{Ty}(e_3); \ v_2 : S_2' \ \text{End}$$

On functor types, subtyping is contravariant in the argument type and covariant in the result. The subtyping is used by the following subsumption rule:

(SUB) $$\frac{E \vdash m : S \qquad E \vdash S <: S'}{E \vdash m : S'}$$

4   Modules in the Kernel

In the type-theory tradition, the kernel of a proof assistant is the type-checker of the calculus implemented in the system. Up to version 7.3 the Coq kernel implemented the type-checker for the calculus of inductive constructions. Now it also implements the type-checker for the module language.

The interface of the kernel to the rest of the Coq system is the abstract type `safe_environment` together with lookup functions and update functions, like `add_constant`, `add_inductive` etc. which return the updated environment only if the given element is correctly type-checked. The kernel is functional i.e. no in-place modification is performed and the update functions return the new environment or fail if type-checking is not successful.

An update function, called with `add_*` E v (q, t), where E is a correct environment, v a name of the new element and (q, t) its body[1], implements the following typing rule:

$$
(\text{ADD}) \qquad \frac{E \vdash \text{ok} \qquad E \vdash q : t}{E; v : t := q \ \vdash \ \text{ok}} \quad \text{if } v \notin E
$$

The left premise denotes the assumed correctness of the input environment E, the right premise denotes the type-checking of the new element, and the conclusion says that the returned updated environment $E; v : t := q$ is correct. It is important to note here that even though the environment sometimes contain implementations, they are never used for typing.

Adding modules requires the function `add_module` to be implemented, together with the module type-checker. Like previous `add_*` functions, this one also can be seen as implementing the rule (ADD), with q a module body, and t a module specification (interface).

However it would be difficult for the user to write the whole definition of a module at once, especially for larger modules containing many definitions and proofs. Moreover, it would contradict the interactive character of Coq.

4.1   Interactive Modules

What seems natural in an interactive theorem prover is *interactive modules*. The user should have a possibility to declare the beginning of a new module, input definitions, declare and interactively prove some lemmas and then close the module, making all the entered definitions and lemmas the components of a new defined module. This is exactly what is implemented in version 7.4 of Coq. The following Coq session (on the left) results in a module body m (on the right) assigned to the name M:

---

[1] For the sake of clarity we ignore the fact that parts of the body may be synthesized.

```
Coq < Module M.                          Struct
Interactive Module M started               Definition T:Set=nat.
                                           Definition x:nat=0.
Coq <    Definition T:=nat.                Definition y:bool:=true.
T is defined                             End

Coq <    Definition x:=0.
x is defined

Coq <    Definition y:bool.
1 subgoal


  ==============================
    bool

Coq <       Exact true.
Proof completed.

Coq <    Defined.
Exact true.
y is defined

Coq < End M.
Module M is defined
```

After closing a module, its components can be accessed using the dot notation:

```
Coq < Print M.x.
M.x = (0)
      : nat
```

A naive way to implement the End M operation would be to recover the whole body of the structure outside the kernel, retract the environment to the one before Module M and call add_module with the reconstructed module body and environment.

Let us see in details what would have to be done on the kernel side in order to perform all this. Let us call E the environment before Module M command. First, during the interactive session, the definitions of T, x, and y would have to be checked by the kernel. After End M the non-critical part of code would reconstruct the module body m and the kernel function add_module would be called with the environment E, the name M and the module body m. Like all add_* functions, add_module would type-check m before returning the new environment, according to the (ADD) rule. Now let us concentrate on the right premise of this rule. In our case q is m and therefore the rule (STRUCT) must be used, all the premises of which already been verified during the interactive phase of module construction.

The naive implementation of module ending would make the kernel redo the job it did just a few moments before. For this reason we decided to turn the beginning and ending of the module into kernel operations. This allows us to eliminate the unnecessary double-checks.

So the interface of the kernel to the rest of the system has been extended with the functions `start_module`, marking the beginning of a module, and `end_module`, implementing (roughly) the rule:

$$\frac{E; v_1 : t_1 := q_1 \ldots v_n : t_n := q_n \vdash \mathsf{ok}}{E; \; V : \mathsf{Sig}\; v_1 : t_1 \ldots v_n : t_n \; \mathsf{End} := \mathsf{Struct}\; v_1 : t_1 := q_1 \ldots v_n : t_n := q_n \; \mathsf{End} \vdash \mathsf{ok}}$$

where V is the module name. The admissibility of this rule follows from the fact, that the only derivation of the premise is through a sequence of (ADD) rules. Their right premises imply

$$E \; \vdash \; \mathsf{Struct}\; v_1 : t_1 := q_1 \ldots v_n : t_n := q_n \; \mathsf{End} \; : \; \mathsf{Sig}\; v_1 : t_1 \ldots v_n : t_n \; \mathsf{End}$$

by an application of (STRUCT). Using (ADD) applied to $E \vdash \mathsf{ok}$ and the above, we get the desired conclusion.

The same interactive mechanism can also be used to declare parametric modules, i.e. functors. Given a signature `SIG` (on the right[2]), one can define an interactive functor (on the left):

```
Coq < Module Two[X:SIG][Y:SIG].              SIG = Sig
Interactive Module Two started                  Parameter T:Set.
                                                Parameter x:T.
Coq <    Definition T:=X.T * Y.T.            End

Coq <    Definition x:=(X.x, Y.x).

Coq < End Two.
Module Two is defined
```

In this case the environment operation performed by the function `end_module` shortcuts not only the (STRUCT) rule, but also (l applications of) the (FUNCTOR) rule, leading to the admissible rule:

$$\frac{E; \; V_1 : S_1 \ldots V_l : S_l; \; v_1 : t_1 := q_1 \ldots v_n : t_n := q_n \; \vdash \; \mathsf{ok}}{\begin{array}{l} E; \; V : \mathsf{Funsig}(V_1 : S_1) \ldots \mathsf{Funsig}(V_l : S_l) \\ \qquad \mathsf{Sig}\; v_1 : t_1 \ldots v_n : t_n \; \mathsf{End} \\ \qquad := \mathsf{Functor}[V_1 : S_1] \ldots \mathsf{Functor}[V_l : S_l] \\ \qquad \mathsf{Struct}\; v_1 : t_1 := q_1 \ldots v_k : t_k := q_k \; \mathsf{End} \; \vdash \; \mathsf{ok} \end{array}}$$

where $V_1, \ldots, V_l$ are formal parameters of the functor, $S_1, \ldots, S_l$ are their module types, and triples $v_i : t_i := q_i$ are functor body components.

The optional element of a module opening declaration is the expected module type. After the following definition:

```
Coq < Module N:SIG.

Coq <    Definition T:=bool.

Coq <    Definition x:=true.

Coq < End N.
```

---

[2] Using the convention described in Sect. 3, `Parameter v:e` is understood as a signature component $v : \mathsf{Ty}(e)$.

the signature of the module body will be matched against the signature SIG and if the matching succeeds, the interface of N will be restricted to SIG. In our example the conversion equalities N.T≈bool and N.x≈true will be forgotten, making both these components abstract.

If a restricting signature is present, the implementation of the end_module function also involves the application of the subsumption rule (SUB).

4.2   Overview of the Environment Structure

In order to implement the function end_module the type representing correct environments has to contain the information of how many definitions must be transformed into structure components, how many module declarations must be turned into functor parameters and (optionally) against what signature the body must be matched.

Therefore the type safe_environment represents in fact a stack of growing correct environments $E_1 \subseteq \cdots \subseteq E_n$. Fortunately, thanks to functional data structures and sharing, the elements of the environment E_1 are not copied in each $E_2, \ldots E_n$.

The operations add_* affect only the last environment, i.e. the update of $E_1 \subseteq \cdots \subseteq E_{n-1} \subseteq E_n$ results in $E_1 \subseteq \cdots \subseteq E_{n-1} \subseteq (E_n; v : t := q)$.

The operations which change the length of the environment stack are of course start_module and end_module. The first one is called with an environment stack $E_1 \subseteq \cdots \subseteq E_n$, a name for the new module V, its parameters $V_1 : S_1 \ldots V_l : S_l$ and optionally output signature S_{out}. It verifies correctness of $S_1, \ldots S_l$ and S_{out} and the fact that names $V, V_1, \ldots, V_l$ are new and returns $E_1 \subseteq \cdots \subseteq E_n \subseteq E_{n+1}$, with $E_{n+1} = E_n; V_1 : S_1 \ldots V_l : S_l;$ STRUCT$\langle V, S_{out} \rangle$, where STRUCT$\langle V, S_{out} \rangle$ is a special mark that is transparent for typing rules. The mark is only used by end_module as a placeholder separating functor arguments from structure components and keeping the optional output signature S_{out}.

The correctness of the new environment follows from the fact that E_{n+1} can be obtained by applying l times the rule (ADD).

The function end_module called with $E_1 \subseteq \cdots \subseteq E_{n-1} \subseteq E_n \subseteq E_{n+1}$, returns $E_1 \subseteq \cdots \subseteq E_{n-1} \subseteq E'_n$ where $E'_n = E_n; V : S := m$ with S and m synthesized from the information contained in E_{n+1}. More precisely, if E_{n+1} is

$$E_n; V_1 : S_1 \ldots V_l : S_l; \text{STRUCT}\langle V, S_{out} \rangle; v_1 : t_1 := q_1 \ldots v_k : t_k := q_k$$

m and S become respectively

$$\mathsf{Functor}[V_1 : S_1] \ldots \mathsf{Functor}[V_l : S_l] \ \mathsf{Struct} \ v_1 : t_1 := q_1 \ldots v_k : t_k := q_k \ \mathsf{End}$$

$$\text{and} \qquad \mathsf{Funsig}(V_1 : S_1) \ldots \mathsf{Funsig}(V_l : S_l) \ S_{out}$$

after checking that $E_n; V_1 : S_1 \ldots V_l : S_l \vdash \mathsf{Sig} \ v_1 : t_1 \ldots v_k : t_k \ \mathsf{End} <: S_{out}$. In case S_{out} is missing, S becomes

$$\mathsf{Funsig}(V_1 : S_1) \ldots \mathsf{Funsig}(V_l : S_l) \ \mathsf{Sig} \ v_1 : t_1 \ldots v_k : t_k \ \mathsf{End}$$

A similar mechanism is also used to implement interactive module types, through the functions `start_modtype` and `end_modtype` and a mark SIG⟨V⟩.

Non-interactive module and module type definitions are implemented through the functions `add_module` and `add_modtype`. Note however that by the time of writing these words, parsing of whole structures and signatures is not implemented. Therefore non-interactive module definitions are basically limited to renamings and functor applications, like

```
Coq < Module DoubleN:=Two N N.
Module DoubleN is defined
```

4.3   Avoiding Name Clashes

The possibility of having nested modules forces us to take care of name clashes. Consider the following nested module:

```
Module F.
  Definition T:=nat.
  Definition x:T:=0.
  Module N.
    Definition T:=bool.
    Definition y:=x.
    Definition z:T:=true.
  End N.
  Definition z:=N.y.
End F.
```

The problem here is the two occurrences of the name T in the scope of the inner module. The simplest solution of rejecting every piece of code having two equal short names would be too restrictive, because the names of module components are important and the user cannot change them arbitrarily.[3] The second solution consisting of hiding completely the previous definition with the new one is also impossible, because the old definition may be accessed indirectly, as shown by our example (the type of y is the first T). Using the Coq tradition to internally represent names together with the section path (`Top.F.T` for the first T and `Top.F.N.T` for the second) does not work well with functors (if F was a functor) and module renamings, like `Module G:=F`.

A correct solution to this problem requires noticing that the name of a component is at the same time a label which has to be visible from the outside of the module and a binder which binds the name used in the rest of the same module. If we distinguish the two names, the binder could get alpha converted (like all other binders), and the label clash is not a problem.

This is the solution proposed in the literature on modules. For example, in the convention of Harper and Lillibridge [HL94], the module type of *F* would look as follows (labels in `typewriter` font, binders in *italics*):

---

[3] This strict policy is applied for functor parameters, since once a functor is defined, its parameters names are no longer important.

Sig
    $T \triangleright T : \star = \mathrm{nat}$
    $x \triangleright x : T = 0$
    $N \triangleright N$: Sig $T \triangleright T' : \star = \mathrm{bool}$ $y \triangleright y : T = x$ $z \triangleright z : T' = \mathrm{true}$ End
    $z \triangleright z : T = N.\mathrm{y}$
End

To calculate the specification of $F.\mathrm{z}$ one has to use the substitution $\{T \mapsto F.\mathrm{T},$ $x \mapsto F.\mathrm{x}, N \mapsto F.\mathrm{N}\}$ on "$: T = N.\mathrm{y}$"[4], obtaining

$$F.\mathrm{z} : F.\mathrm{T} = F.\mathrm{N}.\mathrm{y}$$

Leroy in [Ler94] and in the implementation of Ocaml attaches a unique number to every component name. The name (character string) plays the role of label and the name with the unique number (called identifier) plays the role of binder. In order to calculate the specification of a module component the substitution still has to list the identifiers of all signature components.

The solution we adopted consists in assigning a unique number not to every component name, but only to the leading Sig keyword. The signature of F is then represented internally as follows:

Sig $\boxed{1}$
    $T : \star = \mathrm{nat}$
    $x : \boxed{1}.T = 0$
    N : Sig $\boxed{2}$ $T : \star = \mathrm{bool}$ $y : \boxed{1}.T = \boxed{1}.x$ $z : \boxed{2}.T = \mathrm{true}$ End
    $z : \boxed{1}.T := \boxed{1}.N.y$
End

Now, to calculate the specification of $\boxed{0}.F.z$ one only has to use the short substitution $\{\boxed{1} \mapsto \boxed{0}.F\}$, obtaining

$$\boxed{0}.F.z : \boxed{0}.F.T = \boxed{0}.F.N.y$$

In the above, $\boxed{0}$ is a unique identifier attached to the outer block, as the unique identifiers are not only attached to every Sig, but to every Struct and marks STRUCT$\langle \cdot \rangle$ and SIG$\langle \cdot \rangle$ as well. Moreover we assume that the first element of the environment is the mark STRUCT$\langle \cdot \rangle$ with the self identifier $\boxed{0}$. In other words the environment stack is never empty, and the unique identifier of the current structure or signature is stored in the corresponding mark.

Of course the user never sees these unique identifiers. The name table mechanism, described in Sect. 5.5, efficiently separates user names from internal representation. It is also interesting to note that our unique identifiers bear a lot of similarities to the *self* identifier used in object oriented programming.

---

[4] To be precise, we should have written $\mathsf{Ty}(T)\mathsf{Eq}(N)$ here and similar specifications in the signatures, but they would become completely unreadable.

5   Modules Outside the Kernel

The most important challenge of the introduction of modules in Coq was not the implementation of the type-checking algorithm. Apart from managing the certified environment, Coq has extra-logical features like implicit arguments, an extensible pretty-printer and an extensible parser, databases for automated tactics, etc. They are controlled through commands which can very well be issued inside modules or module types. The management of these features in the presence of modules was technically much more difficult than the modifications in the kernel.

5.1   Overview

The generic mechanisms responsible for the management of extra-logical features of Coq are implemented in the directory **library**. They include:

1. Backtracking and state management
   Backtracking is implemented through the generic extensible mechanisms of *library objects* and *summaries*.
2. Theory file management
   Compiling theory files and loading them, management of dependencies and logical/physical paths.
3. Name visibility management
   Every Coq element has a unique long name, like `Coq.Datatypes.nat` for the type of natural numbers. The validity of its suffixes is stored in the name table, implemented in the file **nametab**.

The module operations on extra-logical features are implemented in a new file **declaremods**. Of course many other files were also modified. Before going into details, let us briefly present the generic mechanisms of Coq.

Backtracking and Library Objects. Since Coq is an interactive proof assistant, it is important to let users correct the mistakes they make. Therefore a backtracking mechanism is implemented in Coq (through the `Reset` command).

The commands issued by the user are pushed on a stack, and from time to time, the full state of the system is pushed there as well. To backtrack to a given point it is enough to "recall" the most recent copy of the state preceding the point and redo the commands following the state and preceding the point. See Fig. 1 for a graphical presentation (copies of the state are marked gray, and regular commands – white).

In order to make this mechanism work properly and be easily extensible, the "commands on the stack" are given a common interface of so called *library objects*[5]. The object method `cache_function` implements the non-functional part of command execution (usually table updates) and is called when pushing the object to the command stack, and while backtracking.

---

[5] In fact for historical reasons, they are not Objective Caml objects.

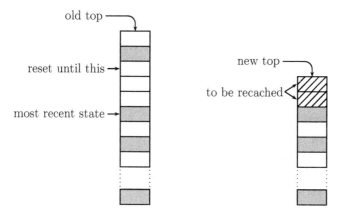

Fig. 1. Backtracking

In previous versions of Coq the other uses of the generic object mechanism was to store and restore (to and from the disk) the extra-logical elements of compiled theory files and to partially control the discharge at the end of a section.

Summaries and State. An important aspect of the implementation of backtracking is the possibility to periodically store the state of the system. Various Coq features require mutable information to work properly, for example the `Auto` tactic uses hint databases, the pretty-printing mechanism uses tables of pretty-printing rules, parsing — of parsing rules etc. Appropriate commands change the contents of these tables, so the contents of each table is a part of the state, and therefore should be stored. Of course copying the contents of each table would waste a lot of memory, so the data-structures used in Coq are all functional and their "copying" is just a pointer copying.

In order to facilitate the addition of new features in Coq, the tables able to store and restore their contents are given a common interface of so called *summaries*. The important remark here is that the global environment is also registered as a summary and managed through the generic mechanism.

5.2   Module Operations on Objects

To understand the issues we had to solve when putting together modules and extra-logical features of Coq, consider the following code which uses `Syntactic Definition` as an example.

```
Coq < Module M.

Coq <    Definition id := [A:Set][a:A]a.

Coq <    Syntactic Definition Id := (id ?).

Coq <    Check (Id O).
```

```
(id nat (O))
    : nat

Coq < End M.

Coq < Check (M.Id true).
(M.id bool true)
    : bool

Coq < Module N:=M.

Coq < Check (N.Id (M.Id None)).
(N.id (A:Set)(option A) (M.id (A:Set)(option A) None))
    : (A:Set)(option A)

Coq < Print N.Id.
 Syntactic Definition N.Id = (N.id ?)
```

When we rebind the module M to a new name N, in the same time we create a new
syntactic definition N.Id, which now is a shorthand for (N.id ?). So the same
mechanism of substitutions that exists in the kernel for module components had
to be implemented for library objects[6]. This mechanism naturally covers objects
defined inside a functor body and used after the functor is applied to a module
(see the example on the left). Moreover, it is possible to attach objects to a
module type. Such objects can be used inside a functor body or attached to a
module defined with that module type (on the right).

```
Coq < Module Type SIG.                  Coq < Module Type OBJECTS.

Coq <    Parameter id : (A:Set)A->A.    Coq <    Parameter id : (A:Set)A->A.

Coq < End SIG.                          Coq <    Syntactic Definition Id :=
                                        Coq <       (id ?).
Coq < Module F[X:SIG].
                                        Coq < End OBJECTS.
Coq <    Syntactic Definition FId :=
Coq <       (X.id ?).                   Coq < Module G[X:OBJECTS].

Coq < End F.                            Coq <    Definition id:=
                                        Coq <       [A:Set][a:A](X.Id a).
Coq < Module M1:=(F M).
                                        Coq < End G.
Coq < Module N1:=(F N).
                                        Coq < Module X.
Coq < Check (M1.FId O).
(M.id nat (O))                          Coq <    Definition id:=
    : nat                               Coq <       [A:Set][a:A]a.

Coq < Check (N1.FId true).              Coq < End X.
(N.id bool true)
    : bool                              Coq < Module P : OBJECTS := (G X).

                                        Coq < Check (P.Id O).
                                        (P.id nat (O))
                                            : nat
```

---

[6] Moreover, the same substitution that is used in the kernel, is also used in the library.

The interface of objects has been extended with a new method `subst_function`, and in order to unify the treatment of objects for simple modules, functors and module types, we introduced a concept of *object closure*. It corresponds to a list of inactive objects that reference module names invalid in the current context, that wait to be substituted once the objects are assigned to an actual module and activated. An object closure is remembered for simple modules because of renamings, for functors because of applications, and for module types because of their possible attachment to modules.

Technically, an object closure is built from a list of objects, a list of bound module identifiers (functor formal parameters), a *self* identifier and a delayed substitution for efficient handling of partially substituted object closures.

5.3   Interactive Modules Revisited

When the user starts a new interactive module, `Declaremods.start_module` is called, which itself calls the kernel function `start_module` in order to start the new module in the global environment. Then, the state of the system is pushed on the library stack together with a special start mark.

Inside the module, user commands are executed and corresponding objects are pushed on the stack and their `cache_function` methods are called.

When the module is ended, `Declaremods.end_module` is called. Its operations are the following.

1. End the module in the global environment,
2. Get objects and the state from the library stack,
3. Compute the object closure,
4. Prepare the module object,
5. Restore summaries except for the environment,
6. Push the module object on the stack.

The operation on the global environment is performed through the kernel function `end_module` (point 1). Then we recover all objects[7] pushed on the stack after the most recent start mark and the state of the system stored at the time of starting the module (point 2).

Next, the object closure of the module is computed (point 3), according to the module specification: If the module was given an output signature when it was started, we take the object closure of the signature. Otherwise the object closure is constructed from the objects recovered in point 2, the list of functor arguments given when the module was started, the *self* identifier of the module body and the empty substitution.

Now, if the ended module is not a functor, the objects from its object closure are substituted (using the method `subst_function`) with the substitution contained within the closure extended with the mapping of the *self* identifier to the name of the module. The object closure and the substituted objects are

---

[7] Intermediate copies of the state stored on the stack inside the module are forgotten.

packaged into a module object (point 4), but before putting it on the command stack, all tables except for the global environment are restored (point 5) to the state recovered in point 2.

Only now, the module object is pushed on the stack and its caching method is called (point 6). It stores the object closure in a table and if the module was not a functor, calls a caching method for every substituted object. This way, if the module has submodules, their objects also get activated.

5.4   Non-interactive Modules

Although the operations described in the previous section may seem complicated, our goal was to maximally unify the object operations for interactive and non-interactive modules (possibly nested), for modules loaded from disk, and for module types, having in mind that all these should cooperate with the backtracking mechanism.

Indeed, the management of non-interactive modules is similar to the points 3, 4 and 6 of the `end_module` operation. Let us take

`Module M:=F N`

as an example, and suppose that the formal parameter of the functor `F` is `X`. The object closure of `M` is constructed from the object closure of `F`, by extending the substitution contained within the closure with the mapping from `X` to `N`[8]. Now the module object is prepared in the same way that in point 4 in the previous section. Once it is pushed on the command stack, the sequence of events is like in point 6 above, with the only exception that the `cache_function` of the module object starts by updating the global environment using the kernel function `add_module`.

Theory files are treated like special modules and their object operations are performed by module functions. Interactive and non-interactive module type operations are very similar to those for modules, but simpler, since only the object closure is important and no objects are substituted.

5.5   Long Names and Suffix Visibility

Since version 7 of Coq, all named elements, like definitions, inductives etc. have unique long names available to the user. For example the long name of the inductive type `list` from the file **PolyList** of the standard library of Coq is `Coq.Lists.PolyList.list`. Of course suffixes of the long name are also valid references to that inductive type. Without modules, suffix validity patterns were very simple: either all suffixes were valid, or all suffixes of length strictly greater than one. In the recent version of Coq, definitions of nested modules, combined with the use of the `Import` command (declaring components of the module to be directly available at toplevel), may lead to arbitrary suffix validity patters.

---

[8] If we had a module renaming, `Module M:=N`, we would take the object closure of N, and if the output type was given, `Module M:SIG:=...`, we would take the object closure of `SIG`.

Validity of suffixes is managed by the file **nametab**, whose function is to maintain the correspondence between user names and internal names. During the implementation of modules, the file **nametab** has been substantially cleaned up and its functionality extended.

6   Conclusions

We have described the implementation of ML-style modules in the Coq proof assistant. Our implementation carefully follows the idea of separating correctness-critical code (the kernel) from the rest of the system.

The modules have been successfully used in several examples, even though some features, like parsing and printing of structures and signatures and precise error messages are still not implemented. In combination with the extraction mechanism capable to produce Ocaml modules from Coq modules (implementated by Pierre Letouzey), Coq may become a very convenient tool to develop certified parametric data structures. For example, a modular formalization of certified dictionaries implemented by binary search trees was realized by Pierre Casteran (contribution **Bordeaux/dictionaries**).

Another interesting example of using modules is KRAKATOA [MPMU03], a Coq frontend to certify JAVA programs. The authors prove quite a few generic properties of Java classes abstractly in a functor, and a user working on a concrete Java program simply applies the functor to a module representing the classes of his program and can conveniently use the properties already instantiated to his particular setting.

An interesting possibility opened by addition of modules is the adaptation to Coq of the EML methodology of gradual construction of functional programs [ST97], which strongly relies on the use of functors. In a proof assistant framework, correctness of refining steps could be established formally, using interactive proofs.

Acknowledgments. The author would like to thank the anonymous referees for their extensive comments, suggestions and numerous corrections.

References

[Chr03]   Jacek Chrząaszcz. Modules in type theory with generative definitions. PhD thesis, to be defended, 2003.

[Coq]   The Coq Proof Assistant. http://coq.inria.fr/.

[Cou97]   Judicaël Courant. A Module Calculus for Pure Type Systems. In *Typed Lambda Calculi and Applications 97*, Lecture Notes in Computer Science, pages 112–128. Springer-Verlag, 1997.

[Cou98]   Judicaël Courant. *Un calcul de modules pour les systèmes de types purs.* Thèse de doctorat, Ecole Normale Supérieure de Lyon, 1998.

[CPM90]   Thierry Coquand and Christine Paulin-Mohring. Inductively defined types. In P. Martin-Löf and G. Mints, editors, *Proceedings of Colog'88*, volume 417 of *Lecture Notes in Computer Science*. Springer-Verlag, 1990.

[DM98]   F. Durán and J. Meseguer. An extensible module algebra for Maude. In
            *In 2nd International Workshop on Rewriting Logic and its Applications
            (WRLA'98)*, volume 15 of *Electronic Notes in Theoretical Computer Science*.
            Elsevier, 1998.
[Fil00]   J.-C. Filliâtre. Design of a proof assistant: Coq version 7. Unpublished,
            2000.
[HL94]   R. Harper and M. Lillibridge. A type-theoretic approach to higher-order
            modules with sharing. In POPL'94 [POP94], pages 123–137.
[Kam00]   Florian Kammüller. Modular reasoning in isabelle. In *17th International
            Conference on Automated Deduction, CADE-17*, volume 1831 of *Lecture
            Notes in Artificial Intelligence*. Springer-Verlag, 2000.
[Ler94]   Xavier Leroy. Manifest types, modules, and separate compilation. In
            POPL'94 [POP94], pages 109–122.
[MPMU03]   Claude Marché, Christine Paulin-Mohring, and Xavier Urbain. The
            KRAKATOA tool for JML/JAVA program certification. submitted, 2003.
[OS97]   Sam Owre and Natarajan Shankar. The formal semantics of PVS. Technical
            Report SRI-CSL-97-2, Computer Science Laboratory, SRI International,
            Menlo Park, CA, August 1997.
[POP94]   *Conference Record of the 21st Symposium on Principles of Programming
            Languages*, Portland, Oregon, 1994. ACM Press.
[ST97]   D. Sannella and A. Tarlecki. Essential concepts of algebraic specification
            and program development. *Formal Aspects of Computing*, 9:229–269,
            1997.

MetaPRL – A Modular Logical Environment*

Jason Hickey[1], Aleksey Nogin[1], Robert L. Constable[2], Brian E. Aydemir[1], Eli Barzilay[2], Yegor Bryukhov[3], Richard Eaton[2], Adam Granicz[1], Alexei Kopylov[2], Christoph Kreitz[2], Vladimir N. Krupski[4], Lori Lorigo[2], Stephan Schmitt[5], Carl Witty[6], and Xin Yu[1]

[1] Department of Computer Science, California Institute of Technology
M/C 256-80, Pasadena, CA 91125
{jyh,nogin,emre,granicz,xiny}@cs.caltech.edu
[2] Department of Computer Science, Cornell University,
Ithaca, NY 14853
{rc,eli,eaton,kopylov,kreitz,lolorigo}@cs.cornell.edu
[3] Graduate Center, City University of New York
365 Fifth Avenue, New York, NY 10016
ybryukhov@gc.cuny.edu
[4] Laboratory for Logical Problems of Computer Science
Department of Mathematical Logic and Theory of Algorithms
Faculty of Mechanics and Mathematics, Moscow State University
Vorob'evy Gory, 119899 RUSSIA
krupski@lpcs.math.msu.ru
[5] Sapient, Presidency Building,
Mehrauli-Gurgaon Road, Sector-14,
Gurgaon-112 001, Haryana, India
sschmitt@sapient.com
[6] Newton Research Labs,
441 SW 41st Street,
Renton, WA 98055
cwitty@newtonlabs.com

Abstract. MetaPRL is the latest system to come out of over twenty five years of research by the Cornell PRL group. While initially created at Cornell, MetaPRL is currently a collaborative project involving several universities in several countries. The MetaPRL system combines the properties of an interactive LCF-style tactic-based proof assistant, a logical framework, a logical programming environment, and a formal methods programming toolkit. MetaPRL is distributed under an open-source license and can be downloaded from http://metaprl.org/. This paper provides an overview of the system focusing on the features that did not exist in the previous generations of PRL systems.

* This work was supported in part by the DoD Multidisciplinary University Research Initiative (MURI) program administered by the Office of Naval Research (ONR) under Grant N00014-01-1-0765, the Defense Advanced Research Projects Agency (DARPA), the United States Air Force, the Lee Center, and by NSF Grant CCR 0204193.

1   Introduction

MetaPRL is the latest in the PRL family of systems [5,11,12,17,18,29,49] developed over the last 25 years. MetaPRL's predecessor NuPRL [5,18] was successfully used for verification and automated optimization of the Ensemble group communication toolkit [14,38]. The Ensemble toolkit [23] is being used for both military and commercial applications; its users include BBN, Nortel Networks and NASA.

The MetaPRL project (which was initially called NuPRL-Light [27]) was started by Jason Hickey as a part of Ensemble verification effort to simplify formal reasoning about the program code and to address scalability and modularity limitations of NuPRL-4. As more effort was put into the system, MetaPRL eventually grew into a very general modern system whose modularity on all levels gives it flexibility to support a very wide range of applications.

MetaPRL is not only a tactic-based interactive proof assistant, it is also *a logical framework* that allows users to specify their own logical theories rather than requiring them to use a single theory. Additionally, MetaPRL is a logical programming environment that incorporates many features to simplify reasoning about programs being developed. In fact, MetaPRL is implemented as an extension of the OCaml compiler [50]. Finally, MetaPRL can be considered *a logical toolkit* that exports not only the "high-level" logical interface, but all the intermediary ones as well. This allows for rapid development of applications that require formal or semi-formal handling of data.

While MetaPRL was written from scratch and without using any of the pre-existing PRL code, it keeps many of the major design principles and concepts of the NuPRL system. For example, the two systems have very similar term syntax and MetaPRL implements several variations of the NuPRL type theory as one of its logics (see Section 5.2).

However, MetaPRL is substantially different from NuPRL and has many new features. In this paper we present an overview of the system focusing on the features that were introduced in MetaPRL and that did not exist in previous generations of PRL systems.

MetaPRL is an open-source software system distributed under the terms of the GNU GPL. Documentation and download instructions can be found at [32].

2   Architecture Overview

At a very high level, the architecture of a tactic-based theorem prover can usually be described as a layered architecture as shown in Figure 1.

The core of the system is its *logical engine*, or *refiner* [10]. It is responsible for performing the individual proof steps (such as applying a single inference rule). Next, there is the lower "support" layer for the logical theories. It usually includes basic meta-theory definitions and possibly some basic proof search mechanisms (such as basic tactics). Finally, at the top of the structure there are the logical theories themselves, each potentially equipped with theory-specific mechanisms (such as theory-specific proof search strategies and theory-specific display mechanisms). In a way, the structure of the prover mimics the structure of an operating system with logical engine being the "kernel" of the system, meta-theory being its "system library" and logical theories being its "user space".

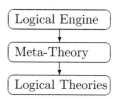

Fig. 1

We intentionally did not include any user interface in Figure 1. The reason for such omission is that often a user interface (such as the NuPRL Editor [5,39] or Proof General [6]) would be a separate package added on top of a formal system, rather than a part of the system itself.

There are two main approaches to building such a prover — one can build a monolithic prover (such as NuPRL-4) or one can build a modular one. There are several advantages in a more modular architecture, especially in a research environment where we want to work on general methodology of formal reasoning.

In a modular system with well-defined interfaces it is easier to try out new ideas and new approaches. This allows for a greater flexibility and also helps in bringing new people (including new students) to the project.

The modular architecture also allows one to have several implementations of some critical module. For example, it is possible to have a generic implementation and at the same time create alternative implementations of some modules that are optimized towards a particular class of applications. This approach is especially useful in the trusted core of the system — there we can have a simple "reference" implementation that is extensively tested and checked for correctness as well as one (or more[1]) highly optimized implementations. Users can develop proofs using the optimized modules and then later double-check them by re-running the proof scripts using the reference implementation. This provides the confidence of knowing that proofs were accepted by *both* implementations.

Similarly to the modularity of the logical engine of a formal system, the modularity of the logical theories supported by a system is also important. Some provers only support reasoning in a single monolithic logical theory, while others, including MetaPRL, not only give their users a choice of which logical theory to use, but also allow users to add their own logical theories to the system. Such systems are often called *logical frameworks* [47].

MetaPRL provides an implementation of the architecture presented in Figure 1. The implementation is highly modular on all levels — from logical engine to logical theories.

The structure of the paper follows the structure of the system. In Section 3 we present the features of the MetaPRL logical engine, in Section 4 we present the features of MetaPRL intermediate layer, and in Section 5 we present an overview of logical theories in MetaPRL. We present the logical toolkit side of the system in Section 6 and provide a brief overview of the related work in Section 7.

---

[1] In fact, in MetaPRL some of the most performance-sensitive modules have up to 6 different implementations.

3   Logical Engine

The core of the system is its *logical engine* or *refiner* [10] that performs two basic operations. First, it builds the basic proof procedures from the parts of a logic. The second refiner operation is the *application* of the basic proof steps producing justifications from the proofs.

The MetaPRL refiner is based on a higher-order term rewriting engine. This rewriting engine is used to apply the rules of the system (including both the axioms and the derived rules described in Section 3.3) by rewriting the current proof goal term into terms representing the subgoals that remain to be proven. The rewriting engine is also used to apply computational and definitional rewrites (see Section 3.4). When a rule or rewrite is defined in a logical theory, the MetaPRL refiner compiles it to a bytecode program [31] that is run whenever the rule or rewrite is applied. This precompilation phase significantly improves performance.

The rewriting engine also has an "informal" mode that is used to convert terms into strings to be displayed to a user (or to be written into a LATEX file). This informal mode is also used to provide generic parsing capabilities and enables users to specify parts of their logical theories in their own notation [21]. The rewriting engine is used to execute parsing derivations based on the formal definition of the notation, which includes the specification of the grammar and the semantic rules associated with each grammar production. For instance, one can define a logical theory to reason about simple functional programs and use actual programming syntax in rewrite rules to specify formal transformations. When experimental parsing capabilities are more tightly integrated into the system, the definitions of the notation will become an integral part of the logical theories making the logical content more apparent and easy to understand.

3.1   Speed

In a tactic-based prover, the speed of the underlying logical engine has a direct impact on the level of reasoning. If proof search is slow, more interactive user guidance is needed to prune the search space, leading to excessive detail in the tactic proofs. And if the system is fast, it allows users to concentrate more on the high-level reasoning leaving it to the machine to fill in the "trivial" details.

MetaPRL was designed with efficiency in mind. In addition, MetaPRL code is highly modular, which has made it easy to improve the efficiency of the procedures along the critical path (the rewriting engine). MetaPRL modularity has also allowed us to replace generic modules with domain-specific implementations that improve performance in some logics. As we explained in Section 2, adding complex optimizations even to the "trusted core" of the system does not increase the potential exposure to bugs since the proofs developed using the optimized refiner can still be double-checked using the slower more trusted implementation.

As a result of our speed-conscious design and implementation (described in detail in [31]) as well as the quality of the OCaml compiler, the MetaPRL logical engine is considerably faster than NuPRL-4. We compared the two systems by writing tactics that implement a simple domain-specific proof search algorithm in each of the systems. We performed several tests in several domains and in all cases MetaPRL was over 100 times faster. And by distributing the system over several processors and several computers we were able to achieve even greater speed-ups.

3.2 Transparent Concurrent and Distributed Refinement

MetaPRL is capable of distributing a proof search over several processors using the Ensemble group communication system [23]. The distribution is transparent for both the tactic programmer and the system user. That is, the tactics are programmed using a language very similar to that of NuPRL without restriction. Processes may join and leave (even fail) at any time, affecting only the speed of the distributed proof search. On a small number of processors, speed improvements are usually superlinear in the number of processors participating in a proof.

The distribution mechanism is described in-depth in [28].

3.3 Derived Rules

In an interactive theorem prover it is very useful to have a mechanism allowing users to prove some statement in advance and then reuse the derivation in further proofs. Often it is especially useful to be able to *abstract* the particular derivation. For example, suppose we wish to formalize a data structure for labeled binary trees. If binary trees are not primitive to the system, we might implement them in several ways, but the details are irrelevant. The more important feature is the inference rule for induction. In a sequent logic, the induction principle would be similar to the following: for an arbitrary predicate P,

$$\frac{\Gamma \vdash P(leaf) \qquad \Gamma, a\colon btree, P(a), b\colon btree, P(b) \vdash P(node(a, b))}{\Gamma, x\colon btree \vdash P(x)}$$

If this rule can be established, further proofs may use it to reason about binary trees *abstractly* without having to unfold the *btree* definition. This leaves the user free to replace or augment the implementation of binary trees as long as she can still prove the same induction principle for the new implementation. Furthermore, in predicative logics, or in cases where well-formedness is defined logically, the inference rule is strictly more powerful than its propositional form. For example, in NuPRL-style type theories certain induction principles can only be expressed as rules and can not be fully expressed in a propositional form.

If a mechanism for establishing a derived rule is not available, one alternative is to construct a proof "script" or tactic that can be reapplied whenever a derivation is needed. There are several problems with this. First, it is inefficient — instead of applying the derived rule in a single step, the system has to run through the entire proof each time. Second, the proof script would have to unfold the *btree* definition, exposing implementation detail. Third, proof scripts tend to be fragile, and must be reconstructed frequently as a system evolves. Finally, by looking at a proof script or a tactic code, it may be hard to see what exactly it does, while a derived rule is essentially self-documenting.

Another advantage of derived rules is that they usually contain some information on how they are supposed to be used. For example, an implication $A \Rightarrow B$ can be stated and proved as an A elimination rule or as a B introduction rule, depending on how we expect it to be used. As we will see in Section 4.2, such information can be made available to the proof automation procedures, significantly reducing the amount of information users have to provide manually.

MetaPRL provides a purely syntactical mechanism for *derived rules*. The mechanism is very general and does not depend on a particular logical theory being used. The key idea of our approach is in using a special higher-order language for specifying rules; we call it a *sequent schemata* language [44]. From a theoretical point of view, we first take some logical theory and express its rules using sequent schemata. Next, we extend the language of the theory with the language of sequent schemata. After that we allow extending our theory with a new *derived rule* $\frac{S_1 \cdots S_n}{S}$ whenever we can prove S from S_i in the expanded theory. We have shown [44] that this mechanism would only allow deriving statements that were already derivable in a conservative extension of the original theory.

In MetaPRL the user only has to provide the axioms of the base theory in a sequent schemata language and the rest happens automatically. The system immediately allows the user to mix the object language of a theory with the sequent schemata meta-language. Whenever a derived rule is proven in a system, it allows using that rule in further proofs as if it were a basic postulate of the theory.[2]

3.4   Computational Rewrites

In MetaPRL it is possible to define not only logical rules, but also logical rewrites. A logical rewrite states an equivalence between two terms is valid in any context. For example, in NuPRL-style type theory, the computationally equivalent terms, such as $\lambda x.A(x)$ B and $A(B)$, can always be interchanged.

MetaPRL also allows "rewrite theorems" (derived rewrites) and conditional rewrites — rewrites that state that two terms can be interchanged in contexts where a certain condition is true. For example, the rewrite $(x \neq 0) \longrightarrow (x/x \longleftrightarrow 1)$ states that in any context where x is known to be non-zero, x/x can be interchanged with 1.

This powerful rewrite mechanism allows MetaPRL users to avoid stating and proving well-formedness subgoals in cases when they are not really necessary.

---

[2] MetaPRL would also allow the reverse order — first state a derived rule, use it, and later "come back" and prove the derived rule. Of course, this means that a proof is not considered complete until all the derived rules used in it are also proven. Such an approach allows one to "test-drive" a derived rule before investing time into establishing its admissibility.

Additionally, the context-independence of rewrites enables us to chain rewrite applications (and rewrite application attempts) in a very efficient manner, making rewrite applications an order of magnitude faster than rule applications.

4 Proof Search Automation

In addition to the logical engine, MetaPRL also provides considerable proof automation, using extensible proof-search procedures coded as LCF-style [20] *tactics*.

4.1 Resources

Often some basic tactics are designed to behave very differently in different contexts. One of the best examples of such a tactic is the *decomposition tactic* [33, Section 3.3] present both in NuPRL and in MetaPRL. When applied to the conclusion of a goal sequent, it will try to decompose the conclusion into simpler ones, normally by using an appropriate introduction rule. When applied to a hypothesis, the decomposition tactic would try to break the hypothesis into simpler ones, usually by applying an appropriate elimination rule.

Even with a fixed base logic, as in NuPRL, these automated procedures need to be updated dynamically as new definitions and theorems are added. In Meta-PRL, with multiple (perhaps conflicting) logics, this has the added complexity that definitions and theorems can be used for automation only in the logic in which they are defined or proved.

MetaPRL automates this process through a mechanism called *resources*. A resource is essentially a collection of pieces of data (with each piece of data residing in a particular logical theory); the resource interface provides an *inheritance* mechanism based on the logical hierarchy (see Section 5.1). Resources are managed on a per-theorem granularity — when working on a particular proof, the resource state reflects everything collected from the current theory up to the theorem being proved, as well as everything inherited from the theories that are ancestors of the current one in the logical hierarchy.

MetaPRL has resources controlling the behavior of the decomposition tactic, of the type inference heuristic, of the term simplifier rewriting tactic, and many others.

4.2 Resource Annotations

When a new rule (or rewrite) is added to a system, new data has to be added to some resources if we want to allow the proof search procedures controlled by those resources to take advantage of the new rule (rewrite). It turns out that most such resource updates are rather uniform. For most MetaPRL resources we have been able to automate these resource insertions by giving the resource updating functions access to the *text* of the newly added rules and rewrites (as opposed to just giving them access to primitive tactics corresponding to those rules and rewrites), essentially creating a *reflective* mechanism. This is possible because all rules and rewrites are expressed in a formally defined language of sequent schemata (see Section 3.3).

From the MetaPRL user's perspective this mechanism has a form of *resource annotations*. When adding a new rule, a user only has to annotate it with the names of resources that need to be automatically improved. Users can also pass some optional arguments to the automatic procedure in order to modify its behavior. As a result, when a new logical object (rule, rewrite, etc) is added to a MetaPRL theory, the user can usually update all relevant proof search automation by only typing a few extra symbols. Moreover, adding new resources is quite easy, and there are many tools that make automation of resource improvements simpler.

For more information on resource annotations, see [43, Section 4.3].

4.3   Generic Tactics

Derived rules and resource annotations combined provide a new way of implementing many complex tactics. Instead of writing large tactics code that may be hard to debug and to understand, MetaPRL users can view a tactic as a number of deterministic sequences of rule applications together with some control information that specifies which sequences get executed and in what order. Deterministic sequences would be implemented as derived rules, and control information would be added as resource annotations on some of the rules. This improves the efficiency of these tactics (applying a derived rule only takes one step of the rewriting engine) and usually makes them easier to maintain.

When a tactic is implemented via resource annotations, most of its code is *generic* and does not depend on particular details of a logical theory. The great advantage of such generic tactics is that they can be implemented once and then reused in a wide range of logical theories with no or a little additional effort. In a logical framework like MetaPRL this leads to a significant degree of code reuse and greatly simplifies the task of automating proof search when new theories are added to the system.

Another approach to creating generic tactics in MetaPRL is turning decision procedures and automated proving procedures into *heuristics*. We observe that proving the decision procedure is correct *in a particular instance* is much easier than proving that it will *always* be correct and the former can often be established automatically. When a decision procedure can be enhanced to output some evidence along with the "yes" answer, it can be turned into a tactic that first executes the enhanced decision procedure and then tries to interpret the provided evidence, turning it into a complete proof. Since tactics go through the logical engine, we now get a decision procedure that does not have to be trusted. This decouples the procedure from the theory it is being used in since we no longer have to keep making sure the procedure correctly matches the theory every time we want to change either the theory, or the decision procedure.

This approach was used by Stephan Schmitt for implementing the JProver decision procedure in MetaPRL. JProver [48] is a complete[3] theorem prover for first-order intuitionistic logic that is based on a strategy called the *connection method* [13,36]. Upon success it generates a sequent proof for the proof goal [37] that may be inspected by a user.

JProver is implemented on top of MetaPRL core in a very generic way [48], using MetaPRL as a theorem proving toolkit (see Section 6) without referring to any specific logical theory. When it finds a proof, JProver outputs a simple generic encoding of the proof that can be easily converted to a tactic in, for example, type theory. Since JProver's output is converted to a tactic and is not "trusted", this allows us to use it even when not all assumptions JProver makes about the underlying logic are actually valid (as it happens in type theory).

Both approaches to generic tactics are essentially replacing a human-intensive approach with a computer-intensive one. In case of an updatable tactic we have the system itself extracting the relevant information from the text of the rules, instead of requiring users to provide it. In case of decision procedures we eliminate the need for manually establishing the validity of a procedure and instead use a computer system for post-processing proofs that come out of the procedure.

5   Logical Theories

MetaPRL *logical theories* (or simply *logics*) can contain the following kinds of objects:

(A) *Syntax definitions* define the *language* of a logic.
(B) *Inference rules* define the primitive inferences of a logic. For instance, the first-order logic contains rules like MODUS_PONENS in a sequent calculus.

$$\frac{}{\Gamma, A \vdash A} \text{ AXIOM} \qquad \frac{\Gamma \vdash A \Rightarrow B \quad \Gamma \vdash A}{\Gamma \vdash B} \text{ MODUS\_PONENS}$$

(C) *Rewrites* (described in Section 3.4) define computational and definitional equivalences. For example, the type theory defines functions and applications with the equivalence $(\lambda x. b[x]) \, a \longleftrightarrow b[a]$.
(D) *Theorems* contain proofs of derived inference rules.
(E) *Tactics* provide theory-specific proof search automation.

In addition to the *formal* objects enumerated above, MetaPRL theories contain *display forms* that describe how the formal syntax should be presented to the user and how to export it to LaTeX. Most theories also contain *literate comments* that are used to generate the documentation for those theories.

An extensive documentation of MetaPRL theories (generated automatically from the literate comments and updated on a regular basis) is available at [30].

---

[3] Since first-order logic is undecidable, JProver will not terminate if the goal cannot be proven and must be interrupted (typically by limiting the maximum proof search depth).

5.1   Hierarchical Theories Mechanism

MetaPRL does not assume any particular theory or logic and allows users to formulate and use different logics and theories. In MetaPRL logical theories are implemented as extensions of ML modules. Each theory is usually a sequence of logical objects (such as rules and definitions) and ML code (such as tactic implementations and resource code). The theories are object-oriented, in the sense that a theory specifies a class that inherits rules and implementations from other classes. All rules (including the derived rules — see Section 3.3) that are valid in a superclass are valid in a subclass.

Such a modular mechanism has many advantages. It allows formulating a new logic by composing pieces (theories) of an existing logic and adding extra theories if necessary. For example, if a user wanted to create a theory based on product types and some extra objects, she can take the product type module from the NuPRL-style type theory implemented in MetaPRL and add other modules if necessary. A nice property of our implementation is that such a user would automatically get not only all the primitive rules about the product types, but also all the theorems about them and all the tactics and resource data (see Section 4.1) needed to work with product types and all the display forms describing how to pretty print product types.

See [27] for a detailed description of the MetaPRL logical framework.

5.2   NuPRL-Style Type Theory

Some of the most powerful and challenging logical theories implemented in theorem provers are various flavors of constructive type theory. MetaPRL is not an exception — its most extensively developed and most frequently used theory is a variation of the NuPRL intuitionistic type theory [18] (which in turn is based on the Martin-Löf type theory [41]).

The MetaPRL implementation of the type theory differs from the NuPRL's one in several major aspects. The most obvious distinction is the extensive use of computational rewrites (including derived ones), derived rules and resource annotations as well as an extensive modularization of the theory.

Another big difference is MetaPRL's approach to formalizing the notion of a quotient type. In MetaPRL the traditional monolithic axiomatization of quotients is replaced by a modular set of rules for a specially chosen set of primitive operations (as described in [42] and [43, Chapter 5]). This modular formalization of quotient types turns out to be much easier to use and free of many limitations of the traditional monolithic formalization. As an illustration of the advantages of the new approach, MetaPRL includes a theory that demonstrates how the type of *collections* (that is known to be very hard to formalize using traditional quotient types) can be naturally formalized using the new primitives.

MetaPRL also includes Kopylov's theory of extensible dependent record types [34]. Record types are an important tool for programming and are essential in formalizing object-oriented calculi [1,19,26]. Dependent record types

may be used to represent modules in programming languages with their specifications. Dependent record types are also used to represent algebraic structures.
In most of the previous approaches, the dependent record type was treated as
primitive. MetaPRL theory defines it using a new type constructor, *dependent
intersection* [34]. Dependent intersection is an intersection of two types, where
the second type may depend on elements of the first one. This type constructor
is built by analogy to the dependent product. It turns out that the concatenation
of dependent records is a dependent intersection. This observation allows us to
define the record type in a very simple way. Our record type has natural subtyping properties and we are able to extend record types. Dependent intersection
can also be used to define a set type. This means that dependent intersection
not only adds support for dependent records, it *simplifies* the theory at the same
time.

While NuPRL uses "trusted" decision procedures to implement some of its
arithmetical reasoning, MetaPRL has explicit axioms with corresponding decision
procedures being implemented as generic tactics (see Section 4.3).

In addition to the purely intuitionistic type theory, MetaPRL also has a theory (implemented as a module extending the standard type theory) that allows
some limited form of classical reasoning [35]. While retaining most of the constructive properties, this theory allows expressing and proving a propositional
analog of Markov's principle [40]. The MetaPRL and NuPRL groups continue to
use purely intuitionistic reasoning for most purposes, however this experimental
theory provides a promising alternative approach to managing computational
meaning of constructive proofs.

5.3   Constructive Set Theory

In [2,3], Aczel introduced Constructive Zermelo-Fraenkel set theory, CZF, and
formulated an embedding of CZF into the Martin-Löf's type theory [41]. Based
on Aczel's work, Hickey formally embedded CZF into the MetaPRL type theory
[29]. Since Aczel's CZF theory is specified explicitly by a collection of axioms,
after sets and these axioms are encoded in MetaPRL's CZF module, we can use
them directly without referring to the type theory.

In [51,52], Yu provided a machine-checked formalization of the basic abstract
algebra on the basis of MetaPRL's CZF implementation. She started by specifying the group axioms as a collection of inference rules, defining a logic for groups.
The formalization of all other concepts in abstract algebra, such as subgroups
and homomorphisms, is based on this group logic. She proved some theorems
of group theory constructively from these inference rules as well as the axioms
of CZF in MetaPRL, and provided an example of a formalization of a concrete
group, the Klein 4-group.

5.4   Other Theories

One of the goals in MetaPRL is to maintain a close connection between the formal
module system and the OCaml programming language. By making the formal

system an extension of OCaml, we provide a path for adding formal reasoning to applications that have been previously developed using standard software engineering methodology. This eases the burden of programming in a formal system because formal tools (for specification, verification, documentation, etc.) need only be learned when the benefits of doing so are desired. The reason is also pedantic: to learn how to program in a formal system, we can first learn how to program informally and then augment our knowledge with a foundational mathematical understanding. The final reason is a matter of bootstrapping: we would like to use MetaPRL to reason about its own implementation but we need an implementation first!

The MC theory is the first attempt at implementing a formal compiler [7]. Terms are used to formally represent the functional intermediate representation (FIR) [25] of the Mojave Compiler Collection (MCC) within MetaPRL, and rewrites are used to give the operational semantics of the FIR. Several tactics allow MetaPRL to transform FIR code through dead code elimination and inlining. Additional ML code informally translates the FIR between MCC's internal representation and the MetaPRL term language.

6   Logical Toolkit

The MetaPRL system provides a large array of efficient modules with well-defined and very generic interfaces covering various aspects of formal reasoning. The exported functionality ranges from very low-level (term syntax, alpha-equality, unification, *etc*) to very high-level (generic proof automation procedures, an ability to reason in various logical theories), and includes a very efficient term rewriting engine. This makes it very easy to use MetaPRL as a general programming toolkit for applications requiring formal methods functionality.

One example of an application developed using MetaPRL as a programming toolkit is the JProver (see Section 4.3) automated prover for first-order intuitionistic and classical logics. Once JProver was implemented[4], it *itself* became a part of the MetaPRL toolkit. As described in [48], this allowed us to integrate JProver into the MetaPRL implementation of the type theory and into the NuPRL system. Later, Guan-Shieng Huang was able to integrate[5] JProver into Coq proof assistant [8] (without any help by the members of the PRL community).

Another example is the Phobos generic parser [21] that is powered by the MetaPRL rewriting engine. Phobos is a part of a compiler [24] for a simple ML-like language, where all program transformations (all the way from parsing to x86 assembly language) are (semi-)formally specified and are executed through the MetaPRL logical engine.

MetaPRL is also being used as a part of the Formal Digital Library (FDL) project being developed at Cornell, Caltech and Wyoming. The first prototype

---

[4] The main JProver developer did not have any previous experience with MetaPRL.

[5] See   http://coqcvs.inria.fr/cgi-bin/cvswebcoq.cgi/checkout/V7/contrib/jprover/README   for more information on Coq JProver integration.

FDL has been built [4] and contains definitions, theorems, theories, proof methods, and articles about topics in computational mathematics and books assembled from them. Currently it supports these objects created with the theorem proving systems MetaPRL, NuPRL and PVS, with intent to include material from other implemented logics such as Minlog, Coq, HOL, Isabelle, and Larch in due course.

The MetaPRL logics that an FDL user is interested in are specified during the build of MetaPRL. After the FDL is connected to MetaPRL, one can retrieve the modules of those logics, and their contents. The data is transferred over TCP sockets in the MathBus interchange format [53]. FDL sends MetaPRL commands that specify what to import and how, and can contain additional evaluation requests. Example commands include listing all modules, retrieving a particular proof in a module, calling the proof engine on a particular proof step, or migrating an entire module, or logic.

For the purpose of the FDL, we typically migrate all the available data. Then, the FDL can check the proofs by calling the MetaPRL proof engine and build the appropriate certificates.

7 Related Work

In parallel with MetaPRL, Cornell PRL group also developed another descendant of NuPRL-4 — NuPRL LPE [5]. These two projects are intended to compliment each other. In particular, NuPRL LPE features a complex implementation of a knowledge base that allows one to store logical objects with arbitrary relations between them — such as, for example, the MetaPRL objects organized in a hierarchy of theories (see Section 5.1). NuPRL LPE's distributed nature allows one to use different logical engines from NuPRL LPE — including the fast logical engine (see Section 3.1) provided by MetaPRL. NuPRL LPE also provides a complex GUI — a logical navigator, which compensates for the lack of an advanced GUI in MetaPRL. NuPRL LPE is currently being used in UAV system protocol verification and in work on practical reflection [9].

MetaPRL has much in common with the Isabelle generic theorem prover [45, 46]. The main differences are the logical foundations and the theory mechanism. We have kept a Martin-Löf style logic, hence the need for computational rewrites. Also, our module mechanism stresses relations between theories, allowing reuse of proof automation.

Harrison's HOL-Light [22] shares some common features with the MetaPRL implementation. Harrison's system is implemented in Caml-Light, and both systems require fewer computational resources than their predecessors.

For a more detailed overview of the work related to some of the individual features of the MetaPRL system, please see the corresponding papers cited above [7,21,24,27,28,29,31,34,35,42,43,44,48,51,52].

References

1. Martín Abadi and Luca Cardelli. *A Theory of Objects*. Springer, 1996.
2. Peter Aczel. The type theoretic interpretation of constructive set theory: Inductive definition. In *Logic, Methodology and Philosophy of Science VII*, pages 17–49. Elsevier Science Publishers, 1986.
3. Peter Aczel and Michael Rathjen. Notes on constructive set theory. Technical Report 40, Mittag-Leffler, 2000/2001.
4. Stuart Allen, Mark Bickford, Robert Constable, et al. FDL: A prototype formal digital library. PostScript document on website, May 2002.
   `http://www.nuprl.org/html/FDLProject/02cucs-fdl.html`.
5. Stuart Allen, Robert Constable, Richard Eaton, Christoph Kreitz, and Lori Lorigo. The NuPRL open logical environment. In David McAllester, editor, *Proceedings of the 17th International Conference on Automated Deduction*, volume 1831 of *Lecture Notes in Artificial Intelligence*, pages 170–176. Springer Verlag, 2000.
6. David Aspinall. Proof General – A generic tool for proof development. In *Proceedings of TACAS*, volume 1785 of *Lecture Notes in Computer Science*, 2000.
   `http://zermelo.dcs.ed.ac.uk/home/da/papers/pgoutline/`.
7. Brian Aydemir, Adam Granicz, and Jason Hickey. Formal design environments. In Carreño et al. [16], pages 12–22.
8. Bruno Barras, Samuel Boutin, Cristina Cornes, Judicaël Courant, Jean-Christophe Filliâtre, Eduardo Giménez, Hugo Herbelin, Gérard-Mohring, Amokrane Saïbi, and Benjamin Werner. *The Coq Proof Assistant Reference Manual*. INRIA-Rocquencourt, CNRS and ENS Lyon, 1996.
9. Eli Barzilay and Stuart Allen. Reflecting higher-order abstract syntax in NuPRL. In Carreño et al. [16], pages 23–32.
10. J. L. Bates. *A Logic for Correct Program Development*. PhD thesis, Cornell University, 1979.
11. J. L. Bates and Robert L. Constable. Definition of micro-PRL. Technical Report 82–492, Cornell University, Computer Science Department, Ithaca, NY, 1981.
12. J. L. Bates and Robert L. Constable. Proofs as programs. *ACM Transactions on Programming Languages and Systems*, 7(1):53–71, 1985.
13. W. Bibel. *Automated Theorem Proving*. Vieweg Verlag, Braunschweig, 2nd edition, 1987.
14. Mark Bickford, Christoph Kreitz, Robbert van Renesse, and Xiaoming Liu. Proving hybrid protocols correct. In Richard Boulton and Paul Jackson, editors, *14th International Conference on Theorem Proving in Higher Order Logics*, volume 2152 of *Lecture Notes in Computer Science*, pages 105–120, Edinburgh, Scotland, September 2001. Springer-Verlag.
15. Victor A. Carreño, Cézar A. Muñoz, and Sophiène Tahar, editors. *Proceedings of the 15th International Conference on Theorem Proving in Higher Order Logics (TPHOLs 2002)*, volume 2410 of *Lecture Notes in Computer Science*. Springer-Verlag, 2002.
16. Victor A. Carreño, Cézar A. Muñoz, and Sophiène Tahar, editors. *Theorem Proving in Higher Order Logics; Track B Proceedings of the 15th International Conference on Theorem Proving in Higher Order Logics (TPHOLs 2002), Hampton, VA, August 2002*. National Aeronautics and Space Administration, 2002.
17. Robert L. Constable. On the theory of programming logics. In *Proceedings of the 9th Annual ACM Symposium on the Theory of Computing*, Boulder, CO., pages 269–85, May 1977.

18. Robert L. Constable, Stuart F. Allen, H. M. Bromley, W. R. Cleaveland, J. F. Cremer, R. W. Harper, Douglas J. Howe, T. B. Knoblock, N. P. Mendler, P. Panangaden, James T. Sasaki, and Scott F. Smith. *Implementing Mathematics with the NuPRL Development System*. Prentice-Hall, NJ, 1986.

19. Robert L. Constable and Jason Hickey. NuPRL's class theory and its applications. In Friedrich L. Bauer and Ralf Steinbrueggen, editors, *Foundations of Secure Computation*, NATO ASI Series, Series F: Computer & System Sciences, pages 91–116. IOS Press, 2000.

20. Michael Gordon, Robin Milner, and Christopher Wadsworth. *Edinburgh LCF: a mechanized logic of computation*, volume 78 of *Lecture Notes in Computer Science*. Springer-Verlag, NY, 1979.

21. Adam Granicz and Jason Hickey. Phobos: A front-end approach to extensible compilers. In *36th Hawaii International Conference on System Sciences*. IEEE, 2002.

22. John Harrison. HOL Light: A tutorial introduction. In *Formal Methods in Computer-Aided Design (FMCAD'96)*, volume 1166 of *Lecture Notes in Computer Science*, pages 265–269. Springer, 1996.

23. Mark Hayden. *The Ensemble System*. PhD thesis, Department of Computer Science, Cornell University, Ithaca, NY, January 1998.

24. Jason Hickey, Aleksey Nogin, Adam Granicz, and Brian Aydemir. Formal compiler implementation in a logical framework. Submitted to ICFP'03. Extended version of the paper is available as Caltech Technical Report caltechCSTR:2003.002, 2003.

25. Jason Hickey, Justin D. Smith, Brian Aydemir, Nathaniel Gray, Adam Granicz, and Cristian Tapus. Process migration and transactions using a novel intermediate language. Technical Report caltechCSTR 2002.007, California Institute of Technology, Computer Science, July 2002.

26. Jason J. Hickey. Formal objects in type theory using very dependent types. In *Foundations of Object Oriented Languages 3*, 1996. Available electronically through the http://www.cis.upenn.edu/ bcpierce/FOOL/FOOL3.html.

27. Jason J. Hickey. NuPRL-Light: An implementation framework for higer-order logics. In William McCune, editor, *Proceedings of the 14th International Conference on Automated Deduction*, volume 1249 of *Lecture Notes in Artificial Intelligence*, pages 395–399. Springer, July 13–17 1997. An extended version of the paper can be found at http://www.cs.caltech.edu/ jyh/papers/cade14_nl/default.html.

28. Jason J. Hickey. Fault-tolerant distributed theorem proving. In Harald Ganzinger, editor, *Proceedings of the 16th International Conference on Automated Deduction*, volume 1632 of *Lecture Notes in Artificial Intelligence*, pages 227–231, Berlin, July 7–10 1999. Trento, Italy.

29. Jason J. Hickey. *The MetaPRL Logical Programming Environment*. PhD thesis, Cornell University, Ithaca, NY, January 2001.

30. Jason J. Hickey, Brian Aydemir, Yegor Bryukhov, Alexei Kopylov, Aleksey Nogin, and Xin Yu. A listing of MetaPRL theories. http://metaprl.org/theories.pdf.

31. Jason J. Hickey and Aleksey Nogin. Fast tactic-based theorem proving. In J. Harrison and M. Aagaard, editors, *Theorem Proving in Higher Order Logics: 13th International Conference, TPHOLs 2000*, volume 1869 of *Lecture Notes in Computer Science*, pages 252–266. Springer-Verlag, 2000.

32. Jason J. Hickey, Aleksey Nogin, Alexei Kopylov, et al. MetaPRL home page. http://metaprl.org/.

33. Paul B. Jackson. *Enhancing the NuPRL Proof Development System and Applying it to Computational Abstract Algebra*. PhD thesis, Cornell University, Ithaca, NY, January 1995.

34. Alexei Kopylov. Dependent intersection: A new way of defining records in type theory. In *Proceedings of 18th IEEE Symposium on Logic in Computer Science*, 2003. To appear.

35. Alexei Kopylov and Aleksey Nogin. Markov's principle for propositional type theory. In L. Fribourg, editor, *Computer Science Logic, Proceedings of the 10th Annual Conference of the EACSL*, volume 2142 of *Lecture Notes in Computer Science*, pages 570–584. Springer-Verlag, 2001.

36. Christoph Kreitz and Jens Otten. Connection-based theorem proving in classical and non-classical logics. *Journal for Universal Computer Science, Special Issue on Integration of Deductive Systems*, 5(3):88–112, 1999.

37. Christoph Kreitz and Stephan Schmitt. A uniform procedure for converting matrix proofs into sequent-style systems. *Journal of Information and Computation*, 162(1–2):226–254, 2000.

38. Xiaoming Liu, Christoph Kreitz, Robbert van Renesse, Jason J. Hickey, Mark Hayden, Kenneth Birman, and Robert Constable. Building reliable, high-performance communication systems from components. In *17th ACM Symposium on Operating Systems Principles (SOSP'99)*, volume 34 of *Operating Systems Review*, pages 80–92, December 1999.

39. Conal L. Mannion and Stuart F. Allen. A notation for computer aided mathematics. Department of Computer Science TR94-1465, Cornell University, Ithaca, NY, November 1994.

40. A.A. Markov. On constructive mathematics. *Trudy Matematicheskogo Instituta imeni V.A. Steklova*, 67:8–14, 1962. In Russian. English Translation: A.M.S. Translations, series 2, vol.98, pp. 1-9. MR 27#3528.

41. Per Martin-Löf. Constructive mathematics and computer programming. In *Proceedings of the Sixth International Congress for Logic, Methodology, and Philosophy of Science*, pages 153–175, Amsterdam, 1982. North Holland.

42. Aleksey Nogin. Quotient types: A modular approach. In Carreño et al. [15], pages 263–280. Available at `http://nogin.org/papers/quotients.html`.

43. Aleksey Nogin. *Theory and Implementation of an Efficient Tactic-Based Logical Framework*. PhD thesis, Cornell University, Ithaca, NY, August 2002.

44. Aleksey Nogin and Jason Hickey. Sequent schema for derived rules. In Carreño et al. [15], pages 281–297.

45. L. Paulson and T. Nipkow. Isabelle tutorial and user's manual. Technical report, University of Cambridge Computing Laboratory, 1990.

46. Lawrence C. Paulson. *Isabelle: A Generic Theorem Prover*, volume 828 of *Lecture Notes in Computer Science*. Springer-Verlag, New York, 1994.

47. Frank Pfenning. Logical frameworks. In Alan Robinson and Andrei Voronkov, editors, *Handbook of Automated Reasoning*, volume 2. Elsevier Science Publishers, 2001.

48. Stephan Schmitt, Lori Lorigo, Christoph Kreitz, and Aleksey Nogin. JProver: Integrating connection-based theorem proving into interactive proof assistants. In *International Joint Conference on Automated Reasoning*, volume 2083 of *Lecture Notes in Artificial Intelligence*, pages 421–426. Springer-Verlag, 2001.

49. The Nuprl Staff. PRL: Proof refinement logic programmer's manual (Lambda PRL, VAX version). Cornell University, Department of Computer Science, 1983.

50. Pierre Weis and Xavier Leroy. *Le langage Caml*. Dunod, Paris, 2nd edition, 1999. In French.

51. Xin Yu. Formalizing abstract algebra in constructive set theory. Master's thesis, California Institute of Technology, 2002.

52. Xin Yu and Jason J. Hickey. Formalizing abstract algebra in constructive set theory. Submitted to LICS conference, 2003.
53. Richard Zippel. MathBus. Available online at http://www.cs.cornell.edu/Simlab/papers/mathbus/mathTerm.htm.

Proving Pearl: Knuth's Algorithm for Prime Numbers

Laurent Théry

INRIA, 2004 route des Lucioles, 06902 Sophia Antipolis France*
Laurent.Thery@sophia.inria.fr

Abstract. In his book "The Art of Computer Programming", Donald Knuth gives an algorithm to compute the first n prime numbers. Surprisingly, proving the correctness of this simple algorithm from basic principles is far from being obvious and requires a wide range of verification techniques. In this paper, we explain how the verification has been mechanised in the COQ proof system.

1 Introduction

There is no relation between the length of a program and the difficulty of its proof of correctness. Very long programs performing elementary tasks could be trivial to prove correct, while short programs relying on some very deep properties could be much harder. Highly optimized programs usually belong to the second category. For example, algorithms designed for efficient arithmetic operations are known to be hard to verify since every single line has been thought in order to minimize execution time and/or memory allocation. Bertot et al. [4] illustrate the difficulty of verifying such algorithms.

In this paper we are interested in an algorithm given by Knuth in his book "The Art of Computer Programming" [12]. This algorithm takes an integer n as an argument and returns the list of the first n prime numbers. The correctness of this simple algorithm relies on a deep property of prime numbers called Bertrand's postulate. The property, first conjectured by Bertrand and then proved by Chebyshev, states that for any integer number $n \geq 2$ there always exists a prime number p strictly between n and $2n$. Proving Knuth's algorithm from basic principles means formally proving Bertrand's postulate. To do so we follow the proof given by Arkadii Slinko [15]. The original idea of this elementary proof is due to Paul Erdös [6]. The proof itself has a very interesting structure. The initial problem in number theory is translated into real analysis, namely analysing the variation of a function. Using derivative and the intermediate value theorem, it is possible to conclude that for n greater than 128 the property holds. To finish the proof, we are then left with the task of individually checking that the property holds for n varying from 2 to 127.

The paper is structured as follows. In Section 2, we show how prime numbers can be easily defined in a prover. In Section 3, we present the algorithm proposed

---

* Currently Visiting Professor at University of L'Aquila, Italy.

D. Basin and B. Wolff (Eds.): TPHOLs 2003, LNCS 2758, pp. 304–318, 2003.

by Knuth. In Section 4, we detail the different logical assertions that need to be attached to the program to prove its correctness. In Section 5, we outline the proof of Bertrand's postulate. In Section 6, we comment on some specific aspects of our formalisation.

2   Prime Numbers

The notion of primality can be defined in a prover in a simple way. Natural numbers are usually defined using Peano representation. In COQ, we have:

Inductive $\mathbb{N} : Set :=$
  $O : \mathbb{N}$
| $S : \mathbb{N} \to \mathbb{N}$.

With this definition, 0,1,2 are represented as O, $(S\ O)$, $(S\ (S\ O))$. The next step is to define the notion of divisibility:

Definition $divides \colon \mathbb{N} \to \mathbb{N} \to Prop := \lambda a, b \colon \mathbb{N}.\ \exists q \colon \mathbb{N}.\ b = qa$.

In COQ, predicates are represented as functions. The predicate $divides$ is a function that takes two natural numbers and returns a proposition. The fact that a $divides$ b is then written $divides(a, b)$ and corresponds to the proposition $\exists q \colon \mathbb{N}.\ b = qa$.

Once divisibility has been defined, we can proceed with primality. A number is prime if it has exactly two divisors 1 and itself:

Definition $prime \colon \mathbb{N} \to Prop := \lambda a \colon \mathbb{N}.$
  $a \neq 1 \wedge (\forall b \colon \mathbb{N}.\ divides(b, a) \Rightarrow (b = 1 \vee b = a))$.

With this definition it is possible to derive some basic properties of prime numbers. Two of them are of special interest in our context. The first one states that all prime numbers are odd except 2. Using the definition of odd number:

Definition $odd \colon \mathbb{N} \to Prop := \lambda a \colon \mathbb{N}.\ \exists b \colon \mathbb{N}.\ a = 2b + 1$.

we have the following theorem:

Theorem $prime2Odd \colon \forall p \colon \mathbb{N}.\ prime(p) \Rightarrow p = 2 \vee odd(p)$.

The second property states that a number n is prime if all the prime numbers less than $\sqrt{n}$ do not divide it:

Theorem $primeDef_1 \colon \forall n \colon \mathbb{N}.$
  $1 < n \wedge (\forall p \colon \mathbb{N}.\ prime(p) \wedge p^2 \leq n \Rightarrow \neg(divides(p, n))) \Rightarrow prime(n)$.

The bound of $\sqrt{n}$ comes from the fact that if n is composite, i.e. $n = pq$, then either p or q must be less than $\sqrt{n}$.

3   Knuth's Algorithm

To express the algorithm given by Knuth and state its correctness, we use the WHY tool [7]. This tool takes a program annotated with logical assertions à

```
parameter n: int
parameter a: array n of int
parameter m,s,i,j:  int ref
parameter b: bool ref

external sqr : int -> int
external mod : int -> int -> int

begin
  a[0]  := 2;
  m := 3;
  i := 1;
  while ((!i) < n) do
    b := true;
    s := (sqr !m);
    j := 0;
    while ((!b) && a[!j] <= !s) do
      if (mod !m a[!j]) = 0
      then b := false
      else j := !j + 1
    done;
    if (!b) then
      begin
        a[!i] := !m;
        i := !i + 1
      end;
    m := !m + 2
  done
end
```

Fig. 1. The Algorithm in WHY

la Hoare [10] and generates a list of verification conditions. Proving all these conditions ensures that all the logical assertions in the program hold. WHY is generic in the sense that it is not linked to a specific prover. Outputs for PVS and COQ are available.

The algorithm written in WHY is given in Figure 1. The syntax of WHY is a subset of the one of the OCAML programming language. In OCAML, a variable that is modifiable has a reference type α *ref*. If x is a variable of type *int ref*, the expression !x denotes the value of x and the statement x := !x +1 increments the value of x by one. Let us explain the program given in Figure 1. It starts with a sequence of declarations:

```
parameter n: int
parameter a: array n of int
parameter m,s,i,j:  int ref
parameter b: bool ref
```

According to these declarations, n is a variable whose value cannot be modified, a is an array that should eventually contain the first n primes, m, s, i and j are modifiable integer variables, and b is a modifiable boolean variable. To write the algorithm, we need two extra functions on integer numbers. Since these functions are not going to be defined, they are declared external:

```
external sqr : int -> int
external mod : int -> int -> int
```

The first one represents the square root, the second one the modulo. For example (sqr 5) and (mod 23 7) are both equal to 2.

The program has two while loops. The outer one fills the array a with prime numbers. For this, it uses a candidate prime number m. The boolean variable b tells whether m is prime or not. If at the end of the inner loop, the value of b is true, m is put in the array. In any case at the end of each iteration of the outer loop, the value of m is incremented by 2.

The inner loop checks the primality of the value of m. For this it makes use of the property $primeDef_1$. The test (mod !m a[!j])=0 is used for checking if a[j] divides m. The real difficulty in proving the correctness of the program lies in the following line:

```
while ((!b) && a[!j] <= !s) do
```

If the guard of the loop had been more defensive, i.e.

```
while ((!b) && j<i && a[!j] <= !s) do
```

the correctness of the program would be a direct consequence of the two properties $prime2Odd$ and $primeDef_1$. As noted by Knuth the test j<i is unnecessary because of the density of prime numbers. To find a new prime number for the location a[i], the program starts from the value a[i-1]+2 incrementing m repeatedly by 2 till a prime number is found. It results that j could exceed i if and only if there was no prime number between a[i-1] and a[i-1]^2. Bertrand's postulate ensures that there is always a prime between a[i-1] and 2a[i-1]. As a[i-1] is prime and thus larger than 1, we have 2a[i-1] $\le$ a[i-1]^2, so j cannot exceed i.

4   Correctness

In order to prove the program given in Figure 1, we have to annotate it with logical assertions. To do so we need some predicates and functions:

```
logic one : bool -> int
logic In : int,array int,int,int -> prop
logic Prime : int -> prop
logic Odd : int -> prop
logic Divides : int,int -> prop
```

The function **one** transforms a boolean into an integer: *true* → 1 and *false* → 0. It is used to express some termination properties of the program.
The predicate **In** is used to express properties of the array: In(n,a,i,j) is equivalent to the fact that there exists an index i ≤ k < j such that a[k] = n. The predicates **Prime**, **Odd** and **Divides** are the usual predicates on integers.

4.1   Preconditions and Postconditions

The only precondition for the program is

```
{ 0<n }
```

It is needed to ensure the correct execution of the statement a[0]=2. The post-condition simply states that at the end of the program a should hold a complete ordered list of prime numbers:

```
{(forall k:int.  (0 <= k and k < n -> Prime(a[k])))          and
 (forall k:int. forall j:int.
        (0 <= k and k < j and j < n -> a[k] < a[j]))          and
 (forall k:int.
        (0 <= k and k <= a[n-1] and Prime(k)) -> In(k,a,0,n))
}
```

4.2   Invariant and Variant for the First Loop

For the first loop

```
while ((!i) < n) do
```

the invariant is a conjunction of three blocks. The first one states that the final assertion holds till i:

```
(forall k:int.  (0 <= k and k < i -> Prime(a[k])))          and
(forall k:int. forall j:int.
        (0 <= k and k < j and j < i -> a[k] < a[j]))          and
(forall k:int.
        (0 <= k and k <= a[i-1] and Prime(k)) -> In(k,a,0,i))
```

The second block keeps the information related to m, i.e. m is odd and in the interval defined by Bertrand's postulate:

```
a[i-1] < m and m < 2*a[i-1] and Odd (m)
```

The last block keeps the information related to i:

```
0 < i and i <= n
```

In order to find the variant that ensures the termination of the first loop, we have to notice that either i gets closer to n or m gets closer to 2a[i-1]. So for a lexicographic order, the pair of these two quantities always gets smaller. This gives us the following variant:

```
variant (n-i, 2*a[i-1]-m) for lexZ
```

4.3   Invariant and Variant for the Second Loop

For the second loop

```
while ((!b) && a[!j] <= !s) do
```

the invariant is a conjunction of two blocks. The first block keeps the information related to j:

```
0 <= j and j < i
```

The second block states that if the boolean b is true we have not yet found a divisor of m and if it is false, a[j] divides m:

```
(if (b)
    then (forall k:int.
              (0 <= k and k < j -> not(Divides(a[k],m))))
    else  Divides(a[j],m))
```

The termination is ensured because j always gets closer to i except when b is set to false:

```
variant one(b)+i-j
```

This ends all the assertions we need to put in the program. The complete annotated program is given in Appendix A.

5   Bertrand's Postulate

Running the WHY tool on the annotated program given in Appendix A generates 18 verification conditions. Only the condition coming from the invariant of the first loop that says that m keeps between a[i-1] and 2a[i-1] is difficult to prove. This is no surprise: to prove it we need a proof of Bertrand's postulate.

   In this section we are not going to present the whole formal proof but only illustrate some of its most interesting aspects. The proof is largely inspired from that given by Arkadii Slinko [15]. Still, it has been slightly modified so to make its formalisation in a prover easier. We refer to the technical report [16] for the details of the proof.

5.1   Number Theory

The main part of the proof consists in proving properties about natural numbers. Primality is a key notion on which we need to be able to compute. For this we turn the predicate into a test function. The primality test $1_p(a)$ is defined as follows:

$$1_p(a) = a \quad \text{if } a \text{ is prime}$$
$$1_p(a) = 1 \quad \text{otherwise}$$

In particular this test is used to express theorems about the product of prime numbers. For example, to denote the product of all prime numbers less than n we simply write

$$\prod_{i \leq n} 1_p(i)$$

Another important notion in the proof of Bertrand's postulate is the one of binomial coefficients. The main step of the proof is to find an upper bound and a lower bound for $\binom{2n}{n}$. The lower bound is given by the following theorem:

Theorem $binomialEven$: $\forall n$: $\mathbb{N}$. $0 < n \Rightarrow 4^n \leq 2n\binom{2n}{n}$.

The upper bound is only valid in a context where there is no prime between n and $2n$ and where n is greater than 128:

Theorem $upperBound$:
$$\forall n: \mathbb{N}. \, 2^7 \leq n \wedge (\forall p: \mathbb{N}. \, n < p < 2n \Rightarrow \neg(prime(p))) \Rightarrow$$
$$\binom{2n}{n} \leq (2n)^{\sqrt{2n}/2 - 1} 4^{2n/3}.$$

In order to define binomial coefficients, we use Pascal's triangle:

$$\binom{0}{a} = 0 \quad \text{if } a \neq 0$$
$$\binom{a}{0} = 1$$
$$\binom{a+1}{b+1} = \binom{a}{b+1} + \binom{a}{b}$$

We then derive the usual closed form:

Theorem $binomialFact$: $\forall n, m$: $\mathbb{N}$. $\binom{n+m}{m} n! m! = (n + m)!$.

Three main properties of binomial coefficients are needed:

Theorem $binomialMonoS$: $\forall n, m, p$: $\mathbb{N}$. $2m < n \Rightarrow \binom{n}{m} \leq \binom{n}{m+1}$.

Theorem $binomialComp$: $\forall n, m$: $\mathbb{N}$. $\binom{n+m}{n} = \binom{n+m}{m}$.

Theorem $primeDiracDividesBinomial$:
$$\forall n, m, p: \mathbb{N}. \, n < p \leq n + m \wedge m < p \Rightarrow divides(1_p(p), \binom{n+m}{n}).$$

The first property is a direct consequence of the definition while the second property follows from the closed form. To get the third property we use the closed form and the fact that, if a prime number divides a product, then it divides one of the elements of the product.

The road to the lower bound theorem $binomialEven$ is rather direct. It starts by proving the binomial theorem:

Theorem $expPascal$: $\forall a, b, n$: $\mathbb{N}$. $(a + b)^n = \sum_{0 \leq i \leq n} \binom{n}{i} a^i b^{n-i}$.

By applying this theorem for $a = b = 1$ we get

Theorem $binomial_2$: $\forall n$: $\mathbb{N}$. $2^n = \sum_{0 \leq i \leq n} \binom{n}{i}$.

Now we have all the ingredients to prove the theorem *binomialEven*. Using the theorem *binomial₂*, we have

$$2^{2n} = \sum_{0 \leq i \leq 2n} \binom{2n}{i}$$

Taking apart the first and the last term gives

$$2^{2n} = 1 + \sum_{1 \leq i \leq 2n-1} \binom{2n}{i} + 1$$

We have $2 \leq \binom{2n}{n}$ and using *binomialMonoS* and *binomialComp* we can prove that

$$\binom{2n}{i} \leq \binom{2n}{n} \text{ for } 1 \leq i \leq 2n - 1$$

Using these two bounds we have

$$4^n \leq \binom{2n}{n} + (2n - 1)\binom{2n}{n} = 2n\binom{2n}{n}$$

The proof of the upper bound theorem *upperBound* is much more intricate. In this paper we only illustrate how the expression $4^{2n/3}$ is derived. It comes from an appropriate upper bound on the product of prime numbers less than $2n/3$. In order to establish this upper bound, we first prove a dual theorem to the theorem *binomialEven* and get

Theorem *binomialOdd*: $\forall n$: $\mathbb{N}$. $\binom{2n+1}{n} \leq 4^n$.

The proof follows the same path as the one of *binomialEven*. We first use the theorem *binomial₂*:

$$2^{2n+1} = \sum_{0 \leq i \leq 2n+1} \binom{2n+1}{i}$$

By keeping only the two middle terms of the sum, we have

$$\binom{2n+1}{n} + \binom{2n+1}{n+1} \leq 2^{2n+1}$$

Using the theorem *binomialComp*, we get

$$2\binom{2n+1}{n} \leq 2^{2n+1}$$

By simplifying by 2 on both sides we get the expected result.

Now it is possible to establish the expected upper bound on the product of prime numbers:

Theorem *prodPrimeLt*: $\forall n$: $\mathbb{N}$. $1 < n \Rightarrow \prod_{i \leq n} 1_p(i) < 4^n$.

The proof is done using complete induction on $<$. First of all, the property is true for $n = 2$. We suppose that the property holds for all $m < n$ and try to prove that the property holds for n.
If n is even, we have

$$\prod_{i \leq n} 1_p(p) = \prod_{i \leq n-1} 1_p(p) \leq 4^{n-1} \leq 4^n$$

If n is odd, we can write n as $2m + 1$ and we have

$$\prod_{i \leq 2m+1} 1_p(p) = \left(\prod_{i \leq m+1} 1_p(p)\right) \ \left(\prod_{m+2 \leq i \leq 2m+1} 1_p(p)\right)$$

Using the induction hypothesis on the left element of the product, we get

$$\prod_{i \leq 2m+1} 1_p(p) \leq 4^{m+1} \ \left(\prod_{m+2 \leq i \leq 2m+1} 1_p(p)\right)$$

From the theorem $primeDiracDividesBinomial$ we know that each element in the product $\prod_{m+2 \leq i < 2m+1} 1_p(p)$ divides $\binom{2m+1}{m}$. So we have

$$\prod_{i \leq 2m+1} 1_p(p) \leq 4^{m+1} \binom{2m+1}{m}$$

It is sufficient to apply the theorem $binomialOdd$ to get the expected result

$$\prod_{i \leq n} 1_p(p) \leq 4^{m+1} 4^m = 4^{2m+1} = 4^n$$

5.2   Real Analysis

The two theorems $binomialEven$ and $upperBound$ give a lower bound and an upper bound for $2n\binom{2n}{n}$ respectively. By composing them, we get the following inequality:

$$4^n \leq 2n\binom{2n}{n} < (2n)^{\sqrt{2n}/2} 4^{2n/3}$$

For n sufficiently large, this inequality cannot hold since elementary function analysis tells us that the left part of the inequality, 4^n, grows much faster than the right part, $(2n)^{\sqrt{2n}/2} 4^{2n/3}$. To prove this formally, we transfer the problem into real analysis. So far all our definitions and theorems have been using natural numbers only. For example, in the previous inequality the operations $\sqrt{\ }$ and $/$ are functions over natural numbers, i.e $\sqrt{6} = 2$ and $7/2 = 3$. Now if we are able to prove that for x real and $x \geq 128$ we have

$$(2x)^{\sqrt{2x}/2} 4^{2x/3} < 4^x$$

where the operations $\sqrt{\ }$ and $/$ are the usual real functions then, because of monotonicity, the inequality over the natural numbers should also hold. This means that the only way the theorem $upperBound$ could still be true is because the assumption that there is no prime number between n and $2n$ is false. So Bertrand's postulate would be true for $n \geq 128$.

To prove the inequality over the reals, we first simplify it using properties of the power function

$$(2x)^{\sqrt{2x}/2} < 4^{x/3}$$

By taking the logarithm on both sides, we have

$$\frac{\sqrt{2x}}{2} \ln(2x) < \frac{2x}{3} \ln(2)$$

By simplifying it again we get

$$0 < \sqrt{8x}\ln(2) - 3\ln(2x)$$

If we set $f(x) = \sqrt{8x}\ln(2) - 3\ln(2x)$, we are left with proving that this function is always strictly positive for $128 \le x$. If we evaluate $f(128)$, we get

$$
\begin{aligned}
f(128) &= f(2^7) \\
&= \sqrt{2^{10}}\ln(2) - 3\ln(2^8) \\
&= 2^5 \ln(2) - 3\,2^3 \ln(2) \\
&= 2^3 \ln(2)(4-3) > 0
\end{aligned}
$$

If we compute the derivative of f we get

$$f'(x) = \frac{8\ln(2)}{2\sqrt{8x}} - 3\frac{2}{2x} = \frac{\sqrt{2x}\ln(2) - 3}{x}$$

It is easy to show that the derivative is positive for $128 \le x$. This implies that the function is positive. The above function analysis demonstrates that Bertrand's conjecture holds for $128 \le n$. Checking individually the cases from 2 to 127 gives us the main result:

Theorem $Bertrand: \forall n: \mathbb{N}.\, 2 \le n \Rightarrow \exists p: \mathbb{N}.\, prime(p) \wedge n < p < 2n$.

6   Some Remarks on the Formal Development

The full development is available at
`ftp://ftp-sop.inria.fr/lemme/Laurent.Thery/Bertrand/index.html`
It is 6000 lines long. The actual proof of the 18 verification conditions is 1000 lines long of which 800 are just the statements of the conditions. The development largely benefits from a previous formalisation of the correctness of the RSA encryption algorithm [3] in which binomials were defined in order to prove Fermat's little theorem. From this previous development 1000 lines were reused.

The really difficult part of the formalisation is the proof of Bertrand's postulate. With respect to the proof on paper [15], we discover that the applicability of two properties should be restricted. The theorem $powerDivBinomial_3$ was clearly not valid for $n = 1$. More interesting was the case of the theorem $upperBound$. In the paper the condition $128 \le n$ was missing. The condition that $n \ge 128$ was only introduced later in the function analysis. In the proof of the theorem $upperBound$ it was wrongly stated that the number of prime numbers less than p was always less than $p/2 - 1$. Spotting such minutiae is a clear benefit of formalising proofs with the help of a proof assistant. It shows that, when possible, a mechanised proof is a valuable companion to a proof on paper.

Formalising the analysis of the function f requires basic notions about the exponential and logarithmic functions. It also needs the fact that a function that has a positive derivative is increasing. This is a consequence of the intermediate value theorem. The most tedious part of the function analysis was actually to prove that the inequality that we had over the natural numbers should also hold for the real numbers. In COQ, natural numbers and real numbers being two separate types, translating statements from natural to real numbers must be justified explicitly.

When trying to prove the property that there is always a prime number between n and $2n$ for $n \le 128$, we took full advantage of the possibility of defining functions that can be directly evaluated inside CoQ. For example, we have defined the function $primeb$ of type $\mathbb{N} \to bool$ and proved its associated theorem of correctness

Theorem $primebCorrect$: $\forall n$: nat.
  if $primeb(n)$ **then** $prime(p)$ **else** $\neg prime(p)$.

This theorem says that if $primeb(n)$ evaluates to $true$ we have a proof of $prime(p)$ and if $primeb(n)$ evaluates to $false$ we have a proof of $\neg prime(p)$. CoQ is based on the isomorphism of Curry-Howard. This means that proofs are programs. So the proof of the theorem $primebCorrect$ is actually a program that, given a natural number n, returns a proof of primality or a proof of non-primality. It means, for example, that since $primeb(11)$ evaluates to $true$ a proof of $prime(11)$ is simply the proof term $primebCorrect(11)$, i.e. the application of the program $primebCorrect$ to the argument 11. Using functions that can be evaluated inside CoQ is interesting because not only it automates proofs but also generates very small proof objects. Following the same idea we have a function $checkPostulate$ with the associated theorem of correctness

Theorem $checkPostulateCorrect$: $\forall m$: $\mathbb{N}$.
  $checkPostulate(m) = true \Rightarrow$
    $\forall n$: $\mathbb{N}$. $2 \le n \le m \Rightarrow \exists p$: $\mathbb{N}$. $prime(p) \wedge n < p < 2n$.

Then to prove the following theorem

Theorem $postulateCorrect128$:
  $\forall n$: $\mathbb{N}$. $2 \le n \le 128 \Rightarrow \exists p$: $\mathbb{N}$. $prime(p) \wedge n < p < 2n$.

we use the previous theorem with a proof of $checkPostulate(128) = true$. Since the function $checkPostulate$ can be evaluated directly inside CoQ, the expression $checkPostulate(128) = true$ is identical to the expression $true = true$. Its proof is an instantiation of the theorem $reflEqual$ that states the reflexivity of equality. The proof term for the theorem $postulateCorrect128$ is then $postulateCorrect(128, reflEqual(bool, true))$.

The formal development also includes the proof of a surprising corollary of Bertrand's postulate suggested to us by Gérard Huet. For any given n, when taking the set of all natural numbers from 1 to $2n$, it is always possible to sort them pairwise in such a way that the sum of each pair is a prime number. For example, with $n = 10$ we have

$$\{ \quad (1,2); \quad (3,4); \quad (5,8); \quad (6,7); \quad (9,14);$$
$$(10,13); (11,12); (15,16); (17,20); (18,19) \}$$

The proof of this corollary is left to the reader and can be found in the file `Partition.v` of our formal development.

7   Conclusions

We believe that Knuth's algorithm is a very nice example of both the complexity and the diversity of program verification. First of all, it is elementary. Prime numbers are among the first examples one encounters when learning programming. They are also a standard example for theorem proving. From the point of view of program verification, Knuth's algorithm shows that adding or removing a single instruction in a program can have a huge impact on the difficulty of establishing its correctness. With the extra test in the second loop, proving Knuth's algorithm correct would be a relatively easy exercise. Note that even if Bertrand's postulate were already in the database of the theorem prover, deriving the correctness of Knuth's algorithm automatically would still require some non-trivial insight. Bertrand's postulate asserts that there is a prime between n and $2n$. In the program what is needed is that there exists a prime between n and n^2.

From the point of view of theorem proving, the interesting part of Knuth's algorithm is the proof of Bertrand's postulate. In order to prove it, we had to derive a fair amount of properties in discrete mathematics. This was no surprise. More surprisingly the final steps required to transfer the problem into real analysis. As we could only assess that the property holds asymptotically, we had to establish that the property holds for an initial segment of the integers. Luckily enough we had only to check the property from 2 to 128. This property has been proved automatically using the evaluation mechanism of functions inside CoQ. It is worth noticing that slightly different versions of the proof exist that give a different initial segment to check. For example in the book "Proofs from THE BOOK" [2] the bound is $4000 \leq n$. The function we have written to solve the problem for $n \leq 128$ is very naïve and uses a brute force method. It would be too inefficient for $n \leq 4000$. A systematic and more efficient method proposed by Harrison and Théry [9] would be to delegate the search for all the necessary primes to an external program and use CoQ only to check the result. Note that a similar method [5] has already been used to get relatively large prime numbers in CoQ.

The main contribution of this work is to present a tour of different formal verification techniques with an elementary example, a proving pearl. The main difficulty of proving Knuth's algorithm correct lies in having all these techniques working together. A much more elaborate proof effort that exhibits a similar diversity of verification techniques is the one described by John Harrison [8]. The fact that it is possible to carry out such kinds of verification in a single system shows how generic provers based on higher-order logics are. Having expressive logics makes them suitable for all different kinds of verification. It also indicates the maturity of theorem provers.

Number theory is an area of interest for theorem proving. For example, Art Quaife [14] shows how it is possible to prove automatically some non-trivial theorems of number theory. More recently, Joe Hurd [11] gives a very nice formalisation of the correctness of Miller-Rabin probabilistic algorithm to check primality. Along this line, the next natural candidate for formal verification is the recent polynomial algorithm to check primality proposed by Manindra Agrawal, Neeraj Kayal and Nitin Saxena [1]. Unfortunately their algorithm relies on much deeper properties than Bertrand's postulate, such as Brun-Titchmarsh theorem. These properties require the formalisation of some fascinating but elaborate tools, such as sieve methods. It is then most likely that mechanising the correctness of such an algorithm will still be a challenge for the next couple of years.

Acknowledgments. The formalisation in this paper was motivated by the preparation of an introductive lecture on Formalised Mathematics that the author gave at the Types Summer School at Giens in September 2002.

When reading the tutorial [15], it became clear that formalising Bertrand's postulate was possible. Many thanks go to Arkadii Slinko for setting up such an interesting web site.

Without the library of real analysis developed by Micaela Mayero and Olivier Desmettre, our work could not have been completed. A special thank goes to Olivier that adapted the library so to include some key properties that were needed in our formalisation.

Jean-Christophe Filliâtre gave us a very reactive support on WHY.

All the formalisation has been done using the neat user-interface PCOQ [13]. Yves Bertot was kind enough to spend some time to update PCOQ with the very latest version of COQ.

References

1. Manindra Agrawal, Neeraj Kayal, and Nitin Saxena. PRIMES is in P. Preprint, 2002, Available at http://www.cse.iit.ac.in/primality.pdf.
2. Martin Aigner and Günter M. Ziegler. *Proofs from THE BOOK*. Springer, 1998.
3. José C. Almeida and Laurent Théry. Correctness of the RSA algorithm. Coq contribution, 1999, Available at http://coq.inria.fr/contribs/summary.html.
4. Yves Bertot, Nicolas Magaud, and Paul Zimmermann. A GMP program computing square roots and its proof within Coq. *Journal of Automated Reasoning*, 29(3–4), 2002.
5. Olga Caprotti and Martijn Oostdijk. Formal and Efficient Primality Proofs by Use of Computer Algebra Oracles. *Journal of Symbolic Computation*, 32(1):55–70, 2001.
6. Paul Erdös. Beweis eines Satzes von Tschebyschef. In *Acta Scientifica Mathematica*, volume 5, pages 194–198, 1932.
7. Jean-Christophe Filliâtre. Proof of Imperative Programs in Type Theory. In *TYPES '98*, volume 1657 of *LNCS*, 1998.
8. John Harrison. Floating Point Verification in HOL. In *Higher Order Logic Theorem Proving and Its Applications*, volume 971 of *LNCS*, pages 186–199, 1995.
9. John Harrison and Laurent Théry. A Skeptic's Approach to Combining HOL and Maple. *Journal of Automated Reasoning*, 21(3):279–294, 1998.
10. C. Anthony R. Hoare. An Axiomatic Basis for Computer Programming. *Communication of the ACM*, 12(10):576–80, 583, October 1969.
11. Joe Hurd. Formal Verification of Probabilistic Algorithms. Phd Thesis, University of Cambridge, 2002.

12. Donald E. Knuth. *The Art of Computer Programming: Fundamental Algorithms*, pages 147–149. Addison-Wesley, 1997.
13. PCoq. A Graphical User-interface to Coq, Available at `http://www-sop.inria.fr /lemme/pcoq/`.
14. Art Quaife. *Automated development of fundamental mathematical theories*. Automated reasoning series: 2. Kluwer, 1992.
15. Arkadii Slinko. Number Theory. Tutorial 5: Bertrand's Postulate. Available at `http://matholymp.com/tutorials/bertrand.pdf`.
16. Laurent Théry. A Tour of Formal Verification with Coq: Knuth's Algorithm for Prime Numbers. Research Report 4600, INRIA, 2002.

A   The Complete Annotated Program

```
{ n > 0 }
begin
  a[0]  := 2;
  m := 3;
  i := 1;
  while ((!i) < n) do
```
$\{$invariant

$(0 < i$ and $i <= n)$ and

$(a[i-1] < m$ and $m < 2*a[i-1])$ and Odd (m) and

$(forall$ k:int.

$\quad\quad (a[i-1] < k$ and $k < m \to not(Prime(k))))$ and

$(forall$ k:int. $(0 <= k$ and $k < i \to Prime(a[k])))$ and

$(forall$ k:int. $forall$ j:int.

$\quad\quad (0 <= k$ and $k < j$ and $j < i \to a[k] < a[j]))$ and

$(forall$ k:int.

$\quad\quad (0 <= k$ and $k <= a[i-1]$ and $Prime(k)) \to In(k,a,0,i))$

variant $(n\text{-}i,$ $2*a[i\text{-}1]\text{-}m)$ **for** $lexZ$ $\}$

```
    b := true;
    s := (sqr !m);
    j := 0;
    while (!b && a[!j] <= !s) do
```
$\{$invariant

$(if$ (b)

$\quad then$

$\quad\quad (forall$ k:int.

$\quad\quad\quad (0 <= k$ and $k < j \to not(Divides(a[k],m))))$

$\quad else$ $Divides(a[j],m))$ and

$(0 <= j$ and $j < i)$

variant $one(b)+i\text{-}j$ $\}$

```
      if (mod !m a[!j]) = 0
      then b := false
      else j := !j + 1
    done;
```

```
    if (!b) then
      begin
        a[!i] := !m;
        i := !i + 1
      end;
    m := !m + 2
 done
end
```
$\{$ *(forall k:int. (0 <= k and k < n -> Prime(a[k])))*   *and*
 (forall k:int. forall j:int.
    (0 <= k and k < j and j < n -> a[k] < a[j]))   *and*
 (forall k:int.
    (0 <= k and k <= a[n-1] and Prime(k)) -> In(k,a,0,n))
$\}$

Formalizing Hilbert's Grundlagen in Isabelle/Isar

Laura I. Meikle and Jacques D. Fleuriot

School of Informatics, University of Edinburgh,
Appleton Tower, Crighton Street, Edinburgh, EH8 9LE, UK
{lauram,jdf}@dai.ed.ac.uk

Abstract. This paper describes part of the formalization of Hilbert's *Grundlagen der Geometrie* in the higher order logic of Isabelle/Isar, an extension of the interactive theorem prover Isabelle. Many mechanized proofs and formalization issues are discussed and the work is compared against Hilbert's prose and also other research in the field.

1 Introduction

Chairs, tables and beer mugs are three objects not usually associated with geometry. However, in an attempt to eliminate the need for intuition in geometric theorem proving, David Hilbert argued that these precise objects could replace points, lines and planes in his axiomatic approach. The now classic *Grundlagen der Geometrie* [5] combined the rules of logic with some "evident truths" or axioms to prove theorems about Euclidean space. It is generally accepted that Hilbert's work managed to eradicate the need for intuition in deriving results. This paper investigates this claim further.

We examine the first three groups of Hilbert's axiomatics, formalized for the first time in Isabelle/Isar. The organization of the paper is as follows: Section 2 briefly explains Isabelle/Isar; Section 3 presents an overview of the *Grundlagen*; Sections 4, 5 and 6 present some of the formal translations of Hilbert's axioms and reveal the important observations from the mechanical proofs; Related work is then detailed in Section 7; Section 8 describes future work and finally some concluding remarks and analysis of the work are given in Section 9.

2 Isabelle/Isar

This section briefly reviews the system and notation used for this work.

2.1 Higher Order Logic in Isabelle

Isabelle/HOL, which embodies higher order logic, is influenced by Gordon's HOL theorem prover [4] which itself originates from a classic paper by Church [2]. It provides an extensive library of theories, a powerful simplifier which accomplishes

D. Basin and B. Wolff (Eds.): TPHOLs 2003, LNCS 2758, pp. 319–334, 2003.

conditional and unconditional rewritings and several generic proof methods, including `blast` and `auto` which attempts to prove all subgoals by a combination of simplification and classical reasoning. These tools greatly help mechanization. As Isabelle/HOL is strongly typed, it ensures that only type correct terms are permitted and thus simplifies the statement of definitions and theorems.

2.2   Notation

Isar [11] is an extension of the generic theorem prover Isabelle [7], which allows more structured, readable proofs to be written. Its declarative nature seems naturally suited to formalized mathematics.

In Isabelle/HOL, "$[-\ \gamma_1;...;\gamma_n\ -] \Rightarrow \gamma$" represents an inference rule with n premises. It abbreviates to $\gamma_1 \Rightarrow (... \Rightarrow \gamma_n \Rightarrow \gamma)$ and means "if $\gamma_1 \wedge ... \wedge \gamma_n$ then γ". This notation shall be used, where necessary, to formally represent the axioms, lemmas and theorems of Hilbert's work. The alternative Isar representation "**assumes** γ_1 and ... and γ_n **shows** γ" will also be used.

It is also possible to name propositions in definitions, lemmas and proofs by "*name: proposition*". The name *?thesis* always stands for the current goal. ".." is an abbreviation for **by**(rule *name*) if *name* refers to one of the predefined introduction rules. Intermediate steps of the proof can be of the form:

from *fact1* **and** *fact2* ... **and** *propositions* (**show** — **have**) *proposition*

3   Hilbert's Axiomatics

In 1899 David Hilbert proposed a new axiomatic approach to elementary geometry. The aptly titled *Grundlagen der Geometrie* (Foundations of Geometry) gave particular emphasis to issues such as axiom classification, independence and minimality. Hilbert was also the first to abstractly link arithmetics and geometry by creating a linear and area calculus system.

Hilbert's axioms were constructed from three abstract beings, or primitives, which he named points $(A, B, C,...)$, lines $(a, b, c,...)$ and planes $(\alpha, \beta, \gamma,...)$. The 'evident truths' about the relations between these primitives were characterised by the axioms, which were classified into five groups: I. Incidence axioms, II. Order axioms, III. Congruence axioms, IV. Parallel axiom, V. Continuity axioms.

In addition to the axioms, Hilbert also included important theorems which could be derived from each group. In this development, mechanizing the theorems often required several pages of proof commands and lemmas. In what follows, rather than giving a complete formalization of each group, we discuss only some of the interesting parts.

4   Group I: The Incidence Axioms

Hilbert's first group of axioms establishes an *incidence* relation between the three primitives. Before these axioms could be formalized in Isabelle it was necessary to declare the three primitives as types, namely `pt`, `line` and `plane`. In Isabelle these types are not defined, so nothing is known about them except that they are nonempty. It was also essential to declare two binary incidence relations:

```
consts on_line :: "[pt, line] ⇒ bool"
consts in_plane :: "[pt, plane] ⇒ bool"
```

The predicates each take two arguments and represent the notion of a point lying on a line and in a plane respectively.

4.1   Some Axioms and Definitions of the First Group

The first two axioms Hilbert presented in the *Grundlagen* were:

Axiom (I,1) *For every two points A, B there exists a line that contains each of the points A, B.*

Axiom (I,2) *For every two points A, B there exists no more than one line that contains each of the points A, B.*

These axioms do not explicitly state that A and B are different points. However, when Hilbert refers to primitives of the same kind they are always assumed to be distinct. Unlike the prose, the formalizations must assert this fact:

```
AxiomI12: "A≠B ⟹ ∃! a. on_line A a ∧ on_line B a"
```

In Isabelle it is possible to combine both axioms in one statement using ∃!, which stands for 'there exists a unique'. It is interesting to note that Hilbert never refers to these axioms in his proofs. An explanation for this is revealed if Hilbert's original edition [6] is consulted: instead of using existential axioms, a constructive approach was initially taken where Axiom (I,1) was written as *"Two distinct points A and B always completely determine a straight line a and we write AB=a or BA=a"*. Hilbert was then able to write AB whenever Axiom (I,1) was applied to points A and B, without explicitly stating the axiom. However, when Hilbert later decided to change his axioms, he kept the proofs as they were, leading to this confusion[1].

Hilbert's third axiom and its formalization are:

Axiom (I,3) *There exist at least two points on a line. There exist at least three points that do not lie on a line.*

```
AxiomI3a: " ∀ a. ∃ A B . A≠B ∧ on_line A a ∧ on_line B a "
AxiomI3b: "∃ A B C. A≠B ∧ B≠C ∧ A≠C ∧ ¬collinear {A,B,C}"
```

Note that `AxiomI3b` is formalized concisely by using:

```
constdefs collinear :: "pt set ⇒ bool"
          "collinear S ≡ ∃a. ∀ A∈S. on_line A a"
```

The remaining 5 axioms of Group I are all relatively straight forward to formalize and we will not examine them due to space considerations.

---

[1] We thank one of the referees for pointing this out for us.

4.2   Some Consequences of the First Group

Hilbert states, without proofs, two theorems as consequences of the above axioms. As an example of the mechanization process in Isabelle/Isar, this section looks at part of Theorem 1 and describes the interesting aspects of its proof.

Theorem 1 *Two lines in a plane either have one point in common or none at all. Two planes have no point in common, or have one line and otherwise no point in common. A plane and a line that does not lie in it either have one point in common or none at all.*

To facilitate mechanization, we split this theorem into four subtheorems, named **onea** to **oned**; **onea** being the first statement in Theorem 1. The second statement was split into two subtheorems.

It is interesting to note that the formalization of **onea** below is not a direct translation of Hilbert's prose. It is a stronger statement as it does not require the lines to be planar. Of course the extra *plane* conditions could be added to the assumptions, but they would be redundant in the mechanical proof.

The proof strategy adopted for this theorem aims to show that if the lines *a* and *b* have two points in common then they cannot be distinct by Axiom (I, 12). The Isar proof, which proceeds by contradiction and uses the definition

```
constdefs pts_of_line :: "line ⇒ pt set"
          "pts_of_line a ≡ {A. on_line A a}"
```

is as follows:

```
theorem onea:
   assumes ab_distinct: "b≠a"
   shows "(∃ A. (pts_of_line a) ∩ (pts_of_line b) = {A}) ∨
              (pts_of_line a) ∩ (pts_of_line b) = {}"
   proof (rule ccontr)
    assume antithesis: "¬ ((∃A. pts_of_line a ∩ pts_of_line b = {A}) ∨
                           pts_of_line a ∩ pts_of_line b = {})"
    from antithesis obtain B where
     "(∀A. pts_of_line a ∩ pts_of_line b ≠ {A}) ∧
       B ∈ pts_of_line a ∧ B ∈ pts_of_line b" by auto
    from this and pts_of_line_def have
    non_intersect: "∀A. {X. on_line X a} ∩ {X. on_line X b} ≠ {A}" and

    B_on_a_and_b: "on_line B a ∧ on_line B b" by auto
    from non_intersect and B_on_a_and_b obtain C where
    C_on_a_and_b: "on_line C a ∧ on_line C b" and
    C_not_B:" C≠B" by auto
    from this and AxiomI12 have
    unique_line_B_C: "∃!l. on_line B l ∧ on_line C l"
    by blast
    from unique_line_B_C and ab_distinct and B_on_a_and_b and
         C_on_a_and_b
    show "False" by auto
   qed
```

As can be seen the Isar proof is relatively structured and readable. It is possible to follow the reasoning, although the actual strategy used for the proof may not be as evident.

Another potential drawback of the current Isar proof is that the user is expected to have a clear idea of what facts need to be derived at each stage of the proof. This can be complicated. In contrast, we believe the procedural style of proof adopted in classical Isabelle allows more proof exploration. In some instances it was easier to prove theorems and lemmas using this older, though mathematically unreadable, style and then convert the proof into Isar.

The proofs of the remaining subtheorems do not bring to light any particularly interesting observations, so they will not be described here.

5 Group II: Axioms of Order

Group II axiomatizes the notion of **between** and consequently describes the idea of *ordering* points on a line and in a plane. To formalize these axioms in Isabelle we declare a ternary betweenness relation:

consts `between :: "[pt, pt, pt] ⇒ bool"`

The notation **between** A B C indicates that the "point B is between the points A and C". Occasionally this may be shortened to (ABC), as used by Hilbert.

5.1 Some Axioms and Definitions of the Second Group

Axiom (II,1) *If a point B lies between a point A and a point C then the points A, B, C are three distinct points of a line, and B also lies between C and A.*

This translates into formal logic as:

```
AxiomII1: " between A B C ⟹
            A≠B ∧ A≠C ∧ B≠C ∧ collinear{A,B,C} ∧ between C B A"
```

Axiom (II,2) *For two points A and C, there always exists at least one point B on the line AC such that C lies between A and B.*

Our first attempt to formalize Axiom (II,2) merely took a direct translation of the English prose. This required the predicate below to represent the line AC:

constdefs `line_of ::"[pt, pt] ⇒ line"`
           `"line_of A C ≡ εa. A≠C ∧ on_line A a ∧ on_line C a"`

The special Hilbert operator ϵ is used in this predicate to represent the line on which the points A and C lie [2] . It also requires that the points A and C are not identical, as a single point cannot determine a line. The use of the Hilbert operator is well defined as Axiom(I,12) states that there exists a unique line determined by any two distinct points.

---

[2] $\epsilon\, x.\ P(x)$ can be read intuitively as 'the x such that $P(x)$ holds'.

We later realised a simpler translation of Axiom (II,2), not involving `line_of`, could be obtained by using the properties of `between` carried in Axiom (II,1).

`AxiomII2: "A≠C ⟹ ∃ B. between A C B"`

Axiom(II,3) shall not be given here. Before Hilbert describes the final axiom of Group II, he gives a few definitions which are needed in the formalization.

Definition. *Consider two points, A and B, on a line a. The set of the two points A and B is called a segment, and will be denoted by AB or by BA.*

It was not clear if Hilbert meant the segment AB was the set $\{A,B\}$ or the set of all points lying on the segment. We decided to formalize the definition in the second way, as the first did not appear to be of any use for the mechanical proofs.

constdefs `segment :: "[pt, pt] ⇒ pt set"`
`        "segment A B ≡ {X. A≠B ∧ (X=A ∨ X=B ∨ (between A X B)) }"`

Definition. *The points between A and B are called the points of the segment AB. They are also said to lie inside the segment AB.*

constdefs `inside_seg :: "[pt, pt] ⇒ pt set"`
`        "inside_seg A B ≡ {X. A≠B ∧ between A X B}"`

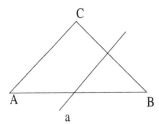

Axiom (II,4) (or Axiom of Pasch). *Let A, B, C be three points that do not lie on a line and let a be a line (in the plane ABC) which does not meet any of the points A, B, C. If the line a passes through a point of the segment AB, it also passes through a point of the segment AC, or through a point of the segment BC.*

Intuitively, this axiom reveals that if a line enters the interior of a triangle, then it also leaves it. Our formalization made use of some newly defined predicates, including: `line_on_plane` which holds if the points of a given line all lie in a given plane and `pts_in_plane` which holds if all the points in a given point set lie in the given plane. Below are two more predicates which were required for the formalization of Axiom (II,4):

constdefs `plane_of :: "[pt, pt, pt] ⇒ plane"`
`        "plane_of A B C ≡ (εz. A≠B ∧ B≠C ∧ A≠C ∧`
`                          ¬collinear {A,B,C} ∧`
`                          pts_in_plane {A,B,C} z )"`

constdefs `line_meets_seg :: "[line, pt, pt] ⇒ bool"`
`        "line_meets_seg a A B ≡ (∃ C∈inside_seg A B. on_line C a)"`

`AxiomII4: "⟦ ¬collinear {A,B,C};`
`            line_on_plane a (plane_of A B C); line_meets_seg a A B;`
`            ¬on_line A a; ¬on_line B a; ¬on_line C a`
`          ⟧ ⟹ (line_meets_seg a A C ∨ line_meets_seg a B C)"`

It is important to notice that the predicate `line_meets_seg` does not hold if the line meets the endpoints of the given segment. Also note that in Axiom (II,4) it is not necessary to state that A, B and C are distinct, as this can be derived from the fact that the three points are noncollinear.

5.2   Some Consequences of the Second Group

Hilbert presented eight theorems which were consequences of the above axioms. Undoubtedly these theorems were much harder to prove formally than those of Group I. Theorem 3 has been chosen as a case study of the mechanical proofs of this Group. Other theorems which shall not be discussed in this paper involve ordering collinear points.

Theorem 3: *For two points A and C there always exists at least one point D on the line AC that lies between A and C.*

theorem three: " $A \neq C \implies \exists\ D.$ between A D C"

As with the formal translation of Axiom (II,2), this formalization is made concise due to the properties of **between**. The *Grundlagen* proof of Theorem 3 is shown below.

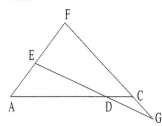

Grundlagen proof:
By Axiom (I,3) there exists a point E outside the line AC, and by Axiom (II,2) there exists on AE a point F such that E is a point of the segment AF. By the same axiom and by Axiom (II,3) there exists on FC a point G, that does not lie on the segment FC. By Axiom (II,4) the line EG must then intersect the segment AC at a point D. □

Hilbert accompanied his proof with the above diagram. Although the mechanical proof follows the same strategy as Hilbert's, it highlights that this diagram allowed Hilbert to make many implicit assumptions.

Several lemmas were required in the Isar proof. These shall not be shown explicitly as it is clear from the Isar proof how each lemma behaves. The Isar proof of Theorem 3 now follows:

theorem three:
    assumes A_not_C : "$A \neq C$"
    shows "$\exists$ D. between A D C"
    proof -
from A_not_C **and** AxiomI3b **and** intro_pt_not_on_line **obtain** E **where**
    A_not_E: "$A \neq E$" **and** E_not_on_AC: "$\neg$on_line E (line_of A C)"
by blast

from A_not_E **and** AxiomII2 **obtain** F **where** AEF:"between A E F" **by** blast
    from this and AxiomII1 **have**
        "$A \neq E \wedge A \neq F \wedge E \neq F \wedge$ collinear{A,E,F} $\wedge$ between F E A" **by** blast
    then have

```
  A_not_F: "A≠F" and E_not_F: "E≠F" and AEF_coll: "collinear{A,E,F}"
by auto

from A_not_C and E_not_on_AC and noncollinear have
  not_coll_ACE: "¬collinear{A,C,E}" by blast
from this and AEF_coll and different_pts have
  F_not_C: "F≠C" by blast
from this and AxiomII2 obtain G where FCG:"between F C G" by blast
from this and AxiomII1 have "between G C F" by auto
from this and AxiomII3 have not_CGF: "¬between C G F" by blast

from FCG and A_not_C and A_not_E and A_not_F and E_not_F and
     AEF and AEF_coll and not_coll_ACE and F_not_C and
     Hilberts_missing_assumptions have
 not_coll_AFC:"¬collinear{A,F,C}" and
 A_not_on_EG: "¬on_line A (line_of E G)" and
 F_not_on_EG: "¬on_line F (line_of E G)" and
 C_not_on_EG: "¬on_line C (line_of E G)" and
 EG_meets_AF: "line_meets_seg (line_of E G) A F" and
 EG_on_planeAFC: "line_on_plane (line_of E G) (plane_of A F C)"
by auto

from not_coll_AFC and EG_on_planeAFC and A_not_on_EG and
  F_not_on_EG and C_not_on_EG and EG_meets_AF and AxiomII4
have EG_meets_AC_or_FC: " line_meets_seg (line_of E G) A C ∨
                      line_meets_seg (line_of E G) F C" by blast

from E_not_F and AEF_coll and not_coll_ACE and F_not_C and
     FCG and E_not_F and AEF_coll and not_coll_ACE and not_CGF and
     line_not_meet_seg have
 "¬line_meets_seg (line_of E G) F C" by blast

from this and EG_meets_AC_or_FC and line_meets_seg_def and
     inside_seg_def obtain X where "between A X C" by blast
thus ?thesis ..
qed
```

By comparing our proof to Hilbert's, it can be seen that there are many differences. Recall that Hilbert's first step used Axiom(I,3) to introduce the point E, with the property that it did not lie on the line AC. Proving this mechanically also required using a lemma called intro_pt_not_on_line, which had to show the existence of the line AC. This lemma also allowed the fact $A \neq E$ to be shown. Despite this being important to the rest of the proof, Hilbert does not prove it explicitly. Instead this fact is assumed to hold through the use of the accompanying diagram. This observation disagrees with popular belief that Hilbert's work does not incorporate diagrammatic reasoning.

Hilbert's strategy of applying Axiom (II,2) to the fact $A \neq E$ is then followed. This introduces the point F such that (AEF). Hilbert then glosses over the fact that Axiom (II,1) needs to be applied in order to derive $A{\neq}F$, $E{\neq}F$ and $collinear\{A, E, F\}$. Once again these facts are implicit in the diagram.

Before Hilbert's next step of applying Axiom (II,2) to obtain (FCG), it is first essential to prove that $F{\neq}C$. This complicates the mechanical proof but reveals the subtle points of reasoning taken for granted. In order to achieve this fact several lemmas were applied; one called `noncollinear` followed by a lemma called `different_pts`. Hilbert then suggested that Axiom (II,3) be applied to show that G did not lie on the segment FC. However, due to the way this axiom is formalized Axiom (II,1) had to be applied first.

The *Grundlagen* proof then applied Axiom(II,4). This was not possible in the mechanical proof until all nine assumptions of the axiom were present. By examining the proof state it was observed that six facts (e.g `not_coll_AFC`, `A_no_on_EG` etc.) still needed to be derived. `Hilberts_missing_assumptions` was a lemma used to achieve this. Its proof was difficult, especially having to show that EG lay on the plane AFC. Hilbert failed to mention these difficulties.

Another major difference between Hilbert's proof and the mechanical one emerged after the application of Axiom (II,4). Hilbert assumes that this axiom shows that EG must intersect the segment AC. He completely ignores the fact that this axiom also shows that EG could intersect the segment FC. This second case has to be shown to be false before the proof is complete. This was a nontrivial task, captured by a lemma called `line_not_meet_seg` used in the proof . The proof of this lemma needed theorem `onea`.

It is interesting to note that the prevailing assumption in mathematics is that Hilbert's proofs seem less intuitive, but have increased rigour. The Isar proof shows that Hilbert's work can be made even more rigorous by machine assistance. Hilbert clearly used a diagram to aid geometric intuition and make many assumptions. This seems to disagree with his claim that no geometric intuition was needed to derive the theorems presented in the *Grundlagen*.

6   Group III: Axioms of Congruence

The third group of Hilbert's axioms introduces the idea of *congruence* between segments and angles. Segment congruence is declared as a primitive relation:

```
consts cong_segs :: "[pt set, pt set] ⇒ bool"
```

6.1   Some Axioms and Definitions of the Third Group

Axiom (III,1) *If A, B are two points on a line a, and A′ is a point on the same or another line a′ then it is always possible to find a point B′ on a given side of the line a′ through A′ such that the segment AB is congruent or equal to the segment A′B′. In symbols $AB \equiv A′B′$.*

The mechanization showed that the phrase *'on a given side of the line'* was crucial to the axiom. The implicit notion of a particular side of the line $a′$, was formalized by showing that two points $B′$ and $C′$ could be found on the line

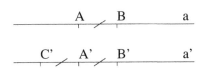

a' such that each point lay on opposite sides of A', and furthermore the segments $A'B'$ and $A'C'$ were both congruent to the segment AB. This is formalized in AxiomIII1.

```
AxiomIII1: "[ A≠B; on_line A a; on_line B a; on_line A' a']
    ⟹ ∃ B' C'.  on_line B' a' ∧ on_line C' a' ∧ between C' A' B' ∧
                cong_segs (segment A B) (segment A' B') ∧
                cong_segs (segment A B) (segment A' C') "
```

The *possibility of* constructing congruent *segments* is achieved by this axiom. The fact that the segment AB has the same point set as the segment BA is trivially proved in Isabelle by expanding the formal definition of segment. This is important, especially when proving the theorems of Group III mechanically.

Due to lack of space, we shall not describe the second and third axioms here. The last two axioms of Group III concern angles. The construction of angles is dealt in the same manner as that of segments. As Hilbert defines an angle in terms of a *ray*, it is first necessary to formalize this concept:

```
constdefs ray :: "[pt,pt] => pt set"
          "ray X A ≡ {P. X≠A ∧ ( P=A ∨ between X P A ∨ between X A P)}"
```

Note that **ray** takes two points; the first being the point the ray emanates from. The use of the **between** relation introduces the concept of the ray having a direction. This is implied by Hilbert in his definition and is important in mechanizing the later theorems.

Definition *Let α be a plane and h, k any two distinct rays emanating from O in α and lying in distinct lines. The pair of rays h, k is called an angle and is denoted by $\angle (h, k)$ or by $\angle (k, h)$.*

The above concept is captured by a relational definition:

```
constdefs angle :: "pt set set ⟹ bool"
          "angle {ray O A, ray O B} ≡ O≠A ∧ O≠B ∧ A≠B ∧
                              ¬collinear{O,A,B}"
```

The predicate **angle** takes two objects of type **point set**, in this case two rays. It is implicit in the fact {ray O B, ray O C} that both rays emanate from the same point. It is also implicit that both rays lie in distinct lines, using the fact ¬collinear{O,A,B}. Notice that it is redundant to state that the two rays lie in the same plane, as it can be shown that the angle must lie in the plane defined by the three points O, A and B. Degenerate and obtuse angles are excluded by Hilbert's definition. Hilbert then defined the notion of the *interior* angle.

Definition *Let the ray h lie on the line h' and the ray k on the line k'. The rays h and k together with the point O partition the points of the plane into two regions. All points that lie on the same side of k as those on h, and also those that lie on the same side of h' as those on k, are said to lie in the **interior** of the angle $\angle(h, k)$.*

This definition proved difficult to comprehend let alone formalize, especially since it was not accompanied by a diagram. Eventually it was decided to express the interior of an angle as:

```
constdefs interior_angle :: "pt set set ⇒ pt set"
        "interior_angle {h,k} ≡
            {P. ∀ A B. pt_on_ray A h ∧ pt_on_ray B k ∧
                angle {h,k} ∧ between A P B }"
```

where `pt_on_ray` is a defined predicate that holds if a point lies on a ray.

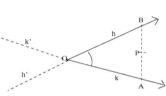

This formal definition is better understood by referring to the diagram. The set of points which are returned are precisely those points which lie between two points lying on opposite rays of the angle. The vertex and the points which lie on the sides of the angle are excluded from the set of interior points.

It is now possible for the primitive relation of angle congruence to be declared:

```
consts cong_angles :: "[ pt set set, pt set set] ⇒ bool"
```

As there is no requirement stating that the two objects of type `pt set set` are angles, this condition must be carried whenever `cong_angles` is reasoned about.

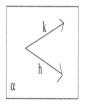
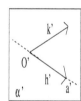

Axiom (III,4) *Let ∠(h, k) be an angle in a plane α and a' a line in a plane α' be given. Let h' be a ray on the line a' that emanates from the point O'. Then there exists in the plane α' one and only one ray k' such that the angle ∠(h, k) is congruent or equal to the angle ∠(h', k') and at the same time all interior points of the angle ∠(h', k') lie on the given side of a'. Symbolically ∠(h, k) ≡ ∠(h', k'). Every angle is congruent to itself.*

Hilbert did not accompany this axiom with the above diagram, but it has been included to aid understanding. Hilbert's second statement is formalized as:

```
AxiomIII4b: " angle {h,k} ⟹ cong_angles {h,k} {h,k}"
```

Before the first part of Axiom (III,4) could be formally represented in Isabelle we defined several predicates: `ray_on_line` holds if all points of a given ray lie on the given line; `angle_in_plane` holds if all interior points of a given angle lie in the given plane; `angle_in_region` holds if all interior points of a given angle are contained in a given point set. The formal translation of Axiom (III,4a) is shown below with another necessary predicate:

```
constdefs region_of_plane :: "[plane, line] ⇒ pt set"
        "region_of_plane α a ≡
            εr. ∀ A B. A≠B ∧ in_plane A α ∧ in_plane B α ∧
                line_on_plane a α ∧ ¬line_meets_seg a A B
                ⟶ A∈r ∧ B∈r"
```

```
AxiomIII4a:"[ angle_in_plane {h,k} α ; line_on_plane a' α';
          ray_on_line h' a' ]
      ⟹ ∃! k'. angle_in_region {h', k'} (region_of_plane α' a')
            ∧ cong_angles {h,k} {h',k'} "
```

Note that a particular region of the plane α' has to be specified with respect to the line a'. This is achieved by the predicate region_of_plane and is a necessary requirement in order to capture the idea that the interior points of $\angle (h', k')$ lie *on a given side* of the line a'. Without this relation it would be false to say that k' was unique. This will prove to be important to the mechanization of theorems in this group.

The second fact to pay particular attention to is that although Hilbert's prose explicitly states that the ray h' emanates from a point O', this seems to be a redundant phrase, and so was left out of this formalization.

Before Hilbert's last axiom of congruence, another definition is given:

Definition *An angle with a vertex B on one of whose sides lies a point A and on whose other side lies a point C will also be denoted by $\angle$ ABC or briefly by $\angle$ B.*

This definition can be associated with the angle of a triangle; a useful fact for formalizing the fifth axiom of this group. Therefore, it was necessary to define the notion of a triangle before formalizing this definition.

```
constdefs  triangle :: "[pt, pt, pt] ⟹ bool"
           "triangle A B C ≡ A≠B ∧ A≠C ∧ B≠C ∧ ¬collinear{A,B,C}"

constdefs angle_of_tri :: "[pt, pt, pt] ⟹ pt set set"
          "angle_of_tri A B C ≡ (εa. triangle A B C ∧
                              a={ray B A, ray B C})"
```

Using this last definition, the angle {ray B A, ray B C} can now be represented in Isabelle as angle_of_tri A B C. This allows certain formalizations to be clearer, as can be seen in the formal translation of Axiom (III,5).

Axiom (III,5) *If for two triangles ABC and A'B'C' the congruences $AB \equiv A'B'$, $AC \equiv A'C'$, $\angle BAC \equiv \angle B'A'C'$ hold, then the congruence $\angle ABC \equiv \angle A'B'C'$ is also satisfied.*

```
AxiomIII5: "[ triangle A B C ; triangle A' B' C' ;
             cong_segs (segment A B) (segment A' B') ;
             cong_segs (segment A C) (segment A' C') ;
             cong_angles (angle_of_tri B A C) (angle_of_tri B' A' C')
          ] ⟹ cong_angles (angle_of_tri A B C) (angle_of_tri A' B' C')"
```

6.2   Some Consequences of the Third Group

Hilbert states several theorems which are consequences of the above axioms. The interesting aspects of the mechanization of Theorem 12 are described next.

Theorem 12 of the *Grundlagen* deals with congruent triangles. It is therefore necessary to first define the notion of a *congruent triangle*.

Definition *A triangle ABC is said to be congruent to a triangle A'B'C' if all congruences* $AB \equiv A'B'$, $AC \equiv A'C'$, $BC \equiv B'C'$, $\angle\, ABC \equiv \angle\, A'B'C'$, $\angle\, BAC \equiv \angle\, B'A'C'$, $\angle\, ACB \equiv \angle\, A'C'B'$ *are satisfied.*

The formalization of this definition is not shown here, but note that it uses the representation `cong_triangles (A,B,C) (A',B',C')` to mean that two triangles, *ABC* and *A'B'C'*, are congruent.

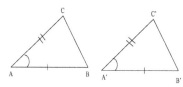

Theorem 12 (first congruence theorem for triangles):
A triangle ABC is congruent to a triangle A'B'C' whenever the congruence $AB \equiv A'B'$, $AC \equiv A'C'$, $\angle\, BAC \equiv \angle\, B'A'C'$ *hold.*

```
theorem twelve: "⟦ triangle A B C; triangle A' B' C';
                 cong_segs (segment A B) (segment A' B');
                 cong_segs (segment A C) (segment A' C');
                 cong_angles (angle_of_tri B A C)
                             (angle_of_tri B' A' C')
             ⟧ ⟹ cong_triangles (A,B,C) (A',B',C')"
```

Hilbert's proof is shown below:

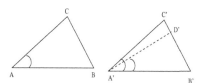

Fig. 1. Diagram accompanying Grundlagen Proof of Theorem 12

By Axiom (III,5) the congruences $\angle\, ABC \equiv \angle\, A'B'C'$ *and* $\angle\, ACB \equiv \angle\, A'C'B'$ *are satisfied and thus it is only necessary to prove the validity of the congruence* $BC \equiv B'C'$. *If it is assumed to the contrary that BC is not congruent to B'C' and a point D' is determined on B'C' so that* $BC \equiv B'D'$ *then Axiom (III,5) applied to both triangles ABC and A'B'D', will indicate that* $\angle\, BAC \equiv \angle\, B'A'D'$. *Then* $\angle\, BAC$ *would be congruent to* $\angle\, B'A'D'$ *as well as to* $\angle\, B'A'C'$. *This is impossible, as by Axiom (III,4) every angle can be constructed on a given side of a given ray in a plane in only one way. It has thus been proved that the triangle ABC is congruent to the triangle A'B'C'.*   □

The mechanical proof of Theorem 12 was a challenging task in Isabelle. Proving that $\angle\, ABC \equiv \angle\, A'B'C'$ and $\angle\, ACB \equiv \angle\, A'C'B'$, was reasonably simple. However, proving that *BC* was congruent to *B'C'* was a lengthy process. As Hilbert suggested, it was assumed that *BC* was not congruent to *B'C'* and a proof by contradiction was carried out. Note that Hilbert introduces a point *D'* so that $BC \equiv B'D'$, but does not state how to achieve this. It was observed that an application of Axiom (III,1) was required. However, an application of this axiom had the effect of introducing the following additional facts into the goal:

```
on_line D' (line_of B' C')     on_line E' (line_of B' C')
between D' B' E'
cong_segs (segment B C) (segment B' D')
cong_segs (segment B C) (segment B' E')
```

Observe that a point E' has been introduced and that two distinct segments, namely $B'D'$ and $B'E'$, can be congruent to BC. This is where the mechanical proof differed from that of Hilbert's (compare Fig. 1 and Fig. 2), where only the case $B'D'$ being congruent to BC is considered.

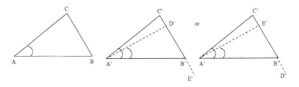

Fig. 2. Diagram accompanying Mechanical Proof of Theorem 12

The *Grundlagen* proof did not explicitly state where the point D' had to lie on the line $B'C'$. This information was implicit in the diagram. Unfortunately the mechanization must consider the possibility that either D' or E' lies on the desired side of the line $B'C'$.

The goal then had to be split into two cases; one case where the ray $B'C'$ was equal to the ray $B'D'$ and one case where the ray $B'C'$ was equal to the ray $B'E'$. This shows whether it is the point D' or the point E' which lies on the desired side of the line $B'C'$.

Another difficulty in the mechanical proof was encountered when applying Axiom (III,4a). In the first case split this required obtaining the fact that $\angle B'A'C'$ and $\angle B'A'D'$ lay in the same plane and more importantly in the same region. Many trivial lemmas were needed to obtain these facts, complicating the mechanization. Interestingly, Hilbert's proof assumed these facts were true.

The previous sections have highlighted a few of the differences between the mechanized and original versions of the *Grundlagen*. Next we examine some related and future work and draw our conclusions.

7   Related Work

The task of mechanizing Hilbert's *Grundlagen* has been attempted before. An alternative approach was proposed by Dehlinger, Dufourd and Schreck [3]. Similar to our research, a mechanical higher-order logical framework was used. However, their work only focused on Groups I and II in Coq and investigated an intuitionistic approach to proving Hilbert's theorems.

The main goal in their work was to investigate constructive proofs for Hilbert's theorems. However, they discovered that most of the theorems could not be proved in this manner. In fact a weaker version of each theorem could be proved constructively, but to yield a complete proof it was necessary to define the excluded middle axiom, or equivalently the axiom of decidability of point equality. This was not necessary in Isabelle as a classical logic framework was used, allowing proofs by refutation. Given the restrictions of their approach, it is hard to compare their formal versions of the axioms, proofs and other concepts with Hilbert's original formulation. Their work also differed from this paper as it did not emphasise any of the implicit aspects of Hilbert's proofs.

It is worth noting that Tarski criticised Hilbert's *Grundlagen* for giving the same importance to the three primitives; points, lines and planes. He built a axiomatization for Euclidean geometry using only points as primitives. Quaife attempted to formalize Euclidean space using this approach [9]. He formally represented it using first order logic in the system OTTER and his development, like ours, suggested that automating geometric proofs is a difficult task.

The formalization of Hilbert's work also relates to the active field of research in mechanical geometry theorem proving (GTP) [10,12]. However, the highly successful coordinate free techniques, such as the signed area method [1], propose axioms that are not claimed to be minimal or complete. This contrasts greatly with Hilbert's *Grundlagen* which was a systematic axiomatic endeavour. For this reason Hilbert's work may be viewed by some as mathematically sounder. By formalizing the *Grundlagen* a more rigorous approach for GTP may emerge.

8   Further Work

We still have to mechanize many of Hilbert's theorems. This will be a challenging task in Isabelle. One problem has already been encountered regarding the formal representation of `ray`. Future work will have to be focused on, where necessary, strengthening definitions or finding alternative mechanical proofs.

Hilbert made the claim that his set of axioms were consistent, in other words no direct contradiction follows from them. One method to check the consistency of the system of axioms is to construct *models* for which all the axioms are verified. We hope to formalize a model for Hilbert's system in Isabelle.

Despite the fact that formalizing Tarski's work in Isabelle would take more effort than formalizing Hilbert's, it would be an interesting task to carry out and compare the two approaches. Using the formalization of Tarski's system, it would then be possible to discover if Hilbert's work could be derived as a consequence.

9   Conclusion

Many mathematicians believe it is impossible to define the properties of mathematical objects simply by establishing a number of axioms and that the axiomatic method is merely a reconstruction of intuitive concepts [8]. Hilbert claimed his *Grundlagen* did not concur with this belief. By formalizing the *Grundlagen* in Isabelle/Isar we showed that Hilbert's work glossed over subtle points of reasoning and relied heavily, in some cases, on diagrams which allowed implicit assumptions to be made. For this reason it can be argued that Hilbert interleaved his axioms with geometric intuition in order to prove many of his theorems. This suggests that his claim may not be not founded.

Although the mechanization of Hilbert's proofs was a long and sometimes tedious process in Isabelle/Isar, it did add rigour to Hilbert's work and reveal the potential ambiguities and omissions contained in many of his definitions, axioms and proofs.

Acknowledgements. We would like to thank the reviewers for their useful comments. This work was funded by the EPSRC grant GR/S01771/01.

References

1. S. C. Chou, X. S. Gao, and J. Z. Zhang. Automated generation of readable proofs with geometric invariants, I. multiple and shortest proof generation. *Journal of Automated Reasoning*, 17:325–347, 1996.
2. A. Church. A formulation of the simple theorey of type. *Journal of Symbolic Logic*, 5:56–68, 1940.
3. C. Dehlinger, J. Duford & P. Schreck. *Higher-Order Intuitionistic Formalization and Proofs in Hilbert's Elementary Geometry*. Automated deduction in Geometry, Springer, pages 306–323, 2001.
4. M. Gordon and T. Melham. *Introduction to HOL: A theorem proving enviroment for Higher Order Logic*. Cambridge University Press, 1993.
5. D. Hilbert. *The Foundations of Geometry*. The Open Court Company, 2001, 11th edition. Translation by Leo Unger.
6. D. Hilbert. *The Foundations of Geometry*. The Open Court Company, 1901, 1st edition. Translation by E. J. Townsend.
7. L. C. Paulson. Isabelle: A Generic Theorem Prover. *Lecture Notes in Computer Science*, Volume 828. Springer, 1994.
8. K. M. Podnieks. *Around Goedel's Theorem*. 2nd edition, Latvian State University Press, 1992.
9. A. Quaife. *Automated Development of Fundamental Mathematical Theories*. Kluwer, 1992.
10. D. Wang. Geometry Machines: From AI to SMC. *Proceedings of the 3rd International Conference on Artificial Intelligence and Symbolic Mathematical Computation (AISMC-3)*, LNCS 1138, pp. 213–239, 1996.
11. Markus Wenzel. *The Isabelle/Isar Reference Manual*. Technische Universität München, 2002.
    http://isabelle.in.tum.de/dist/Isabelle2002/doc/isar-ref.pdf.
12. W. Wu. Basic principles of mechanical theorem proving in elementary geometries. *Journal of Automated Reasoning*, 2:221–252, 1986.

Using Coq to Verify Java Card™ Applet Isolation Properties

June Andronick, Boutheina Chetali, and Olivier Ly

Schlumberger Systems – Advanced Research on Smart Cards

Abstract. This paper reports on the use of the Coq proof assistant for the formal verification of applet isolation properties in Java Card technology. We focus on the confidentiality property. We show how this property is verified by the card manager and the APIs, extending our former proof addressing the Java Card virtual machine. We also show how our verification method allows to complete specifications and to enhance the secure design of the platform. For instance, we describe how the proof of the integrity puts the light on a known bug. Finally, we present the benefits of the use of high order modelling to handle the complexity of the system, to prove security properties and eventually to construct generic re-usable proof architectures.

Keywords: Theorem Proving, Smart Card, Security.

Introduction

A multi-application smart card can hold several applications coming from different vendors of different sectors and possibly loaded after issuance. This implies a new security model that has to assure the card issuer that the embedded applications will not corrupt its system, and the application provider that its applications are protected against the other ones.

In order to face these new security needs Java Card technology strengthens the inherent security of Java technology with a complex mechanism to control the sharing of information and services between on-card applications. This mechanism is known as the *applet isolation principle*, a central security issue in Java Card technology (see [6]). This principle relies on the classical sandbox model of Java security (see [14,10,21]) which consists in partitioning on-card applications into contexts, and verifying accesses across these contexts. This verification is supposed to face two main concepts: the *integrity* and the *confidentiality* of data of applets. Confidentiality (integrity respectively) means that data are protected from any unauthorized disclosure (modification respectively).

The work described here fits in the global objective of proving the correctness of the security architecture of the Java Card platform. It deals with the formal verification of the applet isolation principle. We actually focus on the formal

D. Basin and B. Wolff (Eds.): TPHOLs 2003, LNCS 2758, pp. 335–351, 2003.

verification of the confidentiality property. Our formalization of this property relies on the classical concept of *non-interference* (see [8,9]). We define the confidentiality as a non-interference property between on-card applets, assuming that they do not provide any *shareable interfaces*.

In a former work (see [1]), we proved that the virtual machine ensures the confidentiality property. At this level, confidentiality mainly relies on the firewall mechanism used by the virtual machine which enforces a runtime checking during bytecode interpretation.

Although the virtual machine is central in Java Card technology, it fits however in a complex architecture relying on several other components, also involved in the execution process of an applet. These components are the *API* which provides system services to applets and the *card manager* which is in charge of the communication module, the dispatching of the received commands, the loading of new packages, etc. For instance, some global objects like the APDU buffer, used by the applet to communicate with the external world, are managed by the card manager, outside the control of the virtual machine. Given that the whole security depends on the weakest link, proving the confidentiality at the virtual machine level is not sufficient. Therefore, the next step consists in verifying that the confidentiality property is respected during the whole process of applet's execution including card manager specific operations and API methods executions. The work presented here extends our former work concerning the virtual machine to the card manager and the API. This consists of two main steps: the formalization of the confidentiality property for these components and its formal proof.

The formal verification relies on the formal modelling of the Java Card architecture which has been developed in FORMAVIE project[1] (see [5]). This modelling has been developed within the language of the *Calculus of (Co)Inductive Constructions* and mechanically checked using the Coq proof-assistant (see [17]).

The paper is organized as follows: Section 1 gives an overview of Java Card technology from the security point of view. Section 2 gives a brief account about the formal modelling of the Java Card architecture which has been developed in FORMAVIE project. In Section 3, we describe the proof architecture taking into account the card management on one hand, and the API on the other hand; in particular, we show how we extend the formal statement of the confidentiality to the levels of the card manager and of the API. In Section 4, we point out some results about the integrity property.

Acknowledgement. The authors acknowledge Pr. C. Paulin-Mohring for her advises for this work.

---

[1] FORMAVIE project is an R&D project in the domain of information systems, partially funded by the French government. The partners of the project are Schlumberger Systems, Trusted Logic and the French research institute INRIA.

1   Security in Java Card Technology

1.1   The Java Card Platform

A Java Card based smart card is made of (see [11]):

- The *operating system* and the *native methods*[2].
- The *Java Card virtual machine* whose task is to interpret bytecode programs (the code obtained after Java compilation) and to enforce secure data sharing between Java Card applications at runtime, in particular data confidentiality.
- The *Application Programming Interface* (API for short) which handles Java Card specific features and also provides system services to embedded applications as class or library packages.
- The *card manager* which handles the life cycle of the card and its embedded applications. It is in charge of loading Java Card applications and managing inputs and outputs.
- The *applets* which are compiled Java Card applications.

A smart card communicates with the outside world when inserted into a *Card Acceptance Device* (CAD for short). The CAD supplies the card with power and establishes a data-carrying connection. The communication between the card and the CAD is done by exchanging *Application Protocol Data Units* (APDU for short). An APDU is a data packet containing either a *command* from the host to the card or a *response* from the card to the host.

The card manager is the component which is in charge of the storage of Java Card packages, applet installation and initialization, card resource management, and communications. When the card is inserted into the CAD, first a reset occurs, then the card manager enters into a loop, waiting for APDU commands from the CAD. When an APDU command arrives, the card manager either selects an applet to run as instructed in the command or forwards the command to the running applet (the currently selected applet). By forwarding the command to the currently selected applet, we actually mean requesting from the virtual machine the execution of the **process** method of this applet. Once the processing of the command is finished, the card manager takes back the control and forwards the response to the CAD. The whole process repeats for each incoming command.

1.2   The Java Card Sandbox Model

The *applet isolation principle*, i.e. the *isolation* regarding data access between applets embedded on the same card, is central for the security of multi-applicative smart cards.

To enforce this principle, Java Card security implements a sandbox-like policy. Each applet is confined to a particular space called a *context*, which is associated to its package; and the verification of the isolation between contexts

---

[2] i.e. written in a low level language.

is enforced at runtime by a *firewall* mechanism. More precisely, each package defines a *context* and each applet it contains is associated to this context. In addition, there is a privileged context – the *JCRE context* – devoted to system operations (where JCRE stands for Java Card Runtime Environment).

Isolation of contexts relies on the concepts of *object ownership* and *active owner* which are defined as follows:

- An *owner* is either an applet instance, or the system.
- An object *belongs* to the owner who created it, i.e. the owner which was *active* when it was created. The owner is then unique, determined at the creation of the object and never changed.
- During the execution of a non-static method, the *active owner* is the owner of the object that contains the method[3].
- During the execution of a static method, the *active owner* is the one which was active during the execution of the calling method. There is an exception to this rule: to install a new applet instance, the static method `install` of the class of the applet being installed is called by the system; during this execution, the *active owner* is the applet instance to be created, instead of the JCRE context. Therefore, any applet instance belongs to itself, as all the objects it creates.

During the execution of a method, the *currently active context* is then defined as the context of the active owner (the context of the system being the JCRE context). For instance, when the card manager forwards an APDU command to the selected applet, the `process` method of the applet is invoked and its context becomes the currently active context.

An object can only be accessed by a subject within the same context, i.e. when the object's context is the currently active context. Object accesses *across contexts* are allowed only in the four following cases:

1. Services and resources provided by the system (the *entry point objects*) belong to the JCRE context, but can be accessed by any object.
2. Applets and the system can share data through *global arrays* like the byte array parameter of the method `install` or the APDU buffer. These global arrays can be accessed from any context. However references to them cannot be stored; this avoids their re-use in non specified situations.
3. When the currently active context is the JCRE context, methods and fields of any object can be accessed.
4. Interaction between applets of different contexts is possible via *shareable interfaces*: when a given applet wants to make some methods available for other applets of different contexts, it provides an object whose class implements a shareable interface, i.e. an interface which extends the interface `javacard.framework.Shareable`. Such an interface defines a set of methods, that are the services that the applet in question makes accessible to other applets. These methods can be invoked *from any context.*

---

[3] Let us note that Java Card technology does not provide any multi-thread mechanism.

1.3   The Firewall

To enforce the isolation between the contexts, Java Card technology provides a dynamic check of these rules by the *firewall* (see [11]). This means that for each bytecode instruction (`getfield`, `putfield` ...), a specific set of rules is defined. When the virtual machine interprets a bytecode instruction, it checks that the access conditions specified by the firewall rules are fulfilled. If they are not, a `SecurityException` is thrown.

The execution of a method m of a given applet consists of the interpretation of the successive bytecode instructions of m, including the execution of the methods of the API which are called in m. But the firewall mechanism enforced by the virtual machine only occurs during the bytecode interpretation, i.e. when the virtual machine interprets the methods written in Java. In particular, both the operations done by the card manager and the execution of API methods which are not written in Java are not under the control of the firewall.

On the one hand, the API methods are mostly implemented as *native*[4] methods. For instance, the method `javacard.framework.Util.arrayCopy(...)` is native for obvious performance reasons; while `javacard.framework.JCSystem.beginTransaction()` is intrinsically native because it is a direct request to the system. This implies that firewall rules cannot be directly applied in this context since there is no bytecode instruction interpretation. Moreover no security mechanism is specified for the execution of API methods; decisions are left to the developer. However, such a mechanism is crucial for Java Card security to make sense. For example, let us consider the method `static short arrayCopy(byte[] src, short srcOff, byte[] dest, short destOff, short length)` of the class `javacard.framework.Util`. This method intends to copy an array of length `length` from the specified source `src` to the specified destination array `dest` according to offsets `srcOff` and `destOff`. No security constraints are imposed by the specifications about the owners of `src` and `dest`. Therefore, without any additional constraints on the use of this API method, any applet could steal the contents of any array of any other context, which definitely is contrary to Java Card security goals. Therefore, some security constraints must be added to the specification. In this case, the situation is clear: by extension of the firewall rules, we have to impose that `src` and `dest` both are accessible from the context of execution, i.e. the context of the caller of the method since this last one is static; if not, a `SecurityException` must be thrown.

On the other hand, some information flow may also rely on the operations occuring during the card management. For instance, such a flow could rely on some of the globally shared resources (such as the APDU buffer, or the byte array parameter) used by the card manager to communicate with applets. However, unlike the case of the API, some security rules are specified for the card manager. Still, the fact that these rules are sufficient to ensure the isolation of applets remains to be proved.

---

[4] i.e. written in a low level language.

The purpose here is thus to prove that under suitable conditions, the principle of isolation of applets holds for all the life cycle of a Java Card based smart card, from the card manager specific operations to the interpretation of each bytecode instruction of a method of an applet, including calls to API methods.

2   The Modelling of Java Card Technology

Here we present the formal modelling of the Java Card platform developed in FORMAVIE project (see [5]) on which the proof is based. The JCVM and the card manager have been formally modelled in the Coq system ([17]). This modelling is exhaustive regarding Sun specification (see [11]). Moreover a part of the API has also been modelled.

2.1   The Virtual Machine

The Java Card virtual machine has been modelled as a *state machine*, the JCVM. A *JCVM state* encloses all the data needed by the virtual machine to interpret bytecode instructions. It contains for example a *heap* which is an association table mapping references to object instances. Whereas a *JCVM transition* between two JCVM states represents the execution of a single bytecode instruction. The definition of this state machine is fully described in [1].

2.2   The Card Manager

The card manager is in charge of managing the whole life cycle of the card. The card life is divided into sessions. A session is the period from the time a card is inserted into the CAD and is powered up until the time the card is removed from the CAD. During a session, the card manager is in charge of dispatching the commands it receives and returning the responses to the CAD. The modelling of the card manager thus involves several concepts, depending on the level of abstraction.

At the highest level, the card manager can be seen as a relation between an infinite sequence of commands and an infinite sequence of responses, according to an initial state of the JCVM. In accordance with the partitioning of the card life into sessions, these sequences are represented by streams respectively defined by:

```
Definition card_in := (Stream input_card_session).
Definition card_out := (Stream output_card_session).
```

where `input_card_session` represents a list of *commands* and `output_card_session` a list of *responses*. A response is defined by:

```
Inductive typ_response : Set :=  Success : typ_response
                              | OutData : (list byte) -> typ_response
                              | Atr    : typ_response
                              | Fail   : status_word -> typ_response.
```

```
Inductive response : Set := NoResponse : response
                          | Response   : typ_response -> response.
```

The definition of a command is the generalization of the notion of APDU command (describing only the selection of an applet and a plain command), in order to take into account all the features of the card manager, such as the installation of applets or the loading of packages:

```
Inductive command : Set :=
    Select        : apdu_comm -> command
  | Command       : apdu_comm -> command
  | Load_File     : cap_format -> command
  | Install       : aid -> package_info -> install_params -> command
  | Load_Install  : cap_format -> aid -> package_info ->
                    install_params -> command
  | Reset         : command.
```

The card manager is then represented by the co-inductive type:

```
card_life : card_in -> jcre_state -> card_out -> Prop.
```

where the state records the packages installed on the card, together with the state of the JCVM:

```
Record jcre_state : Set := JCRE_State
    { installed_packages : package_table; execution_state :> jcvm_state }.
```

The card_life is defined as an infinite sequence of sessions. Each session is in turn modelled inductively using the modelling of the dispatching of a single command. This last one is modelled by the predicate[5]:

```
dispatcher: package_table -> jcvm_state -> command ->
            package_table -> jcvm_state -> response -> Prop.
```

that associates to an initial state of the JCVM and a received command, a final state resulting from the execution of this command and an output response to be sent back to the CAD. This predicate takes into account a set of loaded packages and defines a new set of packages if a loading of new packages has occurred.

The execution of an APDU command involves the interpretation of the process method by the virtual machine, including possible calls to API methods. For instance, the receiving of the command Select apdu causes an applet to become the currently selected applet. This applet is the one associated to the AID (Application IDentifier) mentioned in the argument apdu of the command. Prior to the selection, the card manager shall deselect the previously selected applet, by invoking its deselect method. Then it informs the applet of selection by invoking its select method. The applet may refuse to be selected by returning false or by throwing an exception. If it returns true, the actual Select apdu command is supplied to the applet in a subsequent call to its process method. The process method is then interpreted by the virtual machine. The interpretation ends in a final state, returning the result of the method. The card manager analyses this value and sends a response to the CAD.

---

[5] let us note that HOL predicates are encoded as Coq inductive types.

2.3   Modelling the API

The formal specification of each method of the API is defined by pre and post conditions expressed on the JCVM states. These conditions are defined in a relational way as inductive types.

Precondition. For each method, the precondition specifies the necessary conditions on the JCVM state for the method to be invoked. It mainly defines the form of the operand stack, which contains the arguments of the method. In particular, it specifies the types of these arguments.

Postcondition. The postcondition of a method specifies the returned value of the method, together with the JCVM state resulting from the execution of the method. Let us note that the result may be the throwing of an exception. Postconditions of API methods have to specify the resulting JCVM state because some methods of the API are used as system entry points, i.e. they are used to send requests to the system. This is the case of methods of the class `JCSystem`. For instance, methods like `beginTransaction()` or `commitTransaction()` allow applets to use the transaction mechanism, which is managed by the system; therefore, the specification of these methods describe their effects on the state of the system itself, and especially the part dealing with transaction.

Example. Let us consider for instance the method `boolean equals(byte[] bArray, short offset, byte length)` of the class `AID` which checks if the specified AID bytes in `bArray` (the ones starting at `offset` in `bArray` and of length `length`) are the same as those encapsulated in `this` AID object instance. The precondition of this method specifies that at the invocation, the operand stack must have the form:

byte	short	reference	reference	...

where the first item represents `length`, the second one `offset`, the third one `bArray` and the fourth one the reference, let us say `ref`, to the object instance of class AID on which the method is called. On top of the required types, the precondition specifies that `ref` must be different from the `null` reference. The modelling of this precondition in Coq is straightforward and is not described here. Let us note that the precondition does not specify that `bArray` must be different from `null`. Indeed in this case, the specification of the method is that a `NullPointerException` must be thrown by the method; therefore, this is a part of the behaviour of the method which is specified by the postcondition.

The postcondition is defined as an inductive type of signature
`equals_post_cond: jcvm_state -> equals_info -> method_state_result -> Prop`.
This relation specifies the returned value of the method together with the resulting JCVM state from the initial state at method invocation and the arguments. The returned value and the resulting state are both enclosed in a term of type `method_state_result`. The arguments are enclosed in a term of type `equals_info` defined by the precondition from the initial state.

All the postconditions of API methods follow the same scheme; in particular, the signature of each postcondition is the following:
`jcvm_state -> pre_info -> method_state_result -> Prop`
where the type `pre_info` depends on the method being specified.

3 A Formal Validation Method Based on Coq

3.1 Formalization of the Confidentiality

In [1], the confidentiality property has been formally stated at the level of the virtual machine. Here the formalization is extended in order to address the card manager level.

Non-interference. Our modelling of the confidentiality is based on the classical concept of *non-interference* (see [8,9,18]) which states that the confidentiality of data is ensured if the values of these confidential data have no effect on the behaviour of external entities.

In our framework, we consider a context C, a selected applet α not belonging to C and a received command c which does not request the selection of an applet of C (see Remark 2 at the end of this section). We want to verify that there is no disclosure of data of the context C during the processing of c by α. Let $\mathcal{F}_C(s)$ denote the contents of the fields of all objects belonging to C, i.e. the data to be protected, and $\mathcal{F}_{\overline{C}}(s)$ the contents of the fields of all objects *not* belonging to C.

Let us consider two states s_1 and s'_1 of the JCVM that may differ only on data of the context C. This means that we have $\mathcal{F}_{\overline{C}}(s_1) = \mathcal{F}_{\overline{C}}(s'_1)$ and that nothing is assumed on the values of neither $\mathcal{F}_C(s_1)$ nor on the ones of $\mathcal{F}_C(s'_1)$.

Then, the confidentiality is ensured if the two processings of the same command c from s_1 and s'_1 respectively leads to two final states s_2 and s'_2 that may differ only on data of the context C, and to two responses that are equal.

Equivalence of JCVM states. The simple equality of the states up to the confidential data is too restrictive and a notion of equivalent states is in fact needed. Indeed, when the virtual machine interprets the bytecode **new**, it needs a fresh reference. This fresh reference is retrieved from the operating system of the card, whose mechanism is not specified. This operation is non-deterministic. But the execution of the bytecode **new** on two states that are equivalent should lead to equivalent states, even if the fresh references which have been used are different. So, we must consider the equality of terms concerned *up to a one-to-one mapping of references*. But such a mapping can only be defined on references appearing on the heap. Therefore the JCVM state equivalence is only defined for *consistent* states, where a JCVM state is said to be consistent regarding references (consistent for short) if it contains in its data structures only null references or references appearing as index in the heap.

We can now define the equivalence of JCVM states up to one context.

Definition 1 (JCVM State Equivalence up to a Context).
Two consistent JCVM states s and s' are said to be equivalent up to the context C, which is denoted by $s \sim_C s'$, if there exists a one-to-one mapping φ such that all the components of s' except the heap, as well as the objects of the heap not belonging to C, are obtained from their counter-parts in s by replacing any reference ρ by $\varphi(\rho)$. No assumption is done about objects belonging to C.

Hypotheses. Let us now look at the hypotheses we have to assume to state a coherent definition of the confidentiality. We must assume that C does not provide any shareable interfaces, since it corresponds to one of the four cases where access across context is authorized (see page 338). Moreover, α is the selected applet in the initial state s_1 (and thus in s_1'), and therefore we have to suppose that this applet does not belong to C, otherwise the objects belonging to C could be accessed by any applet and in particular by α. For the same reasons, we must assume that the received command does not request the selection of an applet belonging to C. Finally, C must be different from the JCRE context since objects belonging to the JCRE context can be accessed from any context.

Statement. We are now able to state a formal definition of the confidentiality:

Definition 2 (Confidentiality Property).
Let C be a context different from the JCRE context, which does not provide any shareable interfaces. Let s_1 and s_1' be two consistent states such that $s_1 \sim_C s_1'$. Let us assume that the selected applet in s_1 does not belong to C. Let c be a command received from the CAD which is not a command of selection of an applet of the context C. Let s_2 (s_2' respectively) and r (r' respectively) be the state and the response resulting from the processing of c from s_1 (s_1' respectively). Then $s_2 \sim_C s_2'$ and $r = r'$.

Remark 1. This definition specifies the confidentiality at the level of the processing of a single command, i.e. concerning the `dispatcher` predicate. This processing of the command is specified from a JCVM state, according to loaded packages. But the generalization to the card life is easily defined by stating that the executions of the same stream of inputs from two equivalent JCRE states respectively lead to the same stream of output. At this upper level, JCRE states are considered, enclosing the JCVM state and the loaded packages used by the `dispatcher` predicate.

Remark 2. The confidentiality property does not address commands which request the selection of an applet of the context C. The processing of such a command puts into action the applet to be selected, say β, in the context C. In particular, β becomes the active owner and C the currently active context[6]. As mentioned on page 341, the method β.`process(apdu)` is then invoked. During the execution of this method, β can read or modify the data belonging to its own context, i.e., C. Actually β is responsible for protection of its context's data. In particular, it must ensure that no information disclosure may occur through the execution of its method `process` or within the response sent back to the CAD. Since this execution depends on the argument `apdu` for which β is not responsible, β can deny its selection according to its proper security policy defined at the level of the application, and not of the system.

---

[6] See page 338 for the definition of active owner and currently active context.

3.2   Formal Verification

Architecture

The verification of the isolation of applets has to be done at each step of the execution of a command received from the CAD. These steps are the following ones.
1) First, a pre-treatment is performed by the card manager in order to "prepare" the initial state of the JCVM. For instance, if the command has to be processed by the selected applet, the method `public void process (APDU apdu)` of this last one is called with the *APDU object* in argument. This APDU object is an instance of the `APDU` class, created by the card manager from the data contained in the received APDU command. Let us denote by $\overset{CM}{\leadsto}$ such a treatment of the card manager.
2) Then the method (either `process, install, select` or `deselect`) is interpreted by the virtual machine. This interpretation consists of a finite sequence of transitions. Each transition can be either a JCVM transition (denoted by $\overset{VM}{\longrightarrow}$), i.e. the execution of a single bytecode instruction, or a call to a method m of the API (denoted by $\overset{API(m)}{\longrightarrow}$), i.e. a relation between the state at the call of m and the resulting state obtained after the full execution of m.
3) Finally, the card manager performs final operations (also denoted by $\overset{CM}{\leadsto}$) in order to build the response to send to the CAD according to the returned value of the method, and also to prepare the state to receive the following command, including for instance the zeroing of the APDU buffer.

Let us note however that the processing of some commands may not involve the JCVM such as the loading of a new package.

The verification of the isolation at the level of the card manager implies a proof at each step of this process:

$$\ldots \overset{CM}{\leadsto} \overset{c_i}{\underset{r_i}{\bigcirc}} \overset{CM}{\leadsto} \bigcirc \overset{VM}{\longrightarrow} \bigcirc \overset{API(m)}{\longrightarrow} \bigcirc \overset{VM}{\longrightarrow} \ldots \overset{API(m')}{\longrightarrow} \bigcirc \overset{VM}{\longrightarrow} \bigcirc \overset{VM}{\longrightarrow} \bigcirc \overset{CM}{\leadsto} \overset{c_{i+1}}{\underset{r_{i+1}}{\bigcirc}} \overset{CM}{\leadsto} \ldots$$

Concerning the specific operations of the card manager, the verification consists in proving that the processing of commands and the building of the response do not introduce any leak regarding isolation.

Concerning the interpretation of the method, we have to prove that neither the interpretation of bytecode instructions nor the execution of methods of the API violate the confidentiality of data of applets.

Proofs

At the level of the card manager, we have proved the confidentiality property as defined in Definition 2. The proof is done by case analysis on the kind of the received command.

A large number of intermediate lemmas has been needed in order to prove that the confidentiality is preserved during specific operations of the card manager. These specific operations are the ones already mentioned as the loading of new packages, the selection and deselection of applets, the dispatching of commands, the management of APDU buffer, etc ($\sim$ 14000 lines of coq script).

Furthermore the proof architecture is organized around two main lemmas, corresponding to the two kinds of steps needed to process the command.

The first lemma concerns the confidentiality of the execution of one bytecode instruction. It states that, assuming suitable hypotheses (in particular that there is no shareable interface in C), if there are two JCVM transitions $s_1 \xrightarrow{VM} s_2$ and $s'_1 \xrightarrow{VM} s'_2$ such that $s_1 \sim_C s'_1$, then $s_2 \sim_C s'_2$. This proof has already been presented in [1] ($\sim$ 16000 lines of coq script).

Similarly, the second main lemma states that for each method m of the API, if $s_1 \xrightarrow{API(m)} s_2$ and $s'_1 \xrightarrow{API(m)} s'_2$ such that $s_1 \sim_C s'_1$, then $s_2 \sim_C s'_2$ and the results of the executions are the same ($\sim$ 5000 lines of coq script). This proof is presented in detail in the next section.

Confidentiality Property for the API

Here we focus on the execution of API methods. We saw that API methods are specified with pre and postconditions. In particular, for each method, the postcondition specifies the JCVM state resulting from the execution of the method. Therefore, the relation that we denoted by $\xrightarrow{API(m)}$ is defined by the postcondition of the method m. We define a generic confidentiality property for the API as follows:

```
Section ApiConfidentialityProperty.

Variable pre_info : Set.
Variable method_post_condition:
  jcvm_state -> pre_info -> method_state_result -> Prop.
Variable confidentiality_condition: jcvm_state -> pre_info -> Prop.
Variable pre_info_isom: pre_info->(reference->reference)->pre_info.

Definition confidentiality_api :=
  (* equivalent jcvm states at method invocation *)
    (invkst,invkst':jcvm_state)
    (own:owner)(phi:(reference -> reference))
    (jcvm_state_equivalence_up_to_one_context invkst invkst' own phi) ->
  (* equivalent parameters for the method *)
    (inf,inf':pre_info) inf'=(pre_info_isom inf phi) ->
  (* the caller context is not the JCRE *)
   ~(jcvm_caller_context invkst JCRE_Context) ->
  (* the context which must not be accessible *)
    (own:owner) (jcvm_caller_context invkst (Applet_Context own)) ->
    (hiddenown:owner) ~(same_owner own hiddenown) ->
  (* the hypothesis for confidentiality *)
    (confidentiality_condition invkst inf) ->
  (* the execution *)
```

```
(poststate,poststate':jcvm_state)
(res,res':method_result)
(method_post_condition invkst  inf  (Meth_Res poststate  res )) ->
(method_post_condition invkst' inf' (Meth_Res poststate' res')) ->
(jcvm_state_equivalence_up_to_one_context poststate poststate' own phi)
/\ (res'=(method_result_isom res phi)).
```

End ApiConfidentialityProperty.

Remark 3. Since the arguments and the result of a method may contain references, we must consider two executions from equivalents states, but also from equivalent arguments; and we prove that the results are equivalent.

Variables are used to instantiate the property to each method of the API:

- `pre_info` is a type depending on the method; it is designed to enclose the parameters of the method (see page 342).
- `method_post_condition` is the specification of the postcondition of the method.
- `confidentiality_condition` encloses the additional hypotheses, if any, to ensure the confidentiality. It is shown on page 348 that the specification of the security mechanism is not stated concerning the API. Therefore, it may happen that some additional conditions have to be fulfilled in order to ensure confidentiality; they are enclosed in this variable.
- `pre_info_isom` defines a specific equivalence for the type `pre_info` of the parameters of the method.

Remark 4. Here no hypothesis is done concerning shareable interface, since the API does neither provide nor call any.

To prove the confidentiality for the API, we instantiate this definition for each method, and prove it. Let us look at the particular example of the method `boolean equals(byte[] bArray, short offset, byte length)`. The confidentiality property is obtained by instantiating `pre_info` with `equals_info` and `method_post_condition` with `equals_post_condition`. To achieve the proof of the property, we had to assume that `bArray` is accessible from the caller context, which is the instantiation of `confidentiality_condition`. This gave rise to the following result:

```
Theorem equals211_confidentiality:
let confidentiality_condition =
 [invkst:jcvm_state; inf:equals_info]
 (caller_array_access_security_constraints invkst (equalsinfo_arr inf))
in (confidentiality_api
        equals_info equals211_post_cond confidentiality_condition).
```

We do not give the details of the definition of
    `caller_array_access_security_constraints`
which expresses that `bArray` (here (`equalsinfo_arr inf`)) is accessible from the caller context according the security policy to regulate access across contexts (see [11]).

Remark 5. For each method, the instantiation of the variable
    `confidentiality_condition`
actually completes the specification of the method from the security point of
view. Therefore, the collection of these conditions for all the methods of the API
specifies a sufficient security mechanism for the API to enforce the confidentiality
property. This is an important application of this work.

Remark 6. Independently of our work, this condition has been added in Java
Card 2.2 specification (see [12]). However, we also did the proof of the same
property on the models of Java Card 2.2; it is very similar to the one for Java
Card 2.1.1; the only difference is that the security hypothesis is no longer needed.

4   About the Integrity

Concerning the API, a similar method can be used to prove the integrity property; it has been done in the case of the `AID` class.

    The notion of integrity is simpler than the one of confidentiality since its
violation is "observable". Indeed, the integrity is ensured during the execution
of a method if the values of the confidential data at the end of the execution are
the same that the ones at the beginning. Thus, with the notation of Section 3.1,
the integrity for the API can by formally stated as follows.

Definition 3 (Integrity Property for the API).
*Let m be an API method, C a context and s a JCVM state. If the calling context
in s, i.e. the one of the caller of the method m, is different from C and from the
JCRE context, and if $s \xrightarrow{API(m)} s'$ then $\mathcal{F}_C(s) = \mathcal{F}_C(s')$.*

This gives rise to the definition of a generic integrity property to be instantiated
and proved for each method of the API.

Example. Let us look here at the following example, well known from Java
Card technology developer community. Let us consider the method `byte
getBytes(byte[] dest, short offset)` of the class `javacard.framework.AID`
which is supposed to put in the array `dest` all the AID bytes encapsulated
within the `AID` instance from which the method is called (`offset` specifies
where the AID bytes begin within `dest`). Here the security problem concerns
the access to the array `dest`. The basic extension of the firewall rules is not
sufficient to ensure applet isolation. Indeed, this natural extension would be
to allow access to `dest` only if the context of execution of the method is the
JCRE context, or is the same as the context of `dest`. Following such a policy would introduce a security hole. Indeed, `AID` instances are provided by
the system and belong to it. Any applet α can get such an instance, say `a`,
via the method `javacard.framework.JCSystem.lookupAID(...)`. Now, if α invokes
`a.getBytes(dest,offset)`, there is a context switch into the JCRE context
since `a` belongs to the system; this gives to the method all the rights to access
any object in any context. In particular, the method can put the bytes enclosed

in a into dest, whatever the context of this last one is. It particular, even if the context of dest is different from the context of α, the content of dest is erased. In conclusion, α would be able to modify any byte array in an other context in an indirect way via the JCRE context. This is again contrary to Java Card security goals. So, a stronger security rule must be enforced to control the use this method: dest must be accessible from the context of the caller of the method.

This information leak has also been revealed during the development of the proof of integrity. Indeed, the introduction of an additional hypothesis has been necessary to complete the proof:

```
Theorem getBytes211_integrity:
let integrity_condition =
 [invkst:jcvm_state; getbinf:getB_info]
 (caller_array_access_security_constraints invkst (getbinfo_arr getbinf))
in (integrity_api getB_info getBytes211_post_cond integrity_condition).
```

Similarly to the case of the method equals, this rule has been added in Java Card 2.2 specification.

Conclusion

The security mechanism of the API is not specified by Sun specification; it is actually left to the design and implementation stages. The present work proposes a formal method to complete the functional specification of the API in the objective of ensuring the applet isolation. This method is extended to the card management in order to ensure that the confidentiality holds for the whole Java Card platform.

Let us emphasize that the use of a proof assistant handling higher order logic has been crucial in this work. The definition of infinite traces describing the executions of a machine as well as that of propositions over those traces are directly expressed in terms of the mechanisms for supporting co-inductive definitions. Moreover the formalization of the confidentiality property uses quantification on bijections between Java references.

Related Work. In the framework of Java Card technology, the problem of confidentiality has been investigated in [7]. This work concerns applet interactions and focuses on the qualification of admissible information flows. Verification of applet isolation has also been investigated in [13] by setting up a type system at applet source code level to check applet isolation. More generally, formal verification techniques have been investigated for Java source code (see e.g. [19]). These works deal with the application level and not with the underlying system. Our approach is complementary: we focus on the verification of applet isolation at the level of the Java Card platform itself.

Java Card platform security has been investigated in [2,4,3]. In particular, these studies established a correspondence between offensive and defensive Java Card virtual machine. Verification of the Java Card API has also been investigated in [16,15,20]. Here we focus on applet isolation and especially on confidentiality, adding another building block to prove Java Card security.

Future Work. A first direction to investigate is to generalize our result about applet isolation, in order for instance to take into account the case of shareable interfaces. A second direction consists in checking the property for actual implementation of the Java Card platform.

References

1. J. Andronick, B. Chetali, and O. Ly. Formal Verification of the Confidentiality Property in Java Card™ Technology. Submitted at Journal of Logic and Algebraic Programming.
2. G. Barthe, G. Dufay, M. Huisman, and S. Melo de Sousa. Jakarta: a Toolset to Reason about the JavaCard Platform. In I. Attali and T. Jensen, editors, *Proceedings of E-SMART'01*, number 2140 in LNCS, pages 2–18. Springer-Verlag, 2001.
3. G. Barthe, G. Dufay, L. Jakubiec, and S. Melo de Sousa. A Formal Correspondence between Offencive and Defensive JavaCard Virtual Machine. In A. Cortesi, editor, *Proceedings of VMCAI'02*, number 2294 in LNCS, pages 32–45, 2002.
4. G. Barthe, G. Dufay, L. Jakubiec, B. Serpette, and S. Melo de Sousa. A Formal Executable Semantics of the JavaCard Platform. In D. Sands, editor, *Proceedings of ESOP'01*, number 2028 in LNCS, pages 302–319. Springer-Verlag, 2001.
5. G. Betarte, B. Chetali, E. Gimenez, and C. Loiseaux. Formavie: Formal Modelling and Verification of the JavaCard 2.1.1 Security Architecture. In *E-SMART 2002*, pages 213–231, 2002.
6. Z. Chen. *Java Card Technology for Smart Cards: Architecture and Programmer's Guide.* Addison Wesley, 2000.
7. M. Dam and P. Giambiagi. Confidentiality for Mobile Code: The Case of a Simple Payment Protocol. In *13th IEEE Computer Security Foundations Workshop*, pages 233–244. IEEE Computer Society Press, July 2000.
8. J.A. Goguen and J. Meseguer. Security Policy and Security Models. In *Proc. of the 1982 Symposium on Security and Privacy*, pages 11–20. IEEE Computer Society Press, 1982.
9. J.A. Goguen and J. Meseguer. Unwinding and interference control. In *Proc. of the 1982 Symposium on Security and Privacy*, pages 75–86. IEEE Computer Society Press, 1984.
10. G. McGrow and E. Felten. *Securing Java: Getting Down to Business with Mobile Code.* John Wiley & Sons, 1999.
11. Sun Microsystems. *Java Card 2.1.1 Specification.* http://java.sun.com/products/javacard/, 2000.
12. Sun Microsystems. *Java Card 2.2 API Specification.* http://java.sun.com/products/javacard/, 2002.
13. P. Müller and A. Poetzsch-Heffter. A Type System for Checking Applet Isolation in Java Card. In S. Drossopoulou et al, editor, *Proceedings of FTfJP'01*, 2001.
14. S. Oaks. *Java Security.* O'Reilly, 1998.
15. E. Poll, P. Hartel, and de E. Jong. A Java Reference Model of Transacted Memory for Smart Cards. In *Fifth Smart Card Research and Advanced Application Conf. (CARDIS'2002)*, 2002. To Appear. See http://www.cs.kun.nl/VerifiCard/files/publications.html
16. E. Poll, J. van den Berg, and B. Jacobs. Formal specification of the Java Card API in JML: the APDU class. *Computer Networks*, 36(4):407–421, 2001.

17. The Coq Development Team LogiCal Project. *The Coq Proof Assistant Reference Manual.* http://pauillac.inria.fr/coq/doc/main.html
18. J. Rushby. Noninterference, transitivity, and channel-control security policies, December 1992.
19. J. van den Berg and B. Jacobs. The LOOP compiler for Java and JML. In T. Margaria and W. Yi, editors, *Tools and Algorithms for the Constructions and Analysis of Software (TACAS'2001)*, number 2031 in LNCS, pages 299–312. Springer, 2001.
20. J. van den Berg, B. Jacobs, and E. Poll. Formal Specification and Verification of JavaCard's Application Identifier Class. In *Proceedings of the Java Card 2000 Workshop*, 2000. http://www.irisa.fr/lande/jensen/jcw-program.html
21. B. Venners. *Inside the Java Virtual Machine.* McGraw-Hill, 1997.

Verifying Second-Level Security Protocols

Giampaolo Bella[1],[2], Cristiano Longo[2], and Lawrence C Paulson[1]

[1] Computer Laboratory, University of Cambridge
15 JJ Thomson Avenue, Cambridge CB3 0FD (UK)
{gb221,lcp}@cl.cam.ac.uk
[2] Dipartimento di Matematica e Informatica, Università di Catania
Viale A. Doria 6, I-95125 Catania (ITALY)
{giamp,longo}@dmi.unict.it

Abstract. A *second-level security protocol* is defined as a security protocol that relies on an underlying security protocol in order to achieve its goals. The verification of classical authentication protocols has become routine, but second-level protocols raise new challenges. These include the formalisation of appeals to the underlying protocols, the modification of the threat model, and the formalisation of the novel goals. These challenges have been met using Isabelle and the Inductive Approach [14]. The outcomes are demonstrated on a recent protocol for certified e-mail delivery by Abadi et al. [2].

1 Introduction

The development of *security protocols* during the last two and a half decades has mainly focused on the fundamental goals of *authentication*, which confirms the identity of a peer, and of *confidentiality*, which confirms that a message is kept from attackers. Somewhat simplistically, security protocols have often been referred to as *authentication protocols* [9,10]. However, the growth of Internet transactions and distributed computing in general require more sophisticated goals such as *anonymity, non-repudiation* [18], *delegation* [4] and *certified delivery* [2]. No one can predict what security goals will become important next year.

Many recent protocols rely on some other protocol as a primitive. For example, the fair-exchange protocol by Asokan et al. [3] presupposes that the peers authenticate each other by means of an authentication protocol before they engage in a transaction whereby they commit to a contract. The certified e-mail protocol by Abadi et al. requires the establishment of a secure channel between the e-mail recipient and the trusted third party: "in practice, such a channel might be an SSL connection" [2]. But SSL is already rather complicated [15], hence a protocol that employs it becomes even more complicated as a whole, unless we assume that SSL works correctly. These observations inspire our definition of *second-level* protocols.

Definition 1 (Second-Level Protocol). *A second-level security protocol is a security protocol that relies on the goals of underlying authentication protocols in order to achieve its goals.*

D. Basin and B. Wolff (Eds.): TPHOLs 2003, LNCS 2758, pp. 352–366, 2003.

This concept is natural. Any kind of construction customarily makes use of existing constructions, and this process can be iterated. Likewise, our definition can be trivially generalised for n^{th}-*level* protocols, which employ $(n-1)^{st}$-*level* protocols. In turn, classical authentication protocols can be seen as *first-level* protocols, which adopt 0th-*level* protocols, the transfer protocols.

The verification of authentication protocols can be considered mature. Innumerable approaches have been taken [8,11,12,14,16]; a wide variety of protocols can be formalised; the verification is often highly or fully automated. However, second-level protocols raise new challenges for formal verification. We briefly outline them here.

Underlying goals. It is not obvious how to treat the goals made available by the underlying authentication protocols. Should we examine the interaction of authentication and second-level protocols directly, combining them to form one giant protocol? Surely not. Should we instead take for granted the authentication protocols' goals during the verification of the second-level protocols? By following well-established principles of hierarchical verification, we settled for the latter course. The former is conceptually simpler and avoids the danger of missing a low-level interaction between the two levels, but it becomes infeasible as more protocols are combined.

Threat model. Dolev-Yao's threat model is the standard for authentication protocols. It consists of a single attacker who monitors the entire network, reuses the intercepted messages as he pleases, and yet cannot break ciphertexts. But what is the threat model for second-level protocols? Our choice was to limit Dolev-Yao's model as follows. If a second-level protocol rests on some authenticated communication, then the attacker must be prevented from interposing. If that communication is confidential, then the attacker must be prevented from overhearing.

New goals. If we aim at verifying new goals, we must first solve the problem of their formalisation. New security requirements will be increasingly complex and difficult to formalise. Concentrating on second-level protocols, we have found simple formalisations for the goals of certified e-mail delivery, and, most importantly, simple strategies for proving them. They will be presented below. Goals of other second-level protocols may require dedicated treatment.

This paper addresses the challenges given above. We start with the Inductive Approach [14] to protocol verification and make it capable of verifying second-level protocols. Our modifications, described in Sect. 2, are surprisingly simple. The currently formalised network events can be quickly adapted to the new protocols. Then, Sect. 3 describes the certified e-mail protocol developed by Abadi et al. [2]. Sect. 4 introduces our inductive model for the protocol, and Sect. 5 describes our findings. Sect. 6 concludes the paper.

There is little work that is related to ours. Abadi and Blanchet are publishing their verification of the same protocol [1] using Blanchet's verifier [8]. Their study is extremely detailed and mostly automatic, human intervention being required only occasionally. For example, "The fact that messages reach their destination

(...) cannot be taken into account by our verifier, so it cannot prove the required properties in a fully automatic way" [1, p.15]. Both our works appear to confirm that the protocol meets its goals, though a deeper comparison is necessary.

Shmatikov and Mitchell have used model-checking techniques to analyse what we would call a second-level protocol [17]. Their model is kept small to make exhaustive search feasible, and appears to be precisely tailored to the specific protocol under consideration. By contrast, our aim below is to provide a general treatment of second-level protocol verification. Because we use theorem proving rather than model checking, we do not have to limit the size of the model.

2   Modelling and Verifying Second-Level Protocols

Our approach to analysing second-level security protocols is built upon our existing work on analysing authentication protocols [5,14] using inductive definitions. The machinery is mechanised in Isabelle/HOL, so modelling and verifying a protocol in fact involves interaction with that theorem prover.

We outline the original approach (§2.1) and describe how we extended it to cope with second-level protocols (§2.2).

2.1   The Inductive Approach

Our approach is to formalise the system inductively [14]. This defines an operational semantics that has much in common with Lowe's CSP formalisations [13], except that the models are infinite. The participants include the honest ones, who execute the protocol faithfully; one of these is designated as a trusted third party. There is a spy, who eavesdrops on network traffic and might send any messages he is able to generate. We only verify safety properties: for example, we cannot reason about denial of service. Proving a protocol guarantee involves demonstrating that it holds in all execution traces, no matter what the spy does.

Event histories are lists (built in reverse order) containing three kinds of elements.

- The event Says A B X means that A has sent message X to B. However, sending does not imply reception.
- The event Gets B X means that B has received message X from the network. As we normally consider the channel to be unauthenticated, B does not know who sent the message.
- The event Notes A X means that A has stored message X internally. It represents a local state change.

Messages are a recursive datatype that includes the following constructors:

- Agent A denotes the name of the agent A.
- Number N denotes a guessable number, where N is a non-negative integer.
- Nonce N is like Number N but the number is treated as non-guessable; it models long, randomly generated byte strings.

- Key K denotes a key and is treated as non-guessable.
- Hash X denotes the cryptographic hash of the message X.
- Crypt KX denotes encryption of message X with K.
- $\{X_1, \ldots, X_n\}$ denotes the concatenation of the messages $X_1, \ldots, X_n$.

Protocol definitions and proofs involve several additional functions.

- used evs denotes the set of all message components that appear in the trace evs, so Nonce $N \notin$ used evs expresses that N is a fresh nonce.
- parts H denotes the set of all message components (including the plaintexts of encryptions) that appear in the set of messages H.
- analz H is a subset of parts H, namely the components that are effectively derivable from the set of messages H. Plaintexts of encryptions are derivable provided the corresponding key is also derivable.
- synth H denotes the set of messages that can be built up using elements of H and guessable values.
- priEK A and priSK A denote the private keys (encryption and signature) of the agent A.
- pubEK A and pubSK A denote the public keys (encryption and signature) of the agent A.
- symKeys denotes the set of all symmetric keys; the complement of this set denotes the asymmetric keys.
- bad denotes the set of compromised agents (see below).

Fig. 1 presents a trivial authentication protocol and its inductive definition. The latter consists of four introduction rules defining the constant dap, which

$$
\begin{array}{llll}
1. & A \longrightarrow B & : & A, Na \\
2. & B \longrightarrow A & : & \{Na\}_{Kb-1}
\end{array}
$$

```
Nil:     "[] ∈ dap"

DAP1:    "⟦evs1 ∈ dap; Nonce Na ∉ used evs1⟧
         ⟹ Says A B {Agent A, Nonce Na} # evs1 ∈ dap"

DAP2:    "⟦evs2 ∈ dap; Gets B {Agent A, Nonce Na} ∈ set evs2⟧
         ⟹ Says B A (Crypt (priSK B) (Nonce Na)) # evs2 ∈ dap"

Recp:    "⟦evsr ∈ dap; Says A B X ∈ set evsr⟧
         ⟹ Gets B X # evsr ∈ dap"

Fake:    "⟦evsf ∈ dap; X ∈ synth(analz(knows Spy evsf))⟧
         ⟹ Says Spy B X # evsf ∈ dap"
```

Fig. 1. A demo authentication protocol (DAP) and its inductive model

denotes the set of traces permissible with this protocol. By rule *Nil*, the empty trace is permissible. Rule *DAP1* represents the first protocol step: A chooses a fresh nonce and sends it to B. Rule *DAP2* represents the second protocol step: if B receives a suitable message, he signs the nonce it contains using his private key and sends it to A. He doesn't know that the message came from A, but sends it to the principal named in the first component of the message he received. Rule *Recp* says that if a message is sent, it might be received. Rule *Fake* allows the spy to generate a message X using material gleaned from past traffic, and send it to anybody.

2.2   Adapting the Inductive Approach

The Inductive Approach had to be extended to face the three challenges sketched in the introduction, a process that required much thought. However, the extensions turned out to be technically simple and quick to implement.

Modelling the underlying protocols' goals. According to Definition 1, the underlying protocols are authentication protocols. Therefore, the main goals that we need to model are authentication and confidentiality. Other, minor, goals may also be of interest.

Authentication. The sender identity A of a Says $A\,B\,X$ event cannot be altered in the model once that event occurs on a trace. When we formalise an authentication protocol, we must not allow an agent to inspect the sender identity; the originator of a message remains unknown unless it is conveyed by the message itself. We usually formalise message reception using the Gets event, which does not mention the sender. In earlier work [14], we formalised message reception using the event Says $A'\,B\,X$, taking care to ensure that the value of A' (the true sender) was never used.

On the basis of these observations, one strategy to formalising authentication is to allow Says events among rule preconditions. For example, Says $A\,B\,X$ would signify that B can authenticate X as coming from A. This is the right way to model an authenticated channel that does not offer confidentiality, because the spy can read X from the event Says $A\,B\,X$.

Confidentiality. What if the channel must be confidential? We could extend our definitional framework, introducing an additional event ConfSays $A\,B\,X$ for sending a message confidentially. This would require extending the definition of the function knows, which formalises each agent's knowledge. The new event ConfSays $A\,B\,X$ would make X available only to the designated recipient, B. If we include the event ConfSays $A\,B\,X$ as the precondition of a rule and allow other references to A, who is the true sender, then we have modelled an authenticated, confidential channel. If we forbid other references to A, then our confidential channel is unauthenticated. We performed some experiments using the new event but abandoned them when we realised that the original definitional framework was already sufficient to model secure channels.

$$
\begin{aligned}
&1.\ A \xrightarrow{\text{SSL}} B \quad : \quad A, Na \\
&2.\ B \longrightarrow A \quad : \quad \{Na\}_{Kb^{-1}}
\end{aligned}
$$

Nil: `"[] ∈ dslp"`

DSLP1:   `"⟦evs1 ∈ dslp; Nonce Na ∉ used evs1⟧`
         `⟹ Notes A ⦃Agent A, Agent B, Nonce Na⦄ # evs1 ∈ dslp"`

DSLP2:   `"⟦evs2 ∈ dslp;`
         `Notes B ⦃Agent A, Agent B, Nonce Na⦄ ∈ set evs2⟧`
         `⟹ Says B A (Crypt (priSK B) (Nonce Na)) # evs2 ∈ dslp"`

Recp: `"⟦evsr ∈ dslp; Says A B X ∈ set evsr⟧`
         `⟹ Gets B X # evsr ∈ dslp"`

RecpN: `"⟦evsr ∈ dslp; Notes A ⦃Agent A, Agent B, X⦄ ∈ set evsr⟧`
         `⟹ Notes B ⦃Agent A, Agent B, X⦄ # evsr ∈ dslp"`

Fake: `"⟦evsf ∈ dslp; X ∈ synth(analz(knows Spy evsf))⟧`
         `⟹ Says Spy B X # evsf ∈ dslp"`

Fig. 2. A demo second-level protocol (DSLP) and its inductive model

The Notes event formalises an agent's changing his internal state. It has the form Notes $A\, X$, where X is a message (perhaps the result of a computation) being stored for future reference. We can formalise a confidential transmission of a message X from A to B by the event

$$\text{Notes } A\, \{A, B, X\} \tag{1}$$

as demonstrated by rule DSLP1 in Fig. 2. The figure shows a demo second-level protocol that differs from the demo authentication protocol seen above only in the first step, which now takes place over an authenticated, confidential channel. Event 1 must be included as precondition of a new inductive rule formalising reception of the confidential message, because reception is in general not guaranteed even on a confidential channel. The new reception rule must introduce the event

$$\text{Notes } B\, \{A, B, X\} \tag{2}$$

signifying that B receives X confidentially, as demonstrated by rule RecpN in Fig. 2. Event 2 must be included as precondition of the rule formalising B's actions upon reception of the confidential message X. The message is therefore authenticated to arrive from the agent whose identity appears as first component of the noted message. This is demonstrated by rule DSLP2 in Fig. 2.

No additional modification is necessary to the model of a second-level proto-col, as highlighted by a comparison of Fig. 2 with Fig. 1. In particular, the Fake rule remains unvaried. However, some protocols require an additional rule, al-lowing the spy to send arbitrary messages on previously established confidential connections. Such a rule would insert an event of the form Notes Spy {Spy, B, X}. Also, it is important to make sure that other uses of Notes do not involve mes-sages beginning with two agent names, to avoid confusion with our representation of transmission along secure channels.

Guaranteed Delivery. Other minor goals of authentication protocols can be for-malised using similar techniques. For example, distribution of a session key to a pair of agents can be formalised by an inductive rule that gives both agents Notes events containing a key, with a precondition that the key is fresh. Another goal is guaranteed delivery, which can be implemented by sending a message repeatedly until there is an acknowledgement. This goal can be easily formalised by introducing the event for receiving a message at the same time as the event for sending it. Even simpler is just to introduce the former event: the sender magically causes the message to reach the recipient. This formalisation will be vastly used below (§4) to model Abadi et al.'s certified e-mail protocol. With either approach to guaranteed delivery, no reception rule in the style of RecpN (Fig. 2) is necessary.

Notes events are affected by a detail of our model, the set bad of *compromised agents*. These are honest agents that have somehow come under the control of the spy, perhaps through a security lapse. The spy knows their private keys and can read their Notes. This detail is consistent with our use of Notes above, since we can expect the spy to grab anything that a compromised agent receives, even via a secure channel. The model does not constrain bad other than asserting that the spy is in this set.

Traditional authentication protocols are designed to protect honest agents from the rest of the world, and a typical guarantee will hold provided both peers are uncompromised. However, some protocols are intended to protect a principal even from its peer, about whom we make no assumptions. An agent A who executes a non-repudiation protocol or a certified e-mail protocol with B requires the protocol goals *especially* if B is bad.

Let us emphasise what we have provided here, namely a formalisation of the security properties assumed by a second-level protocol. We do not formalise the specific underlying authentication protocol that achieves those properties. Following a hierarchical verification strategy, it is irrelevant what is hidden inside the black box (whether SSL or Kerberos, for example) that is assumed to provide the goals. To our knowledge, this is the first time that principles of hierarchical verification have been spelled out in the context of security protocols.

Adapting the threat model. The threat model formalised in the Inductive Approach is a Dolev-Yao spy (§2.1). He monitors the network traffic by means of knows, can analyse that traffic by means of analz, and can synthesise new messages from the analysed components by means of synth. The spy can send a so formed message X to anyone, as formalised by rule Fake in Fig. 1, which introduces the event Says Spy $B\,X$ in the current trace, B being a free variable.

In principle, it is not obvious what is the threat model for second-level protocols, but we believe that they should still achieve their goals against a Dolev-Yao spy, as illustrated below on the certified e-mail protocol by Abadi et al. Therefore, we decide to maintain the existing spy in such a way that he cannot interfere with the goals of the underlying authentication protocols, though he can execute these protocols himself.

In other words, we analyse second-level protocols under a threat model that is the same as that for authentication protocols, except that it does nothing against those communications that are secured by authentication protocols. Modelling secure communications using Notes events, as explained above, yields this threat model for free — that is, with no changes to our definitional framework.

Modelling and verifying the novel goals. Abstractly, the main goal of certified e-mail delivery resembles a logical equivalence. Given an e-mail m, a sender S and an intended receiver R for m, in the assumption that S sends m to R, it must be the case that R receives m if and only if S obtains the receipt d that R received m.

> *Let evs be a generic trace of the protocol model;*
> *let* Says $S\,R\,X$ *be an event in evs such that X features m;*
> *then*
>
> $$m \in \mathsf{analz}(\mathsf{knows}\,R\ evs) \iff d \in \mathsf{analz}(\mathsf{knows}\,S\ evs).$$

Fig. 3. Abstract formalisation of certified e-mail delivery

The Inductive Approach comes with enough operators to model this goal. Fig. 3 specifies certified e-mail delivery at a very high level. As it is customary, the goal is expressed over a generic trace of events evs of the inductive protocol model. The Says event in the preconditions expresses the role of sender played by S, that of receiver played by R, and features the e-mail m in a form that depends on the specific protocol, such as encrypted or hashed. The delivery receipt, d, is presumably built up from m, S and R. Then, the goal can be expressed as a logical equivalence, one implication for each protocol participant. Most importantly, the formalisation must express that agents who conform to the protocol be protected from agents who do not.

Implication ($\Longrightarrow$) reads as follows: if the receiver can derive the e-mail from the portion he sees of the network traffic on evs, then the sender can derive the corresponding delivery receipt from the portion he sees of the network traffic on evs. This guarantee confirms that the sender never has a disadvantage over the receiver, even if the receiver is able to derive the e-mail off-line from the analysed components.

Implication ($\Longleftarrow$) reads as follows: if the sender can derive a delivery receipt, then the receiver can derive the corresponding e-mail. When the sender submits his delivery receipt to a judge, this guarantee counts as evidence against the receiver. We assume that a delivery receipt involves a digital signature or other mechanism to prevent its being forged; we could explicitly exclude this danger by formalising the precondition as $d \in \mathsf{synth}(\mathsf{analz}(\mathsf{knows}\,S\,evs))$, since the operator synth expresses message creation.

Given a specific protocol, the abstract formalisation of certified e-mail delivery needs to be refined. Despite its nice symmetry, its conclusions are weak because the operator analz represents a potentially unlimited series of decryptions by available keys. A stronger formalisation would replace the use of analz by a reference to a specific protocol message that delivers the required item. The refined Implication ($\Longrightarrow$) says that if the receiver can compute the e-mail by an unlimited amount of work, then the sender has been given the corresponding delivery receipt. The refined Implication ($\Longleftarrow$) says that if the sender can compute a delivery receipt by an unlimited amount of work, then the receiver has been given the corresponding e-mail. Note that we cannot express this refined formalisation unless we know the precise format of the protocol messages.

An additional problem is that, at the time of this writing, we lack techniques for reasoning about the knowledge of agents other than the spy. Specifically, we do not know how to prove anything useful from the assumption $X \in \mathsf{analz}(\mathsf{knows}\,A\,evs)$ unless $A = \mathsf{Spy}$. Sometimes, we can correct the situation by proving something stronger that no longer involves analz. Here is an improved version of Implication ($\Longleftarrow$):

> If a delivery receipt has been created at all, then the receiver has been given the corresponding e-mail.

This version does not refer to the sender. We have strengthened the guarantee while eliminating the need to reason about the sender's knowledge.

We cannot apply this technique to Implication ($\Longrightarrow$) because obviously the message m will have been created. Instead, we are forced to divide Implication ($\Longrightarrow$) into two separate properties. One concerns the spy and is proved by reasoning about $\mathsf{analz}(\mathsf{knows}\,\mathsf{Spy}\,evs)$, which we know how to do. The other concerns an honest agent, and states that if R is given the message (in the normal way) then S has been given the receipt.

Further refinements depend upon the specific delivery mechanism used in the protocol. The e-mail protocol we consider below uses a key to protect the message. Later, R is given this key, so that she can decrypt the message. We therefore refine the statements above, replacing "R has the e-mail" by "R has the key to the e-mail." We can also formalise a further guarantee, namely that the key never reaches the spy. This guarantee, which is of obvious value to both parties, is formalised and proved much as it would be for a typical authentication protocol.

To prove these guarantees, we have been able to reuse the techniques previously developed on a non-repudiation protocol [7], which has the similar aim of protecting one agent from another.

Abbreviations

$$h_S \quad = \quad \mathsf{Hash}(q, r, \{m\}_k)$$
$$h_R \quad = \quad \mathsf{Hash}(q', r', em')$$
$$S2TTP \quad = \quad \{S, k, R, h_S\}_{(\mathsf{pubEKTTP})}$$

Steps

1. $\quad S \; \longrightarrow \; R \quad : \quad \mathsf{TTP}, \{m\}_k, q, S2TTP$

2. $\quad R \; \xrightarrow{\mathsf{SSL}} \; \mathsf{TTP} \quad : \quad S2TTP', \mathsf{RPwd}, h_R$

3. $\quad \mathsf{TTP} \; \xrightarrow{\mathsf{SSL}} \; R \quad : \quad k', h'_R$

4. $\quad \mathsf{TTP} \; \longrightarrow \; S \quad : \quad \{S2TTP''\}_{(\mathsf{priSKTTP})}$

Fig. 4. Abadi et al.'s certified e-mail protocol

3 Abadi et al.'s Certified Email Protocol

Abadi et al. [2] have recently designed a protocol for certified e-mail delivery that appears to have many practical advantages. Although it requires a trusted third party (TTP), this TTP is stateless and lightweight; it never has access to the clear-text of the transmitted messages. The burden on the TTP is independent of the message size. No public-key infrastructure is necessary. The TTP must have signature and encryption keys, but other principals merely share a secret with the TTP, such as a password.

The gist of the protocol is that the e-mail sender sends his e-mail encrypted under a symmetric key to the intended receiver. (This is similar in spirit to the previously mentioned non-repudiation protocol: send the encrypted message first, and the corresponding key only later.) Here, the sender also attaches the symmetric key encrypted under the TTP's public encryption key. Then, the recipient forwards the message to the TTP in order to obtain the symmetric key. (In the non-repudiation protocol, it is up to the sender to lodge the key with the TTP.) As the TTP releases the key, it also releases a certificate documenting the transaction to the sender.

Fig. 4 presents a protocol version, simplifying the headers and authentication options. The fullest authentication option, whereby the receiver should authenticate to both the sender and the TTP, is assumed. Our notation purposely makes no distinction between the various uses of symmetric encryption, asymmetric encryption, and digital signatures by using subscripts in all cases.

In step 1, the sender S sends the receiver R the encrypted e-mail $\{m\}_k$, a query q, and a certificate for the TTP, called $S2TTP$. The query is part of the authentication mechanism between R and S. They are required to agree beforehand on some acknowledgement function to link a query q to its response r. The certificate is encrypted under the TTP's public encryption key, ($\mathsf{pubEKTTP}$), and contains the symmetric key k that protects $\{m\}_k$ along with a hash linking $\{m\}_k$ to the query/response pair.

In step 2, R issues a response r' to the query q' just received, which is not necessarily the same as S's query because the network is insecure. Then, R uses his query/response pair along with the received ciphertext em' to build his own hash h_R. Finally, R wraps this up with the received certificate and with his password RPwd and sends the outcome to the TTP on secure channel. Presumably, R creates this channel by running the SSL protocol with authentication of TTP.

In step 3, the TTP verifies that the received certificate has the expected form by decrypting it by its private decryption key. Then, the TTP authenticates R by the password and verifies that h'_S found inside the ticket matches h'_R. A positive check signifies that S and R agree on the authentication mechanism. If satisfied, the TTP replies to R, delivering the key found inside the ticket. This reply goes along the secure channel created in step 2.

In step 4, the TTP sends the delivery receipt to S. It is the certificate signed by the TTP's private signature key. The TTP is trusted to take this step jointly with the previous one, so as to be fair to both sender and receiver. If the certificate received inside the delivery receipt matches S's stored certificate, then S authenticates R.

The TTP sees the symmetric key k, but not the plaintext message m. This is a desirable goal that reduces the trust in the TTP: it cannot disclose the e-mails even if it later becomes compromised. (Note that a misbehaving TTP could eavesdrop on the initial message from S to R, taking the ciphertext $\{m\}_k$, which he could decrypt once he knows k.) Also, the use of encryption should prevent third parties from learning m. Most importantly, however, the protocol "should allow a sender, S, to send an e-mail message to a receiver, R, so that R reads the message if and only if S receives the corresponding return receipt" [2, §2].

4   Modelling Abadi et al.'s Protocol

Although the protocol does not require a public-key infrastructure, the TTP must have one key pair for encryption and another for signature. Hence, the protocol model requires a treatment of both kinds of asymmetric keys. The protocol also uses passwords to strengthen the authentication of the receiver to the TTP. Hence, a treatment of symmetric keys (shared with the TTP) is also necessary. A complete formalisation of asymmetric keys was developed to verify SET [6], and can be reused here. A formalisation of symmetric keys exists too, and has been used for a number of protocols relying on symmetric cryptography [14]. We have added these extensions to our standard formalisation of public keys, where it can be used for verifying other protocols.

For authentication, R must be able to respond to a query q from S. The original protocol expects S and R to agree off-line on a series of challenge-response pairs. We chose the following implementation of responses:

$$\text{response } S\ R\ q == \text{Hash}\{\text{Agent } S, \text{Key}(\text{shrK } R), \text{Nonce } q\}$$

This explicit definition allows the spy to generate the response if R is compromised.

```
FakeSSL:
  "⟦ evsfssl ∈ certified_mail; X ∈ synth(analz(knows Spy evsfssl))⟧
   ⟹ Notes TTP {|Agent Spy, Agent TTP, X|} # evsfssl ∈ certified_mail"

CM1:
  "⟦evs1 ∈ certified_mail;
    Key K ∉ used evs1;
    K ∈ symKeys;
    Nonce q ∉ used evs1;
    hs = Hash {|Number cleartext, Nonce q, response S R q,
                Crypt K (Number m)|};
    S2TTP = Crypt (pubEK TTP) {|Agent S, Number AO, Key K, Agent R, hs|}⟧
   ⟹ Says S R {|Agent S, Agent TTP, Crypt K (Number m), Number AO,
                Number cleartext, Nonce q, S2TTP|} # evs1
         ∈ certified_mail"

CM2:
  "⟦evs2 ∈ certified_mail;
    Gets R {|Agent S, Agent TTP, em', Number AO, Number cleartext',
             Nonce q', S2TTP'|} ∈ set evs2;
    TTP ≠ R;
    hr = Hash {|Number cleartext', Nonce q', response S R q', em'|} ⟧
   ⟹
   Notes TTP {|Agent R, Agent TTP, S2TTP', Key(RPwd R), hr|} # evs2
     ∈ certified_mail"

CM3:
  "⟦evs3 ∈ certified_mail;
    Notes TTP {|Agent R', Agent TTP, S2TTP'', Key(RPwd R'), hr'|}
      ∈ set evs3;
    S2TTP'' = Crypt (pubEK TTP)
                    {|Agent S, Number AO, Key k', Agent R', hs'|};
    TTP ≠ R';  hs' = hr';  k' ∈ symKeys⟧
   ⟹
   Notes R' {|Agent TTP, Agent R', Key k', hr'|} #
   Gets S (Crypt (priSK TTP) S2TTP'') #
   Says TTP S (Crypt (priSK TTP) S2TTP'') # evs3 ∈ certified_mail"
```

Fig. 5. Modelling Abadi et al.'s protocol (fragment)

Fig. 5 shows the largest fragment of our protocol model, omitting only three classical rules (Nil, Recp and Fake, Fig. 2). Message transmission over a secure channel, which is authentic, confidential and delivery-guaranteed, is formalised by a Notes event of the form (2) discussed above (§2.2). Rule FakeSSL represents the possibility of the spy's opening a secure channel to TTP and sending a fake message. Rule CM1 represents the first protocol message; note that *cleartext* is a part of the message that is given to R immediately. In rule CM2, a Notes event represents R's message to TTP; here Key(RPwd R) is R's password. Steps 3 and 4 are assumed to take place at the same time, so they are formalised by the single rule *CM3*. The TTP checks R's password to authenticate the sender of message 2, but regardless he must reply along the same secure channel. The replies to both S and R are delivery-guaranteed, so the rule introduces an appropriate Notes event for the receiver, and a double Says-Gets event for the TTP's transmission to the sender. That Says event is unnecessary according to our simple formalisation of guaranteed delivery (§2.2), but is retained to preserve a feature of our model: a Gets event is always preceded by a matching Says event.

5   Verifying Abadi et al.'s Protocol

The novel features of this protocol required some new techniques in the verification. However, space limitations force us directly to the final results on certified e-mail delivery, also omitting the classical ones on confidentiality and authentication.

The guarantee for the sender is expressed as two theorems: one for the case when the recipient is the spy and one for honest recipients. The sender does not have to know which case applies.

Theorem 1 (Sender's guarantee: spy).

```
"[Says S R {|Agent S, Agent TTP, Crypt K (Number m), Number AO,
          Number cleartext, Nonce q, S2TTP|} ∈ set evs;
 S2TTP = Crypt (pubEK TTP) {|Agent S, Number AO, Key K, Agent R, hs|};
 Key K ∈ analz(knows Spy evs);
 evs ∈ certified_mail;
 S≠Spy]
 ⟹ R ∈ bad & Gets S (Crypt (priSK TTP) S2TTP) ∈ set evs"
```

This theorem's premises are that the sender has issued message 1 (with the given value of $S2TTP$) and that the session key is available to the spy. The conclusion is that R is compromised, but even in this case, the sender gets the return receipt.

Theorem 2 (Sender's guarantee: honest recipient).

```
"[Says S R {|Agent S, Agent TTP, Crypt K (Number m), Number AO,
          Number cleartext, Nonce q, S2TTP|} ∈ set evs;
 S2TTP = Crypt (pubEK TTP) {|Agent S, Number AO, Key K, Agent R, hs|};
 Notes R {|Agent TTP, Agent R, Key K, hs|} ∈ set evs;
 S≠Spy;   evs ∈ certified_mail]
 ⟹ Gets S (Crypt (priSK TTP) S2TTP) ∈ set evs"
```

In this version, the sender has issued message 1 and R has legitimately received the session key. The conclusion is that S gets the return receipt.

Theorem 3 (Recipient's guarantee).

```
"[Crypt (priSK TTP) S2TTP ∈ used evs;
 S2TTP = Crypt (pubEK TTP)
            {|Agent S, Number AO, Key K, Agent R,
               Hash {|Number cleartext, Nonce q, r, em|}|};
 hr = Hash {|Number cleartext, Nonce q, r, em|};
 R≠Spy;   evs ∈ certified_mail]
 ⟹ Notes R {|Agent TTP, Agent R, Key K, hr|} ∈ set evs"
```

The recipient's guarantee states that if the return receipt exists at all (as formalised by the function used) then R has received the session key.

The development of our proofs has highlighted that an anomalous execution of the protocol is possible. The receiver can initiate a session from step 2 by quoting an arbitrary sender, and by building two identical hashes. The session will terminate successfully and the sender will get evidence that an e-mail he has never sent has been delivered. This is due to the fact that the protocol uses no technique to authenticate the sender to TTP. The anomaly can be solved by inserting the sender's password into the certificate $S2TTP$ created at step 1, so that the receiver cannot forge it.

Another flaw is that S has no defence against R's claim that the message was sent years ago and is no longer relevant. This attack works in both directions: R's claim might be truthful and not believed. Even if S includes a date in the message, he cannot prove that the date is accurate. The obvious solution is for TTP to include a timestamp in the return receipt.

6   Conclusions

We have developed the concept of a second-level security protocol, namely one that uses a first-level protocol as a primitive. We have shown how correctness assertions for second-level protocols can be expressed. The existing primitives of the Inductive Approach already let us formalise such concepts as sending a confidential message, an authenticated message, or a message with guaranteed delivery. As a concrete example, we have specified a certified e-mail protocol and formalised its correctness assertions. We have verified the main guarantees of this protocol.

Acknowledgements. Research was funded by the EPSRC grant GR/R01156/ 01 *Verifying Electronic Commerce Protocols*. Discussions with Martin Abadi, Bruno Blanchet, and Salvatore Riccobene were useful.

References

1. M. Abadi and B. Blanchet. Computer-Assisted Verification of a Protocol for Certified Email. In R. Cousot, editor, *Static Analysis, 10th International Symposium (SAS'03)*, Lecture Notes in Comp. Sci. Springer-Verlag, June 2003. To appear.
2. M. Abadi, N. Glew, B. Horne, and B. Pinkas. Certified email with a light on-line trusted third party: Design and implementation. In *Proceedings of the 11th International Conference on Wold Wide Web (WWW-02)*. ACM Press and Addison Wesley, 2002.
3. N. Asokan, V. Shoup, and M. Waidner. Asynchronous protocols for optimistic fair exchange. In *Proc. of the 17th IEEE Sym. on Sec. and Privacy*. IEEE Comp. Society Press, 1998.

4. T. Aura. Distributed access-rights management with delegation certificates. In J. Vitek and C. Jensen, editors, *Secure Internet Programming: Security Issues with Distributed Mobile Objects*, volume 1603 of *Lecture Notes in Comp. Sci.*, pages 211–235. Springer-Verlag, 1999.

5. G. Bella. Inductive verification of smart card protocols. *J. of Comp. Sec.*, 11(1):87–132, 2003.

6. G. Bella, F. Massacci, and L. C. Paulson. Verifying the SET registration protocols. *IEEE J. of Selected Areas in Communications*, 21(1):77 87, 2003.

7. G. Bella and L. C. Paulson. Mechanical proofs about a non-repudiation protocol. In R. J. Boulton and P. B. Jackson, editors, *Theorem Proving in Higher Order Logics: TPHOLs 2001*, volume 2152 of *Lecture Notes in Comp. Sci.*, pages 91–104. Springer, 2001.

8. B. Blanchet. An efficient cryptographic protocol verifier based on prolog rules. In *Proc. of the 14th IEEE Comp. Sec. Found. Workshop*. IEEE Comp. Society Press, 1998.

9. M. Burrows, M. Abadi, and R. M. Needham. A logic of authentication. *Proceedings of the Royal Society of London*, 426:233–271, 1989.

10. J. Clark and J. Jacob. A survey of authentication protocol literature: Version 1.0. Technical report, University of York, Department of Computer Science, November 1997. Available on the web at http://www-users.cs.york.ac.uk/~jac/. A complete specification of the Clark-Jacob library in CAPSL is available at http://www.cs.sri.com/~millen/capsl/.

11. E. Cohen. TAPS: A first-order verifier for cryptographic protocols. In *Proc. of the 13th IEEE Comp. Sec. Found. Workshop*, pages 144–158. IEEE Comp. Society Press, 2000.

12. F. J. T. Fábrega, J. C. Herzog, and J. D. Guttman. Strand Spaces: Why is a Security Protocol Correct? In *Proc. of the 17th IEEE Sym. on Sec. and Privacy*. IEEE Comp. Society Press, 1998.

13. G. Lowe. Breaking and fixing the Needham-Schroeder public-key protocol using CSP and FDR. In T. Margaria and B. Steffen, editors, *Tools and Algorithms for the Construction and Analysis of Systems: second international workshop, TACAS '96*, volume 1055 of *Lecture Notes in Comp. Sci.*, pages 147–166. Springer, 1996.

14. L. C. Paulson. The inductive approach to verifying cryptographic protocols. *J. of Comp. Sec.*, 6:85–128, 1998.

15. L. C. Paulson. Inductive analysis of the internet protocol TLS. *ACM Trans. on Inform. and Sys. Sec.*, 2(3):332–351, 1999.

16. P. Y. A. Ryan and S. A. Schneider. *The Modelling and Analysis of Security Protocols: the CSP Approach*. Addison Wesley Publ. Co., Reading, Massachussetts, 2000.

17. V. Shmatikov and J. C. Mitchell. Analysis of a fair exchange protocol. In *Network and Distributed System Security Symposium (NDSS-00)*, 2000.

18. J. Zhou and D. Gollmann. A fair non-repudiation protocol. In *Symposium on Security and Privacy*. IEEE Computer Society, 1996.

Author Index